Employment Law
Answer Book

Third Edition

James O. Castagnera, Esq.

THE PANEL ANSWER BOOK SERIES

A PANEL PUBLICATION
ASPEN PUBLISHERS, INC.

Copyright © 1996

by
PANEL PUBLISHERS
A division of Aspen Publishers, Inc.
A Wolters Kluwer Company

36 West 44th Street
New York, NY 10036
(212] 790-2000

ISBN 1-56706-101-X

Printed in the United States of America

About Panel Publishers

Panel Publishers derives its name from a panel of business professionals who organized in 1964 to publish authoritative, timely books, information services, and journals written by specialists to assist business professionals in the areas of human resources, compensation and benefits management, and pension planning and compliance, as well as owners of small to medium-sized businesses and their legal and financial advisors. Our mission is to provide practical, solution-based "how-to" information to business professionals.

Also available from Panel Publishers:

Employment Law Answer Book: Forms & Checklists
COBRA Handbook
Managed Care Answer Book
The Employee Handbook
Compensation & Benefits Management
Employee Benefits Answer Book
Flexible Benefits Answer Book
Flexible Benefits Newsletter
The Americans With Disabilities Act
The Family and Medical Leave Act
State by State Guide to Human Resources Law
Health Insurance Answer Book
Company Policy Manual
Hiring Handbook
Sexual Harassment

PANEL PUBLISHERS
A division of Aspen Publishers, Inc.
Practical Solutions for Business Professionals

SUBSCRIPTION NOTICE

This Panel product is updated periodically with supplements to reflect important changes in the subject matter. If you purchased this product directly from Panel Publishers, we have already recorded your subscription for this update service.

If, however, you purchased this product from a bookstore and wish to receive future updates and revised or related volumes billed separately with a 30-day examination review, please contact our Customer Service Department at 1-800-901-9074 or send your name, company name (if applicable), address, and the title of the product to:

PANEL PUBLISHERS
A division of Aspen Publishers, Inc.
7201 McKinney Circle
Frederick, MD 21701

Preface

To meet the challenges posed by the many dramatic changes in employment law that have occurred during the first half of the 1990s, Panel Publishers developed this comprehensive third edition of *The Employment Law Answer Book*. It is an indispensable resource for employers, human resources managers, labor lawyers, and all professionals who require current, authoritative information about issues that affect employment law. *The Employment Law Answer Book, Third Edition* gives readers cogent explanations of major recent developments in clear, straightforward language. It examines, for example, the requirements of the following far-reaching federal legislation:

- The Drug Free Workplace Act
- The Polygraph Protection Act
- The 1991 Civil Rights Act
- The Family and Medical Leave Act
- The Americans with Disabilities Act

The *Third Edition* also discusses the implications of such national milestones as the following:

- The North American Free Trade Agreement (NAFTA) has added an international dimension to significant aspects of U.S. employment law.
- Organized labor's slide from the political power it wielded at mid-century seems to be bottoming out and there is a resurgence of union militancy in some sectors of the economy.

- Judicial decisions are reshaping the application of laws governing job discrimination, affirmative action, and arbitration of labor disputes.
- President Clinton issued an executive order forbidding companies doing business with the government from permanently replacing striking employees.
- In the midst of national debate about preferences and quotas, the U.S. Supreme Court has signaled its intent to scrutinize affirmative action programs, which could affect job discrimination law profoundly.
- Trade conflict with Japan, China, and other Pacific Rim nations promises to affect the fortunes of U.S. labor unions for at least the remainder of the century.
- The Americans with Disabilities Act (ADA) touches many previously settled aspects of labor and employment law, including collective bargaining, workers' compensation, and unemployment compensation. Its effect on the workplace has yet to be fully realized.

In addition, you'll find valuable information about how to safely handle important issues such as:

- Workplace safety
- Employee theft and dishonesty
- Labor disputes, unions, and employee associations
- Successful "just cause" defenses in recent wrongful termination cases
- Immigration laws and alien rights
- Smokers' and nonsmokers' rights
- New auto emission laws
- Age discrimination
- Drug-free workplace
- Whistle blower protections
- Workers' compensation

Studded with examples, practice pointers, and cases that illustrate these and many more up-to-the-minute issues, the *Employment Law Answer Book, Third Edition* is the one professional reference source you need to answer your employment law questions. It will help you keep abreast of crucial aspects of labor and employment law, from the latest rulings on employee privacy rights (versus the employer's power to protect the company's inventory and intellectual property) to the best new strategies for handling labor litigation.

James O. Castagnera, JD, PhD
October 1995

How to Use This Book

Judicial mandates and legislative changes, such as the Family and Medical Leave Act and the Americans with Disabilities Act, have created the need for more careful recordkeeping, better employment policies and practices, and more sophisticated hiring and firing decisions. The *Employment Law Answer Book, Third Edition* provides comprehensive current information on employment law in an easy-to-use question-and-answer format. It is a quick, ready reference to help you identify problems and possible solutions. Because each organization's circumstances are unique, it is important to remember that these are general answers to common questions and are not intended to replace good legal advice on specific employment problems. Also, employers must be aware of the applicable local laws which vary from one state and city to another.

The *Employment Law Answer Book* uses simple, straightforward language and avoids technical jargon wherever possible. Numerous examples illustrate how different laws have been applied in specific cases. Citations are provided in brackets as research aids to those who wish to pursue particular subjects in greater detail. For additional assistance in locating related topics, there is an extensive system of cross-referencing to relevant material in other sections of the text.

Question Numbers: To make the *Employment Law Answer Book* easy to use, questions are numbered consecutively within each chapter (e.g., 2:1, 2:2, 2:3).

List of Questions: A list of every question in the *Third Edition* follows the Summary Table of Contents to help readers locate specific areas of immediate interest. Subheadings that correspond to chapter subheads organize the questions by topics within each chapter.

Tables of Cases and Codes: Every case cited throughout the cumulative supplement is listed alphabetically by both plaintiff and defendant in the first table following chapter 15 with reference to each question in which it is discussed. Specific Code Sections and state statutes and constitutions are also referenced to question numbers.

Index: The comprehensive index provides a further aid to locating specific information. All references in the index are to question numbers rather than page numbers.

Use of Abbreviations: Because of the breadth of subject area, a number of terms and statutory references are abbreviated throughout *Employment Law Answer Book*. Among the most common of these shorthand references are:

- Code—The Internal Revenue Code of 1986.
- ERISA—The Employee Retirement Income Security Act of 1974, as amended.
- IRS—The Internal Revenue Service.
- DOL—The U.S. Department of Labor.
- COBRA—The Consolidated Omnibus Budget Reconciliation Act of 1985.

About the Author

James O. Castagnera is a lawyer, writer, and teacher. He is currently Professor of Legal Methods at the Widener University School of Law in Wilmington, Delaware, and Adjunct Professor of Legal Studies at the Wharton School of the University of Pennsylvania. He formerly taught labor and emloyment law at the University of Texas in Austin. Mr. Castagnera is the author of five books on human resources law, three of them for Panel Publishers, and also writes a column on human resource and loss prevention issues for *Convenience Store Decisions Magazine.*

Mr. Castagnera holds a law degree with honors and a Ph.D. in Interdisciplinary Studies from Case Western Reserve University in Cleveland. For nearly ten years he was a senior associate with Saul, Ewing, Remick & Saul, a major Philadelphia law firm for which he still consults. He continues to counsel clients on matters involving human resource and intellectual property law. He is an arbitrator with the Philadelphia Court of Common Pleas and the American Arbitration Association, and a member of the American Bar Association's Committee on International Labor Law.

Summary Table of Contents

Table of Contents

Contents

List of Questions

xxv

Employment Contracts and Agreements

Oral Contracts

Written Contracts

Alternative Dispute Resolution

Arbitration

Peer Grievance Review

Covenants Not to Compete and Confidentiality Agreements

Other Employment Relationships

Chapter 3   Hiring and Evaluating Employees

The Hiring Process

Advertising and Recruiting

Applicant Evaluation

Assessing Honesty in Applicants and Employees

Employee Evaluation

Employee Health

Probationary Employees

Performance Evaluations

Discipline

Attendance

Work Rules

Disciplinary Programs and Procedures

Workplace Due Process

Employee Searches and Surveillance

Dishonest Employees

Types of Discrimination Prohibited by Title VII

Racial Discrimination

Discrimination Based on National Origin or Religion

Discrimination Based on Sex

Disability Discrimination

The Americans With Disabilities Act

AIDS in the Workplace

The ADA And Workers' Compensation

Chapter 5 Employee Personnel Files and the Employee's Right to Privacy

Personnel Files

Chapter 6   Security Issues

Employee Honesty and Safety

Chapter 7 Job Safety

OSHA

I

Emergency Planning and Right to Know Act

Smoking in the Workplace

AIDS

Drug Abuse

Minimum Wages

Work Periods

Overtime

Exemptions from FLSA

Compensation and Work Schedules

Withholding

ERISA

Required Insurance

Workers' Compensation Insurance

Chapter 9 Government Contractors

Security Clearances

Affirmative Action

Chapter 10 Public Employees

Collective Bargaining

Federal Employees

Constitutional and Civil Rights

Federal Employees

State Employees

Chapter 11 Labor Unions

Illegal Activities

Disputes and Decertification

Bankruptcies, Mergers, and Acquisitions

Unfair Labor Practices

Chapter 12   Immigration and Naturalization

Immigration Reform and Control Act of 1986

Chapter 13   Employment Termination

Prerequisites and Grounds for Termination

Wrongful Discharge

Plant Closings, Mass Layoffs, and WARN

Termination Interviews and Letters

Chapter 14 Worker Retraining, Quality, and Productivity

Employee Participation Programs

New Developments in Employee Compensation, Retraining, and Welfare Reform

Welfare

Chapter 15 Managing Labor and Employment Litigation

Litigation by Employees against Employers

Chapter 1

The Legal Framework

Unlike the laws of many nations, which developed in statutory form, English jurisprudence evolved from decisions made by judges, compiled and published for future generations. Known as the common law, this body of legal precedents held sway for centuries in Great Britain and its former colony, the United States. Even today, the modern law library's shelves are lined with volumes of U.S. Supreme Court, lower appellate court, and trial court rulings. But beginning with the New Deal of the 1930s, when Congress enacted the Fair Labor Standards Act [29 USC §§ 201–217], the Norris-LaGuardia Anti-Injunction Act [29 USC §§ 101–115], and the National Labor Relations, or Wagner, Act [29 USC §§ 151 *et seq*], labor law joined the area of substantive law increasingly controlled by federal statute.

The National Labor Relations Act was amended and enhanced by the Taft-Hartley Act [29 USC §§ 141 *et seq*] in 1947, and the Landrum-Griffin Act [29 USC §§ 153, 158–60, 164, 186, 187, and 401 *et seq*] in 1959. Then, as labor unions declined in strength and influence, and individual civil rights came to the fore in the 1960s, employment discrimination became the principal focus of congressional action. Title VII of the Civil Rights Act of 1964 contained equal employment opportunity guarantees. [42 USC §§ 2000e–2000e-17] The Age Discrimination in Employment Act [29 USC §§ 621–634] followed three years later.

Job safety was also a concern, especially since unions were less involved in the American workplace. The congressional response to what it perceived as an unacceptable number of on-the-job injuries and deaths was the Occupational Safety and Health Act of 1970. [29 USC §§ 553 and 651–678]

Most recently, the Americans with Disabilities Act [29 USC § 706 and various sections of Title 42 between §§ 12101 and 12213] has filled what many perceived as a gap in the federal antidiscrimination statutory scheme.

In short, while common law, including the evolving law of employment at will, remains a significant part of U.S. labor and employment law, federal and state statutes now have become the predominant influence in the American workplace.

Additionally, for perhaps the first time in American history, U.S. labor law and policy will be propelled in part by international treaty provisions. A labor agreement supplementing the North American Free Trade Agreement (NAFTA) requires the United States and its two North American trading partners to respond to complaints by one another involving the administration of their own internal labor laws to the extent they adversely affect NAFTA's provisions and purposes.

Q 1:1   What were the first antidiscrimination laws?

Shortly after the Civil War, Congress enacted laws to strengthen the Thirteenth and Fourteenth amendments, which outlawed slavery and guaranteed equal protection and due process of the law to all. Commonly called Sections 1981, 1983, 1985, and 1986 (of a particular Title of the U.S. Code of statutory laws), these post-Civil War laws afford individuals the right to sue for protection of certain of their civil rights as follows:

1. Section 1981 provides a cause of action for race discrimination only. However, the U.S. Supreme Court has expanded the statute's protection to include such groups as Arabs and Jews; that is, any group historically perceived to be a separate "race";

2. Section 1983 establishes a cause of action for deprivation "under color of state law" (i.e., this section protects Fourteenth Amendment due-process rights from any action by a state or municipality);

3. Section 1985 proscribes conspiratorial action depriving individuals of their rights, although its scope remains unsettled; and

4. Section 1986 creates a cause of action against individuals who are aware of Section 1985, but negligently fail to take action to prevent the wrongdoing.

The language of these laws is arcane and continues to pose interpretive problems for the federal courts.

Q 1:2   Do any antidiscrimination laws deal with employment?

Yes. Title VII of the Civil Rights Act of 1964 (Title VII) and the Age Discrimination in Employment Act (ADEA) deal with employment discrimination. Title VII makes it illegal for employers to discriminate in employment decisions (including those related to hiring, promoting, paying, terminating, and disciplining employees) on the basis of race, color, religion, national origin, and sex. Title VII also established the Equal Employment Opportunity Commission (EEOC) to help enforce its prohibition against discriminatory employment decisions. The EEOC provides victims of discrimination with a quick and inexpensive method of seeking redress, without obtaining a lawyer.

Q 1:3 What is the ADEA?

The ADEA prohibits employers from discriminating against employees over 40 years of age. Age is unique among the categories protected against discrimination under federal law in that it is the most universal. Consequently, Congress seems to have considered it inappropriate to include age under Title VII. Rather, the ADEA is closely tied in its rights and remedies to the Fair Labor Standards Act (FLSA).

Q 1:4 What are the differences between enforcement of Title VII and the ADEA?

Because the ADEA is related to the FLSA and not directly derived from Title VII, there are several important substantive and procedural differences between them. First, an individual filing a complaint with the EEOC under Title VII must obtain a 90-day "letter to sue" from the agency before taking the case to federal court; the ADEA complainant, however, must wait only 60 days after filing an age complaint with the EEOC before filing suit in federal court without the agency's permission. The discrimination victim filing under Title VII does not have a statute of limitations until the letter to sue is issued by the EEOC, which may be years after the initial filing of the complaint. The ADEA complainant, however, should be aware of the statute of limitations contained in the FLSA, which runs from the date of the discriminatory act (e.g., termination of employment), in spite of filing the EEOC complaint. The FLSA's procedures, including its statute of limitations, govern actions under ADEA.

Q 1:5 What antidiscrimination laws deal with handicapped individuals?

The Rehabilitation Act of 1973 (the Rehabilitation Act) prohibits employment discrimination based on a handicap against persons otherwise qualified to perform a job and applies to all federal contractors and anyone receiving federal financial assistance.

On July 26, 1990, President Bush signed the Americans with Disabilities Act (ADA) and ushered in the most sweeping antidiscrimination law enacted since the Civil Rights Act of 1964. Basically, the ADA expands the scope of the Rehabilitation Act to include most employers. The ADA became effective for employers with 25 or more employees on July 26, 1992; it took effect for employers with 15 to 24 employees on July 26, 1994. In addition, Title III of the ADA, concerning access to public accommodations, became effective January 26, 1992, for older facilities, and on January 26, 1993, for new construction.

Q 1:6   In what areas of employment does the ADA prohibit discrimination?

Discrimination against a qualified individual with a disability is prohibited in all parts of the employment process. The employment process specifically includes, but is not limited to, job application procedures, hiring, advancement, discharge, compensation, job training, recruitment and advertising, job assignments, job classifications, organizational structures, position descriptions, lines of progression, seniority lists, leaves of absence, sick leave, fringe benefits available by virtue of employment (whether or not administered by the employer), employer-sponsored activities (including social or recreational programs), and other terms, conditions, and privileges of employment.

Q 1:7   How will the ADA be enforced?

Title I of the ADA incorporates the powers, remedies, and procedures set forth in the Civil Rights Act of 1964. The EEOC has been designated as the enforcement agency for the ADA. The ADA provides that the powers and procedures available to persons discriminated against because of disability be the same as, and parallel to, those available to persons discriminated against because of race, color, religion, sex, or national origin. Additionally, the Civil Rights Act of 1991 provides that successful plaintiffs suing under the ADA may receive compensatory or punitive damages in some circumstances. For employers that have 25 or more employees, Title I became effective on July 26, 1992; for employers with 15 or more employees, the ADA became effective on July 26, 1994.

Statutory and Regulatory Scheme

Q 1:8   Are there other recent antidiscrimination laws?

Yes. In 1990 Congress passed and the president signed the Older Workers Benefits Protection Act (OWBPA), and a year later Congress passed and the president signed the Civil Rights Act of 1991. The OWBPA was passed in response to a Supreme Court decision that outraged many members of Congress and vocal segments of their constituencies. In *Public Employees Retirement System of Ohio v. Betts* [109 S Ct 2854 (1989)], the Supreme Court held that the ADEA did not forbid age discrimination in the area of employee benefits except in unusual circumstances.

The OWBPA amended the ADEA and expressly rejects the Supreme Court's controversial decision by defining "compensation, terms, conditions or privileges of employment" as including all employee benefits, even those provided under a bona fide employee benefit plan. Consequently, Section 4(a)(1) of the ADEA now forbids discrimination in employee benefits as well as in every other aspect of employment that is not protected by some specific exemption from coverage of the Act.

The law also codifies the concept of "equal benefit or equal cost" as part of the federal regulatory scheme for employee benefits. This concept was rejected by the Supreme Court in 1989 in the *Betts* decision. This principle, which was previously espoused in Department of Labor (DOL) and EEOC interpretive letters, states that a company must provide to its older workers benefits that are at least equal to those provided to younger workers, unless the company can prove that the cost of providing an equal benefit is higher for an older worker than for a younger one. The only exception to this equal benefit or equal cost rule is a voluntary early retirement incentive plan.

The Civil Rights Act of 1991 (CRA '91) was enacted for two major reasons: first, to overrule recent Supreme Court decisions viewed by Congress as unduly restricting employees' causes of action under Title VII, ADEA, and ADA, and second, to expand the range of damages available to victims of job discrimination. CRA '91 expressly overruled *Wards Cove Packing Co. v. Atonio* [490 US 642 (1989)], a Supreme Court decision that had made it almost impossible for plaintiffs to prove job discrimination based on statistical evidence. CRA '91 permits Title VII plaintiffs to demand jury trials and permits juries to award compensatory and punitive damages in addition to back wages.

CRA '91 also expands the rights of federal employees under federal antidiscrimination acts, and extends these statutes' jurisdiction to employees of Congress under a special set of procedures.

Also, private employers with 15 or more employees are subject to the federal Pregnancy Discrimination Act [42 USC § 2000e-2], which prohibits discriminatory treatment of pregnant women. Consequently, employers may not discharge an employee because of pregnancy or treat pregnancy-related disabilities differently from any other temporary disability. Employers should develop a neutral disability and sick-leave policy and make certain that the policy is administered so that it does not discriminate against pregnant women.

One of the most controversial and vexing issues involving CRA '91 has been whether Congress intended it to apply retroactively to cases in which (1) the allegedly illegal conduct occurred prior to the enactment of the statute; and (2) the suit (or discrimination charge before the EEOC) was filed before the effective date of the statute; or (3) a trial was held and the case sent up on appeal before the effective date. Neither the facts nor the law have helped courts in ruling on this issue, which can, of course, affect not only whether the plaintiff gets a jury but also the measure of damages and even some of the legal theories (such as disparate impact) that may be available in the case.

Congressional history has been of little help to the beleaguered courts in resolving the retroactivity question, because some members of Congress have commented that the act was not to be applied retroactively, while co-sponsor Edward M. Kennedy (D-Mass.) has insisted on the Senate floor that CRA '91 was in fact to be applied retroactively. Similarly, Supreme Court cases covering the retroactivity of federal statutes and regulations have traveled down two distinct lines of legal precedents, one favoring retroactivity in most instances, the other saying that retroactive application is the exception and not the rule. [For a fuller discussion of the retroactivity debate, see

Derewicz, "Is CRA '91 Retroactive?" 1 *Employment Law Update* 2 (1992)]

Under former President Bush, the federal executive branch sided with employers, which naturally prefer a nonretroactive statute. Both the U.S. Justice Department and the EEOC lined up with the majority of federal courts, which held against retroactive application of CRA '91. However, it came as no surprise that the Clinton administration moved to reverse that stance early in its term. Thus, a brief signed by the acting solicitor general, and submitted to the Supreme Court, argued:

1. CRA '91's plain language supports retroactivity (see Section 402 of the Act, which simply says that it becomes effective "upon enactment").

2. Congressional history, while confusing and ambiguous, does not clearly come out against retroactivity.

3. As CRA '91 is a remedial law, correcting what Congress considered several overly narrow or unduly harsh interpretations of Title VII and the ADEA, the law should be applied retroactively to provide the greatest amount of relief to victims of unlawful discrimination without regard to the timing of their having suffered discriminatory treatment.

[1993 *BNA Daily Labor Report* 82 (Apr 30, 1993) at 1]

Additionally, the EEOC, in April 1993, voted to rescind its own earlier position favoring only prospective application of the 1991 statute.

In the autumn of 1993, the U.S. Supreme Court heard oral argument in the case of *Landgraf v. USI Film Products.* [968 F 2d 427 (5th Cir 1992), *cert granted*, 113 S Ct 1250 (1993)] In this case, plaintiff Barbara Landgraf worked for USI at its production plant in Tyler, Texas. Landgraf worked the graveyard shift (11 P.M. to 7 A.M.). From September 1984 to January 1986 she was a materials handler operating a machine that produced several thousand plastic bags per shift. During her job tenure a co-worker allegedly subjected her to what the federal trial court described as "continuous and repeated inappropriate verbal comments and physical contact," severe enough to create an illegal "hostile work environment." Her difficulties with the co-worker were aggravated by the fact that the co-worker was the plant's union steward and the repairman who maintained her machine.

Landgraf testified that she reported the harassment to her supervisor but to no avail. She next took her complaints to the plant's personnel manager, who reportedly found four women to corroborate the plaintiff's story. Nonetheless, the offending employee got away with merely a reprimand, although the company's policy on sexual harassment called for "suspension or dismissal." He was technically transferred to another department, but under circumstances that ensured his continuing contact with the plaintiff. Additionally, while the personnel manager advised Landgraf of this action he also told her that she was very unpopular among her co-workers and, in fact, one of her "own worst enemies." After working just two more shifts, Landgraf resigned.

In a bench trial, a U.S. District Judge ruled that, although Landgraf was a victim of sexual harassment, she had not been constructively discharged and therefore had no remedy under Title VII. The U.S. Court of Appeals for the Fifth Circuit, which sits in New Orleans, agreed, and further ruled that the plaintiff had no retroactive right to a jury trial and compensatory or punitive damages under CRA '91. The Supreme Court granted certiorari expressly to resolve the issue of retroactivity, and ultimately decided against retroactivity in most circumstances. [Landgraf v USI Film Products, 114 S Ct 1483 (1994)]

The decision has become the high court's benchmark for retroactivity law involving not only job discrimination, but also all other new federal statutes. [See, for example, O'Melveny & Myers v Federal Deposit Insurance Corp, 114 S Ct 2048 (1994) and McKnight v General Motors Corp, 114 S Ct 1826 (1994)]

Enforcement Agencies

Q 1:9   What is the EEOC?

The EEOC is an independent federal agency charged by Congress with enforcing Title VII, the Equal Pay Act, and the ADEA. The agency operates out of regional offices in major cities across the country, such as Boston, Philadelphia, Atlanta, and Dallas. Intake officers assist employees in filing charges of discrimination, which are then investigated by other EEOC employees. EEOC investigators conduct fact-finding conferences between the parties, subpoena business records, and interview witnesses, all for the purpose of ascertaining whether or not there exists probable cause that federal law was violated by the respondent-employer. In meritorious cases, these investigators attempt to remedy the illegal discrimination through conciliation meetings. In unconciliated, meritorious cases, an EEOC lawyer may sue in federal court on behalf of the original employee.

Q 1:10   What is the DOL?

The DOL is a vast bureaucracy under the Secretary of Labor. DOL's duties span many areas of labor and employment law, including minimum wages and overtime (FLSA); the Occupational Health and Safety Act (OSHA); federal contract programs; labor racketeering; and labor reporting and disclosure (Labor-Management Reporting and Disclosure Act (LMRDA)). In addition, DOL performs a variety of other functions, including research under the auspices of the Bureau of Labor Statistics and the Women's Bureau.

Labor

Q 1:11   Are labor-management relations governed by federal law?

Yes. The Labor-Management Relations Act (sometimes referred to as the Taft-Hartley Act or the National Labor Relations Act (NLRA)) governs an employee's right to join (or not to join) a labor union, and defines what are unfair practices of employers and unions with respect to unionization, economic pressure (e.g., strikes and lockouts), and collective bargaining.

The LMRDA defines the standards to which unions are held as custodians of their member's funds, requires unions to file annual reports with the DOL, and contains a union member's bill of rights. Both the NLRA and the LMRDA are federal statutes that preempt all similar state and local laws. However, they do not apply to public employees or to very small, strictly intrastate companies, which often are covered by analogous state laws.

Wages and Hours

Q 1:12   What federal law covers wages?

The FLSA, enacted in 1938, is the leading federal law regulating minimum wage and overtime compensation. The FLSA also regulates child labor and equal pay for equal work.

Q 1:13   Which employees are covered by FLSA?

In general, three types of employees are covered by the FLSA:

1. Employees engaged in interstate commerce, including import and export;

2. Employees engaged in "the production" of goods for interstate commerce; and

3. Employees in an "enterprise engaged in" interstate commerce.

According to FLSA regulations, the production of goods includes "any closely related process or occupation directly essential" to the production of goods for interstate commerce. With respect to the third group covered by the FLSA, the so-called enterprise test has been very broadly interpreted by the courts, and thus there are few employers today whose employees are not covered by the FLSA.

Q 1:14   How broad is the FLSA's coverage?

The FLSA's coverage is very broad. Over the years, the FLSA has been amended and extended to include most federal employees, state and local government employees, employees of state and local hospitals and educational institutions, and private household domestic workers. If certain employees are not covered by FLSA, it is likely that they are covered by similar state laws that regulate minimum wage and overtime compensation.

Q 1:15   What is the Equal Pay Act?

The Equal Pay Act, an amendment to the FLSA, states that male and female employees who perform the same work for the same employer must receive the same rate of pay.

Q 1:16   Are there any exceptions to the rule that male and female employees receive equal pay for equal work?

There are several exceptions. An employer may pay one employee more than another for the same work based on greater productivity or seniority. Also, if a company has more than one facility and its operations are in different labor markets, wages may vary to reflect labor supply and demand.

Job Safety

Q 1:17   What law governs job safety?

The primary law governing on-the-job safety is OSHA, which was passed by Congress in 1970. Although OSHA has preemptive power when its rules and regulations enter an economic sector (e.g., manufacturing), states are free to pass legislation to fill any vacuums. Additionally, states are invited by Congress to adopt OSHA's standards and create agencies to act in its stead within their boundaries.

OSHA has two broad goals: (1) to assure safe and healthful working conditions for working men and women; and (2) to provide a framework for research, education, training, and information in the field of occupational safety and health.

Q 1:18   What does OSHA require of employers?

OSHA requires employers to furnish their workers with a workplace that is free from recognized hazards that cause, or are likely to cause, death or serious injury. Besides this general duty to furnish a workplace free from hazards, OSHA requires employers to meet various health and safety standards established for particular industries and situations, and to keep records of injuries, deaths, accidents, illnesses, and special hazards in their workplaces.

Q 1:19   What is the Drug-Free Workplace Act of 1988?

The Drug-Free Workplace Act of 1988 [PL No 100-690], which became effective on March 16, 1989, requires federal contractors and federal grant recipients to provide a drug-free workplace. Individuals are required to refrain from unlawful drug-related activities when performing the contract or conducting the grant activity. Federal contractors and federal grant recipients must certify to the contracting or granting agency that they will abide by the requirements of the Act.

Workers' Compensation

Q 1:20   What is workers' compensation insurance?

Workers' compensation insurance, developed at the beginning of this century, is intended to compensate employees for on-the-job injuries, and to provide income when such injuries prevent the employee from working either temporarily or permanently. Workers' compensation laws have been enacted by the states, and although there are differences in the requirements and administration of these laws from state to state, there are also many similarities. It is essential that an employer check the specific compensation law for the state in which the business is located.

Employee Benefits

Q 1:21   Is there a federal law covering pension and employee benefit plans?

Yes. In 1974 Congress enacted the Employee Retirement Income Security Act (ERISA). This comprehensive piece of federal legislation covers not only pension plans, but almost all other employee benefits plans as well.

ERISA imposes standards of conduct and responsibility on pension fund fiduciaries (that is, persons having authority or control over the management of pension fund assets). The law also requires that pension plan administrators disclose relevant financial information to employees and the government. It sets certain minimum standards that pension plans must meet in order to qualify for preferential tax treatment, and it provides legal remedies to employees and their beneficiaries for violations.

Q 1:22 Why was ERISA enacted?

ERISA was enacted in response to numerous instances of pension fund mismanagement and abuse. In some cases, retired employees had their pension benefits reduced or terminated because their pension plan had not been adequately funded or had been depleted through mismanagement. In other instances, employees retiring after 20 years of service were ineligible for their pension benefits because of complex and strict eligibility requirements. ERISA was intended to prevent such abuses and to protect the interests of employees and their beneficiaries.

Q 1:23 Which employers are subject to COBRA?

An employer of 20 or more persons on a typical business day that maintains a group health plan is required to provide continuation coverage. [IRC § 4980B(d)]

Under COBRA legislation, the definition of "employee" can include an independent contractor.

Other Federal Laws

Q 1:24 What are the requirements of the federal polygraph law?

The Employee Polygraph Protection Act of 1988 prevents most private employers from using lie detector tests to screen job applicants or to test current employees. An employer may use such a test only if it reasonably suspects an employee of involvement in a workplace theft or other incident that causes economic loss to the employer.

Q 1:25 What are the purposes of the Immigration Reform and Control Act of 1986?

The Immigration Reform and Control Act of 1986 (IRCA) has three main purposes: (1) to provide a solution for controlling illegal immigration to the United States; (2) to make limited changes in the system for legal immigration; and (3) to provide a controlled legalization program for undocumented aliens who entered the United States before 1982.

Q 1:26 How does IRCA control illegal immigration?

IRCA changed a 1952 federal law that allowed employers to hire illegal aliens without penalty. Under the 1986 law, employers are subject to civil and/or criminal penalties if they hire undocumented aliens or continue the employment of undocumented aliens. Congress believes that most undocumented aliens enter the country in order to find jobs. Thus, it has created a system whereby employers share the responsibility of controlling illegal immigration. An employer that fails to carry out this responsibility, which primarily involves demanding and reviewing suitable identification (e.g., birth certificate, social security card, and driver's license) from all new employees, will be penalized. The philosophy behind this approach is that the imposition of penalties for violating the Act will deter employers from hiring illegal aliens. The employers' reluctance to hire will, in turn, deter aliens from illegally entering the United States.

Q 1:27 Which employees are affected by IRCA?

IRCA applies only to unauthorized aliens hired after November 6, 1986. It does not apply to employees hired before that time.

Family and Medical Leave Act

Q 1:28   What are the major requirements of the Family and Medical Leave Act of 1993?

The Family and Medical Leave Act of 1993 imposes the obligation upon employers of 50 or more employees to provide eligible employees with as much as 12 weeks of unpaid leave in any particular 12-month period. An eligible employee is one who has worked for the employer for at least a year, and who, during the prior 12 months, logged in at least 1,250 hours on the job. Such an employee is entitled to unpaid leave in a 12-week lump, or under certain circumstances in intermittent increments, for his or her own serious illness or that of a parent, child, or spouse, or to care for a child, whether newly born or adopted.

The law applies to private employers as well as state and local government entities and the federal civil service. While the leave itself is unpaid, the employer must continue health insurance coverage throughout the employee's absence. Additionally, upon the employee's return, the employee must be reinstated to the same job or to a job comparable to the one he or she left with no loss of benefits (see chapter 8). The law took effect on August 4, 1993.

North American Free Trade Agreement

Q 1:29   Does NAFTA contain any labor and employment provisions?

NAFTA was supplemented by two side agreements—one on labor and the other on the environment—before it was approved by the U.S. Senate. The North American Agreement on Labor Cooperation calls for the establishment of arbitral panels empowered to consider accusations that may arise out of a "persistent pattern of failure by the [country] complained against to effectively enforce its occupational safety and health, child labor or minimum wage technical labor standards."

Should one of the three NAFTA partners—Mexico, the United States, or Canada—stand accused of such a violation and subsequently fail to agree on a plan recommended by the arbitrators to remedy the violation, then "monetary enforcement assessments" may be imposed. Any such assessments are to be paid into a fund intended to "improve or enhance labor law enforcement in the [country] complained against, consistent with its law."

And, should the offending country fail to pay the assessment into the fund, the supplemental agreement calls for the suspension of NAFTA's trade benefits until payment is made.

Q 1:30   How did the North American Agreement on Labor Cooperation come about?

NAFTA was signed on December 17, 1992, by the United States, Mexico, and Canada. The U.S. House of Representatives approved the agreement on November 17, 1993, and the Senate a short while thereafter. The agreement took effect on January 1, 1994.

To lay the groundwork for this agreement, the Bush administration had responded to vocal opposition by organized labor by entering into negotiation of an understanding with Mexico on key labor issues, including health and safety, formulation and enforcement of fair labor standards, conflict resolution, and labor statistics. The Clinton administration expanded on Bush's initial efforts, creating a three-nation commission to enforce labor standards and worker rights.

The net result is a 43-page side agreement known as the North American Agreement on Labor Cooperation. This supplemental agreement went into effect concurrent with NAFTA itself.

Q 1:31   What will be the short- and long-term impact of NAFTA upon American workers?

Some labor experts contend that NAFTA is having no short-term effects on the American workforce. For instance, one labor lawyer, Frank T. Mamat of Detroit, was quoted shortly before NAFTA's effective date as saying, "I don't think it will have any short-term impact. Based on talks I've had with several people in Congress, staff members and economists, I think that most people who are knowledgeable believe that, if anything, it will preserve American jobs." Executives of one of the big three auto companies had confided to Mamat, he said, that, if not for NAFTA, it would have moved a plant to Mexico in order to take advantage of the burgeoning market for cars in that country. With NAFTA's enactment, however, "it can do that from Michigan." [*CCH Labor Law Reports Insight,* No 376, Issue 86, Nov 1993, at 5]

In October 1994 *The Wall Street Journal* declared that both sides in the debate exaggerated. . . . ["So Far, So Good," *The Wall Street Journal,* Oct 28, 1994, at R1] Furthermore, the *Journal* reported that the news for Yankees was mostly good. "In the first six months of [1994], U.S. exports to Mexico rose 16 percent from a year earlier, to $24.5 billion." [Id] Additionally, said the newspaper, "Fears in the U.S. of huge job losses have subsided. There hasn't been any 'giant sucking sound.' In fact, it seems that Mexican blue-collar workers have far more to fear from efficient U.S. competitors than U.S. workers have to fear from low-wage Mexican ones." [Id]

But not all American workers survived NAFTA's first full year unscathed. A good measure of the negative impact upon American jobs is the incidence of petitions filed with the U.S. Department of Labor by employees claiming to have been displaced by NAFTA competition and seeking retraining plus extra unemployment benefits. [Narisetti, "Not Everybody Wins," *The Wall Street Journal,* Oct 28, 1994, at R10] As of October 1994, 93 such petitions from 20 states had been found to have merit by the DOL; these approved petitions involved some 10,000 workers. [Id]

Q 1:32   Does NAFTA's enactment place American workers' wage and work standards outside the jurisdiction of the NLRA, OSHA, and FLSA?

As a general proposition, treaties between the United States and foreign countries have the force of law, equivalent to statutes passed by the U.S. Congress and signed by the president. Thus, NAFTA in effect stands on a par within our federal legal scheme with the NLRA and other federal labor laws. This proposition also appears to apply to the supplemental "North American Agreement on Labor Cooperation."

> Key among the agreement's objectives is the commitment by the U.S., Canada and Mexico to improve working conditions and living standards; to promote enumerated labor principles; to strengthen labor-management cooperation throughout the trade area; and promote compliance with and effective enforcement

by each country of its labor laws. ["NAFTA's Labor Agreement: Does It Change the Outlook?", 376 *CCH Labor Law Reports Insight*, 86, Nov 1993, at 3]

The supplemental labor agreement was pushed by the U.S. government in an effort to assuage organized labor's fears of, and blunt its objections to, NAFTA. The concern, of course, was with Mexico, where wages are significantly lower than those enjoyed by American workers, and where the record on workplace health and safety has been less than exemplary.

However, it is possible to envision circumstances in which the United States might be the target of a complaint for failure to abide fully by the supplement's goals. For instance, labor-management cooperation, as it is viewed in some parts of the world, is virtually the antithesis of the confrontational approach to collective bargaining in this country. [See, for example, James O. Castagnera, "To Confront or Cooperate? The Lesson of Anthracite Coal," *Labor Law Journal*, Mar 1990 at 158; Datz, "Employee Participation Programs: Are They Lawful Under the National Labor Relations Act?" 8 *Labor Lawyer* 81 (1992); Castagnera and Cihon, "Employee Ownership and Participation Programs in the 1990s," *1993 Wiley Employment Law Update*, chap 9 (1993)]

Furthermore, should the U.S. electorate opt for a Reaganesque Republican president in 1996, the nation could revert to the benign regulatory neglect that characterized the DOL in the 1980s, so that the United States might find itself the target of a complaint from one or another of its North American trading partners. (See Charles J. Morris, "In Search of a National Labor Policy," statement to the Dunlop Commission, in *The Future of Worker-Management Relations*, Jan 1994; Q 11:10.) The 1994 mid-term election placed Republicans in charge of both houses of Congress for the first time in decades. Downsizing the federal bureaucracy to help pay for promised tax cuts and reduce the deficit may well include trimming the DOL.

Whichever party is in power, NAFTA commits each country to respect the others' constitutions and to respect one another's domestic legal standards.

Nevertheless, no participating nation may enforce the labor laws of any other. U.S. workers relocating to their companies' plants in one of the other two NAFTA trading partners may find themselves subject to foreign law in some respects. Such statutes as the CRA '91, however, ensure that U.S. citizens employed by U.S. corporations abroad retain some of the protections from job discrimination and the like that they enjoy in the states. (See Q 4:5.)

Q 1:33   How would a NAFTA trading partner prosecute a labor complaint against one of the other two participating nations?

The North American Agreement on Labor Cooperation calls for "consultations" between NAFTA nations at the federal level "in relation to [a participating country's] labor law, its administration, or labor market conditions in its territory." During any such consultations, every reasonable effort is supposed to be made to resolve the dispute, for example, a complaint the United States might have about wages and working conditions in a Mexican industry competing against its counterpart in America.

If such consultations fail to resolve the matter, either country can request the creation of an Evaluation Committee of Experts (ECE) to "analyze, in a nonadversarial manner, patterns of practice by each country in the enforcement of its occupational safety and health or other technical labor standards as they apply to the particular matter," provided the matter is trade related and subject to mutually recognized labor laws. An independent expert must determine these two threshold issues—trade relatedness and the existence of mutually recognized labor laws—before the ECE may be convened.

"Trade related" means that the dispute involves companies and workplaces providing goods or services that are traded between the two trading partners that have been engaging in the ministerial consultations, or that sell such goods or services in one of the two countries after importing them from the other.

"Mutually recognized labor laws" are all labor and employment laws of the nation subject to the trading partner's complaint. These statutes ostensibly provide rights, standards, and protections that, if the law were appropriately enforced, arguably would resolve the dispute.

The ECE will investigate and produce a report. After that, the consulting countries will have 60 days to make every reasonable attempt to resolve their differences by exploring together "whether there has been a persistent pattern of failure . . . to effectively enforce such standards in respect of the general subject matter addressed in the report."

If this second round of consultations fails to resolve the matter, a special session of the tri-national council overseeing NAFTA may meet within 20 days to convene a five-person arbitral panel to decide whether the country complained against has engaged in a "persistent pattern of failure . . . to effectively enforce its occupational safety and health, child labor or minimum wage technical labor standards in a matter that is trade-related and covered by mutually recognized labor laws."

If the arbitration panel decides this issue in the affirmative, the consulting countries will have 60 more days to work out a mutually acceptable solution. Failing that, the panel could establish a plan and a monetary enforcement assessment, which the offending nation must pay within 180 days. Failure to do so empowers the complaining country to suspend the benefits it would otherwise have to accord the offending nation under NAFTA.

Q 1:34   Will NAFTA's supplemental North American Agreement on Labor Cooperation protect U.S. jobs?

Proponents of NAFTA, including President Clinton, contend that the act will create jobs by (among other things) opening the vast Mexican market to more U.S. goods and services. The labor cooperation agreement is intended to prevent Mexico from becoming a safe haven for companies wishing to exploit low-wage workers while robbing better-paid Americans of their livelihoods. Many vocal critics doubt that the side agreement will succeed in doing this; thus, organized labor was not won over to NAFTA by the negotiation and signing of the supplemental labor accords.

In the words of one knowledgeable commentator, "I think [NAFTA] will have devastating effects on the high-wage, high-tech industries in Michigan that will also be generalized throughout the country. . . . In the long run . . . [A]s the Mexican infrastructure is built up to support the industries that will move to Mexico, that will encourage others to follow. . . . [A]s the Mexicans begin to adapt their educational system and develop a trained work force to perform this kind of work, the process will be accelerated." [376 *CCH Labor*

Law Reports Insight, 86, Nov 1993, at 4, quoting Bruce A. Miller, a Michigan attorney who represents numerous labor unions]

Since the labor accords accompanying NAFTA are aimed at preventing exploitative behavior, they are powerless to prevent such movement of jobs when the host nation (e.g., Mexico) is not only enforcing its own labor laws correctly, but also is improving the quality of its workforce to make it more competitive with respect to jobs at the higher end of the wage and skill scales. Thus, not laws and NAFTA side agreements, but hard-fought competitive efforts, are likely to be the only means of preserving U.S. jobs in the new international environment created by NAFTA.

Data on NAFTA's first year do not indicate any substantial U.S. job losses due to the treaty, but rather reflect increased U.S. exports to Mexico as a consequence of the accord. ["So Far, So Good," *The Wall Street Journal*, Oct 28, 1994, at R1]

Q 1:35   Are there the equivalent of unfair labor practices under NAFTA's side agreement on labor cooperation?

Yes. The U.S. DOL has established a special office to accept such charges. As this edition goes to press, two such charges of anti-union activity have been filed with the office by labor unions against Mexican subsidiaries of major U.S. corporations.

Automobile Emissions

Q 1:36   What is the Employer Trip Reduction Program?

The 1990 amendments to the federal Clean Air Act include a provision aimed at companies operating in areas that have failed to comply with clean air standards. Not surprisingly, these are mainly major metropolitan areas. Corporations employing more than 100 workers at a single location in such densely populated, overly polluted regions must take steps to reduce the number of single-occupancy autos arriving at the workplace during the morning rush hour. The overall goal of this amendment to the Clean Air Act is to reduce the so-called average vehicle occupancy (AVO) in the affected region by 25 percent during the three-year period beginning November 15, 1994.

On that date, large firms in regions subject to the rules were required to submit to their state's department of environmental protection or like agency (or the federal EPA in the absence of an analogous state agency) their plans for fulfilling their statutory obligations. Smaller firms must do likewise by mid-November 1995.

Q 1:37 How does a company formulate such a plan?

First, a multitude of environmental consultants are seeking clients that need to conform to the Act. Chances are your company has received literature from one or more of these consultants, though the literature may have been misdirected and thrown out because the recipient was ignorant of the Act's mandate. Second, numerous local and regional transit authorities have been promoting public transport as an alternative to driving to work. A call to one of these agencies likely will bring in substantial information. Finally, you can contact the federal EPA or an analogous state or municipal agency.

[See, e.g., "Employers Also Face Increased Liability Over Trip Reduction Plan," *PMA Legislative Bulletin*, 30, Apr 29, 1994, at 2]

Employers affected by this aspect of the Clean Air Act amendments should know that if they wish to make public transit vouchers available to their employees as an employment benefit, such vouchers can be obtained from regional transit authorities, are fully deductible by the company as an expense, and are a nontaxable benefit to the employees. For more information, call EPA's Employer Hotline at (800) 355-5000 and ask about "Transit-check."

Q 1:38 What liability risks does the Trip Reduction Program possibly entail?

As large employers gird themselves to implement plans submitted to environmental agencies last November, and smaller companies in affected regions prepare to submit their plans in mid-November 1995, insurers are warning that employer-sponsored car pooling of employees could expose such companies to liability risks in the event that pooling employees are involved in accidents, especially in company owned or leased autos.

[See, e.g., "Employers Also Face Increased Liability Over Trip Reduction Plan," *PMA Legislative Bulletin,* 30, Apr 20, 1994, at 2]

Commuting to and from work is not an activity covered by workers' compensation insurance in most states. Therefore, state personal injury law controls in such cases even with regard to the company's own employees.

Additionally, employers seeking to satisfy the mandates of the Trip Reduction Program or for other reasons have opted to encourage employees to work at home at least a part of the time have not found the employee response to be totally positive. Reports *The Wall Street Journal,* "Hoping for lower costs and higher productivity, more employers are slashing office space and handing employees laptop computers, portable phones and beepers, with orders to work instead from their cars, their homes or their customers' offices." [Shellenbarger, "Overwork, Low Morale Vex the Mobile Office," *The Wall Street Journal,* Aug 17, 1994, at B1]

"Employers are finding that, unlike the voluntary part-time telecommuting programs of the past, plans forcing whole divisions into mobile offices can cause morale problems—and may even provoke valued employees to quit." [Id] And experience has shown that morale problems on the job are quickly followed by litigation problems, whether they be workers' compensation claims, discrimination suits, wrongful discharge actions, or union election petitions to the National Labor Relations Board. The Trip Reduction Program will accelerate the "tidal wave" [id] of corporate shifting to home and mobile office environments; one outcome will be litigation by increasingly disgruntled employees who miss the cocoon of the traditional office environment.

Penalties for Noncompliance

Q 1:39   What are the penalties for noncompliance with employment and labor laws, and what remedies are available to employees?

Penalties and remedies vary from statute to statute and from state to state. A common thread running through a number of these laws (e.g., the NLRA, Title VII, the ADEA) is the "make whole" remedy. The successful employee-claimant or plaintiff is made whole by an award of lost wages and fringe benefits, plus reinstatement if he or she is wrongfully discharged. An applicant who is denied a job on a discriminatory basis may be awarded the position in the company for which he or she applied, or perhaps a comparable position. Under these laws, compensatory damages for pain and suffering (or humiliation) are not available. However, the Civil Rights Act of 1991 does make compensatory and punitive damages available to victims of discrimination under certain circumstances, up to set statutory limits.

Also, some of the older federal civil rights acts [42 USC §§ 1981–1985] apply to race discrimination in employment under certain limited circumstances. These laws, as well as some state antidiscrimination laws, allow juries to award compensation for humiliation, and, in fact, some reported cases reflect substantial (six- and, very occasionally, seven-figure) damage awards under these laws.

Punitive damages (i.e., damages for particularly egregious wrongdoing) are seldom permitted under federal or state labor law; but there are exceptions. For instance, violations of the FLSA and ADEA can be punished by a doubling of the back pay to which the successful claimant is entitled in instances where the employer had no good faith reason, such as advice of counsel, for its violation of the law.

Rather than award damages to successful claimants, some laws, such as OSHA, assess fines against offending employers. OSHA allows substantial fines for willful violations. By leveling a separate statutory maximum fine for each instance in which the OSHA regulations were violated (for instance, for each day or each individual machine), the Administration has been able to hit large corporate offenders (such as foundries accused of repeated lead or mercury poisoning violations) with so-called mega fines, sometimes totaling millions of dollars.

Chapter 2

The Employment Relationship

Chapter 1 discussed the statutory structure upon which U.S. employment law rests. This chapter explores the legal ramifications of creating, memorializing, and maintaining employment relationships.

Employment, the exchange of labor for wages, is among the most enduring and important of human relationships. In ancient and medieval times, it stood in contrast to other economic relationships such as slavery and serfdom. Today, the most legally significant contrast to the employer-employee relationship is the employer-independent contractor relationship. Significant tax and liability consequences flow from this distinction.

Another distinction—between the common-law doctrine of employment at will and an employment contract for a specified duration—has been a lively source of litigation in recent years. Through the evolution from the agrarian to the industrial to the post-industrial workplace, one's job has taken on greater and more complex significance. "Who one is" increasingly depends on "what one does." And few Americans could sustain their lifestyles without a job. These facts of modern life have led courts and legislators to trim and contain the once-dominant doctrine of employment at will. Likewise, the decline of labor unions, chronicled in chapter 11, has made protection of individual employee rights more important.

Q 2:1   What constitutes an employer-employee relationship?

Generally, an employer-employee relationship is created as a result of the terms of an agreement (contract), either oral or written, or is implied by the courts because of the parties' conduct.

When duration of the employer-employee relationship is not defined by either an oral or written agreement, that relationship is said to be one of "employment at will." Employment at will is a rule or presumption created by courts to govern the relationship between employer and employee when there is no other discernible standard. The courts created this doctrine so that, unless an employer and employee had agreed on employment for a fixed period, it could be terminated by either party without any advance notice or reason.

The trend over the past two decades has been away from collective security (i.e., labor unions) and toward a return to individual employment relationships. Legislators and courts have recognized this by giving employees, as individuals, more and more security and protection.

Although there is considerable concern among employees that their rights be clearly articulated in written contracts, they may still possess a contractual relationship with their employers even if it is not reduced to writing.

Q 2:2 Can employment agreements be modified?

Either written or oral contracts can be modified by mutual consent of the parties. In the absence of consent, the court will infer the terms of an oral agreement by examining the behavior of the employer and the employee (see Q 2:39). Thus, the court might examine evidence that indicates the employer's intent to make an employee handbook part of the employment relationship, with changes to the handbook having the effect of modifying the implied employment agreement.

When the agreement is embodied in a written contract, the contract often will contain a clause requiring every modification to take the form of an amendment to be signed by both parties.

Employment at Will

Creating the At-Will Relationship

Q 2:3 What is employment at will?

The term "employment at will" originated during the Industrial Revolution. In its pristine form, employment at will is a type of employer-employee relationship in which workers are free to sell their skills and labor to the highest bidder and move freely from job to job, and in which employers are free to hire and fire employees at will. Employment at will is the opposite of employment for a fixed term.

Q 2:4 What are the legal limits on the at-will relationship?

The at-will concept is limited by employment contracts, federal and state statutes, and public policy.

Employment contracts and statutory restrictions (such as laws covering illegal employment discrimination and the right to join a union) are covered in other sections of this chapter and this book. The focus here is on the court-created limits on what was originally a court-created concept. These common-law limits on employment at will can be divided into two categories:

1. Public policy limitations (see Q 2:13), and

2. The employer's duty of good faith and fair dealing (see Q 2:21).

Q 2:5   Are there any advantages in employment at will to employers?

Because statutes and courts have narrowed employers' unfettered rights to fire employees, employment at will is of limited value. Still, even today most employees are hired with no guarantee of any fixed term of employment. The wide use of this approach suggests that most employers still value their vestigial right to discharge their workers when they deem it appropriate.

Q 2:6   How does an employer know if employment at will is the right choice?

Whether or not the at-will form of employment relationship is right for an employer depends on a number of considerations, including:

- The relevant laws of the state(s) in which the business operates
- The bargaining power of the employees the employer needs to attract and keep
- The corporate philosophy
- The business cycle in the industry and the fluctuations in workforce needs that this cycle may dictate

Q 2:7   Does employment at will rule out written employment contracts?

No. Although many (perhaps most) employees work without written contracts, employment at will can be, and sometimes should be, combined with written terms of employment. For instance, since the courts in a growing number of states have taken over the role that weakened labor unions used to play in protecting workers' job security, many companies have reacted by having job applicants and current employees acknowledge their "at-will" status in writing. This can be done on the employment application or by having the new employee's signature on a receipt for a handbook that includes a notice of the employee's at-will status.

Q 2:8   How can an employer make it clear in a written contract that the employment relationship is at will?

The employer can include a statement in an employment contract that specifies all or most of the employee's terms and conditions of employment. The following is a typical, relatively simple, statement:

> I understand and agree that my employment is for no definite period and may, regardless of the date of payment of my wages and salary, be terminated at any time without prior notice.

Q 2:9   Can a written document alter the at-will relationship?

During 1992 and 1993, courts throughout the country continued to determine when an employee could use a written communication to overcome the presumption that the employment was at will.

The New Jersey Supreme Court ruled that a written statement of the plaintiff's annual salary did not give rise to a year-to-year employment contract. The court made it clear that in the absence of a contract to the contrary, employment is at will, no matter how the salary is laid out in the employee's original offer letter.

The high court expressly overruled an earlier New Jersey decision that had held that a salary expressed in annual terms created a year-to-year contract of employment. Additionally, the new decision definitively established that employment at will is still the rule in New Jersey, an issue that some other recent appellate-level opinions had cast in doubt. The court observed that it is "common business practice to state employee salary, bonus, vacation, sick days and other benefits in annual terms." Most employees fully realize that specifying their salaries "merely determines the method of payment and not the time of employment." [Bernard v IMI Systems Inc, 618 A 2d 338 (NJ 1992)]

A more significant decision, which will have an impact far beyond the court's jurisdiction (because of the effect it will have on employers' formation and administration of employee benefit plans), is a decision of the U.S. Court of Appeals for the Third Circuit, which sits in Philadelphia. The case involved an account executive for an airline who was terminated due to corporate restructuring. Four months prior to his termination, the executive received an employee handbook, which, among other things, outlined the severance benefits to be paid to a terminated employee. Also included in the handbook was the following disclaimer:

> Although it is our present intention to continue these pay practices, employment policies and benefits, we reserve the right, whether in an individual case or more generally, to alter, reduce or eliminate any pay practice, policy or benefit, in whole or in part, without notice.

On May 15, 1989, the executive was notified that his employment would be terminated on the 31st of the month. The severance benefits laid out in the termination letter were substantially less than those in the employee handbook. The executive sued the company, arguing that the severance policy in the employee handbook was a benefit plan covered by the Employee Retirement Income Security Act (ERISA) and not capable of modification by the subsequent termination letter.

The Third Circuit on appeal from the district (trial) court, where the executive had won his case, agreed that the severance policy in the handbook constituted an ERISA plan. But the appellate court diverged from the view of the district judge and held that nothing contained in ERISA forbids an employer from providing benefits on a case-by-case basis, as long as the employer's retained right to do so is explicitly set out in the plan. The court expressly held that with regard to the reserve clause quoted above:

> We find the arguments against enforcing the reservation unpersuasive. First, Air Jamaica's reservation is not an attempt, as the district court asserted, to avoid "award(ing) benefits in accord with this written promise." On the contrary, the reservation is part of the written promise and a limitation upon it. [Hamilton v Air Jamaica Ltd, 945 F 2d 74, 78 (3d Cir 1991)]

The *Air Jamaica* case should be heartening to all employers who worry whether their disclaimers and reservations of rights in employee handbooks will provide protection in court. Clearly, the Third Circuit's opinion will be widely relied upon, predictably even in distant state court cases, for the proposition that even the sweeping preemptive power of ERISA does not overcome the good old common-law, contract principle that an express condition in a contract, if adequately communicated to the other contracting party, will be enforced.

Beware. If the disclaimer or reservation of rights clause is buried in fine print, a court may rule that it was never adequately communicated to the employee who is to be held to its limitations (see Qs 2:33–2:38).

Q 2:10 Can a written disciplinary policy alter the at-will relationship?

An employer's written disciplinary policy has been held to have created an implied contract that employees will be fired only for good cause. An employee, therefore, may have the right to expect that, in light of his or her satisfactory performance evaluations and the absence of any rule violations, he or she will not be fired. [See also, Mitchell v Jewel Food Stores, 586 NE 2d 827 (Ill 1990)]

Terminating At-Will Employment

Public Policy

Q 2:11 What does "public policy" mean?

Public policy is a standard of law that is consistently applied throughout a particular state to such matters as public morals, health, safety, and welfare.

Most state courts will hold that a particular activity or type of behavior is sanctioned (or forbidden) by public policy only if there is some state or federal law dealing with the subject that is being ruled upon. For instance, the courts in almost all states recognize that jury duty is a significant civic responsibility. Therefore, a company that discharged an employee for missing work time to serve as a juror will be held to have violated a clear mandate of public policy.

Q 2:12 How do courts use public policy to restrict or punish at-will firings?

If a company's firing decision hinges on an action that is a violation of public policy, the court will rule that a wrongful discharge took place. For instance, federal law restricts the use of lie detectors, and the law in some states makes it a misdemeanor to require an employee or job applicant to take a polygraph examination as a condition of employment. Assume that an employer suspects one of its supervisors of stealing and tells that manager to take a lie detector test under circumstances that violate federal and/or state laws. If the manager refuses to take the test and is fired for his or her action, the manager can sue the company, asserting that he or she was wrongfully terminated.

On these facts, the court hearing the manager's case is likely to rule that, because the employer's demand appears to have violated a relevant law, the employer should not be allowed to fire the manager for refusing the demand. Therefore, even though technically, under the common law of at-will employment, the company could fire the manager for any reason or no reason, it could not fire the manager for the particular reason of refusing to take the polygraph test. In other words, a discharge for this reason violates a clear mandate of public policy.

Q 2:13 What are some of the most common public policy grounds used by employees to challenge their terminations?

Most wrongful discharge cases involve firings that were ruled illegal because they involved employer retaliation for the following employee actions:

- Absence from work to serve on a jury or as a witness in response to a subpoena [see, e.g., Shea v Rockland, 810 F 2d 27 (2d Cir 1987); Wiskotoni v Michigan National Bank, 716 F 2d 378 (6th Cir 1983); US v Adamita, 3 BNA IER Cases 1770 (SDNY 1988)]

- Filing a claim for workers' compensation [see, e.g., Ford v Blue Cross & Blue Shield of Conn, 216 Conn 40, 578 A 2d 1054 (1990); Twilley v Daubert Coated Products Inc, 536 So 2d 1364 (Ala 1988); Ryherd v General Cable Co, 504 NE 2d 745 (Ill 1986)]

- Refusing to violate a law; for example, by "doctoring" the company's books, or neglecting to report an accident or health code violation to the proper government agency, or whistle-blowing [see, e.g., Schlear v Fiber Materials Co, 574 A 2d 876 (Maine 1990); Wagner v Globe, 722 P 2d 250 (Ariz 1986); Armstrong v American Colloid Co, 721 P 2d 1069 (Wyo 1986)]

However, wrongful discharge can also occur in other instances. In an extreme example of a ruling on public policy, a plaintiff successfully argued that she was fired for refusing to participate in an activity that was tantamount to indecent exposure. [Wagenseller v Scottsdale Memorial Hospital, 710 P 2d 1025 (Ariz 1985)]

Q 2:14 What are the most recent developments in common law with respect to the public policy exception to employment at will?

At last count, only five of the 50 states had rejected a common-law cause of action based upon the public policy exception to employment at will: Delaware, Florida, Georgia, Louisiana, and New York. A handful of other jurisdictions—Maine, Mississippi, Rhode Island—have no definitive, reported decisions from their appellate courts on the question. [BNA, *Individual Employee Rights Manual* at 505:51505:52, July 1992]

Even in these few remaining "holdout" jurisdictions, either the legislature has created express statutory prohibitions against retaliation for the exercise of legal rights (for instance, Florida's voting, jury duty, and whistleblowing statutes contain such express protection for employees exercising those civic rights and duties), or the federal courts in those states have taken the lead in developing a public policy exception to at-will employment. [See, e.g., Kovalesky v AMC Associated Merchandising Corp, 551 F Supp 544 (SDNY 1982)]

Indeed, Georgia and Louisiana appear to be the last two states where public policy seems to have been given no place in the common law of wrongful discharge. Georgia's courts have refused to recognize a public policy exception to the otherwise at-will employment relationship in the following situations:

An employee claimed he was fired just as he was about to uncover criminal activities perpetrated by his supervisor. [Goodroe v Georgia Power Co, 251 SE 2d 51 (Ga Ct App 1978)];

The plaintiff said he was fired by an officer of the defendant corporation as part of the corporation's effort to cover up that officer's illegal activities. [Taylor v Foremost-McKessin Inc, 655 F 2d 1029 (5th Cir 1981)];

The plaintiff-employee claimed to have been fired in retaliation for filing a civil suit against the employer. [Burke v Georgia Power Co, 115 BNA LRRM 4303 (SD Ga 1983)].

Louisiana has always been unique among the jurisdictions contributing to the development of American common law in that it is the only state with a tradition of French, i.e., civil law. Common (court-made, case-by-case) law, as opposed to civil law (based almost entirely upon statute), was a late entrant into Louisiana jurisprudence. Perhaps Louisiana's development along this different path also affected the attitude of its parish and appellate courts, leading to the rejection of a common-law exception to employment at will; under the French approach, such employee protections traditionally should emanate from appropriately passed statutes, not from court decisions, in the first instance.

Whatever the explanation, Louisiana remains recalcitrant toward introduction of a public policy tort action for wrongful discharge. Thus, for example, in *Gil v. Metal Service Corp.* [412 So 2d 706 (La Ct App 1982)], plaintiff's claim to have been discharged for refusing to participate in an illegal act was held to be "appealing . . . (but) not that of a 'whistleblower' who may possibly be protected by constitutional provisions of free speech."

Perhaps the most interesting example of a jurisdiction that has reflected tension between the decisions of the state appellate courts and the state's federal courts is the Commonwealth of Pennsylvania. In *Geary v. United States Steel Corp.* [319 A 2d 174 (Pa 1974)], the commonwealth's highest court started a controversy, while affirming the lower court's dismissal of Geary's case, by observing in passing:

> It may be granted that there are areas of an employee's life in which his employer has no legitimate interest. An intrusion into one of these areas by virtue of the employer's power of discharge might plausibly give rise to a cause of action, particularly where some recognized facet of public policy is threatened.

This bit of dicta (that is, commentary that isn't part of the court's actual decision, and therefore isn't precedent, but that can be persuasive), led the lower appellate court, as well as Pennsylvania's federal courts, to speculate upon what would constitute a clear mandate of public policy capable of supporting this cause of action. [See, e.g., Novosel v Nationwide Insurance Co, 721 F 2d 894 (3d Cir 1983) (insurance agent could not legally be fired for refusing to testify before the Pennsylvania legislature in favor of his employer's position concerning a new no-fault auto insurance bill)] In general, the Pennsylvania Superior Court's decisions tended to take a very narrow view of the public policy limitation upon at-will employment, while the federal courts tended to read the *Geary* dicta more liberally.

Since 1989, the Pennsylvania Supreme Court took two opportunities to review the development of wrongful discharge law in its jurisdiction, and in the process to criticize its federal counterparts for their too-liberal reading of the *Geary* opinion. [Clay v Advanced Computer Applications Inc, 559 A 2d 917 (Pa 1989); Paul v Lankenau Hospital, 569 A 2d 346 (Pa 1990)]

Nevertheless, in a highly publicized and closely watched case, the U.S. Court of Appeals for the Third Circuit in Philadelphia recently reviewed the Pennsylvania Supreme Court's *Clay* and *Paul* decisions and concluded that a plaintiff claiming to have been fired for refusing to submit to a random drug test had enunciated a valid public policy basis for her wrongful discharge action. [Borse v Piece Goods Shop Inc, 963 F 2d 611 (3d Cir 1991)] The outcome of *Borse* will be worth watching because of the employer drug testing issue (see chapter 7) and the failure of the Americans with Disabilities Act to provide protection for current drug abusers (see chapter 4).

The U.S. Court of Appeals for the Third Circuit itself has been at pains to limit its *Borse* decision to the very sympathetic facts of that particular plaintiff's case. For example, a plaintiff who tried to use *Borse* to bootstrap himself past his ex-employer's summary judgment motion and get his ostensible wrongful discharge case was turned back by the appellate court late in 1993. William Clark, chief financial officer of Modern Group Ltd., charged nine officers of Modern with a total of nearly $30,000 in additional income for tax year 1990 based on what Clark said was their excessive reimbursement by the company for the use of company cars. Since these officers incurred the expenses while driving company cars, the plaintiff took the position that the reimbursements were fully taxable as personal income.

When these officers objected to his issuance of IRS W2 forms reflecting the additional taxable income, Clark had refused to budge, despite the fact that his reading of the Internal Revenue regulations was open to debate. The company reversed his decision and fired him. Distinguishing its *Borse* decision, the Third Circuit said, "Clark's case is different. It does not involve any public policy expressed in the common law of Pennsylvania, or otherwise, that could be analogous to the policy in favor of an individual right to privacy which informed our decision in *Borse*. Moreover, we do not think that *Borse* should be extended to create a public policy exception to Pennsylvania's employment-at-will doctrine which would prevent private employers from discharging employees who persist in opposition to company policy based on the employee's own interpretation of ambiguous [laws]." [Clark v Modern Group Ltd, 9 F 3d 321 (3d Cir 1993)]

Meanwhile, some states are pursuing the statutory route to similar employee protections, primarily through so-called lifestyle laws. Among them is New York with its prior history of resistance to the judicial enactment of a public policy exception to at-will employment.

Q 2:15   What are lifestyle protection statutes?

Lifestyle is an ambiguous term that might be loosely defined as:

the way a person conducts his or her private life. . . .

The mission of this legislation is similar to the mission of laws to prohibit religious discrimination . . . and is being pursued in a growing number of states in four principal aspects of private life: (1) marital status, (2) sexual orientation, (3) privacy itself, and (4) use of lawful products. ["State Labor Law Developments," *The Labor Lawyer*, 9, 3, Summer 1993, at 269]

Twenty-nine states have adopted such statutes since 1989. The majority of these laws protect smokers' off-the-job-site enjoyment of tobacco products. But of all such state statutes currently in force New York's lifestyle law enjoyed by far the greatest notoriety in 1994. The Empire State's 1993 statute protects employees from retaliation for legal recreational activities conducted away from work. The new law was not long in effect when the first test case arose involving one of this nation's largest and best-known retail chains.

In *Allen v. Wal-Mart Stores Inc.* [93-CV-0685, FJS-DNH (NDNY)], two Johnstown Wal-Mart store employees—Laurel Allen and Samuel Johnson—are challenging the company's right to fire them pursuant to a corporate "fraternization" policy. The policy, as interpreted by company officials, forbade Allen, who was married but separated from her husband, from dating co-worker Johnson. Soon after Allen and Johnson were fired and had filed their $2 million suit in federal district court, the state's attorney general weighed in on their side with a suit of his own in New York state court. [State of New York v Wal-Mart Stores Inc, 80737/93 (Supreme Ct, Fulton County, NY)]

The suits seem to raise some interesting issues. For example, the New York law only protects *legal* recreational activities. Reportedly, plaintiff Allen was still married, albeit separated from her husband. If her relationship to Johnson included a sexual side, was that adultery? If so, then the pair arguably may have violated a little-enforced, but still valid, New York criminal statute. Can such a technical violation of what admittedly must be an arcane act defeat their cause of action?

Perhaps more to the point, are there public policy grounds for calling these so-called lifestyle laws into question? For instance, six states explicitly protect employees' right to consume alcohol and tobacco before and after their working hours. "At what point, employers ask, does alcohol use off the job increase the potential for workplace injury or violence, and when might a seemingly innocent office romance blossom into a jobsite domestic dispute or provoke a claim of sexual harassment after the relationship sours?" [Randall Samborn, "Love Becomes a Labor Law Issue," *The National Law Journal*, Feb 14, 1994, at 33]

Along with New York, Colorado and North Dakota go the farthest in broadly protecting all legal off-the-job behavior, according to the American Civil Liberties Union's National Task Force on Civil Liberties in the Workplace. Employers' fears that outside activities will spill over into the work environment are not specious. One of Wal-Mart's contentions is that the Allen-Johnson romance affected their job performance; whether this is a post-termination concoction or a genuine basis for discharging them remains for a jury to decide. In 1993 the author defended a client before the Pennsylvania Human Relations Commission in a sex discrimination case stemming from the complainant's termination after her husband appeared at the company's office armed and seeking one of his wife's co-workers, whom he believed was having a relationship with her. These are but

two obvious examples of the predictable inability of people to com-
partmentalize their lives to the extent that employers need not be
concerned about their employees' off-duty activities. The latter example also underlines the fact that lifestyle laws are often treated as
part of the state's antidiscrimination statutory scheme. ["Employees'
Private Lifestyles Getting Protection from State Laws," *1994 Daily
Labor Report* 151 (Aug 9, 1994) at d20]

Add to this the reality that many employers today bear the brunt
of the health insurance burden, and one can appreciate some companies' concerns for employees' use of alcohol and tobacco off, as
well as on, the job. "Coupled with such remedial legislation as the
Americans with Disabilities Act . . . which appears to protect practic-
ing alcoholics who are otherwise fit to perform job tasks . . . the state
initiatives further abridge the power of employers to gather and
record applicant or employee information previously deemed vital to
employee selection and performance management." ["State Labor
Law Developments," *supra,* at 271]

Some commentators have gone so far as to suggest that these state
lifestyle laws, at least the most broadly written ones, may conflict
with such superseding federal legislation as the Omnibus Transportation Employee Testing Act of 1991, which mandates random drug
and alcohol testing of employees in "safety sensitive" jobs operating
airplanes, trains, and trucks. [Id] According to Chicago attorney Burr
E. Anderson in a speech to the American Bar Association's Labor and
Employment Section in August 1994:

> Lifestyle-protection laws can come into conflict with other
> laws. . . . An employer's attempt to avoid sexual harassment by
> prohibiting dating of co-workers can interfere with an em-
> ployee's off-duty personal life. Also, an employer's investigation
> of sexual harassment claims can lead into inquiries about an
> employee's "off-campus" activities and off-duty behavior. Laws
> that mandate employers to conduct investigations, such as
> federally required random alcohol testing of transportation
> employees and state-mandated background checks of child-care
> workers, can lead to intrusion into employees' private, off-duty
> activities. . . . The Department of Transportation's alcohol-test-
> ing regulations use a standard that is lower than most states'
> intoxication levels. . . . A positive test result could reflect an
> employee's off-duty legal use of alcohol. The Occupational
> Safety and Health Administration's efforts to protect against

workplace violence could result in an employer probing an employee's background for potential violence . . . ["Employees' Private Lifestyles Getting Protection from State Laws," *1994 BNA Daily Labor Report* 151 (Aug 9, 1994) at 20]

Finally, these lifestyle laws may limit "some of the deep background investigation employers undertake to avoid liability under the common law theories of negligent hire and negligent retention." [Id] On the other hand, "People have to, in order to maintain any sense of mental balance or integrity, be able to have a sphere in their life where they're not 'on'," according to one commentator on employee privacy rights. [Samborn, *supra*] The issue of employee privacy is one in which a delicate balance between competing interests may have to be calculated carefully on a case-by-case basis. Lifestyle laws will be major factors in this calculus.

Q 2:16   What are "whistleblower" laws?

Both federal and state legislatures have restricted the traditional employment-at-will rule where public health, safety, or ethics in government is involved. The legislation is intended to provide protection for employees who report their employer's statutory violations to appropriate government agencies or authorities. Whistleblower protection is generally limited to good-faith reports of suspected violations.

Q 2:17   What are the provisions of federal whistleblower laws?

A number of federal statutes that protect civil service employees prohibit the government from taking any action against an employee who discloses information he or she reasonably believes reveals a violation of law, mismanagement, waste of funds, abuse of authority, or a substantial and specific failure to protect public safety and health. On April 10, 1989, the Whistleblower Protection Act of 1989 was enacted. [5 USC §§ 7502, 7512, 7521, 7542, 7701, 7703] The Act is designed to protect federal employees from reprisals resulting from whistleblowing on waste, fraud, and unnecessary government expenditures. The Act establishes a Special Counsel's office to act in the interests of these employees. Other federal laws provide whistle-

blower protection to employees in certain private sectors, such as the
nuclear energy industry.

Q 2:18 Can a whistleblower win punitive damages in a lawsuit alleging employer retaliation?

Yes. Early in 1991, the Second Circuit Court of Appeals ruled that
a plaintiff demoted by the New York State Department of Education
after reporting alleged financial wrongdoing was entitled to keep the
punitive damages awarded by a jury. [Vasbrinder v Ambach, 926 F
2d 1333 (1991)]

Punitive damages are awarded on top of compensatory (i.e.,
actual) damages when jurors feel a defendant must be punished for
particularly egregious conduct. In *Vasbrinder*, the plaintiff claimed
his supervisors demoted him after he contacted the FBI about his
suspicions of wrongdoing in a federally funded program overseen by
the Department's Office of Vocational Rehabilitation. According to
the Second Circuit, the trial judge had correctly instructed the jury
that they could award punitive damages if the "defendant's conduct
is shown to be motivated by evil motive or intent, or when it involves
reckless or callous indifference to the federally protected rights of
others." [See 1991 *BNA Daily Labor Report* 51 (Mar 15, 1991) at A-5]

Q 2:19 What must an employee show to prevail in a claim of wrongful discharge under the federal whistleblower laws?

The employee must establish that the following events occurred:

- A protected disclosure was made
- The accused official knew of the disclosure
- Retaliation resulted
- There was a connection between the retaliation and the employee's discharge

Q 2:20 Do the federal whistleblower laws preempt state law claims?

No. In June 1989, the U.S. Supreme Court unanimously held that
Section 210 of the Energy Reorganization Act—the Act's whistle-

blower provision—does not preempt a state law claim of intentional infliction of emotional distress by a worker in the nuclear power industry. [McMonagle v Northeast Women's Center, 493 US 901 (1989)] Two lower courts had previously dismissed the lawsuit of a former General Electric employee who claimed she had been transferred, harassed, and, finally, fired because of her complaint to the Nuclear Regulatory Commission about alleged inadequate clean-up efforts at a nuclear fuel processing plant in Wilmington, North Carolina. In a unanimous decision, Justice Blackmun stated that Congress never intended to preempt all state law remedies when it enacted nuclear safety regulations. The Court held that there was no irreconcilable conflict between Section 210 and a state-law tort claim for harassment.

Good Faith and Fair Dealing

Q 2:21 What is meant by "good faith and fair dealing" in the context of the employer-employee relationship?

"Good faith and fair dealing" is a covenant between employers and their employees, implied by the court whether or not it is actually embodied in an employment contract. It is more easily defined in its breach than in its observance. When an employee's discharge is improperly motivated, as when the employer's purpose is to prevent a salesperson's entitlement to commissions (a common example), the covenant is considered breached. It is the basis for examining the reasons for an employee's dismissal, and for asking whether those reasons show bad faith rather than genuine dissatisfaction with an employee's job performance.

While many courts will punish an employer (through money damages payable to the employee) for violating a clear mandate of public policy in firing that employee, only a few state court systems have so far imposed a duty of good faith and fair dealing on employers. Among those states are Alaska, California, Connecticut, Massachusetts, Montana, and New Hampshire. The courts of a somewhat larger number of states have refused to use an implied covenant of good faith and fair dealing to limit the employment-at-will rule: Arizona, Arkansas, District of Columbia, Hawaii, Kansas, Maryland, New York, Pennsylvania, South Carolina, Tennessee, and Wisconsin.

In many of the remaining states, use of the covenant remains an open issue.

Q 2:22 Are there any limits to the implied covenant of good faith and fair dealing?

Yes. If a company is doing business in one of those states that imposes a duty of good faith and fair dealing on the at-will employment relationship, under the concepts of good faith and fair dealing and public policy, an employee must have been fired for an *inadequate* reason, and not merely because the employer failed to have a *good* reason for the firing. However, from a practical standpoint, if an employer is accused of discharging an employee for a bad reason, the jury is likely to believe the employee, unless the employer can articulate a good reason for the discharge.

Q 2:23 What are some examples of an employer's failure to deal with an employee fairly and in good faith?

The facts of the following two cases illustrate how the implied covenant of good faith and fair dealing was violated. First, in *Khanna v. Microdata Corporation* [170 Cal App 3d 250, 215, Cal Rptr 860 (1985)], a salesman sued his company for commissions that he felt were wrongfully being denied him. On the day his trial started, the company fired him. The court found that the salesman's discharge was unfair and in bad faith, and was intended to punish him for filing his suit. The court rejected the company's argument that the reason the salesman was fired was that the lawsuit was disruptive to operations, since the salesman continued to exceed his sales goals. Additionally, by firing him, the company was able to withhold even more commissions.

In *Gates v. Life of Montana Insurance Company* [638 P 2d 1063 (Mont 1982)], a cashier was called into her boss's office and charged with carelessness, incompetency, and insubordination, and told to resign or she would be fired. The court ruled that a jury should be allowed to decide whether there was a breach of the implied covenant of good faith and fair dealing, because she was discharged without warning and without an opportunity to state her side of the story.

Q 2:24 Have any states joined the ranks of those that recognize an implied covenant of good faith and fair dealing in employment relationships?

A notable recruit to the minority of jurisdictions (currently 14 states) that impose an implied covenant of good faith and fair dealing upon all employment relationships is Delaware. In *Merrill v. Crothall American Inc.* [606 A 2d 96 (Del 1992)], the plaintiff answered the defendant's ad for a temporary employee to help develop a new computer program for the company. At the job interview, he was subjected to a round of interviews that culminated in the company offering him the opportunity to manage plant operations at a Crothall-American client's facility in New York. Merrill testified he was told the job was "permanent." However, little more than three months after he had quit his previous job and relocated to New York City, he was fired for poor performance. He later learned, according to the affidavit of another of defendant's employees, that Crothall had interviewed his replacement just a few weeks after Merrill had moved into the position and that "Dick Merrill was hired (merely) to fulfill the contract (with the New York-based client) . . . until someone else could be hired." On these facts, the Delaware Supreme Court embraced the concept of good faith and fair dealing and held:

> In the absence of statutory or collective bargaining restrictions, the parties to an employment agreement are free to pursue their separate economic goals. . . . [W]e believe, however, that holding an employer to a requirement of good faith when making employment contracts represents a minimal, and wholly justifiable, interference in the management of its business.

In 1994 Wyoming joined the ranks of states imposing good faith and fair dealing upon the employment relationship. The Wyoming Supreme Court even went a step farther and joined the still smaller minority of jurisdictions that permit the recovery of tort, rather than just contract, damages for an employer's breach of the implied covenant of good faith and fair dealing. This means that compensatory, and perhaps even punitive or punishment damages (rarely allowed in straightforward contract cases) will be available to some plaintiffs under the Wyoming high court's ruling. However, the justices were careful to narrow this portion of their opinion, saying:

> A tort, however, requires the presence of a duty created by law, not merely a duty created by contract; and, although a duty of good faith and fair dealing is created by law in all cases, it is only in rare and exceptional cases that the duty is of such a nature as to give rise to tort liability. [Wilder v Cody County Chamber of Commerce, 868 P2d 211, (1994) Wyo LEXIS 9, 9 BNA IER Cases 225, 127 Lab Cases (CCH) P57, 634 (1994)]

The difficulty inherent in the implied covenant of good faith and fair dealing is that while most states require the plaintiff to point to some "clear mandate of public policy" to support a cause of action for wrongful discharge, good faith and fair dealing is (in the eyes of some critics) whatever the judge or appellate court panel believes it to be, based upon those judges' biases and political philosophies. Perhaps this explains why Delaware and Wyoming are only the thirteenth and fourteenth states to embrace this broad limitation upon the doctrine of employment at will.

A number of other states have used statutory enactments to restrict application of the implied covenant of good faith and fair dealing in employment cases. For example, in a series of decisions last year the Supreme Court of Montana held that employee-plaintiffs are limited to the more narrow cause of action stated in that state's relatively new Wrongful Discharge from Employment Act. [Sullivan v Sisters of Charity of Providence of Montana, 1994 Mont LEXIS 267, 51 Mont St Rep 1193 (1994); Boreen v Christensen, 1994 Mont LEXIS 228, 51 Mont St Rep 1014 (1994); Guertin v Moody's Market, 874 P 2d 710, 1994 Mont LEXIS 101, 51 Mont St Rep 407, (1994)]

In Alaska, the supreme court held that a plaintiff's good faith and fair dealing suit, charging his employer with firing him because he reported possible misuse of a trust fund, was preempted by ERISA. [Andrews v Alaska Operating Engineers-Employers Training Trust Fund, 871 P 2d 1142, 1994 Alas LEXIS 29 (1994)]

Q 2:25 What general principles do good faith and fair dealing cases suggest for the at-will employment relationship?

First, the covenant is *implied* by the court. This means that the employer and employee do not have to agree that their at-will employment relationship includes good faith and fair dealing. Instead, the court *imposes* this condition on the employer. Second, a breach of this covenant to deal fairly and in good faith can occur based on either the *why* or the *how* of the discharge. Third, since this exception to the at-will employment rule does not require the court to rely on some clear mandate of public policy (such as a statute), a judge is free to search in almost any area of social customs, standards, and mores to support a decision against the employer. Perhaps this is why so few state courts have as yet adopted this exception to employment at will.

Defending Wrongful Discharge Suits

Q 2:26 How can an employer defend a public policy lawsuit?

Using the example of the polygraph test (Q 2:12), two things should be noted. First, if the company could prove that it fired the manager not because he refused to take an illegal polygraph test, but because the security department's investigation indicated that the manager really was a thief, the public policy limitation would not apply. Second, if the manager had offered to take a lie detector test to clear his name, the public policy problem probably would not have come into play. However, if the illegal demand was made, the employee could sue for wrongful discharge, regardless of whether the state attorney general prosecuted the employer on the criminal offense.

The Future of At-Will Employment

Q 2:27 Does employment at will survive today?

Although the traditional concept of employment at will has been the target of ever-increasing restrictions over the past 20 years, the strongest indication of the viability of the doctrine comes from the National Conference of Commissioners on Uniform State Laws, the prestigious group that drafts and supports uniform acts across the entire spectrum of U.S. law and jurisprudence. This group has drafted a Uniform Employment Termination Act (the Uniform Act), which would permit employers to discharge employees at will, provided there is an individually executed employment agreement that guarantees a minimum schedule of graduated severance payments. If this law were violated by a wrongful discharge, the employee suing under it could get back pay and attorney fees but not compensatory damages (e.g., pain and suffering) or punitive damages. The Uniform Act, if adopted by a state as written, would also disallow "add-on" counts in a wrongful discharge action for such claims as defamation and intentional infliction of emotional distress. Although the proposed Uniform Act does bring severance pay into play, it is, on balance, a conservative measure that would benefit businesses in many states, unlike current, court-made law, which may be much more pro-employee.

In addition, a number of states recently have begun to buck the trend of broadening an employee's opportunity to bring a successful wrongful discharge lawsuit, which began in California and Massachusetts. Notably, the Pennsylvania Supreme Court issued a ringing reaffirmation of employment at will in *Paul v. Lankenau Hospital.* [569 A 2d 346 (1990)] The court reversed a jury's award of more than $400,000 to Dr. Paul, who claimed he was fired for taking property from the hospital after having been given permission to do so. The plaintiff had successfully argued at trial that after allegedly giving him permission to remove the equipment, the defendant-hospital was estopped from firing him since he had relied on the responsible employee's word that he could have the equipment. The Pennsylvania high court reasoned that, as an at-will employee, Dr. Paul could just as easily have been fired the day before he took the machinery home, and for no reason whatever. Therefore, "the doctrine of equitable estoppel is not an exception to the employment-at-will doctrine. An employee may be discharged with or without cause, and our law does not prohibit firing an employee for relying on an employer's promise." [569 A 2d at 348]

Q 2:28　Why have some employers turned away from employment at will?

Some employers voluntarily limit their right to fire at will, whether formally through written policy, or informally by corporate tradition. They do so for a variety of reasons, such as the following:

- Limited availability of employees with the training or talent needed for a particular business

- Avoiding wrongful discharge and discrimination suits
- Avoiding union intervention

Employment Contracts and Agreements

Q 2:29   What constitutes an employment contract?

First, one party must make an *offer* and, second, the other party must *accept* that offer. Further, both parties must *intend* to make a contract.

When a company places a classified advertisement in the newspaper, that ad is not an offer. It is an invitation to qualified, interested readers to submit applications. These applications are not offers either. Only after the applicant has been interviewed, and his or her job references checked, will the employer finally make a job offer that the successful applicant can accept or reject.

To be enforceable, a contract must be supported by *consideration*. This simply means that each party to the agreement gives the other party something tangible, such as money, or intangible, such as a promise to give something in the future. In the case of an employment contract, the employer's consideration is a wage or salary plus fringe benefits. The employee's consideration is performance of the job that the employer needs done.

Q 2:30   Can an employer create an employment contract without intending to?

An employer's immediate reaction, based on the answer to Q 2:29, may be "If I do not *intend* to create a contract, one cannot be created." This is correct, so far as it goes. The problem is that the act of hiring an employee is obviously an intention to create an employment relationship. The issue really is: what terms become part of that relationship? Terms of employment may be embodied in a written contract, or they may be found in the personnel manual or employee handbook. In the absence of these sources, the words and actions of the employer and employee are evidence of the terms of employment.

Q 2:31   How can an employee handbook create an implied contract?

The representations contained in an employee handbook may be construed as factors on which an employee reasonably relied in accepting or continuing employment at a given company. However, the handbook can also be used to spell out the rights and responsibilities of both the employer and employee. As is true of any intention committed to writing, an employee handbook is subject to many interpretations and possible manipulation or exploitation. Accordingly, employers should always use great care when drafting such documents.

Q 2:32   What guidelines can an employer follow to avoid lawsuits stemming from disputes over the terms of employment stated or implied by an employee handbook?

An employer should use the following guidelines to protect itself from litigation:

- Avoid making promises about career opportunities, future compensation, or expected job duties

- If promises are made, use disclaimers such as "unless our plans change," or "if we continue to do as well as we have in the past"

- Describe benefits using words such as "currently," "at present," or "now," and note that plans are "subject to change"

- Include in the personnel manual or employee handbook the statement that employment is "at will" and that "the employee or employer may terminate the employment at any time, and no oral or written promises regarding any terms or conditions of employment can be made, or should be relied upon, except for those made in writing by a designated officer of the organization"

Q 2:33   Will the courts recognize and enforce an employer's disclaimer that a handbook is not a contract?

As noted at Q 2:9, American courts have shown a clear tendency to respect employers' disclaimers and reservations of the right to unilaterally revise their employee handbooks. [See, e.g., Hamilton v Air Jamaica Ltd, 945 F 2d 74 (3d Cir 1991); Doe v First National Bank, 865 F 2d 864 (7th Cir 1989); Pratt v Brown Mach Co, 855 F 2d 1225 (6th Cir 1988); Dell v Montgomery Ward & Co, 811 F 2d 970 (6th Cir 1987)]

However, as one commentator recently noted, "Not all disclaimers . . . can defeat an employee's claim. The legal effect of disclaimers depends on their negating of the reasonableness of the employee reliance on subsequent employer statements or conduct that otherwise might support an inference of acceptance of an employment security promise." [Decker, "Enforcing Employment Handbook Disclaimers—The Days May be Numbered," *1993 Wiley Employment Law Update* 81] One reason some employers get in trouble when trying to enforce their handbook disclaimers is that the disclaimers were deliberately written in ambiguous language because the company did not want to undermine the value of the handbook or employee morale by publishing too blatant a disclaimer or reservation of the right to amend the handbook unilaterally without notice to the workers.

Thus, where a company's handbook gave as one of its purposes the provision of a clear explanation of the corporation's employment policies, a court ruled that whether or not the handbook was an employment contract should be left to the jury to decide. [McDonald v Mobil Coal Producing Inc, 820 P 2d 986 (Wyo 1991)]

Once the employer's policies have been published in the handbook for the purpose of improving employees' performance and behavior, at least one court has refused to permit the company to take them away with other provisions in the same handbook. [Thompson v Kings Entertainment Co, 653 F Supp 871, 875 (ED VA 1987)]

If the disclaimer is not prominently and clearly communicated, a court may refuse to enforce it against an employee. For instance, in one recent case, the following disclaimer was placed near the middle of a "welcome" letter from the company's general manager to all new employees, and was neither underlined, capitalized, nor otherwise made to stand out from the rest of the text:

> [This handbook] is not meant to cover everything and is not intended to be a contract between the Company and its employ-

ees. Rather, the handbook is intended to explain most procedures and policies that we try to operate by.

The court held that this company could not use the handbook as its vehicle for demanding employee loyalty and performance levels, as well as to discourage unionism, and then subtly reserve the firm's right to alter or back off from handbook terms favorable to those same employees. [Arellano v AMAX Coal Co, 6 BNA IER Cas 1399 (D Wyo 1991), *accord*, Jiminez v Colorado Interstate Gas Co, 690 F Supp 977 (D Wyo 1988)]

Late in 1993, the U.S. District Court for the Eastern District of Pennsylvania ruled that a disclaimer in an employee handbook, which denied that the book constituted a contract with the employees, could not prevent a plaintiff-employee from claiming for herself the salary prescribed for her category of employee in that handbook. In the words of one knowledgeable commentator, "Rejecting the employer's arguments, [the court] concluded that the disclaimer could be read as simply reiterating that employees were subject to termination-at-will and did not necessarily bar an employee's claim for a particular salary." [Edward S. Mazurek, "Disclaimer in Company Handbook No Bar to Claim for Specific Salary," Saul, Ewing, Remick & Saul, *Employment Law Update,* Dec 1993, at 2]

An issue that remains controversial is the effect of a disclaimer inserted into a subsequent version of a handbook, months or even years after the employee has commenced work. In *Robinson v. Ada S. McKinley Community Services Inc.* [19 F 3d 359 (7th Cir 1994)], the plaintiff had commenced her employment in 1978, having received an offer letter and a manual, which together provided her protections against the defendant's at-will termination of her employment. Not until 1986 did the employer amend the manual by the addition of a disclaimer of any contractual obligation to follow that handbook's provisions. When the plaintiff, having been terminated, sued to enforce her rights under the original letter and manual received in 1978, the company defended itself on the theory that the plaintiff's decision to continue working after the new manual was released amounted to acceptance of its revisions. The court rejected this contention, saying, such acceptance "cannot be inferred from Robinson's continued work. By continuing to work, Robinson was merely performing her duties under the original contract. According to McKinley's logic, the only way Robinson could preserve her rights under their original employment contract would be to quit working after McKinley unilaterally issued the disclaimer." That, the court concludes, "is ridiculous."[19 F 3d 359, 1994 US App LEXIS 5194, 127 Lab Cas (CCH) P57,646, 9 BNA IER Cases 461 (7th Cir 1994)]

In 1994, other courts rejected disclaimers for more traditional reasons. For example, where a health care provider's handbook did not contain an express disclaimer of contractual effect, the Supreme Court of North Dakota refused to infer such a disclaimer from language in the handbook's termination policy, which said, "[E]mployment in the hospital is based upon mutual consent. Either the employee or the hospital may find it necessary to sever the employment relationship." Rejecting the defendant's reliance upon this provision, the court concluded, "The language. . . . does not rise to the level of a conspicuous and explicit disclaimer. The statements can as easily be construed as consistent with the existence of enforceable contract rights as being inconsistent with their existence. The policies in this case are silent on whether the terms and benefits set out affected or modified the defendants' right to terminate the employment relationship at will." [Osterman-Levitt v MedQuest Inc, 513 NW 2d 70 (1994) ND LEXIS 63, 9 BNA IER Cases 498, 127 Lab Cas (CCH) P57,659 (1994)]

Similarly, where the disclaimer in the employee policy manual was "untitled, in fine print, and on a signature page allegedly unsigned by the plaintiff," it was ineffectual in defeating the contractual rights created by that manual. [Dicker v Middlesex Memorial Hospital, 1994 Conn Super LEXIS 790 (Conn Super Ct 1994)] And, furthermore, a jury in a wrongful discharge action may be entitled to find that a disclaimer in a handbook applied to some provisions, yet may not have been effective to deprive the plaintiff of that handbook's disciplinary policy protections where these were expressly accorded to someone such as the plaintiff, who had been fired for allegedly committing "an immediately terminable offense." [Nicosia v Wakefern Food Corp, 136 NJ 401, 643 A 2d 554, 1994 NJ LEXIS 508, 9 BNA IER Cases 1338 (1994)]

In sum, a disclaimer must be explicit and must be prominently communicated, preferably in the same document it seeks to disclaim, for maximum possibility of enforceability. [See also, Morris v Chem-

Lawn Corp, 541 F Supp 479 (ED MI 1982) (statement in employment agreements that "the Employee's employment with the Company may be terminated by either party at any time" was not explicit as to whether termination had to be for cause or not; therefore the court refused to interpret the agreement as permitting termination for any reason, even absent good cause. See Q 13:2 for a further explanation of "good cause")]

Q 2:34 Will disciplinary rules published in an employee handbook support the denial of unemployment compensation benefits on the basis of willful misconduct?

For an employee to be eligible for unemployment compensation (see Q 8:190) following termination of employment, the reason for the job termination must not have been willful misconduct. The burden of proving willful misconduct for purposes of denying benefits to the separated worker falls on the employer, and unemployment referees typically make this a very heavy burden, often demonstrating a bias in favor of finding that the employee was actually fired because of a downturn in the employer's business or, at worst, because the employee's poor job performance was due to lack of skill rather than willful neglect. Almost uniformly, unemployment referees require employers claiming willful misconduct as the reason for the termination to present documentation of the work rules the employees are alleged to have willfully violated. Where the employer cannot prove that the employee was aware of the relevant disciplinary rule in the employee handbook—i.e., that the rule was clearly written and clearly communicated—willful misconduct will not be found and unemployment benefits will not be denied. [See, e.g., James v Commonwealth of Pennsylvania, Unemployment Compensation Board of Review, 59 Commonwealth Ct 230, 429 A 2d 782 (1982); Decker, "Enforcing Employment Handbook Disclaimers—The Days May be Numbered," *1993 Wiley Employment Law Update* 77, n 52; *accord*, James O. Castagnera, "Unemployment Compensation," *Summary of Pennsylvania Jurisprudence* 2d §§ 4.84 (Law Co-op 1994)]

Q 2:35   What happens if an employer's published employment policies are inconsistent?

The general rule of contract interpretation is that where contract language is ambiguous, the court will interpret it against the party that drafted the language. This rule has been applied in cases of ambiguous or inconsistent language in employee handbooks and other employment documents. [See, e.g., Morris v ChemLawn Corp, 541 F Supp 479 (ED MI 1982) (employment agreements that said either party could terminate employment "at any time," but which failed to say whether "good cause" was required, would not be interpreted against the employee to permit termination for any reason, even absent good cause); Nicosia v Wakefern Food Corp, 136 NJ 401, 643 A 2d 554, 1994 NJ LEXIS 508, 9 BNA IER Cases 1338 (1994) (jury entitled to find that disclaimer applied to some but not all portions of employee handbook)]

In a case where the company placed a disclaimer on the back of its employment application but placed a "termination for just cause only" statement in its handbook, and the employee testified he had never read the disclaimer before signing the job application, the court enforced the "just cause" policy in the handbook against the employer. [McLain v Great American Insurance Co, 208 Cal App 3d 1476, 256 Cal Rptr 863 (1989); *accord*, Dicker v Middlesex Memorial Hospital, 1994 Conn Super LEXIS 790 (Conn Super Ct 1994) (untitled disclaimer, published in fine print on a page the employee was supposed to sign but never did, was to no effect)]

In another case, the court refused to enforce an "employment-at-will" clause in a preprinted employment application that the court found was nothing more than a solicitation of employment offers, and not a contract of employment, and that was not integrated into the employment relationship by language in any of the employer's other documents. [Harden v Maybelline Sales Corp, 230 Cal App 3d 1550, 282 Cal Rptr 96 (1991)]

In a recent federal case out of Pennsylvania, a disgruntled employee succeeded in forcing her employer to pay her the salary outlined in the company's employee handbook, despite the book's disclaimer of contractual significance. In this case the company had established a salary administration program, which eventually was incorporated into a new edition of the employee handbook, along with the statement that, "For personnel being compensated below the mid-point salary of their job classification, the supervisor should ensure that the amount of increase and the timing of increase coincide with the arrival at the mid-point when the employee is adequately competent to perform the required duties." On this language the court held the employee to be entitled to a pay increase. [Mazurek, *supra*, at 2]

Q 2:36 Can a disclaimer or reservation of the right of at-will termination in a handbook contractually supersede a state's statutory or common-law rules concerning wrongful discharge?

As noted elsewhere (see Qs 2:11–2:28 and 13:41–13:47), the courts of many states have limited employers' historic right, absent a contract to the contrary, to terminate their employees at any time and for any reason (i.e., at will). A minority of states have even imposed an implied covenant of good faith and fair dealing upon all employment relationships (see Q 2:24).

Where a particular state's courts, or its legislature by statute, have created employee protection against the employer's right to terminate at will, an attempt to circumvent such common or statutory rules of law may itself violate public policy. An illegal provision in any contract normally is not enforceable; neither is a release from liability given in advance of the wrongful act actually having occurred. Consequently, where a state has set down public policies or common-law rules restricting at-will termination of employment, it is unlikely that an employer will be permitted to overcome such legal rules by means of a provision in an employment contract or handbook, unless an express statutory provision or court decision says that employees are permitted to waive their rights by contract. [See, e.g., Montana Wrongful Discharge from Employment Act, Mont Code §§ 392901 through 392914 (1988) as an example of a statutory definition of what will and will not constitute wrongful discharge in that jurisdiction; see also, the Fair Labor Standards Act, 29 USC §§ 201219, as well as most state workers' compensation laws, as examples of labor laws that cannot be waived by covered employees, even by express contract]

However, worthy of note is the fact that a statute governing termination of otherwise at-will employment also may provide the employer with protection. For example, in a series of cases in 1994, the Montana Supreme Court made it clear that the state's Wrongful Discharge from Employment Act, which does not impose an implied covenant of good faith and fair dealing upon the employment relationship, by implication denies the employee-plaintiff such a cause of action. [Sullivan v Sisters of Charity of Providence of Montana, 1994 Mont LEXIS 267, 51 Mont St Rep 1193 (1994); Boreen v. Christensen, 1994 Mont LEXIS 228, 51 Mont St Rep 1014 (1994); Guertin v Moody's Market, 51 Mont St Rep 407, 874 P 2d 710 1994 Mont LEXIS 101 (1994)]

Consequently, employers drafting and adopting handbooks should carefully scrutinize both the statutory and common law of all states in which the company does business and intends to disseminate the handbook to its employees. Relevant statutory and common-law considerations include each jurisdiction's laws with respect to such things as wages, vacations, and other compensation, all of which should be followed in the handbook's provisions. [Decker, "Enforcing Employment Handbook Disclaimers—The Days May be Numbered," *1993 Wiley Employment Law Update* 72; and see, e.g., the Pennsylvania Wage Payment and Collection Act, 42 Pa Stat Ann §§ 260.1 *et seq*, which classifies vacation pay as wages, but which has been interpreted by the Pennsylvania Department of Labor & Industry to permit an employer in its handbook or other published policy to limit a terminating employee's eligibility for accrued unused vacation, such as by making eligibility contingent upon giving reasonable notice of termination]

Q 2:37 If a company runs the risk of having a handbook enforced against it, is the company better off without one?

Either out of fear that they will be bound by the pro-employee portions of the handbook, to their disadvantage, or simply out of the naive belief that all their employees fully understand their employment policies and rules, some employers state a preference for not having a handbook or policy manual. While this is the individual employer's option, most knowledgeable commentators and counselors advise employers to adopt written employment policies, whether in a fullfledged handbook or otherwise. [See, e.g., Decker and Felix, *Drafting and Revising Employment Handbooks* (1991)]

> Employee handbooks, once considered a frill that only large companies could afford, are now being used by companies of all sizes. They are effective tools for providing employees with information on policies, wages, employee benefits, and a host of other subjects.
>
> Ongoing personal contact between management and employees is an important component of a successful business. However, many managers find that the demands of a growing business curtail the amount of time they can spend getting to know their employees and personally resolving employee problems on a case-by-case basis. Although an employee handbook cannot (and should not) replace personal contacts, it can be used to establish policies and improve communication. This helps the company run more efficiently, because employees who are better informed tend to be more secure, and therefore more loyal and productive.
>
> A comprehensive employee handbook plays a major role in orienting and informing new employees. For experienced employees, it also should serve as a reference for clarification on company policies, benefits, and other issues. [Castagnera, *How to Prepare an Employee Handbook* 3 (Panel Publishers, 2d ed 1988)]

Other reasons often cited as justification for having a handbook are union avoidance and, closely related to that, litigation avoidance. Many times, employees and former employees challenge their employer's actions because those acts appear arbitrary and, therefore, inherently unfair. Employees who feel insecure sometimes turn to a labor union to provide the sense of security that the company has been denying them. Many corporations have drafted and adopted handbooks and policy manuals, often willingly giving up a measure of the discretion available under the at-will employment doctrine, because they want their employees to feel secure in their jobs. Feeling secure, employees are less likely to turn to unionization as an alternative source of job security. Other companies have offered alternative dispute resolution procedures, such as peer review or even binding arbitration (see Qs 2:49–2:57 and 4:120) in their handbooks and policies to discourage or perhaps even forestall employment litigation.

Whether or not litigation and union avoidance are motivating factors, organizational complexity alone justifies, or perhaps even compels, the adoption of handbooks in many organizations. In the words of one vintage management text:

> At any one time, the rights and duties of workers and managers, indeed of all those in the hierarchy, must be established and understood by all those involved in the hierarchy. . . . The industrial system creates an elaborate "government" at the work place and work community. It is often said that primitive societies have extensive rules, customs and taboos, but a study of the industrial society reflects an even greater complex and different set of detailed rules. [Kerry, *Industrialism and Industrial Man* 41 (1960)]

This complexity is the main reason most business organizations have opted to have handbooks, policy manuals, or other sources of written employment policies, despite the fact that the trade-off resulting from their adoption is some loss of managerial discretion.

Recent cases refusing to enforce vague or unfair disclaimers in employee handbooks "should serve as an . . . incentive to employers to review all policies and procedures which are communicated to employees. Employers are cautioned not to place overriding reliance on disclaimers in their handbooks where other terms create reasonable expectation of some specific benefit. Employers should maintain acute sensitivity to the language used when communicating policies to employees to retain the utmost discretion to modify or terminate those policies where appropriate." [Mazurek, *supra*]

Oral Contracts

Q 2:38   What elements create an enforceable oral contract?

In general, if all the basic components of a valid contract are present (offer, acceptance, intention, and consideration), an oral contract is usually enforceable in a court of law. As a general rule, an oral contract of almost any kind is enforceable if it can be proven. For example, if Karen offers to paint Fred's house for $2,000 and Fred agrees, in most, if not all states, Fred and Karen have made a binding oral agreement.

However, in many states, a statute of frauds requires that certain types of contracts, or contracts for longer than one year, be memorialized by a writing. No state's statute of frauds expressly requires that all employment contracts be in writing, but the requirement that contracts that cannot be performed within one year must be written down means that if an executive or sales representative (or any other employee) is offered a contract for a term of more than one year, the parties must memorialize it with a written agreement.

Even in states that have no statute of frauds (e.g., Pennsylvania), oral contracts create problems of proof that make them inadvisable. Enforcement may depend on who the judge or jury decides to believe; problems of proof are often reason enough to reduce an employment agreement to writing (see Q 2:40). Complex employment contracts sealed with only a handshake frequently result in costly litigation.

Q 2:39   Even if an oral employment contract is enforceable in a particular state, should written contracts be used?

There is no single answer to this question. However, some guidelines may help employers to decide which, if any, of their employees should have written contracts. First, the more highly placed the employee, the more he or she should have a written contract, and the more extensive the terms of that contract should be. Second, the greater the employee's access to a company's trade secrets, such as client lists, the more an employer should require the employee to sign at least a written non-competition/confidentiality agreement. This may be a document that even the clerical staff is required to sign.

Q 2:40   Are written contracts of employment preferable to oral ones?

Some employers seem to think they are better off if employment agreements are not in writing. Apparently, they think they are not locked into a contract if it is oral. However, as noted in Q 2:38, courts will generally enforce oral employment contracts. The danger in not

putting the agreement in writing is that if the employment relationship goes sour, the employer and employee may not agree about the
exact terms of the oral understanding. In such a situation, a judge
may leave it up to a jury to hear both views and decide which version
they believe. The best way to be sure this will not happen is to begin
the employment relationship with a clearly written contract.

This is not to say that all employees should have written contracts.
Lower-level clerical and blue-collar workers are usually at-will employees, and, therefore, written contracts are not necessary. Higher-
level employees (managers, administrators, professionals), however,
often demand express agreements. In these situations, legal disputes
can often be anticipated and avoided by spelling out the terms of
employment in a written document, even if this is no more than a
letter from the employer, with the employer's file copy signed by the
new employee.

Q 2:41   Can an employer's gratuitous promises become binding terms of an employment relationship?

Oral promises can create legal difficulties for unwary employers.
Promises can sometimes create contractual obligations, even when
the employer does not intend them to do so. For instance, suppose
an applicant for the job of vice president of finance is told that if she
takes the job, she can look forward to a long and exciting career with
the company. There is no written contract and no fixed period of
employment. But based at least in part on the representations about
a bright future, she sells her townhouse on Society Hill in Philadelphia, quits a good job, and moves to San Diego, where the corporate
headquarters are located.

Three months later, a severe economic downturn forces the company president to cut costs. He suggests that the company treasurer
take over the duties of vice president of finance and that this position
be eliminated to save the salary. Unfortunately, the new vice president of finance must be told that her position is being eliminated.
Soon the company receives a letter from an attorney, retained by the
terminated vice president, stating that his client moved, gave up her
home and job, and relocated because she was promised a bright
future with the firm.

Courts do not like to enforce promises that are not intended to become contracts, and this employer never intended to create a contract with this employee for a term of years. Besides, no specific time was ever talked about. Was the employee entitled to employment at least for a reasonable length of time? Maybe, maybe not. Some of the factors that a judge will look at in resolving this dispute will be the following:

- Were the representations actually promises or just predictions?
- If the representations were promises, did the employer expect or intend them to cause the employee to take actions to her detriment (selling her home, quitting her job, relocating)?
- Did the employee in fact change her position, fully or partly, in reliance on such representations?
- Was the employee behaving as a reasonable person when she changed jobs in full or partial reliance on such representations?

If the answers to these questions are yes, the employer may be liable.

Written Contracts

Q 2:42 What purposes do written employment contracts serve?

In addition to specifying the expectations of both the employer and employee, in terms of both tasks and compensation, written employment contracts also provide for termination policies, buy-out provisions, covenants not to compete, confidentiality agreements, choice of law provisions, and other concerns that are particular to specific employers' practices or professions.

Q 2:43 What parts of an employment contract does the law require to be in writing?

ERISA requires that employee pension and welfare benefit plans be in writing and that summary plan descriptions (SPDs) be made available to employees as well.

The duration of the employment contract usually must be in writing if it is longer than one year.

A covenant not to compete can probably not be enforced against an ex-employee unless it was memorialized in a writing.

Collective bargaining agreements are always memorialized by a written document, and once an agreement has been reached, refusal to sign the written agreement is considered an unfair labor practice.

Q 2:44 What constitutes a written employment contract?

Documents such as covenants not to compete, confidentiality agreements, and bonus and severance plans have all been held to be part of employment contracts by various courts, even if they are not incorporated into a comprehensive contractual document. Consequently, care must be taken to include disclaimers in employee handbooks and personnel manuals if such publications are not intended to be contractual commitments. [See, e.g., Mitchell v Jewel Food Stores, 568 NE 2d 827 (Ill 1990)] On the other hand, if a non-competition or confidentiality agreement (see Qs 2:59, 2:61), which may be a standard company form, is intended to bind the employee contractually, employers should take care that any written contract incorporate such standard company forms by reference.

Q 2:45 What are the components of a written contract of employment?

A written contract can be as simple or complex as the parties want it to be. Regardless of the form the contract takes (e.g., a letter from the personnel director or a more detailed, formal document), the following items should be covered in the agreement:

Nature of the employment. This is a description, usually kept fairly general and limited to one or two paragraphs, of what the employee is expected to do during the course of employment. The following is an example of a clause expressing the nature of employment:

> Employee will be the Vice President and General Manager of Employer's Blackacre facility, with responsibility for the management and supervision of all departments and activities of that facility, as well as for the coordination of the activities of

Employer's Blackacre facility with the activities of the Employer's enterprise as a whole.

Compensation. This section should deal (at a minimum) with the salary or wages the employee will receive: how much, how often, any special components, such as commissions, bonuses, and the like.

Fringe benefits. Although "perks" are part of an employee's compensation, they probably should be treated separately from salary. On the other hand, it is rarely necessary or wise to spell out every benefit in great detail. For instance, it is usually sufficient to state that the new employee will receive pension, health, and other benefits equivalent to those enjoyed by others of similar stature in the organization. The details will be spelled out in the company's employee benefits plans and SPDs.

Term and termination. This area of the employment agreement should focus on two points: (1) the length of employment, if all goes well, and (2) how employment will be terminated if the relationship goes sour.

Written employment contracts might include the following additional clauses:

Choice of law. Employers usually specify that the law of the state in which they are located will apply in interpreting the contract. If the employee will be working at a facility in another state, it may be wise for legal counsel to check contract law in that state for more favorable provisions.

Consolidation clause. The contract should state that it contains all the terms agreed to by the two parties and that no other oral or written negotiations or promises (prior to or contemporaneous with the provisions in the contract) apply.

Amendments. The contract should specify that all changes, extensions, and so forth, must be made in writing and signed by the parties.

Non-assignment. The contract should state that the employee cannot assign the employment contract to another person (i.e., he or she should not be allowed to hire someone to serve in his or her place).

Q 2:46   How can a written contract be terminated?

Although the parties can make any termination provisions they want, the employer will most likely want the option to terminate the contract at its discretion, and, if severance pay is involved, to terminate at a price the company can afford. However, be advised that the law may consider the contract unenforceable if the terms allow the employer to cancel the agreement at any time while denying the employee the same privilege.

Q 2:47   What is a typical termination provision?

A typical provision might be as follows:

> Employer may terminate this Agreement on written notice to Employee 90 days prior to the desired date of termination. In lieu of said notice, Employer may pay employee three months severance pay at his (her) regular monthly salary.

Q 2:48   What if a key employee demands greater employment security beyond at-will employment?

Key employees who are not satisfied to work at will may demand some employment security. Some employment contracts specify duration of employment, such as two years, (rarely more than five). As an alternative, or in tandem with a term of years, a company may limit its discretion to certain specified reasons for termination, such as for "just cause," or for "malfeasance amounting to criminal conduct." The problem with the first of these concepts is that the two parties will rarely agree after the fact on what constituted just cause. The trouble with the latter phrase is that it nearly eliminates the employer's right to terminate the agreement prematurely.

Many companies combine two means of termination: at the employer's discretion with notice and/or severance pay, or without notice/ severance when some mutually agreed-upon level of misconduct is involved. The termination clause may also require the employee to pay a price for early termination. For instance, it might include the following provision:

> Employee may terminate this Agreement on 90-days written notice. Failure to furnish such notice to the Employer shall result

in Employee's forfeiture of his (her) entitlement to a pro-rata share of his (her) annual bonus.

Alternative Dispute Resolution

Discussed below are two forms of dispute resolution to which employers and employees may turn rather than litigation: arbitration and peer grievance reviews. These methods may be specified in employment contracts or in the company handbook.

Arbitration

Q 2:49　Are arbitration clauses in individual employment contracts enforceable?

Under the Federal Arbitration Act [9 USC §§ 1-15] and many analogous state arbitration statutes, arbitration clauses are fully enforceable. Thus, a party to an employment contract containing such a clause can get a court order to compel the other party to submit to arbitration, and the victorious party can sue to enforce the arbitrator's award against a recalcitrant opponent.

The more important issue to employers is whether or not they can divest an employee of the right to sue under the federal discrimination laws by including such an arbitration clause in the employment contract. Arbitration clauses are both standard and extensive in scope in the securities industry, for example, covering approximately 6,000 companies and their 400,000 employees who are registered with this country's stock exchanges. In 1991, the Supreme Court in *Gilmer v. Interstate/Johnson Lane Corp.* [111 S Ct 1647] ruled that the plaintiff was required to arbitrate his age discrimination claim.

Q 2:50　Which employment contracts are covered by the Federal Arbitration Act?

As a general rule, all employment contracts involving companies engaged in interstate commerce are subject to the jurisdiction of the Federal Arbitration Act. Under Supreme Court decisions dating back to the New Deal era, most commercial and industrial activities are considered to be involved in interstate commerce.

Q 2:51 Are there any employment contracts not covered by the Federal Arbitration Act?

Employment contracts involving workers who are directly engaged in transportation (e.g., seamen, railroad workers, airline employees) are expressly exempt from the Federal Arbitration Act. Additionally, the Act exempts businesses so local in nature that they can successfully show that they are not involved in interstate commerce. In today's highly integrated national economy, however, such businesses are extremely rare.

When the arbitration agreement expressly provides that the laws of the state will govern the agreement, the state law of arbitration applies rather than the Federal Arbitration Act.

Q 2:52 Who decides whether or not an employment issue is arbitrable?

Sometimes one party to an employment contract with an arbitration clause will claim that the particular dispute is not arbitrable. For example, an employer may want to arbitrate a disagreement involving a collateral agreement outside the four corners of the employment contract (e.g., a supplemental agreement on bonuses or commissions, or a provision in the employee handbook). The employee may argue that his or her agreement to arbitrate does not include disputes not expressly covered in the agreement. Generally, the arbitrator decides the arbitrability issue before reaching the merits of the controversy. Consequently, if the employer files a lawsuit seeking an order to compel the employee to submit to arbitration, the court will generally limit its inquiry to whether the arbitration clause might arguably apply. If the court finds that the arbitration clause should apply, it will turn over jurisdiction to the arbitrator to settle the arbitrability issue.

Q 2:53   What is the standard for determining arbitrability?

There is no statutory definition of arbitrability that applies to all situations. (If there were, the courts, instead of the arbitrators, would most likely decide arbitrability.) Rather, the intent of the contracting parties controls the question of arbitrability. If the written agreement is ambiguous, the arbitrator must look at other evidence of the parties' intentions at the time they executed the arbitration agreement. This evidence may include the following:

- Other documents, such as letters and memoranda
- Past practice of the parties
- Industry customs
- Reported arbitration decisions interpreting the same or similar agreements
- Oral testimony of the employer and the employee

Q 2:54   Is an arbitration agreement in an employment contract with a foreign employer enforceable in the United States?

If a foreign employer enters an employment agreement with an employee in the United States, the company will probably be subject to the same rules as a domestic corporation, including amenability to a suit to compel arbitration. The issue becomes cloudy when the U.S. citizen is employed overseas. It becomes cloudier when the company is owned by a foreign government. [See 9 USC §§ 201-800)]

Peer Grievance Review

Q 2:55   Are there any alternatives to arbitration to settle employee disputes within a company?

Yes. Some companies have initiated a peer grievance review system. This system, which originated at a General Electric plant in Maryland, has been found to be very effective. Studies under this system show that the decisions have varied little from those resulting from a traditional kind of grievance system. However, the employees interviewed said that they felt they received fairer treatment under the peer review system. As with more traditional grievance and arbitration schemes, peer review typically operates in tandem with a stepped disciplinary program and pre-peer review grievance resolution procedures.

Q 2:56   How does the peer grievance review system work?

As instituted in a number of companies, the system consists of a panel of five members, generally made up of two members of management (one of whom is usually a human resources manager) and three employees who are peers (nonmanagement). The panel members are volunteers who have been trained in the process of dispute resolution, including legal and ethical considerations. Two peer members are chosen at random by the grievant by pulling names out of a box. The two management members and the two randomly selected peers choose the fifth member, who chairs the panel.

Q 2:57   What are the steps in the grievance procedure?

The initial steps in a grievance procedure usually include the following:

- The individual employee presents the claim to his or her supervisor
- A higher management level reviews the written grievance
- The employee submits his or her grievance to the peer grievance review panel

The grievant can either receive assistance from someone in the human resources department, or represent him or herself. Individual grievants may present their disputes, provide comments, and call witnesses before the panel.

The supervisor then presents his or her side. The panel is free to ask questions or call witnesses if it wants additional information.

The panel's decision is made by secret ballot. The decision is final, written, and binding on all parties. The system applies to all employees, including managers, and all participants agree to confidentiality.

Covenants Not to Compete and Confidentiality Agreements

Q 2:58   How can employees be prevented from leaving the company and competing against it?

One way to diminish the employee's desire to terminate employment prematurely, and to minimize the damage if he or she does, is to get the employee's agreement to one or more provisions limiting the employee's ability to use the company's expertise to compete against it. A *covenant not to compete* (also called a non-competition agreement or "non-compete") is a promise that, during the employee's tenure with the company and for a reasonable time afterwards (usually one year), he or she will not engage in any activities that compete for business against the enterprise. A *confidentiality agreement* states that the employee will keep the firm's proprietary information secret; this usually includes customer lists, trade secrets, marketing plans and strategies, and financial information of the company. Often such agreements are included as covenants in a broader employment contract, but they can be separate documents that, if supported by adequate consideration, may be executed or reaffirmed at almost any time during the employment relationship.

Restrictions on competition and the free movement of commerce (such as limits on where an ex-employee may practice his or her trade or profession) are frowned upon by courts when they go too far. Thus, the courts have increasingly held that the geographic scope and the duration of such agreements are the critical factors that affect, and largely determine, the enforceability of a covenant not to compete. [See, e.g., Westec Security Services Inc v Westinghouse Electric Corp, 538 F Supp 108 (ED Pa 1982) (geographic scope); Alexander & Alexander Inc v Drayton, 378 F Supp 824 (ED Pa), *aff'd* 505 F 2d 729 (3d Cir 1974) (duration)] In some states, non-competition agreements are void as violating public policy. In California, almost all restrictions on competition are rendered void by statute. In Delaware, non-competition agreements are unenforceable when applied to physicians.

Q 2:59   What are the legal differences between a covenant not to compete and a confidentiality agreement?

The law treats these two forms of employer protection very differently. The right to keep trade secrets confidential is recognized by both the common law of most states and the enactment of the Uniform Trade Secrets Act by many of them. Consequently, a confidentiality provision in a written employment contract is designed not so much to establish a right, but rather to define and/or expand it, and outline the company's remedies for its violation.

By contrast, restraints on trade and competition are abhorred by the courts, which will not automatically impose this kind of restriction on an employee who leaves the firm. Additionally, judges will not enforce non-competition covenants unless they are reasonable. This means that a non-competition provision in a contract must apply only for a reasonable time after the contract terminates (two years is usually the outer limit) and over a reasonable geographic area. In other words, if the company does business only in Pennsylvania, it probably cannot forbid the employee to seek a job in New York or Massachusetts with a company in the same business.

Q 2:60   Are the courts likely to enforce confidentiality agreements?

This generally depends on the scope, purpose, and duration of such agreements. Although an employer can compel its employees to maintain the confidentiality of the subject matter of their employment, it should exercise care in the scope of the restrictions it puts on employees. For example, courts might not enforce an agreement that prohibits employees from ever disclosing the information acquired in their work. Such agreements should be narrowly tailored to effectuate the employer's legitimately defensible concern. Thus, for example, a car manufacturer does not need to compel its employees to conceal the fact that they work in an automobile factory to protect its legitimate interests. However, the employer is within its rights to compel its employees not to disclose the design specifications of its vehicles or the particular marketing strategies that the company has developed. Agreements that protect these types of concerns will be viewed favorably by the courts.

Q 2:61   What is an example of a reasonable covenant not to compete?

Here is a sample provision that combines reasonableness with sufficient protection for the employer:

> *Non-competition.* Employee agrees that during the term of this Agreement and for a period of _____ years following termination of this Agreement, he or she shall not engage, directly or indirectly, alone or as an officer, director, employee, agent, shareholder, partner, or fiduciary, in any activity similar to or in connection with the activities of the Company within a radius of _____ miles of the Company.

Q 2:62   What remedies are available for breach of a covenant not to compete?

The company can usually seek both money damages for its lost business and a court order to prevent improper competition by the former employee in the future. However, it is important to bear in mind this caveat: Many judges do not believe in preventing employees from going to new jobs, or even starting their own businesses in competition with former employers. Urban courts are usually more likely than rural judges to deny enforcement of non-competition agreements. Nevertheless, the more highly paid and privileged the employee was, the more likely that even an urban court will enforce reasonable contractual restraints on that ex-employee. It is important, therefore, for employers not to overreach new recruits. Ask only for the protection the enterprise will require if the employee leaves the firm. This is the most a judge is likely to give a company anyway.

Other Employment Relationships

Q 2:63   What is the difference between an employee and an independent contractor?

An independent contractor differs from an employee in that the employer does not have control over the work activity of an independent contractor. The employer and independent contractor negotiate a fee for an agreed-on product or service to be delivered at a certain time. The employer also does not make payroll deductions for an independent contractor.

Q 2:64 What does "right to control" mean?

The phrase "right to control" is a simple concept with sweeping impact. Right to control means the authority to direct a worker's activities on the job. When this authority exists, the employer has legal responsibility for the worker's well-being while the employee is undertaking these activities.

Right to control can be illustrated by an example:

> The firm's office manager hires a temporary worker. The "temp" is employed by an employee-leasing company. She receives a paycheck and benefits from that company. The firm pays a fee to the leasing company that is large enough to cover wages plus overhead (i.e., a profit for the leasing company. Because the firm's office manager will direct the temp's work for the time during which she substitutes for the regular secretary, the firm has the right to control her activities, and she is, therefore, its employee for many legal purposes. If the leasing company fails to comply with state and federal minimum wage and overtime laws, for example, or to make proper payments to the federal and state taxing authorities, the firm may be secondarily liable for these amounts.

Q 2:65 What is a joint-employer relationship?

A joint-employer relationship is one in which two unrelated companies together employ a single worker or group of workers. The most important tenets of this relationship are shared management of the employees and participation in creating employment policies. The two most common joint-employer situations involve leased employees and borrowed servants.

When two corporations that make use of and direct the services of a single group of employees are under common ownership, they may be considered a single employer for labor law purposes. When unionized construction companies set up nonunion counterparts, with or without common ownership, to escape their union obligations and be more competitive, the joint-employer structure is called a "double-breasted" operation.

Q 2:66   What are leased employees?

Leased employees work for a leasing or temporary employment service that pays them their wages and benefits. The employees report for work at the client company, where their work activities are directed by the client's managers. In the case of a temporary service, the employment relationship is usually short term; for example, while a regular employee is on vacation or on temporary leave or short-term disability. With employee-leasing companies, the client-employee relationship is more likely to be long term. The client company is often a small firm that turns to a leasing company for its employees because the leasing firm, with hundreds or even thousands of employees, can use economies of scale to maximize compensation packages and minimize paperwork costs.

Q 2:67   What are the advantages of becoming a joint employer through employee leasing?

Employee leasing has caught on in recent years with some smaller enterprises, such as medical partnerships. In addition to the advantage of economies of scale that get subscribers better employee benefits for less money (see Q 2:66), subscribers also save administrative costs in the human resources area. Also, awkward discharge problems can sometimes be avoided because the leasing company can occasionally transfer an undesired employee to another of its subscribers.

Q 2:68   What is a borrowed servant?

A borrowed servant is similar to a joint or leased employee (see Qs 2:65, 2:66). However, as the term suggests, a borrowed servant is on short-term loan from one employer to another, as when a general contractor on a construction site lends a subcontractor a worker to help finish a job.

Q 2:69   What are the employer's legal responsibilities in a joint-employment situation?

Because the firm with the right to control its leased employees is a joint employer with the leasing company, its managers must continue to obey all the applicable job discrimination laws as if the employees were hired directly by the firm. The firm's contract is with the leasing company, but its legal duty extends to the workers as well.

Q 2:70   When might joint-employer status give rise to legal liability?

Legal liability may arise when one of the two joint employers violates a labor or employment law, and the other joint employer is held equally liable. Liability may be joint even though one of the employers is factually innocent.

Liability may also arise in a double-breasted operation (see Q 2:65) if the union challenges the arrangement and the NLRB finds a single- or joint-employer situation. The NLRB's remedy is to extend the union contract to cover the nonunion branch of the double-breasted operation. Usually it is the interchange of workers, equipment, and bids that leads to this overlapping result for the two companies.

Q 2:71   Does the company gain any legal protection by being a joint employer?

The one great advantage joint employers have over non-joint employers is in the area of on-the-job injury. The employer's obligation is limited to insurance under the state workers' compensation statute. Third parties, such as the manufacturer of a machine that injures a worker, may face unlimited liability. But to get this protection in an employee-leasing or other joint-employer relationship, the relevant contract must require workers' compensation coverage.

Chapter 3

Hiring and Evaluating Employees

This chapter describes procedures and programs to recruit and retain qualified employees and to evaluate employee performance. It includes discussions of nondiscriminatory job advertising, appropriate information that can be gathered from the application or interview, methods of evaluating employee performance, work rules, and employee discipline.

Laws tend to circumscribe an employer's discretion. Just as chapter 1 demonstrated how federal and state laws have diminished the historic freedom of employment at will, so, too, do these various laws more specifically restrain what companies can and cannot do and say in hiring and measuring the performance of their employees. But while this chapter charts those legal barriers and pitfalls, it also recommends personnel practices that can help employers use hiring and evaluation as tools for loss prevention and improved productivity.

There are three major ways employers can incur legal liability and financial losses when hiring and evaluating employees: (1) liability to employees and applicants can result from discriminatory hiring practices (see chapter 4) or intrusive investigations, such as polygraph examinations (see chapter 3); (2) liability to customers for negligent hiring (see Q 6:16); and (3) losses caused by employee dishonesty, which are lumped under the euphemistic term *inventory shrink*.

Since (1) above is often at odds with problems (2) and (3), employers frequently find themselves on the horns of an uncomfortable dilemma: if they engage in surveillance and other security steps needed to protect company assets and avoid liability to the public for negligent hiring, they find themselves targeted for lawsuits by disgruntled employees and labor unions who object to what they perceive as intrusions upon their privacy rights. This dilemma has been made more acute in recent years by approximately 30 states that have passed so-called lifestyle laws, which forbid employers from inquiring into or interfering with employees' private activities (such as smoking and drinking) outside the workplace (see chapter 2). One knowledgeable group of commentators recently observed:

> The state privacy laws also limit some of the deep background investigation employers undertake to avoid liability under the common-law theories of negligent hire and negligent retention. An employer owes a standard of care to third parties (including other employees) for injuries caused by a worker who was unfit, and whose lack of fitness was known or should have been known by the employer. ["State Labor Law Developments," 9 *The Labor Lawyer* 3, Summer 1993, at 272; see, e.g., "Right to Privacy in the Workplace Act," Ill Comp Stat, Act 55; New York Labor Law Section 201d 2(b)(c)]

Yet so serious are the issues of inventory shrink and liability to customers and the general public that companies must simply soldier onward, continuing to battle employee dishonesty and unfitness, notwithstanding the concomitant liability risks with regard to their employees themselves. Recognizing both the needs and the risks, *Employment Law Answer Book* devotes substantial space to various aspects of this issue. (See Qs 3:123–3:132, 5:14–5:25, and 6:1–6:11.)

The Hiring Process

Advertising and Recruiting

Q 3:1   What are the legal restrictions on how a company advertises for new employees?

Advertising must not reflect an intention to discriminate on the basis of sex, race, religion, national origin, age, veteran status, or non-job-related disabilities. Therefore, advertisements that read "help wanted—male" are improper. Sex-specific job descriptions, such as "waitresses," "waiters," "busboys," "foremen," "maids," and so forth are also inappropriate. A more subtle example of discriminatory advertising, which is considered suspicious by the Equal Employment Opportunity Commission (EEOC), is the phrase, "college students wanted," because an advertisement worded in this way will very likely discourage older workers from applying for the position.

Q 3:2   Should help wanted advertising include an equal employment opportunity policy?

Yes. The words "equal opportunity employer" should be included, if space permits.

Q 3:3   Are oral promises enforceable between recruiters and employers?

Because employment recruiting (or "head-hunting") is a sale of services, no state's statute of frauds requires that the contract for services necessarily be in writing (see Q 2:38). Furthermore, even if a recruiter cannot prove the existence of an oral agreement with an employer, if the recruiter has helped place a new employee with the company, he or she can collect a reasonable fee under the common-law concept of *quantum meruit*. Under *quantum meruit*, the courts award the fair value of the work performed (even though they find no enforceable contract) so that the party receiving the benefit of the services is not unjustly enriched. The recruiter may win his or her fee from the company in court by (1) showing that he or she was instrumental in making the employment "marriage," and (2) presenting his or her normal fee structure for such a service.

Applicant Evaluation

Q 3:4   Are there questions that may not be asked on an application form?

The EEOC, as well as specific laws in many states, forbids certain types of questions on employment applications. These tend to fall into several general categories:

- Race, age, national origin, religion, marital status, and disabilities
- Military service and criminal records
- Credit history

A good rule of thumb is to review each question on the application form and ask: "Why do I want this information from the applicant?" If there is not a good answer, that item probably should be deleted. At best, it clutters the application process with worthless data; at worst, it may be an unwarranted intrusion into the applicant's privacy.

Q 3:5   Is it appropriate to ask about educational background?

Yes. Applicants may be required to outline their education, and employers may require that applicants have some minimum educational achievement. However, employers must be prepared to articulate the reason that a certain type or level of education is necessary for job success, and they must retain a measure of flexibility in applying that criterion.

For instance, an older employee with work experiences equivalent to a significant education should not be automatically disqualified; a contrary policy may disqualify a disproportionate percentage of minorities or women. In one well-known case, the U.S. Supreme Court ruled that the requirement of a high school diploma for promotion in a large company, without proof that such education was necessary, had illegally relegated most of the company's black employees to the maintenance department, while white employees moved into better paying jobs. [See, Griggs v Duke Power Co, 401 US 424 (1971)]

Q 3:6   May the company inquire into an applicant's health?

The company may ask whether an applicant can perform the essential functions of the job. However, inquiries into past disabilities, such as: "Have you ever missed work due to back pain?" are forbidden. Additionally, even if an applicant identifies a disability, the employer should not reject the application without first investigating a reasonable way to accommodate the applicant's physical limitation.

Q 3:7   May an employer test for AIDS?

Unless the company is in the health care business, it probably has nothing to gain and much to lose by testing for AIDS. Numerous state human rights agencies hold the legal position that AIDS is a disability and that it is illegal to refuse to employ someone who has AIDS, but is healthy enough to do the job. Furthermore, the available tests for AIDS are generally expensive and open to false positive results, so that the expense is often doubled by the need to confirm all positive findings. If a refusal to hire is based on a false positive test result, and the hiring decision becomes known to a third party, a serious defamation case is in the company's future. [CF Doyle v Home Office Reference Laboratory, 1990 US Dist LEXIS 5850 (WD Pa 1990)] And, finally, since AIDS has been perceived as highly correlated with homosexuality, AIDS testing may be interpreted as a form of discrimination based on sexual orientation, which a small but growing number of state laws and city ordinances forbid.

Q 3:8   Are there questions that the Americans with Disabilities Act (ADA) forbids to be included on a job application?

The ADA significantly affects an employer's policies regarding physical examinations and inquiries of job applicants and employees.

Employers may no longer conduct physical examinations or ask any medically related questions prior to offering employment. In other words, application forms that list certain diseases or medical conditions and require the applicant to check those from which he or she suffers, or has suffered in the past, must be modified to remove those questions. The ADA does permit an employer to explain the essential functions of the job for which the person is applying, however, and to ask whether the person can perform those functions with or without a reasonable accommodation. For example, an employer may state that the job involves extensive lifting of heavy objects and ask if the applicant could meet this job requirement, but it may not ask if the person has a congenital back problem. An employer may also ask the applicant to demonstrate an ability to perform the job. If the applicant indicates that he or she can perform the essential functions of the job with an accommodation, the employer may ask how the applicant would perform the job and with what accommodation.

In explaining and interpreting the prohibition against pre-offer medical inquiries, the EEOC has stated that the following application or interviewing questions are forbidden: "Is there any health-related reason why you may not be able to perform the job for which you are applying?" and "How many days were you absent from work because of illness last year?" Also, any question related to an applicant's workers' compensation history is disallowed.

Q 3:9   May the applicant be asked what languages he or she speaks?

Yes, but only if the job requires foreign language skills. If the question is merely part of a stock printed form, or is used as a way to assess achievement, then it is probably better to delete it. However, do not ask an applicant's primary language, as this might be evidence of intent to discriminate on the basis of national origin.

Q 3:10   May the applicant's age or date of birth be asked?

No. That question is evidence of age discrimination. The fact that the company needs this information for benefits purposes is no excuse. The information should be obtained on a separate benefits form after the applicant has already been hired.

Q 3:11   May the company inquire about an applicant's marital status?

An employee's marital status, children, and child-rearing plans are none of an employer's business. Such questions have resulted in employers rejecting female applicants because, claimed the employers, present or future family responsibilities might interfere with job performance.

Q 3:12   May an employer ask about pregnancy or plans to become pregnant?

Generally, no. However, if the job involves exposure to radiation or chemicals that could damage the fetus, an employer may be entitled, or even duty-bound, to alert female applicants. Also, there are a few court cases in which the employer was held to be entitled to refuse employment to a pregnant applicant, or to discharge her as soon as the pregnancy became known, because a lengthy and expensive training period would be interrupted, and rendered useless, by the upcoming pregnancy leave. However, situations such as these are rare.

Q 3:13   Are questions concerning criminal arrest records acceptable?

The EEOC takes the position that, since members of certain minority groups are more likely to be arrested, this inquiry can have an illegal adverse impact upon such groups. Therefore, under Title VII, this question cannot be asked.

Q 3:14   May the applicant be asked about criminal convictions?

As with arrests, the EEOC feels that inquiries regarding criminal convictions can have an adverse impact on minority group members. However, the EEOC and the courts recognize that employers have a legitimate right to know whether an applicant has ever been convicted of crimes. And this concern is particularly significant where cash, drugs, valuable property, or one-on-one customer, patient, or client contacts are involved. Therefore, this question may be asked. However, if the question is included on the application, it should be accompanied by the statement: "Criminal convictions are not an absolute bar to employment, but will only be considered with respect to the specific requirements of the job for which you are applying."

Q 3:15   May applicants be asked about their military records?

This inquiry, if made, should be limited to the relevant skills and training the applicant may have acquired as a consequence of military service. Employers should not inquire into military service in another country. Nor should applicants be asked about the type of discharges they received; if this inquiry is made, it should be accompanied by a statement that a less-than-honorable discharge is not an absolute bar to employment. Care should also be taken when inquiring about reservist and National Guard responsibilities. If employment is denied, there may be the appearance that the applicant's military time commitment was the motive—an illegal reason for denying employment.

Q 3:16   May an applicant be asked to provide references?

It is permissible to request personal and professional references. As more and more former employers are limiting reference information to a mere confirmation of the applicant's dates and position of employment, other character and professional references are assuming increased significance in a meaningful application process. However, two caveats are in order here. First, the employer should not ask references any questions that would be illegal if they were asked of the applicant. Second, the employer must not insist that a character reference be a member of the clergy; such a reference could be viewed by the EEOC as an oblique way of ascertaining the applicant's religion.

Q 3:17   Are reference checks and background investigations permitted?

An employer has the legal right to ask about an applicant's prior employment and to follow up with written or oral inquiries to the previous employers. The problem is that many companies, concerned about lawsuits, have adopted a policy that only verifies the former employee's dates of employment, position, and salary. This is prudent on the prior employer's part, but not very helpful to the potential employer. One solution is to build a relationship of trust with human resources managers at companies in the same line of business, companies that are likely to turn up as prior employers on job applications. Sometimes trade associations or professional organizations can help in establishing these contacts on a social level. A more expensive solution, but often highly effective, is to hire a firm that specializes in background investigations. However, because of the cost, these firms should probably be used only when filling key positions.

Q 3:18   How hard is it to get adequate references from former employers?

Many companies, concerned about defamation lawsuits by former employees, have adopted a policy of responding to reference checks with only the former employee's dates of employment and position held. (The author recommends to his clients that they provide only this factual data.) Apparently this practice has become so pervasive that, according to some attorneys quoted by the Bureau of National Affairs in its *Daily Labor Report* of May 3, 1990, it is nearly impossible for companies to get adequate referrals on job applicants. Yet, according to the *Daily Labor Report*, few lawsuits—such as libel, slander, and invasion of privacy—have resulted from more candid reference replies. (Nevertheless, this author's recommendation stands; these odds are no comfort if one is the unlucky employer who is being sued.) A firm's reference policy will depend on many factors, including: (1) the applicable state's law of defamation (e.g., whether a qualified business privilege is applied to reference checks), (2) the need for quid pro quo referrals from frequently contacted companies, and (3) the reliability of the company's personnel who will respond to such calls.

Q 3:19　May an applicant be asked if friends or relatives work at the company?

Yes. However, this type of inquiry is a double-edged sword for the company. On the one hand, a preference for applicants who are "connected" can have an adverse impact upon minority workers who may already be underrepresented at the company.

Q 3:20　May an applicant be asked if friends or relatives work for a competitor?

An employer concerned about its trade secrets may make this inquiry. And if, for example, the applicant indicates that a spouse is employed at a competing company, this is a legitimate reason to withhold an offer of employment.

Q 3:21　May an employer ask an applicant about clubs and other voluntary associations?

This question should not be included on the application form. It is very likely to reveal the applicant's race, religion, or national origin, while having only a remote relationship to job duties and qualifications. However, an application may ask about memberships in professional societies pertinent to the open position. On the other hand, questions concerning political affiliations are unlawful in some states. [See, e.g., Hutchcraft Van Service, Inc v City of Urbana Human Relations Commission, 433 NE 2d 329 (Ill App Ct 1982); Blackhawk Teachers' Federation v Wisconsin Employment Relations Commission, 326 NW 2d 247 (Wis App 1982); see also, Rutan v Republican Party of Illinois, 497 US 62 (1990)(rejection of job application on basis of party affiliation violated first amendment)]

Q 3:22 May an applicant be asked about personal finances?

Not really. Questions concerning the personal financial status of the applicant—such as credit history, wage garnishment, home and automobile ownership, bank and charge accounts—tend to have an adverse impact upon minority groups and single women. And their relationship to job requirements is tangential at best. On the other hand, an employer frequently does have a legitimate interest in whether an applicant is a stable resident of the community or has the use of an automobile. Inquiries as to how long the individual has lived in the area, and whether the applicant has access to reliable transportation, can elicit the desired information without running a risk of inadvertently violating equal employment opportunity laws.

Q 3:23 May an applicant be asked about credit ratings?

Employers should avoid questions concerning credit ratings. Such questions may have an adverse impact on a particular group in the applicant pool and may result in charges of discrimination against the employer.

Q 3:24 May a company deny employment on the basis of a credit report?

In addition to an adverse impact issue under Title VII, employers must consider the Fair Credit Reporting Act. Although this law is better known for its impact on retail sales and credit cards, there are also sections that deal with background investigations of employment applicants. If an employer denies employment to an applicant on the basis of a credit report prepared by a consumer reporting agency, the employer must advise the applicant of the report's existence, and that it was the reason for denying employment.

Q 3:25 How can a company validate job requirements that it feels are necessary?

This question is addressed in the *Uniform Guidelines on Employee Selection Procedures* developed by the EEOC. Perhaps most significantly, the *Guidelines* outline a procedure known as the "four-fifths rule": The illegal disparate impact of a job test or requirement will be demonstrated when the proportion of applicants from the protected group (e.g., blacks or women) with the lowest selection (or pass) rate is less than 80 percent of the selection (or pass) rate of the group (e.g., whites or males) with the highest selection rate. Since the Supreme Court's June 1995 decision on affirmative action, the entire question on quotas and contract preferences will likely come under fire in state courts and legislatures.

Q 3:26 How does the four-fifths rule work?

Suppose a company gives an aptitude test to all applicants, and requires a minimum score to be considered for employment. And suppose 25 percent of all Hispanic applicants achieve this score, while 75 percent of all white applicants score at least the minimum. The formula is:

$$\frac{.25 \text{ (Hispanic pass rate)}}{.75 \text{ (white pass rate)}} = .33$$

Thirty-three percent is less than 80 percent, therefore, the four-fifths rule is violated and the aptitude test is presumably illegal because it has a disparate impact on a protected group (Hispanics).

Q 3:27 May a company determine height and weight requirements for employees?

Minimum height and weight requirements may be discriminatory. Therefore, such standards must be proven to be job related.

Q 3:28   What sort of validation justifies height and weight requirements?

Statistical evidence correlating height and weight requirements with job performance or safety is acceptable under the *Uniform Guidelines on Employee Selection Procedures*. The evidence must show that applicants who do not meet these requirements could not perform the job adequately and safely.

Q 3:29   May applicants and employees be tested for drugs?

The ADA allows pre-employment drug testing, which may include a urine or blood test that can detect substance abuse. It may also be appropriate to request that an employee be tested if his or her behavior at work suggests the use of drugs or alcohol. Refusal can be characterized as insubordination, resulting in termination of employment. However, random testing of employees without any reason to suspect drug abuse has been ruled a constitutional violation by a number of courts with respect to public employees, and probably is a legally risky policy in the private sector as well.

At present, the status of drug testing in the workplace remains unsettled. However, the ADA clearly provides no protection for current substance abusers.

The courts have responded to drug-testing challenges in a variety of ways. For example, in New Jersey, a municipal drug-testing plan that required police officers to submit urine samples during their annual physical examinations, and that also permitted testing on a random basis, was held not to violate the officers' fourth amendment rights. The Court of Appeals for the Third Circuit held that the administrative search exception to the Fourth Amendment's protection against warrantless searches applied because police officers belong to a pervasively regulated profession, which justifiably reduces their expectation of privacy on the job. [Policeman's Benevolent Association Local 318 v Township of Washington, 850 F 2d 133, 3 IER Cas (BNA) (3d Cir 1988)]

In line with the Third Circuit's decision, the Pennsylvania appellate court upheld Philadelphia's policy requiring police officers to be tested for drug use when there are grounds for reasonable suspicion, and when the officers return from extended leaves or are reinstated, promoted, transferred, or reassigned to special units. In upholding the city's "Directive 55" drug-screening policy, the court concluded that such a policy was "inherently managerial" and therefore within the properly exercisable rights of the police commissioner. [Copeland v Philadelphia Police Dept, 840 F 2d 1139 (3d Cir 1987)]

The U.S. Department of Transportation has put into effect regulations requiring both periodic and reasonable cause testing of truck drivers. [See 49 CFR Part 40 (Oct 1, 1989)] These regulations, which took effect for big trucking companies in December 1989, and for smaller trucking outfits in December 1990, lay out in considerable detail the requisite methods of specimen collection, laboratory analysis, and reporting and disclosure requirements.

Q 3:30   What questions may be asked in a personal interview?

Obviously, questions to avoid on an application form should be avoided in an interview. Many human resources specialists believe that the best way to get useful information is to ask open-ended questions that give the interviewer the chance to evaluate many things at once: specific data about the applicant; the applicant's ability to verbalize thoughts and information; and the applicant's personality and interpersonal skills. Often an applicant will volunteer useful information that, if sought by specific questions, might bring the interviewer close to the borders of illegal inquiry.

Q 3:31   May an applicant be required to acknowledge that, if hired, the employment will be "at will"?

Yes. In fact, a statement such as the following is recommended, if the intention is to create an employment-at-will relationship: "I understand that, if hired, I will be an employee at will; that is, my employment will be for no definite period of time, but rather will be subject to termination by myself or the company at any time for any reason."

Q 3:32   What is estoppel and how does it relate to employment offers?

"Estoppel" is a legal concept under which a binding legal obligation may be created, even though no contract exists between two parties, such as an employer and an employee. As a general rule, a person who should have spoken up and did not, or who spoke mistakenly at an early point, is estopped (or "stopped") from saying the correct thing in court later on.

> **Example.** Kurt and Clara are feuding neighbors. Kurt sees that Clara is having her new garage erected partially on his side of their property line, but maliciously fails to bring this to her attention until the building has been built and the contractor has been paid. Under these circumstances, Kurt may be estopped from presenting proof in court of where the property line falls when he tries to force Clara to tear down the garage.

In the employment context, if, for instance, the company extends an offer of employment, and the applicant resigns from her present position in reliance upon this offer prior to acceptance, the company may be estopped from withdrawing the offer and offering the job to someone else. If and when this sort of estoppel comes into play will depend on the reasonableness and timing of the parties' actions and reactions. For example, if the company promptly notified the first applicant that its offer of employment was withdrawn, and that applicant could then have withdrawn her resignation with regard to her present employer, she could not successfully bind the prospective new employer by refusing to rescind her resignation.

Q 3:33   How is estoppel different from a contract?

A contract—whether or not one of employment—requires an offer (e.g., job offer), acceptance, and some bargained-for consideration. In Q 3:32, the hypothetical human resources manager did not bargain for the applicant to quit her present job, so her resignation was not a legal consideration, and since she hadn't formally accepted his offer, no contract had been formed. But the human resources manager knew that the applicant would resign her position before accepting the offer.

Q 3:34 What is the remedy when an estoppel occurs?

Unlike the legal scheme of some of the labor and employment laws discussed in this chapter, common- (court-made) law does not demand a "make-whole" remedy in an estoppel situation. In other words, turning again to the example in Qs 3:32 and 3:33, the company would not be required to reissue the withdrawn job offer to the disappointed applicant. Rather, the company might be required to respond with compensatory damages (equal to the wages and benefits the applicant lost when she resigned her job) until he or she finds a new position.

Negligent Hiring

Q 3:35 What is "negligent hiring"?

Lawsuits have been brought by victims of criminal, violent, or negligent acts perpetrated by employees whom the employer should not have either hired or retained, where a reasonable background investigation would have revealed a history of violent or aberrant behavior (see Q 3:38).

Q 3:36 What is the best way for employers to avoid negligent hiring suits?

The goal is to avoid hiring the wrong employees in the first place. An employer should examine its screening procedure to see whether it provides a thorough look at an applicant's suitability for employment.

Q 3:37 What tests do courts use to determine whether an employer has acted negligently in a hiring decision?

The employer must satisfy the court that a reasonable investigation of the employee's background was conducted vis-à-vis the job for which the employee was hired. Employers should evaluate this information with regard to the possible risk of harm or injury to co-workers or third parties that could result from the conduct of an unfit employee.

In *Nigg v. Patterson* [806 P 2d 841 (Cal 1991)], a laundromat that hired troubled juveniles through a state-run rehabilitation program was held not to be insulated from a negligent hiring lawsuit by any public policy in favor of such rehabilitation programs. The employee was a resident of a San Diego treatment center, known as Stepping Stones. The plaintiff claimed that, while she was in the laundromat, the young man attacked her with his fists and a hammer. She sued the employer for failure to exercise ordinary care by investigating her attacker's background and discovering his vicious disposition.

The complaint in the case alleges that residents of Stepping Stones were juvenile criminal offenders, and the particular employee had a history of, and propensity for, heavy drug use, extreme violence, and bizarre sexual attacks. The court held that, except for a single unannounced visit to the laundromat by a Stepping Stones counselor, employees there were unsupervised. "It is foreseeable," said the court, "that a business invitee might be injured by an unsupervised employee with vicious propensities, especially where the business is open late at night and the potential for one-on-one encounters is likely."

One of the three judges on the appellate panel filed a dissent, saying he felt it is "hugely unfair" to strap an employer with liability for an employee's aberrationally violent act. In the dissenter's view, Stepping Stones would be treated as an independent contractor, analogous to Kelly Services, thus saving the small businessperson, who owned the laundromat, from liability.

Q 3:38 What are some effective ways to recognize and avoid hiring unfit workers?

Employers should:

1. Inspect the information an applicant provides to determine if there are gaps in employment and other suspicious or unusual entries or omissions;

2. Obtain the applicant's consent to get information from past employers, personal references, and other sources, as well as a

     waiver and release from liability in connection with the reference check;

3. Document efforts to obtain information from each previous source, especially if pertinent information was not obtainable from these sources;

4. Decide whether any information provided by the applicant or learned from previous employers, personal references, or the job interview calls for a criminal record search; and

5. Advise applicants that employment is contingent on a satisfactory reference check.

Assessing Honesty in Applicants and Employees

Q 3:39   What is a polygraph and how does it work?

A polygraph is a device that continuously, visually, permanently, and simultaneously records changes in cardiovascular, respiratory, and electrodermal (electric charges on the skin) patterns. The results of the test are used for rendering a diagnostic opinion regarding a person's honesty.

Q 3:40   Is polygraph testing legal?

Over the past two decades, a number of states have passed laws eliminating or controlling the use of polygraph testing. However, the U.S. Congress has passed a polygraph law that virtually eliminates most employers' use of polygraph testing in the employment context.

Q 3:41   What are the requirements of the federal polygraph law?

The Employee Polygraph Protection Act of 1988 prevents most private employers from using lie detector tests to screen job applicants or to test current employees. An employer may use such a test only if it reasonably suspects that an employee was involved in a workplace theft or other incident that caused economic loss to the employer.

The Polygraph Protection Act includes the following:

1. The law permits private security firms and drug companies to continue administering lie detector tests to job applicants and employees.

2. Federal, state, and local government employers are exempt from the ban, and the federal government is allowed to test private consultants or experts under a national security exemption.

3. Employers are prohibited from disciplining, discharging, discriminating against, or denying employment or promotions to prospective or current workers solely on the basis of lie detector test results. Employers may request that an employee submit to a lie detector exam during an investigation of a workplace theft or other incident that causes economic loss or injury to the employer if: (1) the employee had access to the property under investigation; (2) the employer has a reasonable suspicion the employee was involved; and (3) the employer provides the employee with a written statement giving its reasons for testing particular employees.

4. The law authorizes the secretary of labor, as well as employees and job applicants, to bring civil suits under the Act, and federal courts are given the power to award legal and equitable relief. The Department of Labor (DOL) may seek civil fines of up to $10,000 against employers that violate the law.

5. The law prescribes detailed procedures that employers must follow during any permitted lie detector tests.

6. The law does not preempt any state or local laws or collective bargaining agreements that prohibit lie detector tests or are more restrictive with respect to lie detector tests than the federal law.

Q 3:42 Who is considered to be an applicant for employment under the federal Polygraph Protection Act?

An applicant includes a person being considered for employment for the first time, and also a current employee who holds a job that is not covered by an exception to the Polygraph Protection Act, but who is applying for a job, or is otherwise being considered for a job, whether or not covered by an exception.

Q 3:43   Beside polygraphs, what other "lie detectors" exist?

Other lie detectors include deceptographs, voice stress analyzers, psychological stress evaluators, or any other similar device that is used for the purpose of rendering a diagnostic opinion regarding an applicant's or employee's honesty.

Q 3:44   Is anything excluded from the definition of a lie detector?

Yes. Medical tests used to evaluate the presence of controlled substances are excluded, as are written or oral tests commonly referred to as "honesty" or "paper-and-pencil" tests.

Q 3:45   Which employers are exempt from the polygraph and lie detector-testing prohibitions?

An employer authorized to manufacture, distribute, or dispense a controlled substance may administer a lie detector test to any applicant who would have direct access to the manufacturing, storage, distribution, or sale of any such substances. This exemption does not apply to employers involved in the transportation or storage of these substances. Private employers that provide security and security-related services may test applicants for employment.

In late 1990, the Mississippi Supreme Court held that a state-operated mental health facility was justified in firing two attendants who refused to take a polygraph test after one of their patients had been found to have a mysterious neck injury. The chief justice, writing for the court, stated that the state institution had a duty to the juvenile patient to investigate the injuries "to the fullest extent of the law," and that the plaintiff-employees had an analogous duty to cooperate fully in the investigation. Although the Mississippi decision involved state action and turned on constitutional questions, it is instructive as to how courts can be expected to balance the competing interests at issue when employees are requested to submit to a lie detector test. [Roosevelt Jackson and Annie Grant v Hudspeth Mental Retardation Center, 573 So 2d 750 (Miss 1990)]

Q 3:46   Who are considered employers that provide "security services"?

Under the DOL's regulations implementing the Employee Polygraph Protection Act, a broader definition of the law's security service exemption emerged than had been incorporated in the interim rule in effect for the Act's first two years. Under the interim rule, only armored car personnel, personnel engaged in the design, installation, and maintenance of security alarm systems, and other security personnel (if their responsibilities involved certain specified types of facilities) were covered by the exemption. Under the final regulations, employers providing security services to casinos, racetracks, lotteries, and "other business activities where large amounts of cash are acquired from or dispensed to customers," are also permitted to administer lie detector tests to their employees.

This broader regulation comes in response to the large number of comments (almost half of the total comments) received by the DOL's Wage and Hour Division after publication of the interim rule. Even the sponsors of the security services provision in the Act, Senator Don Nickles (R-Okla.) and Representative Marge Roukema (R-N.J.), criticized the narrowness of the interim rule. On the other hand, the Service Employees International Union wrote in support of the DOL's original definition, adding that it strongly opposed "any attempt to broaden the exemption to include security personnel servicing private homes or businesses."

The final regulation was something of a compromise between the two extreme positions. On the one hand, it clearly expanded the exemption beyond what was permitted under the interim rule. On the other hand, it still does not stretch the exemption so far as to cover all security functions that a security company might possibly perform. In essence, the final regulations extend the exemption to cover security services when they are provided to businesses and institutions in which "cash in effect constitutes the inventory or stock-in-trade."

Q 3:47   What facilities, materials, operations, and assets are Polygraph Protection Act exemptions?

Security services must protect operations, whether privately or publicly owned, that affect the health and safety of any state or its political subdivisions, or the national security of the United States, such as:

- Facilities engaged in the production, transmission, or distribution of electric or nuclear power
- Public water supply facilities
- Facilities that ship or store radioactive or other toxic waste materials
- Public transportation operations
- Operations that provide currency and securities
- Communication facilities
- Hospitals and health research facilities
- Facilities at which large public events are held

Q 3:48   What constitutes an "economic injury" or "loss"?

An economic injury or loss to an employer's business includes theft, embezzlement, misappropriation, or an act of unlawful industrial espionage or sabotage. Unintentional economic losses, such as injury resulting from a workplace accident, do not justify lie detector testing.

Q 3:49   May an employer use the polygraph test when thefts are committed by one employee against another employee?

No. The economic loss must be suffered by the employer, not its employees.

Q 3:50   What constitutes "access to property"?

Access means more than direct physical contact; it includes the opportunity to cause or aid in causing an economic loss or injury. For example, when an employee has the combination to a safe or the ability to falsify records to effectively conceal a loss, he or she has access to property.

Q 3:51   What constitutes "property"?

Property includes not only tangible items, but also intangible items of value, such as technical information, trade secrets, and security codes.

Q 3:52   What "reasonable suspicion" justifies a lie detector test?

An employer's "reasonable suspicion" must have some observable, articulatable basis in fact. Access alone is insufficient to establish reasonable suspicion. It is the employer's burden to establish that reasonable suspicion existed to justify the lie detector examination.

Q 3:53   What information must an employer provide to an employee prior to giving the examination?

The employer must provide a statement that sets forth with particularity the specific activity or event under investigation. The employer must also reveal the basis for testing a particular employee. This written statement must be signed by a person employed by the company who is authorized to legally bind the employer.

The statement must set forth the economic loss or injury suffered by the employer and must indicate that the employee had access to the property that is the subject of the investigation. The employer must also describe the basis of its reasonable suspicion.

Q 3:54   When must this statement be given to the employee who will be tested?

This statement must be given to the employee 48 hours prior to the scheduled examination.

Q 3:55   Must the statement identify any person(s) who provided the employer with information giving rise to its reasonable suspicion?

No. The employer does not have to reveal the names or identities of co-workers or others who provided information.

Q 3:56　What adverse action may an employer take against an employee applying for a promotion on the basis of the lie detector test result?

An employer may take adverse action against an employee only with respect to the prospective position applied for, not the current position the employee holds. For example, an employee attempting to transfer into a security-related position may be denied the transfer if he or she fails a lie detector test, but the test results cannot be used against that person's current employment status.

Q 3:57　Must the employer's adverse action be founded on something in addition to the lie detector test result?

Yes. An employer's adverse action may not be based solely on the results of, or the refusal to take, a lie detector test. The action must also be based on either the employee's statements or admissions, or some bona fide reason, such as the employee's employment history.

Q 3:58　Does the Polygraph Protection Act supersede state or local laws or collective bargaining agreements?

The Polygraph Protection Act does not preempt any provision that either prohibits lie detector tests altogether, or is more restrictive with respect to such tests than the Polygraph Protection Act.

Q 3:59　May an employer ask its employees to waive their rights under the Polygraph Protection Act?

Applicants or employees may not waive any of the rights provided by the Polygraph Protection Act, voluntarily or by contract, unless a specific action or complaint is involved. In other words, an advance general release is void as to later, specific testing situations.

Q 3:60　Are there questions that may not be asked during a lie detector examination?

Yes. Questions concerning the following are prohibited:

- Racial matters
- Religious beliefs
- Political beliefs
- Sexual preferences
- Union affiliation

Q 3:61   Are there regulations regarding the length and frequency of the lie detector test?

Yes. A lie detector test will violate the Polygraph Protection Act if one examiner conducts more than five tests in one day, or if each test does not last at least 90 minutes.

Q 3:62   What types of legal claims can arise from lie detector testing?

Employees have relied on several successful theories to bring lawsuits relating to lie detector testing:

1. *Public policy tort theory.* Some states have recognized a cause of action when a statute prohibits submitting an employee to a lie detector as a term or condition of employment.

2. *Breach of contract.* If the employment relationship is governed by an implied contract not to discharge except for "just cause," the employee may argue that discharge in reliance on the results of a lie detector examination cannot establish "cause."

3. *Invasion of privacy.* The constitutions of several states deal with privacy and may apply to the private sector. [See, e.g., Alaska Const, art I, § 22 (1972); Cal Const, art I, § 1 (1972); Hawaii Const, art I, § 6 (1978)]

4. *Defamation.* A discharge shortly after a lie detector exam could lead co-workers to infer that the employee was terminated because he or she lied, and could result in the publication of a defamatory statement in the workplace. Under the doctrine of compelled self-publication, an employer's liability may extend to instances in which a former employee seeking employment was compelled to reveal that he or she had been fired for failing a lie detector test.

5. *Negligence.* If an employee can prove that the exam is not up to industry standards, the examiner's negligence can be imputed back to the employer.

6. *Intentional infliction of emotional distress.* The issue in this type of litigation is whether the employer's conduct was outside the bounds of "civilized society."

7. *Discrimination.* Employees have made claims that lie detector tests disproportionately fail blacks because of physiological particularities. Other potential claims include sexual discrimination or sexual harassment based on the polygraph examiner's conduct, or offensive questions about sexual preferences and practices.

Q 3:63　What is "negligent administration" of a lie detector test?

Some courts have recognized a duty to administer the lie detector examination with "due care." Failure to administer the lie detector test with appropriate due care may be the basis for a suit based on negligent administration of a lie detector test. An employee may challenge the examination by claiming that a different examiner would have phrased the questions more clearly, interpreted the chart more skillfully, or taken more time. The statutory standard requires a test to last at least 90 minutes. Shorter examinations may be faulted on their length alone.

Q 3:64　May an employee sue his or her employer for negligent administration of a lie detector test?

Yes. Although it is not a common cause of action, several courts have recognized claims by employees for negligent administration of a lie detector test. Considering the federal legislation regarding restricted use of lie detector tests, these claims may become more common in the future.

At least one major state court rejected an employee's tort claim for negligent administration of a polygraph exam in 1990. The New York Court of Appeals held that the employee, allegedly forced to resign after failing a lie detector test, could not sue the private detective agency that administered the test. Writing on behalf of a unanimous bench, Judge Titone said that, while the suit brought by a former United Parcel Service Manager was not preempted by the federal Employee Polygraph Protection Act, the Act nevertheless "greatly diminishes the strength of the arguments for recognizing a new tort remedy at the state level." The New York Court of Appeals reasoned that the federal law establishes sufficient safeguards against improper testing, and provides remedies for those who allegedly are injured by violations of the federal law.

Q 3:65   Has the federal Employee Polygraph Protection Act produced litigation?

The DOL's most significant action under the Act thus far is a $305,000 fine, assessed against the operator of a chain of Wendy's Restaurants in Kansas City, Missouri (WH of KC Inc.), which allegedly required its employees to take illegal lie detector tests. The fine, which was announced by the DOL's Wage and Hour Division in April of 1991, consisted of individual penalties of $2,000 each for a total of 152 allegedly illegal polygraph tests purportedly administered between December 1988, and June 1990. An additional $1,000 penalty was assessed for alleged recordkeeping violations. The company exercised its right to request a hearing before an administrative law judge to contest the penalty. The company claimed that the penalty was based upon improper wording in the notice that was provided to employees prior to administration of the test, and that if the wording was indeed legally incorrect, it was the fault of the firm that administered the lie detector tests.

Q 3:66   Are other types of honesty tests recommended?

Some pencil-and-paper honesty tests are well respected. And although numerous states now forbid, or severely restrict, the use of polygraphs, few have enacted similar restraints on pencil-and-paper tests. However, to avoid invasion of privacy and defamation actions, be sure that the job for which the individual is applying warrants such a test, and keep the test results strictly confidential.

There are basically three types of honesty tests:

1. The *overt integrity test*, which asks about an individual's attitudes toward theft and other illegal activities;
2. The *personality test*, which is intended to predict workplace behavior with respect to dependability, job performance, and drug use as well as honesty; and
3. The *combination test*, which combines both types of questions in an attempt to measure honesty.

Q 3:67   What are the pros and cons of honesty tests?

Generally, these tests come under attack because of the uncertainty of their reliability to accurately measure a person's propensity for honest behavior.

On the other hand, paper-and-pencil integrity tests generally are not prohibited by federal or state law, and they have not aroused the same vociferous animosity and distrust of labor unions, civil liberties groups, and so forth, as have polygraphs. Some well-established testing companies claim high correlations between test results and later employment experience. But it is important to track hiring patterns in relation to test results. If honesty testing leads, for example, to an above-average rejection rate for minority applicants, the test could be held to have an illegal adverse impact on that minority group under federal or state discrimination laws. A second caveat: pencil-and-paper tests may well be the next target of lawyers and organizations that oppose any intrusion into employees' privacy. Some polygraph statutes (e.g., in Massachusetts) may already be broad enough to cover pencil-and-paper tests. Employers should keep abreast of new legal challenges in this area.

Employee Evaluation

Employee Health

Q 3:68   May an employer conduct a post-hire physical examination under the provisions of the ADA?

Once an employer has offered a job to an applicant, it may conduct any medical inquiry or examination as long as it requires the same inquiry and examination of all successful applicants in the same job category. In fact, an offer of employment may be contingent on the results of the medical examination. At this point, questions may also be asked about previous injuries and workers' compensation claims. If the post-offer medical inquiry or exam reveals a disability for which no reasonable accommodation exists, the employer may rescind the employment offer. Also, if the examination reveals a disability that poses a current, significant threat to the health or safety of the individual or to others, which cannot be eliminated or reduced by a reasonable accommodation, the employer may refuse to hire this person.

Q 3:69 Does the ADA permit medical examinations of current employees?

Employees who are injured on or off the job, and become disabled within the meaning of the ADA, may be required to undergo a job-related medical examination. Similarly, employers may require job-related medical examinations of employees returning from workers' compensation or disability leave, as long as the requirement extends to all employees within that category rather than only to those who, for example, had previously lodged insurance claims.

Employers may continue to conduct voluntary medical examinations of their employees as part of an employee health program. Any information learned as a result of a voluntary or involuntary medical examination must be kept confidential and must not be used to discriminate against any employee. Congress carved out two very important exceptions to these restrictions on medical examinations: drug tests and fitness for duty exams. Thus, any practices currently in place regarding drug screening or fitness for duty may remain in place despite the restrictions on other types of medical exams and inquiries.

The ADA also limits medical exams of current employees to those situations where they are job related and consistent with business necessity. The examination may be triggered by some evidence of problems related to job performance or safety. The scope of the examination, however, must be related to the functions of the job in question.

Q 3:70   How is the Drug-Free Workplace Act of 1988 affecting employers?

On November 18, 1988, the Drug-Free Workplace Act became law as part of the omnibus anti-drug legislation approved by Congress. Although the law is complicated, the Office of Management and Budget (OMB) issued guidelines to aid federal agencies in enforcing the statutory requirement that federal contractors and grant recipients maintain drug-free workplaces. Although the rules and considerations embodied in this Act are complex, OMB's guidelines, which are published in the Federal Register, provide a detailed question-and-answer section for implementing the Drug-Free Workplace Act. However, several courts have already been called upon to resolve challenges to the new Act.

Probationary Employees

Q 3:71   What is meant by the term "probationary employee"?

This term typically occurs in union contracts. Most collective bargaining agreements provide for a period of time (usually 30, 60, or 90 days) immediately after a new employee starts on the job, during which time the company can fire the new hire without demonstrating good cause for the termination. The probationary employee has no right to invoke the grievance and arbitration procedure in the contract, and the union usually will not lift a finger to forestall the firing. Many nonunion companies, too, have formal or informal probationary periods. Often the completion of probation is signaled by a performance review and is rewarded by eligibility for certain fringe benefits, such as participation in the company's group health insurance plan.

Q 3:72   Should nonunion companies adopt the concept of "probationary employee"?

Placing new employees on probation for a specified period should be done with great caution. Some employers have mistakenly labeled the next step for the probationary employee as "permanent" employee. Sometimes the result has been a wrongful discharge action by a terminated "permanent employee," who argued that the category signified either lifetime employment or at least a commitment by the company to fire its "permanent" workers only for good cause. This pitfall can probably be avoided by classifying those who have completed their probationary periods as "regular employees," and with company policies clearly spelling out what changes occur in an employee's status upon successful completion of his or her probationary period. Typically, "regular employees" are entitled to specified employee benefits not available to probationers.

Q 3:73   What are the types and terms of probationary employment?

In unionized companies, new hires who successfully complete their probationary periods are admitted to union membership, which brings with it all the rights and obligations contained in the collective bargaining agreement, as well as the union's own constitution and bylaws. Nonunion firms that require new hires to complete a probationary period frequently offer probationers a training and evaluation program during their initiation into the organization. Typically, the end of the probationary period is marked by a formal written performance evaluation, which, if favorable, may result in the new employee's first pay raise.

Performance Evaluations

Q 3:74   What are performance evaluations?

Performance evaluations have almost as much variety as the corporations, partnerships, and other business organizations that use them. Some are objective and quantitative, measuring and assessing the number of sales calls, orders, key strokes, or billable hours the employee has recorded over the evaluation period. Others are subjective and qualitative, requiring the manager or supervisor to judge the subordinate's knowledge, attitude, initiative, cooperativeness, and the like. One popular evaluation method, managing by objectives (MBO), involves interaction of the supervisor and subordinate in setting specific goals for the subordinate to achieve, and then a subsequent mutual evaluation of whether the objectives were in fact attained during the following evaluation period.

Corporations have usually concluded that the more complex and qualitative the job, the more it needs to perform periodic performance evaluations. When most Americans filled slots on assembly lines, managers had little difficulty measuring quantity and quality of performance by such factors as number of parts assembled per hour or day, number of rejects, days absent, etc. Today, even where number of keystrokes or sales calls is a relevant measure, it is desirable that other, more subtle indicators of an employee's contribution be identified and tracked over time. Such measures are rarely, if ever, adequate to assess the employee's total contribution to the enterprise.

Q 3:75 Should companies use performance evaluations?

Yes. Performance reviews, if done well, serve many purposes. They can:

- Establish a formal communication system between managers and subordinates
- Provide an opportunity to commend employees for good service
- Provide a powerful source of documentary evidence to defend wrongful discharge and discrimination suits
- Identify inadequacies and inefficiencies in a company's training and production methods

To fully benefit from performance evaluations, a review procedure must be designed that is right for the organization—and then it must be implemented and maintained properly. A slipshod or irrelevant evaluation system is far worse than none at all, since it will harm employee morale and create unwarranted disparities in evaluation and testing of employees, perhaps resulting in claims of illegal discriminatory motivation.

Q 3:76 Which types of performance appraisals serve which purposes?

A performance appraisal aimed primarily at motivating the company's employees will stress employee involvement, i.e., a role more than just a job. Communication between appraiser and appraised employee, employee input, and appraiser feedback are the linchpins of such a system.

The best example is MBO, an appraisal program in which each employee helps to develop the standards, goals, and objectives against which performance periodically will be measured.

An appraisal program intended primarily to facilitate internal selection and promotion decisions will emphasize comparative performance between and among employees. Employees are ranked against one another in the same job classification. Any budgeted increase in payroll for the department or job classification may be divided up accordingly. Although such a system tends to emphasize administrative convenience over employee motivation, even so, at a bare minimum, either the appraiser or a human resource specialist in the company should review and explain the appraisal to each employee. The use of a graphic rating system scale facilitates a quantitative comparison of employees in the same job classification.

Q 3:77   What are the elements of an appropriate employee evaluation program?

There is no one evaluation program that is right for all organizations, but all employee evaluation programs should have at least the following in common. They should:

1. Evaluate employee behavior and attributes that actually relate to the particular job and the needs of the specific business;

2. Force supervisors to focus on meaningful issues and to provide useful information;

3. Facilitate constructive dialogue between supervisors and subordinates; and

4. Inform the employee of behavior and performance deficiencies in a way that gives the employee a chance to rebut unfair or inaccurate criticism.

Q 3:78   Should objective or subjective criteria be used in the evaluation process?

Objective measurements of employee performance have the advantage of being readily verifiable; for example, a total of the number of drawings a drafter produced or the number of programs a computer programmer created or analyzed. Even with highly sophisticated jobs, some objective measurements are available, such as the number of hours a lawyer bills to clients of the firm, or the number of patients seen by a dentist in a clinic. By contrast, subjective measurements are difficult to verify and to apply uniformly throughout a company, and breed favoritism and prejudice among supervisors. Therefore, to avoid litigation, use objective, quantifiable criteria as much as possible. However, bear in mind that the relationship between the criteria and the job must be validated. Avoid the notion that, because something can be measured, it must be relevant. For example, an evaluation procedure limited to the number of drawings produced by a drafter, but unmindful of the complexity or novelty of each person's work, would be objective, but would not be fair.

Q 3:79   How can subjective performance be evaluated?

One way is to set goals and then see if they have been met. Another is to emphasize performance and behavior, not personal characteristics.

Q 3:80   Can employee attitudes be evaluated?

Employers should avoid focusing on an employee's attitude. Far too often an employee termination or disciplinary problem is explained by saying: "He had a bad attitude," or "She and her supervisor had a personality conflict." This sounds pretty tenuous, if not downright discriminatory, to an EEOC investigator when the supervisor and employee are of different sexes or races. The supervisor's attention should focus on job performance, and be reflected in goals achieved and performance levels reached. This will help keep illegal bias out of the evaluation process.

Q 3:81   How complex should the evaluation form be?

The evaluation form should cover all relevant performance criteria. In general, the more sophisticated the job, the more complex the evaluation. Regardless of length, it should be comprehensible to both evaluator and employee. If the evaluator does not understand the form, he or she cannot administer it properly, or make an effective witness if the company must demand a personnel action based in whole or in part on the evaluation. The less the employee comprehends the evaluation, the more likely he or she is to challenge it.

Q 3:82   How can the company use employee evaluations?

Besides determining the adequacy of employee performance and identifying inadequate performers, evaluations can be used to:

- Teach employees how to improve performance
- Give formal recognition to outstanding performers
- Identify weak departments and programs in the organization
- Promote and demote employees
- Provide a basis for merit pay increases

Q 3:83   May one employee be paid more than another for doing the same job, based on a performance evaluation?

Employees may be paid on the basis of merit, and in many instances this is a key incentive. The critical ingredient is objective evidence of the merit that justifies the pay disparity. If the value of one employee over another cannot be demonstrated objectively, an employer risks being accused of:

1. Violating the Equal Pay Act by paying an employee of one sex more than a co-worker of the opposite sex, simply because one is male and the other female; and
2. Setting salaries in a discriminatory manner on the basis of race, age, or another forbidden factor.

Additionally, in the case of unionized employees, an employer may need to bargain with the union not only about giving merit raises, but also about using evaluation forms in the first place.

Q 3:84   What is a graphic rating scale?

Various relevant characteristics (e.g., quantity of work, quality of work, knowledge of the job, ability to communicate with superiors, subordinates, and/or peers, dependability, initiative, punctuality, problem solving, attention to safety considerations) are listed, usually vertically, along the left-hand side of the form. Across the form will be some sort of scale, usually numerical. For example, the form's instructions may state that a "1" is outstanding or superior and a "5" unsatisfactory. Often, the various criteria will each be accompanied by a short definition. Appraisers may also be asked to add up the various individual ratings and give a total score. The form may also provide space for the appraiser's more subjective or summation-type comments, as well as for the employee's reaction to the appraisal.

Q 3:85   What are the advantages and disadvantages of graphic rating scales?

Graphic rating scales are fairly easy to develop and can be adapted to many types of jobs. However, broad general characteristics (e.g., "leadership" or "problem solving") may prove hard to relate to the actual requirements of specific jobs. Also, the human resource specialist must watch out for common appraiser errors and quirks. For instance, if "1" signifies the best, some supervisors will only award it if the employee "walks on water," while the head of another department may award "1's" more generously. Yet a third manager may feel unfamiliar with a certain employee's work, or be reluctant either to flatter or criticize too strongly; such a supervisor will give everyone "2's" or "3's," i.e., the middle of the range.

Q 3:86   Can legal problems arise when appraisers give inaccurate or inconsistent ratings?

Yes. First and foremost, a rating system that presents criteria having no genuine relationship to actual job requirements may have a discriminatory impact upon a protected group, such as blacks or women, and have no defensible business justification.

Second, appraisers who group subordinates around the middle of the rating scale are creating future difficulties for themselves and the human resource department, because when it comes time to terminate a problem employee, the record of poor performance and appropriate counseling simply will not be there to justify the termination decision.

Q 3:87   What is a behavioral anchored rating scale?

In the behavioral anchored rating scale (BARS) method, the first step is to properly identify the most important parameters of the particular job. Second, these major job dimensions must be accurately described in the performance appraisal form. Third, the appraiser is offered a set of sentences that describe employee behavior with respect to the defined job criterion. These descriptive sentences will range from presenting the least desirable to the most worthwhile characterization of the particular employee's performance in relation to the given job characteristic. The appraiser then picks the sentence that most closely conforms to that employee's performance.

The BARS method can overcome the problems identified in Qs 3:84 through 3:86, because it has been demonstrated to have high validity with respect to almost any job, when properly applied. Although graphic rating scales are easily developed and used by even relatively unsophisticated managers, BARS demands substantial expertise to be administered properly. Thus, not only will BARS strain the human resources component of a smaller corporation to its limits, but even in a larger organization, the exhaustive job analyses demanded to make BARS work may be subject to frequent obsolescence in high technology sectors of the economy.

Q 3:88   What is essay rating?

In essay-type appraisals, the appraisers are basically free to say what they will about their subordinates' strengths and weaknesses. Unless these appraisers are well trained, the results may yield (in a worst-case scenario) "smoking guns" for use by plaintiff-employees in discrimination lawsuits. Even offhanded and seemingly "innocent" observations—such as: "brings a welcome 'woman's touch' to her classroom," or "I'm afraid you just can't teach an old dog new tricks"—can come back to haunt the organization, becoming the centerpiece of a charge of sex or age discrimination. [See, e.g., Price Waterhouse v Hopkins, 104 LEd 2d 268 (1989), where partners' comments on plaintiff's manners and dress helped form the basis of a successful sex discrimination suit]

Q 3:89   What is critical incident rating?

A variation of essay rating is critical incident rating, in which the appraiser keeps a sort of running narrative or log of significant (at least in the appraiser's view) performance events throughout each appraisal period. This approach also requires proper training and orientation for the appraiser. Its advantage over essay rating is that it forces the appraiser to focus on job-related occurrences, rather than allowing the appraiser a license to ramble on and wander down tangential paths.

Q 3:90   What kinds of ranking methods are available?

Several methods of ranking employees within a department, section, or job classification have been developed by human resource professionals and industrial psychologists.

In *paired comparison* ranking, each employee in the group is compared one-on-one to every other employee in the group. This exercise may be performed for as many criteria as are desired and practical. If the job group is big, and there are several significant performance criteria, the task can be time-consuming. But the result can be a fairly solid, quantitative measurement of the strongest, average, and weakest members of the group. On the other hand, the group's overall relationship to the ideal group for doing the particular job remains rather elusive.

In *alternation* ranking, the appraiser picks one member of the job group as "most effective," another as "least effective" in a given criterion, and so forth, moving toward the middle or average point on the spectrum of group members. This method overcomes the danger, presented by more common graphic rating scales, of clustering employees around the median. Also, it is less time-consuming than paired comparison ranking. However, like the paired comparison method, it only tells the company how group members compare to one another, not how they stack up against the competition.

An even easier method is *forced distribution* ranking, which usually requires the appraiser to put a percentage of the group on each rung of the hierarchy; e.g., 10 percent of the group on the highest rung, 20 percent on the next rung, 40 percent in the mid-range, and 20 percent and 10 percent on the bottom plateaus.

Q 3:91   What is peer review?

In a typical peer review system, colleagues are called upon to rate the individual's performance in confidential evaluations and/or deliberations. Usually peer review is only effective in fairly sophisticated professions, such as medicine, law, and college teaching. Confidentiality is critical, and yet in court cases involving tenure, partnership, and staff privilege decisions challenged under state and federal antidiscrimination laws, these rulings have called for confidential deliberations to be revealed.

Discipline

Attendance

Q 3:92   Should a company have a formal attendance policy?

Yes. Many companies, especially smaller ones, believe that an attendance policy is unnecessary, or that a statement such as "Excessive absenteeism may result in discipline, up to and including discharge," is sufficient. Such an approach is seldom adequate. In the absence of specific attendance requirements, supervisors will apply personal standards and will do so unevenly, depending on each supervisor's attitude toward each subordinate. Employees who are good producers, who are difficult to replace, or whom the supervisor likes, will be treated more leniently than those less favorably regarded. The consequence for the company may be charges of illegal discrimination, morale problems, and the possibility of a union-organized effort to correct the inconsistent treatment.

Q 3:93   What aspects of attendance should a policy address?

There are three issues that an attendance policy should address: absenteeism, late arrivals, and early departures. An absence occurs when the employee does not report to work at all. Tardiness can occur at the start of the shift, at the completion of the lunch hour, or at some other break. An early departure involves leaving the job before the end of the employee's normal workday or shift. Additionally, many companies' attendance policies address failure of the employee to call in prior to the start of the workday or shift if the employee is going to be late or absent. However, many other companies deal with this issue not as an attendance policy matter, but as a major or minor disciplinary rule.

Q 3:94   What types of attendance policies exist?

Just as disciplinary policies can be broadly divided into punitive and positive programs, attendance policies can be divided into fault and no-fault policies.

Q 3:95   What is meant by a "fault" attendance policy?

A fault policy is the traditional attendance policy that distinguishes between excused and unexcused absences. Typically, excused absences include sicknesses, for which the employee can produce a doctor's certificate, and bona fide emergencies and justifiable absences or tardiness. Unexcused absences are those that the employer (from the company's subjective perspective) does not deem to be justifiable. Usually, only unexcused absences are counted against the employee with respect to disciplinary action.

Q 3:96   What is a "no-fault" attendance policy?

Under a typical no-fault system, employees are permitted to have a specified number of absences over a given period of time (for example, 12 absences per calendar year). Every absence from work is counted against the employee's allotment, regardless of the reason for the absence. A philosophical basis is that "good" employees will expend their allotment of absences only in bona fide circumstances, and enough absences are allowed that "good" employees will not get themselves terminated for excessive absenteeism.

Q 3:97 How are late arrivals and early departures handled under an attendance policy?

Whether the attendance policy is fault or no-fault, tardiness and early departures are usually counted as partial absences, such as one-half or one-third of an absence.

Q 3:98 What are the advantages and disadvantages of a no-fault attendance policy?

The primary advantage of a no-fault policy is the ease of administration. It is not necessary for the employer to inquire into the reason for the absence. The company need only record the event and keep a running total for each employee. The disadvantage of such a mechanical policy is that employees may feel the policy is too rigid to accommodate special circumstances, and this may be disturbing to employees. The irony is that "good" employees, without attendance problems, seem to experience this state of anxiety at least as fully as "bad" employees who have a history of attendance problems.

Q 3:99 How can the overly mechanical operation of a no-fault attendance policy be diminished?

The impact of no-fault policies can be diminished in a variety of ways. For example, many no-fault policies contain a provision stating that, in meritorious cases, the automatic termination provision (which becomes effective when the employee exceeds the allotted absences) can be waived by the company president or some other high officer of the firm. Other companies exclude certain kinds of absences (example, absence due to work-related injury) from the application of the no-fault policy. Still others count successive days of absence (for example, five days off for a single bout of the flu) as a single occurrence under the no-fault system.

Work Rules

Q 3:100　What are work rules?

A company's work rules are the do's-and-don'ts that its employees are expected to obey in the day-to-day performance of their jobs. They may be promulgated to the employees in an employee handbook, posted on a company bulletin board, or distributed to the employees in the form of memoranda. Depending on the size and culture of the corporation, these rules may be numerous and detailed, or may consist of only a few general guidelines as to what is expected by the employer.

Q 3:101　Should a company have written work rules?

Yes. In today's litigious society, even small organizations made up entirely of professional employees may have employment disputes. Most often, these disputes become lawsuits when the organization terminates, or attempts to terminate, the professional's employment. When this happens, the employer will almost always find it helpful to be able to refer to specific rules of performance or conduct against which the discharged employee transgressed. In the absence of such written rules, the employer risks accusations of discriminatory treatment, inconsistent discipline, and ex post facto justice, along with the morale problems and legal exposure that these accusations create.

Q 3:102　What work rules should a company have?

If the company is small, close-knit, and informal, and particularly if it consists primarily of professional employees, work rules can be limited to a general statement of the company's expectations, perhaps supplemented by a few specific guidelines. For instance, a medical clinic, made up of doctors, nurses, and therapists or technicians, might adopt a general statement about good professional practice and appropriate patient relations, as well as a few specific rules, such as: "Patient records must be kept in absolute confidence. Breach of a patient's right of confidentiality is an extremely serious offense and will result in immediate termination." The larger the organization, and the more blue-collar and lower-level clerical workers employed, the more likely it is that a fairly extensive and detailed set of work rules will be needed.

Q 3:103   How specific and detailed should work rules be?

Some personnel directors and human resources managers seem to believe that a work rule cannot be more than five words in length. The problem with shorthand statements is that they are invariably ambiguous and therefore subject to different interpretations. There is no reason not to outline what is expected of employees, and there are many good reasons for doing so, not the least of which is that employees are more likely to follow understandable rules. With respect to such sensitive areas as alcohol and drug use, a rule running to several paragraphs may be entirely appropriate.

Q 3:104   What types of work rules exist?

Generally speaking, work rules can cover three areas: major offenses, minor offenses, and safety rules.

Q 3:105   What are major disciplinary offenses?

Major disciplinary offenses are those that, on the first violation, result in immediate termination of employment. Generally, these offenses are so serious that even without a written rule an employee would expect to be fired for committing the act. Some examples are: striking a supervisor, being intoxicated on the job, stealing from the company, or committing a blatant safety violation that endangers the employee or co-workers.

Q 3:106   What are minor disciplinary offenses?

Minor disciplinary offenses involve undesirable conduct that is not serious enough to require discharge of the employee, at least not for the first time that the behavior occurs. Furthermore, some of the rules related to the desirable or undesirable conduct are particular to the specific company or industry, and, therefore, an employee might not realize the behavior that is expected in the absence of a written

guideline. Some examples of rules covering minor disciplinary offenses are: those that prohibit wasting time on the job, personal use
of the telephone during working time, and smoking in locations other
than the employee lounge. It is common for companies to adopt a
three- or four-step disciplinary plan, under which each successive
violation of a minor disciplinary rule leads to more serious consequences (for example: oral warning, written warning, suspension
without pay, and, finally, discharge).

Q 3:107   What are safety rules?

Safety rules generally tend to fall into two categories. First, there
are general, common sense rules of safe behavior, such as those that
prohibit "horseplay" on the job, throwing paper or other debris on
the floors, or excessive speed of vehicles in company parking lots.
Second, there are safety rules that are particular to the company's
business activities. For example, a factory or warehouse may have
rules regarding the operation of forklifts and other mobile equipment.

Disciplinary Programs and Procedures

Q 3:108   Are violations of safety rules subject to the disciplinary
procedure?

As a general rule, violations of safety rules are covered under the
major and minor disciplinary rules. Typically, under the heading of
major disciplinary rules, the company will include as a cause for
immediate termination the violation of any safety rule that endangers
the physical safety of the employee or his or her co-workers, or that
results in damage to company property. Under the minor disciplinary
rules (which are subject to progressive, step discipline), the company
may have a rule defining violations that do not endanger the employee or co-workers.

Q 3:109   What disciplinary programs exist?

There are two broad types of disciplinary programs: (1) punitive,
and (2) affirmative, or positive, discipline.

Q 3:110   What is punitive discipline?

A typical punitive disciplinary program covers two types of offenses: major offenses that lead to immediate termination; and minor offenses that are subject to a progressive or step procedure. The first minor disciplinary violation usually results in an oral reprimand; the second, in a written reprimand; the third, in a suspension of one or more days without pay; and the fourth, in termination of employment. The system is called punitive because its objective is to change the employee's behavior by punishing the employee each time an offense occurs. This is the most common system in effect in both union and nonunion companies in the United States.

Q 3:111   What is affirmative (or positive) discipline?

The philosophy of affirmative or positive discipline is that the employee, if given the opportunity to alter undesirable behavior (and assisted by the supervisor), will generally choose to do so. Sometimes, there is little or no difference between punitive and positive disciplinary codes with respect to rules resulting in immediate termination. When an employee commits a serious violation, discharge from employment is the appropriate result under both systems. The real distinction is in the step or progressive system involving minor disciplinary rules. While the progression under a punitive system results in oral and written warnings, suspension without pay, and finally termination, positive or affirmative discipline takes the employee through a series of steps from a dramatically different perspective. Usually, instead of being given a warning, the employee will be asked to verbalize the reasons for the inappropriate behavior, and will then be asked to sign a written proposal or agreement embodying mutually agreed upon behavioral modifications. Generally, the most dramatic difference between the positive and punitive systems is that under an affirmative system, instead of an unpaid suspension, the employee will be given a "decision day" off with pay. During that day, the employee will be asked to consider whether continued employment is in the employee's best interest. Upon return to work, he or she will be asked to state a desire to continue employment and to make the behavior modifications necessary to facilitate continuation of the working relationship. Positive or affirmative discipline has proven to be more attractive and more successful in white-collar (as opposed to blue-collar) work environments, and in nonunion (as opposed to union) workplaces.

Workplace Due Process

Q 3:112   What is "workplace due process"?

The term "due process of law" is derived from the Fifth and Fourteenth Amendments of the U.S. Constitution (see chapter 12). "Workplace due process" is the term often used to denote an employee's right to a fair hearing before discipline or discharge takes place.

Q 3:113   Is workplace due process required by constitutional law?

No. The Bill of Rights in the U.S. Constitution does not extend its reach into the private workplace. However, public employees, such as municipal employees and those working in state hospitals and universities, are entitled to due process of law under the Fourteenth Amendment.

Q 3:114   Should a company have a workplace due-process policy?

Although not required by law to adopt a workplace due-process policy, there are several reasons why a corporation should consider doing so:

1. A grievance procedure and discharge only for good cause are strong selling points pushed by unions when trying to organize employees;

2. Courts and antidiscrimination agencies tend to look more favorably on employers that discharge only after affording their employees the chance to be heard;

3. Employees, especially white-collar workers, expect due process, although it is not imposed on their employers by law; and

4. Employees afforded due process may be less likely to sue. [See Mark J. Keppler, "Nonunion Grievance Procedures: Union Avoidance Technique or Union Organizing Opportunity?" In-

dustrial Relations Research Association, *Proceedings of the 1990 Spring Meeting*, 557-563 (1990)]

Q 3:115   What kinds of due-process programs exist?

Like company work rules, a due-process program can be as simple or as complicated as the employer makes it. As with work rules, the larger the organization, the more formal and structured the program will be. Smaller companies generally opt for relatively simple, informal procedures.

Q 3:116   What is an example of a simple and informal due-process procedure?

The most common due-process procedure is the "open-door" policy. Typically, the written statement of the policy, promulgated to employees, states that managers' doors (often including the president's) are always open to employees having problems and grievances.

Q 3:117   What is an example of a more formal and complex workplace due-process program?

Companies adopting more formal due-process programs often emulate the grievance/arbitration procedures found in typical union contracts. If the union's collective bargaining agreement calls for hiring an impartial arbitrator from the American Arbitration Association or the Federal Mediation and Conciliation Service, the nonunion company's voluntary program may delegate the arbitrator's role to a corporate employee, such as the personnel director or president.

Q 3:118   Is workplace due process final and binding on the employee?

Numerous U.S. Supreme Court decisions have held that arbitration, pursuant to a union contract, is generally final and binding on the aggrieved employee. [See, e.g., United Steelworkers v Enterprise Wheel & Car Co, 363 US 593 (1960); United Steelworkers v Warrior & Gulf Navigation Co, 363 US 574 (1960)] Few court cases suggest that the same may be true of voluntary workplace due process, unless the employee is required to sign a binding agreement to that effect before being allowed to take advantage of the employer's system. In a major policy shift, the U.S. Supreme Court recently held that a stockbroker was required to submit his age discrimination claim to binding arbitration pursuant to his employment contract. [See, Gilmer v Interstate/Johnson Lane Corp, 111 S Ct 1647 (1991)]

Q 3:119   What are some variations on the grievance arbitration model?

Some companies have developed peer review committees. The committee is composed of employees and managers who serve either for a fixed term or for a single grievance. Usually, the committee's duties are limited to review of discharge cases. Other companies hire professional arbitrators, provided by the American Arbitration Association, even if they are not required by a collective bargaining agreement to do so.

Q 3:120   How much power should the grievance committee be given?

If the decision is made to adopt a workplace due-process system with a grievance committee or peer review committee, that committee's power should be carefully and strictly circumscribed. Many employers provide access to the peer review committee only in cases of discharge from employment and only when the discharged employee requests appeal to the committee within a short period of time, such as three days from the date of discharge. It is also common for companies to limit the committee's authority to a yes-or-no answer when asked, "Did the employee violate the rule for which he or she was terminated?" In other words, the committee is not allowed to question or rewrite the rule itself.

Q 3:121 Is an employee entitled to representation during the disciplinary process?

Unlike the constitutional requirement that police give suspects access to attorneys, there is no requirement that an employee subject to investigation or discipline by the employer be given a similar right. However, unionized employees are entitled to be accompanied by a union official (business agent, officer, or steward) to any meeting or proceeding of the employer that could lead to disciplinary action. Some federal and state laws provide a similar right to some public employees. Although it is not recommended that an employee be permitted to bring an attorney into the workplace, some nonunion companies do permit employees to choose a noninvolved supervisor or co-worker to serve as a representative in disciplinary or grievance proceedings.

Q 3:122 How long should disciplinary records be retained?

Most companies drop minor disciplinary infractions and unexcused absences from an employee's record after a specific period of time, such as 12, 18, or 24 months. Nevertheless, a good rule of thumb with respect to disciplinary action is to maintain this information in the file for at least three years. Indeed, in today's litigation-oriented society, it may be wise for an employer to retain information on disciplinary action and unfavorable evaluations of employees throughout the tenure of their employment, plus a period of about three years thereafter.

Employee Searches and Surveillance

Q 3:123 Does an employee have a right against self-incrimination or unreasonable search and seizure?

The Bill of Rights does not cross the threshold of the private workplace. Therefore, an employee subject to a disciplinary investigation does not have a legal right to "take the Fifth Amendment," or to refuse to open his or her locker, lunch bucket, or desk. However, employers are cautioned not to be overly enthusiastic in the pursuit of a disciplinary investigation. Even in the private sector, employees do have some protection under state common laws of defamation, invasion of privacy, and infliction of emotional distress. Cases have arisen in which employees have successfully sued their employers for high-handed and outrageous conduct in their handling of disciplinary investigations. [See, McLain v Boise Cascade Corp, 533 P 2d 343 (Ore 1975)]

Q 3:124 How much privacy must an employee be permitted?

The answer to this question depends on many factors. First, an employee's privacy is dependent on whether the employer is a government agency or a private party. For instance, a professor at a state university may be entitled to constitutional protections that colleagues at a private liberal arts college are not. In other words, it has often been said that the Bills of Rights stops at the factory door (although some labor arbitrators have from time to time tried to invoke Fourth Amendment search-and-seizure rules and the like in deciding grievances).

Second, the collective bargaining agreement, if any, may limit management's right to invade employee privacy. Common law also sets limits on unreasonable invasions of privacy, and the standards vary from state to state. The bottom line is that an employer planning to investigate employee theft (or drug use) on its premises should proceed with great restraint. However, this does not mean that employers can do nothing. They have a right to protect their property, but in enforcing this right, employers must be ever mindful that they are brushing up against some cherished employee rights.

Q 3:125 What procedures should an employer follow if it wants to conduct employee searches?

Employee searches may violate an employee's expectation of privacy. To prevent this from occurring, before implementing an employee search, employers should have reasonable cause.

It is suggested that employers:

1. Defeat employees' expectations of privacy by notifying them that they can expect periodic searches;

2. Conduct nondiscriminatory searches of all workers, including executives;

3. Conduct searches using the least intrusive means possible;

4. Have a union representative present during the search, if applicable; and

5. Suspend and arbitrate prior to discharging an employee who is found guilty of theft or substance abuse.

Q 3:126 Can consent forms protect a company against liability?

Some employers require employees to give advance written consent to potential company searches of an office, desk, locker, or even the employee's car on company premises. Whether this exercise is effective depends on many factors. Public policy in most states does not permit an employee to waive his or her right to challenge future tortious activities by the employer. The employee may later argue that he or she did not sign the form voluntarily because employment (or continued employment) seemed to be at stake. An employee may argue that he or she did not knowingly sign the form because it was hidden in the fine print of a job application or other lengthy document. An employee may also claim that he or she did not anticipate the sort of search that ultimately ensued. Does all this mean employers should not use such consent forms if they plan to search employees for drugs or stolen goods? No. The forms may constitute a useful, maybe even a decisive, defense. But be aware that a consent form will not necessarily avert or win lawsuits.

Q 3:127 How else can an employer lower employee expectations of privacy?

If an employer intends to conduct a search-and-seizure operation under certain circumstances, the policy should be promulgated at the earliest opportunity in the company's employee handbook and other appropriate media. This serves to lower the workforce's expectation of privacy and, thus, the chances of a successful lawsuit based on a tortious invasion of privacy.

Q 3:128   May a company electronically monitor employees?

The answer depends on the kind of monitoring being conducted, why it is being done, and how it is handled.

Concerning the kind of monitoring, many states have wiretap and eavesdrop laws that expressly forbid the secret monitoring of telephone conversations.

With respect to why the employer is monitoring employees, there should be a demonstrable business purpose. For example, personal computers might be monitored to check efficiency, or telephones might be monitored to ensure that proper sales techniques are being used.

Finally, there is the issue of how the employer handles the monitoring. Advance notice to employees may circumvent a wiretap or eavesdrop statute by eliminating the element of secrecy. Notice may also diminish the employee's expectation of privacy, a necessary element in some states' common-law definition of the invasion of privacy tort, as well as in some Fourth Amendment search-and-seizure situations. Also, although employees may not like being monitored, a thoughtful employee communication program may help workers see the need, thus minimizing some of the predictable employee hostility and resentment. Hand in hand with this thought goes another: Monitoring should always be done with as much consideration as possible; for instance, telephone monitoring should not intrude on permissible personal phone calls.

Q 3:129   May a company photograph or film its employees on the job?

A common method of catching thieves in the act is to place a time-lapse video camera with a pinhole lens behind a wall or partition in the vicinity of the suspected employee's cash register, desk, or workbench. There appear to be no reported cases holding this sort of surveillance to be illegal in a private workplace. If the suspected activity occurs, the impact of this evidence can be devastating to the employee in any subsequent court action. However, patience is an essential virtue in surveillance situations, and a deep pocket is a prerequisite for the company that contracts out this work to a private detective agency. Although time-lapse cameras can show time and date on the videotape, many security professionals feel strongly that an operator be present at all times who later can verify the authenticity of the pictures by his or her live testimony. Time-lapse cameras raise another problem—the editing of what may be anywhere from several to many hours of tape so that a judge or jury sees only the critical events or transactions. In short, videotape surveillance can be highly effective, but not in the hands of amateurs.

Dishonest Employees

Q 3:130   Are undercover agents an effective means of detecting employee crime?

When a company is convinced that a thief or drug ring is operating among its employees on its premises, "planting" a detective among the employees may be the most effective means of flushing out the culprits. Detective agencies usually charge an hourly rate for the planted employee; the rate is really a composite of the regular hourly rate received as one of the company's employees, plus a premium to bring the total to the agency's regular rate. Agencies prefer to have the employer's help in establishing a cover story for the detective by setting aside an advertised job opening, accepting his or her application, and interviewing him or her as per the employer's usual practice. Then, as with time-lapse video surveillance, it becomes a waiting game, with the employee-detective being the employer's eyes and ears.

Q 3:131   Should criminal charges be lodged against a dishonest employee?

An employer may want to file criminal charges for a number of reasons: to deter other employees, to involve the criminal justice system in the process of obtaining restitution, or perhaps to establish a record that clearly negates any chance of a defamation or wrongful-termination suit by the discharged employee. Of course, the tactic can backfire if the ex-employee is ultimately acquitted. Sometimes, seeking a windfall and/or vindication, the acquitted employee may bring suit based on some sort of malicious prosecution theory.

Q 3:132   May a company threaten to bring criminal charges to gain some concessions from a dishonest employee?

The threat of criminal prosecution lurks beneath many restitution agreements extracted from thieving employees. From a legal standpoint, it is a misuse of the criminal justice process to use the threat of filing a criminal complaint to extract a confession, a release of claims, or a restitution agreement. Such a threat may itself be a criminal offense.

Q 3:133   Are disciplinary proceedings subject to defamation lawsuits?

Proceedings before a court or administrative agency are protected by an absolute privilege. Thus, while the participants could be subject to perjury charges if they lie, they may not be sued by others for defamation (libel and slander). Private grievance procedures are not covered by such an absolute privilege. However, the common law of most states recognizes a qualified privilege as a shield against defamation lawsuits. This generally means that, unless the employer maliciously lies about the employee, the employee may not later pursue a successful lawsuit for slander or libel. Malice is generally defined as the voicing of untrue statements while either knowing them to be false, or recklessly disregarding information that suggests they are false. One way to avoid liability for defamation is to carefully limit information about a disciplinary proceeding and the underlying facts only to those members of management who need to know. Another possibility is to require the employee to waive defamation claims before permitting that employee to have access to a grievance committee or peer review board.

Q 3:134   Are employees entitled to review their personnel files?

Some states have passed laws that permit employees to review their personnel files. However, these laws tend to be limited in the rights that they give employees. For example, in Pennsylvania an employee may review the file and take notes, but may not demand to remove the file from the premises or to make photocopies of its contents. That state's law also enumerates a number of items in the file that the employer need not let the employee review at all.

Additionally, those who are no longer employees, such as someone who has been fired from a job, do not retain the right to review the file. However, the employer should check state law or consult a knowledgeable attorney about the state's particular requirements, if any (see Qs 5:3–5:6).

Q 3:135 What are returning veterans' reemployment rights?

Most National Guard troops and reservists activated for the war in the Persian Gulf did not run into reemployment problems. However, the unhappy coincidence of an economic recession resulted in some returnees finding their jobs had disappeared in their absence. Decreases in American troop concentrations in Europe and elsewhere will likewise result in some veterans seeking reemployment in the private sector. Meanwhile, a decision of the U.S. Court of Appeals for the Eighth Circuit involving a lawsuit filed several years before Desert Storm and the Soviet Union's demise sheds some light on the returning veteran's reemployment rights. [Leib v Georgia-Pacific Corp, 925 F 2d 240 (1991)]

Statutory reemployment rights for veterans date from the first peacetime draft law in the United States, passed by the Congress in 1940. Section 8 of the Selective Training and Service Act of 1940 provided that a veteran returning from active duty was entitled to reinstatement to the position the veteran had vacated, or be given one of equal seniority. The law stemmed from the aftermath of World War I in which 200,000 veterans wound up jobless and enrolled in Civilian Conservation Corps camps. The legislative history of the 1940 Act reflects the finding: "While employers indicated that when their men went into the service they would receive their jobs back, the men did not get them back when they returned."

The contemporary successor to the 1940 Act is the Veterans' Readjustment Assistance Act of 1974 [38 USC §§ 2021–2026], which provides in pertinent part:

> In the case of any person who is inducted into the Armed Forces of the United States . . . for training and service and who leaves a position . . . in the employ of any employer in order to perform such training and service, and . . . makes application for reemployment within ninety days after such person is relieved from

such training and service . . . shall . . . be restored by such
employer or the employer's successor in interest.

In the Eighth Circuit case, the man returning from the Air Force
found himself a victim of the merger mania of the 1980s; his company
had been acquired and the purchaser refused to recognize his reinstatement rights. Attempting to balance the competing interests of
veterans and corporations, the court found that the balance tipped in
the veteran's favor in this case. The court reasoned that ownership
was all that had changed; plant, equipment, supervision, and composition of the workforce were all about the same. [See Lieb v
Georgia-Pacific Corp, 925 F 2d 240 (8th Cir 1991)]

Losses from Dishonest Employees

The following material is the result of research, including the
annual loss prevention colloquium in Fort Lauderdale, Florida, sponsored by Sensormatic Electronics Corp., a security company providing security systems for the 1996 Olympics in Atlanta.

Q 3:136 How much inventory loss can be attributed to dishonest employees?

According to Richard C. Hollinger, a sociologist at the University
of Florida and head of its Security Research Project, inventory loss
("shrink") in the U.S. retail industry averages about 1.85 percent of
sales per year. With retail sales averaging about $1.2 trillion annually,
shrink amounts to some $22.5 billion. Hollinger attributes 41 percent
of this loss to employees. [Richard C. Hollinger, "Crime in the Workplace: A Multi-Billion Dollar Problem," presentation, Sensormatic
Loss Prevention Colloquium, Fort Lauderdale, FL, Mar 11, 1994]

Similar statistics were reported in 1993 by the Food Marketing
Institute with respect to the supermarket industry. In a survey that
promised employee anonymity, "Forty-four percent of the employees
admitted to cash or merchandise theft. Twenty percent provided an
estimate (in dollars) of the cash and merchandise they typically steal.
These estimates ranged from $26 to $26,000 annually." [London

House and Food Marketing Institute, *Fourth Annual Report on Employee Theft in the Supermarket Industry* (1993) at 17]

Q 3:137 What are the main ways dishonest employees steal from their employers?

According to Hollinger and his colleague, loss prevention specialist Read Hayes, the major types of employee theft are:

1. *Theft of money.* Hayes says, "Theft of money is absolutely pervasive."

2. *Sweethearting*, another name for collusion. One of the conspirators is the employee, the other a friend or relative. The employee, usually working a cash register, under-rings the friend's purchases or permits the relative to go out of the store with items not properly purchased. Variants of this phenomenon may occur at warehouses and other nonretail facilities as well.

3. *Merchandise theft.* In a convenience store or supermarket, the theft may be as seemingly innocent as eating a candy bar every day. But a one dollar candy bar per day times 1,000 employees equals a $365,000 sales loss to a retail chain.

4. *Time theft.* Often overlooked because of its lack of visibility, theft of time includes late arrivals and early quits, fraudulent filling out of time sheets, and goofing off during working hours.

Q 3:138 Do dishonest employees usually limit themselves to one type of dishonest behavior?

To the contrary, while a dishonest employee may begin with relatively minor acts of dishonesty, such as consuming a small amount of inventory during a shift, the "hydraulic effect" soon takes over, according to Hollinger. As in a hydraulic system on a machine, pressure created by one form of dishonesty pushes the employee toward other acts of wrongdoing. Small, irregular acts of dishonesty can blossom into a regular pattern involving two or more of the four main types of employee theft outlined in Q 3:137.

Q 3:139　Why do employees become dishonest?

Most employees are at first uncomfortable stealing from their employers. Consequently, when they begin stealing, usually they develop rationalizations for their dishonest acts. For example, the following are actual employee comments from London House and Food Marketing Institute [*Fourth Annual Report on Employee Theft in the Supermarket Industry* (1993) at 1516]:

> My employer is a large company, and working in a small store I sometimes feel insignificant. The only problem I've had with other employees is when they steal from the company by not working while they are punched in.

> There are many people who employ others at very low wages and then expect these people to perform for them. If you don't pay me one way, you'll pay me another! All is fair in love and war. Treat others as you would have them treat you. If employers were more understanding of the people who earn them their livings, or would put themselves in these people's shoes, they might begin to understand how the other half of the world lives.

> Working for a company that cares only about profit at any cost is difficult. There is a definite loss of communication between the employees and the corporate office. Work rules change frequently. Also, we're expected to put in eight hours of work in just four hours at reduced wages. The company doesn't want to offer medical benefits to part-time people. Because part-timers don't receive benefits, full-time employees who leave are not replaced. A part-time person is assigned to the full-timer's work and is also required to complete his own workload. All this for no pay increase! If the job isn't done in four hours you're written up. The stress is unbelievable.

> The merchandise that is taken in my department is usually samples of products or outdated products that would otherwise be thrown away.

> Management insists on keeping us on a continuously shifting schedule. I'm second from the top in seniority, and even I can't get a schedule that's remotely regular. I don't like working with the public. They're spoiled. If something doesn't go their way, they throw a tantrum, and management will side with them. This is true even if the customer caused the problem! Employees never have management support when it comes to customers.

Q 3:140   Does employee dishonesty correlate positively with employee turnover?

One recent survey found that employees planning to quit their jobs soon admitted anonymously to stealing seven times more from their employers than employees who claimed they had no immediate interest in resigning. [London House and Food Marketing Institute, *Fourth Annual Report on Employee Theft in the Supermarket Industry* (1993) at 14]

Q 3:141   What are the main causes of employee dishonesty?

In addition to employee dissatisfaction (Q 3:139) and plans to quit the job soon (Q 3:140), the other causes leading to employee dishonesty, according to Hayes, are opportunity and low deterrence. When the motivated employee perceives low risk, a theft is likely to occur. Consequently, according to Hayes, employers must communicate the perception that the risks of detection, the thwarting of success, and denial of the benefit of the dishonest act are extremely high. Such communication can begin with an overall loss prevention program that tells the company's employees that the organization cares about its property and the impact that shrink and other losses can have on its bottom line.

Surveillance of Employees

Q 3:142   Is surveillance an effective way of thwarting employee dishonesty?

The effectiveness of employee surveillance seems indisputable. In the words of one of the world's largest vendors of closed-circuit television (CCTV) security systems:

> Recent reports issued by Ernst & Young and the Food Marketing Institute show that retail losses from the cash register can amount to 40 percent to 50 percent of total shrinkage. With Sensormatic's monitoring system, POS/EM, medium-sized retailers, without full-time security staff, can now defend themselves against these losses. Its main feature is TV. . . . POS/EM actually shows you the suspicious transactions as they transpire

using moving pictures. . . . POS/EM provides a video tape recording of unusual exceptions such as voids, no-sales, refunds, and coupon sales as they occur at the cash register. POS/EM also will pick up and record under-rings, like 20 cents for a pack of cigarettes. ["POS/EM Series II Point of Sale Exception Monitoring," Sensormatic Electronics Corp (1994)]

While the foregoing quotation is from a promotional piece, and arguably somewhat self-serving, it nonetheless highlights how the marriage of the personal computer and CCTV enables the security industry to make retail cash registers capable of monitoring unusual point-of-purchase behavior by cashiers, then activating an overhead CCTV to photograph the questionable transaction.

Furthermore, Sensormatic's enthusiasm is echoed by experts in such industries as banking and financial services. Security experts in the world of high finance are wedding CCTV systems to silent alarms, so that TV cameras alerted by alarm buttons switch from time-lapse to real-time photography during a robbery. [Castagnera and Szvetitz, "Tips for Quality CCTV," *Convenience Store Decisions*, Jan 1994, at 20]

In short, electronic media have made employee surveillance a highly sophisticated and effective art, if not quite a science. [Castagnera and Szvetitz, "Reducing Shrink by a Hair," *Convenience Store Decisions*, May 1994, at 18]

Q 3:143 Is computer and closed-circuit TV surveillance of employees a violation of their privacy rights?

As pointed out in Questions 3:128, 3:129, and 5:23, video and computer monitoring usually does not violate employee privacy rights, especially if the employer has lowered the employees' expectations of privacy by notifying them in advance that the monitoring will occur. Furthermore, CCTV monitoring can have the added effect of protecting employees from outside intruders, such as robbers in retail and banking environments.

However, employees and in some cases their labor unions are showing signs of revolting against employer surveillance in the workplace. The revolt is better exemplified by resistance to drug testing than to CCTV or computer marketing. [See Q 7:151; see e.g., National

Treasury Employees Union v Von Raab, 489 US 656 (1989) and
Skinner v Railway Labor Executives' Association, 489 US 602
(1989)(two cases challenging drug testing of federal employees and
employees in a federally regulated industry, respectively; Borse v
Piece Goods Shops Inc, 963 F 2d 611 (3d Cir 1991); see also, Q 5:27,
concerning state protection of employee privacy rights, generally] In
early 1994, "20/20," a network television program, and several radio
shows, focused attention on a union challenge to Pittsburgh's
Monongahela Electric Co., which reputedly was visually monitoring
employee locker rooms. [Castagnera and Szvetitz, "Privacy: The
Coming Confrontation," *Convenience Store Decisions*, Mar 1994, at
24]

The foregoing cases and employee-union activities indicate that,
notwithstanding the safety side effects of CCTV in the workplace,
employers seeking to use this powerful security tool, especially in
tandem with computerized monitoring of cash registers, E-mail (see
Q 5:26), and inventory, must be sensitive to employee privacy concerns.

Just how sensitive employers must be is painfully illustrated by a
jury verdict emerging from an historically conservative jurisdiction
in 1994. On May 9, 1994, a federal jury in Iowa returned a verdict of
$1 million in actual damages and $500,000 in punitive damages
against the Amoco Oil Co., purely on the basis of an alleged invasion
of the employee-plaintiff's privacy; the same jury rejected the plaintiff's principal claims of age discrimination. [Pulla v Amoco Oil Co,
1994 US Dist LEXIS 17145 (SD Iowa, Nov 1994)]

Plaintiff Pulla had been employed for many years by the defendant
company when a co-worker became convinced that he had abused
his sick leave. To prove that he had, the co-worker reviewed the
records of plaintiff's use of his own Amoco credit card. In other
words, the co-worker examined the records of Pulla as a customer of
Amoco, not as an employee, to demonstrate that he was not sick at
home on the days claimed. Apparently these records were later
discussed with other Amoco employees. Pulla claimed in his case,
and the jury apparently believed that, "As a result of what he
discovered about review and use of his credit card records, Pulla
suffered feelings of being watched all the time, and believe[d] that

the credit card records were made available to third parties . . . [and] unfairly cast him in a bad light." [Id at 17144-45]

This is a scary but fascinating case because it illustrates the resources of surveillance available to employers, but also demonstrates how dangerous succumbing to the temptation to make full use of these resources can be. In this case the trial judge, asked to review the trial and the verdict, stated, "[T]he court conducts the appropriate review to determine whether Amoco is entitled to judgment as a matter of law or to a new trial, and concludes that Amoco is not entitled to post-trial relief under either standard." [Id at 17145] What the appellate court may do, assuming Amoco has appealed and not settled the verdict, remains to be seen as this edition goes to press. However, the lesson to be learned is clear: No employer can comfortably assume that because a means of employee investigation or surveillance is available, it should blindly be used without careful consideration of the legal implications.

Chapter 4

Employment Discrimination

Antidiscrimination law is among the most dynamic areas of labor and employment law in America. Since this book was first published in 1988, substantive changes in the statutory law as well as developments in the federal common (court-made) law of employment discrimination have been dramatic.

Three significant new federal statutes have been enacted since 1988, and all of them are covered in detail in the questions below. First is the Older Workers Benefits Protection Act of 1990, which has as its most significant effect the creation of specific steps that an employer must take in order to bind a terminated employee to a valid waiver of that employee's right to sue under the Age Discrimination in Employment Act.

Second, the Americans with Disabilities Act, enacted in July 1990, extends to all disabled Americans protection against job discrimination based upon handicap or physical disability. (The congressional history suggests there are some 46 million disabled people in this country.) Title III of the Act, which covers access to public accommodations, went into effect in January 1992. Title I, relating to employment decisions, took effect for larger companies (those with 25 or more employees) in July 1992. Substantial litigation can reasonably be predicted in light of the Act's high profile in the press and broadcast media and among advocacy organizations, and, in fact, has already begun.

Third, in November 1991, Congress finally passed, and President George Bush signed, the Civil Rights Act of 1991. The act overturns a number of leading Supreme Court decisions that have been reported previously in the annual supplements to this book. Additionally, victims of discrimination who sue their former employers may be entitled to compensatory and punitive damages and a jury trial in federal court, all rights previously denied them under Title VII of 1964 Civil Rights Act.

As befits this highly significant topic, the subject is thoroughly updated in this chapter, with both revised and completely new questions and answers.

Title VII

Q 4:1　What is Title VII?

Title VII of the Civil Rights Act of 1964 (Title VII) is concerned with employment discrimination. It expands the protection extended originally by the post-Civil War antidiscrimination laws [41 USC

§§ 1981–1986] beyond race to sex, national origin, color, and religion. Title VII is enforced by the Equal Employment Opportunity Commission (EEOC), which affords victims of discrimination a relatively quick, inexpensive means of seeking redress, often without the assistance of an attorney.

Q 4:2 What rights were outlined in Title VII?

First, Title VII made it illegal for individuals and companies to discriminate in employment decisions (including those related to hiring, promoting, paying, terminating, and disciplining employees) on the basis of race, religion, national origin, and sex. Second, Title VII established the EEOC to help enforce its prohibition against discriminatory employment decisions.

Q 4:3 Are there special hiring rules under Title VII with respect to native Americans?

Yes. Section 703(i) of Title VII of the 1964 Civil Rights Act has a special exception to the law's general nondiscrimination principles with respect to native Americans. The law allows employers on or near an American Indian reservation to exercise a preference for an individual because he or she is an American Indian living on or near that reservation. In 1990, the EEOC clarified this provision, stating that it is applicable to areas containing large numbers of American Indian tribes or a large native American population where there are no reservations as such, for example, parts of Oklahoma.

Q 4:4 Are foreign companies doing business in the United States subject to the antidiscrimination provisions of Title VII?

Yes. U.S. district courts have held that foreign employers doing business in the United States must do so according to federal laws prohibiting discrimination. [See, e.g., Ward v W&H Voortman Ltd, 46 FEP Cas 1490 (MD Ala 1988)] Early in 1991, the EEOC filed suit against a Japanese-owned employment agency, charging discrimination on the basis of race, sex, national origin, and age. The suit, which was filed in federal court in San Francisco against Interplace/Transworld Recruit, an American-based subsidiary of a Japanese firm called Recruit Company, claims that the defendant violated both Title VII and the Age Discrimination in Employment Act (ADEA). The EEOC alleges that Interplace engaged "in a continuing, nationwide pattern and practice of race, national origin, sex, and age discrimination in its employment referral operations" as well as in its own hiring practices. The complaint also claims that the company deliberately destroyed business records "for the purpose of covering up the extent of its illegal activities and the identities of (the) victims." According to EEOC Vice Chairman Ricky Silberman, quoted in the March 13, 1991, BNA Daily Labor Report, "We have in our possession the proverbial 'smoking gun'—a coding system used by the company on job order forms to indicate client preferences for employees of a particular race, national origin, sex or age."

In another suit directed at a Japanese company operating in the United States, a federal judge ordered Quasar Company of Franklin Park, Illinois, a subsidiary of Matsushita, to pay $2.5 million in damages to a group of U.S. workers dismissed from the company in violation of their civil rights. Wrote Judge Alesia of the U.S. District Court for Northern Illinois:

> Quasar accomplished its discrimination by reserving certain managerial positions for employees of Japanese national origin, by evaluating and paying Quasar's managerial employees of Japanese national origin on an entirely different basis from that used to evaluate and pay Quasar's managerial employees of American national origin, and by exempting all of its employees of Japanese national origin from Quasar's RIF, all without lawful justification.

[Fortino v Quasar Co, No 87-C-4386 1990 *BNA Daily Labor Report*, 751 F Supp 1306 (ND Ill 1990)]

As foreign corporations buy and build more and more enterprises in the United States (ranging from automobile plants and colleges to movie studios and skyscrapers), such lawsuits may increase.

Q 4:5   Are U.S. companies operating overseas subject to the antidiscrimination provisions of Title VII?

In February 1990, the U.S. Court of Appeals for the Fifth Circuit, sitting in New Orleans, held that Title VII does not protect U.S.

citizens working for a U.S. company in a foreign country. By a vote of 9 to 5, the court affirmed the earlier decision of a three-judge panel on the dismissal of the case of Ali Boureslan, a naturalized U.S. citizen, who had charged the Arabian American Oil Company (Aramco) with racial, religious, and national origin bias. [Boureslan v Aramco, 857 F 2d 1014 (5th Cir 1990) *aff'd en banc*)]

This decision ran contrary to the position of the EEOC, which has stated: "if any American corporation operating overseas or a foreign corporation operating in the U.S. or overseas is 'engaged in an industry affecting commerce,' Congress intended there to be Title VII coverage. . . . The Commission therefore has the authority to accept and investigate these cases of employment discrimination." [*EEOC Compliance Manual* at 605:0057]

Some courts have agreed with the EEOC's position. [See Bryan v Intl Schools Services, Inc, 502 F Supp 472 (D NJ 1980), *rev'd on other grounds*, 675 F 2d 562 (3d Cir 1990)] In a worldwide marketplace, the U.S. corporate presence abroad will most likely increase to include, for example, enhanced activity in the East European nations, to name just one significant overseas opportunity. This international expansion emphasizes the urgency employers felt in receiving Supreme Court clarification on this issue.

Such clarification came in March 1991, when the Supreme Court affirmed the Fifth Circuit's *Boureslan* decision. [111 S Ct 1227 (1991)] The Court held that "Title VII does not apply extraterritorially to regulate the employment practices of United States firms that employ American citizens abroad. Petitioners' evidence, while not totally lacking in probative value, falls short of demonstrating the clearly expressed affirmative Congressional intent that is required to overcome the well-established presumption against statutory extraterritoriality." Overruling this decision, Section 109 of the Civil Rights Act of 1991 extends protection of Title VII, as well as the Americans with Disabilities Act (ADA), to U.S. citizens employed by U.S. companies abroad.

Q 4:6   Must a victim of discrimination choose between the post-Civil War discrimination laws and Title VII?

No. In cases in which both laws apply (primarily race discrimination cases), the victim can pursue one or both of these legal avenues, in sequence or concurrently. For instance, the party who alleges discrimination could obtain a lawyer and commence a Section 1981 lawsuit in federal court and also file a complaint with the EEOC under Title VII. Later, these two actions might be joined in a single lawsuit.

Q 4:7 What is the statute of limitations on commencing a lawsuit under post-Civil War laws?

These laws do not contain a time limit, but the Supreme Court has ruled that federal judges should look to the most appropriate state statute of limitations. The Court has also held that the judge should generally apply the limit on personal injury actions, commonly two years, in which case the lawsuit must commence within two years of the alleged illegal act to avoid forfeiting the right to sue.

Enforcement of Title VII by the EEOC

Q 4:8 What is the EEOC?

The EEOC is a quasi-independent federal agency whose purpose is to enforce Title VII. It has offices in most major U.S. cities. These offices consist primarily of investigators who accept discrimination charges from employees and determine whether there is probable cause to believe that the law has been broken, and attorneys who may represent deserving charging parties when the investigators are unable to settle worthy claims of job discrimination.

Q 4:9 What reporting and recordkeeping requirements are imposed by the EEOC?

Employers with 100 or more employees must annually file Standard Form 100 (Employer Information Report EEO-1, available from the Joint Reporting Committee, Federal Depot, 1201 E. 10 S., Jeffersonville, IN 47130) and must retain a copy of the most recent report filed by each reporting unit at the company or division headquarters. The EEOC has not adopted any generally applicable requirement that employers make or keep other employee records, although it has the authority to do so. It may also impose recordkeeping requirements on individual employers or groups of employers whenever it determines that such records are necessary for the operation of the EEO-1 reporting system or to further the purposes of Title VII.

To the extent an employer does generate employee records (including, for example, application forms and records of hiring, promotion, demotion, and so forth), it must retain the records for six months after the personnel action or making of the record, whichever is later. An employer must keep a record of termination for six months from the date of termination. When a charge of discrimination has been filed or an action brought by the EEOC or Attorney General under Title VII, the employer must retain all relevant personnel records until final disposition of the matter. [29 CFR §§ 1602.7, 1602.14 (1988)]

Q 4:10 When can an employee initiate a discrimination complaint with the EEOC?

Usually, the employee must file a discrimination complaint within 180 days of the event (such as termination of employment) claimed to be discriminatory.

Q 4:11 Must an employee always file a discrimination complaint with the EEOC within 180 days?

To eradicate discrimination more effectively, Congress has permitted the states to establish their own antidiscrimination agencies, similar to the EEOC. Most states have done so; these states are called "deferral states." In a deferral state, if an employee chooses to file a discrimination complaint with the EEOC and/or a similar state agency, the law will usually give the employee 300 days to file under Title VII, rather than the usual 180 days.

Q 4:12 What will the EEOC, or a similar state agency, do with a discrimination complaint after it has been filed?

First, a copy of the complaint (or charge of discrimination, depending on the particular agency's nomenclature) will be sent to the employer, who is then required to file a response. Once the employer has answered the complaint, the investigator will usually hold a fact-finding conference to acquire further information about the case.

Q 4:13   Is the EEOC planning to modify how it deals with charges of discrimination?

With only about 170 investigators nationwide, and a backlog of more than 100,000 pending discrimination charges, the EEOC launched a Charge Processing Task Force, under Commission Vice Chairman Paul Igasaki. In late April 1995, the task force made its recommendations for wide-ranging changes in the way charges are processed. The task force had been established in December 1994 by EEOC Chairman Gilbert Casellas and by the third week of April 1995 the full commission had voted to accept the task force recommendations.

First among the changes is that priorities will be set for all charges of discrimination. Those categorized early in the process as having either a high likelihood of merit, or conversely a high likelihood of meritlessness, will be moved quickly through the investigation process. Those cases falling between the two extremes will be handled normally.

Second, the recommendations provide a renewed emphasis on settlement of discrimination claims. Taking its lead from Congress, which in the 1991 Civil Rights Act (see Q 1:8) encouraged alternative dispute resolution techniques (see Q 15:17), the commission has indicated that it will use mediation to settle meritorious claims for less than the make-whole remedy, which the agency traditionally has demanded in so-called "conciliation" proceedings following a finding of probable cause. (See Q 4:16 for an explanation of "probable cause.")

Third, the agency announced its intent to provide more discretion to its attorneys in its ten regional offices in deciding which cases to take into federal court, thus freeing commissioners to deal with broader policy issues.

[See "Casellas Says New Litigation Procedure Will Free Commission for More Policy Work," 1995 *BNA Daily Labor Report* 77, Apr 21, 1995, at 5; "EEOC Adopts Charge-Priority System, Gives General

Counsel More Authority," 1995 *BNA Daily Labor Report* 76, Apr 20, 1995, at 3; Rochelle Sharpf, "EEOC Is Making Sweeping Changes in Handling Cases," *The Wall Street Journal*, Apr 20, 1995, at B6]

Meanwhile, the agency, following some four hours of discussion and debate, deferred deciding whether to change the way it deals with analogous state anti-discrimination agencies (see Q 4:12). Some 48,000 charges are filed with both the EEOC and one of the state agencies that exist in all but a few of the 50 states. While recognizing that greater flexibility of work sharing arrangements with the states, as well as jurisdictional and other procedural questions need to be addressed, the commission decided to defer a vote on task force recommendation. ["Commission Defers Vote on Task Force Report on State, Local FEP Agencies," 1995 *BNA Daily Labor Report* 79, Apr 25, 1995, at d13]

Q 4:14 What is a fact-finding conference?

A fact-finding conference is a formal meeting at which the EEOC or state investigator reviews the discrimination complaint and the employer's response to it in the presence of both parties. Both the employee and the employer have ample opportunity to reply to the other's positions and, using the investigator as intermediary, to solicit additional information from one another. Although no transcript of the proceedings is taken, the investigator or an assistant often takes copious notes. If appropriate, the fact-finding conference is used as a forum for discussing settlement of the complaint between the parties.

Q 4:15 What happens after the fact-finding conference?

Frequently, after the fact-finding conference the EEOC or state investigator will request additional documents or other information from the employer. Then, after reviewing the file, the investigator will rule on whether there is probable cause to believe that the law has been broken.

Q 4:16   What happens if the EEOC or state investigator finds probable cause to believe that the employer has committed illegal employment discrimination?

If the investigator reaches a finding of probable cause, his or her next duty is to try to conciliate the complaint. Conciliation is an attempt to persuade the employer to remedy the illegal discrimination by such actions as back pay and reinstatement.

Q 4:17   What if an employer is suspected by an EEOC or state investigator of violating the law and refuses to conciliate the complaint?

If the employer refuses to resolve the dispute by giving the employee an appropriate remedy, the EEOC investigator can either turn the case over to the agency's litigation department, with the recommendation of a lawsuit on behalf of the complaining employee, or merely issue to the employee a letter to sue, which gives the complainant 90 days in which to locate an attorney and initiate a lawsuit.

Some state antidiscrimination agencies operate in the same manner as the EEOC. Other agencies have the power to conduct a public hearing in front of an administrative law judge, who may give a legal remedy to the employee if the employee prevails at such a trial.

Q 4:18   What if the EEOC or state investigator finds no probable cause to believe that discrimination has occurred?

If the agency investigator concludes that the employer did not violate the law, the investigation will be terminated.

Q 4:19   Does termination of the EEOC or state investigation resolve the employee's discrimination claim?

A finding of no probable cause and termination of the investigation by the antidiscrimination agency does not necessarily resolve the employee's claim. The employee will still be issued a letter to sue, which affords the employee (typically) 90 days in which to find a lawyer and file suit in federal or state court. However, as a practical matter, an unfavorable finding by the antidiscrimination agency generally terminates the employee's claim, either because the employee is discouraged or because it is impossible to find an attorney who will take such a case on a contingent-fee basis. Therefore, it is very important for employers and their legal counsel to make a strong attempt to prevail before the EEOC or the state agency.

Q 4:20 Can the EEOC force an employer to cooperate in its investigation?

Yes. The EEOC has the power to subpoena employer records if the employer refuses to respond to the agency's request for documents and other information pertaining to the discrimination complaint.

Other Antidiscrimination Laws

Q 4:21 Aside from Title VII and the nineteenth-century civil rights acts, what other antidiscrimination laws exist?

At the federal level, the ADEA was passed in the mid-1970s to afford protection to employees between the ages of 40 and 70 and amended in 1986 to extend its protection to employees age 40 and older. In addition, companies that have federal contracts for goods and services are subject to affirmative action requirements and antidiscrimination laws covering veterans and disabled workers. Finally, most states and many cities have passed laws and ordinances supplementing the federal antidiscrimination laws. A few of these states and cities have even expanded the coverage of the federal laws, sometimes including protection for homosexuals, individuals who have AIDS, and other groups of employees who are frequently subject to discrimination. The most recent addition to this panoply of statutes is the ADA.

Q 4:22 Do the remedies differ under these different discrimination laws?

Yes. Title VII calls for a "make-whole" remedy, which places the offended party in the same position as if the discriminatory event had never taken place. This generally includes back pay and reinstatement or promotion. Punitive damages are allowed under the post-Civil War discrimination laws, in addition to compensatory damages, if the jury thinks the employer deserves to be taught a lesson. Enactment of the Civil Rights Act of 1991 also puts compensatory and punitive damages in the picture in some Title VII cases from now on. The ADEA also has a form of punishment damages: the court can award to the employee "liquidated damages," doubling the back pay award.

Q 4:23   Can an employer found guilty of discrimination against an employee be made to pay prospective as well as back pay?

The usual remedy for a successful employment discrimination claim is reinstatement to the job previously held and back pay for the time lost from the job due to the employer's discriminatory act. However, it has been held that in unusual cases where reinstatement to the former job is not feasible because of "great antagonism between the employer and employee," an employee is entitled to "front pay," which is the difference between what the employee is making in a new job and what the employee made in his or her former job, multiplied by the number of years the employee held the job prior to being wrongfully dismissed. [EEOC v Red Baron Steak House, 47 Fair Empl Prac Cas (BNA) (ND Cal June 2, 1988)]

Judicial Enforcement of the Civil Rights Laws

Q 4:24   What constitutes a prima facie case of discrimination?

The Supreme Court has held that a *prima facie* case of discrimination exists if the following are proven:

1. The plaintiff is in a protected class;
2. The plaintiff was qualified for the job or promotion;
3. The qualified plaintiff did not get the job or promotion; and
4. The employer hired or promoted someone less qualified or at least continued to look for qualified people after rejecting the plaintiff.

With minor variations, this formula can be applied to any employment decision, including discipline, termination, and wage increases. [See, e.g., McDonnell Douglas v Green, 411 US 782, (1973); Texas Department of Community Affairs v Burdine, 450 US 248 (1981)]

Q 4:25 Does an employer have to intend to break the law to be guilty of illegal discrimination?

No. One type of discrimination is disparate treatment, which means intentional discriminatory treatment based on a person's race, sex, national origin, color, religion, age, or disability. However, the law also recognizes a form of illegal discrimination based on disparate impact. Illegal disparate impact occurs when an apparently neutral employment policy has a discriminatory (and perhaps inadvertent) impact on one of the protected classes of employees. This cause of action was recently reinvigorated by provisions of the Civil Rights Act of 1991.

Q 4:26 What is an example of disparate impact?

In a classic disparate impact case decided by the U.S. Supreme Court, a company had a rule stating that, except for the maintenance department, employees of all departments must have at least a high school diploma. [Griggs v Duke Power Co, 401 US 424 (1971)] When the case was initiated, many more whites had high school diplomas than did blacks. Consequently, almost all of the positions outside the maintenance department (the lowest department in pay and status in the company) were filled by whites. The Court declared that, although the requirement of a high school diploma was neutral on the surface, it had a discriminatory disparate impact on black workers. Therefore, the policy was a violation of Title VII.

Q 4:27 What does the term "protected group" mean?

A protected group, also referred to as a "suspect class," is a class or substrata of the population that historically has been subjected to discriminatory treatment (e.g., blacks, women, or handicapped individuals). The term has been somewhat broadened in recent years to include so-called reverse discrimination; for example, discriminatory treatment of white males. However, reverse discrimination cases usually are not as closely scrutinized by our courts as are cases involving traditional targets of discrimination, in which discrimination is more strongly suspected by the judiciary.

Q 4:28 Can a policy that has a disparate impact on a protected group ever be legal?

Yes. If a job requirement is a bona fide occupational qualification (BFOQ), it may fulfill legal guidelines even though it has a disparate impact on a certain class of employees. For instance, an airline or police force may be able to demonstrate that mandatory retirement at a given age is required for the effective and safe operation of certain kinds of equipment or to ensure the public safety. Another example is a job that requires heavy lifting; the ability to perform this aspect of the job may be a legitimate requirement even though many females, as well as members of certain ethnic groups, may be disqualified from the position. Similarly, educational requirements and test scores may be permissible if the diploma or test is directly related to the requirements of the job. However, the courts have held that a BFOQ with respect to racial discrimination cannot exist.

Q 4:29 Has the difficulty of proving disparate impact changed over the years?

Yes. In the years following *Griggs v. Duke Power Co.* (see Q 4:24), the judicial climate for enforcing Title VII in the federal courts cooled. After the appointment of several Justices by the Reagan and Bush administrations, an increasingly conservative Supreme Court made it more difficult for an employee to charge his or her employer with employment discrimination. In *Wards Cove Packing Co. v. Atonio* [109 S Ct 2115 (1989)], the Court modified *Griggs* by increasing the burden of proof on an employee charging "disparate effects" discrimination. *Wards Cove* involved Alaskan salmon canneries where unskilled jobs were filled predominantly by nonwhite employees and skilled jobs were filled predominantly by white employees. The employees based their claim of discriminatory hiring practices on this disparity. The Court, however, held that a mere showing of different racial proportions in various jobs was insufficient to support a claim of discrimination by disparate impact. Instead, the workers had to show that the percentage of nonwhites in skilled jobs was out of balance with the percentage of nonwhites who applied and were qualified for the jobs. In this case, the Court held that the workers had not shown the requisite imbalance between the qualified worker pool and the hired skilled work force. Further, the workers were required to point to specific employment practices that had demonstrably caused the disparity; it was not enough to state that "overall practices" caused an imbalance. Finally, even if the workers had proved that specific employment practices had a discriminatory impact (still assuming no intention to discriminate), the employer could defend its actions by providing a reasonable business justification for them; it would be up to the workers to show that the company's explanation was inadequate.

Overruling *Wards Cove*, the Civil Rights Act of 1991 reinstated statistical evidence as a powerful evidentiary weapon for plaintiffs in disparate impact cases.

Q 4:30 What has been the impact of *Wards Cove*?

In *Green v. USX Corp.* [896 F 2d 801 (3d Cir 1990)], the court held that the evidence that USX's hiring practices for unskilled workers at a Pennsylvania plant discriminated against black applicants was good enough to establish liability, even under the Supreme Court's new disparate impact test. *Green* grew out of a 1976 class action against USX's predecessor, United States Steel Corporation, under Title VII on behalf of thousands of black job applicants who had unsuccessfully competed for production and maintenance jobs at the firm's Fairless Works. The court found that the plaintiffs had presented sufficient evidence to support a trial court's finding that the employment interview at Fairless had a disparate impact on black applicants. Consequently, concluded the court, the *Green* plaintiffs had met the *Wards Cove* test.

In early 1991, the Supreme Court held in *United Auto Workers v. Johnson Controls, Inc.* [111 S Ct 1196 (1991)] that the battery manufacturer's policy of not allowing female workers to take jobs because of the effect of exposure to lead on unborn children had a disparate impact on females, and therefore violated Title VII. Labor unions and women's organizations had backed the UAW's suit, viewing such policies as effectively excluding women from better-paying jobs in a wide range of industries. Under Johnson Controls' policy—postured as a facially neutral "fetal protection plan"—the burden was placed on female employees to prove they were infertile before being permitted to work in areas of the plant where they would be exposed to lead. Writing for a unanimous court, Justice Blackmun stated: "Decisions about the welfare of future children must be left to the parents who conceive, bear, support, and raise them rather than to the employers who hire those parents. Congress has mandated this choice through Title VII, as amended by the Pregnancy Discrimination Act (PDA). Johnson Controls has attempted to exclude women because of their reproductive capacity. Title VII and the PDA simply do not allow a woman's dismissal because of her failure to submit to sterilization." In reversing the earlier decision of the Seventh Circuit, which was based on a "disparate impact versus business necessity" analysis, the Court rejected the lower court's view that Johnson Controls' fetal protection policy was in fact facially neutral. Wrote Justice Blackmun: "The bias in Johnson Controls' policy is obvious. Fertile men, but not fertile women, are given a choice as to whether they wish to risk their reproductive health for a particular job." Thus, the Court distinguished this case from *Wards Cove* (see Q 4:29).

One effect of the *Johnson Controls* decision was to offset the *Wards Cove* limitation on plaintiff-employees' reliance on the adverse impact analysis by placing many employer policies, which formerly would have been analyzed under disparate impact, into the category of disparate treatment. When this happens, as in *Johnson Controls*, the employer must show not merely a business necessity for the policy, but must bear the much heavier burden of demonstrating to the trial court a bona fide occupational qualification (BFOQ) to justify the discriminatory effect of the policy.

Whatever vitality as legal precedent *Wards Cove* retained was virtually wiped out by the Civil Rights Act of 1991.

Q 4:31 When subjective or discretionary criteria are used in employment decisions, must an employee prove that the employer intended to discriminate to prevail in a Title VII action?

In the past, courts have applied separate standards to employment decisions that were based solely on objective criteria, such as standardized tests, and subjective criteria, such as personal judgment or the application of inherently subjective criteria. Only when objective criteria were used did courts apply the disparate impact analysis. If an employee could show, to a statistically significant degree, that such objective criteria disproportionately affected a protected class and that such criteria were not related to job performance, a court would find an employer liable under Title VII—even if the employer had not intended to discriminate. However, for cases in which an employer used only subjective criteria, courts would apply a disparate treatment analysis under which an employee had to prove that an employer intended to discriminate. A showing of disproportionate impact alone would not be sufficient.

But the Supreme Court has held that in "mixed" cases, when both subjective and objective criteria are used, the process is correctly considered to be objective, and the disproportionate impact analysis is appropriate. Consequently, to prevail, an employee does not have to prove intent to discriminate. The ruling makes prevailing in mixed cases easier for employees because they no longer have to prove discriminatory intent. Consequently, employers' exposure to successful Title VII claims is increased. [Watson v Fort Worth Bank & Trust Co, 108 S Ct 2777 (1988)]

Q 4:32 If a plaintiff proves a prima facie case of discrimination, does the plaintiff win?

If the employer can prove a bona fide business reason for the allegedly discriminatory decision or action, the plaintiff must then prove that the employer's explanation is no more than a pretext for illegal discrimination. Typically, a plaintiff attempts to prove pretext by some combination of direct and indirect evidence.

Circumstantial evidence may be sufficient to show that the employer's business justification is not reasonably believable, so that the court is left with the presumption that the employer had a discriminatory (and, therefore, illegal) motive. However, sometimes the employer's motive may be mixed; that is, there may have been both a legitimate business reason and a discriminatory motive behind the employment decision. If the plaintiff can't prove that the legitimate business reason offered by the employer is a mere pretext, then most courts require that the plaintiff present some direct evidence that discrimination was also a substantial motivating factor. [See, e.g., Price Waterhouse v Hopkins, 490 US 228, 49 FEP 954 (1989)]

Types of Discrimination Prohibited by Title VII

Racial Discrimination

Q 4:33　What employment decisions and actions constitute racial discrimination?

The most obvious form of racial discrimination occurs when a white person is selected for a position in place of a better qualified person of another race. However, there are more subtle, but equally illegal forms of racial discrimination. For example, selection of one black person over another black because of variation in skin color constitutes racial discrimination. Also, illegal racial discrimination may occur when personal background is treated as a distinct racial characteristic. For example, the Supreme Court has held that if a university discriminatorily treated an Iranian professor, he could sue for racial discrimination. [Saint Francis College v Majid Ghaidan, 107 S Ct 2022 (1987)]

Q 4:34　What new techniques are being used to detect racial discrimination?

Although racial quotas cannot normally be imposed upon employers, the EEOC continues to rely upon statistical evidence to identify and attack apparent patterns of race discrimination. Even though the use of statistics to prove discrimination had been cast in some doubt by certain recent Supreme Court decisions, the viability of such cases was restored by the Civil Rights Act of 1991. In 1993, the EEOC successfully prosecuted a case grounded in statistical evidence against Olson's Dairy Queens Inc.'s operations in the Houston area. The EEOC's statistics were presented at trial by an expert witness and showed that blacks comprised approximately 25 percent of all food preparation and service employees in Houston, yet they represented only 8 percent of the Olson's workforce in that region of Texas. The statistician also testified that between 27 percent and 40 percent of all Houston-area Olson's applicants were black.

Interestingly, Olson's prevailed at trial, the district judge having given credence to Olson's expert, who testified that most people who wanted to work in Dairy Queen-type restaurants were young part-timers living close to the restaurant locations, despite the EEOC's showing that job applications reflected a willingness of black applicants to travel substantial distances for the coveted jobs. [1993 *BNA Daily Labor Report* 81 (Apr 29, 1993) at 1]

In addition to statistics, antidiscrimination agencies are using so-called testers, white and black investigators posing as real job applicants, to uncover subtle instances of race discrimination. In 1993, Brooks Brothers Inc., and a Boston store called Walker's Riding Apparel settled a case with the Massachusetts Commission Against Discrimination in what is believed to be one of the first job bias cases based upon the treatment of applications filed by undercover investigators. Critics of testing complain that the technique is unethical, because the testers don't have any real interest in getting the available jobs. In some sense the method seems to smack of entrapment. At a minimum it wastes the employer's time, since presumably neither the black nor the white tester will accept employment if successful in the application process. Nevertheless, testing has been upheld by the U.S. Supreme Court in the area of housing bias. Critics reply, however, that employment decisions are more complex and do not readily lend themselves to such techniques. [Suskind, "Brooks Bros Settles Job-Bias Suit; Inquiry Used Controversial 'Tests'," *The Wall Street Journal*, Apr 21, 1993, at B7]

In 1993 and 1994 the Massachusetts Commission continued to use bias testing in the Boston area. One six-week testing project resulted in the filing of age discrimination complaints by the state agency against seven employers. Qualified applicants, one between 40 and 65 years old, the other in her 20s or 30s,were sent out in pairs to apply for jobs. As a result of the test, probable cause to proceed was found against Ann Taylor, Gymboree, Shepherds of Australia, and American Personnel, while the investigation continued with regard to other retailers. The Massachusetts commission is reportedly the only antidiscrimination agency currently using such testing to detect employment discrimination, while the NAACP and the Fair Employment Council of Washington (DC) are also said to have tried the technique. ["Employment Testing Reveals Significant Age Bias, Agency Says," 1994 *BNA Daily Labor Report* 13, Jan 20, 1994, at 9]

The point to be taken by employers is that, while the EEOC and its state law counterparts may at times be slow and even appear inept in the processing of routine discrimination charges (see Qs 4:8–4:20 for a description of these routine procedures), at least some of these antidiscrimination agencies (and some private advocacy groups) are using highly sophisticated investigative techniques to identify and attack subtle instances of apparent race discrimination, particularly with regard to the hiring practices of medium to large corporations.

Q 4:35   Have significant monetary awards been made in race discrimination cases in 1994?

Some 13 years after he was fired for admittedly conspiring to falsify an alcohol breath test and also for physically abusing a girlfriend, an African-American state trooper won a $211,000 jury verdict in a Boston courthouse in January 1994. The ex-trooper's attorney succeeded in convincing the jurors that, while his client had done the things of which he was accused by his superiors, the discipline they imposed was far harsher than what white troopers had received for similar offenses. The trooper had worked sporadically as a truck and bus driver following his termination, thereby mitigating the damages; however, the Massachusetts State Police will also have to pay some $70,000 in interest on top of the award if the court withstands any appeals, according to the plaintiff's attorney. ["Federal Jury Awards $211,000 to Black Trooper Fired in 1981," 1994 *BNA Daily Labor Report* 19, Jan 31, 1994, at 10]

The U.S. Court of Appeals for the Seventh Circuit, sitting in Chicago, affirmed in January 1994 a $102,000 back pay award to an African-American salesman from Milwaukee who claimed a constructive discharge based upon racial slurs. Writing for the court,

Circuit Judge Joel M. Flaum observed, "Title VII does not guarantee stress-free employment, but it does protect employees from toiling in a hostile working environment created by their employer's use of racial slurs and epithets." In this case the plaintiff had compiled an outstanding record as a member of the defendant's sales force over some seven years before being promoted to a management post. Thereafter his district manager reportedly subjected him to comments such as, "You black guys are too f_____ dumb to be insurance agents." The plaintiff testified that he took it as long as he could, then quit; the courts concluded that he was entitled to do so under the circumstances. ["Supervisor's Racial Slurs Warrant $102,000 Award to Milwaukee Salesman," 1994 *BNA Daily Labor Report* 5, Jan 7, 1994, at 5]

In New Jersey, a federal judge ruled early in 1994 to allow a plaintiff of Indian ancestry to proceed with his race discrimination claim under the post-Civil War civil rights acts (see Q 1:1), despite the fact that the defendant's supervisor had never met the litigant. The plaintiff, pointing out that he speaks with the pronounced accent characteristic of the Indian subcontinent, says he contacted Anheuser-Busch in response to an advertisement for a brewery job. An assistant manager reportedly called him to inquire about a six-year gap in his resume. The plaintiff claims he explained that his brewing experience had been in India and that for the last half dozen years he had owned and operated a delicatessen that he had recently sold. The manager later sent him a letter which said he wouldn't be hired at "this time." Denying the brewing giant's motion for summary judgment, the trial judge said that a jury might well find that the plaintiff's accent gave away his race, thus entitling him to try and prove at trial that racial bias was the basis for his unsuccessful job application. ["Race, National Origin Bias Claims by Indian Job Applicant Can Proceed," 1994 *BNA Daily Labor Report* 29, Feb 14, 1994, at 13]

The largest verdict in 1994 was awarded by a California jury on June 6 to a plaintiff in a race discrimination and breach of contract case. The jurors handed down a verdict consisting of $1.1 million for the plaintiff's economic losses and a like sum for non-economic damages. The case is on appeal. [Cobb v Univ of S Cal, 1994 Cal App LEXIS 1269 (1994).]

These cases illustrate that while some areas of discrimination law, such as sexual harassment (see below) and the ADA, may grab most media attention, garden-variety race discrimination continues to subject callous and careless companies to major monetary exposure and tenacious litigation when it occurs in the workplace.

Q 4:36   Are there any indications of white backlash to racial discrimination charges in our courts?

The U.S. Court of Appeals for the Fifth Circuit, which sits in New Orleans, turned back an attempt by a white faculty member to prove that her colleagues at a predominantly black university had subjected her to racial discrimination. The clash seems to have stemmed from a long history of disputes between the professor and the institution. In 1986 the plaintiff, a professor of elementary and early childhood education, sued the university's School of Education, complaining that because of her race she was being denied the opportunity to conduct a child abuse clinic. The Title VII action was settled and subsequently dismissed by the federal court.

In 1990 she sued again, this time contending that she had been subjected to numerous acts of disparate treatment on the basis of being white and also contending retaliation for having filed the previous action. After a six-day bench trial the federal judge ruled that, while the plaintiff had failed to prove discrimination, she nonetheless was entitled to back pay in compensation for extra duties she proved she had been required to perform in violation of the earlier settlement agreement.

On appeal, the Fifth Circuit said that, because the settlement agreement had never been incorporated into the earlier federal action (which had been dismissed with prejudice in light of the private settlement contract), the U.S. District Court lacked jurisdiction to decide whether the settlement subsequently had been breached. In other words, the professor's breach of contract charges belonged in a state court of general jurisdiction. Therefore, the appellate court reversed the federal judge on that issue. At the same time, the circuit court affirmed the federal trial court in its finding that the plaintiff had failed to prove her allegations of race discrimination.

In so holding, the Fifth Circuit relied upon its own recent decision as well as that of the U.S. Supreme Court to the effect that a plaintiff alleging discriminatory employment treatment must present some direct evidence of a discriminatory motivation before the burden shifts to the defendant to demonstrate a nondiscriminatory reason for its treatment of the complaining employee. [See Brown v East Mississippi Electric Power Assn, 989 F 2d 858, 861 (5th Cir 1993) ("When a plaintiff presents credible direct evidence that discriminatory animus in part motivated or was a substantial factor in the contested employment action, the burden of proof shifts to the employer to establish by a preponderance of the evidence that the same decision would have been made regardless of the forbidden factor."); Derewicz, "Supreme Court Rules Employees Must Show More Than Pretext in Discrimination Cases," *Employment Law Update*, Saul Ewing Remick & Saul, August 1993, at 1]

The appeals court reached this conclusion notwithstanding evidence in the record that the professor's race most certainly influenced the way she was viewed and treated by some of her African-American colleagues who, according to the opinion of the appellate court, "were race-conscious to the extent that some felt uncomfortable with, and possibly even resented, Dr. Langley's presence at JSU, an historically black institution." For example, the court continued in its opinion, Dr. Langley testified at trial that a colleague had commented that "she doesn't see why black students feel that they need to have white advisors" and that "black people are overlooked at Jackson State to give white faculty more rights." A white colleague testified that their department chair had indicated a preference for an all-black school. This testimony, even if believed, commented the court, did not demonstrate that the school had "actually relied on" race in deciding how it would treat the plaintiff-professor. Therefore, the Fifth Circuit affirmed the district judge's verdict against her on the race discrimination claim. [Langley v Jackson State University, 1994 *BNA Daily Labor Report* 52, Mar 8, 1994, at d33]

In St. Louis a food store fared better in its defamation action against a labor union, that had unsuccessfully attempted to organize its employees. During the course of the organizing effort the union had called the company a variety of names, including "racist." Once the organization effort fizzled, the company sued. Denying the union's motion for summary judgment, the federal court in 1994 ruled that the defamation case should go to a jury for decision following a trial on its merits.

The court observed, "In light of the recent racial disturbances in Los Angeles, the alleged racial polarization in St. Louis, and the fact that these accusations were made in a predominantly Afro-American community, this Court cannot say, as a matter of law that a jury would not find the use of the word 'racist' to be devoid of specific meaning or rendered meaningless by overuse, [and] therefore not defamatory, as the defendant contends." ["Court Permits Jury to Resolve Whether Branding Employer a 'Racist' Is Defamatory," 1994 *BNA Daily Labor Report* 1, Jan 3, 1994, at 3]

The significance of these cases is uncertain. They may suggest something of a reaction among white employers and employees against so-called "political correctness" where race is a motive or a means for giving the defendant's nonwhite constituency an allegedly unfair advantage. Of course, reverse discrimination cases are nothing new, and the foregoing cases may be no more than interesting aspects of 1994 employment law, having no significant meaning as harbingers of a trend. However, other evidence indicates that indeed some sort of backlash is developing. Some journalists are labeling 1995 the "year of the white male as victim. . . ." [Debra J. Saunders, "The Big White Mistake," *The San Francisco Chronicle*, Jan 9, 1995, at A21]

Even some more thoughtful and presumably unprejudiced observers are questioning the unintended outcomes of our job discrimination laws, particularly of affirmative action activities. Russell Roberts of the Olin School of Business at Washington University wondered aloud on National Public Radio on January 9, 1995, whether one unintended outcome of Title VII and its state law counterparts was a reluctance by businesses to hire members of protected classes in the first instance. The most controversial work to emerge during the past year is a book by two Ivy League professors, one a doctor of psychology at Harvard until his recent death, the other a Harvard graduate now a political scientist at the American Enterprise Institute. The book's central thesis is as follows:

> The twentieth century dawned on a world segregated into social classes defined in terms of money, power, and status. The ancient lines of separation based on hereditary rank were being erased, replaced by a more complicated set of overlapping lines.

Social standing still played a major role, if less often accompanied by a sword or a tiara, but so did out-and-out wealth, educational credentials, and, increasingly, talent.

Our thesis is that the twentieth century has continued the transformation, so that the twenty-first will open on a world in which cognitive ability is the decisive dividing force. The shift is more subtle than the previous one but more momentous. Social class remains the vehicle of social life, but intelligence now pulls the train.

[Richard J. Herrnstein and Charles Murray, *The Bell Curve: Intelligence and Class Structure in American Life* 25 (Free Press 1994)]

The authors, having challenged the efficacy and wisdom of affirmative action [Id at 451–58 and 655–63], caused a stir in the news media. For example, one commentator, who challenged The Bell Curve's most controversial conclusions ((1) that average I.Q. is not equal across all races and national backgrounds, and (2) that the differences are the result, primarily, of heredity rather than environment), stated:

Among the ideas that have harmed mankind, one of the most destructive is that the human species is divided into biological units called races and that some races are innately superior to others. Their argument goes like this. Blacks perform more poorly on I.Q. tests than whites, so they must be less intelligent. The I.Q. scores of children correlate with those of their parents, so intelligence must be at least partly governed by genes. Therefore, the I.Q. difference between blacks and whites has a genetic component that cannot be eliminated by society.

[Jim Holt, "Anti-Social Science?" *The New York Times*, Oct 19, 1994, at A23]

The writer of the above-quoted op-ed piece then goes on to challenge The Bell Curve's hypothesis. [Joye Mercer, "A Fascination with Genetics: Pioneer Fund is at center of debate over research on race and intelligence," *The Chronicle of Higher Education*, Dec 7, 1994, at A28] But, while "[o]ne may loathe or share the opinions expressed by [*The Bell Curve*]. . . one thing seems clear: The government or society that persists in sweeping [its] subject matter under the rug will do so at its peril." [Malcolm W. Browne, "What Is Intelligence, and Who Has It?" *The New York Times Book Review*, Oct 16, 1994, at 3]

Q 4:37 Can an employer be held accountable for racially motivated harassment in the workplace?

Yes. Under Title VII a racial harassment action can be brought against an employer when the employee claims that the employer subjected the employee to a racially hostile work environment. To establish a cause of action under this theory, the employee must show:

1. Racially motivated conduct resulting in an unreasonably abusive or offensive work environment that makes the employee's job more difficult, and

2. That the employer tolerated or condoned the situation.

Employers that take reasonable steps to correct and/or prevent racial harassment in the workplace will not be found to have violated Title VII. Consequently, employers should take quick and appropriate action to remedy the situation when they become aware of racially motivated conduct in the workplace that could conceivably constitute harassment.

Discrimination Based on National Origin or Religion

Q 4:38 What is national origin discrimination?

National origin discrimination occurs when an employment event such as hiring is based on the employee's ethnic origins. It should be distinguished from citizenship discrimination, in which an alien is treated less favorably than a U.S. citizen. Under the Immigration Reform and Control Act of 1986 (IRCA), legal aliens who are entitled to work cannot be discriminated against with respect to most jobs.

Q 4:39 What is religious discrimination?

Religious discrimination occurs if employment decisions are based on an employee's religious affiliation or convictions, and also if an employer refuses to reasonably accommodate a worker's religious convictions or obligations.

Q 4:40 What is reasonable accommodation of an employee's religious beliefs?

Section 701 (j) of Title VII requires that, absent undue hardship, an employer must reasonably accommodate the religious needs of its employees. An employer may be required by law to allow an employee to wear a costume, headpiece, or emblem peculiar to a particular religion, or to allow the employee to work out a schedule that permits absence on religious holidays. However, the emphasis is on "reasonable." For instance, a company is not required to force some employees to work every Saturday so that a Seventh Day Adventist can consistently observe the Saturday sabbath. Nor must an employer allow a Muslim to wear a turban in lieu of a hard hat if job safety requires the hard hat.

Firing an employee who refuses to work on his or her sabbath may leave an employer open to a charge of religious discrimination. Before an employer may fire such an employee, it must be sure that no reasonable accommodation of the employee's religious belief is possible without undue harm to the business. In addition, increased costs to the employer, if significant, may constitute undue hardship under Title VII.

Discrimination Based on Sex

Q 4:41 What is sex discrimination?

Sex discrimination exists in a variety of forms. An employment decision based on gender is only one of these forms. Sexual harassment is another, and unequal pay for similar work performed by males and females is a third.

Q 4:42 Are employment decisions that are based on sexual stereotypes actionable under Title VII?

Yes. The Supreme Court has held that an employer's use of sexual stereotypes in deciding whether to make a female employee a partner in an accounting firm could lead to employer liability under Title VII. [Price Waterhouse v Hopkins, 490 US 228, 49 FEP 954 (1989)] In *Hopkins*, the plaintiff was evaluated for partnership consideration, but was turned down. Her job performance apparently was outstanding in most ways; notably, she had brought a $25 million government account into the company's Washington office. But some partners commented that she projected the wrong image of a female partner, comments including suggestions that she wear more makeup and change her hairstyle, even that she enroll in "charm school." But there also was evidence that she interacted poorly with subordinates, a legitimate business reason for denying partnership. Consequently, *Hopkins* is an important case both because it recognizes discrimination based on being the "wrong kind of woman" (or black, or whatever) as illegal under Title VII, and because it lays down the standards for courts in deciding mixed motive cases.

If it can be shown that both permissible and impermissible criteria were used in arriving at an employment decision, an employer is not liable under Title VII if most of the evidence shows that the employer would have made the same decision had it considered only the permissible factors. Clearly, an employer will not prevail in a mixed motive case if it justifies its employment decision with permissible criteria that were not actually used at the time of the original employment decision. To win, an employer must show by the weight of the evidence that a legitimate reason, relied on during the original employment decision and standing alone, would have resulted in the same decision. Without such a showing, an employer will be found liable in a mixed motive case.

Employers should examine their employee evaluation practices to determine whether stereotyped views or notions are present, and if so, remove them.

Q 4:43 May an employer discharge an employee because of pregnancy?

No. Private employers with 15 or more employees are subject to the federal Pregnancy Discrimination Act (PDA) [42 USCA § 2000-2], which prohibits discriminatory treatment of pregnant women. Consequently, employers may not discharge an employee because of pregnancy or treat pregnancy-related disabilities differently from any other temporary disability. Employers should develop a neutral disability and sick leave policy and make certain that the policy is administered so that it does not discriminate against pregnant women.

Some general guidelines an employer can follow are:

1. A pregnant woman may not be denied any job solely because she is pregnant. Any decision made must be based on her ability or inability to perform the work.

2. A pregnant woman may not be required to take a leave of absence if she is able to perform her job duties.

3. A pregnant woman who requests maternity leave is entitled to it on the same basis that leaves are granted for other temporary disabilities.

Q 4:44 Can an employer require a pregnant woman to return to work within a specified period after delivery or after a physician has certified that the woman is capable of returning to work?

Generally, yes, as long as the employer can support such a policy by a business necessity. Courts have upheld policies that require women to return to work within 60 days of delivery or upon certification of capability by a physician.

Q 4:45 Must an employer guarantee to reinstate a pregnant worker in the same position she held prior to maternity leave?

An employer is not required to return an employee to the position she occupied prior to maternity leave (or to any job for that matter) unless the employer's policy promises to do so. However, if the employer guarantees reinstatement in the same job to persons who return to work from disability leave for other nonoccupational illness or injuries, refusing reinstatement following maternity leave would be considered discriminatory. Consequently, an employer that extends reinstatement to employees after medical leaves of absence must pursue the same policy for pregnant women.

Note, too, that some states have passed laws requiring covered employers in those states to guarantee reinstatement following maternity leave, and the Supreme Court has held that these state laws are constitutional. In recent years parental leave bills that would afford such a right to both male and female employees—not only for maternity and paternity purposes, but also to care for an ill child, spouse, or parent—have been introduced repeatedly in both houses of Congress, thus far without success. The following states, the District of Columbia, and Puerto Rico have adopted some form of family, parental and/or maternity leave law or regulation: California, Colorado, Connecticut, Hawaii, Iowa, Kansas, Maine, Maryland, Massachusetts, Minnesota, Montana, Nevada, New Jersey, North Dakota, Oklahoma, Oregon, Rhode Island, South Carolina, Tennessee, Utah, Washington, and Wisconsin.

Q 4:46 When a woman returns to her job after a pregnancy leave, may her seniority or benefits be affected?

No. An employer may not reduce an employee's seniority or benefits due to a pregnancy-related leave of absence.

Q 4:47 May a company lay off a pregnant employee as part of a fetal protection program?

No. *United Auto Workers v. Johnson Controls, Inc* (see Qs 4:28, 4:29.) appears to be a powerful statement by the Supreme Court in favor of a woman's right to decide for herself what reproductive risks she'll run on the job. The decision turns not only on the Court's reading of Title VII; Justice Blackmun's opinion also makes a statement about workplace safety; that is, a company cannot substitute a discriminatory fetal protection policy for its obligation under the Occupational Safety and Health Act (OSHA) to police its premises and keep them free from hazards. Following Johnson Controls, any employer still desirous of implementing or maintaining a fetal protection policy must be prepared to prove that such a policy qualifies as a BFOQ.

Q 4:48   Is it a violation of Title VII to fire an employee who becomes pregnant out of wedlock?

No. In 1990, a U.S. appeals court held that a Puerto Rican bank violated Title VII when it fired an employee who became pregnant from an extramarital affair with her supervisor. The bank apparently had been aware of the affair for several years, but took no action until the employee became pregnant, at which time she and her supervisor, the bank's assistant controller, were fired. In its defense, the bank pointed to its rule requiring its employees to "maintain at all times conduct characterized by decency and public morality." However, the real reason for the dismissal was found to be her pregnancy, and that, in turn, was found to be an illegal discriminatory motive. [Sanchez v Banco Santander Puerto Rico, 52 Fair Empl Prac Cas (BNA) 1444, 53 Empl Prac Dec (CCH) ¶39,900 (1st Cir 1990)]

Sexual Harassment

Q 4:49   What is sexual harassment?

Sexual harassment is either establishing terms and conditions of employment with reference to sexual favors, called quid pro quo sexual harassment, or creating, maintaining, or tolerating a sexually hostile work environment. A hostile, abusive, or offensive work environment as the foundation for a claim of sexual harassment was recognized by the U.S. Supreme Court in *Meritor Savings Bank v. Vinson*. [477 US 57 (1986)] Just how hostile, offensive, or abusive the environment must be to support such a cause of action remains a matter of legal dispute and judicial controversy.

In 1993, the U.S. Supreme Court agreed to review a case to determine whether, to recover damages, a woman must prove that her psychological well-being was affected by the sexual harassment to which she was subjected. In *Harris v. Forklift Systems Inc.* [976 F 2d 773 (6th Cir 1992)], the U.S. appeals court in Cincinnati ruled in favor of a more liberal standard that has also been embraced by three other federal courts of appeals. That standard says that a plaintiff can recover damages under Title VII for sex discrimination if the illegal harassment would have offended a "reasonable victim." Harris, whose lawyers are arguing for the adoption of this more liberal standard, claims she worked as a rental manager for the defendant in Nashville, Tennessee, for two years, until she quit in October 1987 because she could no longer tolerate her co-workers referring to her as, for instance, "dumb ass woman," and asking her whether she had ever offered sexual favors to customers.

The defendant-employer, in its brief in opposition to Harris's successful petition to the Supreme Court for review of her case, suggested that the plaintiff had merely been treated like "one of the boys" enjoying the benefits of workplace camaraderie, and that at times, she herself had used language that "sank below the generally accepted norm."

Assuming that a jury could find that the facts, as Harris presents them, would offend a reasonable person, the Supreme Court was faced with deciding whether such a finding is sufficient, absent real psychological pain or harm, to support a Title VII cause of action. In the words of one commentator, if the Court finds in favor of Harris's position, "[T]he case could greatly increase employers' vulnerability to sex-harassment suits. . . ." or it could be construed as redeeming women's rights. [Barrett, "Justices to Decide Psychological Injury Case," *The Wall Street Journal*, Mar 2, 1993 at A4]

In fact, if an analogy can be drawn between hostile environment sexual harassment cases under Title VII and state tort actions for intentional infliction of emotional distress, then it might seem appropriate for the Supreme Court to hold that a plaintiff should proffer some evidence, typically an expert witness such as a psychiatrist or psychologist, to support the existence of psychological harm before a trial court can find, as a matter of law, that all the elements of the cause of action are present and that a jury is entitled to determine the factual disputes and weigh the worth of the inflicted injuries. Successful prosecution of an emotional distress case usually requires not merely intentional but actually outrageous or egregious behavior resulting in an actual infliction of psychological pain or injury. [See, e.g., Chuy v Philadelphia Eagles Football Club, 595 F 2d 1265 (3d Cir 1979) (team physician allegedly told professional football player, falsely, that he had diagnosed the player as suffering from a fatal disease)]

Indeed, not only is the analogy to intentional infliction of emotional distress arguably apt, but in fact many states have held that a cause of action for such distress may be brought in conjunction with, or even instead of a sexual harassment suit pursuant to state or federal antidiscrimination statutes. However, other states have not gone quite so far. [See, e.g., Clay v Advanced Computer Applications Inc, 522 Pa 86, 559 A 2d 917 (1989) (plaintiffs' sole cause of action on their contention that wife was terminated by their employer as the result of repelling illicit sexual advances was under the Pennsylvania Human Relations Act for sex discrimination)]

In fact, in an opinion penned by Justice Sandra Day O'Connor, a unanimous Supreme Court ruled on November 9, 1993, that for conduct to be actionable under Title VII for creating an "abusive work environment" that conduct need not be so severe as to have caused the plaintiff-employee to suffer psychological injury. In so holding, the majority opinion stated:

> This standard . . . takes a middle path between making action- able any conduct that is merely offensive and requiring the conduct to cause a tangible psychological injury. As we pointed out in *Meritor*, "mere utterance of an . . . epithet which engen- ders offensive feeling in a [sic] employee,' . . . does not suffi- ciently affect the conditions of employment to implicate Title VII. Conduct that is not severe or pervasive enough to create an objectively hostile or abusive work environment, an environ- ment that a reasonable person would find hostile or abusive, is beyond Title VII's purview. Likewise, if the victim does not subjectively perceive the environment to be abusive, the con- duct has not actually altered the conditions of the victim's employment, and there is no Title VII violation.
>
> But Title VII comes into play before the harassing conduct leads to a nervous breakdown. A discriminatorily abusive work envi- ronment, even one that does not seriously affect employees' psychological well-being, can and often will detract from em- ployees' job performance, discourage employees from remain- ing in the job, or keep them from advancing in their careers. [Harris v Forklift Systems Inc, 114 S Ct 367, 370-71 (1993)]

The other woman on the nation's high court, Justice Ruth Ginsburg, filed a short concurring opinion in which she endorsed the Equal Employment Opportunity Commission's argument, filed as a friend of the court, that to have a claim, the employee need only "prove that a reasonable person subjected to the discriminatory conduct would find, as the plaintiff did, that the harassment so altered working conditions as to "ma[k]e it more difficult to do the job." [Id at 372] In other words, while Justice Ginsburg was able to join the unanimous court opinion as it came out in favor of the plaintiff, she seemingly would have endorsed an even more liberal standard under which women could challenge allegedly hostile working environments.

By way of a final note on *Harris*, the refusal to require a plaintiff to prove actual psychological harm or emotional distress would seem to preserve the position of those states which permit a concurrent or alternative state law tort action for intentional infliction of emotional distress in circumstances of very serious sexual harassment.

Q 4:50   Does a supervisor's favoritism toward a woman amount to sexual harassment?

The federal courts are somewhat in disagreement about the answer to this question. In the mid-80s, "[t]he Second Circuit limited the definition of gender discrimination by finding that sex discrimination or sexual harassment does not exist in cases where a consensual sexual relationship is used to affect one's terms and conditions of employment. The Court determined that in those instances where there was an ongoing, voluntary, romantic engagement it would not and should not stretch the breadth and scope of the Title VII definition of sex to include such activity." [Robert F. Conte, "Does a Supervisor's Favoritism Towards a Woman Equal Sexual Harassment?" *Saul, Ewing, Remick & Saul Employment Law Update*, April 1994, at 1]

More recently, a federal trial court, distinguishing such predecessor decisions, held that where one female employee declined her supervisor's invitation to engage in a sexual relationship, only to see the promotion go to a co-worker who complied with his subsequent request, the passed-over employee had a cause of action for sex harassment. [Dirksen v City of Springfield, 842 F Supp 1117, 1994 US Dist LEXIS 1412, 64 BNA FEP Cases 116, 64 Empl Prac Dec (CCH) P43,051 (CD Ill 1994)]

The plaintiff was a secretary in the Springfield, Illinois, Police Department and claimed that the police chief made unwanted physical advances and told her that, if she wanted to be promoted to become his personal secretary, she had to enter a relationship with him. When she declined, his new girlfriend got the job. [Id]

The Dirksen case is but one example of expanding views of sexual harassment that are leading thoughtful employers and others to worry about where this volatile area of the law is headed.

A jury in Puerto Rico in a sex discrimination and sexual harassment trial in mid-1994 brought in a verdict totaling $2.37 million, including $350,000 in punitive damages, as allowed by Title VII as amended by the Civil Rights Act of 1991. (See Q 1:8.) On a motion by the corporate defendant the trial judge granted a remittitur, reducing the total award to $1.5 million and leaving it to the plaintiff to accept the award or face a new trial. [Selgas v American Airlines Inc, 858 F Supp 316, 1994 US Dist LEXIS 10147 (D Puerto Rico 1994)] In the face of such potentially devastating exposure, employers are constantly searching for shields to protect themselves. One such shield is alternative dispute resolution. [See Q 15:17; James O. Castagnera, "Alternative Dispute Resolution: Construction Industry," 52 *Am Jur Trials* 209 (Lawyer's Cooperative, 1994)]

Another shield may be liability insurance. (See Q 4:51.)

Q 4:51   Can a company carry insurance against a sexual harassment claim?

According to Professor James M. Fischer of the Southwestern University School of Law in Los Angeles, many corporations have been prompted to reexamine their liability insurance policies to see if a sexual harassment lawsuit might be covered. Unfortunately, there are several reasons why such a suit may not be.

First, most liability insurance limits its coverage to accidents. While pregnancy can happen by accident, sexual harassment normally does not. And a model policy provision, such as Insurance Service Office 1988 Commercial General Liability Coverage Form CG 00 01 11 88, provides:

> We will pay those sums that the insured becomes legally obligated to pay as damages because of bodily injury or property damage. . . . This insurance applies to bodily injury and property damage only if: (1) The bodily injury or property damage is caused by an occurrence. . . . Occurrence means an accident,

including continuing or repeated exposure to substantially the same general harmful conditions.

Second, many policies contain a standard exclusion for intentional wrongs. With regard to employment discrimination, including sex discrimination, generally this exclusion was sometimes circumvented because the plaintiff, be it the Equal Employment Opportunity Commission or an individual litigant, pleaded the case in the alternative. In other words, the plaintiff accused the defendant of intentional acts of discrimination and then also contended that, even if the company's behavior or personnel policy was neutral on its face, it had resulted in a disparate impact upon the plaintiff or the plaintiff's protected class. Because an unintended, disparate impact is closely akin to common law negligence (as opposed to intentional torts such as assault and battery), the defendant's insurer was obligated to assume the defense.

Although the perpetrator of sexual harassment may be acting intentionally, the company may be able to argue that its failure to detect the illicit acts, or to respond to them properly, was mere negligent behavior, thus circumventing the exclusion in the insurance contract. But where the harasser is a supervisor, as is often the case, such an argument may be futile because the manager may be deemed to represent the corporation.

Third, many states' common (court-made) law holds that public policy is offended by any insurance provision that covers the insured's intentional misbehavior. Consequently, before your company buys an insurance policies designed to cover various forms of employment liabilities, or you agree to pay your insurer a substantially higher premium to buy out those troublesome limits and exclusions, you are well advised to have legal counsel investigate the enforceability of such insurance in the state(s) where your company has employees.

Lastly, it's worth noting that whether your current or future liability policy will cover sexual harassment may depend in part upon the sort of harassment with which your firm is faced. Demanding sexual favors for job advantages, such as a promotion, is the most blatant form of harassment and clearly indicates illegal intent. But the other, more mercurial form of sexual harassment recognized by the law today is the hostile environment variety. What if the basis of the harassment complaint is the display of nude photos by a female employee's male co-workers in the employee locker room or the common use of foul language weighted with sexual innuendo in a supervisor's everyday speech? Such conduct may be more accidental than deliberate. Once again the insurer may be nudged by effective legal arguments to feel compelled to assume your company's defense.

Employers feeling harassed by the threat of sexual harassment suits should confer with their insurers and brokers to determine whether it might make good financial sense to insure against these all-too-common legal liabilities.

Q 4:52 Does the display of pinups in the workplace constitute sexual harassment?

In 1991, a female welder in a shipyard convinced a federal judge that the posting of calendars and posters picturing nude or scantily clad women was sexual harassment made illegal by Title VII. Judge Melton of the U.S. District Court in Jacksonville, Florida, termed the pinups a "visual assault on the sensibilities of women." The lawsuit was pursued on behalf of the woman welder by the National Organization of Women (NOW) Legal Defense Fund. The plaintiff convinced the court that the "nudies" had a "cumulative, eroding effect to the victim's well-being." It may be significant that the offending pictures were posted on the welding shop walls. Possibly the court would have reached a different result if they had been put up in individual employees' private offices, where presumably the plaintiff would not have been subjected to their "cumulative, eroding effect" on her well-being. The Jacksonville district judge stated that the standard for deciding such cases is whether a "reasonable woman" would feel that she was being subjected to a hostile or abusive work environment. [Robinson v Jacksonville Shipyards, Inc, 760 F Supp 1486 (MD Fla 1991)] More recently, a group of female employees of the Adolph Coors Brewing Company sued to compel the company to pull its TV commercials featuring scantily clad women. The plaintiffs contend this image adversely influenced the behavior of their male co-workers toward them and other women in the plant.

Q 4:53   What is the "reasonable woman" test of sexual harassment?

In *Burns v. McGregor Electronic Industries* [1993 US App Lexis 6336 (1993)], the U.S. Supreme Court was faced with the employer's attempt to defend its conduct by pointing to the fact that the plaintiff had appeared as the nude centerfold in Easyrider Magazine. The trial court had ruled against the plaintiff, concluding that her nude appearance in the motorcycle magazine undermined the credibility of her claim that sexual advances by her boss were offensive to her. Disagreeing and remanding for trial, the appellate court stated:

> [Plaintiff's] choice to pose for a nude magazine outside work hours is not material to the issue of whether [she] found her employer's work-related conduct offensive. This is not a case where Burns posed in provocative and suggestive ways at work. Her private life, regardless how reprehensible the trier of fact might find it to be, did not provide lawful acquiescence to unwanted sexual advances at her workplace by her employer.

Q 4:54   Can a group of employees pursue a class action sexual harassment suit against their employer?

In May 1993, the U.S. District Court for the district of Minnesota ruled that a company accused of creating a hostile work environment for its female workers could be subjected to a class action suit brought by a group of these female employees. Finding that a "sexualized, male-oriented and anti-female environment" predominated two of Eveleth Taconite's mines, District Judge Kyle noted that visual references to women as sex objects, such as nude photographs, graffiti, and cartoons, plus frequent comments about female body parts and women's sex lives, poisoned the work atmosphere at the two mines. Breaking new ground, the judge permitted the reasonably offended women to proceed against the company as a class to recover damages against the company. ["Women Employees Win First Sex Harassment Class Ruling," 1993 *BNA Daily Labor Report* 94 (May 18, 1993) at 1] (See also Q 15:16 for a discussion of class action suits.)

Q 4:55 To what extent must a woman resist her boss's attention in order later to pursue a successful sexual harassment suit?

Recent case law indicates that for the reasonable woman (see Qs 4:52, 4:53) to prevail in a sexual harassment suit against an overly attentive boss, a woman must be able to offer evidence that she not only found the advances unwelcome, but also that she clearly communicated her negative reaction to the perpetrator. For instance, in a situation where the boss paid undue attention to his secretary, including "little notes, escorting her to the bathroom or her car, and visiting her both at home and in the hospital," the federal judge ruled against the secretary-plaintiff because she "never made any realistic effort to cut it off." Summarizing the evidence, the court observed, "she indicated that she continually asked him not to touch her and that she attempted to avoid his hugs, yet it seems that her requests were not delivered with any sense of urgency, sincerity, or force." [Louri v Liberian Services, Inc, Fair Empl Prac Cas (BNA) (ED Va 1991)] The bottom line is that mixed signals do not provide the sexual harasser with legally sufficient notice of the offensiveness of his behavior and therefore may not give rise to a Title VII cause of action. Nevertheless, a reasonable employer should promulgate a clear policy forbidding conduct that can give rise to sexual harassment charges and should also give prompt attention to even mild complaints about such behavior from its female employees.

Q 4:56 Which employees are considered victims of sexual harassment?

If granting sexual favors becomes a condition of employment or career advancement, the victims are not only those employees from whom the favors are asked, but also co-workers whose careers suffer because the boss denies them a similar opportunity.

Q 4:57 Is the company responsible for sexual harassment of one employee by another?

When an employee alleges no loss of economic benefits resulting from sexual harassment, an employer will not be found automatically liable for an act of sexual harassment by a supervisor. However, courts will find an employer liable for a supervisor's sexual harassment of a subordinate if the employer had actual knowledge or, given the circumstances, should have had knowledge of the supervisor's actions. Also, an employer will be held strictly liable for a supervisor's discriminatory discharge of an employee if, under common-law principles of agency, the supervisor was acting within the scope of his or her actual or apparent authority.

When the harassment is by a worker on the same organizational level as the person being harassed, the company may not be liable unless the victim complains to upper management. Once a complaint is made, the company must take prompt, effective action in order to avoid liability.

In one case, a district court in New York held an employer liable for sexual harassment by nonemployees. [EEOC v Sage Realty Corp, 507 F Supp 599 (SDNY 1981)] The employer required a female employee to wear a revealing uniform, which prompted customers to make sexually suggestive comments. When the employee refused to continue to wear the uniform, she was fired. The court held that the company was liable because it was aware of the sexual harassment and yet refused to take appropriate action to eliminate it.

Q 4:58   Is the employer ever liable for sexual harassment conducted by a third party not employed by the employer?

The legal foundation for an employer's liability for sexual harassment in the workplace is that the harassing and discriminatory conduct affects the victim's terms and conditions of employment. Obviously, harassment by a supervisor or co-worker can create a hostile work environment; however, such an environment can also be caused by a third party. If an employer tolerates or encourages harassment by outsiders on the employer's premises, then the hostile work environment that results will be the employer's legal responsibility, even though the harassers are not employed by that company. For instance, if a law firm required a female associate attorney to deal with a valued client who sexually harassed the attorney and refused to act upon her subsequent complaints because the firm did not want to jeopardize the client relationship, that law firm could be liable for the damages resulting from the harassment.

On the other hand, suppose that a temporary or leased employee on the company's premises is harassed by one of the firm's employees. This also might result in vicarious liability for the host company. Staying with the law firm hypothetical case, if the firm employed a legal secretary from a temporary agency and she was harassed by the lawyer to whom she was assigned and upon complaining was shipped back to her agency with a bad reference by the law firm's managing partner, the law firm might well be viewed as her joint employer and the unresolved harassment, a violation of Title VII, could be the basis for a case.

Q 4:59   Is the employer ever liable when the plaintiff herself has willingly participated in some of the allegedly harassing conduct?

Ordinarily, when a female employee willingly engages in conduct, such as a consensual affair with a co-worker, even a supervisor, no sexual harassment occurs with regard to that woman. [But see Dirksen v City of Springfield, 842 F Supp 1117, 1994 US Dist LEXIS 1412, 64 BNA FEP Cases 116, 64 Emp Prac Dec (CCH) P43051 (CD Ill 1994)]

However, in 1994, the U.S. Court of Appeals for the Seventh Circuit held General Motors liable for sexual harassment against the lone woman worker in a tinsmith shop, reversing the decision of the trial judge who had exonerated the company. In a decision penned by Chief Judge Richard Posner, not necessarily known for flaming views, the appellate panel ruled by a vote of 2 to 1 that though the woman's conduct might be characterized as "vulgar and unladylike," it was not a basis for firing her. The rowdy behavior allegedly instigated by her demeanor had been blamed upon the plaintiff, who was then the only employee terminated. The appellate judges saw the scenario differently.

"The asymmetry of the positions must be considered," wrote Judge Posner. "She was one woman; they were many men." Her crude and vulgar behavior could hardly have intimidated her male co-workers, he continued. "We have trouble imagining a situation in which male factory workers sexually harass a lone woman in self-defense as it were; yet that at root is General Motors' characterization of what happened here."

["Seventh Circuit Finds GM Liable for Sexual Harassment," 1994 *Daily Labor Report* 140 (Aug 2, 1994) at 1]

Q 4:60 To bring a claim of sexual harassment successfully, must the complainant be the actual subject of sexually suggestive behavior?

No. An employee who was never directly subjected to sexual harassment may nevertheless bring a successful claim for sexual harassment under Title VII. Although not themselves singled out for unwanted sexual attention, if employees can show that co-workers were the subject of such sexually oriented behavior and that as a result those co-workers who complied were granted favored treatment, the employees can allege that the employer created a work environment that was hostile, abusive, and offensive. If the facts support such an allegation, the employer will be liable for sexual harassment under Title VII. In a recent decision, a federal judge in Rhode Island found in favor of two male employees who sued for sexual harassment, claiming the company's general manager compelled them to engage in sexual activities with his female secretary or be fired. [1991 *BNA Daily Labor Report* 159 (Aug 16, 1991)]

Q 4:61 What kind of action must management take in response to a sexual harassment complaint?

The first step is immediate investigation. This should be conducted confidentially to protect the reputation and privacy of both the accuser and the employee accused of harassment. If the investigation supports the victim's charges, effective action to halt the harassment must follow. Disciplinary action may include discharge or transfer of the employees involved. If the harassment was mild and the harasser is an otherwise valued employee, a verbal reprimand may be sufficient for a first offense. Nonetheless, the courts insist that the action must be prompt, effective, and must not leave the victim open to retaliation. Sexual harassment is considered a serious act of sexual discrimination, and serious measures are usually justified to remedy it.

Q 4:62 Should a company have a sexual harassment policy?

A policy dealing with sexual harassment is not a requirement, but it is a very good idea. The policy should contain two parts. Part one should clearly state the definition of sexual harassment (see Q 4:49) and the fact that the company will not tolerate it in any form. Part two should provide a complaint procedure that directs the complainant to the immediate supervisor, unless that manager is the harasser, in which case the victim should be directed to the company president, human resources manager, or other higher official. The policy should provide an assurance of prompt and confidential action.

Q 4:63 Should an employer discourage sexual contact outside the workplace between supervisory personnel and subordinate employees?

A policy that discourages such contact is advisable. An employee who has voluntarily engaged in sexual relations with his or her supervisor may later claim that such relations were unwanted and that he or she was afraid of being fired. Such an allegation constitutes a foundation for a claim of sexual harassment under Title VII, despite the fact that the conduct was voluntary. The Supreme Court has held that the fact that sexual relations were voluntary is not a defense to a Title VII suit for sexual harassment. [Meritor Savings Bank, FSB v Vinson, 106 S Ct 2399 (1986)] The key is whether, albeit voluntary, the relationship was "unwelcome." Supervisors should be especially sensitized to this potential problem regarding subordinate employees.

Q 4:64 Is it a violation of Title VII to promote a spouse or significant other?

Somewhat surprisingly, the EEOC has said in a policy guideline to its field people that sexual favoritism to a spouse or friend "may be unfair," but is not necessarily illegal. Since both male and female workers sometimes suffer disadvantages and unfairness in the workplace "for reasons other than their genders," favoritism based upon a mutually agreeable sexual relationship might not, in and of itself, violate Title VII. However, widespread favoritism of this type in a company could meet the "hostile work environment" test since a supervisor who coerces an employee to grant sexual favors for workplace advantage may give rise to actions by both the victim of the unwelcome advances and his or her co-workers who were denied a fair opportunity to compete.

Q 4:65 Is any general trend discernible in the development of Title VII law on sexual harassment?

The developments discussed in Qs 4:53–4:56 suggest that the emphasis is shifting to "hostile work environment" as the focus of Title VII lawsuits involving sexual harassment. Consenting sexual relationships between co-workers, even when they result in pregnancy or promotion, are not per se illegal violations of Title VII, nor do they clearly call for company discipline. Unwelcome advances or demands, however, as well as inappropriate personal behavior that would offend a reasonable woman, will give rise to Title VII violations.

Many employers discourage sexual relations between supervisors and subordinates. None of these new developments indicates such a rule is either improper or illegal, and it may be the prudent course for companies to follow.

Q 4:66 Will a sexual harassment policy protect a company from legal liability for sexual harassment?

The policy suggested in Q 4:63 is not a guarantee of freedom from liability. Nonetheless, if all employees are aware of the policy, and an employee alleges harassment but does not follow through on the procedures, his or her claim will be considerably weakened. To be fully effective, however, the policy must be promulgated and enforced.

Disability Discrimination

Q 4:67 What is disability discrimination?

The definition of disability discrimination varies somewhat from law to law, but generally covers employment decisions based on an employee's non-job-related handicap. When the employer's decision (e.g., to hire, fire, promote or transfer an employee) is based upon the employee's real or perceived handicap and that disability does not actually impact job performance, disability discrimination occurs. Disability discrimination is not forbidden by Title VII, although many state human rights acts make handicap discrimination illegal.

For many years, federal law forbade handicap discrimination only by government agencies and federal contractors. However, the Americans with Disabilities Act (ADA), passed in 1990, became effective on July 26, 1992, for private companies employing 25 or more workers. Additionally, many state antidiscrimination laws also forbid employment discrimination against the handicapped.

Q 4:68 How do the Vocational Rehabilitation Act of 1973 (Rehabilitation Act) and the ADA define a disabled individual?

The federal definition of a disabled individual has three elements. The disabled person:

1. Has a physical or mental impairment that substantially limits one or more major life activities,
2. Has a record of such an impairment, or
3. Is regarded as having such an impairment.

If an employee or job applicant meets any one of these three definitions, he or she is in the protected group. [See 29 USC § 706(7)(b)]

Q 4:69 Does the Rehabilitation Act apply to private employers?

The Rehabilitation Act, which prohibits employment discrimination based on a handicap against persons otherwise qualified to perform a job, does not apply to private employers. However, all federal contractors and recipients of federal financial assistance are now considered to be public employers for purposes of the Act. Consequently, seemingly private employers, such as hospitals that receive federal financial assistance are subject to the provisions of the act.

Q 4:70　What is a non-job-related disability?

A non-job-related disability is a physical deficiency that impairs a person's daily activities but does not prevent that person from performing on the job. The definition of a non-job-related disability may include a condition that the employer chooses to treat as a handicap, even though the condition does not actually impair the employee's daily life. For instance, if an employer fires a worker because the worker is left-handed, that worker might have an action for handicap discrimination (although in an actual lawsuit, a court rejected this particular legal argument) [De La Torres v Bolger, 610 F Supp 593 (ND Tex 1985)]

Q 4:71　May an employer refuse to hire a person with a non-job-related disability?

In general, courts will uphold an employer's right to deny employment to persons with high blood pressure, epilepsy, or diabetes, as well as alcoholism or substance abuse, if the handicapped individual fails to take steps to correct or control the condition. For example, New York City was able to sustain its decision not to hire a diabetic to drive a garbage truck in Manhattan by proving that permitting a person prone to blackouts to drive a truck that can at times weigh 30 tons constitutes a danger to public safety. The driver not only admitted that his condition had become severe, but also acknowledged his failure to control his condition. [Serrapica v City of New York, 708 F Supp 64 (SDNY), *aff'd without op*, 888 F 2d 126 (2d Cir 1989)]

On the other hand, courts often require employers, under a reasonable accommodation theory, to give the afflicted employee at least one opportunity to get corrective treatment before terminating employment on the basis that the handicap is job-related.

Q 4:72   Is high blood pressure a non-job-related handicap?

In an increasing number of states, high blood pressure is viewed as a handicap. If the condition can be controlled by medication, it probably cannot constitute a bona fide reason to deny employment. But if the worker refuses or neglects to control high blood pressure, an employer may be justified in suspending him or her, or at least transferring the employee from a dangerous job, until the problem is under control.

Q 4:73   Is poor eyesight a non-job-related handicap?

Courts and agencies around the country seem to be divided on whether an employee with poor eyesight should be classified as a handicapped employee. One group holds that simply needing to wear glasses does not make an employee a handicapped individual for purposes of discrimination protection. However, some courts and antidiscrimination agencies have adopted the opposite view that job discrimination based on poor eyesight (such as practiced by some police departments) is illegal. This faction points to modern technological advances in eyewear that undercut the argument that near-perfect eyesight is an appropriate BFOQ. During the hoopla surrounding passage of the ADA in 1990, government sources asserted that some 46 million Americans meet one of the definitions of disabled individual. This astounding figure suggests federal intent to expand prior preconceptions of who is disabled.

Q 4:74   Is pathological gambling a non-job-related handicap?

In 1988, an FBI agent who was fired for gambling with funds he was issued as part of an undercover assignment convinced a federal judge that his compulsive gambling was a handicap under the Rehabilitation Act. [Rezza v US Dept of Justice, 698 F Supp 586 (ED Pa 1988)] After the gambling incident, the agent had entered a 22-day treatment program, and thereafter attended Gamblers' Anonymous twice a week. The Rehabilitation Act specifically covers both "physical and mental impairment," and the implementing regulations cover psychological disorders, mental retardation, emotional and mental illnesses, and learning disabilities. The agent had to satisfy the court that he was actually impaired and that he was otherwise qualified to perform his job. Whether this case will serve as precedent for state courts in determining an addicted gambler's rights under applicable state antidiscrimination laws may turn on how specific state laws and regulations are written. Assuming that compulsive gambling is generally accepted as a genuine mental disorder, there is no obvious reason that it should not be treated as a handicap, as is alcoholism. However, the ADA excludes such mental problems as pyromania and nicotine addiction from its covered disabilities; arguably a gambling addiction likewise is outside the ADA's ambit.

Q 4:75   Is obesity a non-job-related disability?

This is actually two questions. First: Is obesity a handicap? Because it impairs many day-to-day activities, can lead to various diseases and physical problems, and can even reduce life span, a number of courts and agencies have held that obesity is a handicap. Second: Is obesity non-job-related? In general, yes, but the issue of whether personal appearance is an important part of the job remains hotly contested. In one of the most recent decisions on the obesity issue, the California Court of Appeal held that the City of Los Angeles was not guilty of disability discrimination under applicable state law for twice suspending a female paramedic who had put on an extra 100 pounds during her seven years of employment. Calling the city's body weight regulations for paramedics and firefighters reasonable, the court held that at 230 pounds, the plaintiff-employee's condition was job-related in that it impeded her strength, agility, speed, and endurance. Consequently, though her obesity was caused by a thyroid condition beyond her control, the employee could not claim to be a victim of illegal job discrimination. [See 1992 BNA Daily Labor Report, No 87 (May 5, 1992) at A-6]

Q 4:76   Is alcoholism a non-job-related disability?

As in Q 4:75, this question is twofold: Is alcoholism a handicap and is it non-job-related? First, the weight of medical evidence overwhelmingly concludes that alcoholism is a disease, not a personal choice; therefore, it is a handicap. It is, however, related to job performance; if untreated, it invariably has a dramatic, negative effect on job performance. However, this does not mean that an alcoholic employee can be fired. Most states require that the alcoholic be given an unpaid leave of absence for detoxification. The ADA does not protect current untreated alcoholism or drug abuse.

Q 4:77 What if the recovered alcoholic employee returns to work and then reverts to alcoholism?

The law generally demands that an employer give the alcoholic employee only one opportunity to reform. If he or she comes back to work and reverts to alcoholism, discharge is generally appropriate. However, we can expect new challenges to emerge under the ADA.

Q 4:78 Is drug dependence a non-job-related disability?

Like alcoholism, drug addiction is a handicap that will ultimately affect work performance. Some courts and discrimination agencies have held that, as with alcoholics, drug addicts deserve a reasonable leave of absence for detoxification. However, other legal decision makers have held that, because most addictive drugs are also illegal, a lawbreaker is not entitled to such reasonable accommodation. The ADA is clear that current drug abusers are not protected.

The Americans With Disabilities Act

Q 4:79 What is a disability under the ADA?

A disability under the Act is:

1. A physical or mental impairment that substantially limits one or more major life activities,
2. A history of such an impairment, or
3. Being regarded as having such an impairment.

Definitions (2) and (3) can pull people who are not actually disabled under the ADA umbrella. Some examples may be helpful.

Example 1. A worker with a history of back trouble applies for a job. As a result of his preemployment physical examination, the company learns of his history of sprains and strains. The applicant is physically fine now and has not had a back problem for several years, yet he is not hired. He is not disabled in the eyes of the doctor. In the eyes of the law, he is a victim of disability discrimination. Legally, he is one of those estimated 46 million disabled Americans the ADA seeks to protect.

Example 2. A convenience food store manager hires a clerk. On his first day on the job, the new employee tells the cashier he has tested positive as a carrier of the HIV virus. The cashier tells the manager, who finds fault with how the new clerk stocked the shelves and fires him at the end of the day. The fired clerk, too, is not disabled in a strict medical sense. He may have received a false positive test; or if he is an HIV carrier, he still may never develop AIDS. He may even have been joking about the positive test. Whatever the case, he has been treated as if he has a disability. Under the ADA, he is a victim of disability discrimination.

The ADA could cover many other situations where the existence of an actual medical or physical disability is unclear. Workers with high blood pressure controlled by medication, short persons, and persons with unusual birthmarks are all good examples of people with conditions that may not be considered disabilities in a medical sense, but that would be covered under the ADA. If the best qualified applicant for an office receptionist position has a large red birthmark on her forehead, failure to hire that applicant for that reason would constitute disability discrimination. The ADA demands that the disabled person be able to do the job, allowing for reasonable accommodation, without posing an unreasonable danger to himself or herself or to others. The ADA does not permit looking good to be a criterion for hiring.

Q 4:80   How is reasonable accommodation defined under the ADA?

A reasonable accommodation is any change in a term of condition of employment aimed at assisting the disabled employee to do the job. What constitutes a reasonable accommodation is another area of ambiguity, and, therefore, likely litigation. There is a wide range of possible approaches to this concept.

The Pennsylvania Human Relations Act (PHRA) and its implementing regulations do not define reasonable accommodation, opting to leave it to case-by-case development. The PHRA and its regulations say only that the employer need not alter standards of attendance or productivity on the job to accommodate a handicapped worker.

By contrast, the Delaware Handicapped Persons Employment Protection Act is far more specific, enumerating four areas of accommodation that usually will be unreasonable:

1. Providing personal appliances, such as eyeglasses and hearing aids;
2. Reassigning regular duties from the handicapped employee to other workers without giving the disabled worker compensating tasks;
3. Increasing the skill, effort, or responsibility of co-workers in order to lighten the handicapped worker's workload; and
4. Spending more than 5 percent of the handicapped employee's annual salary to make a physical change to accommodate his or her needs.

The ADA takes a middle ground between these two extremes. Reasonable accommodations include job restructuring, part-time or modified work schedules (such as flextime), modification or acquisition of equipment or devices, adjustment or modification of examinations and training materials, and possibly provision of readers or interpreters. At what point the costs of these accommodations becomes unreasonable is unclear under the ADA, but no doubt it is a function of the size and financial wherewithal of the employer, as well as the nature of the accommodation. One other important point is that the suggestion or request for an accommodation must come from the employee or applicant, not the employer.

Q 4:81   How is undue hardship defined under the ADA?

Factors determining whether a reasonable accommodation would impose an undue hardship on an employer include the overall size of the business, the site involved, and the nature and cost of the accommodation needed. Additionally, the number of employees or applicants potentially benefiting from an accommodation may be a relevant consideration in determining undue hardship. Another factor that may be considered in determining undue hardship is the availability of outside funding (from state vocational rehabilitation agencies or from federal, state, or local tax deductions or credits) to pay for accommodations.

The type of business operation also affects whether an accommodation imposes an undue hardship. For example, to implement or maintain physical accessibility for a job applicant or employee who uses a wheelchair might fundamentally alter the nature of a construction site or be unduly costly if the site's terrain and building structure change daily as construction progresses.

The determination of undue hardship is made on a case-by-case basis. The burden is on the employer to demonstrate that the needed accommodation would cause an undue hardship.

According to the Committee on Education and Labor, the definition of undue hardship is intended to discourage an employer who would, for example, otherwise elect to close a store that is only marginally profitable, rather than undertake significant investments to make reasonable accommodations for employees with disabilities. The requirements of the ADA should not result in the closure of a business or in the loss of jobs.

By providing a number of factors to take into consideration in each case, the intent of the ADA is to establish a flexible approach in determining undue hardship.

Q 4:82   In what areas of employment does the ADA prohibit discrimination?

Discrimination against a qualified individual with a disability is prohibited in all parts of the employment process. The employment process specifically includes, but is not limited to job application procedures, hiring, advancement, discharge, compensation, job training, recruitment and advertising, job assignments, job classifications, organizational structures, position descriptions, lines of progression, seniority lists, leaves of absence, sick leave, fringe benefits available by virtue of employment (whether or not administered by the employer), employer-sponsored activities (including social or recreational programs), and other terms, conditions, and privileges of employment.

Employers can, however, continue to use job-related criteria in choosing qualified candidates. For example, the employer may test applicants and employees to determine whether or not they can lift 50-pound boxes if it is required by the position. Similarly, an employer can continue to give typing tests when filling a position requiring that skill.

Section 102(b)(1) of the ADA prohibits the employer from limiting, segregating, or classifying a job applicant or an employee in a way that adversely affects the opportunities or status of the applicant or employee based on that person's disability. Therefore, an employer cannot adopt different pay scales, benefits programs, promotion opportunities, or working areas for employees with disabilities.

Section 102(b)(2) of Title I provides that a covered entity (i.e., a business subject to the ADA) may not participate in a contractual relationship that has the effect of discriminating against qualified applicants or employees. An employer cannot, therefore, enter into a contractual relationship with another company that would have the effect of discriminating against the employer's own employees or applicants. For example, assume that ABC Corporation is seeking to contract with XYZ Company to provide training for ABC's employees. The same responsibilities of accommodation that would apply to ABC Corporation if it provided the training itself also apply in the contractual relationship. Thus, if XYZ Company planned to hold its training program in a location inaccessible to ABC's employees with disabilities, ABC Corporation would have a duty to consider various reasonable accommodations, including asking the training company to identify other sites for the program that would be accessible to these employees, identifying other training companies that use accessible sites, paying to have the training company train the disabled employee elsewhere (either on a one-to-one basis or with other employees who may have missed the training for other reasons), or providing any other accommodation that might result in making the training program available to the employee.

Furthermore, the employer has an affirmative duty to investigate the accessibility of an off-site location that it plans to use for its own employees. In such situations, an employer can protect itself by simply ensuring that the contract with the host facility specifies that the rooms that are to be used for the function (e.g., meeting rooms, exhibit halls, sleeping rooms, and dining facilities) are accessible in accordance with applicable standards. If the facility breaches this accessibility provision, it will be liable to the employer for the cost of any accommodation needed to provide access to the disabled individual during the off-site function.

Q 4:83 Does an employer have the obligation under the ADA to ensure that third parties' behavior toward the employer's disabled employees is discrimination-free?

When the employer has the power to control the third party's behavior (e.g., by contract), the employer may be legally obliged by the ADA to ensure that the behavior is not discriminatory. Section 102(b)(3) of the ADA prohibits employers from using standards, criteria, or methods of administration that have the effect of discrimination or that perpetuate discrimination by others who are subject to common administrative control. For example, an employer cannot enter into a contract for liability insurance with an insurance company that refuses to cover accidents or injuries of persons with disabilities. Nor can the employer refuse to hire a person with a disability because its liability policy does not cover persons with disabilities.

Q 4:84 Does the ADA prohibit discrimination against persons related to or living with a handicapped individual?

Under Section 102(b)(4) of the ADA, an employer cannot discriminate against an employee or an applicant because of an association with a person with a disability. These associations may include family, friends, and people who provide care for persons with disabilities.

This provision applies only when the employer knows of the association with the disabled person and knows of the disability. The burden of proof is on the individual who is claiming discrimination; he or she must prove that the discrimination was motivated by his or her relationship or association with a person with a disability. Therefore, the employer would violate the Act if it discriminated against a qualified employee who did volunteer work with AIDS victims, if the employer knew of the employee's relationship or association with the persons with AIDS or the volunteer organization, and if the employment action was motivated by that relationship or association. Further, it would be illegal for an employer to discriminate against a qualified employee because that employee had a family member or friend who had a disability if the employer knew about the relationship and acted on that basis.

Q 4:85 What are the ADA's job qualification standards with regard to disabled persons?

Section 102(b)(6) of the ADA prohibits the use of qualification standards, employment tests, or other selection criteria that screen out or tend to screen out persons with disabilities, unless the criteria are shown to be job related and consistent with business necessity. The intent is that employment-related tests actually measure what they purport to measure. Thus, it would be discriminatory to administer speaking and listening skills tests to a person with a disability that impairs speech and hearing if the essential functions of the job do not require those skills.

A qualification standard may include a requirement that an individual not pose a direct threat to the health and safety of others. A direct threat is defined as a significant risk to the health and safety of others that cannot be eliminated by reasonable accommodation. The Committee on Labor and Education notes that the definition and standard apply not only to those with contagious diseases or infections, but also to individuals with disabilities.

The ADA's goal is to eliminate instances in which a person with a disability is excluded or found to be unqualified based on stereotypes or fear. Therefore, the ADA prohibits employment decisions based on generalizations about a disability rather than on the facts of an individual case. For example, an employer may not assume that a person with a mental disability or a person who has been treated for a mental disability poses a direct threat to others. In such instances, there must be objective evidence that the person has a recent history of committing overt acts or making threats that caused harm or that directly threatened harm. The determination of a significant risk must be based on the current condition of the applicant or employee.

The decision to exclude cannot be based simply on an elevated risk of injury.

Q 4:86 What are the ADA's requirements regarding preemployment medical examinations?

The ADA will significantly affect an employer's policies regarding physical examinations and inquiries of job applicants and employees.

Employers may no longer conduct physical examinations or ask any medically related questions before offering employment. Application forms that list diseases or medical conditions and require the applicant to check any that pertain must be modified to remove those questions. The ADA does, however, permit an employer to explain the essential functions of the job for which the person is applying and ask whether the person can perform those functions with or without a reasonable accommodation. For example, the employer may state that the job involves extensive heavy lifting and ask if the applicant could meet this job requirement, but the employer may not ask if the person has a congenital back problem. The employer may also ask the applicant to demonstrate an ability to perform the job. If the applicant indicates that he or she can perform with an accommodation, the employer may ask how the applicant would perform the job and with what accommodation.

In explaining and interpreting the prohibition against pre-offer medical inquiries, the EEOC has stated that the following application or interview questions are impermissible: "Is there any health-related reason why you may not be able to perform the job for which you are applying?" and "How many days were you absent from work because of illness last year?" Also, any question related to an applicant's worker compensation history is disallowed. Many employers routinely ask these types of questions, and should be aware that these practices prior to making an offer of employment must change.

Once the employer has offered a job to an applicant, it may conduct any medical inquiry or examination as long as it requires the same inquiry or examination of all employees in the same job category. In fact, an offer of employment may be contingent on the results of the medical examination. At this point, questions may also be asked about previous injuries and workers' compensation claims. If the post-offer medical inquiry or exam reveals a disability for which no reasonable accommodation exists, the employer may rescind the employment offer. Also, if the examination reveals a disability that is a threat to the health or safety of the individual or to others and that cannot be eliminated or reduced by a reasonable accommodation, the employer may refuse to hire the person.

Q 4:87　Are there situations in which an employer may inquire about the nature or severity of an applicant's disability?

There are several instances in which an employer may inquire into the nature or severity of a disability of a qualified individual without being subject to the penalties of the ADA. Such circumstances include (1) when an employer is taking voluntary action to overcome the effects or conditions that will result in long-term opportunities for persons with disabilities, (2) when an employer is taking remedial action to correct the effects of past discrimination, or (3) when an employer is taking affirmative action required by Section 503 of the Rehabilitation Act. Under any of these circumstances, the inquiring employer must make clear that the information requested is intended for use solely in connection with its remedial actions, obligations, or its voluntary or affirmative action efforts and that the information should be furnished on a purely voluntary basis.

Q 4:88　What are the ADA's provisions on illegal drug use?

Section 104(a) of the ADA provides that a qualified individual with a disability does not include an employee or applicant who is a current user of illegal drugs. However, Section 104(b) of the ADA provides that rehabilitated individuals and those in treatment who no longer use illegal drugs and individuals who are erroneously re-garded as illegal drug users are not excluded from the definition of an "individual with a disability." As in all other disability cases, the employee must prove that he or she has a history of a disability or is regarded as having a disability in order to be protected by the ADA.

What if the employer hires a drug abuser and later, after terminat-ing the employee, allegedly for current illegal drug use, the fired employee offers evidence that the problem had been overcome after commencement of employment? This hypothetical does not presume that the ex-employee necessarily did overcome the illegal drug abuse problem, but rather presents a problem of proof: the employer has relied upon illegal drug abuse as the legitimate business reason for terminating the employee, who in turn intends to present evidence of rehabilitation to show that the company's legitimate reason was in fact a pretext for a discriminatory discharge in violation of the ADA.

A recent case interpreting a prohibition against disability discrimination from an Ohio state statute, which is closely analogous to the ADA, suggests an alternative business justification for the legal termination of such an employee. In *Bray v. Forest Pharmaceuticals Inc.* [812 F Supp 115 (SD Ohio 1993)], the plaintiff was employed as a "tablet presser." His job duties included participating in the manufacture of controlled substances and the disposal of defective pills. During the course of his employment, Bray voluntarily admitted himself into a drug treatment program. The company inspected his locker and discovered two pills it manufactured. Based upon this discovery, the defendant-firm fired Bray. Bray sued, claiming he was illegally terminated based on his substance-abuse handicap, in violation of the Ohio statute.

Today, Bray may be able to bring a similar claim under ADA section 104(b), which states: "Nothing in subsection (a) of this section shall be construed to exclude as a qualified individual with a disability an individual who. . .is participating in a supervised rehabilitation program and is no longer engaging in such use; or. . .is erroneously regarded as engaging in such use, but is no longer engaging in such use. . ." Under these provisions of the ADA, as under the Ohio antidiscrimination law, such a plaintiff may well be able to successfully invoke either the shield of involvement in a drug rehabilitation program (note that now the federal Family and Medical Leave Act might be dovetailed into the equation to help ensure a job is waiting for the employee upon completion of the rehabilitation program; see chapter 8) or contend no current drug abuse and ignorance of how the pills got in the locker.

The *Bray* case, however, provides another promising avenue of defense for a corporate defendant, a defense uncovered after the firing. In *Bray*, it was not until the discovery stage of the lawsuit that the employer-defendant found out that Bray had lied about his drug problem when he applied for employment with the drug company. The court granted the company's motion for summary judgment based on this newly discovered evidence. Resume or employment application fraud are deemed by the EEOC and an increasing number of courts as legitimate independent bases for firing employees who otherwise might be protected by federal antidiscrimination statutes.

However, this use of so-called "after-acquired evidence" is a matter of considerable controversy within the federal court system. Late in 1994, for example, the U.S. Court of Appeals for the Third Circuit, which sits in Philadelphia, held that evidence of resume fraud and job misconduct discovered by the employer after the ex-employee had filed employment discrimination charges could not be used to shield the defendant from those charges. The employer's legal theory, accepted by some courts, was that, had it known of the fraud and misconduct, it would have fired the plaintiff for those non-discriminatory reasons. These courts differ somewhat on how the after-acquired evidence should affect the outcome of the case. A unanimous Third Circuit panel wrote that the plaintiff-employee's alleged misdeeds are a "possible wrong against the employer, whereas the employer's discrimination is a wrong against the employee and society at large." Thus, went the panel's opinion, society's need to eradicate job discrimination stands above the employer's private right to discipline or terminate an errant employee, and so the after-acquired justifications for the job termination cannot be used to thwart society's mechanisms for punishing the discriminatory acts of the defendant-company. ["Third Circuit Rejects After-Acquired Evidence Rule," 1994 *BNA Daily Labor Report* 150 (Aug 8, 1994) at 1]

The U.S. Supreme Court heard oral arguments in an "after-acquired evidence" case late in 1994 and had the case under consideration as this 1996 supplement went to press.

Q 4:89 When can resume or employment application fraud be used to justify an allegedly discriminatory job termination?

This is a very tough legal question, involving several difficult legal issues and thus resulting in disagreement among the courts that have confronted it. Deciding whether an employee's false statement on a resume or employment application justifies termination may involve the federal common-law standard for deciding "mixed motive" cases. In the case of *Price Waterhouse v. Hopkins* [490 US 228 (1989)], the U.S. Supreme Court held that an employer could defeat a discrimination complaint by showing that it would have reached the same termination decision on another, legal basis, even if it had not also entertained the alleged illegal motive in making the termination.

The 1991 Civil Rights Act (CRA '91) effectively overruled this aspect of the *Hopkins* decision, when it addressed mixed motive cases in Section 703(m), which states:

> [A]n unlawful employment practice is established when the complaining party demonstrates that race, color, religion, sex, or national origin was a motivating factor for any employment practice, even though other factors also motivated the practice.

Thus, if both a legal and an illegal factor are present in the employment decision, the employer can still be held liable for job discrimination. However, the Section 703(m) advantage to the employee-plaintiff is diluted by Section 706(g)(2)(B), which says that, while the court in such a mixed motive case can issue an injunction against any such further violations of Title VII or the ADA and order the defendant to pay plaintiff's legal fees, the defendant-corporation cannot be assessed compensatory or punitive damages, nor can it be required to reinstate the plaintiff. Thus, proof of mixed motive remains an extremely significant defense in job discrimination cases.

Furthermore, as in the *Bray* case, a court must decide what weight to give the resume fraud when evidence of it has been discovered only after the allegedly illegal firing. Building upon the guidance in Section 706(g)(2)(B) quoted above, the EEOC and some federal courts have decided that an employer's proof of resume fraud, even though it is acquired only after the fact, will cut off the employee's entitlement to the remedies of Title VII and the ADA or at least any entitlement to a prospective remedy, such as front pay or reinstatement. The reasoning behind this conclusion is that even if the employer acted illegally in terminating the employee, because it did not know of the resume fraud until the lawsuit caused it to thoroughly investigate the plaintiff's background and employment history, after the fraud was discovered the employer would have fired the plaintiff on that independent basis. Thus, at a minimum, liability for the discriminatory firing ought to be cut off as soon as the employer discovers the independent grounds of resume fraud. Note that this line of reasoning strongly suggests that companies are well advised to have explicit, written rules against resume and application fraud that call for immediate discharge at whatever stage in the employment relationship the fraud may be uncovered (see Q 4:89, above, and chapter 5).

Q 4:90 What does the ADA say about drug testing?

Under the ADA, employers may test their employees for the use of illegal drugs. An employer may terminate or refuse to hire someone whose test indicates the presence of an illegal substance. However, it would be a violation of the ADA to discriminate on the basis of prescription drugs taken by individuals with disabilities who are under the care and supervision of a licensed health care professional.

Q 4:91 How is the ADA enforced?

Title I of the ADA incorporates the powers, remedies, and procedures in the Civil Rights Act of 1964. The EEOC has been designated as the enforcement agency for the ADA. The ADA provides that the powers and procedures available to persons discriminated against based on disability be the same as, and parallel to those available to persons discriminated against based on race, color, religion, sex, or national origin. For employers that have 25 or more employees, Title I became effective in 1992; for employers with 15 to 24 employees, the ADA became effective in 1994. Additionally, the Civil Rights Act of 1991 provides that successful plaintiffs suing under the ADA may receive compensatory or punitive damages in some circumstances.

Q 4:92 What potential benefits will there be for employers under the ADA?

The ADA aims to tap an apparent reservoir of underutilized workers. This approach may work, not only because the ADA forces businesses to assess handicapped applicants more objectively, but also because the wide publicity the new law has been receiving will encourage handicapped people who have heretofore been reluctant, possibly due to past discrimination, to enter the workforce.

Q 4:93 How may an employer proceed if it wishes to use medical examinations to show that an employee is unfit for duty or has breached the employer's policy regarding intoxicants?

An employer that conducts medical examinations of employees must be extremely cautious to avoid violating the employees' personal rights. An employer should have a clear policy regarding prohibited conduct and the circumstances under which medical examinations will be given. The examination should be justified by a valid business reason. Once this is established, the examination should be administered on a nondiscriminatory basis.

Before an employee is required to undergo an examination, he or she should be apprised of the reasons for the examination and be given an opportunity to discuss them. If an employee agrees with the employer that a problem exists, a medical examination may not be necessary.

An employer should have the employee sign a consent form to help avoid liability for charges of assault and battery and/or invasion of privacy. The employer should select a qualified physician who is licensed to perform any necessary tests. It is a wise policy to insure the physician and/or require him or her to carry adequate insurance.

An employer must keep all results regarding the examination strictly confidential to avoid infringing unnecessarily on an employee's right to privacy. It is a good idea to allow an employee an opportunity to submit independent medical opinions for consideration before any decision is made. Additionally, the ADA must now be considered (see Q 4:86).

Q 4:94 Has the enactment of the ADA resulted in substantial amounts of new employment discrimination litigation?

During the first year after the employment provisions of the ADA went into effect in July 1992, 13 percent of the EEOC's caseload consisted of ADA-based charges. The agency has been slow in processing those complaints, mainly due to administrative problems, such as the challenge of coding and classifying the multitude of medical conditions that charging parties are claiming come under the act's protection. However, in those cases that have been resolved by the agency in favor of the employee, average settlements are in the $14,000 range, second only to average conciliation awards under the Age Discrimination in Employment Act. During the first seven months that the EEOC accepted ADA charges, 5,500 were filed under the ADA nationally, with 1,200 of those coming in February 1993 alone, nearly double the number of charges filed with the agency in the previous October. [1993 *BNA Daily Labor Report* 58, Mar 29, 1993, at 1]

In fiscal 1993, the EEOC took in a record 88,000 discrimination charges, an increase of 22 percent over the prior year. The increase, contends the agency, is largely attributable to the ADA. A total of 15,274 charges of disability discrimination accounted for 17.4 percent of all charges filed in fiscal 1993. Total amounts recovered by the agency for claimants amounted to $161 million during that fiscal year, down somewhat from the approximately $188 million mark reached in each of the two preceding years. Of that $161 million, $126.8 million was won in the administrative proceedings, and $34.2 million was accumulated for claimants through agency litigation in federal courts. ["Charges of Disability Discrimination Boost EEOC Intake by 22% in Fiscal '93," 1994 *BNA Daily Labor Report* 9, Jan 13, 1994, at 4]

In fiscal 1994, which ended on October 1, 1994, EEOC attorneys filed 373 lawsuits, down from 401 in the previous year. Only 35 of these suits were filed pursuant to the ADA. However, this number represents a sharp jump from the four such suits brought by the agency's lawyers in fiscal 1993. Total recovery for plaintiffs via lawsuits by the EEOC totaled $29.2 million, also down from fiscal 1993, when total recoveries amounted to $34.4 million. Altogether in fiscal 1994, including settlements achieved on behalf of charging parties at the agency level, the EEOC claims to have recovered more than $175 million in monetary benefits for alleged discriminatees in fiscal 1994. ["EEOC Attorneys Filed 373 Substantive Suits in Fiscal '94, Down Slightly From a Year Ago," 1994 *BNA Daily Labor Report* 238, Dec 14, 1994, at 1]

According to agency Deputy General Counsel James Neely, the large increase in ADA suits reflects the large number of ADA charges filed annually with the commission. "ADA has become a large part of our workload," he said. [Id]

Q 4:95   Have juries begun awarding substantial damage amounts in ADA cases?

In *Wessel v. AIC Security Investigations Ltd.* [(ND Ill March 1993)], the first reported jury verdict awarded under the employment provisions of the ADA resulted in $572,000 in damages to a plaintiff who claimed he had been fired because he had brain cancer. Besides the substantial size of the jury verdict, employers should note a number of other aspects of this case.

As a result of the EEOC's limited resources, it rarely brings suit for cases involving single acts of discrimination. Historically, the EEOC has preferred to use its limited legal staff to pursue class actions; yet this case was brought on the employee's behalf by the EEOC. This fact appears to indicate a keen interest on the agency's part to enforce the new law. [See Q4:94, above.]

Additionally, take note that the case was filed in November 1992 and came to trial a mere four months later in mid-March 1993. This time line is extraordinary, even for a federal (as compared to a state) civil action. More federal judges and jurisdictions are adopting what the legal profession terms "rocket dockets" to move litigants through preliminary phases of their cases rapidly. Defendants and their counsel, who once relied in unfavorable cases upon "wearing the plaintiff down" by delay and inactivity over years of grinding litigation, now often find they are denied this tactic.

The third aspect of this verdict deserving of employers' close analysis is the structure of the damage award. It illustrates how a court and a jury, intent upon punishing what they perceive to be a guilty employer, can creatively collaborate to increase the bottom-line verdict beyond what the act itself, in conjunction with the damages provisions of CRA '91, appears to contemplate. In the words of one commentator:

The $500,000 in punitive damages included in the March 18 award nearly doubles the top amount of $300,000 generally available under the ADA and the Civil Rights Act of 1991, because the jury assessed separate awards of $250,000 against the owner and the [company]. The jury also awarded $22,000 in back pay and $50,000 in compensatory damages.

[1993 *BNA Daily Labor Report*, 52, Mar 19, 1993, at 1]

In *Wessel*, the EEOC charged the defendants with firing the executive director when he was diagnosed as having an inoperable brain tumor. According to the commission, the plaintiff was fired "not because of his inability to do his job, but because of predictions about his future health problems and because of stereotypical fears about disability." As for the verdict, the agency's general counsel observed, "The EEOC's primary goal is to educate businesses regarding their responsibility under the Americans with Disabilities Act. This verdict should distinctly accomplish that goal."

The ADA became effective July 26, 1994 for employers of 15 to 24 employees. Attorney General Janet Reno announced in August 1994 her department's intent to intensify educational as well as enforcement efforts. Meanwhile, the EEOC has received more than 30,000 disability discrimination charges since the ADA became effective, and these charges constitute almost 20 percent of the commission's workload. ["More Activism, Awareness Mark ADA as Law Extends to Smaller Employers," 1994 *BNA Pension & Benefits Reporter*, Vol 21, No 31, Aug 1, 1994, at 1512]

Back problems have been a major source of ADA charges with the EEOC, amounting to one in five agency cases. Neurological impairment comes in at number two, followed closely by emotional and psychiatric problems at 11 percent of total discrimination charges. [Id] Given that back pain and emotional and psychiatric problems are the hardest to diagnose and the easiest to fake of all health-related problems, one might well wonder about the legitimacy of these numerous charges of disability discrimination. As Professor Russell Roberts of the Owens School of Business at Washington University in St. Louis has observed, discrimination cases increasingly are a sort of lottery for disappointed employees to enter. [Russell Roberts, Commentary, *Morning Edition*, NPR, Jan 9, 1995]

Q 4:96   Do the federal antidiscrimination laws allow naming individual owners and managers as defendants and assessment of damages directly against these individuals?

As in *Wessel* (Q 4:95), individual managers and owners can be named as defendants and assessed damages individually in employment discrimination cases. This is possible because the federal antidiscrimination laws generally define the term "employer" broadly. For example, the ADA, under which *Wessel* was tried, states:

> The term "employer" means a person in an industry affecting commerce who has 15 or more employees for each working day in each of 20 or more calendar weeks in the current or preceding calendar year, and any agent of such person. [42 USC § 12lll(5)(A)]

This definition is virtually identical to the definition of employer in the 1964 Civil Rights Act [42 USC § 2000e(b)], the Fair Labor Standards Act [29 USC § 203(d)], the Equal Pay Act, and the Age Discrimination in Employment Act. Therefore, in the words of the Fair Labor Standards Act, employer-defendants can include "any person acting in the interest of an employer."

With respect to allegedly discriminatory discharges and other employment actions (e.g., hiring and promoting), the EEOC and the courts consider whether individuals sought to be named as defendants were in fact the decision makers "acting in the interest of the employer." Thus, if human resources professionals and managers at various levels in the corporate hierarchy are the decision makers, they may be appropriate targets for individual liability under these antidiscrimination acts. (In the area of sexual harassment, lower-level employees, including the complaining worker's co-workers, may share liability with the corporation.) However, passive shareholders, who do not participate in the management of the organization, typically will retain their traditional immunity from suits against the corporate entity in which they hold shares.

Why would plaintiffs' counsel and the EEOC want to name and seek damages from individual managers of corporate defendants? In personal injury claims, individual employees often remain unnamed in complaints because they are considered to be largely judgment-proof. One reason, well illustrated by *Wessel*, is that multiple defendants may enable a sympathetic jury to circumvent the compensatory and punitive damage caps set by the CRA '91. Second, while in personal injury cases plaintiffs are often looking to the corporate defendant's liability insurance to make good on the claim, insurance coverage in discrimination cases, while not unknown, is relatively rare. Plaintiffs and their attorneys want to be able to dip into as many pockets as possible to recover damages. Third, in situations in which the corporate defendant is in bankruptcy or receivership or is otherwise defunct, individual defendants may offer the only "full pockets." Finally, naming managers as individual defendants can be an effective "divide and conquer" tactic, causing one or more of the individual defendants to elect to cooperate with the EEOC or the plaintiff's attorney against the corporate opponent in return for release from individual liability.

In a recent decision, a three-judge panel of the U.S. Court of Appeals for the Ninth Circuit disagreed on individual liability with regard to Title VII and the ADEA. Two of the judges held that a plaintiff-employee cannot sue supervisors or co-workers, because an employer is not covered by these acts unless that employer has a minimal number of employees. (Title VII applies to employers of 15 or more [42 USC § 2000e(b)], while the ADEA covers employers of 20 or more. [29 USC § 630(b)]) The majority also expressed doubts about whether the word "agent" was intended to include a supervisor or other employee of the corporate defendant. In dissent, the third panel member pointed in particular to the ADEA's close relationship to the Fair Labor Standards Act, which, as pointed out above, clearly includes supervisors as employers potentially liable for unpaid wages of their subordinates. Additionally, the judge pointed to the CRA '91, which expressly affixes individual liability for intentional discrimination. [1993 *BNA Daily Labor Report* 77, Apr 23, 1993, at 1]

By contrast there are situations in which only the individual employee-defendant will be liable, and not his employer. Given employers' justified concern about sexual harassment liability (see Qs 4:49–4:58), a case decided by the Missouri Court of Appeals in 1994 is of interest. The court's decision states, "We hold that [the psychiatric practice-] employer is not liable under respondeat superior for damages resulting from Dr. Bouzrara's sexual relations with plaintiff P.S. because he was not acting within the scope and course of his employment as a therapist." [PS v Psychiatric Coverage LTD, 1994 Mo App LEXIS 1443 (1994)] While not a Title VII case, this

Missouri decision does reflect a reluctance on the partt of at least some judges to hold the employer responsible for everything that an employee may do to or with a co-worker or customer of the company.

Q 4:97　Does a policy barring "light duty" violate the Americans with Disabilities Act?

In 1994 the U.S. Department of Labor (DOL) ruled that a blanket refusal to permit disabled employees to perform in "light duty" jobs illegally discriminates against handicapped workers under the terms of the federal Rehabilitation Act of 1973. The fact that management feared problems with the union if it unilaterally instituted light duty opportunities was speculative and thus insufficient to overcome the proscriptions of the federal statute. ["Policy Barring 'Light Duty' Violates Rehabilitation Act," 1994 BNA Daily Labor Report 32, Feb 17, 1994, at 2]

Since the ADA closely tracks many of the requirements of the Rehabilitation Act, which applies only to government entities and contractors, the federal courts have frequently followed the earlier act's lead in interpreting the newer federal statute. Consequently, we can conclude that the "light duty" rule enunciated by DOL, if accepted by the courts for purposes of the one law, will also be applied with equal force under the other.

Q 4:98　What are the rules governing preemployment inquiries under the ADA?

In mid-1994 the EEOC issued Enforcement Guidance on preemployment disability-related inquiries and medical examinations, aimed at assisting its own investigators in their legal analyses of such inquiries and exams. The guidance document presents a lengthy list of questions labeled "disability-related inquiries" and therefore deemed illegal if asked before a conditional offer of employment is made. According to labor lawyer Robert F. Conte, "The ADA's prohibition against pre-offer inquiries and medical exams is designed to prevent discrimination against those with 'hidden' disabilities like cancer, mental illness, heart disease, and AIDS." [Robert F. Conte, "EEOC Issues Guidance on Pre-Employment Inquiries Under the

ADA," *Saul, Ewing, Remick & Saul Employment Law Update* (J.O. Castagnera, editor), July 1994, at 1]

"Disability-related questions which are prohibited. . . include asking an applicant whether he or she has a particular impairment which constitutes a disability under the Act." [Id] Additionally, the following questions are examples of impermissible pre-offer inquiries:

1. How many days were you sick last year?
2. Have you ever filed for workers' compensation?
3. How much alcohol do you drink each week?
4. Have you ever been treated for alcohol-related problems?
5. Have you ever been treated for mental health problems?
6. What prescription drugs are you currently taking?

Observes Conte, "Because each of the above questions specifically seeks information regarding an employee's status as an individual with a disability, they are [all] prohibited at the pre-offer stage." [Id] Beyond identification of specific questions that are prohibited, the EEOC guidance provides the general criterion that, if the employer might reasonably expect a preemployment question to reveal the existence of a disability, that question is prohibited until a tentative offer of employment is made. Of course, the tentative offer may be conditioned upon the applicant's ability to perform the job.

That last observation raises the issue of reasonable accommodation. (See Q 4:80.) If at the pre-offer stage the applicant requests a reasonable accommodation in order to be able to perform the job, then the employer may ask that applicant to document the disability involved. "Accordingly, the applicant may be required to provide documentation from an appropriate professional stating that he or she has a disability." [Id]

With respect to absenteeism and tardiness concerns, the employer may state its attendance requirements and inquire whether or not the applicant will be able to meet them.

The guidance also elucidates employers' obligations with regard to medical exams under the ADA. "Although it is clear that an employer may not require or conduct medical examinations before an applicant has been given a conditional offer of employment, the question of when an examination is 'medical' has been unclear." [Id at 3.] The agency defines medical exams as procedures or tests that "seek information about the existence, nature, or severity of an individual's physical or mental impairment," or that seek information regarding an individual's physical or psychological health. (See, generally, Qs 3:69, 4:86, 4:93, 4:107.) Factors for EEOC investigators to consider under the new guidance include:

- Whether the test is administered or interpreted by a health care professional

- Whether the test is invasive

- Whether the test measures psychological or physiological response rather than the applicant's performance of a job task

- Whether the test normally is administered in a medical setting

- Whether medical equipment or devices are used to give the test

Many employers currently administer psychological tests, often including an I.Q. component. The EEOC apparently does not attack I.Q. testing. "The EEOC's guidance instructs that psychological examinations would be considered medical examinations to the extent that they provide evidence concerning whether an applicant has a mental disorder or impairment as characterized by the American Psychiatric Association." [Conte, supra, at 3]

The EEOC guidance does not forbid pre-offer testing for illegal drug use. And if the same test should inadvertently and unintentionally reveal use of legal drugs, the ADA has not been violated. However, pre-offer testing for alcohol use probably is not legal for two reasons. First, the tests, requiring the analysis of blood, urine, or breath, are all deemed to be invasive. Second, alcohol, while frequently abused, is a legal drug. Consequently, companies are well advised not to conduct pre-offer alcohol tests. [Id at 4.]

Post-offer physicals and medical tests are legal under the ADA, according to the EEOC Guidance. "The EEOC cautions, however, that job offers which are conditioned on the results of medical examinations. . . must be bona fide job offers." [Id] All relevant non-medical information on the candidate must have been evaluated before the offer was made.

Post-offer medical information can be shared only with corporate decision makers who have the need to know. And it must be kept strictly confidential.

AIDS in the Workplace

Q 4:99 Is AIDS a protected disability?

AIDS is considered to be a non-job-related handicap by most relevant federal and state agencies under most working conditions. This position has been strengthened by a report issued by the Centers for Disease Control (CDC) of the U.S. Public Health Service, which has concluded that AIDS cannot be transmitted in any of the typical workday situations. More specifically, the CDC position maintains the AIDS can be transmitted only through a limited number of body fluids, notably blood and semen. Tears, breath, and saliva are believed to be incapable of communicating the disease. Consequently, the CDC has stated that casual contact in the workplace does not pose a danger to healthy employees. Therefore, many state human relations agencies have held that someone who has AIDS but who is otherwise capable of performing the job cannot be terminated on the basis of the virus. [See, e.g., Cain v Hyatt Legal Services, 734 F Supp 671 (ED Pa 1990), holding that AIDS is a disability protected under the Pennsylvania Human Relations Act]

Q 4:100 Are persons with AIDS or AIDS-related complex (ARC) or carriers of the HIV virus handicapped under the Rehabilitation Act?

Yes. The Supreme Court has ruled that those with contagious diseases are handicapped for purposes of the Rehabilitation Act. [School Bd of Nassau County v Arline, 107 S Ct 1123 (1987)] In *Arline*, the contagious disease was tuberculosis, but the Court's ruling can be applied to cases involving AIDS and other infectious diseases. The Court's decision has been applied to reinstate a teacher who had been dismissed because of having AIDS and to find as handicapped carriers of the HIV virus who are perceived as dangerous and are consequently discriminated against. Therefore, persons with AIDS, as well as those who are HIV carriers with no symptoms but who are treated as being impaired, are all covered persons under the Rehabilitation Act.

The Justice Department has also taken the position that Section 504 of the Rehabilitation Act covers all people with AIDS and that no justification exists to single out AIDS as a basis for discharge. This Justice Department opinion supersedes an opinion issued earlier that said that if an employer feared AIDS might be contagious, it could lawfully discriminate against the affected individual.

The extension of protections under the Rehabilitation Act does not mean that federal employers or federally financed programs cannot, in individual circumstances, exclude an AIDS-infected individual from the workplace. If an individual poses a threat to the health and safety of others or is unable to perform his or her job or satisfy the requirements of the work program, that individual can be excluded if there is no reasonable way to accommodate these health and safety performance conditions. These legal principles are likely to be applied under the ADA as well.

Q 4:101   Are private employers free to discriminate against persons with AIDS or ARC or carriers of the HIV virus?

No. An employer that is not within the scope of the Rehabilitation Act may not treat persons with AIDS or ARC or carriers of the HIV virus differently from those free of the disease. Many state and local governments have passed laws that specifically prohibit discrimination against people with AIDS or ARC or HIV-positive persons, and the ADA extends such protection nationwide.

Q 4:102   Do persons with AIDS or ARC, or who carry the HIV virus, constitute a direct threat to the health or safety of other workers?

No. The Rehabilitation Act exempts from coverage those handicapped individuals who present a direct threat to the health or safety of others in the workplace. However, because those with AIDS or ARC or carriers of the HIV virus are considered in most cases to present no direct threat to the health or safety of others, they are not exempt and must be treated like everyone else. The same holds true under the ADA. (See US Department of Health and Human Services, "Summary: Recommendation for Preventing Transmission of Infection with Human T-Lymphotropic Virus Type III/Lymphadenopathy-Associated Virus in the Workplaces," MMWR, vol 34, no 45 (1-15-05) at 681-686, 691-695)

Q 4:103   Has the federal government taken a firm position on the AIDS issue?

To the contrary, various segments of the federal government dispute among themselves as to what the federal position on AIDS should be. The CDC believes that only in limited workplace settings such as hospitals, where interchange of blood is likely, must employees take unusual precautions in dealing with infected individuals. In contrast, the Justice Department under President Ronald Reagan made an official statement that reasonable fear of contagion was a valid defense to a discrimination charge involving AIDS. The Supreme Court has not ruled on a case directly involving AIDS. However, in a 1987 decision involving a Florida school teacher with tuberculosis, the Court stated that the presence of this disease did not automatically disqualify the teacher from performing the job, even in a classroom full of children [School Bd of Nassau County v Arline, 107 S Ct 1123 (1987)] The decision is viewed by many as the Supreme Court's de facto position on AIDS as a handicap under the Rehabilitation Act (see Q 4:99).

OSHA issued its final rule on bloodborne pathogens effective 90 days after the December 6, 1991, publication date. This rule is directed at minimizing health care workers' exposure to the hepatitis and AIDS viruses. The rule, which covers approximately 5.6 million workers, is expected to prevent about 9,000 infections and 200 deaths annually, according to OSHA. Among the more than half-million establishments covered by the rule, in addition to health care facilities, are medical and dental labs, nursing homes, blood collection facilities, funeral services, emergency response facilities, correctional facilities, and law enforcement agencies. The rule "will protect all employees who could reasonably be expected to come into contact with human blood and other potentially infectious materials in the course of their work." The total estimated annual costs of enforcing the rule will be about $821 million, according to OSHA. The largest costs will be for providing disposable protective equipment (e.g., gloves, masks, gowns) to employees, at an estimated $334 million per year.

Q 4:104   Have private companies taken a firm position on the AIDS issue?

The private sector of our society is too large and diverse to speak with one voice. Last year, however, a group of major corporations met in New York City under the banner of the Citizens Commission on AIDS and endorsed the following principles:

1. People with AIDS or HIV infection are entitled to the same rights and opportunities as people with other serious or life-threatening illnesses.

2. Employment policies must, at a minimum, comply with federal, state, and local laws and regulations.

3. Employment policies should be based on the scientific and epidemiological evidence that people with AIDS or HIV infection do not pose a risk of transmitting the virus to co-workers through ordinary workplace contact.

4. The highest levels of management and union leadership should unequivocally endorse nondiscriminatory employment policies and educational programs about AIDS.

5. Employers and unions should communicate their support of these policies to workers in simple, clear, and unambiguous terms.

6. Employers should provide employees with sensitive, accurate, and up-to-date education about risk reduction in their personal lives.

7. Employers have a duty to protect the confidentiality of employees' medical information.

8. To prevent work disruption and rejection by co-workers of an employee with AIDS or HIV infection, employers and unions should attempt to educate all employees before and following an incident.

9. Employers should not require HIV screening as part of general preemployment or workplace physical examinations.

10. In those special occupational settings where there may be a potential risk of exposure to HIV (for example, in health care, where workers may be exposed to blood or blood products), employers should provide specific, ongoing education and training and the necessary equipment to reinforce appropriate infection control procedures and ensure that they are implemented.

Q 4:105 What should an employer do, and not do, if it discovers that an employee has AIDS or ARC or is an HIV carrier?

The employer and its agents must not allow the information to be circulated to other employees. Allowing such dissemination can result in a "public disclosure of private facts" action against the employer, which may result in punitive in addition to actual damages. An employer must keep such information strictly confidential.

Some problem cases involving AIDS may be resolved by allowing the employee to work at home or transfer to a different department. Although these measures may be offered to an employee, they may not be forced on him or her under most circumstances.

A key problem in dealing with AIDS in the workplace is lack of understanding. Mediation, rather than litigation, is the preferable method for resolving disputes involving the disease. Generally, an AIDS education presentation should be incorporated into the regular training program rather than introduced as a separate agenda. Bringing in someone to talk about only AIDS in a small company of 30 employees may engender fear of who, if anyone, has AIDS. The city of Philadelphia, for example, has enacted an ordinance mandating such education as part of any routine training program.

Q 4:106 How should a company go about developing an AIDS policy?

An employer might create a committee of upper management, supervisors, and employees that meets and discusses its concerns regarding AIDS and potential methods of resolving the issues. It is important for upper management to participate in order to send the right kind of message to employees. The committee should draft a proposal and issue a final plan company-wide. The proposal should identify those within the company who need to know if or when an employee has contracted AIDS. Assurances of the strictest confidentiality should be guaranteed.

An employer should deal with AIDS by developing:

- A well-advertised, well-understood policy
- A core advisory team with key personnel who will become knowledgeable on the issues
- A benefits protocol involving insurance, disability, and Social Security benefits and rights
- A communications strategy on how management should respond when an employee identifies himself or herself as HIV positive
- An educational program that includes a medical overview on AIDS and information on employee-employer rights and responsibilities
- A resource and referral service to let employees know what resources are available to them

Q 4:107 Should an employer test job applicants for AIDS?

No, unless the employer is a health care provider. The test is expensive and is not always reliable. If a person is inactively carrying the virus, any action that the employer takes in response to a positive test can expose the employer to liability for disability discrimination, defamation, and invasion of privacy. However, if a company's benefits package provides life and health insurance, the insurance carrier may require an AIDS test of the new employee.

Q 4:108 May an employee with AIDS be discharged because co-workers refuse to work with that person?

There is no clear-cut answer to this question. It has been suggested that disciplining employees for refusing to work with a person who has AIDS could be a violation of the National Labor Relations

Act (NLRA), which protects concerted activity, even if the employees are not unionized. This might seem to justify discharging an employee who has AIDS. A more accurate legal view, however, is that refusal to work with an AIDS virus carrier is probably not reasonable concerted activity and, therefore, is not protected by the NLRA. If an employer is faced with a work stoppage or walkout, perhaps it is advisable to attempt negotiation of a termination agreement with the AIDS carrier whereby the employer in effect pays the employee to remove himself or herself from the workplace. The employer should seek legal counsel as quickly as possible. In short, an employer who terminates an employee for unreasonably refusing to work with an AIDS victim is within its legal rights to do so, while terminating the AIDS victim, if that employee remains willing and able to perform the job, violates the ADA.

Q 4:109 Does the ADA require employers to pay for AIDS-related health care?

Since the publication of the second edition of this book, the hottest issue to emerge under the ADA has placed the EEOC on a collision course with not only corporate America but organized labor as well. The issue is whether the ADA prevents a group health insurance plan, either employer- or union-administered and funded, from reducing major medical benefits for employees suffering from AIDS. To understand how this issue has developed and has reached the current high level of controversy, it is necessary to revisit *McGann v. H&H Music Co.* [946 F 2d 401 (5th Cir 1991)], a U.S. appeals court decision that interpreted the Employee Retirement Income Security Act of 1974 (ERISA), not the ADA.

In *McGann*, the plaintiff-employee had AIDS. When the company learned of his condition, it amended its self-funded group health insurance plan to limit major medical benefits for AIDS-related health care services to a maximum of $5,000, instead of the $1 million cap applicable to all other major medical claims. McGann sued, arguing discriminatory treatment under applicable provisions of ERISA. The Fifth Circuit disagreed, holding that because the reduced cap on AIDS-related claims applied to all employees, it was not discriminatory, and therefore was legal. The court added that health insurance benefits are normally not "vested" under ERISA and, therefore, can

be altered by the employer as long as the alteration is not discriminatory. The Bush administration urged the U.S. Supreme Court to
deny certiorari of the case, arguing that it was really an ADA question. The Court did in fact decline to review the Fifth Circuit's
decision in *McGann*.

The EEOC has now entered the fray with a preliminary finding by
its District Director for New York that a labor union violated the ADA
when it amended its health insurance plan to exclude payment of
expenses arising out of treatment of HIV, AIDS, or AIDS-related
complex conditions. A joint union-management benefit fund has
initiated a lawsuit in the U.S. District Court for the Southern District
of New York, sitting in Manhattan, challenging the EEOC's preliminary position. The particular benefit fund, which covers some unionized asbestos and construction workers in New York, claims to have
lost $19.7 million since 1990 due to huge health care bills. Moreover,
there have been few large construction jobs to help keep the coffers
filled. The benefit fund asserts that it cut reimbursement not only for
HIV- and AIDS-related conditions, but also for routine checkups,
eyeglasses, dental care, and organ transplants.

The EEOC District Director, whose position undoubtedly reflects
the agency's preliminary position on this issue, wrote, "The commission's investigation finds respondent's medical insurance appears, on
its face, to violate the [act]. . . .the commission has determined that
respondent has no viable defense to the charge of discrimination."
[District Director's Determination, Charge No. 160-93-0419 (Jan 28,
1993)]

Q 4:110   What are the most recent developments regarding AIDS in the workplace?

As discussed above (see Q 4:109), the EEOC has taken the position
that altering a group insurance policy to lower benefits for employees
with HIV or AIDS, as compared to other illnesses, is illegal discrimination under the ADA. This agency position differs from and is
philosophically, if not legally, opposed to a recent U.S. appeals court
decision that found such discriminatory treatment not to be the sort
of discrimination that violated the provisions of the ERISA. [See
McGann v H&H Music Co, 946 F 2d 401 (5th Cir 1991)] The Supreme

Court refused to review *McGann*, but will probably finally determine the correctness of the EEOC's position under the ADA, as a result of a case on this same subject, currently in the U.S. District Court for the Southern District of New York in Manhattan.

Meanwhile, in mid-1994 the EEOC also took on The Laborers District Council Building and Construction Health and Welfare Fund in the U.S. District Court for the Eastern District of Pennsylvania. The fund, following the example approved in *McGann*, had amended its medical plan to cap lifetime benefits for HIV-related illnesses at $10,000. In January 1995 the EEOC and the union fund reached a settlement and the court entered a consent decree under which this cap was dropped. The decree requires the fund to amend its plan immediately to eliminate the discriminatory cap and also forbids any reinstatement of such a cap absent federal legislation expressly authorizing such differentiation. ["Union Health Fund Agrees to Drop AIDS Cap," 1995 *BNA Daily Labor Report* 5, Jan 5, 1995, at 2]

AIDS in the workplace remains a topic of great concern to the news media and the general public. For example, a case in which an attorney claimed to have been fired by his firm because he was diagnosed with AIDS was dramatized in a major motion picture. The case, *Cain v. Hyatt* [734 F Supp 671 (ED Pa 1990)], involved a nationwide chain of legal clinics and was a pre-ADA case of first impression, holding that the Pennsylvania Human Relations Act viewed AIDS as a protected disability, a position taken under the federal Rehabilitation Act and numerous state antidiscrimination acts by courts across the country in recent years. [See, e.g., Chalk v US Dist Ct, Cent Dist of Cal, 840 F 2d 701 (9th Cir 1988); Martinez v School Board, 861 F 2d 1502 (11th Cir 1988); Thomas v Atascadero Unified School Dist, 662 F Supp 376 (CD Cal 1986); Barton v New York City Commission on Human Rights, 531 NYS 2d (NY Sup Ct 1988); Poff v Caro, 228 NJ Super 370 (1987); Benjamin R v Orkin Exterminating Co, 390 SE 2d 814 (W Va 1990); Cronan v New England Telephone, 41 BNA FEP Cas 1273 (Mass Superior 1986)]

The legal battles over AIDS in the workplace are not likely to subside in light of an increasing awareness among doctors and scientists that no quick cure for AIDS is in the offing. Writes one journalist who specializes in viruses and other health issues:

More than a decade into the pandemic, drugs have been found to fight many of the infections people with AIDS develop. But only a small number of drugs approved for use in the U.S. . . . attack the virus directly. And over time HIV outsmarts each of them by generating resistant strains. Researchers hope to develop a more effective combination of drugs, each targeting a different part of the virus. Meanwhile they are testing more than a dozen potential vaccines, but no one expects an effective shot against AIDS to be available before the end of the century.

[Peter Jaret, "Viruses: On the Edge of Life, On the Edge of Death," *National Geographic*, July 1994, at 84]

Age Discrimination

Q 4:111   Who is protected by the ADEA?

In a recent decision, a U.S. appeals court looked through the form into the substance of a relationship and held that a salesman, who operated as a corporation and appeared to be an independent contractor, could nevertheless pursue an Age Discrimination in Employment Act claim against a private corporation. Reversing the lower court's dismissal of the ADEA lawsuit, the appellate court weighed the salesman's act of incorporation against the facts that he received salary and benefits from the company and that he engaged in sales for no other "clients" in deciding that, on balance, he was indeed an employee and not an independent contractor. [1993 *BNA Daily Labor Report* 35, Feb 24, 1993) at 1] Although the decision appears to be a first under the ADEA, the court's reasoning is well within the traditional parameters of labor and employment law (see Qs 2:63–2:71). This line of legal reasoning, which places substance ahead of form, ignores how the parties label the relationship (employee versus independent contractor) and goes to the bundle of sticks actually comprising the relationship. In particular, the company's right to control not only what the independent contractor does, but also the how, when, and where it's done is of prime importance. Whether the individual received a salary or merely commission, does similar services for other companies, has employees, and provides the work space and the tools for them are also factual items to be resolved in reaching a determination.

ADEA claims continue to account for major jury verdicts, though this form of alleged discrimination seems eclipsed in the media, the courts, and the EEOC by ADA claims in the second half of the decade. (See Q 4:94.) For example, a New Jersey jury recently awarded an age discrimination plaintiff nearly $500,000 plus interest. [Abrams v Lightolier Inc, 841 F Supp 584, 1994 US Dist LEXIS 4900, 65 BNE FEP Cases 1149 (1994)] Additionally, since health problems tend to plague older workers more frequently than younger ones, some claimants predictably are filing ADA charges, either in lieu of or in conjunction with ADEA claims, thus masking the continued strength of the ADEA issue in employment discrimination law.

Q 4:112 Is there any protection against discrimination based on age for employees under 40 years old?

A few states have passed age discrimination acts that forbid disparate treatment on the basis of age for all employees. The courts have held that these laws are not preempted by federal law.

Q 4:113 Is the ADEA part of Title VII?

No. The ADEA was passed as a separate law several years after Title VII was enacted and is more closely related to the Fair Labor Standards Act (FLSA).

Initially, ADEA was enforced by the DOL, while Title VII has always been enforced by the EEOC. However, when the ADEA was later amended, responsibility shifted to the EEOC. The EEOC investigates age discrimination complaints in much the same way that it investigates other accusations of discrimination. The time limitation for filing the complaint and other details are essentially the same as those under Title VII (see Qs 4:1–4:7).

Q 4:114 Are there any differences between enforcement of Title VII and enforcement of ADEA?

Because the ADEA is related to the FLSA and not directly derived from Title VII of the 1964 Civil Rights Act, there are several important substantive and procedural differences between them. First, an individual filing a complaint with the EEOC under Title VII must obtain a 90-day letter to sue from the agency before taking the case into federal court; the ADEA complainant, however, must wait only 60 days after filing an age complaint with the EEOC before filing a suit in federal court without the agency's permission. The discrimination victim filing under Title VII does not have a statute of limitations until the 90-day letter to sue is issued by the EEOC, which may be years after the initial filing of the complaint. The ADEA complainant, however, should be aware of the statute of limitations contained in the FLSA, which runs from the date of the discriminatory act (e.g., termination of employment), not from when the EEOC complaint was filed.

The ADEA derives its limitation of actions provision from the FLSA. Litigants can sue under the FLSA for willful violations of the law within three years of the illegal action. Nonwillful violations must be pursued within two years of their occurrence. The same is true under the ADEA. These time periods run from the date of the last illegal action, despite timely filing of a complaint with the EEOC.

Q 4:115   What is a willful violation of the ADEA?

At one time, some U.S. appellate courts recognized such a low degree of willfulness that almost every violation of the ADEA could be interpreted by a jury as willful. The standard used by these courts implied that a violation of the ADEA was willful if the employer knew or should have known that the ADEA was applicable. The Supreme Court rejected this view and now holds that a willful violation of the ADEA occurs if age discrimination knowingly takes place or if there is a reckless disregard of whether the employment decision might involve a violation of ADEA. [McLaughlin v Richland Shoe Co, 486 US 128 (1988); Trans World Airlines Inc v Thurston, 469 US 111 (1985)] These cases rejected a more liberal definition of willfulness, which had been enunciated by some U.S. appeals courts, in favor of the standard that the employer's actions are willful if the employer is found either to have known or at least to have shown reckless disregard for whether the ADEA or FLSA would be violated by the employment action.

Because *McLaughlin* and *Trans World Airlines* rejected a more lenient standard, some federal courts have felt that these two Supreme Court pronouncements do not prohibit holding employees to an even more stringent standard for proving willfulness, under which the ADEA can result in doubling of damages assessed against the employer, as well as the expansion of the statute of limitations from two to three years. These courts have required the plaintiff to prove that the employer's conduct was "egregious" or "outrageous." The courts reason that double damages are analogous to punitive damages under common law, and most courts require outrageous conduct before punitive damages can be awarded.

In January 1993, the U.S. Supreme Court again took up this thorny issue, hearing oral argument in *Biggins v. Hazen Paper Co.* [112 F 2d 3035 (1992)], a case in which the appellate court accepted the "knew or showed reckless disregard" standard and thereby rejected the employer's plea for the tougher standard requiring some evidence of outrageous conduct.

In April, a unanimous Supreme Court expressly adopted the "knowing or reckless disregard" standard put forward by the employee-plaintiff's counsel and thereby rejected a tougher, punitive damages-style standard. Expressly reaffirming *Trans World Airlines v. Thurston*, Justice O'Connor's opinion rebuffed the employer's contention that its conduct had to be outrageous or egregious before double damages can be awarded. [1993 *BNA Daily Labor Report* 75, Apr 21, 1993, at 1] Presumably, this standard will control both the double-damages provision and the statute of limitations under the ADEA. By contrast, it is worth noting that willfulness comes into play as a meaningful concept under the closely related FLSA only with regard to the three-year (as opposed to two-year) statute of limitations for willful as opposed to non-willful violations of that act. Thus, with respect to unpaid minimum wages and overtime premiums, the FLSA says simply: "Any employer who violates [either of these provisions] shall be liable to employees affected in the amount of their unpaid minimum wages, or their unpaid overtime compensation . . . and in an additional equal amount as liquidated damages." [29 USC § 216(b)] The congressional notion behind this liquidated damages provision is that the employee should be compensated for the time during which the claim was prosecuted, when the employer actually had possession and use of the employee's unpaid wages.

Willfulness is punished under the FLSA by permitting the employee to go back three as opposed to two years (for nonwillful violations) in collecting unpaid wages. Liquidated damages can only be avoided under the FLSA where the violating employer can demonstrate to the court's satisfaction that it acted in good faith when failing to pay required overtime or minimum wages (see Q 8:49). Thus, even under *Biggins*, employers face an easier time in trying to avoid double damages under the ADEA than they do under the FLSA.

Q 4:116   What is the Older Workers Benefits Protection Act (OWBPA)?

In 1990 Congress passed OWBPA. As has frequently happened in the history of labor and employment law, this legislation was passed in response to a Supreme Court decision, the outcome of which outraged many congressmen and important segments of their constituencies. In *Public Employees Retirement Sys of Ohio v. Betts* [109 S Ct 2854 (1989)], the Court held that the ADEA did not forbid age discrimination in the area of employee benefits except in unusual circumstances. On September 24, 1990, the Senate approved OWBPA by an overwhelming 94 to 1 majority. The House of Representatives approved the measure by a margin of 406 to 17. OWBPA was subsequently signed into law by President George Bush, thus overturning *Betts*.

OWBPA expressly rejects the Supreme Court's controversial decision by defining "compensation, terms, conditions or privileges of employment" as including all employee benefits, even those provided under a bona fide employee benefit plan. Consequently, Section 4(a)(1) of the ADEA now forbids discrimination in employee benefits as well as in every other aspect of employment that is not protected by some specific exemption from coverage of the Act.

The law also codifies the concept of "equal benefit or equal cost," as part of the federal regulatory scheme for employee benefits. This concept was rejected by the Supreme Court in 1989 in *Betts*. Previously espoused in DOL and EEOC interpretative letters, the principle of equal benefit or equal cost holds that a company must provide to its older workers benefits that are at least equal to those provided to younger workers, unless the company can prove that the cost of providing an equal benefit is higher for an older worker than for a younger one. The only exception to this equal benefit or equal cost rule is a voluntary early retirement incentive plan.

Q 4:117 What are OWBPA requirements with regard to early retirement incentive plans?

OWBPA sets out the following rules for voluntary early retirement incentive plans:

1. When such a plan is challenged in court, the burden is on the employer to prove that its conduct does not violate OWBPA. This is a very different burden of proof than that set out under Title VII and the other discrimination acts discussed in this chapter.

2. The company may set a minimum age as a condition of eligibility for either a normal or an early retirement benefit.

3. The company may provide pension subsidies to subsidize regular pension benefits. For example, it may make bridge payments until the early retiree becomes eligible for Social Security benefits.

4. No discrimination based on age is permitted with respect to severance pay when employees are terminated. However, a company may offset severance payments, including up to 52 weeks of supplemental unemployment compensation benefits paid until the employee is eligible for a pension, by the value of any retiree health benefits that the pensioner is entitled to as well as any immediate and unreduced pension benefits that the terminated employee can get. OWBPA provides specific rules for determining the value of retiree health benefits under this deduction. Furthermore, if immediately available pension benefits are actuarially reduced, a pro rata reduction in the authorized deduction is also required.

5. The company may reduce long-term disability benefits by a like amount of pension benefits that the retiree elects to receive or that he or she is eligible to receive after attaining the latter of age 62 or normal retirement age.

6. The company may implement a new disability plan that reflects OWBPA's requirements, and then give employees the option of

being covered under either the old or the new plan. Old plans are thus grandfathered in for employees who elect the old plans or who fail to make an election.

Q 4:118 What does OWBPA say about waivers and releases of age discrimination claims?

In a case that received much publicity, the Sixth Circuit Court of Appeals found that a waiver and release agreement executed by the corporation's in-house legal counsel was not binding upon him. [Runyan v Natl Cash Register Corp, 787 F 2d 1039, *cert denied* 479 US 850 (1986)] Since that decision, labor attorneys and human resource professionals have struggled with various forms of waivers and releases, some of them laying out in excruciating detail precisely what the signing employee will be waiving and trying to ensure that the signer does so willingly and knowingly. OWBPA has apparently resolved this controversial dilemma by laying out six requirements for a valid waiver under the ADEA:

1. The waiver of ADEA claims must be part of an overall agreement between employer and employee, written in plain, everyday English.

2. The waiver section of the agreement must specifically refer to rights or claims arising under the ADEA, not just make a general reference to discrimination laws or federal laws or the like.

3. The waiver cannot be prospective, that is, it cannot seek to waive rights or a cause of action that may arise due to the company's actions or behavior after the date the agreement is signed.

4. The employee must receive good consideration (i.e., a thing of value) for executing the waiver, and that consideration must be given by the company in addition to anything of value (such as severance benefits under a preexisting severance policy) that the employee would have been entitled to without signing the waiver.

5. The employee must be told in writing that he or she should consult an attorney before executing the agreement.

6. The employee must be given reasonable time in which to decide whether or not to execute the waiver. This reasonable time can

range from 21 to 45 days, depending upon the circumstances under which the agreement is signed.

Q 4:119 Does the ADEA recognize disparate impact?

Yes. A company policy that appears to be neutral may actually violate the ADEA if it has a disparate, negative impact on a protected group of employees. An example is a company decision to cut the budget by releasing all managers earning in excess of $50,000 per year. This policy appears to be neutral because highly paid executives, regardless of age, are involved; however, the impact will most likely fall most heavily on older members of the management team. The reason is obvious: higher salaries usually come with age, experience, and longer tenure with the firm. Thus, some courts have held that such a salary reduction plan is a violation of the ADEA. Note, too, that because the disparate impact was probably an unintended offshoot of cost cutting, this strategy would probably be a nonwillful violation of the ADEA.

In what was described as a "major victory for the EEOC," a U.S. district judge in Chicago ruled that it will permit a jury to decide whether a company's policy of passing by job applicants with extensive experience or high prior salaries has an illegal adverse impact upon older workers. In a case filed by a 63-year-old drama teacher against the Francis W. Parker School, a private K-12 institution, the principal told the plaintiff he could not afford him. The Parker School then proceeded to hire an applicant with just one year of experience for a salary of $22,000. In this case, as in other recent cases (see Q 4:34), the EEOC brought suit on behalf of the 63-year-old prospective employee and used statistics to demonstrate that applicants over 40 were 4.2 times more likely to be disregarded in the school's application process than applicants below the protected age range, thereby establishing its prima facie case. [1993 BNA Daily Labor Report 70, Apr 14, 1993, at 1]

The agency went on to lose that case at the district court level. And late in 1994 the U.S. Court of Appeals for the Seventh Circuit affirmed the district judge's grant of summary judgment for the school, stating:

Ultimately, the EEOC must show that Parker's rationale is pretextual and that the salary system is predicated on some stereotype, conscious or unconscious. Otherwise, summary judgment in favor of Parker is proper. [citation omitted] The EEOC has not alleged how Parker's salary system might be a subterfuge for the belief that older teachers are less effective than younger teachers. The EEOC contends only that Parker's system disproportionately affects older applicants. As the district court held, this statistical correlation alone is insufficient to sustain a finding of ADEA liability. For these reasons, the decision of the lower court granting summary judgment in favor of Parker is affirmed.

[Equal Employment Opportunity Comm v Francis W Parker School, 1994 US App LEXIS 29366, 66 BNA FEP Cases 85 (7th Cir. 1994), *reh denied*, 1994 US App LEXIS 32729 (1994)]

Q 4:120   Can an employee sue for age discrimination under the ADEA even if he or she refuses to arbitrate the dispute?

Yes. In 1988, the U.S. District Court for the District of New Jersey held that, even though an employee had an arbitration clause in his employment contract, he could ignore the clause and sue under the ADEA. [Nicholson v CPI Intl, 46 Fair Empl Prac Cas (BNA) (D NJ 1988)] This decision seemed to be a logical extension of the Supreme Court's 1975 ruling that a unionized worker is entitled to pursue a Title VII discrimination claim, whether or not the underlying grievance is subject to arbitration. [Emporium Capwell v Western Addition Community Org, 420 US 50 (1975)]

In 1990, however, the Fourth Circuit Court of Appeals opened a split among the federal courts by concluding differently. Resolving what it perceived as a battle between the ADEA and the Federal Arbitration Act, the court held that an employee who had agreed in his employment contract to arbitrate all disputes must do so. He could not sue in federal court at his sole discretion. Meanwhile, the Third Circuit Court of Appeals Philadelphia affirmed the Nicholson decision. Thus, it was up to the Supreme Court to resolve this split among the appellate courts.

In May 1991, the Supreme Court resolved the conflict in favor of the Fourth Circuit's approach. By a vote of seven to two, the Court held that the stockbroker-plaintiff was bound by his promise in his employment contract to arbitrate any and all disputes during the course of his employment, even though the ADEA appeared to apply to his case. The Court rejected the employee's argument that the employer's bargaining power dwarfed his own, especially at the time he was being hired. Justice White's majority opinion notes that at age 62 the employee was an experienced businessman, and there was no evidence in the record to suggest that he was coerced or defrauded into accepting the arbitration provision. [Gilmer v Interstate, 111 S Ct 1647 (1990)]

Gilmer is a marked departure from the Court's 1974 decision in *Alexander v. Gardner Denver Corp.*, which held that an arbitration clause in a collective bargaining agreement—and even an arbitration pursuant to it—could not deprive a unionized employee of the right to pursue an action under Title VII for employment discrimination. The *Gilmer* decision leaves Alexander undisturbed; apparently the court sees a significant difference between a collectively bargained grievance/arbitration provision negotiated on behalf of an employee by the union and an arbitration clause in an employment agreement entered into by an experienced and knowledgeable employee on his or her own behalf. In the latter situation, the arbitration clause likely will control.

Q 4:121 Are the damages a plaintiff receives in an age discrimination claim subject to income taxation?

No. In 1989 the U.S. Tax Court held that damages awarded in a suit filed under the ADEA are subject to income taxation. The court agreed with the IRS that compensation for lost fringe benefits is taxable income, even though the underlying fringe benefits would not have been included in gross income. The court hinted that liquidated, or double, damages (allowed under the ADEA for willful violations) might not be taxable, but it was not considering this question. [Wirtz v Commr, 56 TCM 1596 (1989)]

However, in 1990, the U.S. Court of Appeals for the D.C. Circuit reversed the Tax Court and held that neither back pay for lost wages nor liquidated damages is taxable. The court found that ADEA actions are, by nature, personal injury claims and, therefore, plaintiffs' awards cannot be taxed as income.

The Equal Pay Act

Q 4:122　What is the Equal Pay Act?

The Equal Pay Act is an amendment to the FLSA. It states that male and female employees who perform the same work for the same employer must receive the same rate of pay.

Q 4:123　Are there any exceptions to the rule that male and female employees receive equal pay for equal work?

Yes, there are several exceptions. An employer may pay one employee more than another for the same work based on greater productivity or seniority. Also, if a company has more than one facility and its operations are in different labor markets, wages can vary to reflect labor supply and demand.

Q 4:124　What is comparable worth?

Comparable worth is a relatively new theory, which states that employees who perform duties of comparable value, difficulty, or sophistication should receive comparable pay.

Q 4:125　How does the comparable-worth theory support a claim of sex discrimination?

Plaintiffs have asserted the comparable-worth theory in cases in which large employers, notably state and city governments, have widely disparate pay scales between job categories historically filled by male workers and those historically filled by female employees. Note that comparable-worth plaintiffs have not necessarily asserted that the defendant-employer intentionally hired only males or females for certain jobs. Rather, the chief argument has been that predominantly male jobs are better paid not because these jobs are more valuable, but because male employees are able to command higher wages in the job market.

Q 4:126 Does comparable worth continue to be a viable theory of sex discrimination?

Comparable worth seems to have lost some of its former vitality as an approach to sex discrimination, in part because a number of courts have rejected the theory, usually following long and expensive lawsuits. [See, e.g., State County & Municipal Employees v Washington, 770 F 2d 1401, 38 BNA FEP Cas 1353 (9th Cir 1985)] There have also been a few victories for the concept, especially in cases involving government employers. [Connecticut State Employees Assn v Connecticut, 31 BNA FEP Cas 191 (D Conn 1983)]

It is difficult for plaintiffs to establish the comparable worth of different jobs. Even when comparable worth can be demonstrated, the court may require the litigants to show that the employer purposely structured the pay scales with gender in mind, or that women were discouraged from competing for the higher paying positions. In general, women workers continue to find the Equal Pay Act—which calls for equal pay between the sexes for substantially the same work—a more efficacious route to recovery of damages.

Q 4:127 How does the comparable-worth theory relate to the Equal Pay Act?

The comparable-worth theory attempts to expand the coverage of the Equal Pay Act. The Equal Pay Act requires only that male and female workers, doing the same job for the same company at the same location, must, if all else is equal (e.g., seniority), receive the same wage. Comparable-worth enthusiasts compare different job classifications to other, unrelated, classifications (for example, chemists to accountants, secretaries to custodians) to determine whether each job group is of equal worth and, if so, equally compensated.

Q 4:128 Has comparable worth been accepted by the American legal system?

No. After protracted litigation, most comparable-worth cases have resulted in defeat for the plaintiff. Still, a few have had favorable

outcomes, and comparable-worth lobbying has led some state legislators to fund studies on the subject and even to raise the wages of
some female-dominated public-employee positions.

Comparable worth has had little impact on private companies thus
far.

Affirmative Action

Q 4:129　Do government contractors have a special obligation to eliminate job discrimination?

Yes. A company wishing to do business with the federal government, whether to provide goods, services, or both, must be prepared
to fulfill affirmative action requirements. Similarly, many state and
local governments impose such requirements on companies that
contract with them (see chapter 9).

Q 4:130　What are the goals of affirmative action laws and regulations?

The general goal is to make better use of members of the minority
workforce in the contractor's performance of its federal contracts.
Specific goals will depend on the representation of qualified minority
group members in the geographic area in which the individual contractor operates.

Q 4:131　What is the source of a government contractor's affirmative action obligation?

The earliest, and still the most important source is Executive Order
No. 11246, promulgated by President John F. Kennedy. Other laws
and regulations now supplement this executive order.

Q 4:132　What restrictions or requirements are included in Executive Order No. 11246?

First, it forbids discrimination by federal government contractors
and subcontractors. This was more significant prior to enactment of

Title VII, but it is still important today because a contractor's violation of the order can result in contract debarment. Second, the order requires affirmative action by the contractor.

Q 4:133 What is the government contractor's affirmative action duty?

The duty consists of formulating a plan having goals and timetables and making a good faith effort to achieve those goals within the established time frame. A government contractor must also make sure that any company to which it subcontracts also fulfills this affirmative action duty.

Q 4:134 What congressional legislation has increased the federal contractor's original duties under Executive Order No. 11246?

Section 503 of the Rehabilitation Act requires contractor accommodation of handicapped workers when the contractor has a service, supply, or construction contract with the government in excess of $2,500. Section 504 of the Act imposes a similar duty on recipients of federal financial assistance. Title IX of the Education Amendments of 1972 extends affirmative action duties to colleges and universities that receive federal funding. The Vietnam Era Veterans Act extends the affirmative action duty to Vietnam-era disabled veterans, making the scope of the federal contractor's duty broader than a private employer's Title VII obligations in two important ways: first, the duty is affirmative, not merely a negative prohibition on discrimination; second, the contractor's duty goes beyond discrimination based on sex, race, color, national origin, religion, and age to include the handicapped and many veterans.

Q 4:135 Who enforces the federal contractor's affirmative action duties?

This task has been given to the Office of Federal Contract Compliance Programs (OFCCP) in the DOL.

The OFCCP coordinates the various components of the federal bureaucracy to ensure that government contracts contain affirmative action requirements. The OFCCP investigators audit contractors to determine whether they have written affirmative action plans and whether they are making good faith efforts to meet the goals and timetables in these plans for hiring and promoting minorities, women, disabled individuals, and veterans. The OFCCP accepts and investigates complaints from applicants and employees who believe that the company has not lived up to its affirmative action obligations. The OFCCP can recommend debarment of contractors that are found to have violated affirmative action obligations.

Q 4:136   What is an affirmative action plan?

An affirmative action plan is a detailed plan of action whose purpose is to increase the representation of minority groups among the employees of a corporation, government agency, or nonprofit institution.

Q 4:137   Are hiring quotas legal?

Hiring quotas are legal under some circumstances. If a company is found guilty of discrimination in a lawsuit, the court can order the company to engage in affirmative action as part of the remedy of the lawsuit. Such a plan may necessitate a hiring quota. Also, public and private employers may be permitted to adopt hiring quotas to correct past discrimination and to assist the various groups that were previously discriminated against. Even then, strict quotas of various minority groups may be illegal.

Q 4:138   Are any private employers required to adopt affirmative action plans?

Corporations that bid for and receive government contracts are usually required to adopt affirmative action plans as a contract requirement.

Q 4:139   When and how should a company create an affirmative action plan?

The first time a company bids for a government contract, it should check the specifications of a plan or ask the contracting officer whether an affirmative action plan is necessary. If a plan is necessary and the company wins the contract, the plan should be initiated. If the company does not have an in-house human resources or equal employment opportunity specialist, a consultant or labor lawyer should be hired.

Discrimination and Immigration

Q 4:140   May a company discriminate against alien workers?

Under IRCA, it is illegal to discriminate against alien workers who are legally in this country and legally entitled to work here. (See chapter 12 for a complete discussion of immigration issues.)

Q 4:141   What is the process for bringing a claim of discrimination under IRCA?

A complaint must be filed with the Office of Special Counsel for Immigration-Related Unfair Employment Practices (Special Counsel) within 180 days of the alleged discriminatory act. Each charge must be investigated within 120 days of its filing to determine whether there is reasonable cause to believe the charge is true. If the Special Counsel finds reasonable cause, a hearing before an administrative law judge will be scheduled. If, as a result of the hearing, an employer is found in violation of IRCA's antidiscrimination provisions, sanctions will be imposed.

Q 4:142   Who can file complaints alleging discrimination based on national origin or citizenship status?

The Special Counsel will accept complaints only from a person who is a U.S. citizen or from a legal alien who evidences intention to become a U.S. citizen.

Q 4:143   May an employer be subject to duplicate actions regarding discrimination before the EEOC and the Special Counsel?

No. IRCA specifically states that charges of discrimination cannot be filed with both the EEOC and the Special Counsel. An employee must choose one forum.

Q 4:144   May employers mandate English only as the language of the workplace?

The debate about English only in the workplace continues within the broader conflict over what will be the official language in some states. The large Spanish-speaking populations of Florida, Texas, and California (three of the most populous states) have been agitating for wider recognition of their native tongue as being on at least an equal footing with English. Predictably, this has evoked a reaction from some members of the English-speaking population, such as the U.S. ENGLISH Foundation, which supports California Proposition 63, an initiative that would declare English to be the state's official language. Meanwhile, the courts continue to adhere to the rule that an English-only workplace rule must be supported by business necessity.

In practice, in many U.S. jurisdictions the preprinted portions of pleadings (such as the notice on the face of the complaint concerning the time allowed to answer) are printed in both English and Spanish. Recently, a deputy clerk challenged the Los Angeles Municipal Court's English-only rule, and in *Mun Court of S.E. Judicial Dist v. Gutierrez*, [109 S Ct 1736 (1989)] enforcement of the rule was enjoined.

Q 4:145   What remedies are available to alien workers who are the victims of illegal discrimination?

Under IRCA, aliens legally entitled to employment who are discriminated against because they are aliens can obtain the remedies of employment and back pay. Additionally, the discriminatory employer may be ordered to keep records of alien applications and hiring history for up to three years and to pay civil penalties of from $1,000 to $2,000 per individual against whom discrimination took place.

Q 4:146   May an employer hire illegal aliens?

IRCA reaffirmed the historic illegality of hiring illegal alien workers. Under IRCA, federal officials will be less likely to overlook traditional, common violations of the law, such as those in the agricultural and garment industries. Penalties are more severe as well, with fines ranging up to $10,000 per illegal alien in the workplace for repeat offenders.

Q 4:147   May an employer give preference to a citizen over an equally qualified alien?

Yes. A provision of IRCA states that it will not be considered an unfair immigration-related employment practice if an employer prefers a citizen over an equally qualified alien. However, if an alien entitled to employment in the United States is better qualified than a particular citizen, giving preference to the citizen may constitute impermissible discrimination.

In May 1991, INS Commissioner Gene McNary issued an order that enforcement of employer sanctions be accorded top priority within his agency, at least until September 1991. As quoted in the May 20, 1991, BNA Daily Labor Report, McNary commented, "At this juncture, with the employer sanctions provisions institutionalized as part of immigration law for more than four years, it is appropriate to reassess the focus of our enforcement strategy."

In 1990 Senator Edward Kennedy, Chairman of the Senate's Immigration Subcommittee, criticized Commissioner McNary's proposal of an extended outreach program to make companies and other employers more aware of their obligations under IRCA. INS investigators had in fact spent substantial amounts of time during the past four years educating employers. McNary's 1991 order stated that these same enforcement officials must now cease all such educational activities. The clear message from the INS is that it is now time for companies with employee alien workers to comply with the law.

Q 4:148   Can a company ask an alien employee to indemnify it against liability under IRCA?

No. IRCA permits a fine of $1,000 per individual in cases in which the employer has required an alien employee to post an indemnity bond. This prohibition does not extend to performance clauses in contracts between two contracting parties, such as a fruit grower and labor agent.

Q 4:149   Must a company verify a job applicant's eligibility for employment under IRCA?

Yes. An employer must require documentary evidence (such as a birth certificate, Social Security card, driver's license, or green card) and keep a record of this verification.

Q 4:150   Does IRCA require verification of all job applicants?

Yes. An employer that verifies eligibility of only "foreign-looking," "foreign-sounding," Spanish-surnamed, or dark-complexioned applicants is guilty of illegal discriminatory treatment of such applicants.

The ADA And Workers' Compensation

Q 4:151   Why does the Americans with Disabilities Act present new risks for employers with workers' compensation claims to address?

As pointed out by one group of experts writing for Panel Publishers:

> The employee who becomes disabled because of a work-related injury obviously was performing his or her job prior to the injury. This proves he was qualified and could perform the essential functions of the job. These are two necessary prerequisites in the definition of "disability" according to the ADA. Clearly, the employer knows about the nature of the employee's impairment because of the workers' compensation process, so if the employee is fired or demoted, these actions constitute

discrimination and grounds for a complaint. [Bannon et al., *Special Report: How to Cut Workers' Compensation Costs* (1993) at 21]

In other words, the company that fires or refuses to reinstate an employee with a bad heart or a back injury who received workers' compensation benefits will look guilty going into any subsequent lawsuit. After all, if the employee's job performance, independent of the disability, was substandard, the company could have been expected to have disciplined that employee before the compensation claim occurred. And the corporation can hardly contend that it acted in the absence of knowledge of the worker's health problem. These factors do not automatically subject the employer to ADA liability; an employer has the right to terminate a disabled employee who, even with reasonable accommodation, can no longer perform the essential functions of the job. But the foregoing circumstances do make any firing of or refusal to reinstate the claimant appear suspicious.

Panel's compensation experts go on to state: "Because of the increase in workers' compensation litigation, there is already attorney involvement, which gives the individual easy access to legal advice regarding discrimination."

These experts are correct. A typical law firm specializing in representing workers' compensation claimants will seek tort claims and other types of legal actions that will enable the lawyers to enhance their statutorily limited workers' compensation fees with more handsome contingent-fee arrangements with their clients.

Q 4:152 How do employers deal with the danger of ADA actions by workers' compensation claimants?

Assume that an employee has been away from work due to a heart attack, serious back injury, or other job-related disability for which the company's carrier has paid workers' compensation benefits. Can the company replace that employee either before or after the worker is ready to return to work? Under the federal Family and Medical Leave Act, the ill or injured worker usually will be entitled to 12 weeks of unpaid leave, regardless of whether the disability is work-related. (See Qs 1:28, 8:209 et seq.) Under this federal law, at the end of the 12 weeks the employer must reinstate the worker to the same or a substantially similar job as was vacated during the disability.

Should the injured or ill employee be unable to return to work at the end of the 12-week leave period, the company may be able to replace that employee permanently on the basis of legitimate need to fill the vacancy in more than a temporary or make-do fashion. The risk here is that the replacement will be viewed either as retaliation for the employee's use of the workers' compensation claim process or as subterfuge for eliminating an ailing worker. In fact, the incentive against such a subterfuge is that it creates a tremendous incentive for the disabled worker to "milk" the compensation claim for all it may be worth. Nonetheless, the company is well advised to create a paper trail, fully documenting its legitimate need to put a permanent replacement in the disabled worker's former post.

Should the worker return to work, the company is entitled to have the job performed at about the same level of competency as before the injury or accident. The difference is that the returning compensation claimant will be entitled to reasonable accommodation of any remaining disabling condition, upon the employee's request for such accommodation. (Reasonable accommodation is defined in Q 4:80.) What accommodation is reasonable will depend upon the nature of the job, size of the company, cost of the accommodation, and other factors.

Furthermore, a disabled worker can be required to perform only the essential functions of the job. Therefore, an employer might wisely anticipate problems involving returning compensation claimants and other disabled employees by undertaking a so-called "functional job analysis."

To ensure compliance with the ADA, it is important to determine essential functions accurately by performing a complete functional job analysis. This essential step should begin with a meeting between managers, supervisors, workers, human resources personnel, and the individual performing the job analysis to list possible activities that may be considered essential functions of the occupation in question. The essential function task force encourages open dialogue among the various company representatives to ensure accuracy of the stated job functions. In this way unrealistic standards can be exposed and appropriately modified to reflect the day-to-day activities of the job. . . . It should cover the following areas with regard to workers' compensation issues:

- Work site, workstation, environment, tools
- Manual material handling tasks and what is required
- Positional tolerances
- Ambulation activities and on what type of surface, (e.g., stairs, rough ground)
- Hand coordination and strength required
- Physical attributes
- Sensory activities
- Length of day, tasks, breaks, work-week sequence

[Id at 25-26]

Such a functional job analysis can be translated into a functional job description. [Id at 26.] Then, applicants as well as returning compensation claimants can be tested against the job analysis functions. For applicants, such testing must come after a conditional offer of employment. For returning claimants, the test should be a universal company policy, or at least a policy applied uniformly to all claimants in a particular classification of jobs that may lead to injuries; in other words, a single claimant should not be singled out for post-reinstatement testing. Similarly, it is legally safest to subject all applicants to post-offer testing, if any are to be so tested.

Additionally, experts recommend case management while the worker is away due to the disability. [Id at 29; Marion, "Case Management: Crucial Aid to Law," 3 *Advance for Physical Therapists* 7 (1992)]

Q 4:153 Are there any recent federal court decisions which illustrate the interaction between the ADA and state workers' compensation laws?

A number of 1994 decisions help highlight issues that arise from the interplay of the ADA and various state workers' compensation statutes:

In *Flasza v. TNT Holland Motor Express* [1994 US Dist LEXIS 1760 (ND Ill 1994)], the plaintiff claimed that after he was hired as a dock worker in July 1992 the defendant fired him a month later, after its background investigation revealed that Flasza had filed a number of workers' compensation claims in previous employment. Clearly, if Flasza had been fired for filing such claims and not for any present inability to perform his job (with or without reasonable accommodation), then arguably the ADA was violated by the trucking firm.

Conversely, if, as the defendant contended, Flasza had been fired for "resume fraud" (i.e., lying on his job application), then the company was entitled to terminate him for that dishonest act. [See Washington v Lake County, 969 F 2d 250, 255 (7th Cir 1992)] As with Flasza's contention that he was fired for filing workers' compensation claims, the company's contention of resume fraud revolves around the background investigation that purportedly resulted in plaintiff's discharge. A fair reading of the court's published opinion in this case suggests that the allegedly fraudulent statements involved the plaintiff's job experience and qualifications, not his physical fitness or past compensation claims history.

Consequently, the court in essence held that the case should move forward toward a resolution of this factual dispute between the parties. If the plaintiff ultimately can prove to a jury that he was fired for past injuries and workers' compensation claims, then he should obtain a remedy under the ADA. But if the company can convince the jurors that Flasza lied on his application, inflating his qualifications for the position, then a defense verdict would be appropriate.

Austin v. Owens-Brockway Glass Container Inc, [1994 US Dist LEXIS 846, 145 BNA LRRM 2445 (WD Va 1994)] is a somewhat complicated case, involving a workers' compensation claim, a collective bargaining agreement, and the ADA. The disabled plaintiff was away from work at a time when, according to the company, her equipment cleaner/oiler-greaser job classification was eliminated. The company claimed the other person in that position was reassigned. Conditionally released by her physician, the plaintiff requested and was denied a light-duty assignment, which she contended the company was obliged to provide.

After challenging the denial of light duty in this federal court case, the company moved to dismiss, contending that Austin and her attorney had failed to file a discrimination charge with the EEOC first, which is an administrative prerequisite to a lawsuit (see Qs 4:8–4:20). Austin and her counsel countered that they had tried several times to get the local EEOC office to accept their proffered charge of disability discrimination, but without success, before turning to the court.

The company, however, also contended that the applicable labor contract covering Austin required her to have recourse to the grievance and arbitration procedures before coming to federal court to challenge the light duty denial. The U.S. Supreme Court has in fact sent clear signals in recent years to the lower federal courts that binding arbitration, where accepted as an alternative dispute resolution process in private employment contracts, must be pursued even in the face of discrimination claims. [Gilmer v Interstate, 111 S Ct 1647 (1990), thoroughly discussed in Qs 11:56, 13:2, 13:3, 15:3] It's not so clear whether the arbitration provision of a collective bargaining agreement will be to the same effect, since older Supreme Court cases seem to preserve the unionized employee's right to pursue an EEOC remedy simultaneously or subsequently.

In this case, however, the court concluded that: "Because plaintiff's complaint was subject to mandatory arbitration, the Gilmer line of cases applies here. Accordingly, because plaintiff did not utilize the grievance procedures available in the April 1, 1993-March 31, 1996 Union Shop Contract, Summary Judgment will be granted in favor of the defendant."

Finally, in *Hartman v. City of Petaluma Police Dept* [841 F Supp 946 (ND Cal 1994)], a former rock-and-roll musician challenged denial of his application to join the defendant police department. The PD turned the rock-and-roller away because of his prior drug problems. Contending that any addiction was confined to the past, the plaintiff argued a violation of the ADA. The defendant responded in a summary judgment motion that plaintiff's downplaying of the extent of his past problems was again an example of resume fraud. Concluding that, as a matter of law, the police could prove that the plaintiff's gross understatements of his prior drug dependency in his application materials was the real reason he was turned away, the court granted summary judgment to the defendant PD on the ADA claim.

Turning then to a pendent state claim of intentional infliction of emotional distress, the court also dismissed that claim, contending it was barred by the exclusivity provisions of California's workers' compensation law, citing *Livitsanos v. Superior Court* [828 P 2d 1195 (1992)] for that proposition. How the workers' compensation act comes into play here is unclear; the plaintiff was never hired by the police force in the first place. The court bolstered this argument by adding that the facts pleaded in support of the emotional distress claim did not appear to be sufficiently outrageous to support such a tort claim anyway.

Chapter 5

Employee Personnel Files and the Employee's Right to Privacy

The generation that read Orwell's *1984* and Huxley's *Brave New World* as teens has come of age in the electronic future. While it may not be the high-tech horror show Orwell envisioned, Big Brother is indeed often watching. Worldwide computer networks accumulate and disseminate information about everyone.

Ours is also a litigious age in which workers seem ever-more willing to sue on the slightest provocation. Clients and customers, too, are quick to sue when a company's employees injure them in some way. For these reasons, more and more employers are inclined to take advantage of the full panoply of public records available about a prospective employee. Applicants often are asked to agree to drug screening or psychological testing. The Polygraph Act and the Americans with Disabilities Act have drastically reduced the use of pre-hire lie detector and physical examinations, but the concerned and determined human resources manager can still access large amounts of data to help evaluate applicants.

The understandable desire on the part of employees to protect their privacy, and the equally understandable need of employers to protect their companies, have created tension in the workplace. This chapter deals with these conflicting objectives and suggests some methods of attaining them.

Personnel Files

Q 5:1   Does federal law require an employer to maintain personnel files?

Federal law does not require that an employer maintain personnel files per se. However, many federal labor and employment laws require specified records to be maintained for minimum periods to aid the government agencies assigned to enforce these statutes.

The Fair Labor Standards Act (FLSA). FLSA requires employers to maintain wage records for at least three years. Such records must contain at least the following information:

- Each employee's name, home address, date of birth (if under 19), gender, and occupation
- Hours worked daily and total for each workweek
- Straight-time earnings and overtime premiums per week
- Total additions to and deductions from each week's pay
- Date of each payment of wages and the period covered by the payment

Some supplementary records (e.g., wage rate tables and work schedules) must be preserved for two years.

The Equal Pay Act. According to the Equal Employment Opportunity Commission (EEOC), this Act requires preservation of those records previously listed under the FLSA, plus any additional records describing and explaining the payment of higher wages to one sex than to another, for two years.

Title VII of the 1964 Civil Rights Act (Title VII). The EEOC does not demand that any particular records be maintained under this statute, but any employer who chooses to keep personnel records (such as applications and other documents reflecting hiring, promotion, demotion, transfer, layoff, discharge, compensation, training, or disciplinary decisions), must preserve these records for six months from the date they are created or the date of the personnel actions they memorialize, whichever occurs later in time. Also, if a charge of discrimination is filed by an employee against the employer, the foregoing records must be maintained until the litigation is resolved. (Indeed, with regard to any employment-related litigation, an employer-defendant runs the risk of serious legal sanctions for the purposeful destruction of relevant records.) Employers with 100 or more employees must prepare and file Standard Form 100 (Employer Information Report—EEO-1) annually.

The Age Discrimination in Employment Act (ADA). The ADA requires retention of records for three years that reflect each employee's name, address, date of birth, occupation, and rate of pay or salary per week. The following records must be retained for one year:

- Documentation of failure to hire
- Promotion, demotion, transfer, training, layoff, recall, and termination records
- Recruitment records per labor unions (e.g., hiring halls), employment agencies, and search firms
- Tests and test scores
- Physical examination results
- Advertisements and notices of position openings, training opportunities, or overtime availability

The Occupational Safety and Health Act (OSHA). OSHA requires employers to maintain medical records and records of exposure to toxic substances, radiation, and so forth, for the employee's entire job tenure plus 30 years. Additionally, employers must maintain workplace accident records.

The Immigration Reform and Control Act (IRCA). IRCA requires that a federal Form I-9 be completed by the company and the employee together at time of hire. (See chapter 12 for a complete review of this law.) Individuals recruited or referred for employment must also complete I-9s; if such an individual is not hired, the I-9 must be retained for three years. If the candidate is hired, the I-9 must be held for three years after the hire date or one year following subsequent termination, whichever limit is later.

The Employee Polygraph Protection Act. This Act requires that records of lie detector tests be preserved for three years. These records include the following:

- The employer's written verification required by the Act
- The test's written questions
- All opinions, reports, and charges resulting from the test

As this summary suggests, a good policy for employers is to maintain all legally mandated personnel records for at least three years from the date of their creation.

Q 5:2   What is the legal definition of personnel file?

While there is no single, standard legal definition, the one contained in the Pennsylvania "Inspection of Personnel Files" Act is reasonably representative:

> If maintained by the employer, any application for employment, wage or salary information, notices of commendations, warning or discipline, authorization for a deduction or withholding of pay, fringe benefit information, leave records, employment history with the employer, including salary information, job title, dates of changes, retirement record, attendance records and performance evaluation. [43 Pa Cons Stat Ann § 1321 (1978)]

Q 5:3   Do employees have the right to review their personnel files?

Just as there is no federal law specifically requiring the maintenance of personnel files, no federal law gives employees the right to review such files. Using the example of the Pennsylvania Act, the following suggests procedures for the review of an employee file:

An employer shall, at reasonable times, upon request of an employee permit that employee to inspect his or her own personnel file used to determine his or her own qualifications for employment, promotion, additional compensation, termination or disciplinary action. The employer shall make these records available during the regular business hours of the office where these records are usually and ordinarily maintained, when sufficient time is available during the course of a regular business day, to inspect the personnel files in question. The employer may require the requesting employee to inspect such records on the free time of the employee. At the employer's discretion, the employee may be required to file a written form to request access to the personnel file. This form is solely for the purpose of identifying the requesting individual to avoid disclosure to ineligible individuals. To assist the employer in providing the correct records to meet the employee's need, the employee shall indicate in his written request, either the purpose for which the inspection is requested, or the particular parts of his personnel record which he wishes to inspect. [43 Pa Cons Stat Ann § 1322 (1978)]

Q 5:4 How many states have enacted laws allowing employees access to their personnel files?

To date more than 20 states have enacted such laws. And about half of these states permit employees not only to review, but also to revise or at least offer corrections to the information therein. Some state laws allow the employee to submit an explanatory or corrective statement that must be made a part of the file.

Q 5:5 Who owns an employee's personnel file?

As is the case with virtually all company documents, a personnel file is the property of the company. However, as a practical matter, because the materials in the file are personal, employees often feel that such files belong to them. Thus, even in the absence of a state law mandating employee access, reasonable access is perhaps a desirable policy for the sake of employee morale.

Q 5:6   Are there any parts of the personnel file that the employer need not allow an employee to inspect?

The Pennsylvania Act, a representative example of most other state personnel file acts (see Qs 5:2 and 5:3), excepts certain confidential information from the employee's review:

> The term "personnel file" shall not include records of any employee relating to the investigation of a possible criminal offense, letters of reference, documents which are being developed or prepared for use in civil, criminal or grievance procedures, medical records or materials which are used by the employer to plan for future operations or information available to the employee under the Fair Credit Reporting Act. [43 Pa Cons Stat Ann § 1321 (1978)]

Thus, even in states that allow employee access to personnel files, that right to access is not absolute. Therefore, employers should not only be aware of the existence of such a statute wherever they have employees, but they should also know precisely what is and is not included in the definition of personnel file in each instance where such a law exists.

Q 5:7   Must companies make other corporate records, besides their own personnel files, available to employees and their attorneys?

Employees may be entitled to access to records other than their own personnel files in some cases:

> *Health-related information.* One state court has awarded punitive damages against employers who concealed medical evidence, reflecting symptoms of asbestosis, from the affected workers. [Millison v E I duPont de Nemours & Co, 501 A 2d 505 (NJ Super Ct 1987)] This decision suggests that, even if the health-related information (such as an environmental consultant's dust tests) is not employee-specific, concealment of the information may increase exposure to punitive damages.

> *Information on third parties in workers' compensation suits.* In workers' compensation cases, the employer's insurance carrier may encourage (or even require) the employer to cooperate in the injured employee's third-party claim (e.g., against the

manufacturer of the piece of machinery that caused the injury), to protect the insurance carrier's subrogation interest.

Benefits and pension plan information. The Employee Retirement Income Security Act of 1974 (ERISA) allows employee-participants access to benefit and pension plan information. Participants and beneficiaries of employee stock ownership plans may also have rights to corporate records under Securities and Exchange Commission regulations.

Q 5:8 What is a protective order?

Federal and state rules of civil procedure governing the conduct of lawsuits almost uniformly say that courts can fashion an order to protect both parties and nonparties from unduly burdensome, harassing, and embarrassing discovery activities. A protective order is one common way for a court to do this. A typical protective order involving employee files might include the following restrictions:

- Contents that are clearly irrelevant to the lawsuit will be identified, but not turned over to the requesting party
- Only the requesting party and his or her attorneys will review the files that are produced
- All files will be returned to the producing corporation upon the final resolution of the lawsuit

Q 5:9 What are some records employers may optionally maintain in employees' personnel files?

Besides records that employers must maintain by law (see Q 5:1), optional materials most employers find helpful in personnel files fall into four general categories:

- Preemployment documents (job applications, resumes, references, credit and criminal checks, medical examinations, and test results)
- Benefits administration materials (demographic data, insurance choices, payroll deduction authorizations, pension plan information, insurance claims, sick leave, and vacation schedules)

- Employment history
- Disciplinary history

Access to Personnel Files by Third Parties

Q 5:10 When should the company make employee records available to third parties?

Although employees are ordinarily allowed by law and/or company policy to view and even copy their own personnel files (see Qs 5:3–5:5), they are not accorded automatic access to the personnel files of co-workers, even when they sue the company. To the contrary, a corporate defendant should make every effort to protect and preserve the privacy interests of its other employees who are not parties to the lawsuit. In this regard, the employer should not voluntarily release the contents of these files, but should await service of a proper subpoena or request for production of documents. Then, corporate counsel may still wish to negotiate a stipulation for entry of a protective order (see Q 5:8) before releasing copies of these files.

Q 5:11 Do unions have a right of access to members' personnel files?

As the legally certified collective bargaining agent of the employees in a particular bargaining unit, under appropriate circumstances, it may be an unfair labor practice for an employer to deny the union's request for certain information in one or more members' personnel files. For example, a union representing an employee challenging discipline or discharge under the grievance/arbitration provision of the collective bargaining agreement usually has the right to review the grievant's disciplinary records. And if that union is negotiating wages, benefits, or working conditions, access to pertinent personnel records may be required of the company under its duty to bargain in good faith. Records involving health and safety concerns may also be subject to union review upon the union's appropriate request.

Retention of Personnel Files

Q 5:12 How long should optional materials be maintained in personnel files?

The three-year guideline for retention of legally mandated materials (see Q 5:1) is not necessarily appropriate for every optional record an employer or its human resources department may choose to maintain. Some records, such as job applications, probably should remain in an employee's file for as long as the employee is with the company and for as long thereafter as the file itself is retained. Others, such as vacation and personal leave records, might safely be discarded at the end of the fiscal or calendar year (assuming such fringe benefits cannot be carried over into succeeding years).

Q 5:13 How long should disciplinary records be maintained?

The answer to this question will vary, depending on whether a collective bargaining agreement is implicated and on the company's own disciplinary procedures. For example, if either a collective bargaining agreement or the company's disciplinary scheme specifies how long an infraction can be considered in a subsequent termination decision or remain in the employee's file before it is expunged, the disciplinary records must be retained for at least that length of time.

The corporate culture and, more broadly, the community's culture, may also be significant considerations. Where the union or the workplace is militant or the community has a high per capita number of lawyers or a judicial system clogged with personal injury and employment cases, a company's human resources department may be more cautious about culling aging disciplinary records than a company in a more conservative, perhaps predominantly rural, community where such lawsuits are relatively rare.

Employee Privacy

Q 5:14 What is invasion of privacy?

Four distinct torts of invasion of privacy have emerged over the years:

1. Intrusion upon the plaintiff's seclusion or solitude or into his or her private affairs;

2. Public disclosure of embarrassing private facts about the plaintiff;

3. Publicity, the effect of which is to place the plaintiff in a "false light" in public; and

4. Appropriation of the plaintiff's name or likeness without his or her permission, to the pecuniary advantage of the defendant.

Q 5:15   Why has invasion of privacy become a major legal issue in employment law today?

Drug testing has given rise to a rash of litigation based upon common-law and constitutional law theories of privacy rights. [See, e.g., Luedtke v Nabors Alaska Drilling, Inc, 768 P 2d 1123, 4 BNA IER Cas 129, 79 ALR 4th 75 (Alaska 1989) (based upon Alaska Constitution Art I, § 22, which reads in pertinent part, "Right of Privacy. The right of the people to privacy is recognized and shall not be infringed"); Hennessey v Coastal Eagle Point Oil Co, 589 A 2d 170, 6 BNA IER Cas 513 (NJ Super 1991) (plaintiff argued that random drug testing violated employees' right of privacy under state common law)] As a general rule, preemployment drug tests and drug tests following workplace accidents or based upon supervisors' reasonable suspicion of workplace drug abuse are viewed as reasonable by the courts, while random testing usually is not. The courts also consider the employer's rationale for requiring a test—hazardous working conditions, for example, tend to justify testing.

Even when drug testing may be justified by circumstances, the manner of testing must also be considered. While employers appropriately may be concerned with preventing employee cheating on these tests, procedures such as videotaping or personally observing the employee providing a urine sample, for instance, may give rise to a separate violation of that employee's privacy interest.

Q 5:16   What is constructive defamation?

One novel theory of defamation is analogous to constructive discharge (see chapter 13) and therefore is sometimes labeled "constructive defamation." In pleading a constructive discharge, the employee-plaintiff contends that the employer made working conditions so intolerable that the only choice was to resign. In a constructive defamation claim, the ex-employee argues that in seeking unemployment compensation benefits and a new job, he or she had no choice but to reveal the reason given by the defendant-former employer for the firing—in effect forcing the dischargee to defame himself or herself.

A second form of constructive defamation, more commonly asserted and accepted by the courts, consists of public behavior by a supervisor or security guard that has the effect of creating a false impression in the minds of third parties who observe the conduct. Employee-plaintiffs have successfully complained of such employer conduct as having security padlock their offices and escort them by the arm from the company's premises. Security guards' searches of employees' lockers and cars, as well as the sudden termination of an employee in the course of a company-wide theft investigation or other internally publicized investigation, have also given rise to claims of constructive defamation.

Q 5:17   How can a company protect its employees' privacy rights and guard against defamation suits with respect to personnel files?

Corporations should consider adopting and enforcing a personnel files/privacy policy, which is published in the firm's employee handbook or policy manual. Below is an example of such a policy:

> In recognition of the individual employee's right to privacy, the company has adopted these principles:
>
> 1. The company will request only that information required for business or legal purposes.
>
> 2. The company will protect the confidentiality of all personal information in its records.

3. The company will limit the availability of personal information to those company officials with a business "need to know."

4. The company will refuse to release information to outside inquirers without the employee's written approval.

5. The company will require each employee involved in recordkeeping to adhere to these policies and practices, and violations will result in disciplinary action.

6. Each employee has the right to be given immediate access to personal information regarding him or her in company records, and to correct inaccurate information or express disagreement with material contained therein.

Collecting and retaining personal information. The company will follow the requirements of equal employment opportunity laws and other federal regulations regarding the collection of information from job applicants and employees. Appropriate information will include the following:

- Application forms, references checklists and forms, interviewers' reports, and test results
- Letters of commendation
- Written performance evaluations
- Notices of suspension, disciplinary action, or termination for the past two years
- Attendance records, including leaves of absence

The company will not collect or retain the following information in personnel files:

- Lists of hobbies and outside activities
- Marriage certificates, birth certificates, or other documents for which the company has no business need to know
- Information on an employee's creditworthiness and financial standing

Review of records. The human resources department will review each employee's file annually, and remove and destroy inappropriate or outdated information. Managers and supervisors will review each employee's file before each performance evaluation and destroy outdated and inappropriate information. In addition, managers and supervisors can keep only the following information in their possession:

- One year's attendance records
- Most recent performance evaluation
- Information related to an employee's job performance since the last performance review

Company access to employee records. Access to employee records is restricted to the following:

- Human resources department employees with a business need to know
- An individual employee's direct supervisor or departmental manager with a business need to know
- Company executives with a business need to know

Employee access. An employee may examine his or her personnel records. Records exempt from this inspection include potential job assignments or predictions of future salary and personnel planning information. Regarding any item in the file, an employee has the right to correct the item, ask for its deletion, or write a statement of disagreement with the item, all in the presence of a human resources representative. However, the employee may not actually remove any item from the file.

Disclosure of employee information. All requests for information about a current, retired, or terminated employee must be referred to the human resources department. The human resources manager may disclose to prospective employers dates of employment, final title or position, job location, and, with the employee's permission, a five-year employment and salary history.

Information will also be given in response to duly authorized requests from law-enforcement agencies, including investigations, summonses, subpoenas, and judicial orders. The company need not inform an employee that personal information has been disclosed to law-enforcement agencies if the information is related to an investigation into the employee's on-the-job conduct, especially when the employee's actions may endanger other employees or company security and property.

Of course, in adopting any such policy, the company must confirm with legal counsel that the laws of each state in which the firm does business do not accord employees greater access or privacy rights than are reflected in the policy.

Background Investigations

Q 5:18 Can an employer perform background checks on applicants without violating their privacy?

Employers can, and sometimes do, perform extensive background checks, especially with respect to applicants for high-level or highly sensitive positions. While a release, usually included on the job application, permitting the company to do so is desirable, it is not mandatory for many types of background checks. The most common kinds of background checks include credit checks, consumer reports, and public record checks.

Employers should take into consideration the Fair Credit Reporting Act (FCRA) when conducting a credit check. Although this law is better known for its impact on retail sales and credit cards, it also contains sections that deal with background investigations of employment applicants. If employment is denied to an applicant because of a credit report that was prepared by a consumer reporting agency, the prospective employer must advise the applicant of the report's existence and that it was the reason for denying employment.

Some employers require applicants and employees to consent, in writing and in advance, to a credit check or a search of an office, desk, locker, or even an employee's car that is parked on company premises. The effectiveness of obtaining this consent depends on a number of factors. Public policy in most states bars an employee from waiving the right to pursue actions for future wrongful activities by the employer. The applicant or employee may later argue that signing the form was not voluntary, because employment (or continued employment) seemed to be at stake; that the form was not knowingly executed, because it was hidden in the fine print of a job application or other lengthy form; or that he or she did not anticipate the sort of background check or search that ultimately ensued. This does not mean that employers should not use such forms. The form may constitute a useful—even decisive—defense, but it is no guarantee against lawsuits.

Q 5:19 What should the employer tell the applicant about background checks that it intends to perform as part of the application process?

An example of the notification an employer might give on the application form itself is the following:

> This is to inform you that as part of our procedure for processing your employment application or in making this application for employment, it is understood that an investigation may be made whereby information is obtained through personal interviews with your neighbors, friends, or others with whom you are acquainted. This inquiry includes information as to your character, general reputation, personal characteristics, and mode of living. You have the right to make a written request within a reasonable period of time to receive additional, detailed information about the nature and scope of this investigation.

The purpose of such a notice is to help insulate the company from a subsequent suit by the applicant for invasion of privacy or defamation. While the applicant's tacit, or even explicit, agreement to such a background check is no guarantee against a later lawsuit, it certainly provides an extra level of defense should a disappointed job seeker attempt legal redress because the prospective employer based its negative hiring decision on unfavorable information discovered during the inquiry.

Q 5:20 What is a consumer report?

A consumer report is any written, oral, or other communication of any information by a consumer reporting agency that bears on an individual's creditworthiness, credit standing, credit capacity, character, general reputation, personal characteristics, or mode of living, and is expected to be used in whole or in part in establishing the individual's eligibility for, among other things, employment. (Employment experience information that an employer may seek from an applicant's previous employer does not fall within the definition of consumer report.) Generally speaking, a consumer reporting agency is any firm that is regularly engaged in the practice of assembling credit or other information about individuals for the purpose of furnishing consumer reports to third persons.

An investigative consumer report is a consumer report or a part of a consumer report that is based on personal interviews with neighbors, friends, associates, or knowledgeable acquaintances of the individual being investigated and that contains specific factual information on the individual's credit record.

If an employer needs to know a great deal about a person's background, it may hire an investigative agency to prepare a consumer report on an applicant. The agency may report on police records, lifestyle, personal reputation, and other items. However, an employer's use of these reports is limited to some extent by the FCRA, which provides that whenever an employer plans to have an agency investigate a job applicant, it must notify the applicant in writing that a report is being prepared and that the applicant has the right to know what kind of information the employer is looking for.

An employer is not required to notify a job applicant or existing employee when it seeks a consumer report from a consumer reporting agency. Nor is an employer required to give notice when it seeks an investigative consumer report on individuals or employees in connection with any hiring, promotion, transfer, reassignment, or retention decision for which the individual or employee has not specifically applied. Rather, the disclosure obligation arises whenever an employer uses an investigative consumer report in connection with an employment purpose (e.g., hiring, promoting, transferring) that the employee or applicant has specifically requested.

Q 5:21   What is included in a public records check?

Information available in public records (e.g., criminal convictions, histories of alcohol and drug abuse, involvement in excessive litigation) can reveal much about an applicant. Yet, public records are often overlooked by employers.

There is no central repository for all public records, but the employer can determine where to go and what is required to obtain various types of records. The following types of public records may be valuable in conducting a background check on an employee:

- Criminal records
- Driving records

- Federal and state court records

With employee theft costing companies billions of dollars annually, it is clear that checking applicants' criminal records may be helpful in selecting honest employees. Moreover, increasing numbers of employers are being held liable when employees whose backgrounds show certain types of criminal activities commit similar crimes during the course of their employment. A criminal record check prior to hiring could prevent this type of liability.

The EEOC has ruled that an applicant cannot be denied employment solely because of a criminal record if the nature of the crime is not relevant to the job. For example, a construction contractor hiring a common laborer probably should not be concerned that the applicant was once convicted of illegally shooting a deer out of season. But the EEOC recognizes that a criminal record should prevent employment in certain circumstances. For instance, an applicant convicted of "kiting" bad checks can properly be rejected for a retail cashier job. An employer should monitor whether a criminal record check of applicants would have the effect of excluding otherwise qualified applicants for non-job-related crimes and, if it does, whether there is a real business necessity for conducting the check.

Although employers often rely on the applicants themselves to supply information about prior criminal convictions, many states protect individuals from this kind of disclosure. Even if state law permits an employer to ask an applicant about criminal convictions, there are reasons why an employer might not want to rely on the applicant alone to supply this information. By checking criminal records, an employer can not only obtain more accurate information, but can also check whether an applicant has been completely candid about his or her background.

An employer that denies employment or promotion, in whole or in part, on the basis of information obtained through a criminal record check will be subject to the disclosure requirements of the FCRA. Under this law, employers must disclose to the applicant the name, address, and telephone number of the agency reporting the criminal record and must give the employee the opportunity to inspect the report.

Despite these limitations, for employers that wish to conduct criminal record checks, there are two basic ways to accomplish them. First, every state (except Nevada) has a central repository for criminal records. Contacting a central repository has the advantage of saving time, particularly if the applicant has lived in several locations in a single state. Bear in mind, however, that the records of a central repository are often incomplete and limited to certain types of convictions (such as felonies). Further, the records can be inaccurate, failing to distinguish between convictions and acquittals or failing to even record a conviction. Also note that in many states, the central repository can be contacted only by certain classes of employers.

Second, criminal records can be obtained by contacting individual counties. Although these records are limited to criminal activity within each county, they usually offer more complete data. Counties are also more cooperative with employers, and many of them do not charge fees for the records. Unlike the central repositories, more than 1,500 counties across the country handle employers' telephone requests. Of course, there are some drawbacks to the county-by-county search. The biggest drawback is that many applicants will have lived and worked in several locations within a state, and checking each county can be cumbersome and may leave gaps in the applicant's record.

Since both of the above-mentioned methods of checking criminal records have advantages and drawbacks, a combination of the two methods could be used to make the check as accurate and complete as possible. A third option for the employer is to retain an investigative service. Every major city has a number of such firms, which specialize in providing personal background information quickly and inexpensively to their clients. All such a service needs to get started is the name and Social Security number of the applicant to be investigated.

Driving records from a state's department of motor vehicles are another valuable source of background information, including all traffic violations and driving-related offenses as well as the identifying information contained on drivers' licenses. Seemingly mundane information, such as a full name, date of birth, address, and physical description, may be helpful in verifying the identity of an applicant. Although it may seem odd to have to confirm the identity of an applicant as part of a background check, there have been many cases in which employers have hired individuals who were not who they purported to be. (For example, two foreign employees of the same company, working at different retail locations, shared one Social Security number.) Checking the driving records against the information supplied by the applicant can reveal an incorrect or falsified employment application. Information such as date of birth may also be important in obtaining other records about an applicant, such as criminal records.

Moreover, the kinds of traffic and safety violations noted in applicants' driving records may reveal more serious problems. For instance, if an applicant's license is suspended or expired, this fact may even disqualify the candidate from a position, if it involves driving. A driving record that shows several driving-while-intoxicated (DWI) convictions might indicate that the applicant has an alcohol or drug abuse problem that could affect job performance. This kind of preemployment information can be invaluable in pinpointing potential problem employees before a job offer is extended.

Checking federal court records is relatively simple if the applicant's business and personal residence addresses are known. Although the United States is divided into 93 federal court districts, each district is contained within a single state's borders. Three types of records can be checked: civil cases, criminal cases, and bankruptcy cases. Most of these records are available to the public, and checking them can identify any legal or financial problems an applicant has had if the problems led to lawsuits. Because civil and criminal records are usually kept separate from bankruptcy records, employers should be sure to check the appropriate court for the records that are desired. Note, however, that a provision of the federal Bankruptcy Act prohibits an employer from discriminating against an employee or applicant solely because the individual has filed for bankruptcy. This provision is in keeping with the general bankruptcy policy of giving bankrupt individuals a fresh start.

State court proceedings are also a matter of public record. Because most state court systems are divided by county, searching for state court lawsuits usually involves a courthouse-by-courthouse inquiry. It comes down to a dollars-and-cents business decision: Does the business and/or the position to be filled justify the time and expense of sending an investigator to search for the information?

Surveillance

Q 5:22 Can a retail company "shop" its own stores without invading its clerks' rights of privacy?

Yes, most (if not all) retail corporations regularly conduct "shops" of the company's own stores to test the honesty of store managers and clerks. No employee privacy right is invaded by this activity.

Q 5:23 Can a company conduct videotaped surveillance of its employees?

As a general rule, videotaping employees at the job site does not violate their privacy rights. However, there are some exceptions to this general statement. Videotaping employees engaged in union activity will be an unfair labor practice if the purpose is to intimidate or retaliate against them; however, videotaping illegal strike activity for purposes of obtaining an injunction or suing for damages may be legal, albeit such filming often inflames an already volatile situation. Videotaping employees giving urine samples during drug testing (although intended to guard against cheating) violates the employees' privacy rights.

Q 5:24 May a company eavesdrop on or record employees' telephone calls?

Many states have enacted wiretap laws that may make it illegal to eavesdrop on employee telephone calls. However, these laws usually involve only surreptitious monitoring of calls. In some companies, where telephone solicitation or taking orders is a substantial part of the business, such laws (if arguably applicable) may be satisfied by advising employees in advance that their telephone performance will be randomly monitored.

However, in 1993, a federal judge in Salt Lake City dismissed the invasion-of-privacy claim of a police dispatcher whose personal telephone calls were surreptitiously recorded, resulting in his being disciplined for violating a work rule against abuse of the communications systems for personal purposes. Holding that the officer had no reasonable expectation of privacy, the judge said: "The Constitution does not prevent a public employer from making reasonable demands of its employees during business hours in an attempt to perform its work in an efficient, effective manner." The plaintiff had discussed a co-worker's marital problems. When that co-worker reported for her shift and reviewed the tapes, she complained to their supervisor. Facing discipline, the offending dispatcher resigned and sued. But the court rejected her claim. ["Monitoring Phone Calls Held No Breach of Privacy," 1993 *BNA Daily Labor Report* 57 (Mar 26, 1993) at 1; see also Q 5:27 and Qs 10:27–10:30]

Q 5:25 How should a company deal with a dishonest employee after he or she has been identified?

Once an employee has been identified as being dishonest, the most difficult task is determining how to deal with him or her. Should the employer confront the employee with its findings, demand restitution of the cash or goods embezzled, or fire the employee?

It is imperative that the employer give the employee a chance to explain what appears to be a dishonest act. It may be that what appeared to be theft is a fully justified transaction. The suspected employee must have a chance to defend himself or herself. (This is sometimes called "workplace due process." See chapter 3.)

When confronting the employee, the employer should present its findings in a very matter-of-fact fashion. Incriminating statements should be avoided. If the factual sequence is well presented, it can only point to the commission of a crime and will speak for itself. Then, the employee should be asked whether he or she has an explanation for the findings. It is highly improbable that a dishonest employee will readily admit to any misconduct. Employers should be aware of certain attitudes that are generally manifested by dishonest employees during confrontations, such as the following:

- Overreacting or just the opposite, being extremely polite and calm
- Difficulty in recalling events or too precisely recollecting them
- Excessive specificity in denying the wrongdoing
- Attacking the firm's policies and procedures

An employer is strongly encouraged to seek legal advice if it suspects dishonest activity on the business's premises. Employees have certain rights under the law, and an inadvertent deprivation of these rights could have significant legal implications for the employer. For example, if an employee who is being questioned is represented for collective bargaining purposes by a union, the Supreme Court has held that the employee has the right to union representation at any investigative interview that the employee reasonably believes may result in disciplinary action against him or her. The employer's failure to allow the union to attend is considered an unfair labor practice. [NLRB v Weingarten, Inc, 420 US 251 (1975)]

Although there is no sure way to stop all employee invasion of privacy/defamation suits, reasonable behavior will certainly help minimize the company's exposure.

Q 5:26   What is the Electronic Communications Privacy Act and how might it apply to employee privacy rights?

The Electronic Communications Privacy Act (ECPA) of 1986 comprehensively amended Title III of the Omnibus Crime Control and Safe Streets Act of 1968. [18 USC §§ 25102520] In the words of one commentator:

> The ECPA . . . added a new chapter to the federal wiretap statutes to govern access to electronically stored data. The impetus for the legislation derived, in large part, from a 1985 congressional agency study that used compelling language to describe the threat to civil liberties presented by unregulated intrusions into electronically transmitted communications. . . . The statute needed broadening if it clearly was to bring E-mail and other electronic communications within its purview. [Baumhart, "The Employer's Right to Read Employee E-mail: Protecting Property or Personal Prying?" 8 *The Labor Lawyer* 924, Fall 1992]

ECPA defines electronic communication to include "any transfer of signs, signals, writing, images, sounds, data, or intelligence of any nature transmitted in whole or in part by a wire, radio, electromagnetic, photo-electronic or photo-optical system that affects interstate or foreign commerce." Clearly included in this definition is E-mail, which the federal government has described as a data processing system employing communications technology to transmit mail in electronic form. "If desired, the electronic output can be printed out in hard copy and delivered by the (U.S. Postal Service) or private carrier. But electronic mail also permits terminal-to-terminal communication where the message is never in paper form." [Office of Technology Assessment, *Federal Government Information Technology: Electronic Surveillance and Civil Liberties*, 45 (1985)]

With the proliferation of personal computers in the workplace, E-mail has become commonplace. Employers may have many motives in wanting to monitor or peruse their employees' use of this electronic service. For instance, companies have an interest in ensuring that expensive equipment and services, as well as their employees' time, are being used for company business and not personal activities. Yet, some legal commentators have contended that ECPA and/or some state wiretap acts (see Q 5:24) may render such monitoring or eavesdropping illegal:

> [T]o blindly adopt the view that the statute imposes no access limitations on employers who possess their own systems ignores Congress' stated intent to procure parity in the protection of personal communications, regardless of the medium of transmission. [Baumhart at 926]

Others have expressed the view that employers are free under federal law to monitor employees' E-mail at will. [See Hernandez, "ECPA and Online Computer Privacy," 41 *Fed Communications L J* 17, 39 (1988)] In fact there is little federal court case law to guide employers with regard to ECPA's impact upon employee privacy rights. However, ECPA and most analogous state statutes recognize consent as a means of overcoming their prohibitions upon electronic eavesdropping; consequently, where corporations advise employees in advance of their intent to monitor E-mail, telephone calls, and the like, a good argument may exist for the inapplicability of any of these statutory prohibitions. Such a notice might be contained in the employee handbook and acknowledged by the employee signing an appropriate form following review of the document. (See Qs 2:31 and 2:32 for more on the contractual nature of employee handbooks and the use of reservation of rights clauses in such booklets.)

The decision that likely stands as a leading case in this area, at least for the immediate future, was reached by a panel of three judges with U.S. Court of Appeals for the Fourth Circuit in Richmond, Virginia, in October 1994 and rehearing was denied by the full court in January 1995. [Sanders v Robert Bosch Corp, 38 F 3d 736, 1994 US App LEXIS 30314, 10 BNA IER Cases 1 (4th Cir 1994), *reh'g en banc denied*, 1995 US App LEXIS 1439 (4th Cir 1995)] Plaintiff Beverly Sanders was a security guard for a firm named Guardsmark Inc. in South Carolina. Guardsmark had contracted to provide security services to the defendant company. From 1985 to 1990 Sanders worked as a rent-a-cop for Bosch at its Charleston plant. Unbeknownst to Sanders, Bosch had installed a 24-hours-a-day "voice logger" that recorded all the telephone conversations that took place on certain phone lines leading into the security office. When Sanders discovered that her calls were all recorded she sued under the wiretap provisions of the ECPA.

Bosch defended on the basis that recording telephone conversations was necessary because of alleged bomb threats it reported receiving. The trial judge ruled that these threats did not place the defendant under the business-use exception to the wiretap prohibitions. The business-use exception is an "ordinary course of business" exception. [ECPA § 2510(5)(a)(i)] Since "no bomb threats were received throughout the period that recordings were made," two members of the three-judge appellate panel affirmed the trial judge's ruling on this crucial point. [1994 US App LEXIS 30314, *14] These judges were also made suspicious of defendant's motives because the evidence indicated that "there were telephones readily available to the guards which were not recorded and to which their officers who knew about the recording could have directed them for their personal calls." [Id] This evidence led the judges to wonder whether the company's real motive—or at least one of its motives—was in fact to record surreptitiously the personal calls of Guardsmark employees.

Thus the jury was permitted to award damages to Sanders. However, employers requiring the ability to monitor employee calls can take heart from the trial judge's narrow construction of the damage provisions of the ECPA. Jury instructions were structured so as to prevent the award of damages for periods when the system was not recording due to design defects and also to prevent the award of any punitive damages to Sanders. [Id at *17] These jury instructions were confirmed by the appellate panel. Additionally, Judge Widener of the panel published a lengthy dissent, thus somewhat undercutting the force of the majority opinion. Nonetheless, the Fourth Circuit refused to rehear the case before the full court. The decision is likely to be a leader until a more erudite opinion is honed by another tribunal.

Q 5:27 Do state constitutions protect the privacy rights of employees of private corporations?

Ever since the U.S. Supreme Court found a constitutional right of privacy to be implicitly contained in the Bill of Rights over two decades ago, the issue of privacy has loomed in American law and public policy as a sort of question mark. The Drug Free Workplace Act, which mandates certain forms of drug testing programs by government contractors (see Qs 7:138–7:151), OSHA's AIDS enforcement procedures in the workplace (see Qs 7:103–7:137), and the proliferation of computers, car phones, and other electronic devices capable of casual monitoring have combined to make employee privacy a question urgently needing more definitive answers than those given by the legislatures and courts to date. Indeed, the time may be ripe for a comprehensive national policy on employee privacy rights.

The Bill of Rights of the U.S. Constitution applies only to actions by the federal government. Also, the due process and equal protection clauses of the Fourteenth Amendment apply only to actions by state and local governments. Therefore, while public employees enjoy these constitutional rights with respect to their federal, state, and municipal employers (including public schools, colleges, and universities), the old saying in labor law has always been that "The Constitution stops at the private employer's front door."

However, ten states now grant citizens a constitutional right of privacy (Alaska, Arizona, California, Florida, Hawaii, Illinois, Louisiana, Montana, South Carolina, and Washington), and at least one, Alaska, has extended this privacy right into the private workplace.

In *Soroka v. Dayton Hudson Corp.* [1 Cal Rptr 2d 77 (1991), *rev granted*, 4 Cal Rptr 2d 180 (1992)], the court held that neither a public nor a private employer may invade the privacy of its employees absent a compelling interest in doing so. In this case, the court found that a department store's interest in the emotional stability of its security guards was not sufficiently compelling to warrant psychological testing.

More frequently, privacy right challenges have arisen in recent years in the context of drug testing by private companies (Q 7:151). But, interestingly, no court in California or elsewhere has followed, or apparently even cited, *Soroka* since it was handed down. And, although the California Supreme Court agreed to review the case in 1992, no decision has been reported out of the state's highest tribunal. In short, the decision's impact upon the developing common law of this country seems to have been modest. Indeed, it has become one small part of the evolving body of court-made employment law. This observation, however, should not be interpreted as suggesting that privacy has ceased to be a cutting edge issue among employees and citizens in general.

Q 5:28   Is there a growing backlash against employer surveillance?

The techniques of workplace surveillance are becoming ever more sophisticated. For example, leading security equipment firms have recently begun marketing systems that combine electronic cash registers, closed-circuit television, and the computer in the selective surveillance of retail store cashiers. [See Q 3:142; Castagnera and Szvetitz, "Tips for Quality CCTV," *Convenience Store Decisions*, Jan 1994, at 20]

Thus, employers should not be surprised to encounter a backlash by employees, organized labor, and legislators responsive to labor unions and other employee advocacy groups. In 1994, a major power company in Pittsburgh videotaped its employee locker rooms. The incident led to a talk show on Pittsburgh's KDKA radio station, during which callers aired questions and concerns about workplace surveillance. "Based on the number of callers to that program, many people share a concern about this red-hot issue." [Castagnera and Szvetitz, "Privacy: The Coming Confrontation," *Convenience Store Decisions,* Mar 1994, at 24]

To date, the workplace privacy issue has tended to play itself out around the even more volatile issue of drug testing. Numerous lawsuits have pitted the employer's interest (indeed, the company's obligation) regarding a safe workplace against the employee's desire to protect privacy. [See, e.g., National Treasury Employees Union v Von Raab, 489 US 65 (1989); Skinner v Railway Labor Executives Association, 489 US 602 (1989); Borse v Piece Goods Shops Inc, 963 F 2d 611 (3d Cir 1991); Hennessey v Coastal Eagle Point Oil Co, 589 A 2d 170 (NJ Sup 1991); Jennings v Mince Technology Labs Inc, 765 SW 2d 497 (Tex Civ App 1989); see also, Qs 6:5 and 7:151]

However, as closed-circuit television (CCTV) is teamed with the computer and other electronic systems to enhance employers' ability to watch employees' on-the-job activities, the emphasis can be expected to shift to outcries against "Big Brother" (or more aptly "Big Boss") watching and listening. [Castagnera and Szvetitz, "Privacy: The Coming Confrontation," *supra*, at 24] The U.S. Congress may be positioned to lead the charge against workplace CCTV activities.

Retail loss-prevention programs could be severely hampered by legislation in subcommittees in the House of Representatives and Senate. As Morrison Cain, vice president, legal and public affairs, International Mass Retail Association (IMRA), Washington, D.C., said:

> The Privacy for Consumers and Workers Act (HR 1900, S 984) was not written specifically to limit loss prevention efforts. But critics say that, as drafted, the bill would severely restrict retailers' ability to use electronic monitoring technology for security and data collection purposes. . . . The genesis of the bill was very specific—to remedy alleged telephone monitoring abuses in telecommunications. [See Q 5:24] Indeed, the driving force behind the proposed legislation since its inception in 1991 has been unions representing telecommunications workers . . . . [But o]pponents of the bill says its sponsors cast their nets too wide. Instead of defining specific practices that you could build a consensus on, they started out with the premise that all electronic monitoring is bad.

> Objections to the proposed legislation stem from its all-inclusive definition of electronic monitoring. As written, the definition

encompasses some of the most effective loss prevention and information gathering devices used in retail, including CCTV, point-of-sale exception monitoring and productivity software. ["The Battle Over Electronic Monitoring: Proposed Legislation Takes on Criticism from Retailers," *Chain Store Age Executive*, Jan 1994]

While security firms and other opponents of the legislation point to inventory shrinkage (see chapter 3) and other justifications for electronic and CCTV surveillance of employees, proponents including the American Civil Liberties Union have testified to horror stories aimed at garnering support for the bills.

"We have had nurses discover hidden video cameras in their shower room. We have had employees whose offices have been bugged. We have had employees whose phones have been tapped," testified the ACLU in congressional hearings. ["Pros, Cons of Privacy Bill Explored During Senate Hearing," 1993 *BNA Daily Labor Report* 119, June 23, 1993, at 3; see also, "Bosses with X-ray Eyes," *The Recorder*, Aug 4, 1993, at 8]

This legislation, if ultimately enacted, may shift the present precarious balance away from employers' use of CCTV and electronic monitoring, just as the federal Employee Polygraph Protection Act of 1988 made use of lie detectors in the workplace impractical, if not always outright illegal, for most businesses (see Qs 3:39–3:65). However, until such a law is enacted and signed, "an employer undertaking a surveillance program must weigh the intrusion against the justification for it." [Castagnera and Szvetitz, "Privacy: The Coming Confrontation," *supra*]

The prospects for enactment probably suffered a serious blow when the Republican Party captured the two houses of Congress in November 1994. But notwithstanding the new, predictably pro-business orientation of the U.S. Congress, cases continue to come down that indicate a willingness of private citizens to challenge what they view as invasions of their privacy and to seek substantial damages for such perceived intrusions. For instance, an important nonemployment case, which employers should note with caution, is *Ayeni v. CBS Inc.* [848 F Supp 362, 1994 US Dist LEXIS 3023, 22 Media L Rep 1466 (EDNY 1994)] According to the court's statement of the facts of this rather unusual case, a U.S. Treasury agent, investigating one plaintiff's husband's alleged involvement in a credit card fraud scheme, obtained a warrant to search the plaintiff's apartment for evidence of such activities. The suspect's wife and child were subjected to the search by six Treasury agents but were not targets of the investigation. Along with the half-dozen agents, a camera crew for a CBS show called "Street Stories" entered the apartment and were not even identified by the government officers as CBS television people. Mrs. Ayeni, "clothed only in a dressing gown," and her son were subjected to videotaping.

"The CBS crew followed and taped the agents as they searched the apartment and the Ayenis' belongings. They took close-up pictures of the interiors of closets, personal letters, family pictures. . . ," according to the court. The court went on to hold that the Treasury agent's permitting CBS to enter and videotape the plaintiffs' premises went way beyond the scope of the government's search warrant. However, because the camera crew was acting behind the shield of the search warrant, the videotaped pictures were a seizure under the Fourth Amendment of the U.S. Constitution. Thus the camera crew, present only to take pictures so they could "titillate and entertain others," was a violation of the plaintiffs' constitutional and statutory rights. [1994 US Dist LEXIS 3023, **13]

The court continued, "CBS had no greater right than that of a thief to be in the home, to take pictures and to remove the photographic record." [Id at **16] The district judge therefore denied the defendants' motion to dismiss the Ayenis' legal action. The decision sounds a cautionary note to all employers using video for worker surveillance. The American home is most certainly more sacrosanct than the workplace, and the resident's expectation of privacy more sacred and more reasonable than that of the worker in the workplace, but an expectation of privacy can adhere to the workplace, and especially certain parts of it, such as showers and bathroom facilities, locker rooms, and even private offices. The outrage of the district judge in the *Ayeni* case is clear and sounds a warning that those on the judicial benches may react in human terms to allegations by employee-plaintiffs of unreasonable video intrusions into their working lives.

Chapter 6

Security Issues

In many businesses, employee theft is the single major source of business losses, accounting for 60 percent to 90 percent of losses. The fact that an employee is part of the business machinery provides him or her with numerous opportunities to steal from the business that other individuals (customers, vendors) never have.

The incentive to steal includes the employee's perception that the internal management of the business is superficial, chaotic, and full of potential loopholes. The employee's perception of the system determines the amount of risk he or she will take in committing a crime against the employer. Therefore, increasing the employee's risk exposure is generally the best deterrent to crime. By enhancing an employee's perception of how the company's management and security systems operate, employers can send clear deterrence signals.

Technological advances have expanded opportunities for theft by making valuable proprietary information on floppy disks easily portable.

We see this subject as so important that portions of several chapters in this work have been devoted to aspects of it, including, notably, "Dishonest Employees" in chapter 3 and "Background Investigations" in chapter 5. These sections should be consulted along with the more extensive and detailed consideration of this significant topic in this chapter.

Employee Honesty and Safety

Honesty

Q 6:1   What are the types of employee theft?

Types of employee theft vary according to the types of businesses involved. Each business seems to have a pattern of conduct that dishonest employees tend to follow. If the business in question is one in which cash is readily available to the employee, for example, the focus will be on ways that cash can be diverted. If, instead, employees work at loading terminals, the techniques scrutinized are those that employees may use to hide and remove merchandise. Therefore, depending on the nature of the employer's business, employee theft can include such acts as invoicing goods below established prices and getting cash kickbacks from customers; pilfering merchandise covered by doctored inventory lists; placing orders for side business; and using company time and facilities for personal projects.

Some illustrations, drawn from the author's own experiences in investigating and combating employee theft, may be helpful:

Example. Mabel was a 20-year employee of a major department store chain. She was working as a cashier in the bargain basement of the chain's center-city store. The company's security department regularly monitored such computerized data as merchandise returns, over-rings on the cash registers, and the like, all tell-tale signs of employee theft. As a result of this regular monitoring, security noticed a steady increase in the rate of returned merchandise rung up on Mabel's register during her shifts over a period of months. The head of security for the chain authorized a follow-up investigation, including surveillance. The surveillance consisted of positioning a "pinhole" video camera inside a closet in the vicinity of Mabel's register during her eight-hour shift on a Friday evening. While under video surveillance that evening, Mabel sold a dress to a bargain-basement customer for $10. The videotape showed her placing the dress in the store bag and placing the $10 bill in her register. It also showed her flipping the customer's sales receipt onto the floor behind her counter instead of placing it in the customer's bag along with the dress. Later that evening, Mabel took the time to police her area, picking up the scrap paper that was scattered around the floor. In the process she retrieved the sales receipt for the $10 dress. A little later, Mabel wrote up a "return" slip for the dress, stapled the return to the receipt that she should have placed in the customer's bag, and rang up the return on her register. She then took $10 from the register's cash drawer and placed it in her own purse, from which it was recovered by security at the end of Mabel's shift, when she was escorted back to the security office and interviewed.

Example. Bill was an outside salesman for a company which sold and serviced faxes and copiers. One day, while having lunch in a downtown diner owned by the father of a college friend, his friend sat down at Bill's table to say "hi" and in the course of the conversation mentioned his dad's need for a fax machine in the restaurant's office. After lunch, Bill called an acquaintance, Joe, a former service rep for Bill's employer. Joe, after leaving Bill's company, went into business for himself, dealing in and servicing used faxes and copiers. Bill told Joe of his friend's need. Joe agreed to meet Bill after work at the diner, where together they sold the owner a used fax, which Joe delivered and installed a couple of days later. The diner's check went to Joe, who later gave Bill a commission in cash.

Example. Mary was a secretary for one of a firm's top executives. Ms. Exec traveled a lot and relied on Mary to keep on top of her travel itinerary and her expenses. Sometimes Ms. Exec, while out of town, called Mary and gave her rush assignments to get out, which frequently required Mary to come in early, work through her lunch hour, or stay past quitting time which, under company policy and the Fair Labor Standards Act (see Qs 1:12–1:16), permitted Mary to put in for overtime pay. Because the firm required overtime and expense sheets to be submitted not later than the Wednesday prior to each payday and Ms. Exec traveled so much of the time, she authorized Mary to sign Ms. Exec's initials on overtime and expense sheets. Meanwhile, Mary, forced to operate on her own and unsupervised for so much of the time, developed some bad habits. For instance, knowing that her over-time claims would seldom be scrutinized by Ms. Exec even if her boss happened to be in the office on the day they were due, Mary stopped keeping exact records of the extra hours she worked. Instead, when the overtime sheets came due every two weeks, she estimated the time she had put in after hours and over lunch. She estimated a little high, just to be sure she wasn't inadvertently cheating herself out of some premium pay. She also developed the habit of "goofing off" during some mornings when Ms. Exec was out of town. Then, when Ms. Exec called in for her morning messages and gave Mary some new instructions, Mary would work through her lunch hour in order to get caught up, taking an hour in overtime pay in the process. Finally, when Ms. Exec fell behind in getting her expense sheets to Mary, rather than bother Ms. Exec for the information, Mary would estimate the expenses for the two-week period, again estimating a little high, just to be on the safe side. In all these instances, the extra cash ultimately ended up in Mary's checking account. Eventually, having the extra cash, like taking a drug, became an addiction for Mary. She began to put through overtime and expense sheets regularly for nonexistent expenses and work performance. When the firm instituted a new, computerized reporting procedure, which required all executives to review overtime and expense claims quarterly, and Ms. Exec finally was forced to focus on her numbers, she became suspicious of Mary, who was eventually caught.

Example. Joe was a buyer for a printing company. Over the years he developed a close relationship with the salesman for a large paper supplier. Over a lunch, picked up by the salesman on his expense account and including several drinks, Joe was confronted with the proposition that, if he would direct more of his company's purchases of glossy, coated papers to his friend's firm, the friend would make it worth Joe's while. Although a little "buzzed," Joe made a show of rejecting this suggestion. The friend did not press the issue. A few weeks later, Joe placed a large order for some expensive, coated paper stock with the salesman's company. A pair of season tickets to the New York Giants arrived in the mail a few days later at Joe's home with a nice note from his salesman-friend. Joe hesitated, but decided to keep the tickets rather than offend him. The next time he put in a big order, a VCR arrived by UPS. Once again Joe hesitated, but decided to keep the gift. After all, he reasoned, he only placed the orders because the price was right. However, as time passed Joe found himself placing the orders even when the price was no longer right.

Example. Ernie was a maintenance engineer, one of about a dozen, employed by the management company that ran a high-rise office complex in downtown Philadelphia. A model employee, he was seldom late for work, volunteered for more than his share of overtime, and happily worked weekends and holidays. About a year after Ernie started working in the building, tenants periodically began reporting thefts. The thefts mainly involved PCs and related computer equipment and typically occurred on holiday weekends. After several such occurrences, the management firm hired a security specialist to quietly investigate the problem. The investigator painstakingly correlated thefts with employee time records. By this process, she was able to ascertain that only three of the 12 maintenance engineers were on duty every weekend when the thefts happened. During the next holiday weekend, the investigator stationed herself in her car outside the building every night of the three-day weekend between 11 P.M. and 2 A.M., and monitored the building's activities on her CB radio. In the wee hours of Labor Day morning, her tenacity paid off. Over her radio came a request from Ernie to the guard on duty in the control room to give Ernie access to the freight elevator, which he asked to have directed to the 15th floor. Half an hour later the investigator entered the building and scanned the parking garage, where she identified Ernie's pickup truck. Secured under a tarp in the back of the truck were nine PCs. Subsequent investigation revealed that they had been taken from a tenant's offices on the 15th floor.

Example. Dr. No directed international financial research for a major econometric forecasting firm headquartered in Boston. For some time, he desired to start his own boutique forecasting firm. He finally went so far as to incorporate a company, using his home address as the place of incorporation. Requested by an investment banking firm to provide a proposal for a project involving the forecasting of the future prospects of the junk bond market, he dutifully prepared such a proposal and sent it off to the bankers. He then prepared a second proposal on the stationery of his new company, had his brother-in-law sign it as "executive vice president" of the new corporation, and sent it to the investment banking firm with a lower bottom-line price to the investment bankers.

As earlier indicated, all of these examples are drawn from actual cases. They barely scratch the surface of the ingenuity with which employees with saddening regularity seek to steal from their employers, and too often succeed. The questions and answers that follow are aimed at advising employers about what they legally can do to prevent, detect, and punish such crimes against their businesses.

Q 6:2 What telltale signs indicate employee dishonesty and theft?

It is first advisable to distinguish between the signs that may be discoverable in the work environment and those signs that may become evident through direct observation of the employee's behavior. The objective signs that an employer should be mindful of will depend on the type of business involved. For any given type of operation, there is going to be a "best" (i.e., least risky) stealing technique. Leaving aside the specific nature of the given business, an employer can focus on the types of goods that may be targets of theft and then examine how these goods may be dishonestly removed.

Money's fungible character, which makes it impossible to identify the owner, makes cash a prime target for theft. In most retail operations, cash has to be removed from a register; the employer's inquiry, then, is how would the money be removed from the register without the employer knowing about it? After money has been diverted, the only way to reconcile the figure that the register displays with the amount of money left in the drawer is to artificially reduce the amount from sales actually made. To do this, the employee usually must fail to ring sales in an amount equaling the value of the money diverted. The following are some of the signs that an employee has failed to ring up sales:

Shortages or Overages of Cash. A cash overage is as much a red flag as a cash shortage. The only difference between the two is the timing by which the stealing scheme is carried out. In a cash shortage, the cash is first removed from the drawer; the employee later makes up for the discrepancy by under-ringing subsequent sales. If the register audit shows an overage, this may be evidence that the employee has already reduced the amount from sales rung, intending to remove the money later. Unannounced register checks can spot shortages or overages before the employee has finished manipulating the cash and sales.

Early or Late Checkouts. To conceal their strategies, dishonest employees check out earlier or later than their co-workers to "fix" the registers and avoid the unwanted company of other employees.

Unusual Register Readings. This may involve either the frequency of certain register receipt readings (e.g., an unusual number of refunds) or the types of readings (e.g., no sales, cross-readings, returns, and voids).

Statistics point out that losses due to employee theft tend to be higher in the distribution and supply sectors than in the service and transport sectors. If the targeted items are supplies and merchandise, the following should be viewed as warning signals:

Out of Place Personal Belongings. The presence of employees' belongings that are not usually kept in their work areas can be a signal that merchandise is being concealed and removed by hiding it in the personal belongings.

Odd Parking Habits. The removal of a considerable amount of merchandise or a single large item will usually entail the use of a vehicle. An employee's car that is not parked in its regular parking space (which should be located so that carrying stolen merchandise to the car is not feasible) could be a signal that the owner of the car intends to perform an unlawful act. Even if the employee justifies this habit on the basis of health-related factors (e.g., difficulty in walking long distances), any irregular parking arrangement should be carefully scrutinized.

Unusual Placement of Trash Cans. This may indicate that trash cans are being used for concealment and transportation of merchandise.

Irregular Visits to Controlled Areas. Records of visitors to restricted areas may show an unusual pattern of visits. Further examination may indicate that certain visits occur only at specific hours. Unless the pattern is justified by a sound reason (e.g., the need to check on certain items delivered at a certain hour), this pattern may indicate a conspiracy to steal between the visiting employee and the employee on the shift at that hour, or a pattern of conduct aimed at evading security controls.

Early or Late Checkouts or Checking. As with cash thefts, dishonest employees may check out early or late to avoid other employees who might see them stealing merchandise and supplies.

Q 6:3 What techniques can prevent or detect employee theft?

Loss prevention and security experts have suggested that the following corporate policies may be advisable to prevent and detect employee theft, and thus keep it from adversely affecting the company's bottom line:

1. View the security department as a potential profit center. In the words of one loss control specialist, "A dollar in new sales may yield a nickel to the bottom line after deductions for cost of goods, labor, rent, utilities and other expenses. . . . But a dollar not lost to (inventory) shrink or robbery falls directly to the bottom line." [Castagnera and Szvetitz, "Survival of the Safest," *Convenience Store Decisions*, Jan 1992, at 24]

2. Consider security a bona fide career path and seek out experts with appropriate education and sophistication, not just ex-cops and retired army military police personnel.

3. Involve the security department in all forms and sources of loss, rather than relegating it to supervising security guards and monitoring alarms and TV cameras.

4. Integrate the security function with purchasing, accounting, human resources, and the general counsel's office.

[See, generally, C. Higgins, "Security—Contribution to Corporate Profits," *Security in the Year 2000* (NY: American Management Association 1990) at 103]

Q 6:4   What guidelines exist for preventing employee theft?

Loss control experts suggest the following checklist to prevent employee theft:

- Conduct regular audits on the performance of the company
- Keep complete and up-to-date records of all the company's transactions, goods, routes, and inventories
- Implement a uniform system for reporting matters handled by employees
- Limit access to supply and storage areas
- Set established procedures to handle routine operations that are performed by employees
- Stress the importance of observing company procedures
- Set up a decentralized operating system for each of the company's units (e.g., have one person handle accounting and another take care of billing; have one group handle deliveries and a different group be responsible for shipping)
- Consider using electronic security systems and undercover spies

Q 6:5   How does an employer spot dishonest employees?

As illustrated in Q 6:1, many electronic devices, such as pinhole video cameras, closed-circuit TVs, and CB radios are readily available to investigators. In addition, employer's can monitor all manner of functions and activities on employees' PCs. However, in availing itself of these myriad devices, an employer must be mindful of the potential for violating an employee's privacy rights. (This issue is covered by Qs 5:22–5:27.) Additionally, use of the polygraph, or lie detector, is subject to federal (and often state) statutory restrictions (see Qs 3:39–3:67). Finally, searches and surveillance of employees can give rise to legal liability if inappropriately performed (see Qs 3:123–3:129).

Under proper professional and legal supervision, the employer has an amazing array of devices and techniques available for spotting dishonest employees from the application stage of the employment relationship onward. These include at least the following:

- Arrest and conviction records (see Qs 3:13, 5:21)
- Attitude and honesty tests (see Qs 3:66, 3:67)
- Blood and urine tests, and even brain scans, to detect drug abuse (see Qs 3:70, 4:90, 7:138–7:151)
- Computer monitoring of everything from productivity of typists to employee's E-mail activities (see Qs 5:26, 5:27 and Qs 6:18–6:20)
- Credit reports (see Qs 3:23, 3:24)
- Telephone monitoring (see Q 5:24)

This list is far from exhaustive. (See, e.g., Hartsfield, *Investigating Employee Conduct* (1991) at 1, for a list of still more exotic methods of spotting dishonest employees, such as "drug-sniffing dogs.") Again, it's worth emphasizing that federal and state statutory and common law must be scrutinized carefully for limitations or outright prohibitions of any particular technique. For example, a federal court in Pennsylvania recently held that the commonwealth's public policy against invasion of privacy was offended by an employer's insistence upon a drug test, and that the offense gives rise to a cause of action for wrongful discharge. [See Borse v Piece Goods Shop Inc, 963 F 2d 611 (3d Cir 1991), discussed in detail at Q 2:14]

Q 6:6   How do you legally detect a dishonest employee at the application stage?

Nearly 30 percent of all job applicants falsify some portion of their employment applications. One-third of all employees also steal at their workplaces. Do the same one-third who lie on their applications turn out to be the workplace thieves? This correlation is difficult to make, but logic suggests that if a new hire is dishonest coming through the door, that person will remain a dishonest employee until the day she or he goes out the back door. Consequently, good sense dictates detecting the dishonest applicant before that applicant is an employee of the company.

The background check is the way to accomplish this legally. As suggested above (Q 6:5) the amount of information available today is remarkable. In fact, some employers make their jobs easier in this regard by requiring the applicant to provide vital background information. For example, some employers require all applicants to request a police check before being hired. The police check is required to cover the applicant's home town or county. If the applicant has been a resident there for less than six months, a police report from the previous place of residence also will be demanded, according to Deborah Glacken, Corporate Director of Loss Prevention, Dairy Mart Convenience Stores.

Bruce Marks, Director of Operations for Employment Screening Inc., says, "In [some industries] about 12 percent of all criminal record checks come back with positive results."

Q 6:7   Are criminal record checks legal?

Not only is a criminal record check easy, inexpensive and effective, it is legal. No recent cases have been uncovered in which such a check is declared by a court to be per se illegal. The EEOC historically has indicated some concerns about the possible disparate impact of questions about police records upon certain minorities (see Qs 3:14, 3:15).

However, this concern can be addressed and defused by focusing upon convictions as opposed to mere arrests and upon serious crimes as opposed to minor juvenile scrapes and misdemeanors. [Castagnera & Szvetitz, "The Search for a 'Hire' Authority," *Convenience Store Decisions*, Jan 1995, at 38]

Indeed, some recent case law suggests that under some circumstances employers may owe their clients the duty of checking employees' possible police records. For example, in a case in which a major hotel chain was joined as a defendant in an action by a female guest who was raped on a date with a hotel employee, the court observed that:

> Ms. Jackson's claim that the Hilton Hotel breached its duty to exercise reasonable care in hiring employees is based primarily on her contention that the Hilton Hotel failed to make a routine check of police records or to administer polygraph examinations to discover that Ferrand had a criminal record including theft, felony theft of stolen merchandise, carrying a concealed weapon, and other crimes. [Jackson v Ferrand, 1994 La App LEXIS 3579 (Dec 28, 1994)]

While noting that the federal Employee Polygraph Protection Act of 1988 (see Qs 1:24, 3:40–3:62) made the use of a lie detector a questionable practice, the court observed that, "[T]he employer might engage in a routine check of police records, or some other reasonable screening method might be employed." [Jackson v Ferrand, 1994 La App LEXIS 3579 at *30]

Q 6:8   Is it better for an employer to subcontract security rather than maintain a security department of its own?

Several key considerations come into play in answering this question. First, the company must decide how it intends to do business in general. Some firms tend to run lean and mean, outsourcing all but their core business functions. For such companies, security is clearly at the periphery and should be subcontracted. For other firms, such as retailers, integration of loss prevention with purchasing, financing, and human resources may dictate an in-house operation. [See Castagnera and Szvetitz, "Survival of the Safest," *Convenience Store Decisions*, Jan 1992, at 24]

Second, companies must balance the tradeoffs between employees and independent contractors (see Q 2:63 for a discussion of the difference between an employee and an independent contractor). If a security guard who is the company's employee is injured on the job by an intruder, the guard's remedy against the company would be limited to benefits provided by workers' compensation insurance (see Qs 8:172–8:186). If the guard is employed by an outside agency, the negligence of the company where that guard is injured may support a cause of action against that contracting company.

On the other hand, if the guard engages in misconduct with regard to visitors to the company, such as a false arrest, his liability may be covered by the subcontractor who provided him, either through insurance or an indemnification clause in the contract. Additionally, guards who don't work out must be terminated by the agency at the contracting company's request; thus, the subcontractor usually has to take the heat for claims of wrongful or discriminatory discharge.

Third is the issue of control. A corporation that does not want to be deemed an employer or joint employer of the security guards or loss control specialists for which it has contracted will want to avoid exercising a right of control over them. Yet, under some circumstances such aloofness from the security professionals' day-to-day conduct may be impossible as a practical matter. There is no easy answer, but such issues must be carefully considered in deciding how to set up a security and loss prevention activity at any business site.

Q 6:9 Can an employer insure against the potential wrongdoing of its subcontracted security force?

While an employer who elects to subcontract security functions will want to seek indemnification from the subcontractor (probably accompanied by proof of the subcontractor's adequate liability policies naming the employer as an added insured party), a professional negligence policy can include subcontractors, and for a large firm employing a much smaller security company may be advisable, given that the employer-corporation will be perceived as the deep pocket. However, most liability policies do not automatically cover subcontractor behavior, and some policies actually expressly exclude such coverage. Consequently, it is critical to explicitly demand such coverage if it is desired. [See Hanover Insurance Co v American Engineering Co, 33 F 3d 727, 1994 US App LEXIS 25422 (6th Cir 1994)]

Q 6:10 How does an employer deal with a dishonest employee after detection?

In addition to the rights of unionized employees to have a union representative present at any interview or proceeding when faced with disciplinary investigations, known as Weingarten Rights, other laws may give rise to employee rights, even though the employee is guilty of theft or other dishonest acts. If the dishonesty is a consequence of a mental disorder the Americans with Disabilities Act (ADA) (see Qs 6:7, 4:79–4:96) and analogous disability discrimination laws in some states may afford such an errant employee the right to a reasonable accommodation of the disease or disorder. While the ADA expressly does not provide any protection to current abusers of illegal drugs and controlled substances, the antidiscrimination act of a particular state in which a company does business may view drug addiction differently; therefore, the laws of all jurisdictions where the company does business must be kept in mind when confronting the drug abuse problem on a company-wide basis.

Care must also be taken not to defame the suspect. Even a guilty employee may sue the company, if the investigation brands him or her a thief in the public eye. For instance, in the example of the long-time employee of the department store chain presented in Q 6:1, despite the videotape of her illegal behavior and a subsequent confession obtained at the close of her shift, the company chose to show leniency on the basis of her 20 years of service. It did not prosecute (see Q 6:11), nor did it oppose her unemployment insurance claim, although she was clearly guilty of intentional misconduct (see Q 8:190). This leniency emboldened the ex-employee, who sued for wrongful discharge, defamation, and intentional infliction of emotional distress. She eventually withdrew the action short of trial, but she cost the company thousands of dollars in legal fees and much anxiety about the efficacy of its security program in the meantime.

While prosecution is the recommended response to employee theft in most instances (see Q 6:11), employers are cautioned against misusing the threat of prosecution to obtain some concession, such as restitution from the culprit. Many states consider it a crime to use the threat of prosecution for private ends. It may be better to initiate an arrest or criminal complaint, then consider any offer from the employee or his or her legal counsel to drop the charge in return for a restitution agreement.

Beware of false imprisonment and related tortious conduct. False imprisonment can be claimed by an employee who is forced, by physical contact or threats, to remain in the security office or elsewhere on the employer's premises against his or her will. While reasonable force can be used to detain a suspect while awaiting the arrival of the police, detaining the employee for questioning, especially if for a long period of harsh interrogation, will support a legal action later on against the company and its security forces who engage in such behavior. [See, e.g., Lansburgh's Inc v Ruffin, 373 A 2d 561 (DC App 1977)] This tort goes hand in glove with intentional infliction of emotional distress, defamation, and wrongful discharge.

Public employers must pay particular attention to their employees' constitutional rights against unwarranted searches and seizures, self-incrimination, and the like (see Qs 10:27–10:31). As a "state actor" a public employer, when engaged in the investigation of a theft or other dishonest employee behavior, will be viewed by the courts as more closely analogous to the police and thus held to tougher standards of behavior than private employers in such circumstances.

In sum, dealing with a dishonest employee demands discretion, sophistication, and subtlety. Heavy-handed or ill-conceived conduct can result in lawsuits that can be far more expensive than the loss occasioned by the theft. Nevertheless, the company that chooses to ignore theft may find itself being slowly nibbled to death by dishonest employee behavior. Consequently, following detection, the dishonest employee must be dealt with appropriately.

Q 6:11   Should you prosecute any employee-thief?

First, no thief should be detained unless a company's employees, security, or outside security personnel have strong eyewitness evidence of the thief's guilt. If guilt is nearly certain, prosecution should follow; this will tend to discourage a countersuit by the apprehended thief. Failing to prosecute can lead the thief to believe that the company is uncertain of the facts, and to pluck up his or her courage and take a shot at vindication and a financial windfall in civil court. Second, criminal prosecution has the effect of sending a message to the company's other employees that the company is serious about preventing inventory loss.

Q 6:12   How can an employer guard against allegations of defamation when conducting an employee termination for theft or other dishonest behavior?

Experts concur that the following five-point checklist should be followed when firing an employee for theft or dishonesty:

1. Conduct as careful and thorough an investigation as possible, using outside experts if necessary, and be sure of the facts before confronting and removing the guilty worker.

2. When making a record of the investigation and when confronting the culprit, stick closely to the facts and stay away from innuendo and suppositions.

3. Only those managers and co-workers with an absolute need to know should be filled in about the reason for and the details of the termination.

4. Don't try making an example of the employee, except by arrest and prosecution.

5. If an announcement must be made for its deterrent value, be cautious of the wording, have it reviewed by legal counsel, and limit distribution as far as possible without defeating its purpose.

The significance of observing these guidelines is underlined by a case that attained great notoriety in Philadelphia in late 1994 and early 1995. A well-known Philadelphia law firm fired an associate attorney, allegedly for dishonest conduct. Later it transpired that the plaintiff was HIV positive and he claimed in his federal lawsuit against his former employer that he was terminated because the firm was aware of his medical condition. Claiming primarily that the law practice fired him because he was HIV positive, the plaintiff presented the defendant with a wide-ranging complaint containing numerous causes of action, including claims under the ADA, ERISA, the Pennsylvania Human Relations Act, and state tort law involving invasion of privacy, intentional infliction of emotional distress, conspiracy and defamation. [Doe v Kohn Nast & Graf, PC, 862 F Supp 1310, 1994 US Dist LEXIS 11148 (ED Pa 1994)]

Plaintiff John Doe's defamation claim in this case went right to the heart of the law firm's defense against his claim that he had been fired because of his medical condition. According to the federal judge assigned to the case, who denied the law firm's motion for summary judgment, "[S]ome firm employees testified that they heard the plaintiff was fired because confidential documents were found in his office." [Id, at 1994 US Dist LEXIS 11148, **49] The "confidential documents," retorted the plaintiff, were none other than medical records concerning his supposedly confidential HIV condition, which he claimed to have discovered on the desk of the firm's managing partner. Thus, the plaintiff turned the defendant firm's defense around and used it as an additional weapon with which to attack the attorneys' decision to let him go. Furthermore, the federal court refused to dismiss the defamation claim relating to plaintiff's alleged misappropriation of these documents, which apparently went to the heart of his disability discrimination case against his former employer. Rather the court concluded:

> Neither is summary judgment appropriate with respect to plaintiff's allegations that the defendants defamed him by telling others that he left because he had misappropriated confidential documents. In Pennsylvania, the dismissal of an employee for theft can constitute . . . a cause of action for defamation. (citations omitted) In some instances, mere conduct, without verbal communication to the effect that the dismissed employee was a thief, may support a suit for slander. [Id]

And, in fact, this rule of law applies with equal force in the majority of the states and territories of this nation.

Safety

Q 6:13 Does an employer have a duty to maintain a safe workplace?

Yes. The common law and OSHA, as well as a growing number of analogous state statutes, require employers to maintain safe workplaces.

Injuries suffered in the course of employment, whether due to the negligence of a co-worker or even the employee's own negligence, are generally covered by workers' compensation insurance. The workers' compensation laws of virtually all the states limit the employer's liability to the benefits permitted under those laws, thus providing employers with immunity from liability for various torts. But a number of state workers' compensation laws do not provide this immunity when the injury is not the result of an accident, but of some deliberate act of the employer. (Note that for these purposes, a corporation is a legal entity that acts through its human entities, so that a supervisor's illegal act can be treated as the employer's act.) In some jurisdictions, this intentional-tort exception to workers' compensation coverage has been extended to situations in which the company has exposed its employees to a known and virtually certain hazard, such as asbestos. In other states, the courts have thrown out these kinds of suits. [See, e.g., De Maio v Travelers Ins Co, 1992 Conn Super LEXIS 12(1992); Allen v Southwest Salt Co, 718 P 2d 1021 (Ariz 1986); Johns-Manville Products Corp v Superior Court of Contra Costa County, 612 P 2d 498 (Cal 1980)]

Q 6:14   What is criminal endangerment of employees?

The stated purpose of OSHA is to assure safe and healthful working conditions to workers and to preserve the nation's human resources. It is a comprehensive and complex regulatory body of law, designed primarily to prevent injuries in the workplace. OSHA authorizes and encourages the promulgation of safety standards and the issuance of citations, in order to prevent deaths or injuries from occurring.

OSHA has several levels of penalties, depending on the type of violation. Violations are categorized as serious, repeated, willful, criminally willful, and other. Violations designated as "other" are essentially inconsequential. Serious violations bring a $1,000 fine per occurrence. Repeated and willful violations are on a par with one another and can bring up to a $10,000 fine per occurrence. Criminally willful violations involve the death of an employee and can result in prison terms for managers, as well as substantial fines.

In addition to OSHA's penalties, a number of states have entered the arena of workplace safety not only by promulgating their own occupational safety and health acts (which was expressly permitted and even encouraged by Congress in passing OSHA), but also more recently in prosecuting offenders. In recent years, a number of cases have achieved notoriety. Perhaps the most noteworthy was the prosecution of the Pymm Thermometer Company and the Pymm brothers who owned it. [People v Pymm, 76 NY 2d 511, 14 OSHC (BNA) 1833 (1990), *aff'g* 515 NYS 2d 949 (1987)]

The Pymm Thermometer Company kept a warehouse in the factory basement where workers, allegedly unprotected by OSHA-mandated breathing apparatus, were required to work with mercury. Mercury build-up in the human body can cause severe damage to the nervous and reproductive systems. When OSHA inspectors visited the facility, they were never shown the basement room. Only when a permanently disabled former Pymm employee saw the OSHA inspectors outside the facility and advised them of the room's existence did the inspectors discover, inspect, and cite Pymm for OSHA violations. Thereafter, the Brooklyn District Attorney's Office charged Pymm with the crime of recklessly endangering its workers, for which a jury convicted it.

The appellate division of the New York Supreme Court recently held that the criminal conviction of Pymm Thermometer and the Pymm brothers was not preempted by the criminal provisions of OSHA. [546 NYS 2d 871 (App Div 1990)] Consequently, criminal behavior by companies and their managers and owners is subject to prosecution under both OSHA and state criminal statutes. Neither of these criminal provisions is frequently invoked. As the facts in the Pymm case suggest, behavior has to be pretty outrageous before a district attorney will step in. But in worst-case scenarios, a company's managers, by their actions on behalf of the company, can bring the full weight of criminal law down on a firm and its owners.

Q 6:15   Do employers risk liability for negligent hiring?

An employer's concern with crime and safety does not stop with protecting the employer's own property and proprietary information. An employer has duties to protect its employees, business visitors, and anyone with whom its workers come into contact on its behalf. Under some circumstances, an employee's crime can become a company's crime.

The following is an example of an employer's liability for negligent hiring.

Example. The owners of the Commodore Apartments hired a maintenance man who had recently been released from a state mental hospital, where he had been treated for about a month. Shortly after he was hired, the maintenance man sexually assaulted a female tenant. She sued the owners, arguing that they "knew, or should have known, that the employee possessed dangerous, immoral and perverted propensities." The jury awarded the tenant $175,000 against the landlord-owners. [See Heifetz v Philadelphia State Hospital, 482 Pa 386, 393 A 2d 1160 (1978)]

This case illustrates that the law expects an employer to maintain a safe workplace not only for its employees, but also for all who may come on the premises.

An employer's responsibility for its employees' actions does not end at the boundaries of its business property. If an employee commits a crime in the course of employment, while away from the premises, this too could cause the company civil liability. For example, if the driver of a company's delivery truck assaults a loading dock supervisor at a customer's warehouse over whether or not he dropped off the correct order, this fight might be closely enough connected to the driver's course of employment to hold his employer liable for the supervisor's injury.

Q 6:16   Can an employer be held liable for the crime of a third party against an employee?

Typically, employers are required to carry workers' compensation insurance (Qs 8:172–8:186) which, in return for the ease with which injured employees can obtain benefits, provides the employer immunity from suit. For example, if a retail clerk is the victim of a violent robbery and later sues the robber, the employer-retailer cannot be joined as a defendant either by the employee or the thief.

However, a minority of states permit employers to opt out of the workers' compensation scheme and subject themselves to the normal common-law causes of action available to any negligence victim against a business. Texas is a notable example of such a jurisdiction. Due to the rising cost of workers' compensation insurance, an increasing number of companies have taken the option in recent years. Some employers have come to deeply regret this decision.

For example, in Texas, a couple of cases involving convenience store chains rocked the state, when juries granted enormous compensatory and punitive damage awards in particularly egregious situations. In 1992, a Texas jury awarded $4.5 million in compensatory and punitive damages to the family of a clerk whose mutilated and molested body was found in the woods a couple of weeks after she vanished from her night shift in one of a small chain of stores. Arriving around 8 A.M., police on routine patrol found her car in the store parking area, her purse under the counter, and a hamburger burned to a cinder on the grill. The store was unlocked and lit, but there was no sign of the clerk. The abductor was never apprehended but her next of kin brought an action against the chain of stores. Their attorneys successfully argued that had the chain not removed the silent alarm system that had been in place, the clerk would be alive.

[Castagnera and Szvetitz, "Ill Fitting Suits," *Convenience Store Decisions,* May 1992, at 26]

A jury in Beaumont, Texas, gave $30 million in compensatory and punitive damages in 1992 to a convenience store clerk who was raped twice in her store by the same assailant. The jury was apparently impressed by the woman's testimony that prior to the first assault she had asked to be moved to a store in a safer neighborhood and after the first assault she requested increased security. Both requests, as far as the jury was concerned, received inadequate responses from the store's management. The result was a large damage award, subsequently reduced by the trial judge to around $17 million. [Stewart, "Jury Awards $30 Million to Twice-Raped Clerk," *Houston Chronicle,* Apr 13, 1993, at A33]

The Texas Supreme Court made such verdicts doubly frightening for employers by holding, upon review of the first of these cases, that the plaintiff's four security, alarm, and law enforcement witnesses met the minimal standard of providing "some evidence" upon which the jury properly could conclude that the convenience store was negligent in removing its alarm system and that that action was a proximate cause of the abduction, rape, and murder of the clerk on whose behalf the action was brought. [Havner v E-Z Mart Stores Inc, 825 SW 2d 456 (Tex 1992)]

With regard to the second of these two cases, Norman Bates, President of Liability Consultants in Framingham, Massachusetts, commented upon the $30 million verdict, "No one knows why, but Texas juries seem to view being a victim of crime as akin to winning the lottery." [Claudia H Deutsch, "Returning to the Scene of the Crime, to Sue the Owner," *The New York Times,* June 3, 1994, at B8]

Finally, where an employee is viewed by state law to have been borrowed from a subcontractor or other third-party employer, worker compensation may be no shield to unlimited tort liability. Thus, if an employer is using workers provided by a temp agency, security forces from a "rent-a-cop" company (see Q 6:8), or loaned employees from a subcontractor, and such an employee is victimized by a criminal, the employer may find itself an appropriate defendant accused of failing to take all reasonable precautions to prevent the crime from occurring on its premises.

[Jennifer P Heimmel, "The Workers' Compensation Act Is No Bar to Tort Action Against Employer of a Special Employee," *New Jersey Lawyer,* Feb 13, 1995, at 17; see, e.g., Volb v GE Capital Corp, 139 NJ 110, 651 A 2d 1002, 1995 NJ LEXIS 8 (1995)]

Q 6:17 What are some widely recognized robbery prevention techniques that protect employees in business establishments, while also protecting the corporation's assets?

Numerous techniques have been developed over the years by corporations concerned with reduction or possible elimination of robbery as a source of resource loss and endangerment of their employees, including the following:

Discouraging Robberies and Minimizing Losses:

1. Keep the cash on hand—in registers, cash drawers, and the like—to a minimum; $50 during daylight hours and even less if the establishment is open after dark (frequent bank deposits or cash-control safes are the preferred methods of accomplishing this goal);

2. If there is a safe on the business premises, keep it locked at all times, even though this can entail some minor inconvenience and inefficiency;

3. Acknowledge every customer of the business, as well as vendors, as they enter the establishment. Make eye contact. Let the person know that the employee is alert and could identify the visitor to police later on;

4. Keep the establishment well lit after dusk, back rooms and warehouse areas well illuminated at all times, and if it is a retail establishment, keep the front windows and the sales counters unobstructed from outside view, such as by passing police cruisers;

5. In retail establishments, clerks should not stay behind their counters, but should circulate around the store, cleaning and straightening up inventory and appearing active and alert;

6. Employees should be instructed to watch for and report suspicious activities;

7. The company should advertise its security procedures. This can include decals on doors and signs in parking areas notifying visitors that security systems are in place, and public relations efforts to tell the general public through the news media that the company cares about, and invests in, employee safety and security; and

8. Train employees, and retrain them regularly, on security procedures.

Reacting to a Robbery:

1. The employee should cooperate and try to remain calm;

2. The employee should make no sudden moves or unusual hand gestures;

3. Any movements the employee must make should be explained to the robber in a calm voice, e.g., "I'm getting a bag in which to put the money";

4. If there is more than one employee on the premises, but only one is visible at the time, that employee should advise the robber of the presence of another;

5. The employee should activate the alarm, if there is one, only if that can be done safely; usually it is preferable to press the alarm button or dial 911 after the robber has left (if only a pay phone is available, a quarter should be kept taped to the bottom of the phone for this purpose);

6. The employee should try to get a good description of the robber, but without staring;

7. The employee should also try to recall the type, color, and license number of the criminal's vehicle, if the robber used a car;

8. As the car departs from the premises, the employee should note the direction of travel away from the scene; and

9. If the robber showed a weapon, the employee should note, at least in general, the type of weapon.

Procedure After a Robbery:

1. Lock the door of the store, warehouse, or other facility subjected to the robbery;

2. Call the police (even if there is an alarm, if it has not been activated yet, and if a phone is available on the premises, it's preferable to call the police and give some details over the telephone);

3. The employee should call an appropriate company manager, and if unavailable, keep calling until a corporate official is reached;

4. Keep people from disturbing areas where the criminal may have left fingerprints or other clues that may help the police to apprehend the robber;

5. Cooperate fully with the police;

6. Do not disclose the amount of money or what other property was stolen except to the police and company management.

Computer Security

Q 6:18   Is employee computer crime a major problem for businesses?

Like all significant technological advances, the computer has created new opportunities for criminals, vandals, and unethical employees. And this, in turn, has created new challenges for U.S. law. Piracy of computer software, malicious insertion of a computer virus, and theft of trade secrets stored in computer memories are a few of the major problems that characterize the computer revolution.

Employees, customers, and business associates are most often the only people who have sufficient knowledge to use a firm's computer programs effectively, and, in many instances, may have been instrumental in developing the programs. Therefore, these are the individuals likely to be involved in any software theft. By the same token, in companies that buy and use computer programs developed for them by others, if anyone is going to vandalize the company's system or steal its proprietary database, it is likely to be one of its own disgruntled or departing employees.

Therefore, computers raise two sets of security concerns: those that affect only companies that develop and market computer software, and security issues that all users of computer equipment need

to consider. However, many of the issues that trouble software producers are also of interest to employers that are merely users of
computer equipment.

Q 6:19   What is computer vandalism and what impact can it have on the employer?

Computer vandalism can take a variety of forms. At its least sophisticated level, such vandalism may be accomplished by spilling a cup of
coffee over a keyboard. More sophisticated vandals may alter data in data
bases, or program confusing or contradictory commands. At its highest
level, computer vandalism has taken the form of so-called viruses, which
in effect are commands programmed into computer networks that cause
them, typically, to erase some or all of their hard-drive memories at a
given time and date or upon receipt of a particular signal. This may be
the perpetrator's notion of a practical joke, which results in short-term
inconvenience, or it may be sinister sabotage that causes massive, costly,
long-term loss of a company's data. In either case, inserting a virus
requires substantial computer knowledge.

A destructive virus is just one way a malicious or dishonest
employee can wreak havoc. According to an information security
specialist with a Los Angeles firm, "For the most part, we see an
insider who has decided he can use the company computer for more
than what the company intended." Embezzlement is a perfect example: A company had $7 million in gross sales annually. All of its
inventory and shipping records were kept in a computer. A three-em-
ployee staff maintained all the data. The group leader was not even
a full-fledged computer programmer, but he understood what the
computer could do. He told the computer that a certain quantity of
goods was destroyed in transit. The computer showed less inventory
on the shelves. The employee then shipped the "invisible" goods off
to a third party. The shortage did not reappear until the company's
year-end inventory. By that time the loss was between $70,000 and
$90,000. The employee was fired, but the company did not prosecute.

What are the answers to these problems? Experts have devised a
number of approaches. One is off-site storage of backup data, which is
expensive. However, the employer is guarded not only against employee
mischief and computer viruses, but also against flood, fire, and pestilence.
Off-site storage probably will not prevent embezzlement.

Q 6:20   What are some ways to prevent computer crime?

Computer security experts recommend the following steps to prevent computer crime:

1. Formulate a written policy for responsible computer use by employees. Some companies allow personal use; most do not. Employees need to know what they may and may not do on their office computers. The discipline should be spelled out, so that the consequences of computer misuse are clear.

2. Train employees and, as far as possible, provide them with user-friendly programs. Some employee sabotage unquestionably comes from frustration.

3. Institute a "clean desk" policy. Do not allow employees to leave disks and tapes lying around on their desks or elsewhere in the office.

4. Test the system regularly; do not wait until a large loss shows up.

5. Restrict access, distribution, and off-site use of hard copy. If, for instance, hard copies of customer lists are allowed to float freely around the office, an employee who walks out with one in his or her briefcase may later maintain that confidentiality was lacking to support a trade secret argument.

Copyright and Trade Secrets

Q 6:21   What are copyright and trade-secret laws?

Copyright and trade-secret laws are the two big guns in the software company's security arsenal. These laws derive from two different sources and protect two different things.

Copyright is governed by federal statute. [17 USC §§ 101 et seq] Trade secrets are protected by state law—frequently common law, rather than statutory. [See, e.g. Uniform Trade Secrets Act; for discussions of common-law protection of trade secrets and the difference between a trade secret and common-law copyrights, see Brignoli v Balch Hardy & Scheinman, Inc, 645 F Supp 1201 (SDNY 1986); Warrington Associates, Inc v Real-Time Engineering Systems, Inc, 522 F Supp 367 (ND Ill 1981); Data Mgmt v Greene, 757 P 2d 62 (Alaska 1988)] Because of the tremendous investment involved in developing a software package, whether it is a computer game or a word-processing program, software companies naturally want all the protection they can get from both federal and state sources. The potential difficulty with this is that federal law usually preempts or supersedes state law. Thus, the question is whether a software company can copyright a package and then get the additional protection that might be available under the common law of trade secrets.

At least one aspect of this concern was put to rest by cases decided in the 1980s. In *Warrington Associates, Inc. v. Real-Time Engineering Systems, Inc.*, the court differentiated what federal copyright law protects from what state trade secret law shields from disclosure, noting that an analysis of the interests secured by copyright and trade secret law made it clear that the two claims are not equivalent.

Copyright protection extends to the way an author expresses an idea. In contrast, the protection provided by the common law of trade secret misappropriation extends to the very ideas of the author, subject to the requirement that the ideas have some originality and are as yet undisclosed or disclosed only on the basis of confidentiality. The practical distinction between the two interests, the judge felt, was "manifest."

Q 6:22   What is a work for hire?

Ordinarily, whenever an author expresses an idea, the expression, though not the underlying idea, is automatically and immediately accorded copyright protection. The author can enhance this protection by registering the work with the U.S. Copyright Office. Virtually any sort of written work or computer program can be copyrighted, including sales brochures, employee handbooks, and instruction manuals for a company's products. Obviously, when a company's employees produce these works in the normal course of their employment, neither employer nor employee intends for the copyright protection to descend upon the employee, albeit that employee is without a doubt the author. Similarly, when companies turn to outsourcing, hiring consultants, computer programmers, systems analysts, and other independent contractors to author software works, the intent of the parties is usually that the copyright on the finished product will belong to the company that is paying the contractor to perform the work.

Both of these situations are provided for under the federal copyright act. [See 17 USC § 101] Under the federal law a "work made for hire" is defined as either a work created by an employee within the scope of employment or a work ordered or commissioned under the terms of a written agreement that expressly identifies the project as a work for hire. Whether or not an employee has created a work within the scope of employment is determined within the parameters of the common law definition of that term. The term "course of employment" comes up in many contexts. For example, it has been defined as "(a) requirement that to be eligible for workers' compensation benefits, an employee must have been injured while serving the employer's business." [Cihon and Castagnera, *Labor and Employment Law* 626 (1992)] However, what the employer's business is and when the employee ceases to be serving it are additional concerns. For instance, a computer programmer hacks around at home and develops a software program that would be of value to his or her employer. If it had been developed between 9:00 A.M. and 5:00 P.M., it would clearly constitute work for hire, but if the programmer is paid a salary and sometimes works overtime hours without additional compensation, should the program developed at home belong to the company? Obviously the employee will argue that it was done during free time, and may even assert that the PC belongs to him or her, and that copyright resides with him or her as well. The corporation, therefore, is well advised to deal with such eventualities with express terms contained in an employment contract or a handbook, the terms of which are acknowledged by each employee receiving a copy. [Sample Form 67 in J. Castagnera, *Employment Law Answer Book: Forms & Checklists* (New York: Panel Publishers, 1993) should be reviewed as a basis for such a protective provision]

Q 6:23   What is the statutory definition of a work made for hire?

Section 101 of the federal Copyright Act [17 USC § 101] defines a work made for hire as

> (1) a work prepared by an employee within the scope of his or her employment; or (2) a work especially ordered or commissioned for use as a contribution to a collective work, as part of

a motion picture or other audiovisual work, as a translation, as a supplementary work, as a compilation, as an instructional text, as a test, as answer material for a test, or as an atlas, if the parties expressly agree in a written instrument signed by them that the work shall be considered a work made for hire.

Q 6:24 Are an academic's writings created in a university setting considered to be work made for hire with ownership vesting in the college or university where the work is done?

Section 101 of the Copyright Act [17 USC § 101] must be read in tandem with Section 201(b) [17 USC § 201(b)], which states that with regard to works prepared within the scope of an employee's employment, ". . . the employer or other person for whom the work was prepared is considered the author for purposes of this title, and, unless the parties have expressly agreed otherwise in a written instrument signed by them, owns all the rights comprised in the copyright."

In light of these provisions of the federal act, a professor's scholarly writings may well be works made for hire, the copyrights for which adhere to the university which requires such scholarly efforts as a prerequisite to attaining tenure in today's "publish or perish" academic environment. [See Dreyfuss, "The Creative Employee and the Copyright Act of 1976," 54 *U Chi L Rev* 590 (1987); DuBoff, "An Academic's Copyright: Publish or Perish," 32 *J Copyright Society* 17 (1984); Simon, "Faculty Writings: Are They 'Works Made For Hire' Under the 1976 Copyright Act?," 9 *JC & UL* 485 (198–283)] However, at least one federal court has rejected a university's effort to press such a theoretical claim for a work which actually was prepared by the professor using the plaintiff university's funds. [Weinstein v University of Illinois, 811 F 2d 1091 (7th Cir 1987)]

Indeed, the university and the professor may not be the only parties with reasonable claims to the academic employee's efforts. The faculty member may be preparing a textbook, chapter, or article under contract to a publisher, which contract identifies the work as a work for hire or expressly provides that the copyright for the finished product will reside in the publisher. The academic's rights may include royalties, fees, a combination of the two, and typically the right of first refusal with regard to updates, supplements, and subsequent editions, if any.

Perhaps due in part to *Weinstein,* in part to publishers' prior claims to many academic efforts, and in part to issues of faculty morale and academic freedom, universities have not pressed claims very often thus far. However, rising costs of maintaining and updating college library collections are leading many institutions of higher learning to examine alternatives to purchasing scholarly books and periodicals from publishing companies. Proliferation and maturation of computer networks such as the Internet also provide impetus to identify innovative solutions to rising library costs. "Rising library costs and the increasing reach of computer networks have led administrators at major research universities to consider fundamental changes in scholarly publishing." [DeLoughry, "Remaking Scholarly Publishing," *The Chronicle of Higher Education,* Dec 15, 1993, at A15] Presumably, as universities play a greater hands-on role in scholarly publishing, their claims to copyrights will become stronger and more aggressively asserted.

Q 6:25 Can an independent contractor be treated as an employee with respect to a work made for hire under the auspices of the federal Copyright Act?

In general, U.S. labor law, including our common law, draws a distinction between an employee and an independent contractor (see Qs 2:54–2:62). However, cases interpreting Section 101 of the Copyright Act (see Q 6:23, above) have tended to blur the distinction with regard to works made for hire. In fact, a leading federal case has held that an independent contractor is an employee for purposes of the employer's ownership of the copyright, when the independent contractor's work has been supervised by the commissioning party, i.e., the purported employer. [Aldon Accessories Ltd v Spiegel Inc, 738 F 2d 548 (2d Cir), *cert denied,* 469 US 982 (1984)] This case in effect stretches the so-called "right of control" test of employee versus independent contractor status (see Q 2:64).

Q 6:26 Is Congress planning to change the rules governing works for hire?

Under legislation working its way through the House and Senate early in 1995, copyright protection for work for hire will be extended an additional 20 years, from the current 75 years to a maximum of 95, assuming the legislation is enacted. The change is part of a broader extension of copyright protections aimed at bringing U.S. copyright law into line with rules in effect in the European Community. Songwriters and other individual creative talents will be entitled to receive royalties for their works for the life of the artist plus an extra 70 years for the artist's heirs, which is also a 20-year increase over the time extended to such works under present American law. [Dennis Wharton, "Hatch Gets on 'Right' Bandwagon," *Daily Variety,* Mar 2, 1995, at 7]

Trade Secrets and Confidentiality Agreements

Q 6:27 What is a trade secret?

The term "trade secret" has been given a very broad meaning in U.S. common law. As defined by the case law, and sometimes the statutory law, of most jurisdictions, a trade secret can be almost any piece of proprietary information that is possessed by a company and is useful to it in competing against other firms in the same industry or business. The Uniform Trade Secrets Act, which has been adopted by a number of states, gives this definition:

"Trade Secret" shall mean information including a formula, pattern, compilation, program, device, method, technique or process, that:

(a) derives independent economic value, actual or potential, from not being generally known to, and not being readily ascertainable by proper means, by other persons who can obtain economic value from its disclosure or use; and

(b) is the subject of efforts that are reasonable under the circumstances to maintain its secrecy.

A trade secret does not have to be so unique that it can be patented. On the contrary, trade secrets usually are not patentable, but are sufficiently unique to the possessor that even reverse engineering or other types of careful investigation will not reveal the secret process or procedure to competitors. Some patentable trade secrets, like certain soda pop formulas, were never patented by the holders because they did not want the process or formula to become a part of the public domain when the patent expired.

Q 6:28　Is a customer list a trade secret?

A customer list can constitute a trade secret. In fact, the confidentiality of customer lists when an employee moves from one competing firm to another is at the heart of most trade secret lawsuits. To be a trade secret, a customer list must contain information (e.g., renewal dates of insurance policies, customer requirements, unusual pricing arrangements) that could not be ascertained from public records, such as telephone books or Dun & Bradstreet reports. Also, the possessor of these trade secrets must take reasonable steps to maintain secrecy. For example, computer printouts might be made available to employees on a need-to-know basis, with no access by salespeople, brokers, or the like to customers or clients not actually serviced by those employees.

Q 6:29　How can a company protect its trade secrets?

A company that wants the law's protection of its proprietary information must engage in self-help to protect its trade secrets from misappropriation by departing employees and other third parties. With the proliferation of personal computers, the tendency is to permit every employee to have access to any program or piece of information stored in the system. The wiser course may be to limit some employees' access to certain programs, such as customer lists, or even to bar their access altogether.

Litigation frequently arises in such industries as insurance brokerage firms in which the life-blood of the business is client contacts. Good producers are constantly being wooed by competing brokerage houses and headhunters. Although the competition is bargaining for the producer's talent, needless to say, it also hopes that he or she will bring some business along. Consequently, it makes sense for a brokerage house to restrict each producer's access to only those current accounts and active prospects with which he or she is directly involved.

Similarly, if the trade secret is a formula or process, only a limited number of employees should have access to it. Some companies have even gone so far as to give each employee only a piece of the total puzzle.

High-tech industries, particularly the computer industry, are susceptible to "pirating" of employees. Here, as with any area involving fairly sophisticated research and development, a special challenge is presented because a company sometimes simply does not know everything on which a particular researcher or team is working. When a scientist or team jumps to a competitor (or, more likely in the computer industry, starts its own competing business), and a great idea suddenly springs full blown onto the market, the problem is to prove that the idea was in the works at the previous company and belongs to that company.

Employers should take care to obtain from their employees at the time of job termination all manuals, handbooks, customer lists, and other documents containing proprietary information. And when it becomes clear that an ex-employee has misappropriated and is making use of proprietary information, the employer should be prepared to invest the time and legal fees to vindicate its right to the trade secrets.

Q 6:30 How has the developing case law dealt with employers trying to protect their trade secrets?

In October 1992, the following appeared in a feature story in *The Wall Street Journal:*

> [T]wo men left their dinners, drove six miles to the headquarters of the software company Borland International, Inc., and stepped into one of the strangest and most controversial legal disputes in high technology annals.

> On a large boardroom table were laid copies of 12 computer messages that a Borland executive, Eugene Wang, had sent to Borland's archrival, Symantec Corp., in nearby Cupertino. Earlier that day Mr. Wang had shocked Borland by announcing his decision to defect to Symantec. The Borland executives in the

boardroom that evening believed they had found evidence that
Mr. Wang had conveyed important trade secrets to Symantec.

[Yoder, "High-Tech Firm Cries Trade-Secret Theft, Gets Scant
Sympathy," *The Wall Street Journal,* Oct 8, 1992, at A1]

The article recounts in graphic detail the shenanigans of computer
software specialists who reputedly leapfrog from company to company across California's Silicon Valley. As the story's headline suggests, corporations that cry foul over this game of musical jobs are
viewed by many rivals as interfering with fair, albeit rough-and-
ready, competitive practices. However, according to *The Wall Street
Journal* article: "As software industry executives debate the case,
there are signs that some have begun questioning the prevailing
ethical atmosphere surrounding recruiting practices." (An interesting
aside is that Borland was able to piece together what the departing
Mr. Wang was up to by accessing MCI Communications Corp's MCI
Mail unit for Wang's E-mail. The legality of this tactic is discussed in
detail in Q 5:26; see also, Perritt, "Electronic Workplace and Employment Law," 1993 *Wiley Employment Law Update* (NY: John Wiley &
Sons 1993) at 177; Baumhart, "The Employer's Right to Read Employee E-Mail," 8 *Labor Lawyer* 4, Fall 1992, at 924]

The developing common law of the 1990s indicates that what
courts protect as legitimate trade secrets will depend not only upon
how carefully the company strives to guard against misappropriation,
but also (particularly in cases concerning employees who can't help
being exposed to proprietary information in their day-to-day employment activities) the culpability of the defendant accused of stealing
information. Where the confidential information can be developed
from independent sources, albeit only through an investment of time
and energy, and where the departing employee can't help carrying
some information inside his or her head, a judge is less likely to
prevent the defendant from using that knowledge for his or her own
and/or the new employer's benefit. ["Are Your 'Trade Secrets' Adequately Protected?," 10 *Labor & Employment Law* 1, Mar 1993]

BIEC International Inc. v. Global Steel Services Ltd. [791 F Supp 489
(ED Pa 1992)] is a recent decision that well illustrates these two
central legal considerations of trade secret enforcement. In this case,
a licensor of information and services involving a corrosion-resistant
coating for steel sued several highly placed executives who had

departed to start their own competing business. The plaintiff asked the federal judge to protect two areas of proprietary information: the company's products and services and its customer mailing list.

The district judge found that the knowledge compiled and sold to customers by BIEC included components that were not readily discoverable even by an experienced expert in the industry at large. Thus the court held that the defendants enjoyed an unfair trading advantage by being able to walk off with this information, thereby avoiding the investment of time and money any other would-be competitor would have to put into matching BIEC's product.

The court also issued a preliminary injunction preventing use of the mailing lists. However, the order expressly excluded information contained in the departed employees' personal files, as these consisted of names and addresses of major manufacturers whose identities were widely known and easily discoverable, as well as the defendants' personal contacts, which the Pennsylvania courts refuse to classify as the employer's trade secrets.

In finding, for the most part, for the employer, the court particularly noted the plaintiff's consistent, conscientious efforts to maintain the secrecy of its proprietary information. Of even greater significance is that, as part of the relief granted, the federal judge forbade the defendants from competing with the plaintiff for a period of time, notwithstanding the unenforceable nature of the noncompete provision in their employment contracts (which said the noncompete was effective only if they had been terminated "for cause"). The court reasoned that, if the defendants were allowed to compete at all, inevitable disclosure and use of plaintiff's trade secrets would occur, thus negating the value to the plaintiff of any of the other restraints placed upon the defendants by the court's order (see Qs 6:35–6:41 for an extended discussion of noncompetition agreements).

Q 6:31   What is a confidentiality agreement?

A confidentiality agreement is an employer's attempt to embody in a written, signed document its common-law right (and, sometimes, enhanced rights) to protect and benefit from its trade secrets. Sometimes, this agreement will impose specific obligations on the employee, such as the following:

1. To cooperate in obtaining patents and copyrights;

2. To turn over to the employer all company materials in the employee's possession at the time of job termination, regardless of the circumstances of the termination; and

3. To maintain the secrecy of proprietary information for a stated period of time following termination of employment.

Some companies have tried to deal with problems of pirating by having employees sign confidentiality agreements.

Frequently, a confidentiality agreement will be presented to the employee along with a covenant not to compete. It is not uncommon for an employment contract to contain both of these elements. In fact, this is the most frequent context in which they arise (see chapter 2).

Beyond protecting an employer's trade secrets, a confidentiality agreement may also be directed at protecting the proprietary information of the company's clients. This is an important aspect of any confidentiality agreement, especially if the employer is a medical, legal, or accounting firm. Subcontractors who work for major corporations may be required to swear their employees to secrecy before these employees are allowed to work at the prime contractor's job site. Similarly, government contracting may require special confidentiality provisions, which may go hand-in-hand with security clearances.

Q 6:32　Can a confidentiality agreement "create" trade secret protection?

According to one commentator:

> Computer companies, rebuffed in a spate of recent copyright cases, are discovering there is more than one way to protect their software. Many companies . . . have been able to use contract, trade secret and patent law to compensate for recent decisions denying them as much copyright protection as the companies sought.
>
> [Moses, "When Copyright Law Disappoints, Software Firms Find Alternatives," *The Wall Street Journal*, May 4, 1993, at B6]

Similarly, when some of a company's valued inside information falls short of the common law definition of trade secrets (see Q 6:21), the company may use employment contracts to have new hires acknowledge the proprietary status of that information and agree not to misappropriate it for their own or a future employer's use. If these contracts are supported by adequate consideration, such as a signing bonus, a promotion, discretionary salary increase, or improvement in benefits, a valid contractual restraint upon the employee results. It is a restraint that probably need not be proven reasonable by the employer in order to establish its enforceability, a legal fact distinguishing it from common law requirements for the enforcement of noncompetition agreements (see Q 6:36).

In other words, employers whose legal counsel fear that their proprietary information may fall short of trade secrets status can contract with their employees to accord the information a level of protection not automatically available by operation of the law. This tactic can also save litigation costs if a departing employee violates the agreement because problems of proof at trial are greatly simplified: the company attorney need only prove to the court's satisfaction that the information misappropriated by the defendant-employee fits the description in the contractual provision. The employer need not prove that it meets the test enunciated in the jurisdiction's numerous, and perhaps ambiguous or contradictory, common-law decisions defining trade secrets.

Q 6:33   What legal action can protect trade secrets?

A company whose trade secrets are being misappropriated by an ex-employee or a competitor has the right to go into state (or possibly federal) court and seek a variety of remedies. With respect to lost income (e.g., lost commissions or sales), monetary damages are available to the company. Perhaps of greater significance is the availability of so-called equitable relief, such as an injunction (i.e., court order) that requires the competitor or the ex-employee to do any or all of the following:

- Disgorge to the company its client lists, formulas, or other trade secrets
- Refrain from making use of this information in the future

- Give up the new business that was acquired as a consequence of misappropriations

The larger question is whether a court will enforce a confidentiality agreement (or a covenant not to compete, for that matter). The answer varies markedly from one court to another, and even from one individual judge to another. Most courts recognize the protectability of trade secrets. It is in the area of noncompetition agreements that employers have some difficulty. An important factor in obtaining all of the relief sought is to get into court as soon as the violation is discovered or at least as soon as the violator has been contacted and he or she has given an inappropriate response. An employer that is slow to defend its rights may be held guilty of unreasonable delay in which case it will be denied full remedy by the court.

Q 6:34   Can a company seeking to protect its trade secrets from employee misappropriation resort to criminal prosecution?

The Borland-Symantec case, referenced in Q 6:30, aptly illustrates the efforts of an employer seeking to use the criminal code in tandem with the civil remedies outlined in Q 6:33 to secure complete protection of its valued trade secrets while also striving to deter future miscreant activities by its remaining employees. As this supplement went to press Borland International reportedly continued to press its criminal complaint against its allegedly disloyal former executives. [Jim Nash, "Borland Shakeup Continues," *The Business Journal*, Feb 14, 1994, at 3; Steve Higgins, *Investor's Business Daily*, Apr 5, 1994, at 4]

Although a dearth of reported appellate legal decisions suggests that the criminal law has been little used in the past to prosecute thefts of trade secrets, a number of state criminal codes expressly outlaw trade secret misappropriation, while in other jurisdictions general theft statutes may be readily applicable to such employee dishonesty. By way of example, California—home of the Silicon Valley, from which the Borland case comes—has the following criminal statute in its code:

> Every person is guilty of theft who, with intent to deprive or withhold from the owner thereof the control of a trade secret,

or with an intent to appropriate a trade secret to his or her own use or to the use of another, does any of the following:

(1) Steals, takes, carries away, or uses without authorization a trade secret.

(2) Fraudulently appropriates any article representing a trade secret entrusted to him.

(3) Having unlawfully obtained access to the article, without authority makes or causes to be made a copy of any article representing a trade secret.

(4) Having obtained access to the article through a relationship of trust and confidence, without authority and in breach of the obligations created by such relationship makes or causes to be made, directly from and in the presence of the article, a copy of any article representing a trade secret.

[13 Cal Stats Ann § 499c]

New York's larceny statute singles out "secret scientific material" for protection, defining this as:

[A] sample, culture, microorganism, specimen, record, recording, document, drawing or any other article, material, device or substance which constitutes, represents, evidences, reflects, or records a scientific or technical process, invention or formula or any part or phase thereof, and which is not, and is not intended to be, available to anyone other then the person or persons rightfully in possession thereof or selected persons having access thereto with his or their consent, and when it accords or may accord such rightful possessors an advantage over competitors or other persons who do not have knowledge or the benefit thereof.

[NY Criminal Code § 155.00(6)]

Pennsylvania's theft of trade secrets law has a similarly extensive definition section:

"*Trade secret.*" The whole or any portion or phase of any scientific or technical information, design, process, procedure, formula or improvement which is of value and has been specifically identified by the owner as of a confidential character, and which has not been published or otherwise become a matter of general public knowledge. There shall be a rebuttable presumption that scientific or technical information has not been published or otherwise become a matter of general public knowledge when the owner thereof takes measures to prevent it from becoming available to persons other than those selected by him to have access thereto for limited purposes.

[18 Pa Stats Ann § 3930]

Delaware's statute is typical of those jurisdictions expressly outlawing trade secret theft with regard to how seriously its violation is viewed; having defined property expressly to include trade secrets [11 Del Code § 857(4)], the code states that such "[t]heft is a class A misdemeanor, unless the value of the property received, retained or disposed of is $500 or more, in which case it is a class G felony." [11 Del Code § 841]

In short, clearly the major commercial jurisdictions—such as, California, New York, Pennsylvania, Delaware—have criminal codes capable of accommodating trade secret prosecutions. Equally clear is the capability of high-tech companies to pursue unfaithful employees into not only civil, but also criminal judicial venues.

> Lawyers in high tech are becoming almost as common as entrepreneurs and engineers. . . . Membership in the Computer Law Association . . . has tripled in the last several years. . . . In a survey by the Software Publishing Association, one in four software companies with at least 100 employees said that they had been involved in a legal conflict in the past year." [Steve Higgins, "Executive Update: Litigation," *Investor's Business Daily*, Feb 25, 1994, at 4]

While "the misappropriating party has not normally been exposed to criminal liability for wrongfully taking a trade secret . . . [and] the enactment of state statutes specifically making the misappropriation of trade secrets a crime has been a relatively recent development, prosecutions for the theft of trade secrets . . . have been brought under federal and existing state statutes, as well as under trade secret theft statutes." [Donald M Zupanec, "Criminal Liability for Misappropriation of Trade Secret," 84 ALR 3d 967, 97172; see 18 USC § 2314 (transportation in interstate commerce of goods "stolen, converted or taken by fraud"); see, e.g., People v Serrata, 62 Cal App 3d 9 (1976) (rejecting defendant's plea for reversal of his conviction for theft of trade secrets on the ground of discriminatory enforcement of the statute)]

In light of all of the above, we may anticipate increased prosecution of disloyal employees who misappropriate the proprietary information of their employers in high-tech industries, including the biomedical, computer, pharmaceutical, and entertainment industries.

Noncompetition Agreements

Q 6:35   What is a noncompetition agreement?

A noncompetition agreement is a promise made by one person or company to another person or company not to engage in the same business, usually for a specified period of time in a specified geographic area. Noncompetition agreements (also called covenants not to compete, or "noncompetes") are usually entered by the seller and the buyer of a business or by an employee and a company requiring a covenant.

Unlike confidentiality agreements, noncompetition agreements are not derived from a common-law right such as the inherent right of a company to protect and benefit from its own trade secrets. Because only a few states have passed statutes regulating such covenants, their application and enforceability are generally matters to be determined by state common law.

Although a company can usually expect a sympathetic response to a lawsuit that is aimed at protecting its trade secrets from misappropriation, this may not be true when it comes to enforcement of a noncompetition agreement. Many judges and courts are loath to enforce noncompetition agreements executed by employees because many times they will greatly inhibit an employee's ability to earn a living and care for his or her family.

The general rule is that, although the law does not favor restraints on trade, promises not to compete are not necessarily invalid if they are part of otherwise valid relationships. Such so-called ancillary covenants not to compete will be upheld if they are found to be reasonable. According to Section 188 of *Restatement (Second) of Contracts*, prepared by the American Law Institute, such a covenant may not be reasonable if (1) the restraint is broader than necessary to protect the legitimate interests of the employer, or (2) the employer's need for protection is outweighed by undue hardship to the employee and/or the likely injury to the public. It should be noted that neither reasonableness nor hardship is amenable to a black-and-white test. A court will evaluate them within the broader business, employment, and social contexts. [See, e.g., Auto Club Affiliates v Donahey, 281 So 2d 239 (Fla 2d Dist Ct App 1973) (former employee has a legitimate interest in maintaining a livelihood); Lewmor, Inc v Fleming, 1986 WESTLAW 1244, 12 Del J Corp 292 (Del Ch 1986) (court may take into consideration any harm enforcement of non-competition agreement may cause to general public); Iredell Digestive Disease Clinic v Petrozza, 373 SE 2d 449 (1988) (3-year, 20-mile radius were reasonable restrictions, but were not upheld against defendant because enforcement would have left community with only one gastroenterologist)]

Some countries, such as Mexico, have a strict rule against noncompetition agreements. Similarly, some states have outlawed certain kinds of noncompetition agreements as detrimental to the public good. For example, Delaware recently passed a statute making noncompetition agreements illegal in the health care professions. California, Michigan, Louisiana, North Dakota, and Oklahoma strongly restrict noncompetition clauses. [Cal Bus & Prof Code § 16600 (1987); Mich Comp Laws Ann § 445.774(a) (1989) (the Michigan amendment retains an early statutory prohibition with respect to noncompetition agreements entered into prior to 1985, but permits reasonable noncompetition agreements entered after March 29, 1985); La Rev Stat Ann § 23:921 (1989); ND Cent Code § 9-08-06; Okla Stat title 15, §§ 217-219 (1981)] Because of the different treatment that each jurisdiction gives to them, noncompetition agreements should contain a clause declaring which state's laws will govern the enforcement of the agreement.

A noncompetition agreement that is executed in conjunction with the sale of a business is, from a legal perspective, different from one that is executed in conjunction with employment (see chapter 2). The seller of a business gets a premium price for that business, based on the value of the goodwill. In many cases, if not all, goodwill is nothing more than a customer base. Consequently, any sensible buyer will insist that the sale agreement contain a noncompetition provision. As a general rule, such provisions are fully enforceable.

Q 6:36 What are the requirements for enforceability of noncompetition agreements?

The noncompetition agreement must be reasonably necessary for the protection of the employer. In other words, if an employee operated on a relatively low level in the organization and did not leave with any proprietary information, the court will be reluctant to find that such an employee can provide a competitor with an unfair advantage that justifies preventing that employee from taking any job he or she wants to. Courts have recognized confidential information, trade secrets, and the uniqueness of services rendered by the employee as sufficient to warrant a noncompetition agreement.

The agreement must be reasonable regarding time and geographic limitations. Even if the employer can demonstrate a need for protection because of the unfair advantage an ex-employee can give a competitor, its protection cannot be limitless. With respect to time, the courts have held that a former employer is entitled to only the time necessary to solidify its relationships with customers and clients that were serviced by an ex-employee. [See, e.g., Blair Design & Constr v Kalimon, 366 Pa Super 194 530, A 2d 1357 (1987); Toch v Eric Schuster Corp, 490 SW 2d 618 (Tex Civ App 1972)] As a general proposition, one to two years is considered a reasonable time. Anything beyond that will require greater persuasion by the employer to convince the court that it is necessary. With respect to geography, in this national and, often, worldwide marketplace, courts are still reluctant to prevent a former employee from competing nationwide or worldwide. Generally, a restriction will be considered reasonable if it encompasses the geographical area in which the employer is engaged in business or in which the employee had carried on activities on behalf of the employer. [See, e.g., Allen v Rose Park Pharmacy, 237 P 2d 823 (Utah 1951) (court looked to "the normal shopping habits of the public" in deciding what was a reasonable restriction); Toulmin v Becker, 124 NE 2d 778 (Ohio Ct App 1954) (Ohio and Michigan comprised a reasonable geographic restriction where the parties to the suit were patent attorneys and the plaintiff-employer's clients were heavily concentrated in those two states)] Some companies have been successful in limiting their noncompetition agreements to a list of clients specifically served or prospected by the ex-employee during his or her last year or two with the company, regardless of the customers' or prospects' geographic locations.

Almost all jurisdictions require that a noncompetition agreement be ancillary (i.e., connected) to a larger agreement. This means that the agreement must be entered into in conjunction with the commencement of employment or the according of some new benefit, such as the admission of the employee into the company's preferred stock program.

The more specialized the restricted activity is, the greater the possibility of enforcing the noncompetition agreement. To illustrate, in *Reed, Roberts Assoc. v. Strauman* [40 NY 2d 303, 386 NYS 2d 677, 353 NE 2d 590 (1976)], a company tried to enforce a noncompetition agreement against a former employee who had agreed that at no time for a period of three years from the date his employment was terminated would he engage in any business of the same type. As a key employee in charge of internal administration, the employee was privy to sensitive and confidential information. After 11 years with the employer, the employee left the firm and formed a company (located in the same municipality) that was in direct competition. The New York Court of Appeals affirmed the trial court's finding that the employee's services were not extraordinary or unique and that an injunction against the former employee operating the competing business was not appropriate. The court concluded:

- The former employee's knowledge did not qualify for protection as a trade secret

- There had been no commercial piracy of customer lists

- The services involved were not sufficiently unique or extraordinary to warrant enforcement of the covenant

Strauman illustrates how tough-minded some courts can be about restricting a worker's ability to practice his or her trade or profession. The activity restricted should not be different from or broader than the activity performed for the former employer.

The noncompetition agreement must be supported by consideration. This can be the initial employment of the employee, even if that employment is at will. A growing number of states hold that if employment is at will, the covenant must be entered into at or near the initiation of employment.

Q 6:37   How might a court reform an unreasonable noncompetition agreement?

Previously, if a noncompetition agreement was overly broad, a judge was not only permitted, but was in fact required, to tear it up. Today, most states permit judges to rewrite defective noncompetition agreements with reasonable terms. This is the so-called rule of reasonableness that some state courts have used to rewrite unreasonable agreements to achieve a balance between the employer's and employee's interests.

"Blue penciling" is another approach courts have used. This is the process by which judges sever an offending noncompetition clause from an employment agreement so that the agreement can be enforced. Blue penciling thus allows a judge to convert an unenforceable agreement into an enforceable one. Further support for blue penciling is provided by the standard severability clause generally found in employment (and other) contracts. Blue penciling is not viable, however, when the provision that should be stricken is such an integral part of the agreement that its deletion will change the meaning of the whole document. Alabama, Colorado, Massachusetts, Minnesota, New York, Oregon, Pennsylvania, Tennessee, Texas, and Washington are among the states that permit blue penciling. [See Mason Corp v Kennedy, 244 So 2d 585 (Ala 1971); National Graphics Co v Dilley, 681 P 2d 546 (Colo App 1984); Shipley Co v Clark, 728 F Supp 818 (D Mass 1986); Klick v Crosstown State Bank of Horn Lake, 372 NW 2d 85 (Minn Ct App 1985); Deborah Hope Doelker Inc v Kestly, 87 AD 2d 763, 449 NYS 2d 52 (1st Dept 1982); Lavey v Edwards, 505 P 2d 342 (Ore 1973); Sidco Paper Co v Aaron, 351 A 2d 250 (Pa 1976); Central Adjustment Bureau v Ingram, 678 SW 2d 28 (Tenn 1984); Martin v Linen Systems for Hospitals, 671 SW 2d 706 (Tex Ct App, 1st Dist 1984); Knight, Vale & Gregory v McDaniel, 680 P 2d 448 (Wash 1984)] When drafting noncompetition agreements, the employer should have an attorney check the approach used by the court that will eventually review the employment restriction.

The potential for enforcement difficulties does not mean that a company should not use noncompetition agreements. If a company has customer relationships that require this kind of protection, noncompetition agreements should definitely be used. Many times, the mere existence of such an agreement will chill the enthusiasm of an employee who would otherwise sell his or her knowledge and contacts to the opposition, and once such an agreement has been successfully enforced by a company, other employees are discouraged from violating their noncompetition agreements if and when they leave.

Q 6:38   What should be included in employee noncompetition agreements?

A noncompetition agreement should reflect that it is entered into in connection with or ancillary to employment, the sale of a business, or some other larger agreement. The employment contract's preamble can spell out in detail the circumstances underlying the execution of the agreement. The consideration being given to the employee should be recited and acknowledged in the agreement. The length of time and scope of coverage should be specifically spelled out. Neither the time nor geographic limitations should be unreasonable. The agreement should also provide that the noncompetition covenant is a material condition of the agreement.

It is important to note that the enforceability of these covenants depends heavily on the wording of the provisions. The more sparingly the covenant is used, the more respect it is likely to receive before a judge.

The agreement should also state what remedies are available to the employer. For example, it might provide for liquidated damages in the event that actual damages are difficult or impossible to ascertain; which state's law will apply; and, if desired, which courts will have jurisdiction over any disputes. Unless otherwise stated, the enforceability and the validity of these covenants will be governed by the law of the place where the contract was executed and where it is going to be performed. If the place of execution and the place of performance differ, there is no clear-cut answer, and the intent of the parties (if it can be determined) will determine the jurisdiction. Therefore, if the contract is executed in one jurisdiction but the parties seem to have relied on the law of the place of performance, the latter law will apply; or, if the places of performance are spread across more than one jurisdiction, the law of the place where the contract was made will govern. Moreover, courts have held that the law of the place of performance will control when the law of another jurisdiction has been made applicable by contractual provision, but the restrictive covenant is repugnant to the public policy of the place of performance. In short, an employer that fails to make an informed choice of law and put it in the agreement risks losing its protection due to the vagaries of state law that it never knew were in the picture.

In the case of large businesses, it is a good idea to include in the employment contract an assignability clause, which allows the employer to assign the benefits of the restrictive covenant, as part of the business's goodwill, if the business is merged or sold.

Q 6:39   Which employees should be required to sign noncompetition agreements?

There is no general rule as to which employees should or should not be required to sign noncompetition agreements. At one end of the spectrum, there is probably no reason to ask a janitor or a secretary to execute such an agreement, and it is unlikely that the typical court will enforce it. At the other end of the spectrum, the director of research and development, top sales people, and other high-level employees should almost certainly be subjected to noncompetition agreements. The need for confidentiality or noncompetition agreements should be determined on a case-by-case basis in most companies.

Noncompetition agreements should be required from employees who are likely to have substantial customer contacts that would allow them to build up client relationships and take the customer base with them to a competitor. Frequently, these are employees who have access to trade secrets, such as customer lists, containing special information that would give a competitor an unfair competitive advantage.

The noncompetition agreement should address the issue of solicitation by the ex-employee as well as the possibility of voluntary transfer of the company's customers. Limiting the noncompetition clause to solicitation can leave the employer vulnerable to passive and unspoken solicitation. This unspoken invitation should be contemplated and provided for, especially in situations in which personal relationships with clients are an essential part of the employee's duties and the client-employee relationship has been financially established and fostered at the employer's expense. Therefore, it is advisable to include in the agreement a restriction on rendering services to the employer's customers, whether the client contact at the new employment is induced or is just the result of a voluntary and unsolicited preference. Cases in a number of states have enforced this kind of restriction. [See, e.g., Wood v Clark, 1986 WESTLAW 1160 (Del Ch 1986) (insurance broker prohibited from doing business with clients of his former employer); Eastern Distrib Co v Flynn, 567 P 2d 1371 (Kan 1977) (customer contacts prohibited during the term of the agreement)]

Ironically, sometimes the fact that an employee does not deal with confidential information makes a noncompetition agreement more essential. For instance, if the employee has access to trade secrets, and this proprietary information (such as customer lists) is essential to the employee's ability to compete against the employer on behalf of himself or herself or a competitor, the common law provides a remedy (see Q 6:39).

However, if the only knowledge that the employee takes away is training and experience in the business or profession, this alone does not constitute a protectable trade secret of the former employer. For example, if a company's business is shipping and the employee works as a dispatcher, the fact that he has received training and experience in dispatching trucks does not mean that he has been entrusted with a trade secret. He has merely been given the opportunity to learn a trade, which is something different in the eyes of the law. If the company's customers are readily ascertainable from the local phone book, the employer may not have a customer list that constitutes a trade secret (although the company's rates may constitute proprietary information). In such a situation, if the employer does not want that employee to go to work for a competitor, it may try to enforce a noncompetition agreement supported by appropriate consideration. The employer takes its chances with the courts in this case, but at least it has made the effort to protect its interests.

Q 6:40 What remedies are available for an employee's breach of a noncompetition agreement?

As with the breach of a confidentiality agreement, a former employer can seek monetary damages for lost business, as well as an injunction forbidding the employee from violating the noncompetition agreement for a reasonable period of time. The injunctive remedy is sometimes perceived as a more suitable remedy than damages, since damages can be quite difficult to assess and the employer's injury may be irreparable without the injunction.

Some courts have held that an immediate injunction is appropriate, even without proof of damages, because irreparable injury can be presumed in the form of lost business, the total amount of which is unpredictable. [See, e.g., Whitmyer Bros v Doyle, 274 A 2d 577 (NJ 1971); Standard Register Co v Kerrigan, 119 SE 2d 533 (SC 1961)] Furthermore, if a noncompetition agreement is judicially rewritten to save its enforceability, an injunction may be the only remedy available, since many courts will not award compensatory damages arising from the employee's activity prior to the judicial modification of the covenant.

When an employee is going through a customer list and rapidly stealing business away, a temporary restraining order (TRO) might be obtainable from a judge without having to present witnesses. Usually a TRO is good for five to ten days, pending the holding of a full adversarial hearing with witnesses and legal arguments on both sides. When time is of the essence, a TRO may be the answer.

If damages are the only remedy sought for breach of a noncompetition agreement, the agreement will stand or collapse as written. Damages may be stipulated as a certain percentage of the value of benefits received by the employee or new employer. The agreement itself may also provide for liquidated damages, but such damages present the disadvantage of possibly excluding injunctive relief. The judge may hold that liquidated damages are a stipulation of a specific sum of money that is the only amount that may be recovered in lieu of performance.

The employment contract might include a provision stating that if there is a breach of the noncompetition clause, the employee's severance payments will be forfeited and retained by the employer. Once again, state case and statutory law should be consulted when relying on any forfeiture provisions. Some benefits (e.g., those covered by ERISA) cannot be included in this type of provision.

Although as previously mentioned, noncompetition agreements are not derived from a common-law right, employees are bound by a post-resignation duty of loyalty. If this duty is breached, the action arising from the breach of the noncompetition agreement may also seek remedies in tort deriving from the breach of common-law fiduciary duties.

A lawsuit brought against a former employee to enforce a noncompetition agreement almost always names the individual's new employer as a defendant too. Usually, lawyers for the plaintiff company will accuse the new employer of tortious interference with contract, the contract being the noncompetition agreement between the ex-employee and the plaintiff. The complaint may also allege unfair trade practices or similar wrongful conduct by the new employer. Interestingly, even if a restrictive covenant is found unenforceable against the departing employee, some judges may still impose liability on the new employer. Of course, if the new employer has interfered with a contract that has already been declared unenforceable, the court will not find the new employer liable.

The goal of any such lawsuit is to force the new employer to disgorge all profits that it has realized due to its wrongful competitive advantage (provided by the plaintiff's former employee) and to have the court order constrain not only the employee's activities but also the defendant company's ability to benefit unfairly from hiring that employee away.

However, it may be best not to include the new employer as a co-defendant because of the possible financial hardship that the employee may confront if he or she has to defend himself or herself without any financial aid from a co-defendant. This argument seems to be stronger if the size of the new employer's concern is modest. The more powerful the new employer's concern is, the more probable that the employee will get financial support to pay legal fees, even if the new employer is not joined as a co-defendant.

Q 6:41   What litigation considerations should an employer review before deciding to enforce a noncompetition agreement?

What a plaintiff is theoretically entitled to obtain in court, and what, as a practical matter, it can and will obtain from a particular trial judge can vary widely. On one end of the judicial spectrum are judges who believe that noncompetition agreements are harmful to the public good. These judges will grasp almost any reason to tear up a noncompetition agreement and refuse to enforce it. On the other end of the spectrum, there are judges who believe that a contract is a contract. These judges will fully enforce a noncompetition agreement without any hesitation at all. Most judges will try to do what seems right under the facts and circumstances of the particular case.

Finally, the employer should be aware of counter-claims. Many lawyers and companies today believe that the best defense is a strong offense. They will search for reasons to assert counterclaims, such as a claim for unpaid wages or benefits, accusations of defamation or trade disparagement, tortious interference with the new employment contract between the defendant company and the ex-employee, or some other creative legal theory. Although a defendant is not allowed to file a frivolous counterclaim and there are penalties for doing so, such as the award of the other side's attorney's fees, employers should be aware of this possible response when contemplating court actions to enforce noncompetition or confidentiality agreements.

Q 6:42   Does an employer need to secure all forms of protection, copyright, trademark, trade secret, and noncompetition agreements with all its employees?

The answer to this question depends in part on the nature of the company, its products or services, and the level of employee with whom the employer is concerned. After examining these employer-specific issues, it's vital to understand that each of the four forms of protection is unique and protects different company assets and/or protects them in different ways:

> *Copyright:* As explained in preceding questions, as well as Q 6:21, copyright protects the expression of ideas and is governed by federal statutory law, which permits the registration of the copyright with a federal agency specifically designated for this task.

Trademark: Trademarks are also governed by federal law, although not exclusively, and are registered with the federal trademark and patent office. States are not entirely preempted from playing a role in trademark registration. A company that has developed strong consumer identification for its distinctively designated product will want to protect that identification by registering the trademark. Some of the factors to be considered regarding trademark registration are:

1. A mark must not be generic or purely descriptive (Note: e.g., Employee Benefits Counselors; this doesn't mean a company can't call itself Employee Benefits Counselors, Inc., under state corporate law; to the contrary, some companies do exist with precisely such names, they just can't convert such a designation into a registered trademark);

2. A mark won't pass muster for registration if it is geographically descriptive, such as Santa Fe Tacos;

3. A mark cannot be deceptively descriptive, such as Hawaiian Pineapple Surprise for a product containing no Hawaiian pineapples or Butterbrick as a mark for a product that actually isn't butter at all;

4. Given names won't make it either, so an employer who calls the company Joe's Towing and Autobody probably can't prevent an ex-employee from opening his own Joe's Towing across the street;

5. Surnames, geographic names, and descriptive names can all develop a special "secondary meaning" that raises them to the level of registerable trademarks through heavy investment in advertising and promotion; an obvious example is McDonald's (a group of former McDonald's employees couldn't open a competing McDonald's restaurant across the street from their old employer);

6. Scandalous words and pictures cannot be registered; for instance, a graphic nude photo was recently rejected by the trademark and patent office; and

7. National flags and emblems aren't eligible for copyright registration, nor are names that are confusingly close to existing, well-established trademarks, such as KoKoKola.

Patents: While copyrights protect unique expressions of ideas, and trademarks protect unique labels for products and ideas, patents protect unique ideas themselves. The patent application process can be long and extremely expensive. Only attorneys specially qualified and licensed are allowed to practice before the U.S. Patent Office. Furthermore, the close cooperation of a company's research and development employees is frequently essential to the successful application of a new patent that comes out of the lab. Consequently, an upfront contractual agreement between scientists and other researchers may be essential. [See J. Castagnera, *Employment Law Answer Book: Forms & Checklists*, New York: Panel Publishers (1993) § 6:04] Failure to have such written understandings has caused numerous universities to lose substantial income when faculty members have gotten patents of their own for ideas resulting from university-related functions or facilities.

Trade Secrets: As the name suggests, trade secrets differ significantly from patents, copyrights, and trademarks because of their secrecy. Why would a corporation keep information secret rather than register it and gain the benefits of the particular type of registration (which may include *prima facie* evidence of ownership, punitive damages, and attorney's fees in enforcement litigations)? In some situations, such as client lists, not only does there exist a question of whether the information or the expression of it is sufficiently unique to meet federal registration requirements, but once the information is registered, it is part of the public record and can be accessed even if it isn't precisely copied. In other words, such information is only a valuable asset of the company so long as it remains out of public records and hidden behind closed doors.

Noncompetition Agreements: These agreements (discussed in Qs 6:35–6:41) protect corporate goodwill by giving the employer a reasonable time to substitute a new employee, such as a sales representative, before the outgoing employee can capitalize on this same set of relationships by working for or becoming a competitor. Obviously, such customer relations cannot be copyrighted, trademarked, or patented, but require their own special form of protection. Since customers and customer lists go hand in hand, lawsuits to enforce noncompetition clauses frequently contain trade secret misappropriation claims as well.

A company selling sophisticated products and services may need all the foregoing forms of protection to keep its top-ranked employees from running off with the heart of its business. [See, e.g., Moses, "When Copyright Law Disappoints, Software Firms Find Alternatives," *The Wall Street Journal,* May 4, 1993, at B6; Yoder, "High-Tech Firm Cries Trade-Secret Theft, Gets Scant Sympathy," *The Wall Street Journal,* Oct 8, 1992, at A1] In this tricky area of employment law, legal counsel is necessary for drafting, reviewing, and ultimately enforcing such agreements.

Chapter 7

Job Safety

An employee's right to healthful working conditions is ensured primarily under the Occupational Safety and Health Act and administered by the Occupational Safety and Health Administration (OSHA, or the Administration). As advances are made in science and technology, the Act's reach has extended to limit workers' exposure to new hazards and to require employers to comply with more stringent regulations for a safe work environment. For example, OSHA released blood-borne disease regulations in reaction to the HIV/AIDS epidemic (see Q 7:123). This chapter covers OSHA standards and procedures; right-to-know requirements that govern the manufacture, importing, distribution, and handling of chemicals; cigarette smoking in the workplace; and AIDS in the workplace.

Along with the enactment of OSHA, other social forces have converged to make safety one of today's most significant employment issues. For instance, the U.S. Supreme Court's decision in the *Johnson Controls* case (see Q 7:154), rejected the company's OSHA-derived defense to plaintiffs' accusation of sex discrimination—that the employer had deprived females of desirable jobs based on its fetal protection program. The Americans with Disabilities Act similarly shifts responsibility for the disabled employee's safety from the paternalistic employer to the employee herself (see chapter 4). Such developments make it more difficult than ever before for employers to balance safety concerns and other, potentially conflicting issues.

OSHA

Q 7:1   What law governs job safety?

The primary law governing on-the-job safety is the Occupational Safety and Health Act (the Act), which was passed by Congress in 1970.

Q 7:2   What was Congress's intent in enacting the Act?

During the late 1960s, approximately 14,500 workers were killed each year as a result of occupational or industrial accidents. Many others were exposed to hazardous substances and contracted diseases related to their working conditions. Congress passed the Act to limit workers' exposure to occupational hazards.

Q 7:3   What are the goals of the Act?

The Act has two broad goals: (1) to assure safe and healthful working conditions for working men and women; and (2) to provide a framework for research, education, training, and information in the field of occupational safety and health.

Q 7:4 What does the Act generally require of employers?

The Act requires employers to furnish their workers with a workplace that is free from recognized hazards that cause, or are likely to cause, death or serious injury.

Q 7:5 What is a "recognized hazard" under the Act?

A recognized hazard under the Act is a condition that is known to be dangerous, taking into account the standard of knowledge of that particular industry. The condition does not necessarily have to be hazardous to every employee on the job to meet this definition. Another important point is that it is not necessary that the employer have actual knowledge of the existence of the hazardous condition for that employer to violate the Act. Rather, it is sufficient to show that through the exercise of reasonable diligence the employer could have discovered the hazard.

Q 7:6 What is a worksite analysis?

A worksite analysis is a means of identifying hazards. It consists of regular safety and health inspections, a system through which employees can notify management about potential hazards without fear of reprisal, investigation of accidents and averted accidents, and identification of injury and illness trends with common causes. Employers may conduct worksite safety and health surveys; analyses of facilities, processes, materials, and equipment; and routine job-hazard analyses to identify hazards.

Q 7:7 How can hazards be prevented or controlled?

To prevent or control current or potential hazards identified by the employer, OSHA guidelines recommend establishing procedures using engineering techniques, safe work training, provision of personal protective equipment, and administrative controls. Other than procedural safeguards, the guidelines suggest that employers maintain facilities and equipment, plan and prepare for emergencies, and establish a medical program, including on-site first aid and nearby emergency medical care.

Q 7:8   What should safety and health training encompass?

OSHA guidelines suggest that information employees need will vary, but that each employee should at least be informed about the general hazards and safety rules of the worksite; specific hazards, safety rules, and practices related to particular work assignments; and actions the employee should take in the event of an emergency.

Safety and health training of supervisors should include the information employees need, as well as information about safety and health management responsibilities.

Q 7:9   In addition to the employer's general duty under the Act, does the employer have any specific responsibilities?

Besides the general duty to furnish a workplace free from hazards, the Act requires employers to meet various health and safety standards established for particular industries and situations and also to keep records of injuries, deaths, accidents, illnesses, and special hazards in their workplaces.

Q 7:10   Does OSHA have any regulations involving shutdown of equipment while under repair?

In mid-1988, OSHA issued its long-awaited rules on lockout/tagout procedures to prevent the unexpected energizing, start up, or energy release of equipment that is shut down for repair or maintenance. According to OSHA, in many industries, 10 percent of serious accidents may be prevented by these regulations. Experienced labor, personal injury, and product liability lawyers agree that a frequent source of injuries and lawsuits is absence of fail-safe devices to shut down machinery during unjamming or similar activities. OSHA estimates that 122 fatalities and 60,000 injuries will now be avoided each year.

Q 7:11   What are the major elements of an effective occupational safety and health program?

According to OSHA guidelines, an effective occupational safety and health program has four elements:

1. Management commitment and employee involvement;

2. Worksite analysis;

3. Hazard prevention and control; and

4. Safety and health training.

Q 7:12   What measures can an employer take to ensure management commitment and employee involvement?

To ensure management commitment and employee involvement, OSHA guidelines recommend that employers:

- Articulate a worksite policy on safety and health

- Establish a clear goal for the program and identify objectives to meet the goal

- Make visible the involvement of top management in implementing the program

- Encourage employee involvement in the structure and operation of the program and in decisions that affect employee safety and health

- Divide all program responsibilities among management, supervisors, and employees

- Provide adequate authority and resources to individuals with program responsibilities

- Make individuals with program responsibilities accountable

- Review program operations annually

Q 7:13 Does OSHA provide any voluntary guidelines for employers seeking to improve their employees' working conditions?

Yes. In January 1989, OSHA issued voluntary guidelines that are appropriate for most employers. The guidelines are designed to encourage management practices that will prevent occupational injuries and illnesses. OSHA advises employers to establish comprehensive occupational safety and health programs that provide systematic policies, procedures, and practices. The voluntary guidelines do not apply to employers in the construction industry.

Q 7:14 To whom does the Act apply?

The Act applies to all employees of companies that engage in business affecting interstate commerce. This coverage is extremely broad and reaches almost all employers and employees in the United States and its territories, with very few exceptions. The Act does not apply to federal and state governments in their capacities as employers, to domestic servants, or to the self-employed.

Q 7:15 Are there any exemptions from the Act?

The Act contains no specific, industry-wide exemptions. However, if some other federal agency exercises authority to prescribe or enforce standards or regulations on job safety and health, the Act is preempted by that law. For this exemption to apply, the alternative law must have the safety of workers as one of its intentions, and the agency responsible for that law must have set regulations or standards applying to specific working conditions that might otherwise be covered by the Act. For example, workers on off-shore oil platforms are covered by health and safety regulations enacted and enforced by the U.S. Coast Guard and the U.S. Geological Survey.

Q 7:16 How is the Act administered?

OSHA is the principal agency created to enforce the Act. It is an independent agency within the Department of Labor (DOL), and has the authority to promulgate standards, conduct workplace inspections, issue citations when violations occur, and recommend penalties. Additionally, the National Institute of Occupational Safety and Health (NIOSH) is an agency created by the Act to conduct research and promote the application of that research to ensure that no worker will suffer diminished health, reduced functional capacity, or decreased life expectancy as a result of the work experience. NIOSH provides technical assistance to OSHA through investigations and recommends standards for adoption by that agency. Finally, the Occupational Safety and Health Review Commission (OSHRC) is a quasi-judicial agency created by Congress to adjudicate contested enforcement actions by OSHA. While OSHA may issue citations and recommend penalties, only OSHRC can assess and enforce the penalties. OSHRC has three members who are appointed by the president for overlapping six-year terms, plus a number of administrative law judges (ALJs) who have lifetime tenure. OSHRC decisions can be appealed to appeals courts throughout the United States. Under 29 USC § 660(a), an appeal may be taken to the circuit court of appeals with jurisdiction over the territory in which the violation allegedly occurred or where the employer maintains its principal place of business, or the U.S. Court of Appeals for the District of Columbia Circuit.

Q 7:17   What standards are set by OSHA?

To provide hazard-free workplaces for all workers, the Act requires the secretary of labor, through agency administration, to create and disseminate interim, permanent, and emergency standards.

Q 7:18   What are interim standards under the Act?

During the first two years after the passage of the Act, the secretary of labor had power to issue interim standards. They were generally drawn from or modeled after preexisting industry consensus standards. The secretary of labor was not required to hold public hearings or other formal proceedings in adopting these consensus standards. Many of them remain in effect today, while others have been revoked or modified.

Q 7:19   What are permanent standards under the Act?

Permanent standards can be either newly created or revised interim standards. In either case, they are developed by OSHA and NIOSH and are often based on suggestions made by interested parties such as companies, employees, states and cities, and labor unions. Once OSHA has developed a rule that it has proposed for a permanent standard, the secretary of labor publishes a notice in the Federal Register. This notice will include the reasons for adopting, changing, or revoking the standard. Interested parties are then allowed 30 days to submit written objections, comments, and data relating to the proposed standard. An interested party may also request a public hearing, and the secretary of labor has to publish a time and date for that hearing in the Federal Register. After this process has been completed, the rule (often in modified form) may become a permanent standard.

Q 7:20   What are emergency standards under the Act?

Under special circumstances, the secretary of labor may avoid the procedures described in Q 7:19 and issue temporary emergency standards. This may occur when the secretary believes that employees are exposed to grave dangers from toxic substances. Actual injury does not have to occur before a temporary emergency standard may be promulgated. Emergency standards take effect immediately on publication in the Federal Register. However, after publication, the secretary of labor must follow the procedures for formal adoption to convert an emergency standard to a permanent standard. This must be done within six months after publication of the emergency standard.

Q 7:21   How does a person or company appeal an OSHA standard?

Once a standard has been promulgated (i.e., officially announced) by the secretary of labor, any persons adversely affected by it can file a challenge to the validity of the standard. Such a challenge must be filed with an appropriate federal appeals court before the sixtieth day after the issuance of the standard. The appeals court reviews the standard and will uphold it if substantial evidence supports it. The secretary of labor has the burden of demonstrating that the standard was set in response to a significant risk of material health impairment. The secretary must show that a finding was made before the standard was adopted, indicating that the standard was appropriate or reasonably necessary to protect workers form a significant risk.

Q 7:22 How are the concepts of technological and economic "feasibility" used by OSHA?

OSHA gives the secretary of labor the power to issue standards regarding the amount of toxic material or harmful physical agent that an employer can allow to come in contact with its employees. The standard the secretary chooses must adequately assure, to the extent feasible, that no employee will suffer material impairment of health or functional capacity as a result of exposure to the hazard, even if the employee is regularly exposed. Feasibility must be examined from two perspectives: technological feasibility and economic feasibility.

At least one federal appellate court has held that technological feasibility under the Act is a "technology forcing" concept. [United Steelworkers of America v Marshall, 647 F 2d 1189 (DC Cir), *cert denied,* 453 US 913 (1980)] This means that OSHA may impose a standard that only the most technologically advanced plants in an industry have been able to achieve. Furthermore, OSHA may force an industry to develop and diffuse new technology to satisfy precise permissible exposure limits to toxic materials or harmful physical agents, if the administration can present substantial evidence to show that companies that act vigorously and in good faith can develop that technology.

Economic feasibility means that the cost of meeting a standard set by OSHA bears a reasonable relationship to the standard's benefits, despite the fact that the survival of some companies within an industry may be threatened. The standard does not have to be drafted by the secretary in such a way that it guarantees the continued operation of any individual employer.

Q 7:23 Does the Act require the secretary of labor to engage in cost-benefit analysis with respect to its standards?

No. Although the secretary of labor has the burden of proving both technological and economic feasibility, the DOL is not required to provide a cost-benefit analysis.

Q 7:24 Is it possible for a company to get a variance from an OSHA standard?

If a company, or a class of employers, believes that an OSHA standard is inappropriate to a particular situation, an exemption or variance may be sought. This variance can be either temporary or permanent.

Q 7:25 Under what circumstances will OSHA grant a temporary variance?

A temporary variance may be granted if the company is unable to comply with the standard by its effective date because of unavailability of professional or technological personnel or of materials or equipment necessary to comply with the standard. The company must show that all possible actions have been taken to protect employees and that all remaining actions necessary for compliance are being undertaken. Such a temporary variance can be granted only after the affected employees have been notified of the request and given an opportunity to be heard. A temporary variance can be granted for a one-year period and can be renewed for two subsequent six-month periods.

Q 7:26 Under what circumstances will OSHA grant a permanent variance?

A permanent variance is granted if a company establishes that its procedures provide as safe and healthful a workplace as the OSHA standard would provide. As with an application for a temporary variance, the affected employees must be informed of the request and given a chance to be heard.

Q 7:27 Is there any other kind of variance permitted under the Act?

The secretary of labor has the authority to issue experimental variances that involve new or improved techniques to ensure workers' safety and health.

Enforcement

Q 7:28 Are there any recordkeeping requirements under the Act?

Employers with eight or more employees must keep records of occupational injuries and illnesses and file periodic reports on these to the Administration. Occupational injuries must be recorded if they result in death, loss of consciousness, medical treatment other than minor first aid, one or more lost workdays, the restriction of work or motion, and/or transfer to another job. A covered employer must maintain accurate records of employee exposure to potentially toxic materials. Any employee or representative of the employees can request an OSHA inspection if he or she believes that a violation of an OSHA standard exists and threatens physical harm or imminent danger.

Q 7:29 What rights do employees have under the Act?

Employees have the right to a workplace free from recognized hazards. Additionally, employees are protected from retaliation or discrimination by their employers as a result of exercising any rights that are granted under the Act. Employees have the right to refuse to work under a dangerous condition.

Q 7:30 Must employees comply with certain procedures before they refuse to work under a dangerous condition?

Before an employee can exercise the right to refuse to work under a dangerous condition, the employee must attempt to have the company correct the hazardous condition. Furthermore, the dangerous condition triggering this employee right must be such that a reasonable person, under the same circumstances, would conclude that there is a real danger of death or serious injury.

Workplace Inspections

Q 7:31 Does OSHA provide for workplace inspections?

OSHA standards are enforced by the Administration by means of physical inspections of workplaces. Practical realities of large numbers of workplaces and limited budgetary appropriations have forced the Administration to prioritize the inspection process. The following is a list of types of investigations, in order of priority:

- Claims of imminent danger
- Fatal and catastrophic accidents
- Complaints filed by employees who allege hazardous working conditions
- Inspection of high-hazard industries
- Random general investigations

Q 7:32 Is an OSHA inspector required to present a search warrant before entering a workplace?

No. An OSHA compliance officer conducting an inspection may enter, without delay and at reasonable times, any factory, business establishment, construction site, or workplace that is covered by the Act. This inspection can include all relevant conditions, structures, machines, apparatus, devices, equipment, and materials on the site. The compliance officer has the authority to question in private any employer, owner, operator, agent, or employee.

Q 7:33 If an OSHA inspector appears at a workplace, what rights does the employer have regarding the inspection?

An employer has the right to accompany the inspector during the physical inspection of the worksite. A representative authorized by the employees may also accompany the inspector. At least one federal appellate court has ruled that having an employee representative accompany the OSHA inspector is an absolute right and is not within the discretion of the compliance officer. [Chicago Bridge Co v OSHRC, 535 F 2d 371 (7th Cir 1976)]

Penalties

Q 7:34 What penalties and remedies does the Act provide?

If an inspection leads to the discovery of a violation of an OSHA standard, the company is issued either a written citation describing the nature of the violation or a notice of a *de minimis* violation. A *de minimis* violation is one that has no direct or immediate relationship to the health or safety of the workers in that workplace, and no citation or proposed penalty is included. However, if the citation is for other than a *de minimis* violation, it will contain a time frame in which the company must abate the hazard, and often will include a monetary penalty.

Q 7:35 How is a company notified of a citation under the Act?

If a citation is issued by OSHA following an inspection, the employer must be notified by certified mail within a reasonable time, not later than six months after the violation was identified.

Q 7:36 Can a company contest an OSHA citation?

A company has 15 working days from receipt of an OSHA citation to notify the Administration of its intention to contest either the citation and/or the proposed penalty.

Q 7:37 What happens if a company does not contest an OSHA citation?

If the employer does not contest an OSHA citation, the citation becomes final and is not subject to any other appeal or review in any other court or agency.

Q 7:38 How much time does an OSHA citation allow an employer to abate a hazard?

The citation must provide for a reasonable time to achieve abatement—usually not more than 30 days. The company is required to post the citation (or a copy of it) in a prominent place at or near the area at which the violation exists or occurred. The employees, or their representative, can then file a notice challenging the abatement period set in the citation if they believe it to be too long.

Q 7:39 Must an employer challenge both the citation and the penalty?

Yes, although the company may challenge the penalty and citation separately. However, if the company chooses to contest only the penalty, the violation itself is not subject to later review, even within the context of that penalty challenge.

Q 7:40 What happens if an employer challenges an OSHA citation?

If a company challenges an OSHA citation or the assessed penalty or abatement period in the citation, a hearing will be held in front of an ALJ who will make findings of fact and conclusions of law that either affirm, modify, or vacate the citation. The judge's order becomes final within 30 days after it is filed with OSHA unless, within that time, a member of OSHRC exercises the statutory right to have the decision reviewed by the full Commission. Also, any party to the proceeding can file a petition requesting discretionary review. The final order of the Commission can be appealed to a U.S. appeals court.

Q 7:41 Can an employer defend itself against an OSHA citation by showing that it is impossible to comply with a standard?

A company has an absolute defense to a citation if it can prove that compliance with the standard is impossible. However, that a standard is merely impractical or difficult to meet will not excuse a company from compliance with that standard.

Q 7:42 What happens if a cited employer fails to abate the hazard in the time allowed by the OSHA citation?

If the violation is not corrected in the time allowed by the citation, the company is notified by certified mail of its failure to abate and of the proposed penalty. This notice and proposed penalty are final unless the company files a notice of contest within 15 working days. If the order is not contested, it is deemed final and is not subject to any subsequent judicial review.

Q 7:43 What if an employer has made a good-faith effort to comply with the abatement requirement in the citation?

If an employer has made a good-faith effort to comply with the citation's abatement requirements, but the abatement has not occurred because of factors beyond reasonable control of the employer, a petition for modification should be filed. If the Administration or an employee objects to the extension or modification, a hearing must be held in front of OSHRC.

Q 7:44 What should a company's petition for modification of an abatement requirement state?

The petition must state in detail the steps that have already been taken by the employer to abate the hazard, the additional time necessary to abate, the reasons that additional time is necessary (including unavailability of technical or professional personnel or equipment), and the interim steps that are being taken to protect the employees.

Q 7:45 What happens if an employer fails to correct a citation violation after the citation has become final?

In this situation, a fine of up to $1,000 per day can be imposed on that company. If it is later found that the violation was willful and it caused the death of any employee, a fine of up to $10,000 a day plus six months' imprisonment of the employer may be assessed.

Q 7:46 May an employer whose conduct does not meet OSHA requirements be subject to penalties other than those provided by the Act?

In February 1989 the Illinois Supreme Court—the highest court yet to consider the question—ruled that the Act does not prevent the state from prosecuting an employer under state criminal laws for conduct that was also regulated by OSHA and federal law. The court based its decision in *Illinois v. Chicago Magnet Wire Co.* [534 NE 2d 962 (Ill 1989)] on the fact that OSHA encourages the states to develop their own occupational safety and health plans. The court noted that criminal charges do not impose new responsibilities on employers, but instead impose additional sanctions for improper conduct that "threatens or results in serious physical injury or death to workers." According to the court, state penal sanctions would serve as retribution, as well as a deterrent, keeping employers from violating safety standards. [Chicago Magnet at 966] The Illinois Supreme Court's decision has spurred prosecutors in other states to plan criminal prosecutions of violators of the Act. The Illinois Supreme Court's decision was in agreement with the Department of Justice's position on the issue. However, in April 1991, following an eight-month, nonjury trial, Chicago Magnetic Wire Company and five company executives were acquitted by a Cook County circuit judge. In rendering his verdict, the judge said that the State's Attorney proved only that the company's Elk Grove Village plant was "noisy, dirty, hot and noxious." But the prosecutors, he ruled, had failed to prove that these conditions had made employees sick. This case was the second setback for Illinois prosecutors seeking to establish that workplace safety violations can sustain criminal charges. In January 1991 a state appeals court overturned the convictions of three business executives for the death of an employee, Stefan Golab, from cyanide poisoning at Film Recovery Systems, Inc., a suburban Chicago company. [Illinois v O'Neil, 550 NE 2d 1090 (Ill App Ct 1990)]

Q 7:47 What is the future of workplace safety criminal actions?

In light of the acquittals in *Chicago Magnet Wire* and the overturned convictions in *O'Neil* (see Q 7:46), prosecutors may be discouraged from pursuing many such criminal actions in the future. The Chicago Magnet Wire trial was years in the making and lasted some eight months when it finally occurred in 1991. This suggests that state attorneys and prosecutors in other jurisdictions will see the Cook County experience as a legal experiment in which substantial human and tax resources were expended on a losing cause.

Q 7:48   What is the state's role in the Act's scheme?

The Act requires the Administration to encourage the states to develop and operate their own workplace safety and health programs. If the state decides to do so, its program must be at least as effective as the federal plan. When a state plan is accepted by the Administration, it is monitored shortly after its approval to determine that it is in compliance, and the Administration retains discretionary enforcement authority for three years. The state safety agency must file quarterly and semiannual reports with the Administration. The Administration will determine whether the state program is sufficiently effective to be delegated full authority or whether federal enforcement should be reinstituted in that state. Once the state is fully certified, it is still required to change its standards to conform to any changes made in the federal standards, unless there is some compelling local reason against making the change.

Q 7:49   Have any states instituted their own OSHA-type programs?

The Act expressly permits states to establish their own agencies for enforcement purposes. A few states have done so. However, no trend in picking up this regulatory function is discernible that could be compared to the almost unanimous creation of antidiscrimination agencies across the 50 states, mirroring the federal Equal Employment Opportunity Commission (EEOC).

Hazardous Materials

Q 7:50   What does "right to know" mean?

Both the Administration and many states have taken action to ensure that information about chemical hazards is conveyed to employees who must handle these chemicals. This type of legislation is commonly called right to know. The primary source of right-to-know requirements is the Administration, which enforces them by requiring employers to provide comprehensive hazard communication programs involving the labeling of containers that hold hazardous chemicals, employee training on the handling of such chemicals, and to create and disseminate Material Safety Data Sheets (MSDS) with exhaustive information on the particular chemical.

Q 7:51   Who must comply with OSHA's hazard communication program?

Initially, the Administration issued regulations that applied only to chemical manufacturers and importers and manufacturers that handled hazardous chemicals in their manufacturing processes. This limitation on the coverage of federal right-to-know regulations had two important results. First, many states and cities were lobbied intensively by unions and other interested parties, and in response to that political pressure adopted their own standards to cover the service and construction industries. Second, a federal court of appeals held that, while the state and local regulations were not preempted to the extent that they dealt with areas of the economy not covered by the federal regulations, the Administration should promulgate regulations for these other parts of the economy. [New Jersey Chamber of Commerce v Hughey, 774 F 2d 587 (3d Cir 1985)]

Q 7:52   Has OSHA's hazard communication standard been extended beyond the manufacturing sector?

Late in 1988, the Third Circuit Court of Appeals in Philadelphia, which had earlier ordered OSHA to extend its regulations beyond the manufacturing sector, approved OSHA's expanded standard. In doing so, the court lifted an earlier stay that had prevented OSHA from applying that standard to companies in the construction industry.

Q 7:53   What are a company's obligations under the federal right-to-know regulations?

Obligations can vary drastically depending on whether a company is a chemical manufacturer, importer, or distributor, or is merely a user of hazardous chemicals. The greatest burden under the federal right-to-know regulations is placed on chemical manufacturers, importers, and distributors. Chemical manufacturers and importers must assess the hazards of the chemicals that they sell. A chemical manufacturer is any company with a workplace in some other country in which chemicals are produced with the intention to supply these chemicals to distributors or purchasers inside this country. The distributor's obligation is more limited than that of a manufacturer or importer; it must simply transfer required information to purchasers.

Q 7:54   What obligations do the users of hazardous chemicals have under the federal right-to-know regulations?

Companies that are not chemical manufacturers, importers, or distributors have a more limited obligation under the federal regulations. These employers must ensure that labels on incoming containers of chemicals are not removed or defaced, that MSDS are obtained and are maintained in a readily accessible location in the workplace, and that the company's employees receive the information and training needed for their protection should a spill or leak occur.

Q 7:55   What chemicals are regulated by federal right-to-know regulations?

The Administration's hazard communication rules apply to every chemical known to be present in a workplace, as well as those chemicals that employees may be exposed to either under normal conditions or in a possible emergency. A chemical is considered to be any element, chemical compound, or mixture of elements and/or compounds.

Q 7:56   Has OSHA made any changes in chemical exposure limits during the recent years?

In what some observers describe as the Administration's most significant rulemaking to date, OSHA, in 1989, lowered the permissible exposure limits for about 400 chemicals. The exposure limits were reduced based on recommendations by the American Conference of Governmental Industrial Hygienists and the NIOSH. The recommendations reflect newly available medical and health information.

Many larger manufacturing and chemical companies have reported little impact, because they claim to be complying already with analogous standards of the American Conference of Governmental Industrial Hygienists. In contrast, smaller companies, such as family-owned firms, may be having some trouble meeting the more stringent limits. The new rules cover many of the most common workplace chemicals, including chloroform, carbon monoxide, hydrogen cyanide, and wood dust. The standards became effective March 1, 1989, with a six-month phase-in period. Employers are permitted to comply with the new limits by using a combination of controls, including engineering, workplace practices, and respiratory protection.

Currently, OSHA lacks an automatic review mechanism that would allow the limits to reflect scientific data as they become available. Without such a mechanism, periodic reviews are required. One problem with a system requiring periodic reviews is that, until the reviews are made and revisions implemented, OSHA regulations can contain some standards that are outdated and unsafe.

Q 7:57 Are there chemicals that federal right-to-know regulations do not cover?

The federal right-to-know regulations do not apply to hazardous wastes under the Solid Waste Disposal Act, which is administered under regulations of the Environmental Protection Agency (EPA). The regulations also do not apply to tobacco and tobacco products; wood and wood products; food, drugs, cosmetics, and beverages in retail establishments that are packaged for sale to customers; food, drugs, and cosmetics that are brought into the workplace by employees for their own use and consumption; substances that are really consumer products and are used in the workplace in the same way that they are used in the home; drugs in final form for administration to a patient in a health care facility; and finally, articles that may have been created with hazardous chemicals but that, in final form, are not dangerous (e.g., plastic parts that contain chemicals that in their free form are dangerous).

Q 7:58 How are hazard determinations evaluated under the federal right-to-know regulations?

Chemical manufacturers and importers are responsible for evaluating the chemicals that they produce or bring into the country to determine whether these chemicals are hazardous. The companies that use the chemicals are not required to perform independent evaluations unless they voluntarily choose not to rely on the manufacturer's or importer's assessment. Chemical manufacturers and importers must identify and consider the available scientific evidence. As far as health hazards are concerned, evidence that is statistically significant and based on at least one positive study conducted in accordance with established scientific principles is enough to establish hazardous effect. Additionally, chemical manufacturers and importers must defer to two sources on hazardous chemicals, whether or not they agree with them. The first is a list of toxic and hazardous substances in the Administrations' General Industry Safety and Health Standards. The second source is the American Conference of Governmental Industrial Hygienists' publication, *Threshold Limit Values for Chemical Substances and Physical Agents in the Work Environment.* Finally, the National Toxology Program's annual report on carcinogens, the International Agency for Research on Cancers monographs, and the Toxic and Hazardous Substance Regulations in the Administration's general industry standards identify chemicals as carcinogens (cancer-causing chemicals); manufacturers and importers must then treat such chemicals accordingly.

Q 7:59   Do employees have the right to see the results of studies by chemical manufacturers?

Yes. Employees have the right to see this information, including written descriptions of the way in which the manufacturer conducted the evaluation.

Q 7:60   What is a written hazard communication program?

The Administration requires employers to develop and institute a written hazard communication program in the workplace. This written program must describe the way in which the employer plans to implement right-to-know regulations with respect to labels and other kinds of warnings, MSDS, and employee training. The written program must also include a list of all the hazardous chemicals known to be present in the workplace, with a cross-reference to the relevant MSDS. The program must state how the employer will inform its employees of hazards associated with performing nonroutine tasks, as well as chemicals that are carried in unlabeled pipes in their work areas. This written program must be available on request to employees and their designated representatives, as well as to the Administration and the director of NIOSH.

Q 7:61 How must chemicals be labeled under the right-to-know regulations?

Manufacturers, importers, and distributors of chemicals must make sure that each vessel containing a hazardous chemical is labeled, tagged, or marked with the identity of the hazardous chemical and the name and address of the manufacturer, importer, or other responsible party.

Q 7:62 Are companies other than chemical manufacturers and importers obligated to label hazardous chemicals?

All employers must ensure that containers of hazardous chemicals that come into their workplaces are labeled, tagged, or marked with the identity of chemicals in the container and the appropriate hazard warnings.

Q 7:63 What must be contained on an MSDS?

Each MSDS must be in English and contain the following information:

- The identity of the chemical (which is equivalent to that on the label affixed to the container)
- The chemical and common names of the substance (within the limits of trade-secret law)
- A listing of the ingredients in the chemical if it is a mixture
- An indication of the ingredients that have been identified as carcinogens or that present other specific hazards
- The specific hazards of the ingredients in a chemical mixture

Q 7:64 Is any of the information from completed MSDS, emergency and hazardous chemical inventory forms, or toxic release forms available to the public?

Yes. Information from MSDS is available to the public upon request to the local emergency planning committee. Information from emergency and hazardous chemical inventory forms is available to the public upon written request to the local emergency planning committee or state emergency response commission. Information from toxic chemical release forms is available to the public from the administrator of the EPA, who is responsible for maintaining a national toxic chemical inventory computer database.

Q 7:65 Do the states have a role in right-to-know legislation?

Although OSHA regulations intersect almost all sectors of the economy and preempt to a large extent the states' role in this area, many states and localities have their own right-to-know laws and ordinances. Typically, these provisions require that information on hazardous chemicals be available to local safety forces and health care providers. Since these provisions are directed to a different group of people from those targeted by the OSHA regulations (which target a company's workers), these state laws and ordinances are not preempted by federal law at the present time. An employer must be aware of the existence of such laws in the state or community in which the business operates.

Emergency Planning and Right to Know Act

Q 7:66 What is the purpose of the Emergency Planning and Community Right to Know Act?

The Emergency Planning and Community Right to Know Act [42 USC §§ 11001-11050 (1986)] is designed to avert catastrophe if unacceptable levels of hazardous substances are released into the environment. The Act mandates decentralized emergency planning and institutes reporting requirements.

Q 7:67   What emergency planning measures are mandated by the Emergency Planning and Community Right to Know Act?

The Act calls for states to establish state emergency response commissions, emergency planning districts, and local emergency planning committees. The Act requires states to prepare comprehensive emergency response plans and emergency planning notification. Additionally, the Act includes provisions for emergency training and emergency system review.

Q 7:68   How are state emergency response commissions, emergency planning districts, and local emergency planning committees established?

The governor of each state appoints members to a state emergency response commission. Appointees should have technical expertise in the emergency response field, if practicable. The state emergency response commission designates emergency planning districts and appoints members to emergency planning committees.

Q 7:69   What are the responsibilities of the state emergency response commissions?

State emergency response commissions must designate emergency planning districts, appoint local emergency planning committees, supervise and coordinate the activities of the local emergency planning committees, establish procedures for receiving and processing public requests for information, and designate an information coordinator.

Q 7:70   Who must be included in local emergency planning committees?

Local emergency planning committees must include representatives from the fields of law enforcement, civil defense, fire-fighting, first aid, and health; local environmental, hospital, and transportation personnel; members of the broadcast and print media and community groups; representatives of state and local officials;

and owners and operators of facilities that use extremely hazardous substances.

Q 7:71   How many local emergency planning committees must be established?

One local emergency planning committee must be established for each emergency planning district.

Q 7:72   What are the responsibilities of the local emergency planning committees?

Local emergency planning committees must prepare comprehensive emergency response plans, review the plans annually or as required by changed circumstances, establish procedures for receiving and processing public requests for information, and designate an information coordinator.

Q 7:73   What emergency planning notification is required by the Emergency Planning and Community Right to Know Act?

The Act requires owners or operators of facilities that have extremely hazardous substances in excess of the established threshold to notify the facility's state emergency response commission that the facility is subject to the requirements of the Act.

Q 7:74   What provisions must be included in emergency response plans?

Emergency response plans must include provisions that identify facilities subject to the requirements of the Act within the emergency planning district, routes used for the transportation of extremely hazardous substances, and at-risk facilities near facilities subject to the requirements of the Act. Plans must also include:

- Response procedures to be followed in the event of a release of extremely hazardous substances

- Provisions for designating community and facility emergency coordinators

- Notification procedures that coordinators must follow to inform a designated individual and the public that a release has occurred

- Methods for determining that a release has occurred and those who will be affected by it

- Descriptions of emergency equipment subject to the requirements of the Act

- Methods for identifying those responsible for the equipment and facilities, evacuation plans, training programs, and methods and schedules for exercising the plan

Emergency response plans must be made available to the public.

Q 7:75   When must emergency notification be provided?

Emergency notification must be provided immediately after the release of an extremely hazardous substance occurs. Facilities that use, produce, or store a hazardous chemical must provide emergency notification when:

1. The Comprehensive Environmental Response, Cooperation, and Liability Act of 1980 (CERCLA) [42 USC §§ 9601-9675 (1986)] requires notification of the national response center;

2. The release is not permitted by CERCLA; or

3. The administrator of the EPA determines that notification is required. Notification must also be provided when designated amounts of substances not requiring CERCLA notice are released.

Q 7:76   Are there any exceptions to the notification requirement?

Yes. Notification is not required when a release results in exposure only to people within the facility's site.

Q 7:77   What is a "release" within the meaning of the Emergency Planning and Community Right to Know Act?

A release occurs when any hazardous chemical, extremely hazardous substance, or toxic chemical is spilled, pumped, poured, emitted, emptied, discharged, injected, leached, dumped, or disposed or leaks or escapes into the environment. Disposal of materials that have first been enclosed in containers is included in the definition.

Q 7:78   To whom must emergency notification be provided?

Emergency notification must be provided to the community emergency coordinator for the local emergency planning committee of any area likely to be affected by the release and to the state emergency planning commission of any state likely to be affected by the release.

Q 7:79   What information must emergency notification provide?

Emergency notification must provide information about the nature of the release and the released substance; health risks, medical advice, and precautionary measures relevant to the release; and the name and telephone number of a person to contact for additional information.

Q 7:80   What reporting requirements are imposed on owners or operators of facilities subject to the requirements of the Emergency Planning and Community Right to Know Act?

The owners or operators of facilities subject to the requirements of the Emergency Planning and Community Right to Know Act must provide MSDS and emergency and hazardous chemical inventory forms to the appropriate local planning committee, the state emergency response commission, and the fire departments with jurisdiction over the facilities. Toxic chemical release forms must be provided to the administrator of the EPA and the state official designated by the governor.

MSDS and emergency and hazardous chemical inventory forms provide information about the types, quantities, and location of hazardous chemicals present at the facility. Toxic chemical release forms provide information about the manufacturing, processing, or use of toxic chemicals in excess of the statutorily established threshold amount. Additionally, toxic chemical release forms must provide information about the facility's principal business activities, waste treatment or disposal methods, and the amount of the toxic chemical entering the environment.

Q 7:81 Does the Emergency Planning and Community Right to Know Act require owners or operators of facilities subject to the requirements of the Act to provide any information directly to members of the public?

Yes. Owners or operators of facilities subject to the requirements of the Act are required to provide the specific chemical identity, if known, of any hazardous or toxic chemical or extremely hazardous substance to any health professional who requests such information in writing, provides a written statement of need (for diagnostic or treatment purposes), and provides a written confidentiality agreement.

Q 7:82 How may the owner or operator of a facility subject to the requirements of the Act comply with the mandated reporting requirements without disclosing trade secrets?

The specific chemical identity of a hazardous or toxic chemical or an extremely hazardous substance may be withheld if it is established to be a trade secret. In place of the withheld specific chemical identity, the owner or operator must provide the generic class or category of the hazardous or toxic chemical or extremely hazardous substance.

Q 7:83 Is OSHA enforcing the Emergency Planning and Community Right to Know Act?

Yes. The Administration is enforcing this Act, and is requiring covered companies to have plans in place in accord with the Act until the implementing regulations are promulgated. Where OSHA inspectors find employers lacking in this regard, the Administration is not only requiring future compliance but is also issuing citations and leveling fines.

Smoking in the Workplace

Q 7:84   Is smoking in the workplace regulated by law?

In recent years an increasing number of states and municipalities have passed laws and ordinances governing at least some aspects of workplace smoking. These laws may be divided into several categories:

- Laws that are primarily intended to protect customers, clients, and patients, such as those mandating nonsmoking areas in restaurants, which have become quite common in this country; obviously, these acts and ordinances affect where employees, as well as customers, of eating establishments may light up
- Laws limiting or forbidding smoking in publicly owned or operated facilities
- Most common of all, fire codes and safety standards which forbid smoking not for health, but rather for safety (e.g., fire prevention) reasons
- Far less common, but of increasing importance, statutes and ordinances requiring employers to maintain smoke-free areas in their workplaces or to establish smoking lounges to which use of tobacco products must be limited

Q 7:85   Does the common law affect the rights of smokers and nonsmokers?

In a number of state lawsuits, nonsmokers have attempted to vindicate their rights to a smoke-free workplace. Almost all of these lawsuits have been brought by individuals with severe allergies to smoking or significant respiratory problems that were badly aggravated by smoke in their workplaces. The factual circumstances of these cases have varied, as have the courts' responses. While U.S. courts generally agree that workers are entitled to a workplace free from hazards, judicial discord exists concerning whether or not a particularly sensitive individual should be accorded special protection. [See, e.g., Barbosa v Sec'y of Health & Human Services, 923 F 2d 840 (1st Cir 1990); Lyons v Heritage House Restaurants, 432 NE 2d 270 (Ill 1982); Millison v EI DuPont, 545 A 2d 213 (NJ 1988)]

The increasingly confrontational stance of smokers versus non-smokers is aptly illustrated by a new California case in which the city of Los Angeles published an ordinance prohibiting smoking in restaurants. The Los Angeles Hospitality Coalition, self-described as "including restaurants, hotels, motels, tobacco manufacturers, beverage manufacturers, food companies, night clubs and many other concerned citizens," sought to block the ordinance's enforcement. The Coalition hired a firm called American Petition Consultants to circulate a petition for a referendum to repeal the ordinance. Among those entities contributing funds to the effort, according to the court, were Lorillard Tobacco ($16,716), Miller Brewing ($10,000), R.J. Reynolds Tobacco ($76,276), and Kraft General Foods ($10,000). The county clerk rejected the petition based on another county ordinance, which requires circulators of petitions to be county residents. The Coalition sued for a writ, citing the First Amendment free speech and association guarantees, to force the county to put the referendum on the ballot. The trial court granted the writ. The county appealed, joined by such intervenors as Americans for Nonsmokers' Rights. The California appeals court reversed, ruling that the county ordinance requiring petitioners to be resident was not unconstitutional. The writ was rescinded. [Browne v Russell, 28 Cal App 4th 940H; 1994 Cal App LEXIS 937, 94 Cal Daily Op Service 7256 (1994)]

Q 7:86 Can discrimination law be involved in the workplace smoking controversy?

Both smokers and nonsmokers have potentially valid arguments in the area of discrimination law. With respect to smokers, the argument may be that smokers are addicted to tobacco and therefore are entitled to reasonable accommodation as handicapped individuals. With respect to nonsmokers, the discrimination argument would seem to be limited to those individuals who are so seriously affected by tobacco smoke in the air that they can be classified as disabled workers. Again, reasonable accommodation may be required. In fact, in one federal case, it was held that a government employee was entitled to disability income benefits after he quit working due to his intolerance of secondary tobacco smoke in the work area. [Parodi v Merit Systems Protection Board, 690 F 2d 731 (9th Cir 1982)]

Q 7:87   Does OSHA require elimination of smoking in the workplace?

OSHA does not regulate smoking in the workplace, and OSHA has not classified tobacco smoke as a hazardous substance in a workplace context.

Q 7:88   Can an employee who voluntarily leaves the job due to tobacco smoke collect unemployment?

The Pennsylvania Commonwealth Court, in what appears to be the only case of its kind, held in 1981 that an employee who left his job because of the presence of tobacco smoke in the workplace had not "involuntarily" been separated from his employment. [Ruckstuhl v Pa Unemployment Comp Board of Review, 57 Pa Cmwlth 302, 426 A 2d 719 (1981)] Therefore, the court sustained the decision of the Unemployment Compensation Board of Review denying the employee benefits.

Q 7:89   Is there a constitutional right to a smoke-free workplace?

No. The Bill of Rights of the U.S. Constitution applies only to actions taken by federal, state, and local governmental agencies—not the private workplace. Even in the case of public employees, various lawsuits attempted under the First, Ninth, and Fourteenth Amendments have met with negative reactions in the federal courts, which uniformly appear to have held that a public employer's refusal to prohibit smoking in the workplace does not violate any constitutional provisions.

Q 7:90   Can the prohibition of smoking in the workplace violate a collective bargaining agreement with the union?

Two issues are involved: (1) whether banning smoking in the workplace is a mandatory subject for bargaining under a collective bargaining agreement, and (2) whether an employee fired for violating a smoking ban in the workplace can be considered terminated for just cause under the typical labor contracts. It might be possible for a union or an employee to file an unfair labor practice charge if the employer put a smoking ban into effect with respect to the unionized members of the workforce, although the National Labor Relations Board (NLRB) has not ruled on this issue.

Arbitrators who review the termination of employees who violate a smoking ban typically consider whether the rule is reasonably related to the safe and efficient functioning of the workplace; whether the rule has been properly promulgated and the employee was given enough time to become familiar with it; whether it has been made clear that discipline, including discharge, is a consequence of breaking the rule; whether the rule has been applied in an evenhanded manner to all employees; and whether the discipline that was applied by the employer in the particular case was too severe for circumstances.

Q 7:91　Can an employer legally institute a smoking ban?

Yes. Currently, it appears that employers have the legal right to mandate smoke-free workplaces. The number of employers that ban or limit cigarette smoking on the job has increased steadily in recent years.

An increasing number of employees are affected by smoking bans because of the size of some of the organizations that have adopted antismoking policies. Among those on the list are the U.S. Department of Health and Human Services, with 120,000 employees; Bell Telephone of Pennsylvania in Philadelphia, with 20,000 employees; Honeywell, Inc., of Minneapolis, with 19,000 workers; and Johns-Manville of Denver, Colorado, and other cities, with 1,000 workers. In addition, public laws banning smoking have supplemented policies of private businesses and have made it more difficult for cigarette smokers to indulge their habit in public.

Q 7:92　Is the smoke-free-workplace movement causing a backlash?

Yes. Smokers are beginning to react with arguments, ranging from the contention of some that the smoking habit should be classified as a non-job-related disability, to the assertion of some sort of a constitutional right to light up. These arguments have met with little sympathy in U.S. courts.

Conversely, reports released by the EPA in 1991 may have the effect of spurring fresh efforts by concerned employers and non-smoker advocates to eliminate tobacco totally from the workplace. Two recent draft reports from the EPA on environmental tobacco smoke (ETS) have inspired the Administration to begin gathering data of its own on whether indoor tobacco smoke should be regulated as a workplace hazard. Should OSHA ultimately decide to regulate workplace smoking, Executive Director of the Smoking Policy Institute, Bob Rosner, was quoted in the *BNA Daily Labor Report* on January 25, 1991, as seeing three options from which the Administration is likely to choose to abate the hazard: (1) smoke-free workplaces; (2) smoking rooms with "beefed up" ventilation; or (3) separate smoking rooms with no ventilation changes.

Q 7:93   Is it advisable for a company to mandate a smoke-free workplace?

An outright ban on smoking may appear to be the simplest solution, but it raises some problems. For example, if an employer refuses to hire a smoker, the applicant may claim that he or she is being discriminated against on the basis of a disability (i.e., dependence on tobacco). Employers should consult with legal counsel before firing or refusing to hire a smoker.

Negligence in employment lawsuits have been brought by non-smoking employees who assert that an employer has a duty to provide a smoke-free workplace. The success of such claims depends in large part on individual city or county smoking ordinances. Some ordinances, such as the one enacted by New York City, have a $500 maximum penalty per violation. Ordinances of this type are likely to increase the probability of lawsuits by nonsmokers.

Q 7:94   May a company refuse to hire smokers?

Some companies have concluded that, while they will "grandfather" current smoking employees (i.e., permit them to continue smoking in the workplace), the company will not hire new employees unless they agree not to smoke in the workplace. While this approach solves the morale problem of current employees who smoke, it still presents the risk of a discrimination action by an unsuccessful applicant who claims to be addicted to cigarette smoking.

Q 7:95 How can a company accommodate both smokers and nonsmokers?

A variety of policies have been adopted by companies that have decided not to ban smoking in the workplace, but nevertheless intend to respect the rights of nonsmokers. One approach is to restrict smoking to certain areas. Areas involving customer contact are often declared smoke free, as are employee common areas, for example, employee cafeterias, washrooms, corridors, and stairwells. Some companies restrict smoking to the employee's immediate work area and then provide the employee with an air cleaner for the smoker's individual office or work space. Some companies take another approach, allowing nonsmokers to post a sign (uniformly provided by the personnel department) on their office doors or in their work areas banning smoking from that particular work station.

Q 7:96 Are there any new developments regarding smoking in the workplace?

On January 5, 1993, the U.S. Environmental Protection Agency (EPA) issued a report linking the inhalation of passive tobacco smoke by nonsmokers to lung cancer and other ailments. However, the EPA reportedly will leave it to private plaintiffs to vindicate their own rights, using the agency's research to support the causal connection between their health problems and secondary cigarette smoke.

Lawsuits have tended historically to fall into three categories, none of which have been particularly successful:

1. Workers' compensation claims brought by employees claiming occupational diseases resulting from exposure to co-workers' tobacco smoke;

2. Lawsuits directed at tobacco companies by people contending exposure to cigarette smoke in various locations, not necessar-

ily just their workplaces, has caused them to contract lung cancer or some other disease; and

3. Damage suits by customers in restaurants and other business establishments where they claim to have experienced an adverse reaction, such as an asthma attack, due to secondary smoke from employees or other customers.

[See LeDuc, "NJ Smoking Death Suit Dismissed," *Philadelphia Inquirer,* Nov 6, 1992, at A1; see also generally, Jenkins, The Litigators 121 (1989) for a good overview of the usually fruitless efforts by lawyers and plaintiffs to recover against the cigarette industry for diseases allegedly caused by primary or secondary tobacco smoke]

Despite the failure of most such actions to win damages, chiefly due to the difficulty of creating a convincing causal link between lung cancer and secondary or passive tobacco smoke, some large companies have recently joined the ranks of those that have created smoke-free, or nearly smoke-free, work environments (see Qs 7:93–7:95).

Meanwhile, in 1994 OSHA issued an Indoor Air Quality (IAQ) Rule covering "all indoor or enclosed workplaces under OSHA jurisdiction." After the proposed rule was published in the Federal Register, six months of public hearings held around the country ended in mid-March 1995. The record then remained open for further comments until July 3, 1995.

IAQ as it now stands covers three main areas of indoor air pollutants:

Sick Building Syndrome. According to OSHA this is a "not well defined disease with well defined causes . . . [I]t appears to be a reaction, at least in part, due to stimulation of the common chemical sense, to a variety of chemical, physical, or biological stimuli. Its victims display all or some of the patterns of irritation of the mucous membranes and the worst affected individuals have neurological air symptoms as well."

Building Related Illness. This means "specific medical conditions of known etiology which can often be documented by physical signs and laboratory findings," including respiratory allergies, humidifier fever, and Legionnaire's disease.

Environmental Tobacco Smoke. According to one commentator, "This is an extremely controversial area since many workers smoke and the tobacco industry continues to assert ETS does not represent a risk to nonsmoking co-workers." [Stuart J Lieberman, "OSHA's Indoor Air Quality Proposals Could Choke Employers," *New Jersey Lawyer,* Mar 27, 1995, at 14]

Q 7:97   What will OSHA's Indoor Air Quality Rule require, if adopted?

If ultimately adopted (see Q 7:96), IAQ would require employers to:

- Establish a written IAQ compliance program

- Appoint a person to ensure compliance

- Produce a narrative description and schematic of each building's heating and air conditioning system

- Provide information on the normal operation and performance criteria of heating and air conditioning systems, and a written maintenance program which is "preventive in scope"

- Maintain a log of employee complaints and symptoms

- Use general or local exhaust ventilation when housekeeping and maintenance activities involve equipment or materials that "could be reasonably expected to result in a hazardous chemical or particular exposure to employees working in other areas of the building"

- Maintain relative humidity below 60 percent in buildings with mechanical cooling systems

- Monitor carbon dioxide levels

- Maintain a written record of related building inspections and maintenance activities

- Make alterations in response to employee complaints and adverse inspection evaluations.

Q 7:98   What does OSHA's proposed Indoor Air Quality Rule say about tobacco smoke?

If ultimately adopted, the IAQ rule would require employers to establish designated smoking areas in all enclosed workplaces where smoking is permitted. All such designated areas would have to be enclosed and ventilated directly to the outdoors.

Q 7:99   What new laws have been enacted regulating workplace smoking since the last edition of this book?

In New York City, Mayor Rudolph Giuliani signed a tough new ordinance in January 1995. The Smoke Free Air Act, which took effect on April 10, 1995, bans smoking—with some exceptions—in a range of public venues, including many restaurants and retail stores. The new law replaces a less stringent ordinance. It toughens workplace rules in two significant ways: all employers, not just those employing 15 or more workers are covered, and smoke-free work areas become mandatory rather than contingent on whether non-smokers took offense to the secondary tobacco smoke at the jobsite. Furthermore, the Big Apple's new ordinance defines "place of employment" more broadly than its predecessor to include lounges, rest rooms, cafeterias, conference rooms, gyms, copy and fax rooms, and elevators.

A regulation promulgated under the Maryland Occupational Safety and Health Act, aimed at controlling workplace tobacco smoke, came under a lawsuit aimed at enjoining its enforcement in 1995. COMAR 09.12.23 is aimed at all Maryland employers to eliminate smoking from all enclosed work spaces and to require "No Smoking" signs in all covered work areas. As with OSHA's proposed IAQ rule (see Q 7:97), the Maryland regulation applies to a wide variety of employer facilities, including company cars and trucks commonly occupied by more than one employee. Rejecting a challenge to the new regulation by a group of Maryland employers, the court found that the rule was justified by findings that secondary smoke in the workplace is a health hazard and that the OSHA Commission carefully complied with all procedural rules, according due process to all interested parties through public hearings and the like in 1994, before adopting the measure. Consequently, the prelimi-

nary injunction, granted by the court below, which in effect pre-
vented commission enforcement of the rule, was vacated by the
Maryland Court of Appeals. [Fogle v H & G Restaurant, 1995 Md
LEXIS 24 (Ct App 1995)]

Q 7:100   What are the latest developments in the struggle over rights between smokers and nonsmokers?

While the large cigarette manufacturers have withstood repeated
attacks by attorneys (see Q 7:96), nonsmokers' rights groups, and
health advocacy organizations for decades, events during the past 24
months suggest that the onslaught against the industry is growing in
strength, variety, and determination.

In April 1994 a class action suit was filed in the U.S. District Court
for the Southern District of New York (in Manhattan) by the shareholders of Philip Morris, the world's largest tobacco company. The
action alleges that the company inflated the price of its stock by
misleading investors and regulators about the safety of its cigarettes.
The lawsuit was filed in the wake of a February 28, 1994, report on
ABC's "Day One" news show that Philip Morris and the other big
tobacco companies had deliberately manipulated the levels of nicotine in their cigarettes in order to keep smokers addicted. Philip
Morris has responded with a $10 billion libel suit against the network.
[Maria Mallory, "Is the Smoking Lamp Going Out for Good?" *Business Week,* Apr 11, 1994, at 30]

Two weeks after the ABC broadcast, *The New York Times* ran a
story saying that a 1983 study by the Philip Morris Research Center
allegedly had concluded that nicotine is addictive. The shareholders'
suit claims that Philip Morris stock began to tumble after the ABC
broadcast, plummeting from a high of $58 per share on February 25
to a closing price of $50.625 on March 31.

According to the shareholders' class action complaint: (see Q
15:17) for an explanation of a class action suit):

> Defendants [top officers of Philip Morris are also named as
> parties to the action] engaged in a course of conduct that was
> designed to, and did deceive the investing public concerning
> the current and future profitability of the company's tobacco
> operations.

Defendants' scheme was rooted in their public statements . . . that cigarettes are not addictive, despite the company's own undisclosed evidence to the contrary.

[Gail Appleson, "Stockholder Sues Philip Morris On Nicotine Study," *Chicago Sun-Times,* Apr 6, 1994, at 60]

In California, an advertising campaign against cigarette smoking, publicly financed through a 25-cent-per-pack state tax, began in 1990. Nearly five years later the campaign has been credited with a 27 percent decline in cigarette consumption in the state. That translates into a 1.1 billion-pack decrease in sales during that period. While cigarette smoking overall is declining across the country, this precipitous drop is three times faster than the national average.

With regard to teenagers—whose increasing use of cigarettes is contrary to the downward national trend—the California campaign is credited with stopping the increase in tobacco use by young people. According to Professor Michael Begay of the University of California's Institute for Health Policy Studies in San Francisco, "That in itself should be counted as a victory." [Andrea Adelson, "A Campaign Aimed at Teenagers Is at the Forefront of California's $499 Million Battle Against Smoking," *The New York Times,* Apr 5, 1994, at D21]

In New Orleans, a team of 25 plaintiffs' attorneys, led by Melvin Belli, began a second class action suit aimed at all the major tobacco companies, seeking $5 billion in damages on behalf of all smokers ever addicted to nicotine.

The flamboyant trial attorney told the news media, "We will prove that the tobacco industry has conspired to catch you, hold you, and kill you . . . all without a moment of remorse or self-examination." Like the New York action described above, Belli's suit says that the tobacco giants manipulated nicotine levels in cigarettes to promote addiction. ["Cigarette Makers Sued by All Ever Addicted to Nicotine; Hearing Set for April 13," *Legal Intelligencer,* Apr 4, 1994, at 6]

As this 1996 publication went to press, the federal judge assigned to the case had approved its class action status. "The plaintiffs' class [includes] every American ever allegedly addicted to cigarettes." [Furfaro & Josephson, "New York's Smoke-Free Air Act," *New York Law Journal,* Mar 3, 1995, at 3]

In 1996 the state of Florida filed suit against the tobacco industry, seeking reimbursement of $4.4 billion in Medicaid costs alleged to have been incurred in the treatment of tobacco-related illnesses. [Id]

In New Jersey, the Supreme Court held on March 31, 1994, that the state's municipalities can pass ordinances outlawing cigarette machines in order to protect the health of their minors. The decision upheld an ordinance enacted by the community of East Brunswick, which had been challenged by a group of vending machine companies on the basis of the equal protection and due process clauses of the 14th Amendment. [Rocco Cammarere, "Cigarette Machines Can Be Outlawed," *New Jersey Lawyer,* Apr 4, 1994, at 12]

Although we surely have not heard the last from smokers' rights advocates, the four cases reported above indicate that the tide may be turning in favor of the anti-tobacco forces. A recent survey seems to support this conclusion. A poll released by *Time* magazine and CNN in early April 1994 indicated that most Americans now favor at least some restriction on smoking in public places. The survey showed that some 58 percent of all Americans have smoked at some time in their lives, yet two thirds of those polled wanted smoking confined to designated rooms or areas in eateries and in the workplace. A third of those queried would ban smoking in public places and workplaces entirely. A mere 10 percent were opposed to any restrictions on smokers' rights. ["Poll: Americans Favor Antismoking Rules," *United Press International,* Apr 9, 1994]

However, smokers may have a congressional ally in Senator Nancy Kassebaum, new chair of the Senate Labor and Human Resources Committee in the wake of the GOP election triumph of November 1994. Kassebaum clearly wishes to trim back OSHA's regulatory activities, specifically targeting the agency's Indoor Air Quality Rule (see Q 7:98) as one proposal that may be unduly expensive and intrusive in her view. ["Sen. Kassebaum: A Moderate Reformer Charts New Course for Labor Committee," *1995 BNA Daily Report for Executives* 6, Jan 10, 1995, at 6]

Q 7:101   How is the tobacco industry responding to the onslaught against smoking?

The tobacco industry has never been passive in the face of attack. Lawsuits brought by cancer victims claiming their disease was caused by cigarettes have always been met by vigorous, and usually successful, defenses. [Jenkins, *The Litigators* (NY: Doubleday 1989)] The industry's reaction to the latest assault is no exception. For example, Philip Morris, accused by an ABC program of concealing research results on nicotine addiction, has retorted with a $10 billion libel suit against the network. [Maria Mallory, "Is the Smoking Lamp Going Out for Good?" *Business Week,* Apr 11, 1994, at 30]

As an industry, tobacco generates $45 billion annually in revenue. And while growth may be stymied by anti-smoking efforts in the United States, overseas growth—albeit with weaker profit margins— is proceeding apace. In fact, while many American industries find overseas markets difficult to penetrate, the tobacco business is seeing its exports grow at the rate of 6 percent to 8 percent per year. [Id] For example, as China was once a vast market for English opium, today that country has been called "the most cigarette addicted nation in the world." ["Can China Kick the Habit?" *Nova* (PBS, Apr 12, 1994), as quoted in *Philadelphia Inquirer TV Week*, Apr 10-16, 1994, at 30; see also, Castagnera, "Connecting Up In the American Century," *Philadelphia Lawyer,* Winter 1991, citing Chesneaux et al., *China from the Opium Wars to the 1911 Revolution* (1926)]

With enormous, albeit contracting, revenue, the tobacco industry will continue to fight back. For instance, tobacco company attorneys successfully blocked an effort in a Connecticut federal court test case in March 1994 to force Wendy's, Burger King, and McDonald's to ban smoking on their restaurants' premises. [Mallory, *supra*] However, a similar effort to block a regulation in Maryland in 1995 failed. [Fogle v H & G Restaurant, 1995 Md LEXIS 24 (Ct App 1995)]

Nonetheless the tobacco industry continues to commission and publicize studies disputing the hazards of secondary smoke in work-places and public venues. Thus, for example, in opposition to OSHA's proposed Indoor Air Quality Rule (see Q 7:98) R. J. Reynolds ran full-page ads contending that nonsmokers on average are exposed only to the equivalent of one-and-a-quarter cigarettes per month in their places of employment. [Stuart J Lieberman, "OSHA's Indoor Air Quality Proposals Could Choke Employers," *New Jersey Lawyer,* Mar 27, 1995, at 14]

Q 7:102   What is the federal government's position on smoking in the workplace?

The U.S. government has always been of two minds where tobacco use is concerned. While the Department of Agriculture has provided farm supports and subsidies to tobacco farmers, the surgeon general has issued warnings about cigarettes' danger to smokers' health; these warnings are now required on all packs and advertising. Cigarette ads have been banned for years from television. But the tobacco lobby is still powerful on Capitol Hill.

Thus, while in 1984 Congress amended the Cigarette Labeling and Advertising Act to require manufacturers to list all cigarette ingredients on the packs, the makers successfully argued that disclosure of the list—reportedly containing some 700 ingredients—would mean divulging trade secrets. Consequently, one official at the U.S. Department of Health and Human Services is the sole keeper of the top secret list. ["Cigarettes Can Kill You—Just Look at the Ingredients," *National Public Radio Morning Edition,* Apr 8, 1994]

U.S. Representative Ron Wyden of Oregon stated: "According to these lists, cigarettes contain ingredients so toxic that you could not dump them in a landfill under the federal environmental laws. These lists show that the federal government is allowing toxins to be delivered directly to the bloodstream via the lungs, the most efficient delivery system that nature has ever devised." [Id]

Meanwhile, the U.S. Department of Labor came forward in 1994 with a proposal for a virtual ban on smoking in this country's six million or so private workplaces. [Mallory, *supra*] Numerous companies and office buildings throughout the nation have already gone smoke-free. Rain or shine, snow or sleet, we all witness workers on the sidewalks in front of their workplaces, puffing their precious cigarettes. Many have come to accept the inconvenience with a philosophical shrug of the shoulders.

OSHA's Indoor Air Quality Rule (see Q 7:98) has come under fire, however, from the new chair of the Senate's Labor and Human Resources Committee, Senator Nancy Kassebaum (see Q 7:101).

As with health care in general, the federal government confronts a variety of political, ethical, and business forces that must be considered as it lumbers haphazardly toward a policy consensus on cigarette smoking in the workplace.

AIDS

Q 7:103   Does OSHA have any special rules regarding health care workers who may be exposed to the AIDS virus?

In February 1990, the DOL's Office of Health Compliance Assistance issued extensive "Enforcement Procedures for Occupational Exposure to Hepatitis B Virus (HBV) and Human Immunodeficiency Virus (HIV)." These procedures apply to OSHA workplace inspections and citations for safety violations. These procedures stem from September 1986, when OSHA received a petition from various labor unions that represented health care employees to develop standards that would help protect their members from blood-borne diseases. Such standards are still in the development stage; according to the DOL, "the Agency has concluded that the risk of contracting hepatitis B and AIDS among members of various occupations within the health care system requires an immediate response through a variety of existing mechanisms."

Q 7:104   Is AIDS still a significant workplace safety issue?

To date, neither a cure nor a vaccine has been developed for AIDS. As far as the scientific community knows, contraction of AIDS is ultimately fatal in all instances, although an HIV-infected person may carry the virus in a dormant state for a decade or more before it moves into its more virulent and eventually fatal forms. [See, generally, Greenhill, "AIDS: The Biological Mechanisms," *Trauma* 59, Apr 1991; Langone, *AIDS: The Facts* (1991)] Thus, AIDS remains, quite rightly, a cause of fear among Americans. Unfortunately, many times AIDS is a cause of irrational fear, which can result in workplace problems beyond the legal issues posed for employers by this dreaded disease.

On the legal front, the Americans with Disabilities Act (see Qs 1:5–1:7) unquestionably protects HIV positive applicants and employees from job discrimination (see Qs 4:99–4:110). However, a recent federal appellate court case, interpreting ERISA, gave employers the right to revise their major medical benefits to guard against the enormous health care costs associated with the treatment of the symptoms of AIDS (see Qs 4:109, 8:198). As a result, other federal courts and the Equal Employment Opportunity Commission quickly turned to the ADA as the source of protection for AIDS victims in the workplace, rejecting ERISA as the sole source of guidance on health insurance for the AIDS issue.

Only in the health care industry itself have OSHA and the federal Centers for Disease Control (CDC) taken an active role in promulgating and enforcing rules to protect workers and patients (see Qs 7:109–7:129). However, despite these laudable government efforts, AIDS in the health care industry remains a highly controversial topic, as newspapers and magazines report sensational incidents, such as that of a dentist reportedly infecting his patients and a surgeon insisting upon the right not to make full disclosure of his HIV-positive condition. Such sensational cases, not surprisingly, have produced litigation. [See, Estate of Behringer v Medical Center at Princeton, 249 NJ 597, 592 A 2d 1251 (1991); Daniels, "HIV-Infected Professional, Patient Rights, and the 'Switching Dilemma,'" 267 *JAMA* 1368 (1992)]

For employers in all other industries, an ever-growing body of medical and legal opinion holds that the risks posed by an HIV-positive employee to co-workers and customers is minimal to nonexistent. [See, e.g., CDC, *General Recommendations and Guidelines*, Nov 15, 1985; National Academy of Sciences, *Confronting AIDS: Directions for Public Health, Health Care, and Research 1986* (1988); Langone, *AIDS: The Facts* (1991); Cain v Hyatt, 734 F Supp 671 (ED Pa 1990) (attorney with AIDS posed no threat to co-workers and clients and was protected from employment discrimination under the Pennsylvania Human Relations Act; for further discussion of this case, see Q 4:110)]

Almost without question, any corporation of significant size will, and probably already has, run up against AIDS-infected applicants or employees. Faced with the discrimination and benefits issues discussed above, as well as safety concerns of its employees, all employers must be better educated with respect not only to AIDS, but also other diseases such as hepatitis B.

Q 7:105   What are HIV, ARC, and AIDS?

In a very real sense AIDS is not so much a disease in its own right as the catalyst for a syndrome or combination of opportunistic diseases, which invade and eventually destroy the victim's body, because the body's protective immune system has been destroyed by the AIDS virus. This typically occurs in three distinct stages.

Initially, the victim's body is invaded by the human immunodeficiency virus (HIV). This initial HIV infection can have a long latency period, perhaps as long as a decade. The victim may suffer an initial illness and then appear to recover completely, or may exhibit no early signs of illness at all. While at this stage the individual is not considered to have AIDS, that person will test HIV-positive, is a carrier of the virus, and can transmit it to others (see Q 7:106).

The second stage of AIDS is labeled AIDS-related complex, or ARC. ARC is a somewhat poorly defined, intermediate stage of the fatal cycle, during which some of the characteristics of the final AIDS syndrome are apparent. Generally, however, the illnesses that beset the patient at this stage of the cycle are not life-threatening.

In the final stage of the AIDS cycle, the diseases that attack the victim are of the life-threatening variety, including Karposi's sarcoma, virulent forms of pneumonia, chronic diarrhea, and a dramatically decreased ability to fight off even the mildest infections. This is the stage of the disease characterized by dramatic weight loss and ultimately death.

[See, generally, Greenhill, "AIDS: The Biological Mechanisms," *Trauma,* Apr 1991, at 59; Langone, *AIDS: The Facts* (NY: Little, Brown 1991); Frumkin & Leonard, *Questions & Answers on AIDS,* (NY: Medical Economics Books 1987); Johnston and Hopkins, *The Catastrophe Ahead* (NY: Praeger 1990); Haseltin and Wong-Staal, "The Molecular Biology of the AIDS Virus," *The Science of AIDS,* Piel ed, (NY: WH Freeman & Co 1989)]

Q 7:106   How is HIV transmitted?

There are three recognized methods of transmitting HIV:

- Sexual contact, which includes the transmittal of body fluids (although saliva is not included in the list of transmitting fluids)

- Infected blood, transmitted to the victim such as via blood transfusion, special blood-derived products used by hemophiliacs, or needles shared by intravenous drug users

- By an infected mother to her baby during the perinatal period

HIV cannot be transmitted by:

- Casual contact, such as a handshake or a friendly kiss

- Food prepared by the HIV-infected person

- Saliva or perspiration

- Clothing or other objects worn or handled by the HIV carrier

- The infected person's breath, cough, or sneeze

In fact, HIV is an extremely fragile virus. Even in blood and other bodily fluids that are known to transmit the virus in quantities sufficient to cause infection, brief exposure to the open air will result in the destruction of most of the virus before infection of a new victim can occur.

Q 7:107   Is an HIV-infected employee capable of working?

The nationally publicized saga of Magic Johnson, the professional basketball player who announced he had tested HIV-positive, is the perfect illustration of the fact that a victim of HIV can lead a near-normal life for an indefinite period, potentially a decade or more. Just as Johnson was able to participate in the 1992 Olympics, HIV carriers can perform their jobs without any diminution in the quality or quantity of their output. As the federal Centers for Disease Control and Prevention and other medical experts have found, there is no risk to co-workers or customers of the company (except in the health care industry; see Qs 7:109–7:123). Courts have held that to deny HIV-infected persons employment constitutes illegal disability discrimination. [See, e.g., Cain v Hyatt, 734 F Supp 671 (ED Pa 1990)]

Q 7:108   How is a person tested for HIV infection?

Blood tests that screen for the presence of AIDS (HIV-1) antibodies are available. One common test, the Enzyme-Linked Immunosorbent Assay (ELISA), produces a relatively large number of false-positive results, but is recognized as a good initial screen. However, when a positive result is obtained by using the ELISA, it should be followed up with a more sensitive, confirming test, such as the Western Blot Analysis, to corroborate the presence of the HIV antibodies in the person's bloodstream. Note that these tests detect the presence of antibodies (or HIV seropositivity), meaning that the victim's body has produced a product intended to combat HIV; by implication, the presence of the virus is assumed, although a small body of scientific evidence has arisen recently suggesting the possibility of the AIDS syndrome in the absence of HIV. (Regarding whether and when an employer might be entitled to require that an applicant or employee be tested for HIV, see Q 4:107.)

Q 7:109   Which health care workers are covered by OSHA's AIDS enforcement procedures?

The AIDS enforcement procedures apply to virtually all employees of health care facilities, including physicians, nurses, dentists, dental workers, optometrists, podiatrists, chiropractors, laboratory and blood bank technologists and technicians, research laboratory scientists, phlebotomists, dialysis personnel, paramedics, emergency medical technicians, medical examiners, morticians, housekeepers, laundry workers, and others whose work may involve direct contact with body fluids from living individuals or corpses.

Despite this seemingly sweeping definition, the procedures state, just one page later, that "ward clerks and administrators have virtually no increased risk of contact with body fluids (and) are thus at no greater risk of contracting blood-borne diseases than other members of the general population."

Q 7:110   Can health care professionals transmit AIDS to their patients?

Very rarely, a health care professional can transmit AIDS to a patient. A series of somewhat sensational cases have highlighted this rare, but nonetheless frightening, possibility of transmittal. [See, Karassik and Kayser, "AIDS and the Health Care Provider," *The Health Lawyer* (1992)]

Q 7:111 Are health care institutions required to know if their employees have AIDS?

Neither the CDC nor OSHA mandates AIDS testing (see Qs 7:121–7:123). "On the contrary, mandatory testing of health care workers for HIV antibody is specifically not recommended for reasons relating to cost, delay in seroconversion, privacy and consent." [Krebs-Markrich, "The HIV-Infected Health Care Worker in the Hospital," *1993 Health Law Handbook* (Gosfield, ed) 196] Health care institutions are required to inquire into the health of physicians seeking clinical privileges [see Joint Commission on Accreditation of Healthcare Organizations, Accreditation Manual for Hospitals, 1992, medical staff standard 2.4.1.3], and the CDC does require such workers who perform invasive procedures to know their own HIV status. [See, Centers for Disease Control, "Recommendations for Preventing Transmission of Human Immunodeficiency Virus and Hepatitis B Virus to Patients During Exposure-Prone Invasive Procedures," *Morbidity and Mortality Weekly Report* 40, No RR8 (1991)] Nonetheless, when hospitals become aware of a worker's HIV-positive status in a manner that the employee considers an invasion of privacy (see Q 5:14) or breach of confidentiality, or acts on such knowledge to terminate or restrict the activities of that employee, litigation can result. Some examples are:

> *In re Milton S. Hershey Medical Center* [595 A 2d 1290 (Pa Super Ct 1991)], where a resident physician was accidentally cut by the attending physician during an invasive procedure. He later voluntarily submitted to HIV testing, informed the hospital of the positive result, and took a voluntary leave of absence.

> *In re Westchester County Medical Center* [Docket No 915042, Decision No CR 191, Appeals Board, Department of Health and Human Services (April 20, 1992)] concerned the decision of a major New York hospital to prohibit an HIV-positive pharmacist from preparing medications that were intended to be injected into patients. The pharmacist brought an administrative action under the Rehabilitation Act of 1973 (see Qs 1:5, 4:100), pleading disability discrimination. The administrative law judge ruled

against the hospital's argument that these preparations constituted exposure-prone, invasive procedures, and stated:

> None of Westchester County Medical Center's witnesses
> . . . could do more than speculate as to the theoretical
> chain of events by which [the pharmacist] might commu-
> nicate the virus. None of these witnesses could point to a
> study or studies which verified that [the hospital's] infec-
> tion scenario represented anything more than a theoretical
> possibility. None of these witnesses could identify evi-
> dence that showed that there was a realistic probability
> that [he] would ever contaminate a parenteral product
> with his own blood.

In another case, the estate of a health care worker sued the
former employer, which had learned of the employee's HIV
status while the employee was actually a patient in the hospital,
and which had then breached the employee's privacy right as a
patient. [Estate of Behringer v Medical Center at Princeton, 249
NJ Super 597, 592 A 2d 1251 (1991)]

Q 7:112 Should a health care institution reveal a health care professional's HIV-positive status to its patients who may be served by that professional?

The 1991 Guidelines issued by the CDC recommend that:

> [P]rospective patients of HIV- or HBV (hepatitis B)-infected
> health care workers should be notified of the HIV or HBV status
> of the infected health care worker before undergoing invasive,
> exposure-prone procedures.

This recommendation, which sets the rights of the patient directly
against the privacy rights of the worker, set off a firestorm of debate
when it was announced by the CDC. At least one influential commission soundly rejected the recommendation, stating:

> The Commission believes that a blanket policy of disclosure of
> the health care provider's HIV status to patients would not only
> fail to make the health care workplace safer, it would also have
> a deleterious impact on access to health care. ["Preventing HIV
> Transmission in Health Care Settings," *Report of the National
> Commission on AIDS,* July 1992, at 28]

Federal law requires the states to certify to the secretary of health
and human services that they have adopted the CDC Guidelines or

substantially equivalent guidelines of their own. [42 USC § 300ee(2)(1991)] Some states have adopted the CDC Guidelines almost verbatim. [See, e.g., Iowa SB 2323 (1992)] Other states have elected to go their own way on the issue of patient information. New York is a good example:

> [R]equiring health care workers to inform patients or employers that they are HIV or HBV positive would only serve as a deterrent to workers seeking voluntary testing and medical evaluation. It would also endanger the professional careers of competent and needed health personnel who pose no risk to patients.
>
> [New York State Department of Health, *Policy Statement and Guidelines*, Aug 1992]

With regard to the impact of revelation of HIV-positive status upon the professional's career, the case of *Estate of Behringer v. The Medical Center at Princeton* [249 NJ Super 597, 592 A 2d 1251 (1991)] is telling. In this case, the patient was diagnosed as being HIV-positive when he was an inpatient at the hospital where he was employed. After a brief absence from his practice, Dr. Behringer returned to discover that numerous colleagues and patients had learned of the laboratory test results. As time went on, his practice diminished substantially. Meanwhile the hospital's trustees voted to adopt an "informed consent" form that would be presented to patients before undergoing surgery by an HIV-positive surgeon. As a consequence, no patients agreed to undergo a surgical procedure performed by any such physician, and, therefore, in the words of the New Jersey appellate court, the special consent form became a "*de facto* prohibition" of doctors such as Behringer from the practice of surgery in the defendant hospital. Nevertheless, the court decided to uphold the hospital's decisions to (1) adopt the special "informed consent" form and (2) suspend the plaintiff's surgical privileges. In so holding, the superior court stated that while the requirement the consent form imposed upon the doctor:

> may not be surmountable absent further education of both the public and the medical community about the realities of HIV and AIDS . . . the difficulties created by the public reaction to AIDS cannot deprive the patient of making the ultimate decision where the ultimate risk is so significant. . . . Where the ultimate harm is death, even the presence of a low risk of transmission justifies the adoption of a policy which precludes invasive procedures when there is 'any' risk of transmission. . . . The

ultimate risk to the patient is so absolute, so devastating, that it is untenable to argue against informed consent combined with a restriction on procedures which present 'any risk' to the patient. [Behringer at 1283]

Q 7:113   Are there any precautions involving health care workers on which all governmental agencies and policy-making groups agree?

In the words of one knowledgeable commentator, "Despite the considerable variability in their respective guidelines, the CDC, the commission, published state guidelines, and professional associations appear to speak with one voice concerning the need for universal precautions and enforcement of vigorous infection control procedures in health care institutions." [Krebs-Markrich, "The HIV-Infected Health Care Worker in the Hospital," *1993 Health Law Handbook* (Gosfield, ed) at 294] According to this commentator, these various agencies and commissions agree on at least the following standards:

1. Hospitals and other health care institutions should have appropriate infection control procedures in effect.

2. These institutions should also monitor compliance with these procedures.

3. They should likewise enforce the procedures, including by means of all necessary and appropriate disciplinary action (necessary and appropriate disciplinary action could include restriction or denial of clinical privileges and reporting of violations to the proper state or professional enforcement bodies).

Q 7:114   What types of inspections do OSHA AIDS procedures call for?

The procedures modify OSHA's usual inspection practices in a number of ways. First, all health service providers (Standard Industry Code (SIC) 80) and funeral homes and crematories (SIC 7261) from a list, such as *Dun's Marketing Service*, shall be placed in a pool by each OSHA regional administrator. (Establishments with fewer than 11 employees are excluded.) A list of inspection targets will be randomly drawn from the pool. This list will be narrowed by some additional bureaucratic procedures.

When one of these targeting facilities is visited, the inspector will locate the administrator, medical director, or other person in charge and present his or her appropriate credentials. If the inspector is refused admission, the next step will be to get a search warrant. The inspection will then focus on areas of "primary concern" (e.g., emergency rooms, operating rooms, direct patient care areas, laboratories, and X-ray facilities). "Secondary areas" are laundry and housekeeping facilities.

Q 7:115   What documents will an OSHA inspector want to see during an AIDS inspection?

The OSHA inspector will be particularly interested in the establishment's infection control (IC) program and its injury records. An IC program will normally be a written policy "relating to the control of infectious disease hazards where employees may be exposed to direct contact with body fluids." As to recordkeeping, the new OSHA procedure makes the following observation:

> Needle sticks, like any other puncture wound, are considered injuries for recordkeeping purposes due to the instantaneous nature of the event. Only those work-related injuries that involve loss of consciousness, transfer to another job, restriction of work or motion, or medical treatment are required to be put on the OSHA 200 form. Use of prescription medication (beyond a single dose for minor injury or discomfort) is considered medical treatment. Therefore, any needle stick requiring medical treatment, e.g., gamma globulin, hepatitis B immune globulin, hepatitis B vaccine, etc., shall be recorded. In addition, since this type of treatment is considered absolutely necessary, and must be administered by a physician or licensed medical personnel, such an injury cannot be considered minor.

Q 7:116   What if a facility does not have a formal IC program for hepatitis and AIDS?

If there is no written IC program, the inspector will determine the effectiveness of the facility's program by interviewing employees and inspecting the premises. Even with a formal, written IC Program, it is likely that the inspector will conduct a walk-through examination of the facility and informally interview employees.

Q 7:117   What will the OSHA inspector's walk-through inspection be like?

During the walk-through examination, the inspector will spot check various areas of the facility to ensure that the IC program is actually in place, is operating as documented, and is effective.

Q 7:118   Where can an employer get information on the requirements for an acceptable IC program?

The requirements specifically identified by OSHA's February 27, 1990, instructions are found in the Code of Federal Regulations. [29 CFR § 1910.132(a),(c); 29 CFR § 1910.22(a)(1),(2); 29 CFR § 1910.141(a)(4)(i),(ii); and 29 CFR § 1910.145(F)]

Depending on the level of in-house expertise, employers may want to consult legal counsel or an OSHA-oriented consulting firm for additional information on acceptable IC Programs.

Q 7:119   What is OSHA's citation policy with respect to AIDS and hepatitis inspections?

Citations will normally be issued for violations found in the following areas: personal protective equipment, housekeeping, sanitation and waste disposal, and accident prevention signs and tags.

In addition, health care facilities, like all employers, come under OSHA's general duty to maintain a safe workplace.

Q 7:120   Is AIDS transmittable in the workplace?

In most workplace situations AIDS cannot be transmitted. This conclusion is based on evidence that the AIDS virus can be passed from one person to another only by means of certain bodily fluids such as semen and blood. Since the likelihood of exchanging these kinds of fluids in the work environment is minimal, the conclusion is that AIDS cannot readily be transmitted in the workplace and, therefore, does not pose a hazard therein. The prevalent theory is that such acts as shaking hands, sneezing, or coming into contact with a victim's saliva are insufficient to transmit the disease.

Q 7:121 What are the recommendations of Centers for Disease Control (CDC) of the U.S. Public Health Service?

First, it is important to note that CDC does not impose mandatory obligations on employers. CDC's recommendations emphasize that AIDS is a blood-borne and sexually transmitted disease and is not spread by casual contact, such as a handshake or a kiss. CDC does not recommend routine testing of employees for the AIDS virus, and such testing could lead to legal liability for employers. CDC recommendations concentrate on health care facilities, where it is felt that employees are at a much greater risk of exposure to the AIDS virus. CDC has also examined the risk of exposure to AIDS for food-service and personal-service workers.

Q 7:122 What does CDC recommend with respect to health care professionals?

CDC recommends "universal precautions" for health care workers who have contact with patients, patients' blood or other bodily fluids, and corpses. Nurses, doctors, dentists, laboratory and blood bank technologists, and dialysis personnel are the primary groups considered; paramedics, emergency medical technicians, morticians, and other workers in a health care setting are also taken into account. Universal precautions means that certain precautions should be taken whether or not the particular patient is known to be or suspected of being an AIDS carrier. All bodily fluids and blood should be treated as if potentially infective (and indeed there are other diseases, such as hepatitis B, that can be transmitted in much the same way). CDC recommends that health care workers avoid injuries from needles, scalpels, and other sharp instruments during procedures as well as during the cleaning and disposal of such instruments. Needles should not be recapped, bent, broken by hand, or otherwise handled in a way that might result in a cut or abrasion. Syringes, needles, scalpel blades, and other disposable sharp instruments should be put in puncture-resistant containers for disposal. Health care workers should use "barrier precautions" such as gloves when touching blood, body fluids, and mucous membranes. The gloves should be changed and discarded after each contact with a patient. Masks, protective eyewear, face shields, gowns, and aprons should be worn in any procedure that might generate droplets of blood or bodily fluids. Hands and other skin surfaces should be washed immediately and thoroughly after contamination with blood or bodily fluids. Direct mouth-to-mouth resuscitation should be avoided by using mouthpieces, resuscitation bags, and similar types of ventilation devices. Pregnant workers are advised by CDC to pay particular attention to these kinds of precautions.

Q 7:123 What do OSHA's new blood-borne disease rules require?

Under these new rules, the employer must:

1. Provide the hepatitis B vaccine and vaccination series free of charge to all employees who risk occupational exposure to blood-borne pathogens;

2. Develop written exposure control plans that are designed to minimize or eliminate risk of exposure;

3. Provide engineering controls such as puncture-resistant containers, work practices such as hand washing, and appropriate personal protective equipment;

4. Initiate post-exposure evaluation and follow-up for all employees who are exposed on the job, plus preventive treatment and counseling;

5. Post, where appropriate, hazard communications such as warning labels and signs identifying containers and work areas which may contain potentially infectious materials; and

6. Maintain records of medical information on employees who have been exposed to potentially infectious materials for the duration of each employee's job plus 30 years.

Q 7:124   How did OSHA's blood-borne disease rules come about?

These rules, briefly outlined at Q 7:123, were issued by OSHA not only because of the risk to health care workers of contracting AIDS, but also because of the increased incidence of hepatitis B among health care workers and the American population in general. The hepatitis B virus, or HBV, was not viewed as a risk in the United States until the late 1970s. HBV afflicts literally hundreds of millions world-wide, particularly in Asia, and its incidence is rising rapidly in the United States, although the much lower, but still highly significant incidence of AIDS (about 1.5 million estimated carriers of HIV in the United States in 1995) has commanded most media and public attention. It was these increasingly serious statistics that prompted OSHA to shift from earlier, voluntary instructions to the mandatory rules, which became effective March 6, 1992. [See 13 *BNA OSHA Rep* 765 (Dec 8, 1983); 56 Federal Register 64006 (1991); OSHA Instruction CPL 22.36 (Nov 30, 1983).]

While less frequently fatal than HIV, HBV is a far more resilient pathogen that has been known to survive for up to a week in dried blood at room temperature, and that, in contrast to HIV, can be readily transmitted in human saliva as well as even minute quantities of blood. Today it is estimated that as many as 3,000 Americans die annually of cirrhosis of the liver as a result of chronic HBV infection. [Casey, "Navigating the Arteries of OSHA's Blood-borne Pathogens Standard," *1993 Health Law Handbook* (Gosfield, ed) at 266]

While there has for some time been a vaccine to prevent contraction of HBV, it is relatively expensive and has not received wide-spread distribution in the United States. As recently as two years ago, a Hepatitis B Foundation was founded for the express purpose of funding research to find a cure for HBV.

Q 7:125   How many employees are covered by OSHA's blood-borne disease rules and at what annual cost to their employers?

These rules apply to about 5.6 million workers, about 78 percent of whom are engaged in health care occupations working in 511,755 business establishments and institutions. [56 Federal Register 64038, 64041] Morticians are also among those covered by the rules (see Q

7:127; other occupational categories viewed by the CDC to run some risk are listed at Q 7:128). Annual estimated compliance costs have been put at $813 million with the average being pegged by OSHA at about $1,200 for each individual physician's office and $900 for each dentist's office. [18 *BNA OSHA Rep* 1445 (1989); 56 Federal Register 64063, 64066]

Q 7:126 What are the penalties for violating OSHA's bloodborne disease rule?

OSHA permits the secretary of labor to impose a fine as high as $70,000 for each willful or repeated violation, and as high as $7,000 for every nonserious violation of its provisions. [29 USC § 666(a)(c); Q 7:34] Where a willful violation results in the death of an employee, an additional $10,000 fine plus—and, more significantly—a six-month prison term for responsible company officials are among potential penalties. [29 USC § 666(e)] Finally, OSHA citations are admissible in some jurisdictions as evidence of negligence in subsequent civil lawsuits for compensatory and punitive damages. [See, e.g., Rolick v Collins Pine Co, 975 F 2d 1009 (3d Cir 1992); Pratico v Portland Terminal Co, 783 F 2d 255 (1st Cir 1985); Wiersgalla v Garrett, 486 NW 2d 290 (Iowa 1992); Bellamy v Federal Express Corp, 749 SW 2d 31 (Tenn 1988); Sanchez v Galey, 112 Idaho 609, 733 P 2d 1234 (1986); see also Q 7:46, concerning potential criminal liability under state law for workplace safety violations]

Q 7:127 What precautions should morticians take?

The precautions outlined in Q 7:123 with respect to health care workers should be practiced by morticians as well.

Q 7:128 Which personal-service workers must be mindful of AIDS contamination?

The workers that CDC has identified in this category include hairdressers, barbers, masseurs and masseuses, cosmetologists, and a variety of other occupational groups whose work involves close contact with the skin and other parts of clients' bodies. Although the risk of contamination in these occupations is considered by CDC to be much smaller than with health care employees, the possibility of transmitting the disease exists if either the worker or the client has an open lesion or cut that could leave blood on an instrument. Sterilization appears to be the answer, especially in a case of tattooing, ear piercing, or acupuncture. When possible, disposable instruments should be used on only one customer and then discarded in an appropriate manner.

Q 7:129 What precaution does CDC advise with respect to food-service workers?

CDC does not recommend that persons infected with the AIDS virus be routinely restricted from working in the food and beverage industries. Appropriate standards for the preparation of food and sanitation of the work areas should, of course, be followed. Any food contaminated with blood (e.g., as the result of an employee cutting himself or herself while preparing the food) should be discarded under any circumstances.

Q 7:130 Are restaurant workers and their customers at risk from employees who have tested HIV-positive?

As noted at Q 7:129, the CDC does not recommend any special precautions concerning HIV in the food service industry. It sees no danger of spreading the infection in that environment. When the Americans with Disabilities Act was being debated in Congress, an effort was mounted by certain factions of the restaurant industry to carve out of the act an exemption with regard to HIV-positive employees attempting to continue working in that line of business. Resisting this lobbying effort, Congress made it clear that AIDS is a protected disability under the ADA, and made no exception to this general principle with regard to restaurants and other food services. [HR Rep No 485, 101st Cong, 2d Sess, pt 2 at 5152 (1990)] Thus, while under the act the secretary of health and human services is mandated to develop a list of communicable diseases that will disqualify food handlers from employment, this list will not include HIV. [See 29 CFR § 1630.16(e)(1); 56 Federal Register 22726 (51691); Research Institute of America, *Analysis of the Americans with Disabilities Act and the EEOC Regulations* (Aug 1991) § 403]

Nevertheless, some litigants have attempted to argue, usually without success, that state health department regulations forbidding the employment of workers with infectious diseases [see, e.g., 35 Pa Stat Ann § 655.7] require the release from employment of HIV-positive employees. [See MAE v Doe & Roe, 388 Pa Super 589, 566 A 2d 285 (1989); Stark, "A Restaurant Manager with AIDS Sues over Firing," *Philadelphia Inquirer*, Apr 6, 1990, at B1; Kaufman, "Settlement is Reached in Case of a Worker Fired for Having HIV," *Philadelphia Inquirer*, Dec 31, 1992, at B3] At this writing, it appears that trade associations representing restaurateurs and others involved in policy-making roles for the restaurant industry have accepted the proposition that HIV is a protected disability and does not pose a threat to co-workers and customers of the establishment employing a person so afflicted.

Q 7:131   What are the most recent developments concerning AIDS in the workplace?

The film *Philadelphia* was both a major media event and a major political event in 1994. Actor Tom Hanks garnered his first Academy Award for best actor as the Philadelphia lawyer fired by a big law firm after contracting AIDS. The film was rather loosely based upon, or at least inspired by, a real case that was tried before Senior U.S. District Judge Raymond Broderick in Philadelphia's federal court a few years earlier. [Cain v Hyatt, 734 F Supp 671 (ED Pa 1990), discussed in Q 4:99] While the film was generally well received, one criticism was of its portrayal of AIDS victims as plaintiffs encountering great difficulty obtaining legal counsel; the Hanks character is turned away by more than a half dozen attorneys before a lawyer played by Denzel Washington takes his case. In fact, advocacy organizations such as the AIDS Law Project of Pennsylvania and attorneys eager to do pro bono work have for years been espousing the cause of HIV-positive and AIDS-afflicted workers. [See, Castagnera, "Pro Bono: Committed to the Cause," *The Pennsylvania Lawyer*, July 1993] Nonetheless, *Philadelphia*, while no doubt benefiting Hanks and his cohorts the most, probably did some good with regard to raising the public consciousness about this serious workplace issue.

Whether the success of *Philadelphia* will increase the incidence of AIDS litigation, as the Justice Clarence Thomas hearings heightened

Americans' sensitivity to sexual harassment, remains to be seen. Perhaps the most noteworthy legal action of 1994 was *Tischler v. Dimenna* [*New York Law*, Mar 10, 1994, at 21], a case being pursued in the New York Supreme Court for Westchester County, brought by a woman against the estate of her deceased lover, who died of AIDS. The plaintiff, alleging legal theories of intentional tort and negligence, is seeking $1 million from the decedent's estate, contending that he knew he was HIV-positive but continued having unprotected sex with her without advising her of his condition. In March 1994 the plaintiff withstood the defendant-estate's motion for summary judgment; the court held that an AIDS-phobia claim is a sustainable cause of action in New York.

According to the plaintiff's allegations, from February 1980 until the summer of 1989 she engaged in unprotected sexual relations with her lover, now deceased. Only in the summer of 1989, she says, did the couple make sporadic use of condoms. She further alleges that her lover told her from his deathbed in December 1991 that he had become infected with HIV sometime in 1990, the year his best male friend died of AIDS. However, the plaintiff contends that she cannot be certain that her lover's infection occurred only after their own relationship had cooled in 1989. Consequently, she has submitted to repeated tests for the presence of the virus in her own blood. While these tests have all come back negative, her answer to defendant's interrogatory concerning physical harm states:

> Since December 1991, plaintiff has suffered from extreme physical distress arising from fear that decedent's conduct toward plaintiff is the functional equivalent of a death sentence. Distress has led to high blood pressure, severe headaches, and resulting neck pain, at various times, constant upset stomach and resulting diarrhea, sleepless nights, and occasional nightmares. [Tischler v Dimenna, Interrogatory No 130]

The plaintiff elaborated upon her fears as follows:

> All conditions arise from fear; a fear of dying prematurely and grotesquely as a result of being infected with HIV or AIDS, a fear of discovery by my employers, leading to dismissal and resulting financial impoverishment, a fear that every head cold and runny nose is the beginning of the end, and a fear that any future relationships with any male will terminate once plaintiff discloses what has happened to her. [Id, Interrogatory No 135(e)]

The defendant-estate moved the court for summary judgment on two grounds: (1) the plaintiff really has suffered no physical injury as a result of the decedent's failure to reveal his condition or take precautions with her sooner and (2) under the New York dead man's statute, an interested survivor cannot testify on her own behalf about what the decedent said or didn't say, since the deceased obviously cannot refute the allegations.

Engaging in an extensive analysis of legal precedents involving AIDS, phobia cases, mental distress, and the duties of sexual partners, the court concluded that:

> Plaintiff has made the requisite showing in opposition to the motion for summary judgment to establish *prima facie* her claim of emotional distress for the fear of contracting AIDS. The law recognizes that the decedent owed a duty to plaintiff not to intentionally or negligently inflict mental distress. The plaintiff has proven probable exposure to the disease. Whether defendant did knowingly or negligently expose plaintiff are questions for the jury. Similarly, plaintiff's knowledge, actual or constructive, of decedent's condition and his liaison with another man as well as participating in unprotected sexual activity are for the triers of the facts on damages. Additionally, as in other cases where probabilities must be weighed [citations omitted], the issue of the reasonableness of the plaintiff's fear and for what period of time that fear is compensable are questions for the jury after hearing her testimony and upon full review of actual medical testimony.

One may well wonder what will be the impact of this decision upon workplace cases involving exposure to HIV. Clearly, in cases where the HIV-positive employee is able to perform the job and there is no realistic risk of infecting co-workers or customers [see Q 7:130 concerning restaurant workers; *Mae v Doe & Roe,* 388 Pa Super 589, 566 A 2d 285 (1989); Castagnera, "Pro Bono: Committed to the Cause," *The Pennsylvania Lawyer,* July 1993], the HIV-positive employee's privacy will take priority over the unrealistic fears of others, and the employer will be obliged to honor that privacy right.

But, as the judge in *Tischler v. Dimenna* notes, in work environments such as hospitals, where infection with HIV is a much more realistic possibility, issues of phobia and employer candor make for more difficult cases, and the law is struggling to do justice on a case-by-case basis. [See, e.g., Johnson v West Virginia University

Hospitals, 413 SE 2d 889 (W Va Supr 1991); Lubowitz v Albert Einstein Medical Center, 623 A 2d 3 (Pa Super 1993); Keris v Hartley, 21 Cal Rptr 621 (Ct App 1993)]

If any trend can be discerned in 1995 it is that the dichotomy between the health care industry and all other segments of the U.S. economy with regard to the treatment of HIV-positive employees is widening on the litigation front. Two early 1995 court decisions confirm the judiciary's willingness to support health care employers against the claims of HIV-positive health care professionals, while a case concerning testing of police candidates indicates courts' reluctance to extend the support into non-health care sectors.

In Richmond, Virginia, the U.S. Court of Appeals for the Fourth Circuit affirmed a district court's earlier decision barring a resident neurosurgeon's claims against a Baltimore hospital under the Americans with Disabilities Act and the Rehabilitation Act based upon his suspension from duties after he tested HIV-positive. [Doe v University of Maryland Medical System Corp, US Ct App 4th Cir No. 94-1462 (Apr 4, 1995).] Although "Dr. Doe" contended that the risk of his transmitting the AIDS virus to a patient was "infinitesimal," the court disagreed, holding that "Dr. Doe does pose a significant risk to the health and safety of his patients that cannot be eliminated by reasonable accommodation. Although there may presently be no documented case of surgeon-to-patient transmission, such transmission clearly is possible." [Id]

In Chicago, a district judge found that a former lab technician, who claimed to have received poor performance evaluations, to have been passed by for promotions, and to have been denied a pay increase, all because he was HIV-positive, had failed to prove a violation of the Americans with Disabilities Act. Judge Rubin Castillo ruled on the defendant's motion for partial summary judgment that the plaintiff had failed to adduce any evidence that his appraisal was not a legitimate evaluation of his performance, or indeed that the employer even knew of his HIV status when the appraisal was rendered, resulting in denial of a pay hike and promotion. [RGH v Abbott Laboratories, 1995 US Dist LEXIS 1860 (ND Ill 1995)]

The Chicago Police Department in February 1995 settled an action brought against it by the American Civil Liberties Union, which had challenged the department's right to test new recruits for the AIDS virus. Under the settlement agreement, recruits will neither be tested nor will they be asked to disclose that they are HIV-positive. Additionally, Mayor Richard Daley issued an executive order early in 1995 denouncing AIDS discrimination and denying to other city departments the right to inquire or test for HIV. ["Chicago Police Department Settles HIV Discrimination Suit with ACLU," *1995 BNA Daily Labor Report,* No 34, Feb 21, 1995, at d6]

Q 7:132 Should an employee with the AIDS virus be restricted in the use of any of the facilities in the workplace?

CDC takes the position that there is no reason to prevent AIDS carriers from using telephones, toilets, cafeterias, or other common facilities. Certainly any common area that is contaminated with blood (such as a sink used in the administration of first aid) should be cleaned and sterilized immediately in all cases, not merely in a case in which an employee is suspected of being an AIDS carrier.

Q 7:133 Should the confidentiality of an AIDS carrier be maintained by the employer?

Unquestionably, if an employee voluntarily informs someone at the company of a positive antibody test or an active AIDS condition, or if the employer gets this information from an insurance form, the information should be maintained in strictest confidence. State law may require confidentiality for medical information. Furthermore, legal liability for invasion of privacy and defamation provides additional legal impetus for the employer to respect the privacy and confidentiality of someone who has AIDS or who is HIV positive.

Q 7:134 What should a policy regarding AIDS in the workplace cover?

An AIDS policy should include the following:

- The facts about AIDS and the limited ways that it can be transmitted in the workplace
- The company's position on testing (which should be that testing will not be conducted except in unusual circumstances)

- A notice that reasonable accommodation will be made to enable a person with AIDS to perform his or her job, if possible
- A description of the company's educational program on AIDS

Q 7:135   What educational program should a company have?

The kind of time and money a company decides to invest in an AIDS education program will depend on the company's size and resources, and the likelihood that AIDS will become an issue in the workplace. Many larger companies have quite sophisticated and extremely effective AIDS education programs. These companies have taken the view that in order to effectively reach all employees, the use of several media of communication is desirable. For instance, a Philadelphia pharmaceuticals company developed a policy stating that it would not test for AIDS, nor would it discriminate against employees who have AIDS. The company then proceeded to announce this policy and the facts about AIDS in a newsletter, in a personal letter to employees (with a brochure) sent to the employees' homes, with a videotape, in face-to-face seminars, and, finally, in the employee handbook.

Q 7:136   What rights do employees have with respect to co-workers who have AIDS?

Under the Act, the employer has a general duty to furnish a workplace free from recognized hazards, and employees have the right to refuse to work in the face of uncorrected hazards. Furthermore, under the National Labor Relations Act (NLRA), employees (whether unionized or not) have the right to engage in concerted activity to protect themselves. With respect to AIDS, both of these laws would require that employees have at least some reasonable basis for their refusal to work with someone who has AIDS. Arguably, if the employer has properly attempted to educate employees and there is no factual basis to believe that a hazard exists, the Act and NLRA would not seem to protect from employer discipline those employees who refuse to work. However, the employer should handle employees' concerns with care. For instance, an arbitrator in Minnesota reinstated a prison guard who had been fired for refusing to perform pat-down searches of prisoners because of his fear of

AIDS. The arbitrator found that this fear was partially generated by a memorandum distributed in the prison by its warden. Also, the arbitrator took into account that the warden changed his policy and began permitting other guards to wear gloves during pat-down searches after the guard had been fired. Thus, if the company has not taken appropriate steps to allay the unreasonable fears of employees, these fears may rise to the level of reasonableness, and NLRA and the Act may provide some protection to employees under such circumstances.

Q 7:137 Do employees have the right to know that co-workers have AIDS?

There is no legal right, either under right-to-know regulations or other laws, for employees to know that a co-worker has AIDS. To the contrary, statutes involving confidentiality of medical information, plus the common law of privacy and defamation, may create a right for the employee with AIDS to keep this information confidential.

Drug Abuse

Q 7:138 What is the Drug-Free Workplace Act of 1988?

The Drug-Free Workplace Act of 1988 [L 100-690] is a federal law that requires federal contractors and federal grant recipients to provide a drug-free workplace or, if they are individuals, to refrain from engaging in unlawful drug-related activities when performing the contract or conducting the grant activity. Federal contractors and federal grant recipients must certify to the contracting or granting agency that they will abide by the requirements of the Act. The Act became effective on March 16, 1989. Any entity, other than an individual, that desires to be considered a responsible source of government contract supplies, for purposes of being awarded a contract for goods or services in the amount of $25,000 or more, must certify to the contracting agency that it will provide a drug-free workplace.

Q 7:139 What actions must an employer take to provide a drug-free workplace within the meaning of the Act?

To provide a drug-free workplace within the meaning of the Act, an employer must meet seven requirements. The employer must

1. Publish a statement notifying employees that engaging in unlawful drug-related activity is prohibited in the workplace— the statement must also specify what actions will be taken if employees violate the prohibition;

2. Establish a drug-free awareness program for employees;

3. Provide each employee engaged in the performance of a government contract or grant with a copy of the published prohibition statement;

4. Include in the published prohibition statement notice that employment on the government contract or grant is conditioned on the employee abiding by the terms of the statement and notifying the employer within five days of any criminal drug statute conviction for a workplace violation;

5. Notify the contracting or granting agency within ten days of receiving notice, from an employee or otherwise, of such a conviction;

6. Either impose sanctions up to and including termination on any employee who has been convicted for the workplace violation of a criminal drug statute or require that the convicted employee participate in a federal, state, or agency-approved drug abuse assistance or rehabilitation program; and

7. Make a good faith effort to maintain a drug-free workplace.

These requirements apply to federal contractors and federal grant recipients.

Q 7:140 What constitutes unlawful drug-related activity within the meaning of the Act?

The unlawful manufacture, distribution, dispensing, possession, or use of a controlled substance constitutes unlawful drug-related activity within the meaning of the Act.

Q 7:141   Must employers make reasonable efforts to provide employees with a drug-free workplace?

The Drug-Free Workplace Act of 1988 requires all federal contractors and federal grant recipients to make a good-faith effort to maintain a drug-free workplace. In so doing, employers must prohibit unlawful drug-related activities on their premises. Employers must also notify employees of the prohibition and the penalty for violating it, require employees to notify the employer within five days of their criminal conviction for a drug violation occurring in the workplace, and discipline any such employees or require that they attend a drug rehabilitation program. Furthermore, federal contractors and federal grant recipients must certify that they will not unlawfully manufacture, distribute, dispense, possess, or use a controlled substance in the performance of a contract or during the conduct of any activity funded by the grant.

Q 7:142   What information must a drug-free awareness program provide to employees?

A drug-free awareness program must inform employees about the dangers of workplace drug abuse; the employer's policy of maintaining a drug-free workplace; drug counseling, rehabilitation, and assistance programs available to employees; and penalties that may be imposed for drug abuse violations.

Q 7:143   What actions may be taken against a federal contractor or federal grant recipient failing to abide by the drug-free workplace requirement?

Failure to abide by the drug-free workplace requirement may result in the suspension of payments under the contract or grant, termination of the contract or grant, or suspension or debarment of the contractor or grant recipient. These actions are not mutually exclusive; any combination may be taken in response to a single incident. These measures, or any combination thereof, may also be imposed if a contractor or grant recipient provides the contracting or granting agency a false certification, or if the contractor or grant recipient fails to make a good-faith effort to provide a drug-free workplace.

Q 7:144   What is the effect of debarment?

A federal contractor or grant recipient that has been debarred will be ineligible for the award of any federal agency contract or grant and for participation in any future federal agency contract or grant for a period of up to five years.

Q 7:145   What will indicate that a federal contractor or grant recipient has failed to make a good-faith effort to provide a drug-free workplace?

If a number of employees of a government contractor or grant recipient are convicted for workplace violations of criminal drug statutes, it may indicate that the contractor or grant recipient has not made the required good-faith effort to provide a drug-free workplace.

Q 7:146   What special procedures must be followed before measures can be taken against a federal contractor that violates the Drug-Free Workplace Act?

Before measures can be taken against a federal contractor, a contracting officer must make a written determination that cause for action exists. A contracting officer must initiate an appropriate proceeding to determine what, if any, measures should be taken. The contracting agency must conduct the proceeding in accordance with its own procedural rules and those of the federal acquisition regulation. The procedural rules of the federal acquisition regulation are designed to provide a full and fair proceeding. Requirements include the provision of notice and the opportunity to respond in writing or in person.

Q 7:147   Is there a time limit within which an employer must respond to an employee who has been convicted of a workplace violation of a criminal drug abuse statue?

Yes. An employer must either impose sanctions or require participation in a drug abuse assistance or rehabilitation program within 30 days after receiving notice from an employee of a conviction.

Q 7:148 Will action always be taken against a federal contractor or grant recipient that has failed to abide by the drug-free workplace requirement, failed to make a good-faith effort, or made a false certification?

No. Action may be waived if the head of the contracting agency determines that taking action would result in severe disruption of the agency to the detriment of the federal government or the public. The head of the granting agency may also waive action if he or she determines that taking action would not be in the public interest.

Q 7:149 Does the Drug-Free Workplace Act mandate employee drug testing?

No. The Drug-Free Workplace Act does not generally require drug testing of government contractor employees. However, the Department of Defense (DOD) has issued interim regulations that require contractors to establish workplace drug testing programs or appropriate alternatives. Any drug testing an employer institutes should be only to uncover illegal drug use by employees in sensitive positions (e.g., an employee who has been granted access to classified information or whose job the contractor believes to involve national security, health, or safety or that demands a high level of trust and confidence). The contractor may also institute drug testing when it has a reasonable suspicion that an employee uses illegal drugs, when an employee has been involved in an accident or unsafe practice, as part of a follow-up to rehabilitation for past drug use, or as part of a voluntary employee drug-testing program. A contractor is required to follow the DOD regulations if the contract involves access to classified information, the contracting officer determines that the regulations are necessary for protecting national security, health, and so forth, and the contract obligations (or the pertinent part thereof) are to be performed in the United States.

Q 7:150 Do the provisions of the Drug-Free Workplace Act or the DOD interim rules provide for mandatory penalties for employees who refuse to participate in a drug testing program?

Neither the Act nor the DOD interim rules require that a contractor penalize an employee for failure to participate in a drug testing program the contractor institutes. However, a contractor runs the risk of making a false certification if it does not make a good-faith effort to maintain a drug-free workplace; this effort may include a notation that certain employees refuse to participatein an otherwise valid drug-testing program.

Q 7:151 Will mandatory testing of employees or penalties for refusing to participate in a test subject a contractor to a possible lawsuit by an employee?

Several courts have held that mandatory drug testing is a violation of an employee's right of privacy. Some courts also find that random or mandatory drug testing is an unreasonable search and seizure under the Fourth Amendment. However, other courts have held that testing and other searches based on a reasonable, individual, and particularized suspicion are valid and constitutional. Still other courts have found that an employer was liable for a tortious invasion of employee's privacy, among other things, for firing an employee who refused to participate in a drug test. [See National Treasury Employees Union v Von Raab, 489 US 656 (1989) (mandatory drug testing impacts on federal employees' Fourth Amendment rights, but under at least some circumstances the government-employer's interest in testing outweighs the employee's constitutional rights); Skinner v Railway Labor Executives' Ass'n, 489 US 602 (1989) (Fourth Amendment applies to railroad administration regulations but tests following train accidents were reasonable under the circumstances); see also, Luedtke v Nabors Alaska Drilling, Inc, 768 P 2d 1123 (Alaska 1989) (random drug tests by private employer unsuccessfully challenged as violations of employee's privacy rights under Alaska constitution; Jennings v Mince Technology Labs, Inc, 765 SW 2d 497 (Tex Civ App 1989) (random drug test not tortious invasion of employees' privacy); but see Hennessey v Coastal Eagle Point Oil Co, 589 A 2d 170 (NJ Super 1991)(urine testing may implicate employees' privacy rights); Luck v Southern Pacific Transportation, 218 Call App 3d 1 (1990) (where employee was not involved in dangerous or safety-related work, unwilling participation in random urinalysis was invasion of privacy); Borse v Piece Goods Shop Inc, 963 F 2d 611 (3d Cir 1991) (employee fired for refusing to sign waiver permitting urinalysis drug test and/or search of personal property at workplace may have wrongful discharge claim under Pennsylvania's exception to at-will employment doctrine)]

Other Hazards

VDTs

Q 7:152 Are employees who work with video display terminals (VDTs) exposed to special risks?

VDT users have reported repetitive motion injuries, musculoskeletal problems, and eye-focusing problems. Although employees who work with VDTs are exposed to the small amounts of radiation that the VDTs emit, scientific research on the effects of VDT radiation is inconclusive. For example, a study of female telephone operators, published in the March 14, 1991, issue of the *New England Journal of Medicine* found no correlation between VDT exposure and spontaneous abortion by pregnant workers. In the article, the researchers stated, "we found no increase in the risk of spontaneous abortion associated with the occupational use of VDTs. We did not observe an increased risk associated with three different measures of VDT use or with the VDT model used, after adjusting for confounders, or after accounting for more than one pregnancy in the same woman." So it appears that at least one common misperception about VDT use has been banished.

Q 7:153 How can an employer decrease the risks faced by employees who work with VDTs?

To the extent that modest health risks may in fact exist, an important way employers can decrease the risks faced by employees who work with VDTs is to adjust the work environment. Eye problems can be alleviated by decreasing the illumination in work areas, because overhead fluorescent lighting tends to be very bright compared to a VDT's dark screen. Musculoskeletal problems, including back and neck aches, can be alleviated by using adjustable office equipment, which allows each employee to set his or her chair, keyboard, and screen at a comfortable level. Employers that are concerned about potential radiation exposure problems may want to obtain newer VDTs, which emit less radiation than older models.

Fetal Protection

Q 7:154   Can companies enforce fetal protection policies?

No. In its decision in *UAW v. Johnson Controls, Inc.*, [111 S Ct 2238 (1991)] the Supreme Court in March 1991 held by a five to four vote that an employment policy that barred fertile females from jobs that might harm a fetus violated Title VII of the 1964 Civil Rights Act.

Q 7:155   Did Johnson Controls' fetal protection policy constitute a bona fide occupation qualification (BFOQ)?

No. The Supreme Court majority in *Johnson Controls* held that the employer did not promulgate a policy that fell within the "essence" or "central mission" of its business. That central mission, the Court held, was manufacturing batteries, and the Court found no evidence in the record to support an argument that fertile women were less efficient workers in this enterprise than anyone else. The company's concern for possible prenatal injury from exposure to lead, no matter how sincere, did not demonstrate that its fertile female employees could not do the job. Therefore, the firm's fetal protection policy, which excluded fertile females from jobs involving exposure to lead did not meet the legal test of a BFOQ.

Q 7:156   What other company arguments did the Supreme Court reject in the *Johnson Controls* case?

In ruling that the company's fetal protection policy was illegal, the Court rejected an argument that increased health care claims involving reproductive health hazards would indirectly hurt consumers by pushing up the price of the company's product. All such direct and indirect economic concerns were rebuffed by the Court. This conclusion by the Court seems to be in accord with federal policy under the Act, which has long held that hazard abatement cannot be limited by a showing that the weakest firms in an industry may not be able to afford the required abatement measures. The message of *Johnson Controls* seems to be that, if women wish to work in potentially hazardous occupations, companies (and perhaps, ultimately, consumers) will have to bear the added expense to make the worksite reasonably safe for this class of employee.

Lead

Q 7:157   How serious a hazard is lead in the U.S. workplace?

While *Johnson Controls* is a landmark Supreme Court decision chiefly for what it says about the rights of women employees, the opinion also put the spotlight on one of the most deadly health hazards in our environment: lead.

Lead is a metal that occurs naturally in the earth's crust. It is used in a multitude of products: batteries, industrial paints, solder, and some glass and plastic products. Before medical science understood that lead builds up in the human body and can destroy organs (notably the nervous system), it was used in household plumbing, paint, and wallpaper.

Employees at risk of lead poisoning include not only those employed in battery plants, such as in the *Johnson Controls* case, but also construction workers who must either apply or remove lead-based paints (or perhaps weld steel that has been painted with such paints), and foundry workers who melt down scrap metals that carry lead components or lead paint.

Q 7:158   What precautions can employers take to protect employees against lead poisoning?

Safety precautions include respirators; strict work rules about eating, showering, and changing clothes at the job site; blood tests; and, ultimately, temporary removal from the site(s) of lead exposure until the employee's blood lead level has dropped back into a safe range. OSHA regulations provide detailed guidelines for implementing and monitoring these precautions effectively. Furthermore, OSHA has leveled some of its heaviest fines, in recent years, along with multiple willful citations, upon employers in industries who must deal with lead.

Chapter 8

Employee Compensation and Fringe Benefits

Employee compensation is a highly complex aspect of employment law involving legal wage restrictions that apply to a wide variety of occupations and compensation methods. This chapter describes the provisions of the Fair Labor Standards Act (FLSA) that apply to minimum wage and compensation for overtime, as well as the permissible exemptions from minimum wage and overtime regulations. Employees' rights and remedies are also described, and those pertaining to child labor laws.

Although employers generally are not required by law to provide fringe benefits to employees, there are sound reasons for doing so. A well-thought-out fringe benefit plan can give employers a competitive edge in attracting and retaining qualified employees. Once a plan is established, the employer must comply with legislative provisions that apply to the maintenance of the plan and the distribution of benefits. This chapter covers the legal requirements that apply to employee benefits plans, particularly pension plans and compliance with the Employment Retirement Income Security Act (ERISA): insurance benefits; employee time off and extended leaves of absence; and ERISA provisions that apply to employee welfare benefit plans.

The performance of a company's executives can relate directly to the company's profit margin. Employers, therefore, have developed methods of compensation by which executives' earnings are correlated to the company's earnings, often by some form of ownership interest. This chapter describes effective planning techniques and strategies for compensating executives: stock options; executive perks; executive severance agreements; and deferred compensation plans.

Fair Labor Standards Act

Wages

Q 8:1 Must employers follow certain guidelines when compensating employees?

Yes. Wages paid to employees are largely regulated by federal and state wage laws. These laws typically set minimum wage rates and overtime compensation that must be paid to those employees who fall under the protection of these statutes.

Q 8:2 What federal law covers wages?

FLSA, enacted in 1938, is the leading federal law regulating minimum wage and overtime compensation. The Act also regulates child labor and equal pay for equal work.

Q 8:3 What employees are covered by FLSA?

FLSA is very broad in its coverage. Over the years, the Act has been amended and extended to include most federal employees, state and local government employees, employees of state and local hospitals and educational institutions, and private household domestic workers. If certain employees are not covered by FLSA, it is likely that they are covered by similar state laws that regulate minimum wage and overtime compensation.

In general, three types of employees are covered by FLSA:

1. Employees engaged in interstate commerce, including import and export;
2. Employees engaged in "the production" of goods for interstate commerce; and
3. Employees in an "enterprise engaged in" interstate commerce.

The production of goods, according to FLSA regulations, includes "any closely related process or occupation directly essential" to the production of goods for interstate commerce. With respect to the third group covered by FLSA, the so-called enterprise test has been very broadly interpreted by the courts, and thus there are very few employers today whose employees are not covered by FLSA.

Q 8:4   Are any categories of employees exempt from FLSA coverage?

Despite the broad categories of employees covered by FLSA and comparable state laws, certain types of employees are generally exempt from these laws. These exemptions are based on the nature of the work performed. Executives, administrators, professionals, outside salespersons, and a few other types of employees may be excluded from minimum wage and overtime compensation requirements, provided these employees meet certain standards set forth in the implementing regulations.

Minimum Wages

Q 8:5   What are minimum wages?

Minimum wages are the gross minimum hourly rates employers may pay protected workers, as set by federal wage and hour laws. In 1938, when FLSA was passed, the minimum wage was set at $0.25 per hour over the course of the next seven years.

After vetoing Congress's first attempt in nine years to raise the minimum wage, President Bush signed a second, compromise minimum wage act in November 1989. As of April 1, 1990, the federal minimum wage increased to $3.80 per hour. On April 1, 1991, the minimum hourly wage became $4.25. However, the law also allowed for a sub-minimum training wage of $3.35 per hour, which rose to $3.61 on April 1, 1991. Under the law, only 25 percent of an employer's workforce could be paid the training wage at any one time and only until this part of the law expired in 1993.

Since 1991 the federal minimum wage has remained at $4.25 per hour. Meanwhile a report released by the U.S. Department of Labor's Bureau of Labor Statistics (DOL's BLS) in June 1995 indicated that the number of working families living in poverty in America had increased since the late 1980s, standing at 7.5 percent of all working families in this country as of 1993.

Reacting to this report, House Minority Leader Richard Gephardt commented on June 19, 1995, that the then-pending GOP budget proposals would result in "the greatest redistribution of income from working families to the wealthy since the days of the Robber Barons."

The BLS study states that in 1993, 40 million people in the U.S. were living in poverty, representing 15 percent of the population. At the time, the government's poverty line was set at $14,763 annual income for a family of four.

Such figures have led some states to reexamine their minimum wage requirements. [See, e.g., *BusinessWeek*, July 20, 1995] Under FLSA, Congress has not preempted such state participation in setting minimum wages as long as state variations from the federal norm represent more, not less, favorable treatment of workers than the federal statute and regulations provide at any given time. Thus a state may require employers within its borders to pay a higher minimum wage than is currently required by the federal law. However, such states run the risk of alienating businesses which have the option of locating in other jurisdictions.

Q 8:6 Could a company be required to pay more than the minimum wage set by FLSA?

A provision of FLSA says that if a state wishes to require a higher minimum compensation than that demanded by the federal law, the state legislature may do so. While most states have their minimum wage rates set at $3.61 (the training sub-minimum as of April 1, 1991), as determined by FLSA, a number of states have set the minimum higher. If a company employs workers in one of those states, it must pay the higher minimum wage to employees working in that state.

Q 8:7 How are employees' earnings computed for purposes of determining minimum wage compensation?

The concept of a minimum wage, that no one should receive less than a specified hourly rate of pay for the work performed, is relatively simple. However, payment of the minimum wage may be complicated, depending on the method of compensation used by an employer (for example, hourly, weekly, or monthly). Some employees, such as machinists, are paid a piece-rate wage, earning a set amount for each piece completed. Others may rely largely on tips from customers or on sales commissions as a percentage of their compensation (see Q 8:10).

Q 8:8   What monetary equivalent may be included in wages for purposes of computing minimum wage compensation?

FLSA includes reasonable costs to the employer for furnishing an employee with board, lodging, or other facilities as wages, if such board, lodging, or other facilities are customarily furnished by the employer to its employees. The employee must not only receive the benefits of the board, lodging, or other facilities, but must also accept these benefits voluntarily. If such benefits are provided by an employer but are not used by an employee or are accepted under coercion, the costs of these benefits cannot be added to an employee's earnings.

Q 8:9   Can an employee voluntarily agree to certain deductions from his or her minimum wage compensation?

FLSA allows for some voluntary deductions, such as union dues, from an employee's pay. Other deductions, however, are not permitted. For example, some retail employers deduct from an employee's pay any shortages from the employer's cash register (regardless of the cause of the shortage). Such deductions are invalid if the deduction would bring the employee's earnings below minimum wage. (Of course, if the employer and employee have agreed to deducting only shortages caused by misappropriation or theft of funds by the employee, the agreement would not violate FLSA provisions.) Similarly, deducting from an employee's pay the cost of tools or gear necessary for the job is illegal if the wage falls below minimum as a result.

Q 8:10   Are salaries, piece rates, and commissions subject to minimum wage calculation?

FLSA provides employers enough flexibility to allow for these different methods of compensation, as long as the overall compensation of employees complies with the minimum wage standards. If an employee receives tips from customers, for example, an employer is permitted to reduce the minimum wage paid to that worker by up to 40 percent, with the understanding that the difference will be made up by tips received by that employee. Similarly, the earnings of employees compensated on a piece-rate basis must average out to at least the minimum wage, provided that the time period over which the earnings are averaged is no longer than a single seven-day, 40-hour workweek. Thus, the earnings of an employee paid on a piece-rate basis may be less than the minimum wage for any single hour, provided that the total earnings for the week average out to the minimum wage. Similarly, an employer may reduce the minimum wage paid to a salesperson and make up the difference with commissions.

Work Periods

Q 8:11   For what time periods should employees be compensated?

This question arises in two types of worker situations: (1) workers who are paid on an hourly basis and who are not compensated for scheduled work breaks but work through their scheduled breaks; and (2) workers who are on call (i.e., required to be available in the event of an emergency, but who may spend a portion of that time waiting to be called by not actually performing their normal work duties). This latter situation typically involves health care workers, such as ambulance drivers.

Q 8:12   Must employees be paid during work breaks?

As a general rule, breaks of less than 30 minutes must be paid work breaks, although in some circumstances the Department of Labor (DOL) permits uncompensated breaks of somewhat shorter duration if the employer can show that workers are truly permitted to use the time for their own relaxation. For most employment situations, it is recommended that all breaks of less than 30 minutes be compensated.

Q 8:13   Must lunch breaks be paid?

Lunch breaks of at least 30 minutes duration need not be paid time, unless the employee is forced to remain at the work station to (possibly) perform tasks (for example, answer the phone or wait on customers).

Q 8:14   Must on-call time be paid?

This depends on whether the employee is free to use the on-call time to personal advantage or must remain in one location (at the hospital, firehouse, home) and await calls. As a general rule, if the employee can go out to a restaurant, the movies, and so forth (wearing a beeper, for instance), the time need not be compensated unless there is an actual call. However, like most questions in wage and hour law, this rule may vary on a case-by-case basis.

Q 8:15   What is a workweek?

A workweek must consist of seven consecutive days. The workweek is not required to start or end on any particular day of the calendar week. The starting day of the workweek may be changed as long as the change is not intended as a means to avoid paying overtime.

Overtime

Q 8:16   Who is entitled to overtime compensation?

Employees covered by FLSA or comparable state laws who are not otherwise exempt from these provisions are entitled to overtime pay, at one-and-a-half times their regular pay, for hours worked in excess of 40 hours per workweek.

Q 8:17   What hours should be counted toward overtime eligibility?

Hours worked in excess of 40 hours per workweek should be counted as overtime. In general, preliminary or post-work activities, such as employee travel to or from work, should be included in compensable time only if such compensation is called for under contract or is generally provided for by the customs or practices of the business or industry. If an employee is assigned duties while commuting to and from work (for example, pickups and deliveries), this time may have to be included in the workweek total. For on-call employees, compensable overtime should be evaluated on the same basis as regular compensation. If on-call employees are not required to be present at their workplace at all times and are free to attend to personal business when not actually working, the nonworking hours probably need not be included as compensable overtime. This may not be the case, however, if on-call employees are required to remain at their workplace at all times while on call or are otherwise prevented from engaging in personal pursuits when they are not working.

Q 8:18   Are salaried employees entitled to overtime compensation?

Yes. If the company pays the employee a salary, an employee is entitled to one-and-one-half times his or her regular rate of pay (time-and-a-half) for the number of hours that exceeds the 40-hour workweek. To compute this, the company must determine the employee's hourly rate (usually by dividing the number of hours worked into the salary).

Q 8:19   What is a fluctuating workweek plan?

As indicated in Q 8:18, the usual method of calculating overtime entitlement for salaried employees is to divide the hours into the salary, and pay time-and-a-half for hours in excess of 40. However, other options are available under the wage and hour regulations. One of these is called the fluctuating workweek plan. Under this plan, an employer can agree with an employee that the employee will receive a salary for all straight-time hours worked in any given work. Thus, the employee's hourly rate will vary from week to week. For example, suppose an employee is paid $400 per week. Under the normal situation, as described in Q 8:18, the employee's salary would cover 40 hours of work, and the rate would be $10 per hour. For each additional hour of work, the employee would be entitled to an additional $15 of pay. However, under a fluctuating workweek plan, if the employee worked 50 hours, that employee's straight-time wage rate for that week would be $8 per hour ($400/50 hours). Therefore, that employee would be entitled to $12 per hour only for each hour in excess of 40.

Q 8:20   What is a Belo agreement?

The Belo agreement derives its name from an important U.S. Supreme Court decision that defined the instances in which an employee need not be paid overtime. [Walling v A H Belo Corp, 316 US 624 (1942)] The Court held that an employer may pay an employee a straight salary for all hours worked, whether this includes more or less than 40 hours in a given workweek if:

- The employee works fluctuating hours that vary above and below

- A written agreement exists between the employer and employee

- The fluctuations are irregular and cannot be predicted

Q 8:21   Must a company pay employees overtime if the employees are paid by a rate other than hourly or salary (for example, tips or piece rate)?

Yes, if the employee is not otherwise exempted from coverage under FLSA, the employee is entitled to time-and-a-half for hours worked in excess of 40, regardless of the method of compensation. The DOL provides detailed regulations and guidelines for calculating overtime under atypical situations, and the Wage and Hour Administration of DOL should be contacted if questions arise concerning overtime to employees compensated by piece rate, tips, or some other method.

Q 8:22   If an employee works two different jobs at the same company, and his or her workweek totals more than 40 hours for the two jobs, must the employee be paid overtime?

Generally speaking, such an employee must be paid time-and-a-half for all hours in excess of 40, notwithstanding the fact that the employee may have worked the two different jobs at two different wage rates. The DOL provides formulas for melding two different rates to determine an appropriate overtime rate. These formulas are fairly complex, and the Wage and Hour Administration should be contacted if questions arise regarding such a situation.

Exemptions from FLSA

Q 8:23 Are there any exemptions to minimum wage and overtime standards under the FLSA?

Yes. Four general categories of employees are exempt: executives, administrators, professionals, and outside sales persons.

The FLSA contains a potpourri of other total and partial exemptions. In many cases, these exemptions reflect political issues that were important to certain congressional leaders at one time or another. Thus, special rules apply to various industries and activities, such as fire and police forces; retail and service establishments; hospitals; domestic service; the tobacco industry; and interurban transportation. Also, the rules are somewhat different for companies operating in Puerto Rico, the Virgin Islands, and American Samoa.

Q 8:24 What is meant by a bona fide salary?

Receipt of a bona fide salary is a threshold requirement for exemption from eligibility for premium pay. In other words, no matter how well an employee's job fits into one of the exemptions—executive, professional, administrator, or outside salesperson—the exemption will not apply if the employee is paid by the hour.

Rather, the employee must receive a salary on a weekly or less frequent (for example, biweekly or monthly) schedule. Furthermore, the salary must not be subject to reduction due to absences from the job. Thus, the company cannot dock a salaried employee for arriving late or leaving early. This is the quid pro quo for being able to require that same employee to work late and on the weekend without having to pay any extra beyond the salary itself. [29 CFR § 541.118]

Q 8:25 Can a company ever make a deduction from an employee's salary without destroying the employee's exempt status under the FLSA?

The regulations of the Wage & Hour Division of the DOL allow for deductions from salary when "the employee absents himself from work for a day or more for personal reasons other than sickness or accident. Thus, if an employee is absent for a day or longer to handle personal affairs, his salaried status will not be affected if deductions are made from his salary for such absences." [29 CFR § 541.118(2)]

A recent decision from the U.S. Court of Appeals for the Seventh Circuit in Chicago aptly illustrates when deductions do change an employee's status from exempt to nonexempt:

> From April 23 to Oct. 7, 1984, Klein was on a formal discipline plan for tardiness. If Klein was more than ten minutes late a fourth time after three verbal and written warnings, she would be suspended for one day; if late a fifth time, she would be terminated. She was put on a similar plan for behavioral problems. Klein was never suspended in this period. Then on September 27, 1989, Klein was suspended for being rude, abrupt, and irritable to fellow staff members, as well as for an incident with a patient's visitor. Klein was paid for one hour of work on September 27, but was not paid for the other seven hours of the suspension. Klein was again suspended on January 31, 1990, for three days, for performance problems, specifically being rude, argumentative, and stomping around the unit, as well as being rude to a patient's son and not assisting another patient who was walking unsteadily. Klein was paid for one and one-half hours of work on January 31, but was not paid for the remaining hours of that shift or the next two days. Klein received a six-day suspension beginning on August 26, 1990, for poor judgment and an unsafe nursing practice when she failed to respond properly to a patient who was causing problems, as well as questioning the amount of medication another patient should receive. Following a series of serious safety problems occurring on September 27, 1990, Klein was suspended on September 28 until she was terminated on October 3, 1990, for job performance and conduct problems.
>
> [Klein v Rush-Presbyterian-St. Luke's Medical Center, 990 F 2d 279, 28182 (7th Cir 1993)]

Klein sued her hospital-employer, but not for wrongful discharge or employment discrimination. Instead she brought a claim for overtime pay under the FLSA [29 USC § 201219 (1988)], contending that, while she had been classified as an exempt employee and paid a salary, the monetary deductions that came along with her sundry suspensions had converted her into a non-exempt worker entitled to 1.5 times her regular rate of pay for all overtime she had worked during the statutory two-year period of her claim. The Seventh Circuit agreed with her. [Klein v Rush-Presbyterian-St. Luke's Medical Center, 990 F 2d at 28587] In fact, *"Klein* is just one of a series of recent cases in which employers have been found to have violated the overtime provisions of the FLSA by classifying as exempt employees who are not, according to DOL regulations, paid on a salary basis." [Lawrence Peikes, "Tightening the White-Collar Exemptions—The Courts Breathe New Life into the Fair Labor Standards Act," 10 *The Labor Lawyer* 1, Winter 1994, at 122, citing Shockley v City of Newport News, 997 F 2d 18 (4th Cir 1993); Kinney v District of Columbia, 994 F 2d 6 (DC Cir 1993); Martin v Malcolm Pirnie Inc, 949 F 2d 611 (2d Cir 1991), *cert denied*, 113 S Ct 298 (1992)]

The salary test can be a trap for unwary employers. For example, government contractors must require their employees to account for the actual hours they work on government projects, segregating these hours from work done on other company matters. This can lead to treating such employees in effect as hourly workers. For instance, in one celebrated case a few years ago, the defendant's engineers, accountants, architects, scientists, supervisors, and administrative employees—earning between $30,000 and $70,000—were held to be nonexempt and therefore entitled to overtime compensation for hours worked in excess of 40 each workweek, notwithstanding their substantial "salaries." The court in this case reasoned that because they were required to account for their hourly activities and were regularly docked for hours away from work, they were not salaried employees at all. [Martin v Malcolm Pirnie Inc, 949 F 2d 611 (2d Cir 1991), *cert denied*, 113 S Ct 298 (1992)]

The main issue addressed in *Martin* was "whether [Malcolm Pirnie], by subjecting grade 6 through 9 employees to pay reductions as a result of part-day absences, had converted these employees from salary based to hourly employees." [Id at 614] As the Seventh Circuit did in *Klein*, the *Martin* panel of appellate judges answered this question in the affirmative.

Klein and *Martin* follow a clear path marked by federal precedents from around the nation, which have held that "[s]ubjecting an employee's pay to deductions for absences of less than a day, including absences as short as an hour, is completely antithetical to the concept of a salaried employee." [Abshire v County of Kern, 908 F 2d 483 (9th Cir 1990), *cert denied*, 498 US 1068 (1991)]

Q 8:26   Besides executives, administrators, professionals, and outside salespersons, what are some of the other exemptions from the overtime requirements of the FLSA?

As noted at Q 8:23 in the main volume, the FLSA contains a potpourri of total and partial exemptions that were put into the act because of political and economic interests. These include:

1. Employees in retail and service establishments whose regular hourly rate is greater than 1.5 times the applicable minimum wage and who receive commissions that amount to more than half their total compensation in a typical month [29 USC § 207(i)];

2. Employees in health care institutions need not receive time and a half for hours worked in excess of 40 in a single workweek, if they receive overtime pay for hours worked in excess of 8 in a given day and in excess of 80 in any two-week period [29 USC § 207(j)];

3. Police and firefighters are covered by a somewhat complex formula for overtime entitlement. This formula looks to a 28-day cycle of employment. Special detail work by such safety forces is also subject to special treatment under the act. [29 USC § 207(p); see Q 10:41 for a more detailed discussion of how public employees are treated by federal wage and hour laws; see also, Garcia v San Antonio Metropolitan Transit Authority, 469 US 528 (1985)];

4. Employers in the tobacco industry can hire workers to assist in auctioning tobacco for up to 14 weeks at a time without paying premium pay, if such employees receive not less than 1.5 times the applicable minimum wage [29 USC § 207(m)];

5. State and local government agencies may provide workers with compensatory time off at the rate of 1.5 hours for every hour of overtime worked in lieu of paying premium pay [29 USC § 207(o); see also Q 10:41 and Garcia v San Antonio Metropolitan Transit Authority, *supra*]; and

6. An employer is permitted to employ a worker for up to ten hours above the normal 40 in the workweek for the purpose of providing that employee with remedial education leading to a high school equivalency certificate, or to improve the employee's literacy and other basic skills, so long as the remedial training is not to give the employee the specific skills of a particular job. [29 USC § 207(q)]

Q 8:27   What are FLSA standards for exemption of executive employees?

FLSA regulations provide two different tests to be used to determine whether employees are executives and therefore exempt from overtime and minimum wage protection. The "short test" applies to employees who earn more than $250 per week. To be an executive employee under the short test, employees earning more than $250 per week must meet two requirements: (1) Their primary duty must be management; and (2) they must regularly direct the work of at least two other employees. Under the FLSA, "primary duty" means that the major part, or over 50 percent (the "50 percent rule") of the employee's time must be devoted to management duties. Some courts, however, merely require that, for purposes of the short test, an employee's management duties must be the employee's principal or chief duties, not necessarily constituting over one-half of the employee's time.

Employees earning more than $155 but less than $250 per week must meet the requirements of the "long test" to be exempted as executives. The long test requires that employees meet the two requirements of the short test in addition to the following:

1. They must have the authority to hire or fire employees or to make recommendations that are given "particular weight" as to the hiring, firing, or disciplining of other workers;

2. They must customarily and regularly exercise discretionary powers in their work; and

3. They must not spend more than 20 percent of their time in any week on activities that are not directly or closely related to their management duties.

Q 8:28 What is nonexempt work?

The DOL regulations state that nonexempt work "is easily identifiable where, as in the usual case, it consists of work of the same nature as that performed by the nonexempt subordinates of the 'executive.' " [29 CFR § 541.111(b)] However, the regulations also state that nonexempt work is "more difficult to identify in cases where supervisory employees spend a significant amount of time in activities not performed by any of their subordinates and not consisting of actual supervision and management."

When the nonexempt work is the same as that performed by the executive's subordinates, such as stacking shelves and operating the cash register in a convenience food store, the DOL will make sure that a low-paid manager isn't spending more than 40 percent of the workday doing such tasks; for a manager earning at least $250 per week the test will be whether or not management remains that manager's "primary duty." (Note that for a low-paid manager in a business other than retail, only 20 percent of total work can be nonexempt in order to retain the executive exemption.)

When the nonexempt work, such as routine clerical tasks, is not the same as that normally performed by the executive's subordinates, the DOL will look at whether these nonexempt tasks are directly and closely related to the exempt work performed by the executive. The DOL's Wage & Hour Division will also give weight to whether or not the nonexempt tasks are only occasional in their occurrence. For instance, the DOL recognizes that while "[I]t might be possible for the executive to take one of his subordinates away from his usual tasks, instruct and direct him in the work to be done, and wait for him to finish it. . .[i]t would certainly not be practicable, however, to manage a department in this fashion." Consequently, occasional, even if regular, nonexempt work should not affect the integrity of the executive exemption.

Q 8:29   What is the "sole charge" rule with respect to the executive exemption from the FLSA?

An employee who is the only supervisor at an independent establishment or a physically separated branch facility may be a bona fide executive for purposes of exemption from the FLSA, despite the fact that the employee spends more than half the time performing nonexempt work at that facility. This special subcategory of the executive exemption pops up most often in the retail industry, where companies are often at many locations, whether these locations consist of convenience food stores, gas stations, restaurants, or some combination of these types of enterprises. Because the executive must be in sole charge of the establishment, this subcategory of the executive exemption by definition can apply to only one employee at any particular location. Additionally, the employee "must ordinarily be in charge of all the company activities at the location where he is employed. If he is in charge of only a portion of the company's activities at his location, then he cannot be said to be in sole charge of an independent establishment or a physically separate branch establishment." [29 CFR § 541.113(e)]

Some Wage & Hour Opinions issued over the years by the Wage & Hour (W & H) Administrator of the DOL are helpful in understanding the value and the limits of the sole charge concept:

> Where a company provided contract security guard services at a customer's facilities, and so-called installation supervisors were placed in charge of the guard company's activities and employees at the customer's facility, the W & H Administrator held that "the premises of a customer being serviced by an independent contractor (such as a contract guard service) would not constitute an independent establishment or a physically separate branch establishment of the contractor." [Opinion WH 91, signed Nov 6, 1970 by Wage & Hour Administrator Robert D Moran] The opinion's reasoning in rejecting the sole charge exemption turns upon a strict reading of the regulatory requirement that the employee must be in charge of one of the employer's facilities, not a facility owned by a customer.

> Where a resident manager was in charge of the overall operation and maintenance of a particular apartment complex owned by the employer, but a rental agent, who was not supervised by the resident manager, was also employed at the apartment house, the DOL declined to apply the sole charge exception to the

resident manager, because he "is not in charge of all the company activities at his location and since the one function over which he has no responsibility is such a significant and integral part of the employer's activities at the 'establishment.'" [Opinion WH373 signed by Assistant Wage & Hour Administrator Herbert J Cohen on Feb 20, 1976 (emphasis in original)]

Gas station managers were found by the DOL to meet the requirements of the sole charge test where (1) their method of compensation was salary plus commission with guaranteed earnings in excess of the minimum weekly salary amount, (2) they regularly supervised two or more full-time employees or full-time equivalents, and (3) these managers were in charge of essentially all the functions at the gas stations placed in their charge. [Opinion WH420 signed by Acting Wage & Hour Administrator Warren D Landis on June 9, 1977]

Q 8:30   What is the DOL's definition of two full-time equivalents?

Since a bona fide executive must regularly supervise two or more employees to qualify for the overtime exemption to the FLSA, companies operating numerous small locations or departments with few employees sometimes encounter difficulty in meeting the test. For example, where a gas station manager regularly supervised one attendant who worked 40 hours per week and another who regularly worked only 20 hours, the DOL ruled that the manager was not a bona fide executive employee. [Opinion WH-463, signed by Wage & Hour Administrator Xavier M Vela, Aug 21, 1978]

However, in situations such as many offices staffed by clerical employees and secretaries, the fact that a full-time employee only normally works 35 or 37.5 hours per week will not result in the DOL counting such employees as anything less than full-time equivalents, provided they are receiving employee benefits available to the company's regular full-time workers.

Q 8:31   Are working foremen bona fide executives under the FLSA?

The DOL's regulations identify two types of working foremen who ordinarily are not exempt from the overtime provisions of the FLSA:

- Working foremen, sometimes called strawbosses or gang leaders, who work beside their coworkers, performing the same tasks as they perform
- Working foremen who, while they don't work alongside their subordinates, perform routine, nonexempt tasks of their own

The DOL gives some examples of the latter type of working foremen, as follows:

> Typical of employees in dual jobs are: (1) Foremen or supervisors who also perform one or more of the "production" or "operating" functions, though no other employees in the plant perform such work. An example of this kind of employee is the foreman in a millinery or garment plant who is also the cutter, or the foreman in a garment factory who operates a multiple-needle machine not requiring a full-time operator; (2) foremen or supervisors who have as a regular part of their duties the adjustment, repair, or maintenance of machinery or equipment. Examples of this category are the foreman-fixer in the hosiery industry who devotes a considerable amount of time to making adjustments and repairs to the machines of his subordinates, or the planer-mill foreman who repairs the machines and grinds the knives; (3) foremen or supervisors who perform clerical work other than the maintenance of time and production records of their subordinates; for example, the foreman of the shipping room who makes out the bills of lading and other shipping records, the warehouse foreman who acts as inventory clerk, the head shipper who also has charge of a finished goods stock room, assisting in placing goods on shelves and keeping perpetual inventory records, or the office manager, head bookkeeper, or chief clerk who performs routine bookkeeping. [29 CFR § 541.115(c)]

In all these examples, if the nonexempt work consumes most of the employee's time, that employee will not qualify for the executive exemption from the FLSA, regardless of how well the employee is compensated in salary.

Q 8:32   Are executive trainees considered to be bona fide executives under the FLSA?

A trainee learning to become an executive, such as a manager/trainee working under the tutelage of a store manager in a convenience food store, is not a bona fide executive if that trainee is not in fact performing executive functions, such as supervising the store's employees. [29 CFR § 541.116]

Q 8:33   What are FLSA standards for exemption of administrative employees?

As with executive employees, FLSA regulations set forth a short test and a long test to determine whether employees are administrators exempt from overtime and minimum wage provisions. The short test applies to those employees who earn more than $250 per week. Employees are exempt under the short test if their primary duty consists of either: (1) The performance of office or non-manual work directly related to the management policies or the general business operations of their employer or their employer's customers; or (2) the performance of administrative functions of school systems or educational institutions that are directly related to the instruction or training carried on in such systems or institutions.

The long test applies to employees who earn more than $155 but less than $250 per week. These employees are exempt if they meet the requirements of the short test and if they:

- Customarily and regularly exercise discretion and independent judgment
- Regularly perform, under general supervision only, specialized or technical work that requires training
- Perform special assignments
- Regularly assist an employer or person in an administrative or executive capacity
- Do not devote more than 20 percent (40 percent for employees of retail establishments) of time in a workweek to activities not directly related to their performance of administrative duties

Q 8:34   Who are bona fide administrative employees under the FLSA?

The Wage & Hour Administrator of the DOL has identified three general types of bona fide administrative employees:

1. The assistant to a proprietor or to an executive or administrative employee. Typical titles of persons in this group are executive assistant to the president, confidential assistant, executive secretary, assistant to the general manager, administrative assistant, and, in retail and service establishments, assistant manager and assistant buyer. [29 CFR § 541.201(a)(1)]

2. Employees who can be described as staff rather than line employees, or as functional rather than departmental heads. They include, among others, employees who act as advisory specialists to the management. Typical examples of such advisory specialists are tax experts, insurance experts, sales research experts, wage-rate analysts, investment consultants, foreign-exchange consultants, and statisticians. [29 CFR § 541.201(a)(2)] Other examples under this category are credit managers, purchasing agents, buyers, safety directors, labor relations directors, and others in charge of so-called functional departments.

3. Those who perform special assignments. Among them are a number of persons whose work is performed away from the employer's place of business. Typical titles of such persons are lease buyers, field representatives of utility companies, location managers of motion picture companies, and district gaugers for oil companies. This classification also includes employees whose special assignments are performed entirely or partly inside their employer's place of business. Examples are special organization planners, customers' brokers in stock exchange firms, so-called account executives in advertising firms, and contact or promotion persons of various types. [29 CFR § 541.201(a)(3)]

Q 8:35 Is a job title a sufficient yardstick of whether or not an employee is a bona fide administrator under the FLSA?

No. To the contrary, the DOL's regulations are replete with warnings that job titles alone are not sufficient to establish employees' administrative status: "It should be particularly noted that this is a field which is rife with honorific titles that do not adequately portray the nature of the employee's duties." [29 CFR § 541.201(3)(i)]

The employees for whom exemption is sought under the term "administrative" have extremely diverse functions and a wide variety of titles. A title alone is of little or no assistance in determining the true importance of an employee to the employer or his or her exempt or nonexempt status under the regulations. Titles can be had cheaply and are of no determinative value.

[29 CFR § 541.201(b)(1)]

Q 8:36   What kinds of work must an employee perform to be classified as a bona fide administrator under the FLSA?

As with executives, administrators' primary duties must be non-manual and nonroutine in nature. Additionally, under this exemption, the exercise of discretion and independent judgment becomes a very important determinative factor:

> In general, the exercise of discretion and independent judgment involves the comparison and evaluation of possible courses of conduct and acting or making a decision after the various possibilities have been considered. The term . . . moreover, implies that the person has the authority or power to make an independent choice, free from immediate direction or supervision and with respect to matters of significance. [29 CFR § 541.207 (a)]

Q 8:37   Are academic administrators classified as bona fide administrative employees under the FLSA?

In general, yes. Administrative personnel in the employ of elementary and secondary school systems, institutions of higher education, and most other educational establishments meet the requirements for this exemption. Special education schools, such as those for the mentally handicapped or the gifted, public as well as private schools, and nursery schools (at least those under the auspices of the state) are all typically included. [29 CFR § 541.215] However, private day care centers and preschool programs are not noted in the regulation, and therefore owners and operators of such facilities are cautioned to take special care before including their employees in this category of exemption.

Q 8:38   What are FLSA standards for the exemption of professional employees?

Professional employees are those employees engaged in the practice of law or medicine or who are teachers in a school system or educational institution. These employees are automatically exempt from minimum wage and overtime standards, regardless of salary level. Other types of employees may be considered professional employees and may be exempt if they earn more than $250 per week and meet the two requirements of the short test: (1) They must perform work requiring advanced education in a field of science; and (2) they must work as a teacher in a school system or educational institution.

The long test is applied to employees who earn between $170 and $250 per week. The requirements of the long test include those of the short test as well as the following:

- The employee's work must require the consistent exercise of discretion and judgment
- The work must be predominantly intellectual, varied in character, and its output must not be standardized in relation to a given period of time
- The employee must not devote more than 20 percent of his or her time in a workweek to activities that are not an essential part of, or incident to, the employee's professional duties

Q 8:39   What is meant by the term "learned professions" under the professional exemption to the FLSA?

To qualify as a "learned profession," an occupation must meet the following criteria:

1. Knowledge of an advanced field of science or learning that is usually acquired through a prolonged course of study, as distinguished from a general academic or liberal education or apprenticeship program.
2. The knowledge must not be attainable at the high school level.
3. The knowledge must be in a field of science or learning, not in the so-called mechanical arts.

4. The knowledge must be obtained in a prolonged course of study. At least this must be the customary way of obtaining it; most lawyers have gone to law schools, but even in the late-20th century there remain a few states where a person may clerk for a lawyer and thus achieve some or all of the education required for admission to the bar (such a lawyer is nonetheless viewed as a bona fide member of a learned profession).

[29 CFR § 541.301]

Q 8:40   Is the number of recognized learned professions expanding for purposes of the professional employee exemption?

The DOL has recognized in its regulations that:

> [The] areas in which professional exemptions may be available are expanding. As knowledge is developed, academic training is broadened, degrees are offered in new and diverse fields, specialties are created and the true specialist, so trained, who is given new and greater responsibilities, comes closer to meeting the tests. [29 CFR § 541.301(e)(2)]

The regulations warn employers: "However, just as an excellent legal stenographer is not a lawyer, these technical specialists must be more than highly skilled technicians."

The regulations distinguish between an employee who may become a bona fide executive by virtue of working up the ladder, and a bona fide professional who rarely, if ever, achieves this status without formal study:

> Many employees in industry rise to executive or administrative positions by their natural ability and good common sense, combined with their experience with a company, without the aid of a college education or degree in any area. A college education would perhaps give an executive or administrator a more cultured and polished approach, but the necessary know-how for doing the executive job would depend upon the person's own inherent talent. The professional person, on the other hand, attains his status after a prolonged course of specialized intellectual instruction and study. [29 CFR § 541.301(e)(2)]

Q 8:41   What are the recognized "artistic professions" for purposes of the professional employee exemption?

The DOL regulations speak of "such fields as music, writing, the theater, and the plastic and graphic arts." [29 CFR § 541.302] The work must rely primarily upon "the invention, imagination, or talent of the employee." The DOL has experienced particular difficulty in determining the exempt or nonexempt status of announcers on radio and television:

> The determination of the exempt or nonexempt status of radio and television announcers . . . has been relatively difficult because of the merging of the artistic aspects of the job with the commercial. There is considerable variation in the type of work performed by various announcers, ranging from predominantly routine to predominantly exempt work. The wide variation in earnings as between individual announcers, from the highly paid "name" announcer on a national network who is greatly in demand by sponsors to the staff announcer paid a comparatively small salary in a small station, indicates not only great differences in personality, voice and manner, but also in some inherent special ability or talent which, while extremely difficult to define, is nevertheless real . . . . The determination of whether a particular announcer is exempt as a professional employee must be based upon his individual duties and the amount of exempt and nonexempt work performed, as well as his compensation. [29 CFR § 541.302(d)]

The foregoing analysis is helpful to all employers of members of the so-called artistic professions in that it suggests (1) that the DOL will not simply look to a job description or label, but will weigh the creative versus the routine tasks performed by the artist/employee and (2) that size of the employee's compensation may also be a determinative factor under this subcategory of exemption.

Q 8:42   Are outside salespersons exempt from the minimum wage and overtime provisions of the FLSA?

Yes, if the salesperson is employed in, and regularly engages in, making sales or obtaining orders or contracts at a location other than the employer's place of business, and if he or she does not spend more than 20 percent of his or her time per workweek on duties other than sales.

Q 8:43   What are "sales" for purposes of the outside salesperson exemption under the FLSA?

Under the FLSA, "sale" or "sell" includes any sale, exchange, contract to sell, consignment for sale, shipment for sale, or other disposition. [29 USC § 203(k)] The regulations and wage and hour opinions distinguish sales from such related activities as driving, promoting, and clerical tasks, which typically must not exceed 20 percent of the salesperson's chores, although incidental driving (i.e., not to deliver product, but merely to get from one sales call to the next) is not counted for purposes of this determination, regardless of how it compares to actual selling time. [92 *BNA Wage and Hour Manual* 752 (Apr 24, 1976)]

Q 8:44   What is meant by the term "outside" salesperson?

A bona fide outside salesperson must be customarily and regularly away from the employer's place of business. [29 CFR § 541.502(a)]

> Characteristically the outside salesman is one who makes his sales at his customer's place of business. This is the reverse of sales made by mail or telephone (except where the telephone is used merely as an adjunct to personal calls). Thus any fixed site, whether home or office, used by a salesman as a headquarters or for telephonic solicitation of sales must be construed as one of his employer's places of business, even though his employer is not in any formal sense the owner or tenant of the property. It should not be inferred from the foregoing that an outside salesman loses his exemption by displaying his samples in hotel sample rooms as he travels from city to city. [29 CFR § 541.502(b)]

Q 8:45   Are public employees treated differently from private sector employees under the DOL's approach to the so-called "white collar" exemptions to FLSA?

Recognizing that many public-sector employers are obligated by statutory or constitutional provisions to deduct salary from state and local government employees for missed hours of work, DOL in 1992 issued a "Final Rule on FLSA Exemptions for Public Employees," [57 Fed Reg 37,677] that preserves the exempt status of public executives, administrators, and professionals who are paid a salary that is subject to hourly deductions due to statute, ordinance, regulation, policy, or practice.

> Why did DOL revise the salary test applicable to public-sector employees, but not private-sector employees? . . . DOL expressed fear that recent judicial applications of the regulations' 'salary test' (see Q 8:25) created potential for 'enormous, unforeseen liability' against public employers that 'may threaten their fiscal integrity. [56 Fed Reg 45,825 (1991)]

Of course, private employers may find themselves no less exposed to "enormous, unforeseen liability," as when a federal government contract requires accounting for all hours worked and leads the contractor to deduct for brief absences that cannot be covered by accrued leave time. [Id at 132, citing Reich v Malcolm Pirnie Inc, 821 F Supp 905 (SD NY 1993) in which the court awarded a class of well-compensated, "salaried" claimants a total of $515,455.50 in back pay plus prejudgment interest, under just such government contracting circumstances] Thus, the DOL's favoritism toward public as opposed to private employers appears grounded in a faulty distinction between these two sectors.

Q 8:46   What is the DOL's "window of correction"?

Under DOL regulations [see 29 CFR § 541.118(a)(6)], an employer who makes an impermissible deduction from an exempt employee's salary, which could have the effect of destroying the exemption (see Q 8:25) can correct the error and bring the company back into compliance with regard to that employee. This "window of correction" will not apply in every case; rather, the rule reads as follows:

> [I]nterpretations will depend upon the facts in the particular case. Where deductions are generally made when there is no work available, it indicates that there was no intention to pay the employee on a salary basis. In such a case the exemption would not be applicable to him during the entire period when such deductions were being made. On the other hand, where a deduction not permitted by these interpretations is inadvertent, or is made for reasons other than lack of work, the exemption will not be considered to have been lost if the employer reimburses the employee for such deduction and promises to comply in the future. [Id]

Q 8:47   What are the most common mistakes that employers make with regard to the FLSA exemptions from minimum wage and overtime pay requirements?

In the author's experience, the most common mistake of employers operating in white collar environments is to treat all employees as if they were exempt. Since many employers pay secretaries on a salary basis, it is often assumed, erroneously, that overtime obligations may be ignored. In one company, the personnel department had actually issued a memorandum to all its employees, advising them that "from now on there will be no distinction made between exempt and nonexempt employees." Obviously the company was not empowered to repeal the federal statute!

Such serious errors are mitigated most often by the fact that many of these errant corporations operate their offices on a 37.5 hour workweek, so that even when their salaried secretaries do work a few extra hours in a given week, they do not end up working more than the 40 hours that would be covered by their straight time pay anyway. Nevertheless, a problem can arise either when a nonexempt employee is in fact regularly working more than a 40-hour workweek, or when an employee is fired, embittered, and claims she or he was regularly surpassing the 40-hour limit without receiving suitable compensation. Since most such employers also are violating the FLSA by not requiring the keeping of time records for such nonexempt salaried workers, an embittered ex-employee is very likely to win on this kind of claim, even though that person may be lying.

A second common error is to use payroll deductions as a means of recovering cash register losses, lost time for which the employee has not accrued sufficient paid leave, and a multitude of other reasons. The result can be to take the employee down below the minimum wage or to destroy the salary status upon which an executive, administrative, or professional exemption must be based. Employers are better advised to use their disciplinary system to control such problems as absenteeism and register shortages, thus keeping in compliance with the requirements of the FLSA.

Q 8:48 What remedies are available to an employee if an employer fails to comply with minimum wage and overtime provisions?

An employer that fails to comply with federal or state minimum wage and overtime compensation laws may be ordered to change its compensation practices to conform to legal standards. In addition, the employer may be required to pay, as damages, the amount of minimum wages and overtime compensation wrongfully withheld. An employer may also be required to pay additional damages (e.g., liquidated) damages as a penalty for noncompliance.

Violations and Penalties

Q 8:49 What are liquidated damages?

Liquidated damages are assessed at an amount equal to the minimum wage and overtime compensation wrongfully withheld. Thus, if an employer, in violation of federal or state wage laws, failed to pay an employee $5,000 in minimum wages and overtime, the employer may be liable to pay $10,000 in damages, comprising $5,000 in withheld compensation and $5,000 in liquidated damages. An employer may also be required to pay the legal fees incurred by an employee seeking minimum wage and overtime compensation.

An employer may avoid assessment of liquidated damages if the employer can demonstrate that it acted in good faith when failing to pay minimum wages or overtime and had a reasonable basis for believing that there was no violation of any federal or state regulation. The employer must show that it honestly intended to ascertain and follow the applicable wage laws. A plea of ignorance will not suffice.

Q 8:50 Who can sue an employer for minimum wages and overtime?

FLSA provides a cause of action both to the wronged employee and to the secretary of labor. If the secretary of labor brings a legal action against the employer, the employee's right of action is automatically terminated by the filing of the secretary's lawsuit. Subsequently, the employee must depend on the secretary's attorneys to collect the wages due.

Q 8:51   What is the statute of limitations for the employee or the secretary of labor in collecting back pay?

The FLSA has a two-year statute of limitations on collecting back wages for nonwillful violations of the law and goes back three years for willful violations.

Q 8:52   What is a willful violation of the FLSA?

If an employer knowingly violates FLSA regulations or demonstrates "reckless disregard" for its rules, regardless of whether its conduct violates the Act, the employer is guilty of a willful violation. This will extend the statute of limitations to three years for purposes of collecting back wages. With respect to liquidated damages, the U.S. Supreme Court and other federal courts have indicated that a more specific standard may be applied before assessing such damages, similar to the standard required for assessing punitive damages under common law.

Q 8:53   Has the term "willful," as used in the FLSA, changed recently?

In 1988, the U.S. Supreme Court adopted the definition of a willful violation of the FLSA most employers favor. [McLaughlin v Richland Shoe Co, 486 US 128 (1988)] An employer is guilty of a willful violation, triggering a three-year statute of limitations, only when it acts with actual knowledge or reckless disregard of whether its compensation scheme violates the FLSA. The Court rejected the DOL's suggestion that willfulness is present when the employer knows that the FLSA may apply but proceeds without a reasonable basis for believing its procedures are in compliance with the law. The six justices who made up the majority felt that this sanction was punitive in nature and, therefore, should be triggered only when a company has a fairly high level of culpability.

Q 8:54 When will an employer be required to pay an employee double damages under the FLSA?

Section 216 of the FLSA [29 USC § 216] states that any employer who violates the overtime or minimum wage provision of the Act "shall be liable to the employee or employees affected in the amount of their unpaid minimum wages, or their unpaid overtime compensation . . . , and in an additional equal amount as liquidated damages." Read in a vacuum, this provision would permit the successful employee-plaintiff to receive double damages in every successful lawsuit for back wages. However, to clarify and amend the FLSA, in 1947 Congress passed the Portal-to-Portal Act [29 USC § 260] which provides employers with some relief from FLSA Section 216's liquidated damage provision. While double damages are intended to compensate the successful employee-litigant for the wait and difficulty in collecting the back wages, Section 260 states: "If the employer shows to the satisfaction of the court that the act or omission giving rise to such action was in good faith and that he had reasonable grounds for believing that his act or omission was not a violation of the Fair Labor Standards Act of 1938 . . . , the court may, in its sound discretion, award no liquidated damages." The court also is accorded discretion to award liquidated damages of less than 100 percent of the back wages won by the successful employee-plaintiff.

Child Labor

Q 8:55 What laws restrict the use of child labor?

It is common knowledge that child labor was one of the worst abuses of many industries during the nineteenth and early twentieth centuries. Besides FLSA, virtually every state has laws controlling the use of child labor. Child-labor legislation focuses chiefly on two issues: (1) the number of hours that children are employed, and (2) the type of work that they perform.

Q 8:56 How do the various state laws on child labor interact with provisions of the FLSA?

The child-labor provisions of the FLSA apply in every state. However, if the state law offers greater protection to its children, the state law supersedes any lesser protections afforded by the FLSA.

Q 8:57 Are there any other federal laws that deal with child labor?

In addition to the FLSA, there are three other important federal laws that deal with child labor:

1. The Walsh-Healey Act sets wage and hour standards under federal supply contracts.
2. The Mineral Land Leasing Act, which applies to mines that are operated on lands leased from the federal government.
3. The Interstate Commerce Act has regulations limiting the employment of children as drivers in interstate commerce.

Q 8:58 How do the federal child-labor laws regulate the labor of children?

Federal laws deal with the problem of child labor on an occupational, rather than an industrial basis. This means that, in general, children are not forbidden to work in any particular industry. Rather, the kinds of jobs that they might do are limited by the law. Generally, dangerous jobs cannot be performed by children. Other jobs are acceptable but must be performed only outside of regular school hours and only for a limited number of hours per day.

Q 8:59 What are the penalties for violating child-labor laws?

Violation of child-labor laws can result in fines and, in very serious cases, imprisonment.

Q 8:60 Is the DOL becoming more zealous in enforcing child-labor laws?

Yes. Child-labor violations have become a high-profile issue in the 1990s. In some respects, this seems almost anachronistic, conjuring up visions of "breaker boys" in the coal fields of nineteenth-century Pennsylvania or Kentucky, but, in fact, the proliferation of fast-food restaurants and convenience stores has created a demand for teen-aged employees. When the labor pool is small, companies may be tempted to employ teenagers too many hours and to ignore their operation of dangerous equipment, such as meat slicers. Responding to a perception of widespread abuses, the DOL investigated some national fast-food restaurants, notably Burger King, during the past year, citing them for serious violations of the child-labor laws.

On a completely different industrial front, a one-day "blitz" of 1,890 child labor investigations was conducted across the country in the garment trade and migrant labor camps, according to congressional testimony by Assistant Secretary (for employment standards) William C. Brooks.

The clear message to employers is not to take child labor laws for granted.

Compensation and Benefits

Q 8:61 What are the recent trends in employee compensation?

A study by the Bureau of National Affairs (BNA) reported that a favorite vehicle of financially troubled companies is an employee stock ownership plan (ESOP). Automatic pay increases seem to have given way to merit pay procedures. Many companies are introducing gain-sharing plans to encourage managers and rank-and-file employees to cooperate and work together to improve productivity. Two-tier pay plans, once very much in vogue (especially in tandem with concessionary collective bargaining) seem to be losing their luster. On the other hand, lump-sum bonuses in lieu of pay increases—which unions at one time seemed strongly to resist—now seem to be catching on, turning up in about one-third of all union contracts.

Q 8:62   What is the federal income tax status of employer-provided educational assistance?

Prior to changes in the tax law in 1988, payments to employees of up to $5,250 per year for tuition, fees, books, supplies, and so forth could be excluded from gross income under an employer's educational assistance program. [IRC § 127] For tax years beginning after 1988, however, tax-free treatment of payments under an educational assistance program is not available. Educational assistance that is not excludable under other sections of the Code—for example, Section 117 (qualified scholarships), Section 132 (employee fringe benefits), or Section 162 (trade-or-business expenses)—is includible in gross income and subject to federal income tax and employment taxes.

Q 8:63   How are dependent care expenses treated for federal income tax purposes?

Under Code Section 129, employers are allowed to exclude dependent care benefits of up to $5,000 annually from employees' gross income, for federal tax purposes. Additionally, the code permits married couples to claim a tax credit for child-care and dependent-care expenses, when one spouse works full-time and the other works at least part-time or is going to school.

Q 8:64   What is a DCAP?

A DCAP is a written nondiscriminatory plan pursuant to which an employer provides to an employee, on a tax-free basis, child or dependent care services. The amount excludable from gross income is limited to $5,000 ($2,500 for married individuals filing separately). Furthermore, the amount excluded from the employee's income in any taxable year cannot exceed the employee's earned income for the taxable year or, if the employee is married at the end of the year, the lesser of the employee's or the spouse's earned income.

To claim the exclusion, an employee is generally required to include on his or her tax return the name, address, and taxpayer identification number of the person performing the child or dependent care services.

Amounts that are excluded from gross income under a DCAP will directly offset dependent care expenses that could otherwise be available for purposes of the dependent care credit.

Q 8:65   What is the dependent care tax credit?

Code Section 21 provides an income tax credit with respect to dependent care expenses a taxpayer incurs in order to be gainfully employed. The dependent care expenses must be incurred with respect to a "qualifying individual," which is defined as a dependent under age 13 for whom the taxpayer can claim a dependency exemption, a dependent who is physically or mentally incapable of caring for himself or herself, or the taxpayer's spouse if he or she is physically or mentally incapable of caring for himself or herself.

Taxpayers with adjusted gross incomes of $10,000 or less are allowed a credit equal to 30 percent of employment-related expenses. For taxpayers with adjusted gross incomes of from $10,000 to $28,000, the credit is reduced by one percentage point for each $2,000 of adjusted gross income, or a fraction thereof, above $10,000. The employment-related expenses that will qualify for the credit may not exceed the employee's earned income for a taxable year, or, if the employee is married at the end of the year, the lesser of the employee's or the spouse's earned income. These expenses are further limited to $2,400 per year ($4,800 for two or more qualifying dependents). Furthermore, the credit is unavailable for any qualifying dependent care expenses for which payments or reimbursements have been made by an employer under a DCAP.

Q 8:66   What are 404(c) plans?

A pension plan meeting the requirements of ERISA Section 404(c) permits its participants to determine how their accounts will be invested. For this reason such a plan is called "self-directed."

Q 8:67   Is a participant in a self-directed (404(c)) plan a plan fiduciary?

No. Even though such participants make investment decisions, they do not become plan fiduciaries under ERISA. Although a fiduciary is defined under ERISA as "any person" who exercises discretionary authority or control over the disposition of plan assets, ERISA Section 404(c) has carved out an exception to this broad proviso. Consequently, fiduciary responsibility remains with the plan's normal fiduciaries; however, their burden is somewhat lightened by ERISA Section 404(c)—while they still must prudently select the range of investment options available to plan participants, they do not share liability with those participants for bad investment decisions or improper acts the latter may perform.

Q 8:68 Are there any limits to how employees can invest their accounts in 404(c) plans?

Yes. First, the plans' fiduciaries select the investment categories from which employee participants must choose. At least three diversified categories must be offered. Second, not only are the participants limited to choosing from among these core (and possibly other) categories, but additionally, the plan will also limit the frequency with which participants can move the money in their accounts from one category of investment to another. Third, the plan may limit the number of categories of investments into which each participant can divide an account at any one time.

Q 8:69 How much diversity will a 404(c) plan provide?

Typically, a plan under ERISA Section 404(c) will provide a range of choices from very conservative, but relatively low-yield option(s) to one or more providing at least the potential for higher yield at an enhanced risk. Usually the greater the risk of the investment vehicle, the more often participants will be permitted to transfer the assets in their accounts. The same frequency of transfer accorded higher-risk investments must also be accorded to the least risky and those in between.

Q 8:70 What was the Executive Life Insurance Company crisis?

Companies controlling overfunded pension plans frequently have been tempted to tap the excess funding and channel it back into operating capital. If done properly, this can be perfectly legal under ERISA regulations. While the transaction is complicated and requires expert handling, basically it involves two main steps: (1) termination of the existing overfunded pension plan, and (2) the purchase of annuity contracts to ensure that plan participants and beneficiaries realize their vested rights. In shopping for such annuities during the 1980s, many companies discovered that a California-based insurance company named Executive Life was able to undercut the competition where the cost of the annuity contracts was concerned. Executive Life was able to match competitors' promised returns on investment at lower contract cost to the purchasing companies because the money was heavily invested in "junk bonds." Like the whirlpool of a sinking ship, the dive of Drexel Burnham Lambert into bankruptcy and the shudders that ripped through the "junk bond" market placed Executive Life in such a precarious financial condition that the California Insurance Commission placed the company in conservatorship on April 11, 1991, and cut benefits to retirees owning Executive Life's annuity contracts by 30 percent.

Q 8:71 Are companies that terminated retirement plans and purchased annuities from Executive Life liable to their retirees for lost pension benefits?

The federal Pension Benefit Guarantee Corporation (PBGC) has taken the position that if the company purchasing the annuity fulfilled all its fiduciary obligations under ERISA rules when doing so, then neither the company nor the PBGC is liable to retirees thereafter. However, the DOL has determined that some companies did not fulfill their fiduciary duty in selecting Executive Life as the insurance carrier from which to buy their retirees' annuities. For example, in a suit filed in June 1991 against Pacific Lumber, the DOL asserts the company overruled the recommendation of an outside consultant in choosing Executive Life over carriers more highly rated in the consultant's report. Other companies have also been sued by the DOL for breach of fiduciary duty in the wake of the Executive Life debacle.

Q 8:72 Are any other insurance companies experiencing difficulties similar to those encountered by Executive Life?

Subsequent to placing Executive Life Insurance Company into conservatorship in April 1991, the California Insurance Commission also imposed a conservatorship on San Diego-based First Capital Life Insurance Company. Meanwhile, the state of New Jersey in July 1991 took control of Mutual Benefit Life Insurance Company. Knowledgeable commentators do not believe that the problems encountered by these insurance carriers herald a new wave of failures analogous to the savings and loan crisis. However, more insurance companies may require governmental intervention before the bad decisions and excesses of the past decade are overcome.

Q 8:73 What is the fiduciary duty of an employer that desires to terminate a pension plan and purchase annuities?

The DOL's position is that when the excess funding following plan termination is going back to the company, and the plan fiduciaries are closely associated with that same employer (for example, members of management), then those fiduciaries must do a careful and thorough investigation with a view to buying the safest annuity policy, that is, the policy most likely to pay benefits in the future. The rationale for this tough standard is that any savings realized by the purchase of a less expensive annuity policy will benefit the company, not the participants and beneficiaries of the plan.

Q 8:74 What is a Form 5500?

Companies offering benefit plans governed by the ERISA are required to report annually to the DOL, using Form 5500. Form 5500 is filed with the Internal Revenue Service (IRS) along with a company's annual tax return. The IRS makes the initial review and, if an error is uncovered, sends out up to two letters requesting voluntary correction. If the errant employer ignores these letters, the file is forwarded to the DOL, which sends out a third letter. The employer must comply with this demand within 45 days. Otherwise, a penalty will be assessed by the DOL, absent a reasonable excuse. The fine can be a maximum of $1,000 per day from the date filing was first due. In practice, the DOL's fines have averaged around $70,000.

Q 8:75 What information is reported on Form 5500?

Form 5500, and the abbreviated Form 5500C/R for plans with fewer than 100 participants, require information about a plan's contribution, participation, and investment activities sufficient to permit the DOL and the PBGC to monitor the plan's compliance with ERISA regulations. In addition to filing the form itself, plan administrators must sometimes attach various schedules, such as Schedule A (benefits provided by an insurance company), Schedule B (actuarial information if the plan is a defined benefit plan), Schedule C (service provider and trustee information), and schedules for other special situations.

Executive Compensation

Q 8:76   Is executive compensation different from compensation for rank-and-file employees?

Yes. Executive compensation differs not only in amount, but also in purpose. Consequently, the method of compensating the company's executives differs dramatically from the way in which rank-and-file employees are compensated.

Q 8:77   How does the purpose of compensation for executives differ from that for rank-and-file employees?

Frequently, an executive's compensation is geared (at least in part) to the success of an enterprise and his or her contribution to that success. Often, executives must take greater risks in order to realize greater rewards. Incentives and bonuses are common components of executive compensation plans. This reflects the close relationship between performance and reward that exists for executives.

Q 8:78   How is the method for compensating executives different from that for compensating rank-and-file employees?

Rank-and-file employees usually receive an hourly wage or a weekly, biweekly, or monthly salary derived from an hourly rate. Executives receive a salary that is not geared to hours worked. In addition, executives may have other components of compensation that fluctuate dramatically with the enterprise's performance and thus provide them with substantial opportunities for capital accumulation.

Q 8:79   Can shareholders challenge executive compensation?

The company's shareholders can always initiate a derivative action in court to challenge the amounts or kinds of executive compensation, regardless of whether the IRS disallows a corporate deduction for executive compensation. This can occur in either a publicly held company or a closely held company. Shareholders may challenge expensive management schemes to avert or discourage takeover bids. To the extent that "golden parachute" programs for management are a part of such schemes, they may be targets of shareholder challenges. In closely held companies, a more typical shareholder complaint is that shareholder-managers deplete the profits for their own salaries and benefits, while dividends are kept at low levels to the detriment of inactive shareholders.

Q 8:80   Are tax savings for executives a factor in setting a compensation strategy?

Tax considerations are always a major aspect of executive compensation planning, but never more so than since Section 162(m) was added to the Internal Revenue Code of 1986 by the Omnibus Budget Reconciliation Act of 1993 (OBRA '93). This section denies deductions to publicly traded companies for compensation paid to executives in excess of $1 million per top executive annually. This controversial section brings under its broad umbrella most forms of executive compensation, including

- Base salary
- Cash bonuses
- Stock bonuses
- Stock options
- Restricted stock
- Other equity-based forms of remuneration

Section 162(m) applies to tax years beginning after January 1, 1994. Covered executives under the provision include the chief executive officer and all other executives whose compensation must be reported to shareholders under the Securities Exchange Act of 1934 because they are among the top four highest-paid officers of the company.

Section 162(m) has five exclusions from its income calculation:

1. Income paid under contracts signed before February 17, 1993;
2. Nontaxable fringe benefits;
3. Payments to and from a qualified pension plan;
4. Certain amounts payable only on a commission basis; and
5. Performance-based compensation

Of these five exclusions, performance-based income is clearly the most significant. Compensation is performance based if:

- The compensation is payable only upon achievement of pre-established, objective performance goals set by a compensation committee of the board of directors
- The plan is reviewed and approved by the shareholders
- The compensation is paid only after the committee certifies that the goals have been met

Q 8:81 How do life insurance policies fit into executive compensation planning techniques?

Life insurance policies serve a variety of purposes in a company's executive compensation program. Insurance policies have been used by companies as a means of building up a tax-free fund to cover liabilities for executive benefits. For instance, "key-person policies" are used to provide the corporation with a benefit at the death of one or more top executives. The benefit may enable the company to cover its obligations to the key manager's estate (such as unfunded, vested pension obligations) or to buy out corporate stock held by the executive.

Life insurance policies are the most popular internal company investment to cover liabilities for executive benefits to date; however, lower tax rates under the Tax Reform Act of 1986 will reduce the leveraging that previously resulted from the tax-free inside buildup of the policy and the tax-deductible interest on policy loans. At any rate, life insurance policies can be attractive vehicles to help companies (especially smaller ones) shoulder their executive compensation burden.

Q 8:82   What professional input is needed for executive compensation planning?

A comprehensive executive compensation plan is a product of team effort. Whether comprising in-house or outside professionals, the executive compensation team requires legal, accounting, investment, and human resources expertise. The team must be able to ascertain the demands of the labor market; identify the compensation vehicles (such as stock options, life insurance policies, salary, and incentive bonuses) that best suit the company and the owners and managers; and decipher the provisions of the Tax Reform Act of 1986, ERISA, and other relevant federal and state laws in terms of matching human resources needs with the company's financial capabilities.

Q 8:83   Does public relations fit into executive compensation planning?

First, public relations is an essential component of compensation strategy in terms of justifying executive packages to shareholders and debt holders who frequently question this area of business expense. Second, internal communications may include explaining to executives the value of the various components of their packages, as well as the company's reasons (for example, general business climate, corporate growth plans, and industry competition) for maintaining these components at certain levels. At times, it may also be necessary to justify executive compensation to rank-and-file employees.

Q 8:84   Are U.S. executives still the most highly compensated in the world?

In 1993, the nation's top executives sustained their status as world beaters in the compensation department. Walt Disney's Michael Eisner was the untouchable champion at $203 million, primarily in the form of capital gains realized from the exercise of stock options. The Travelers' Sanford Weill weighed in second at a hefty $52.6 million. "Chief executives' salaries and bonuses rose 8.1 percent in 1993, matching the brisk 8.1 percent pace seen in 1992, and mirroring an 18.9 percent improvement in corporate profit." [Joann S Lublin, "Looking Good: For CEOs, the Pay Gains Haven't Stopped. It's Just the Packaging that has Changed," *The Wall Street Journal*, Apr 13, 1994, at R1]

In 1994 and 1995 this trend continued unabated. In fact, even executives who failed were well rewarded. For example, when the chief executive officer of W.R. Grace & Co. was forced to resign, following a report by a former federal judge confirming that "grounds existed to find that [the CEO] had sexually harassed certain employees of the company," the board of directors proposed "a severance package of $20 million." [Diana B Henriques, "Sexual Harassment and A Chief Executive," *The New York Times,* Mar 30, 1995, at D1, D7]

Neither violating federal employment discrimination laws nor failing to perform seems to affect this nation's top executives. *The Wall Street Journal* commented on this phenomenon, suggesting, "Call it the Glass Floor. Like the Glass Ceiling, it is an invisible barrier standing between those at the very top and the rest of the world. But where the glass ceiling supposedly keeps those below from rising up, the glass floor seems to keep those lucky beings at the top from plunging down." [Amanda Bennett and Joann S Lublin, "Failure Doesn't Always Damage the Careers of Top Executives," *The Wall Street Journal*, Mar 31, 1995, at A1] The article goes on to cite example after example of top executives who have cruised from failure to failure and set-back to set-back, growing ever wealthier in the process.

Not only are CEOs earning more than ever, but Uncle Sam is taking less than ever from them each April 15. "For more than 30 years, members of Congress and presidents . . . have enacted one law after another to create two separate and distinct tax systems: one for the rich and powerful—call it the Privileged Person's Tax Law; another for everyone else—call it the Common Person's Tax Law. They have taken tax and economic policies that once nurtured the growth of history's largest middle class and replaced them with policies that are driving the nation toward a two-class society, eroding living standards for most Americans and causing—for the first time since the Depression—a decline in the population sandwiched between the haves and the have-nots." [D Barlett and J Steele, "Social Insecurity: How the Tax System Is Destabilizing America," *Philadelphia Inquirer Magazine*, Apr 10, 1994, at 12; see also Q 14:20; Robert B Reich, *The*

Work of Nations: Preparing Ourselves for 21st Century Capitalism (1991)]

The median family income in 1993 was $38,000. A typical taxpayer around this income range and with a family to support paid about 20 percent of his or her income in taxes for 1992. By contrast, George and Barbara Bush in 1991 "[w]ith an income of $1.3 million . . . paid . . . total tax payments—federal income tax, Social Security tax, state and local income tax, personal property tax and real estate tax—[of] $293,083. Their overall tax rate: 18.1 percent. [Barlett and Steel, *supra,* at 13]

The apparently growing gap between the wealthiest Americans, including well rewarded corporate executives, has become a focus of many social commentators, who have decried the damage that this phenomenon is doing to the social fabric of the United States. [See, e.g., Herrnstein and Murray, *The Bell Curve: Intelligence and Class Structure in American Life* (1994); Christopher Lasch, *The Revolt of the Elites And the Betrayal of Democracy* (1995); James O Castagnera, "Millionaire's Strike Sounds Sour Note," *Philadelphia Daily News,* Aug 12, 1994, at 38]

But what of the courts and the government agencies charged with the oversight of corporate responsibility? Outcries by academics and other social commentators avail little if regulatory bodies approve such dramatic windfalls and rewards.

Excessive executive compensation is at times subject to court challenge by corporate shareholders. However, U.S. courts have proven themselves reluctant to intervene when the judges are placed in the position of serving as super-directors of the company. For example in a 1994 case in Delaware's Chancery Court, alleging excessive executive compensation, the tribunal approved a settlement in the face of strong opposition from objecting members of the shareholder-plaintiff class. The court in so holding observed:

> The Court is satisfied that the excessive compensation claims have been adequately investigated and reasonably compromised. Excessive compensation claims are difficult to prove at trial, largely because executive compensation is a matter ordinarily left to the business judgment of a company's board of directors. (citations omitted)

> The compensation at issue was recommended by a committee
> consisting of a majority of disinterested outside directors and
> the committee received advice on executive compensation from
> independent experts . . . . The principal reason for the huge
> sums of money some of the individual defendants received in
> the early 1990s was the dramatic increase in the market price
> of [the corporation's] stock . . . due in large part to the stellar
> performance of the corporation. [Lewis v Hirsch, 1994 Del Ch
> LEXIS 68, Fed Sec L Rep (CCH) P98,382 (1994)]

However, a more active role by the Securities and Exchange
Commission (SEC) has lead major accounting firms, such as KPMG
Peat Marwick, to opine that "[c]ompensation committees have
greater accountability for their actions and, consequently, have taken
an increasingly active role and placed greater emphasis on designing
a compensation package that accurately reflects a company's financial performance." [" 'Excessive' Compensation Seen Declining Due
to Changes in Regulations, Attitudes," *BNA Daily Report to Executives,* Mar 2, 1995, at d70] Additionally, the IRS has proposed rules
that, if adopted, would disallow deductions from annual compensation in excess of $1 million. And, finally, the GOP-controlled Congress
may decrease capital gains taxes. [Id] All of this is likely to combine
to make stock options the preferred method of providing executives
with the kinds of large rewards that have been reported above. Stock
options in fact were the means by which Disney's Eisner realized
most of his $200 million dollar windfall. Thus, most likely those
executives who try to realize large rewards through salaries will be
penalized, especially in times of poor company performance, while
those who run the risk of reaping rewards via stock options will pass
judicial and SEC scrutiny, and be handled more gently at tax time by
the IRS as well.

Q 8:85 Are executive stock options subject to any new accounting rules?

In early 1993, the FASB voted 6 to 1 to require corporations to
deduct the value of employee stock options from earnings. Some
companies claimed that pretax earnings could drop from 4.5 percent
to 10 percent per year as a consequence of the accounting move. This
would seem to be particularly true for firms that give options to a
relatively broad spectrum of employees, and some have threatened

to abandon such plans if FASB in fact ultimately institutes this new accounting rule. At present, this change in accounting procedure is set by FASB to take effect for financial statements issued in 1997 or later. (See Q 8:80 for more on this issue.)

In 1994, the drumbeat in opposition to this FASB proposal grew louder as the board conducted hearings around the nation concerning the controversial rule change. FASB "ended a series of hearings March 25 and 26 [in California], as chief financial officers and high-tech executives urged the board to consider the social and monetary impacts of expensing stock options. During the last in a series of public hearings, witnesses testified in San Jose . . . that FASB Exposure Draft 127C would hinder development, harm lower-level employees, impair startup companies' ability to attract venture capital and talented employees, and confuse stockholders" in the Silicon Valley. ["FASB Urged to Consider Social, Monetary Impacts of Stock Options Plan," *BNA Daily Report for Executives*, Mar 29, 1994, at G59]

While Silicon Valley has become shrouded in "[t]he myth of a couple of hardworking, enterprising individuals who turn a hobby in the garage into a multibillion dollar enterprise," [Id] the reality is that hundreds of thousands of workers in California's high-tech enclaves are earning a mere $15,000 to $20,000 per year. It's unclear how many of these rank-and-file (often female, frequently Hispanic) employees share in employee stock ownership plans or stock options. But to the extent they do, such an equity stake could significantly supplement low wages and salaries. Indeed, such opportunities to share the fates of their fledgling enterprises may be key to preserving the U.S. middle class in an era of declining real wages from the halcyon days of U.S. dominance in heavy industry and capital goods manufacturing. [See generally, Reich, *The Work of Nations, supra*]

"Saying 'options are the lifeblood of Silicon Valley,' Intel Chairman Gordon Moore told the board that 'I believe they should not be sacrificed for accounting purity, if purity is possible. And I don't believe purity is possible.' " [*BNA Daily Report for Executives, supra*]

Meanwhile, FASB's threat notwithstanding, stock options remained in 1994 the way the nation's top executives achieved mega-compensation packages, in some instances amounting to tens (and in one case, hundreds) of millions of dollars (see Q 8:84.) "Some business leaders are skipping salary raises amid good times. More

CEOs now collect stock awards only if they significantly drive up their company's share price—rather than just coming to work. Others have begun to give up their generous cash bonuses for stock." [Joann S Lublin, "Looking Good: For CEOs, the Pay Gains Haven't Stopped. It's Just the Packaging that has Changed," *The Wall Street Journal*, Apr 13, 1994, at R1] And corporate directors, too, are receiving stock options in lieu of increased monetary compensation, regardless of FASB's unpopular proposal. [Lublin, "Director's Cut: More Companies Are Giving Stock Options to Outside Board Members in Lieu of Cash," *The Wall Street Journal*, Apr 13, 1994, at R5]

In December 1994, the FASB voted again, this time reversing its 1993 decision to require recognition of expense stemming from employee stock options. One major source of pressure credited with the FASB reversal was a looming Congressional threat to pass legislation giving the SEC the power to approve or to deny all FASB actions. Indeed, soon after the vote was announced, the SEC sent a letter to FASB congratulating it on the change of direction and concurring "in the Board's conclusion that the time has come to . . . ensure that investors and other end-users of corporate financial statements have prompt access to the option valuation information that will be supplied under the FASB's final Statement on Financial Accounting Standards." Those disclosure requirements—FASBs compromise with the many critiques of its earlier rule—will be as follows:

- Value stock options on the grant date using an option pricing model
- Disclose the fair value either in notes to financial statements or formally recognize the value in those statements
- Disclose the major assumptions made in valuing the options

[*BNA Daily Report for Executives*, Apr 10, 1995]

Q 8:86 Can a tax-exempt corporation jeopardize its status by overcompensating its executives?

Code Section 501(c)(3) requires that a tax-exempt entity:

- Operate exclusively for one or more exempt purposes enumerated in the Code
- Serve a public as opposed to a private interest

- Allow no portion of its net earnings to benefit any private shareholder or other insider who is in a position to access the entity's assets and funds for personal gain

In other words, assets cannot inure to an insider's private gain without jeopardizing the corporation's tax-exempt status. The IRS has said the purpose of this proscription is "preventing dividend-like distributions of charitable assets or expenditures to benefit a private interest." The IRS continued, "Inurement is likely to arise where the financial benefit represents a transfer of the organization's financial resources to an individual solely by virtue of the individual's relationship with the organization, and without regard to the accomplishment of the exempt purposes. [See, IRS GCM 39862; Frazier & Levan, Tax Issues Affecting Physician Recruitment and Development, *The Health Law Newsletter*, Apr 1993, at 1]

By way of illustration, consider the situation of a tax-exempt hospital, an entity that may be vulnerable to IRS attack in the current climate of health care reform (see Qs 8:196, 8:197). The IRS maintains that physicians are insiders under Code Section 501(c)(3), and therefore in their dealing with a charitable hospital are subject to the inurement prohibition.

However, the IRS General Counsel has made it clear that:

> [E]ven though medical staff physicians are subject to the inurement proscription, that does not mean that there can be no economic dealings between them and the hospital. The inurement proscription does not prevent the payment of reasonable compensation for goods or services.

Obviously, with physicians (as with other insiders, such as the executive director of a charity), the pivotal issue becomes what is reasonable compensation.

Whether a particular compensation package passes the reasonableness test will be decided by the IRS on all the surrounding facts and circumstances:

> Provided the arrangement has all the earmarks of having been negotiated at arm's length as a means of providing reasonable compensation, without any potential for reducing the charitable services or benefits otherwise being provided, such [an] arrangement should not result in private inurement.

In our example of the charity hospital:

1. The employment of the particular physician, whether as a true employee or as an independent contractor with staff privileges, should fit the staff development plan of the hospital in particular or a documented community health care need in general;

2. The hospital should treat the arrangement as an investment and put a cap on it;

3. The investment should be linked in appropriate documentation to some measurable benefit of bringing the doctor on board; and

4. Negotiation of the compensation package must truly be at arm's length.

Even where bona fide arm's-length negotiation has occurred (see Q 8:87), certain compensation arrangements are deemed by the IRS to be per se inurement arrangements. While fixed compensation packages and fee-for-service arrangements will usually pass IRS muster if in line with what is being paid in the industry or the geographic region, percentage-of-net-revenue arrangements in some sort of joint venture context have been held by the IRS to be per se private inurement, thereby jeopardizing the hospital's federal tax-exempt status.

Furthermore, the IRS in 1995 is considering rules which, if adopted by the agency, would forbid deductions from compensation in excess of $1 million per year. [" 'Excessive' Compensation Seen Declining Due to Changes in Regulations, Attitudes," *BNA Daily Report to Executives*, Mar 2, 1995, at d70]

Q 8:87   What is arm's-length negotiation with regard to an executive compensation arrangement?

For purposes of the private inurement test of tax-exempt status of a nonprofit corporation (see Q 8:86), the IRS has given a good working definition of arm's-length negotiation of executive compensation packages. This definition may be of use in the for-profit sector also:

• More than one person representing the corporation is involved in the negotiations

- The compensation package is then approved by an independent committee or the board of directors
- The executive receiving the package has little or no control over the corporation and the negotiation and approval process
- There is a reasonable relationship between the size of the aggregate compensation package and the responsibilities that come with the executive's position
- The corporation has relied on comparative data in the industry or the region, as well as independent advisers, such as compensation consultants and attorneys, in justifying the compensation package
- If the package is being paid by a taxable organization, it will qualify for treatment as an ordinary and necessary expense of the corporation under Code Section 162

Q 8:88   How does executive compensation compare to that of ordinary employees in major corporations?

According to Secretary of Labor Robert Reich the typical CEO of a "core American corporation" in 1960 earned about $190,000, or approximately 40 times the wages of that company's average worker on the factory floor. With a maximum tax rate of 90 percent, that executive's take-home pay was only around 12 times what the folks on the shop floor were carrying home. But by 1988 the average CEO of a major U.S. corporation was earning $2.025 million, or 93 times what the average employee in the same big company was pulling down. With a top marginal tax rate of only 28 percent, a CEO's take-home pay was about 70 times that of the rank-and-file at the company. [Reich, *The Work of Nations: Preparing Ourselves for 21st Century Capitalism* at 204 (1991)] What does this trend mean? Reich concludes:

> There had been [a] constraint on high earnings, which . . . gave way by the 1990s. At mid-century, the compensation awarded to top executives and advisers of America's core corporations could not be grossly out of proportion to that of low-level production workers. It would be unseemly for executives who engaged in highly visible rounds of bargaining with labor unions, and who routinely responded to government requests to moderate prices, to take home wages and benefits wildly in

excess of what other Americans earned. Unless white-collar executives restrained themselves, moreover, blue-collar production workers could not be expected to restrain their own demands for higher wages.

Management may be well-advised to note that not only the Clinton administration, but also significant segments of the nation's news media seem to have discovered in 1994 a growing gap between what top managers and directors take home in their pay envelopes and what the folks out on the shop floors and office cubicles collect in wages and salaries. Journalists have begun complaining of what they perceive as tax inequities, too. [See, e.g., Barlett and Steele, "Social Insecurity: How the Tax System Is Destabilizing America," *Philadelphia Inquirer Magazine*, Apr 10, 1994, at 12]

In 1995, other voices were raised decrying compensation inequality. Two which received particular attention were Professors Richard Herrnstein and Charles Murray who, in their controversial book, *The Bell Curve*, claimed, "From the end of World War II until the early 1970s, average family income rose. Then in 1973, median family income hit a peak. Part of the reason for the subsequent lack of progress has been the declining real wages for many categories of blue-collar jobs." [at page 516]

This point is confirmed by the Bureau of Labor Statistics (BLS), which reports that, between 1992 and 1993 alone, median U.S. family income dropped by $700 to $36,959.

Whether such perceived and actual inequities will result in a resurgence of unionism is highly speculative (see Q 11:8). Broadening employees' equity in the enterprises that employ them, such as through ESOPs (see Qs 8:168–8:171), has been proposed by some experts as a better solution. [See, e.g., Alan Hyde, "In Defense of Employee Ownership," *Chicago-Kent Law Review*, 1991, at 159]

Compensation and Work Schedules

Q 8:89   What are merit pay procedures and are they legal?

Merit pay, as the name suggests, is tied to performance, as compared to the across-the-board increases typically mandated by collective bargaining agreements. Merit increases are almost never entirely open-ended. Rather, supervisors are usually allowed to recommend raises within the parameters of a company-wide policy. First, such a policy will prescribe when such raises can be given (typically in conjunction with an annual or semi-annual performance review). Reviews may be staggered according to employees' anniversary dates of hire or fulfillment of a probationary period. Alternatively, some companies conduct all annual reviews at a particular point in the calendar or fiscal year. From accounting and cash-flow standpoints, each alternative offers advantages and disadvantages; the same is true from the human resources perspective. Conducting all reviews during approximately the same time frame allows easier oversight and helps the human resources staff monitor relative uniformity of standards and results across departments. Staggering reviews according to anniversaries permits each supervisor to give each subordinate greater personal attention, but probably makes the human resources staff a bit more difficult in both tracking anniversary dates and monitoring relative uniformity of standards within and across departments.

Relative uniformity of standards is legally significant because disparate treatment of minority or female employees may result in discrimination charges. Worth noting in this regard is that merit pay programs do not automatically violate the federal Equal Pay Act. Although that law requires that women and men who do essentially the same work receive the same pay, the Act expressly permits discrepancies in compensation reflecting such differences as seniority, skill, and productivity. Thus, justifiable differences in merit increases are legal under the Equal Pay Act. Nonetheless, discrepancies in increases between, for example, blacks and whites, or females and males that cannot be explained by productivity or other performance records may violate Title VII of the Civil Rights Act of 1964. Similarly, a divergence of merit increases that is unfavorable to older workers may be *prima facie* evidence of age discrimination in violation of the Age Discrimination in Employment Act (ADEA); however, if a job category has a salary ceiling that older employees have already attained (or nearly attained), this may constitute a business justification for such a discrepancy.

Q 8:90   What is the difference between a merit and a promotion increase?

Merit increases are made within the salary range of the employee's present job. A promotion increase, as the term suggests, occurs with a job promotion. Typically, the newly promoted employee moves to the bottom rung of the range for the new position.

Q 8:91   What are some legal and labor implications of salary ranges?

A few years ago the concept of comparable worth called into question how salary ranges were set between the sexes. Although the Equal Pay Act requires that men and women receive the same pay within the same job classification (except for merit increases and differences justified by seniority), proponents of comparable worth have asserted that men and women doing jobs of comparable difficulty and significance should receive the same compensation. In their view, the problem arises from some jobs (for example, maintenance mechanic) being traditionally filled by males, while others of similar significance (for example, secretary) are predominantly filled by females. Where the salary range for maintenance mechanics surpasses that of secretaries, comparable worth enthusiasts contend that Title VII is violated due to the disparate impact upon female employees. Most courts faced with this theory during the 1980s rejected it, unless the plaintiff proved that the employee purposely skewed the salary ranges to favor its male employees.

From the labor standpoint, employers commonly are concerned that their salary ranges are competitive in the industry, if employees in the relevant job classifications are in demand. Nonunion employers, especially in highly unionized industries, often want to keep their salary ranges competitive to keep their employees from wanting to form unions.

Both with respect to comparable worth and considerations of competition, companies sometimes conduct salary surveys on their own industry to see where they stand across a geographic region.

Q 8:92   Has there been a shift in companies' employment practices with respect to full-time versus part-time employees?

Some studies conducted during the past several years indicate that more and more employers are turning to part-time and temporary employees to supplement their regular workforce. According to the BLS, the 1970s saw the start of a trend toward what the BLS terms "involuntary part-timers." What the BLS means by this term is that, while there have always been some employees who wanted to work part-time, some six million part-timers in the U.S. workforce would take full-time jobs if they could find them. Many employers have found part-time employment the solution to keeping wage and benefit costs under control, and to providing flexibility in shifts and work schedules.

Q 8:93   To what compensation and benefits are part-time employees entitled?

Like full-time workers, part-timers are entitled to the minimum hourly wage set by federal law or any higher minimum hourly rate set by an individual state's minimum wage law. Federal law also requires companies to make social security contributions on behalf of part-time employees. Under ERISA requirements, part-time employees who work at least 20 hours per week, or 1,000 hours per year, must be allowed to participate in the company's retirement plan, if any. But part-timers can be, and frequently are, excluded from such expensive benefits as health insurance.

Q 8:94   Can an employer ever pay sub-minimum wages?

Under the DOL's interim rules on sub-minimum training wages, a company can (under appropriate circumstances) pay the lower rate to an employee who is under 20 years of age for up to 90 days of on-the-job training. This rule is in accord with the 1989 amendments to the FLSA. There are, however, a number of regulatory requirements. For instance, the "total period that an employee may be employed at the training wage by any combination of employers may not exceed a cumulative total of 180 days." Therefore, an employer should know a trainee's employment history prior to paying sub-minimum training wages.

Q 8:95   What does "contingent workforce" mean, and why is it of interest to legislators concerned with employee benefits?

The contingent workforce comprises the growing number of part-time and temporary employees filling jobs in the United States.

Concerned members of the U.S. House of Representatives have proposed a "Part-Time and Temporary Workers Protection Act," aimed at requiring companies that use these so-called contingent workers to give them their fair share of core benefits, such as health and life insurance and pension plans. Although workforce flexibility is welcome in our economy, a bifurcated workforce is not. The fact that two-tiered wage provisions have lost their earlier luster in the unionized sector suggests that the groundswell will increase on behalf of minimum benefits for contingent workers. One survey showed 630,000 contingent workers in the temporary help industry alone, and discovered that only about one-fourth of them were getting employer-paid (at least in part) hospitalization and major medical insurance, and only about one-fifth were receiving life insurance coverage.

Withholding

Q 8:96 What deductions does the law commonly require from an employee's paycheck?

Federal law requires both employers and employees to contribute into the social security system. The Internal Revenue Code (the Code) requires employers to withhold from their employees' paychecks income tax deductions in accord with reasonable estimates as to what their ultimate annual tax obligations are likely to be. Many states and municipalities also impose income taxes for which deductions must be taken.

Federal labor law permits employers to withhold union dues, pursuant to an appropriate clause in a collective bargaining agreement, with each member's written authorization.

Federal law also allows pretax deductions for employee pension plan contributions and employee contributions into other welfare benefit plans, such as health insurance in the context of so-called cafeteria plans.

Q 8:97 How can an employee affect payroll withholding?

Upon initial employment, every employee completes a W-4 form, reflecting the number of deductions the employee claims (for example, the employee plus a dependent spouse and children). This determines the percentage of pay the employer will withhold from each paycheck. The employee is permitted to fill out and sign a new W-4 form at any time. Within limits, as a practical matter, an employee who, for example, anticipates extraordinary deductions from income for the given year may increase the number of claimed dependents so as to decrease income tax withholding from the paycheck.

Employees can also determine, up to specified legal limits, their percentage of contributions to employer-sponsored 401(k) plans, cafeteria plans, and savings plans.

Q 8:98 What are the legal penalties for improper withholding?

Employers who fail to withhold income and social security taxes (for example, because they have incorrectly categorized their employees as independent contractors) may ultimately be held personally liable to the IRS for such deductions. With respect to an employer's own obligation to pay payroll taxes, failure to do so is an offense not even dischargeable in bankruptcy. Furthermore, corporate officers may be held personally liable for such taxes, if they are responsible for the company's failure to set aside and turn over such taxes.

Q 8:99 Must an employer take tax deductions from employees' bonuses and severance payments?

Yes. Bonuses and severance payments to terminated employees constitute income realized by these employees, and, therefore, all appropriate payroll deductions are generally demanded by law. However, since Social Security contributions are required only from approximately the first $48,000 of an employee's compensation annually, a bonus or severance payment that goes above that ceiling need not be assessed for Federal Income Contributions Act (FICA) purposes.

Q 8:100 What are fringe benefits?

Fringe benefits can mean virtually any emolument of employment that an employee receives beyond a basic salary, including pensions, various types of insurance (health, life, or disability), paid vacation, company cars, paid sick leave, and expense accounts.

Q 8:101   What is the current status of Code Section 89?

Code Section 89 created broad nondiscrimination requirements applicable to employer-sponsored health and group life insurance plans. However, its quantitative testing procedures proved overly complex and burdensome. Increasing frustration among employer groups and employee benefits practitioners resulted in the introduction of several measures aimed toward modification or outright repeal. Regulations issued by the Treasury Department in March 1989 fueled the fire. Perhaps sensing an open revolt, the Treasury Department repeatedly delayed the provision's effective date. On November 3, 1989, President Bush approved H.R. 2989, temporarily prohibiting the use of Treasury appropriations for the enforcement of Code Section 89.

Q 8:102   What happened to the Code Section 89 nondiscrimination rules?

As a result of the repeal of Code Section 89, predecessor nondiscrimination rules for welfare benefit plans have generally been reinstated. Group term life insurance plans, self-insured medical plans, cafeteria plans per Code Section 125, dependent care plans, education reimbursement schemes, group legal services, and voluntary employees' beneficiary associations (VEBAs) all fall under these earlier rules. On the other hand, there are now no nondiscrimination rules for insured medical plans. However, to reiterate, the old rules under Code Section 105(h) are reinstated for self-insured medical plans. Under Section 105(h), a self-insured health care plan must not discriminate in favor of highly compensated individuals as to eligibility to participate or in terms of benefits provided.

Q 8:103   Is a company legally required to provide its employees with fringe benefits?

No. There is no federal law that requires an employer to give employees any specific fringe benefits, and for the most part, state laws do not require payment of fringe benefits. There are, however, a few exceptions to this general rule. For instance, at least three states currently require employers to provide pregnant employees unpaid maternity leave with guaranteed job rights thereafter. [California Fair Employment and Housing Act §§ 12945, 12945.2 (Family Rights Act of 1991); New Jersey Family Leave Act, 34 NJ Stats §§ 11B-1–11B-16 (1990); Montana Human Rights Act, 49-2-310] Some states mandate severance pay in the case of plant closings. [See, e.g., 26 Maine Stats §§ 625-B(1)–625-B(6)] Generally, however, the decision to provide fringe benefits is left to the individual employer or to collective bargaining between the employer and the employees. Once such a bargain is made, however, federal and state law can come dramatically into play. Therefore, the decision to provide fringe benefits, and the nature of the fringe benefits to be provided, should not be taken lightly.

ERISA

Q 8:104   Is there a federal law covering pensions?

Yes. In 1974, Congress enacted ERISA. This comprehensive federal legislation covers not only pension plans, but almost all other employee benefits plans as well.

Q 8:105   Why was ERISA enacted?

ERISA was passed in response to numerous instances of pension fund mismanagement and abuse. In some cases, retired employees had their pension benefits reduced or terminated because their pension plan had not been adequately funded or had been depleted through mismanagement. In other instances, employees retiring after 20 years of service were ineligible for pensions because of complex and strict eligibility requirements. ERISA was intended to prevent such abuses and to protect the interests of employees and their beneficiaries.

Q 8:106   How does ERISA protect employee pension plans?

ERISA imposes standards of conduct and responsibility on pension fund fiduciaries (i.e., persons having authority or control over the management of pension fund assets). The law also requires that pension plan administrators disclose relevant financial information to employees and the government. It sets certain minimum standards that pension plans must meet in order to qualify for preferential tax treatment, and it provides legal remedies to employees and their beneficiaries for violations.

Q 8:107   To whom do the ERISA provisions apply?

ERISA applies to qualified pension plans (those plans that meet the requirements of the Code and are eligible for special tax considerations that are established by employers). It covers almost all employers except federal, state, and local government entities and tax-exempt churches; plans maintained solely to comply with a state worker compensation, unemployment, or disability insurance law; and plans that are maintained by multinational corporations primarily for the benefit of nonresident aliens.

Q 8:108   What are the main features of ERISA?

The two main features are the imposition of standards for fiduciary responsibility and the setting of minimum standards for pension plan requirements.

Q 8:109   Are employee benefits covered by ERISA?

Fringe benefits are referred to as employee welfare benefit plans under the Act. Some ERISA provisions apply to such plans, while others do not. For example, fringe benefits normally do not vest (as pension benefits do). On the other hand, employers are required to develop, maintain, and administer welfare benefit plans with the same high level of responsibility with which pension plans are maintained.

Q 8:110   What sort of fringe benefits make up employee welfare benefit plans?

Such diverse fringe benefits as severance pay and the continuation of health insurance for retirees have been held by various courts to come under the provisions of ERISA. Thus, at the very least, these benefits cannot be administered in an arbitrary and capricious fashion by the employer, even if the employer has made no contractual commitment to the employees with respect to these benefits.

Q 8:111   Can a creditor garnish an employee's welfare plan benefits?

Although ERISA regulations prevent creditors from garnishing or attaching an employee's pension benefits, the U.S. Supreme Court last year held that the same protection does not extend to other welfare benefit plans. [Mackey v Lanier Collections Agcy & Serv Inc, 486 US 825 (1988)] In other words, if a creditor can garnish the money under a state garnishment statute, ERISA does not preempt such garnishment. For example, an employee's vacation or holiday pay is not protected from a garnishment order, even though the Act clearly covers this benefit for other purposes.

Q 8:112   Can an employee execute a binding release of vested pension rights under ERISA?

ERISA's anti-alienation provision [29 USC § 1056(d)] prevents most creditors from attaching or garnishing an employee's pension benefits (see Q 8:112). This is so even if the employee attempts to assign or alienate them. Therefore, logic might suggest that an employee likewise cannot execute a binding release and relinquish a vested right in a pension plan. However, the U.S. Court of Appeals for the Third Circuit in 1993 reached a contrary conclusion in a case in which the employee released his ERISA rights as part of a broad release in a severance agreement. The appeals court overturned the trial judge's order that Philadelphia National Bank (PNB) pay plaintiff William McVeigh some $51,000 from the estate of John T. Dorrance, who had employed McVeigh as a pilot of Dorrance's personal aircraft for nine years. When Dorrance died in April 1989, he had 25 employees. PNB offered each a lump-sum severance payment, using the formula of a month's pay for each year of service to the decedent. The release in the severance agreement was a broad one that expressly included claims under "any retirement plan." The court found nothing in ERISA to make such a provision in a termination agreement invalid. [1993 *BNA Daily Labor Report* 63 (Apr 6, 1993) at 1]

Fiduciaries

Q 8:113   Who is a fiduciary under ERISA?

A fiduciary can be any person exercising discretionary authority or control regarding the management of the benefit plan or the disposition of the plan assets. It can also be anyone who renders or has the authority or responsibility to render investment advice (for which he or she is compensated) with respect to any of the money or other property of the plan. Anyone who has any discretionary authority or responsibility in the administration of the plan is also a fiduciary. Consultants and advisors are not normally considered fiduciaries by the law but may be found to be fiduciaries if their expertise is used in a managerial, administrative, or advisory capacity with respect to a plan under the Act. ERISA requires that all pension plans designate at least one fiduciary to manage and control the plan's operation.

Q 8:114   What liability does a nonfiduciary advisor have under ERISA?

Nonfiduciary advisors to pension plans are usually referred to as "service providers" under ERISA. These service providers can conceivably include attorneys, accountants, actuaries, money managers, and consultants, this latter term being a sort of "catch all" for advisors who may not fit into any of the foregoing standard categories. The issue of nonfiduciary service provider liability has never been explicitly covered in ERISA or its amendments.

Q 8:115   Have the courts provided any definitive guidance on the question of fiduciary liability?

Since ERISA was enacted in 1974, a number of federal courts have touched upon the issue, but thus far no case law has definitively decided it. However, in February 1993, the U.S. Supreme Court heard oral argument in *Mertens v. Hewitt Associates* [124 LE 2d 161 (1993)], which resulted in definitive guidance on this longstanding question.

Mertens required the high court to evaluate the merits of a decision from the U.S. Court of Appeals for the Ninth Circuit concerning the conduct of an actuarial firm. The plaintiffs are participants in the Kaiser Steel Corporation Retirement Plan. They alleged that Hewitt Associates acted imprudently when the firm set actuarial standards to be used in evaluating the plan's funding status. Kaiser's steel business had been substantially reduced in recent years, with one result of the reduction in operations being a large number of early retirements. The bottom line for the plan was predictable increases in outlays of benefits. The plaintiffs argue that Hewitt failed to impose upon the plan actuarial assumptions that properly reflected these increased obligations, but instead allowed the plan administrators to choose from among a range of actuarial assumptions to suit Kaiser's financial concerns. The motive plaintiffs attached to this accusation is that Hewitt didn't want to jeopardize a lucrative consultancy relationship with Kaiser.

Kaiser selected a set of actuarial assumptions that resulted in severe underfunding of the plan and, ultimately, its assumption by the PBGC. After the PBGC intervened, the participants, including the plaintiffs, received significantly lower benefits than they would have been entitled to had the plan been kept properly funded.

Plaintiffs' legal argument was that ERISA's 1989 amendments reflected a congressional intent to extend liability for a breach of fiduciary duty to service providers, such as Hewitt, who knowingly participated in, or facilitated, the breach. They point to Section 502(1) of the act, which states that the secretary of labor may bring a legal action against a nonfiduciary service provider. Their contention is that by implication a private plaintiff has been accorded the same standing in federal court. In rejecting this legal theory, the Ninth Circuit turned to a case called *Nieto v. Ecker*, [849 F 2d 868 (9th Cir 1988)] in which the plaintiffs went after an attorney who had been retained to pursue delinquent contributions to a pension fund, and who billed, and was paid by the plan, for legal services, but failed to prosecute the appropriate collection actions. Eventually the fund ended up underfunded due to the trustees' failure to procure the necessary level of contributions. In *Nieto* the appeals court refused to infer remedies other than those expressly provided by ERISAs provisions.

In contrast, *Freund v. Marshall and Ilsley Bank* [485 F Supp 629 (WD Wi 1979)] is a case in which the federal judge looked to the common law of trusts for guidance concerning nonfiduciary advisors and concluded that liability could be affixed to such service providers in private civil actions. The court concluded that:

> The intent of Congress was to federalize the common law of trust and apply it to ERISA plans. . . . In view of the expressed Congressional intent in enacting ERISA . . . the Court is fully empowered to award the relief available in traditional trust law against nonfiduciaries who knowingly participate in a breach of trust.

However, in May 1993, in a 5 to 4 decision in the *Mertens* case, the Supreme Court majority held that:

> [P]ension plan recipients cannot recover money damages from outside advisers, such as actuaries, accountants or attorneys, who have aided in a breach of fiduciary duty by a plan trustee. . . . To make outside advisers liable for money damages would upset the balance between ERISA's competing goals of benefiting employees and containing pension costs. [Mertens v Hewitt Associates, 113 S Ct 2063 (1993)]

Interestingly, the majority opinion, penned by Justice Scalia, seemed to assume that service providers could be fiduciaries. But, taking an economic approach to the case, the Court concluded:

> Exposure to [monetary] liability would impose high insurance costs upon persons who regularly deal with and offer advice to ERISA plans themselves. There is, in other words, "a tension between the primary [ERISA] goal of benefiting employees and the subsidiary goal of containing pension costs." (citation omitted) We will not attempt to adjust the balance between those competing goals that the text adopted by Congress has struck. [Id]

Thus, on the basis of cost-benefit analysis and the apparent plain meaning of the statute, the Court concluded that ERISA denies a monetary remedy against service providers, albeit they may have been fiduciaries of the plan, under the facts of *Mertens*.

Q 8:116   What are the fiduciary responsibilities under ERISA?

The fiduciary responsibilities required under ERISA are as follows:

- All pension plans must be in writing and must provide a written procedure for establishing and carrying out a funding policy that is consistent with the plan's objectives and the law's requirements
- The plan must specify the manner in which contributions to the fund and payments from the fund will be made
- The plan must describe the procedure for allocating responsibility for plan administration and operation
- The plan assets must be held in trust
- There must be a procedure for handling claims made by participants and beneficiaries

Q 8:117   To what standards are fiduciaries held under ERISA?

Fiduciaries are held to the common law of the "prudent man rule"; that is, the fiduciary must act "with the care, skill, prudence, and diligence that a prudent man acting in a like capacity and familiar with such matters would use in the conduct of an enterprise of like character and with." Although this may sound rather vague, there are a few specifics that can clarify this definition. For instance, fiduciaries must discharge their duties solely in the interest of the participants and their beneficiaries for the exclusive purpose of providing benefits to them and defraying the reasonable expenses of the plan. A fiduciary must diversify the plan's investments to minimize the risk of large losses, unless under particular circumstances it would be more prudent not to diversify.

Q 8:118   What behavior must a fiduciary avoid under ERISA?

A fiduciary or other person with an interest in a plan normally cannot engage in selling or leasing property to or from the plan, extending credit to the plan, or furnishing goods, services, or facilities to the plan. ERISA also prohibits the transfer of plan assets to, or for the use of, a person with an interest in the plan. Indeed, fiduciaries cannot use or deal with the assets of the plan for their own interests at all. Fiduciaries are also forbidden to receive any consideration or to benefit personally from persons who deal with the plan in connection with any transaction that involves the plan's assets. The plan cannot invest more than 10 percent of its assets in the securities or property of an employer of the participating employees, and such investments must still meet the prudent man rule, as outlined in Q 8:117.

Q 8:119   Who constitutes a person with an interest in a plan under ERISA rules?

ERISA defines a person with an interest in the plan to include a fiduciary, a person providing services to the plan, an employer whose employees are covered by the plan, or an owner having 50 percent or more interest in such an employer.

Q 8:120   What liability does a fiduciary face for breaching a fiduciary duty?

A fiduciary is liable for any losses resulting from the breach of any duties, responsibilities, or obligations to the plan. The fiduciary must refund any profits made through personal use of the plan's assets. The fiduciary may be subject to any other equitable or remedial measures that a court may deem appropriate, including removal of the fiduciary.

Q 8:121   Can a fiduciary be liable for the breach of duty by a co-fiduciary?

There are three circumstances under which a fiduciary might be liable for the wrongful acts of a co-fiduciary:

1. Knowingly participating in, or trying to conceal, a wrongful act or omission of another fiduciary;
2. Enabling another fiduciary to commit a breach by failing to comply with his or her own fiduciary responsibilities; and
3. Failing to make reasonable efforts to remedy a breach by another fiduciary once he or she becomes aware of it.

Q 8:122 Can a fiduciary avoid liability through an exculpatory clause in a plan?

No. Exculpatory clauses, which seek to protect fiduciaries from liability for breaches of their duties, are generally held to be void as being against public policy. A fiduciary can procure insurance against liability for breach of duty; however, if the plan provides such insurance for the fiduciary, the insurance company must be allowed to recover from the fiduciary any amounts paid out under the policy.

Q 8:123 Are fiduciaries responsible for events occurring before and after their tenure as plan fiduciaries?

No. Fiduciaries are not responsible for other people's breaches of fiduciary duties that occur either before or after they themselves are fiduciaries of the plan.

Q 8:124 Does ERISA require fiduciaries to be bonded?

Yes. ERISA requires that every fiduciary and every person who handles assets of a plan be bonded in an amount equal to at least 10 percent of the funds or assets that person will handle, but not less than $1,000 and not more than $500,000. The form of the bond must be approved by the secretary of labor and must provide protection to the plan against any loss caused by fraud or dishonesty of the bonded official.

Q 8:125 Are there any exceptions to ERISA bonding requirement?

Generally, no bonding is required for the administrator, officers, and employees of a plan under which only the general assets of a union are used to pay the benefits. However, no bond is required of a fiduciary that is a U.S. corporation exercising trust powers or conducting an insurance business, if this corporation is subject to supervision or examination by federal or state authorities and, at all times, has combined capital and surplus in excess of minimum set by regulation, provided that the minimum is not less that $1 million. Additionally, ERISA allows a plan administrator to apply to the secretary of labor for an exemption from the bonding requirement on the ground that the overall financial condition of the plan is sound enough to provide protection for the participants and beneficiaries without bonding.

Q 8:126   Who enforces ERISA's fiduciary duty requirements?

The fiduciary duty provisions of ERISA are enforced by the DOL. Also, plan participants and beneficiaries have the right to attempt to enforce their own rights through plan grievance procedures, and once those are exhausted, through court actions. The DOL is authorized to bring a lawsuit against a fiduciary who breaches any duties, obligations, or responsibilities under the Act. Plan participants or beneficiaries bringing such a lawsuit, if successful, may also recover legal fees and costs. The IRS may impose and collect an excise tax against a plan receiving preferential tax treatment if the plan engages in prohibited transactions. Alternatively, the secretary of labor can level a civil penalty against the plan for the same types of violations.

Benefit Plans Under ERISA

Q 8:127   What types of pension plans does ERISA recognize?

ERISA recognizes defined benefit plans and defined contribution plans.

Q 8:128   What is a defined benefit plan?

A defined benefit plan is a pension plan that ensures that eligible employees or their beneficiaries will receive a specified monthly income for life.

Q 8:129   How does ERISA ensure that eligible employees or their beneficiaries will receive a guaranteed benefit under a defined benefit pension plan?

ERISA provides an insurance plan to guarantee the benefits under a defined benefit plan. That insurance plan is administered by the PBGC, which is a quasi-independent governmental entity created by ERISA and financed by a premium levied against employers. The

PBGC was created for the purpose of insuring employees against the loss of their benefits when a defined benefit plan is terminated. The PBGC collects a premium towards an insurance fund from employers offering pensions with defined benefits. If an employer is unable to meet the payment requirements of a defined benefit plan, the PBGC will pay monthly benefits to the participating employees up to a maximum monthly amount.

Q 8:130   Is the PBGC's insurance sufficient to cover the obligations of all of the defined benefit plans in the country?

No. Despite the substantial sums of money that have been raised by the PBGC through employer premiums, the insurance fund is inadequate to cover all potential liability under defined benefit pension plans.

Q 8:131   What is a defined contribution pension plan?

Defined contribution plans are plans under which an employer makes a fixed-share contribution to a retirement account for each employee. These funds are invested on behalf of the participating employees, who receive the proceeds on retirement.

ERISA Pension Rules

Q 8:132   Are defined contribution plans insured by the PBGC?

No. The pension benefits under a defined contribution plan are not insured against failure of the company and are not covered by the PBGC.

Q 8:133   Do pension plans receive preferential tax treatment under ERISA?

Pension plans can receive preferential tax treatment if they are "qualified plans"; that is, if they meet certain minimum requirements set forth by ERISA.

Q 8:134   What is vesting?

Vesting is the legal event that makes an employee's entitlement to plan benefits nonforfeitable. Vesting applies only to pension plans, and not to other employee benefits plans. However, an employer can be committed to continuing other kinds of benefits plans. For example, an employer might contractually promise employees that health insurance benefits will continue after retirement. Once such a promise is made and the employee retires, the employer may find it difficult to renege on that promise legally.

Q 8:135   What are ERISA vesting requirements?

Pension benefits are vested when an employee has a nonforfeitable right to those benefits, even if the employee, at the present time, has no legal right to collect them or is not employed by that particular employer at the time of retirement.

Q 8:136   Can a company ever reduce an employee's pension benefits on account of other benefits received by the employee on retirement?

Yes. Even though an employee has the vested right to enjoy pension plan benefits after the required amount of time, under some circumstances the amount of benefits that the company must pay that employee may be reduced on a dollar-for-dollar basis as a result of benefits received by the employee from some other program. For instance, some pension plans take into account social security payments received by employees when they calculate the monthly pension benefits to be paid. Under ERISA, a qualified plan can offset $83\frac{1}{3}$ percent of social security payments received by the employee. This right to offset benefits against money paid from other sources is known as integration of benefits. Legal counsel should be consulted to determine which benefits from other sources may or may not be integrated with the company's pension plan benefits.

Q 8:137   Can benefit plans covered by the ERISA be modified orally?

Oral modification of benefit plans has been rejected under ERISA rules. Under preempted state law, an employer used to be able to argue that if it made oral representations to an employee about benefits, the employee could not later deny or contradict those oral representations. But now, when ERISA applies, changes to a written plan must likewise be in writing.

Q 8:138 Does ERISA create minimum funding requirements for pension plans?

Companies with tax-qualified pension plans must set aside enough money each year to cover the benefit liabilities that accrue under the plan during a particular year. These monies are maintained in a funding standard account (i.e., an account that is charged annually with amounts that must be paid in order to meet minimum funding standards). ERISA also requires payment of pay-service costs, that is, the costs of earned benefits that had been unfunded prior to passage of the law. These must be paid according to a formula on a year-by-year basis as well. Liability due to experienced gains and deficiencies of the plan must be amortized in equal installments over no more than 15 years. (Determination of these experienced gains or losses and evaluation of the plan's liabilities must be made at least every 3 years. Net losses due to faulty actuarial assumptions must be amortized over 30 years.)

Q 8:139 Does discrimination law come into play with respect to pension plans?

Qualified pension plans are not allowed to discriminate in favor of the officers, shareholders, or highly compensated employees of the company. Discrimination is prohibited with respect to benefits, contributions, and coverage of employee classifications. A plan, however, can be limited to salaried or clerical workers; that is, wage-earning (hourly) employees cannot be excluded from the plan. Contributions and benefits of employees must bear a uniform relationship to their total compensation.

Q 8:140 Does ERISA create any reporting and disclosure requirements?

Pension plan administrators have a number of reporting and disclosure obligations under ERISA. The idea behind these requirements is to provide the government and the plan participants with the information needed to enforce and protect participant rights, ensure nondiscriminatory operation of the plan, bring to light prohibited transactions, and give advance warning of a possible plan failure.

Q 8:141 What information must a pension plan provide to its participants?

A pension plan must provide participants and beneficiaries with a summary plan description (SPD). This description must contain: the name and address of the plan and its administrator and trustee; requirements for participation; vesting and disqualification rules; procedures for presenting claims; and procedures for appealing the denial of a claim. Also, the plan must provide participants and beneficiaries with a summary of any significant (material) modifications to the plan and a summary annual report.

Q 8:142 What information must the pension plan provide to the DOL?

A pension plan must file an SPD similar to the one that it gives to participants and beneficiaries, and a summary of any material modifications that are made to the plan. Additionally, the PBGC requires a detailed annual premium filing form and a notice of any "reportable event"; that is, changes reducing payable benefits, inability to pay the benefits that are due, failure to meet a minimum funding standard, or a transaction with an owner. If a plan intends to terminate, a notice of that intent must be filed with the PBGC at least 10 days before the termination is effective. Also, very detailed financial disclosure forms must be filed with the IRS each year.

Plan Termination

Q 8:143 Can a company terminate a pension plan?

Yes, ERISA allows for the termination of virtually any existing pension plan, provided that the company follows the laws that protect the beneficiaries of the plan and those with vested rights in the plan.

Q 8:144   What steps are required to terminate a pension plan?

First, the notice of intention to terminate the plan must be filed with the PBGC not less than ten days before the termination takes effect. The PBGC will then step in to ensure that all rights are protected in the wake of the plan's termination.

Q 8:145   What does the PBGC do when a plan is terminated?

When a plan is unable to meet its obligations to its beneficiaries, the PBGC will pay minimum monthly benefits to those receiving payments under the plan.

Q 8:146   Upon termination of a pension plan, how are the plan's assets allocated?

ERISA outlines a list of priorities for the allocation of a terminated plan's assets:

- Voluntary employee contributions
- Required employee contributions
- Benefits to participants who have been receiving benefits for at least three years
- All other insured benefits
- All other nonforfeitable benefits
- All other benefits
- If the assets are insufficient to handle all of the claims within any one of the classes, then the assets are allocated on a pro rata basis within the last subclass that receives benefits under the allocation

Q 8:147   If a pension plan has insufficient assets to satisfy claims, is the employer held liable?

The employer will be liable to the PBGC for 100 percent of the underfunding. However, this liability is limited to 30 percent of the employer's net worth. This liability constitutes a government lien against the employer's property and is treated as a federal tax lien.

Q 8:148 Is the owner of a corporation automatically the alter ego of the company for pension payments?

During the past two years, a number of courts have considered whether an officer-shareholder or a related company can be held liable for a company's deficient pension contributions. In 1989, one U.S. appeals court ruled that the president and sole shareholder of a company in default on its pension funds was not personally liable to make up the deficiencies. Four multiemployer pension plans had sued the company for claimed arrears. The corporation declared bankruptcy, and a federal judge ruled that the president-sole shareholder had to pay arrears. The appellate court overruled the judge, finding that neither the plain meaning nor the legislative history of the ERISA calls for an alter-ego interpretation. [Scarbrough v Perez, 870 F 2d 1079 (6th Cir 1989)]

Similarly, the Seventh Circuit Court of Appeals held that former corporate officers of a defunct corporation could not be held personally liable, absent circumstances calling for "piercing the corporate veil," for delinquent contributions to plumbers' union pension and welfare funds. [Plumbers' Pensions Fund v Niedrich, 891 F 2d 1297 (7th Cir 1989), *cert denied*, 110 S Ct 2169 (1990)] However, this same court concluded differently in a case where the nonunion half of a "double-breasted" trucking and excavating operation was found to be the alter ego of the unionized firm. The excavator's labor contract with the Teamsters Union required weekly pension contributions for three drivers. The owner first tried to talk the Teamsters into canceling the contract out of business necessity. When the union refused, the owner's started up the nonunion firm and took over the hauling operations, and pension contributions stopped. Even though the new firm's trucking operations were later diversified, the court found it was started up only to avoid the pension obligations. Therefore, the court found one company to be the alter ego of the other and ordered it to make the contributions current. [Cent States Pension Fund v Sloan, 902 F 2d 593 (7th Cir 1990)]

Q 8:149 Can a company that terminates a plan recover surplus funds in that pension plan?

If there are surplus funds in a pension plan after it has been terminated and the appropriate allocations have been made, the employer can recover that surplus under certain circumstances. The conditions for recovering the funds are as follows:

- All liabilities to participating employees and beneficiaries under the plan must have been satisfied

- The recovery of surplus assets must not violate any section of the law

- The pension plan must provide that the employer may recover surplus funds

Q 8:150   Can an employer withdraw from a multiemployer pension plan?

When ERISA was first enacted, multiemployer pension plans were not covered at all. However, the Multiemployer Pension Plan Amendments Act of 1980 extended the PBGC's authority to these kinds of plans. Under the amendments, an employer wishing to withdraw from a multiemployer plan must pay its proportionate share of any unfunded vested benefits in the plan. The calculations of unfunded vested benefits and the employer's individual share are very complex, involving a rolling five-year experience period. The main point is that some employers have been unpleasantly surprised to discover just how large their withdrawal liability had grown over time. For instance, a client who was trying to sell his business and who was asking $500,000 for the business learned that his withdrawal liability from the Teamster's Pension Plan Fund for Philadelphia and vicinity was almost half the asking price for the business.

Enforcement and Penalties

Q 8:151   Who enforces ERISA?

Responsibility for enforcing ERISA is spread among a number of governmental entities. Fiduciary duties and reporting requirements are enforced by the DOL. The IRS enforces minimum vesting and participation requirements and imposes tax penalties for funding violations and prohibited transactions. The PBGC steps in when a plan is terminated and ensures that the beneficiaries do not lose their benefits. Finally, individual participants and beneficiaries may act as "private attorney generals" by bringing lawsuits to enforce their rights.

Q 8:152 Are there criminal penalties for violating ERISA?

Yes. ERISA provides criminal penalties for willful violations of reporting and disclosure requirements. A person who willfully violates one of these requirements may be subject to a fine of up to $5,000, a prison term of up to one year, or both. Corporate and union fiduciaries may be subject to a fine of up to $100,000.

Q 8:153 What civil actions can be brought against a pension plan under ERISA rules?

A participant or beneficiary in a plan can sue if the plan administrator fails to furnish information to which that person is entitled. A civil suit can also be brought to recover benefits that are due under a plan. A participant may collect up to $100 a day in penalties from an administrator who fails to provide, on request, the information to which the participant is entitled. Participants, beneficiaries, and the secretary of labor may bring lawsuits to clarify rights to future benefits, to enjoin a violation of ERISA or the terms of a pension plan, and to obtain relief from a breach of fiduciary duties.

Q 8:154 When does the statute of limitations begin to run on an ERISA claim by a pension?

In 1989, the U.S. Supreme Court refused to review a lower court's decision that the statute of limitations begins to run anew each time an employer sends a pensioner another incorrect pension check. The case involved retired General Vice President Frank Meagher of the International Association of Machinists. Meagher retired from the union in 1977 and sued in 1986, when the pension fund's trustees amended the plan to eliminate a "living pension" provision pegged to increases in staff salaries. [Int'l Ass'n of Machinists v Meagher, 490 US 1039 (1989)]

Q 8:155　What courts have jurisdiction over ERISA lawsuits?

The federal courts have exclusive jurisdiction over all lawsuits that are brought under ERISA except for actions to recover benefits or to clarify the right to future benefits, which can be brought in state or federal court. A qualified pension plan must provide a method for claims resolution. Participants and beneficiaries must exhaust these plan procedures and remedies for resolving claims before going to court.

Q 8:156　Can fringe benefits vest?

Although fringe benefits do not vest in the same manner as do pension benefits under ERISA, something analogous to vesting can occur if an employer promises not to revoke those benefits. For example, if an employer promises current employees that their health insurance will be continued at the company's expense after retirement, this promise arguably can never be revoked, since the retirees have fulfilled every requirement needed to gain entitlement to this continuing benefit.

Q 8:157　Are there any circumstances under which an employer must offer benefits to nonemployees?

Yes. Under the provisions of the Consolidated Omnibus Budget Reconciliation Act of 1986 (COBRA), group health insurance continuation coverage is mandated for employees and their dependents who would otherwise lose their group plan eligibility. Essentially, COBRA provides that when a "qualifying event" occurs (for example, dismissed or voluntary departure) an employer must offer the affected covered employee and/or qualified beneficiary the option to continue to receive health coverage under the employer's group health plan. The coverage must be offered to the employee at a rate that does not exceed 102 percent of the total cost of providing coverage to similarly situated beneficiaries for whom a qualifying event has not occurred.

Q 8:158   Can an employer terminate or modify welfare benefits being paid to its retirees?

Over the past several decades, numerous companies have provided their retirees with various welfare benefits, either voluntarily or through collective bargaining agreements. Most frequently employers provided their retired workers with continued health insurance, typically supplementing Medicare. Often at the time such benefits were accorded, the cost of the insurance premiums was merely a fraction of the firm's total payroll and perks package. As the cost of health insurance has skyrocketed over the years, as more employees retire, and as retirees live longer than they used to, the burden of these premiums has in some instances become overwhelming. Additionally, FASB has come to require these obligations to be reflected as corporate obligations, thus sometimes affecting financial considerations such as the corporation's ability to borrow, issue new debt securities, and maintain the value of their stock. Consequently, "[o]ver the past ten years, numerous court decisions have addressed pensioners' challenges to employers terminating retiree insurance benefits." [William T Payne, "Lawsuits Challenging Termination or Modification of Retiree Welfare Benefits: A Plaintiff's Perspective," 10 *The Labor Lawyer* 1, Winter 1994, at 91]

"When the retirees challenge the employer's action, courts must decide whether coverage was meant to be a 'vested' lifetime benefit (not subject to reduction), or whether it was meant to be 'gratuitous,' subject to termination at the will of the employer." [Id] Since ERISA does not mandate vesting of welfare, as opposed to pension, benefits, the issue of lifetime entitlement depends upon contract. Whether or not the employer formed a binding and enforceable contract with the employee to continue a welfare benefit for life after retirement may depend upon statute or the common law of contract.

Where a collective bargaining agreement is involved, Section 301 of the Labor Management Relations (Taft-Hartley) Act (LMRA) will be relevant to the lawsuit. [See, e.g., UAW v Yard-Man Inc, 716 F 2d 1476 (6th Cir 1983), *cert denied*, 465 US 1007 (1984)] Beyond ERISA and the LMRA, principles of common law contract interpretation will be relevant. Additionally, the federal courts seem to infer an intent to continue the benefits when faced with ambiguous situations. [Payne, *supra*, at 103]

Some of the factors which may give rise to such an inference of lifetime coverage include:

- Oral or written statements to retirees
- Statements and proposals made during contract negotiations
- Continuation of insurance during strikes
- A cost analysis prepared in preparation for a plant shutdown
- Changes or the lack of changes in the benefits of former retirees, and whether or not any such changes were contested
- Failure by the employer to disclose a limitation on the benefit in a summary plan description

[Id at 107–09]

As an interesting aside, at least one corporation came up with a creative solution to funding its retiree health insurance obligations in the present decade. Procter and Gamble prevailed upon the IRS to approve a plan under which such benefits are being funded from the company's ESOP. Known as an HSOP, the plan is thus far the first and last such scheme approved by the IRS as a qualified plan. After issuing the approval, the federal revenue folks announced that they will not approve another until P&G's plan has been more fully observed and evaluated.

Employee Stock Ownership Plans (ESOPs)

Q 8:159   What is an ESOP?

Generally speaking, an employee welfare benefit plan is classified as an ESOP if it is tax-qualified under Code Section 401(a), and if it is intended primarily for investment in the employer's qualifying securities. It is, in fact, "a special breed of qualified retirement plan." ESOPs are distinguishable from other types of employee ownership, including stock bonus plans, employee stock purchase plans, and worker cooperatives.

Q 8:160   What are the different types of ESOPs?

Experts typically divide ESOPs into three general types: ordinary or nonleveraged, leveraged, and tax credit (see Q 8:162). There are a number of components that all ESOPs have in common. Perhaps most fundamental of all is the Treasury Department regulation requiring that if a plan is to be an ESOP, the plan documents must expressly say so. Additionally, the plan participants (i.e., the employees) must have individual accounts with employer contributions allocated to these accounts on a pro rata basis. These accounts must be held in a trust. The trust must have one or more trustees. An ESOP's trustees have the exclusive authority to manage the plan's assets, with two possible exceptions. The plan can provide that, first, the trustees are subject to a fiduciary's authority, and, second, the named fiduciary may have the power to appoint an investment manager.

As suggested above, an ESOP is distinguishable from a stock bonus plan primarily in that ESOP contributions consist of, or are invested in (overwhelmingly, if not always exclusively), the contributing employer's securities, while the trustees of a "standard" stock bonus plan would be considered imprudent in making such an investment (which might cost the plan its tax qualification). Nonetheless, an ESOP is a variation of a tax-qualified stock bonus plan, or a combination stock bonus and money purchase plan under the Code.

Q 8:161   How does ERISA apply to ESOPs?

Basic ERISA concepts, discussed above, should be kept in mind and reviewed if necessary.

> ESOPs are not appreciably different from other kinds of benefits plans in terms of how participant rights are defined or enforced. Participants may receive whatever benefit the plan instrument provides. Basic ERISA structural requirements apply to ESOPs, requiring a written plan, summary plan descriptions, reports to the Department of Labor, and published claims and appeals procedures. [H Perritt, Jr, *Employee Benefits Claims Law and Practice*, 1990 at 47]

Additionally, an ESOP is subject to ERISA fiduciary rules. However, the application of these rules to ESOPs distinguishes ESOPs from other benefit plans. All plans must have one or more fiduciaries, who "jointly or severally shall have authority to control and manage the operation and administration of the plan." Usually the employer is a fiduciary. In unionized firms this role may be shared with the union or vested in a plan committee staffed jointly by labor and management. Drawing upon the lessons learned from the history of pension fund mismanagement by companies and unions—which was a prime motivation for ERISA enactment—such fiduciaries are typically forbidden from investing in the contributing employer's stock, real estate, or projects. ERISA prohibits certain transactions by fiduciaries or persons with an interest in the benefit plan. Fiduciaries are forbidden to engage in self-dealing with the plan (i.e., dealing with the assets of the plan for their own interest). They are prohibited from receiving any consideration or personal benefit in connection with a transaction involving plan assets. And ERISA prohibits a plan from investing more than 10 percent of its assets in the securities or property of the employer whose employees are participating in the plan.

It is the latter restriction—investment in more than 10 percent of the employer's assets—that by an ESOP's very nature does not pertain. However, the requirement that fiduciaries manage plans prudently and for the exclusive purpose of benefiting the participating employees is still applicable with full force. But applying these tests to ESOPs has proven difficult. With other plans, the test is quantitative (i.e., the 10 percent rule). Since this test is inapplicable, some sort of qualitative test must be substituted. Development of this qualitative test of fiduciary prudence and exclusive purpose has been further complicated by the IRS's recognition that an ESOP is a "technique of corporate finance." Thus, the company can benefit from the ESOP, not just in terms of employee incentive, but more directly, as when a leveraged ESOP's loans help refinance the corporation. The quid pro quo is that a "purpose of an ESOP is to provide stock ownership interests for participants." Thus, the interests of the employer-company and employee-participants must be kept in balance, and this task falls primarily upon the federal courts.

Q 8:162 How does the Code affect ESOPs?

There are at least nine distinct tax benefits that historically have flowed from ESOPs:

1. Employee tax credits equal to the value of the stock contributed;

2. Tax-exempt financing of leveraged ESOPs;

3. Deferral of gains of stock sales to an ESOP, if the profits are reinvested in other qualified securities;

4. Assumption of estate taxes by an ESOP buying securities out of that estate;

5. A concomitant reduction of the decedent-shareholder's taxable estate;

6. A corporate tax deduction for dividends paid on the ESOP's stock;

7. Excise and income tax exemptions on reversions, if such a reversion was transferred to an ESOP by January 1, 1989;

8. Deductible contributions to repay principal owed on a leveraged ESOP; and

9. Greater allowable employee contributions to ESOPs than to any other defined contribution plan.

These nine historical ESOP tax advantages can be grouped into three general areas of advantage: (1) tax credits and deductions for the corporation; (2) tax benefits for employees; and (3) corporate owner's estate-planning opportunities.

Q 8:163   Will a company's tax advantages differ depending upon the type of ESOP established?

Yes. In the case of a nonleveraged ESOP to which the employing corporation contributes stock (or cash for the ESOP to buy the company's stock), the company can deduct its contributions from income.

If the ESOP is leveraged, the securities obtained by means of loan proceeds are held in a suspense account as collateral. As the loan is paid down by means of the employer's cash contributions, stock is released from the suspense account and ceases to be collateral. As the stock is released, it is allocated among the participating employees. Several significant safeguards and limitations are aimed at ensuring the soundness of leveraged ESOPs:

- It must be either a tax qualified stock bonus plan, or a combination stock bonus and money purchase pension plan

- It must principally invest in specified employer securities

- Participating employees must have specified voting rights with respect to the stock held on their behalf

- Ultimate distribution to participants must usually be in the form of stock, rather than cash

A third variety of ESOP is the tax credit ESOP, or TRASOP. Originating in the Tax Reduction Act of 1975, the TRASOP was essentially a defined contribution plan that gained the company an additional 1 percent tax credit, when all criteria were met. The Tax Reform Act of 1976 modified the relevant rules to enable employees to realize an additional 0.5 percent qualifying investment tax credit. A more significant modification was accomplished by the Economic Recovery Tax Act of 1981 (ERTA). ERTA converted the TRASOP from an investment-based tax credit to a payroll-based tax credit. In other words, the extra tax credit was untied from the investment in qualified securities, and tied to the amount of compensation paid to participating employees. With the conceptual change came a concomitant acronym change: PAYSOP. The credit was now equal to 0.5 percent of total payroll of participating employees.

Finally, the Tax Reform Act of 1986 eliminated this ten-year-old tax credit with respect to compensation paid (or accrued) after December 31, 1986. However, unused TRASOP or PAYSOP credit can still be carried forward.

Q 8:164   Is there a limit to the deduction an employer can take for contributions to an ESOP?

The limit on employer deductions for ESOP contributions is 15 percent. However, an ESOP combined with a money purchase pension plan offers a 25-percent limit. Additionally, the IRS places a ceiling of 25 percent on deductions for contributions to all of the employer's defined contribution plans in total. The 25-percent ceiling applies to an employer's contributions to pay down the principal on a leveraged ESOP; however, there is no such limitation on deductions of employer contributions to pay the interest on the leveraged ESOP's loan.

Q 8:165   Do ESOPs offer any tax benefits to lenders?

A commercial lender that makes a "securities acquisition loan" to enable an ESOP to acquire employer securities may be able to exclude from income up to 50 percent of the interest the lender earns on such a loan. Banks, insurance companies, regulated investment companies, and other corporations actively engaged in the business of lending money are among the commercial lenders that can take advantage of the opportunity.

A securities acquisition loan can be a loan made for the initial acquisition of employer securities or an immediate allocation loan to an employer, who within 30 days of closing on the loan transfers employer securities of equal value into the ESOP.

The Code was amended in 1989 to require that a loan made after July 10, 1989, be treated by the IRS as a security acquisition loan only if, after the ESOP acquires the securities sprung loose by the loan, it ends up owning at least 50 percent of all of the employer's stock. However, certain nonvoting, nonconvertible preferred stock is ignored in calculating the ESOP's 50-percent ownership requirement. Similarly, the commercial lender can lose its 50-percent income exclusion during any later period during which the ESOP fails to own at least 50 percent of the relevant corporate stock. While some preferred stock is not counted toward this 50-percent figure, securities issued by a member company in a controlled group will be counted as a safeguard to an employer effort to circumvent this qualification requirement.

The period during which the commercial lender can exclude income from the loan is usually seven years, or for a refinancing, the length of the original loan if longer than seven years. The refinancing cannot be used to extend the exclusion period under the original securities acquisition loan. Securities acquisition loans can be transferred or sold to other commercial lenders, and the exclusion will follow. In fact, even if the original holder of the loan was not qualified for the exclusion, a qualified buyer can still take advantage of the exclusion following the transfer.

Q 8:166   Do ESOPs offer any tax benefits to the company's owners and their estates?

Yes. An ESOP can enable the owner to enjoy the fruits of ownership now, as well as defray the estate's expenses later.

During his or her lifetime, a major shareholder is allowed to make a tax-free "rollover" of his or her closely held corporate securities, so that the gain on the shares sold to the ESOP is tax-deferred, provided:

1. The seller conveys to the ESOP at least 30 percent of the outstanding company stock;

2. He or she reinvests the sale proceeds in securities of some other U.S. company; and

3. The ESOP holds the seller's stock for at least three years.

But there is a simple way for the seller to enjoy the sale proceeds immediately, without forfeiting any tax deferral benefits. The individual takes the proceeds of the stock sale to the ESOP, reinvests in other securities as required, then borrows against those new securities to raise money for whatever purpose the seller wishes. (This transaction is somewhat analogous to the ubiquitous home equity loan, wherein the homeowner adds a second mortgage to a principal or secondary residence, uses the loan proceeds in virtually any way at all, and takes a legitimate tax deduction for the interest payments on the loan.)

A shareholder of a closely held company may also provide the estate with a substantial benefit by establishing the ESOP prior to demise. Absent establishment of the ESOP, at death, the stock is likely to be valued for estate tax purposes based on a compromise between the IRS valuation expert's appraisal and that of the estate's own expert. In establishing the ESOP prior to the owner's death, it will have been necessary to hire an independent appraiser to set fair market value; later on, it is likely the IRS will not challenge this evaluation.

After the owner's death, additional tax advantages may accrue to the estate by means of stock sales to the ESOP. At one time, 50 percent of the proceeds of a qualified sale of employer securities to the ESOP could be deducted from the gross value of the estate as a whole, and the ESOP was permitted to assume some of the estate's taxes. This tax advantage was diminished in 1987 and eliminated in 1989.

Nevertheless, a stock sale to an ESOP can be of great aid to an estate, especially if the bulk of the decedent's wealth consisted of the stock of the closely held corporation. Assume that the estate is cash poor, has failed to meet the IRS requirements for spreading its estate tax payments over 15 years, and has also failed to meet the Code's requirements for redeeming a portion of the deceased's stock for payment of the taxes and administrative expenses of the estate. Under this scenario, the estate's sale of some stock to anyone but an ESOP is likely to yield proceeds that will be taxed as a dividend. Sale to the ESOP, on the other hand, may result in no gain at all, since the fair market value upon the owner's death is likely to equal the sales price to the ESOP. The estate will have raised the cash needed to pay its taxes.

Q 8:167   How does the Code treat ESOP dividends?

Dividends paid to shareholders ordinarily are not deductible from income by the corporation; furthermore, the shareholder must treat them essentially as ordinary income for tax purposes. Dividends paid by an employer or dividends for securities held by an ESOP may be deductible if (1) paid in cash directly to ESOP participants or their beneficiaries; (2) paid to the ESOP and distributed to participants and beneficiaries within 90 days of the end of the ESOP's plan year; or (3) used to pay principal and interest on an exempt loan taken out to purchase the employer securities to which the dividends are attributable. Even if the ESOP plan permits participants to decide whether or not to receive cash payment of dividends, the employer can deduct the dividends paid to those participants who actually elected to receive them.

The employee who receives such a dividend payment, whether directly from the employer or as a subsequent distribution by the ESOP, is taxed on the income received, but is not subject to the 10-percent excise tax that typically pertains to early withdrawals or distributions from tax-deferred retirement plans. The employer reports the deductible dividends on Form 1099-DIV. The employees report it on their tax returns as a plan distribution and not as investment income.

As noted previously in this chapter, there are limits on the employer's tax-deductible annual contributions to an ESOP. It is worth adding that dividends are not viewed as part of this annual contribution. Consequently, where participants can and do elect to reinvest their dividends, this presents a way to effectively increase annual contributions.

Q 8:168   Are ESOPs prospering or declining in America?

Researchers from Rutgers University in New Jersey published a report that they had found 10,000 employee ownership companies in the United States, involving 10.8 million participating employees, equaling about 12.5 percent of the private sector workforce. These employees share 3 percent of the value of all private and publicly held stock in the country. Nine thousand of the firms owned wholly or partly by their employees were closely held corporations with a total of about 6.5 million employees and a market value of $20 billion, which is estimated to be about 1.7 percent of the market value of all the corporate stock in this country. The remaining 1,000 firms identified by the Rutgers researchers were publicly traded companies whose ESOPs had a total of 4.3 million participants holding stock valued at $100 billion, or 2.3 percent of the market value of all stock in the United States. [See, Blasi and Kruse, "Strategic Problems and Tactical Promise: Unions and Employee Ownership," *Labor Law J*, Aug 1991, at 499-500; Blasi and Kruse, *The New Owners: The Mass Emergence of Employee Ownership in Public Companies and What It Means to American Business* (1991)]

Q 8:169   Are ESOPs proving to help improve productivity in American companies that have instituted them?

There is a growing body of evidence, albeit much that is anecdotal, that giving employees a stake in their corporations by means of ESOPs does improve productivity and generate enhanced corporate loyalty. For example, at the Ninth Annual Conference on Employee Ownership and Participation held in San Francisco, a copper mining company located in Michigan's upper peninsula reported:

> People take greater care of and interest in property they own. We are able to get the same productivity with 1,000 workers after the [ESOP] as we'd gotten with 1,600. [We] don't need to see actuarial tables. It's obvious . . . that you get increased productivity with employee ownership, unless you try hard to screw it up.

> ["Large Employee-Owned Firms Tell ESOP Success Stories," 1990 *BNA Daily Labor Report* (Apr 24, 1990) at 2]

ESOPs and other employee-ownership schemes are also increasingly a refuge for displaced workers who have discovered that repositioning in the traditional workforce is difficult or impossible in the present business climate. A good recent example is Kiwi International Air Lines, a "startup born out of the rubble of deregulation" of the airline industry. Based in Newark, New Jersey, Kiwi last year joined the ranks of about 150 regional air carriers operating in U.S. markets. The new company's target markets are "leisure flyers and business travelers who want service superior to standard coach and a low, uncomplicated fare structure." All of the owner-employees average 20 years experience in the industry, most at such defunct major carriers as Midway, Pan Am, and Eastern. Reportedly, they have invested more than $5 million of their own money in the venture. [Velocci, "Kiwi Takes Special Steps to Survive Among 'Sharks,' " *Aviation Week and Space Technology* at 44 (1992)]

Thus, such employee-owned and operated ventures are taking up some of the slack that federal retraining programs and the like (see Qs 14:1–14:7) have been unable to handle.

Q 8:170   Can an ESOP overcome the problem posed by the National Labor Relations Act's (NLRA) prohibition on labor-management cooperation programs that are in fact illegal, company-run labor organizations?

As discussed in Qs 11:105–11:110, the National Labor Relations Board (NLRB) recently held that some labor-management cooperation programs violate the NLRA's prohibition of company-dominated unions. However, shortly after the NLRB made this pronouncement in the widely publicized Electromation decision [309 NLRB 163 (1992)], the General Counsel of the NLRB issued a memorandum to the federal agency's field offices, advising them that a committee concerned exclusively with managerial functions may escape the Electromation restrictions. [1993 *BNA Daily Labor Report* 78 (Apr 26, 1993) at 1] By way of example, General Counsel Hunter cited teams composed of employees, divided according to job assignments, who reach group consensus on such things as job assignment and rotation and the scheduling of overtime. They would be legal even if they involved direct communication between managers and subordinates on these decisions. In essence, Hunter seems to have suggested that such employees would fall outside the labor act because they would be functioning as managers of the enterprise. [See, 29 USC § 152(3) (excluding supervisors from the definition of "employee" for purposes of protection under the NLRA); NLRB v Yeshiva Univ, 444 US 672 (1980) (university faculty members are managerial employees, and thus fall outside the labor act, when they exercise discretion within established employer policies and are aligned with the management of the organization)] Since such managerial functions typically go hand-in-hand with total employee ownership of the enterprise, ESOPs appear to be a valuable component of any employee participation program that seeks to steer clear of labor law illegalities.

Q 8:171   Are rank-and-file employees making money by participating in ESOPs?

Many early efforts at broad-based employee enterprise ownership by means of ESOPs were bailouts of troubled corporations, coupled with deep-seated labor-management hostility, which posed rocky roads for the employees (and perhaps their unions) to traverse merely to keep the companies afloat and perhaps bring them back to a fragile state of financial health. [See, e.g., *In re Rath Packing*, 48 BR 315 (ND Iowa 1985) and 38 BR 552 (ND Iowa 1984), as well as Hammer, "The History of the Rath Buyout: A Role Expectations Analysis," 38 *Industrial Relations Research Association Proceedings* 206 (1985); Weirton Steel, Div of Nat'l Steel Corp, 259 NLRB 666 (1981), *enf denied*, Weirton Steel v NLRB, 689 F 2d 504 (4th Cir 1982), Bauman v Bish, 571 F Supp 1054 (ND W Va 1983) and Gilliam v Indep Steelworkers Union, 572 F Supp 168 (ND W Va 1983); see also, Castagnera and Cihon, "Employee Ownership and Participation Programs in the 1990s," 1993 *Wiley Employment Law Update* § 9.109.11]

Some success stories are beginning to emerge from the American industrial heartland, which bode well for the future of ESOPs as one method of providing employees with the employment and financial security that seemingly had been lost in this era of international competition, mergers, downsizing, and reengineering (see generally, chapter 14).

For instance, rank-and-file workers who participate in the ESOP at Oregon Steel Mills, Inc., in Portland, have in many instances become millionaires thanks to the successful leveraged buyout of their company. Oregon Steel is the successor to Gilmore Steel Corporation, a troubled company that ten years ago was about to close its doors when, following a year-long strike that failed to result in contract concessions, management led the leveraged buyout and extended 100 percent ownership to the firm's employees. Surviving the mid-1980s steel slump, the company went public in 1988 and since then has modernized and competed profitably, and its worth and the price of its common stock have soared. Employees whose stock had been worth only pennies suddenly are very well off. "[L]ast year, Oregon Steel had net income of $36.9 million, or $1.97 a share, on revenue of $489.4 million. The company's profits per ton are among the best in the industry. It has no debt and its productivity is double the industry average. Its average pay of $50,000 . . . is 25 percent higher than the industry average." [Milbank, "Here Is One LBO Deal Where the Workers Became Millionaires," *The Wall Street Journal*, Oct 27, 1992, at A1]

Required Insurance

Workers' Compensation Insurance

Q 8:172   What insurance must a company provide to its employees?

The only mandatory insurance required by federal, and most state, laws is workers' compensation insurance. Although Congress has been considering a law to require health insurance benefits for employees, this has not yet been enacted. Few, if any, states require such insurance. Likewise, life insurance and disability insurance generally are not mandatory.

Q 8:173　What is workers' compensation insurance?

Workers' compensation insurance was developed at the beginning of this century and is intended to compensate employees for on-the-job injuries and to provide income when such injuries prevent the employee from working either temporarily or permanently. Workers' compensation laws have been enacted by the states, and although there are differences in the laws and their administration from state to state, there are also many similarities. It is essential that an employer check the specific compensation law for the state in which the business is located.

Q 8:174　How does an employee qualify for workers' compensation benefits?

In order to collect workers' compensation benefits, an employee must be injured in the course of employment. If the employee is injured at home, over the weekend, or while on vacation, the employee cannot collect benefits under the workers' compensation system. Additionally, under most state workers' compensation laws, the injury must have occurred by accident. If the employee is injured by the intentional act of the employer or some other person, many state systems will not provide compensation benefits.

Q 8:175　Is an employee entitled to workers' compensation benefits if the on-the-job injury is the result of negligence?

Yes. A worker who is injured because of either his or her own or someone else's negligence can still collect workers' compensation benefits. Only intentional injuries, either self-inflicted or caused by another, may be excluded from the workers' compensation system.

Q 8:176　Is it mandatory for an employer to participate in a workers' compensation program?

Not all states require employers to participate in their workers' compensation insurance programs. Texas, for example, is one of the atypical states in which many employers have exercised their statutory option to opt out of the program. However, the alternative is to subject the company to all the risks of ordinary, common-law liability actions. The result in recent years has been some stunningly large liability awards against private employers in favor of injured employees or their families.

For instance, in March 1993, a Jefferson County, Texas jury awarded a convenience store clerk, who was raped twice in a two-week period by the same robber, $30 million in compensatory and punitive damages. The liability was jointly apportioned to both the robber-rapist and E-Z Mart Stores, Inc., the employer-defendant. The trial judge reduced the award to about $17 million. Prior to the first robbery and rape, the plaintiff-clerk had requested to be transferred from the Beaumont store because it was in a high crime neighborhood. Following the first sexual assault, she asked for more security; according to her attorney, she wanted the doors locked in the dead of night. The company failed to comply with any of these requests. Agreeing that E-Z Mart was negligent, the jury made the massive award. Had the defendant opted into the state's workers' compensation system, the plaintiff's damages against it would have been limited to benefits prescribed by the statute. [See also, Castagnera and Szvetitz, "Ill-Fitting Suits," *Convenience Store Decisions*, May 1992, at 26 (for more examples of large liability awards against employers who opted out of workers' compensation systems)]

Another way in which an employer can step out from behind the shield of the workers' compensation law, even though a participant in the program, is by entering into a contract under which the employer assumes the liability for a third party's negligence. [See, e.g., Snare v Ebensburg Power Co, 1993 Pa Superior LEXIS 4102 (1993)] Thus, for example, a company planning to make major renovations to its offices might include a clause in its contract with the builder to indemnify it against all injuries caused to the company's employees by the builder's workers. Such a contractual condition would be a separate basis for the employer-company's liability to its employees, and one that falls outside the protections and limitations of the workers' compensation scheme.

Q 8:177　What if a company does not participate in workers' compensation?

Different states provide different penalties for failure either to carry workers' compensation insurance or to be properly self-insured. In some states, the employer is responsible for workers' compensation benefits as if the company were self-insured under the auspices of the law. In other states, failure to properly provide workers' compensation insurance can result in the employer being exposed to a lawsuit by the employee without any limitation on possible damages.

Q 8:178　Is workers' compensation more beneficial to the employee than a traditional common law personal injury lawsuit?

One of the main reasons that the states have adopted the workers' compensation concept is that, prior to this type of law, employees found it very expensive, time consuming, and difficult to successfully sue their employers. Employers would defend such lawsuits by arguing that the employee had assumed the risk of his or her job, that the employee had been negligent, or that the employee had been injured by the negligence of a co-worker and therefore the company was not responsible. All of these traditional defenses have been eliminated by the workers' compensation laws, and thus an employee is entitled to benefits even if he or she is injured due to the employee's own negligence or that of a co-worker. Furthermore, workers' compensation benefits are usually paid promptly by the insurance carrier or the employer and cannot be arbitrarily terminated by the insurer without appropriate legal process.

Q 8:179　Are there any advantages to the employer in participating in a workers' compensation plan?

The workers' compensation laws provide that participating employers have limited liability; that is, their damages are limited to the payment schedules provided under the law. This is generally preferable to personal injury law, under which a jury can award vast sums of money to injured plaintiffs.

Q 8:180   What benefits can an employee receive under a typical workers' compensation law?

As a general rule, state workers' compensation laws provide for two types of benefits. First, weekly or biweekly salary supplements are payable to employees who are permanently or temporarily disabled, whether the disability is total or partial. These benefits may have some time limitation, but generally continue for the duration of the disability. By contrast, workers who suffer the loss of a body part may receive, under some state laws, a scheduled lump-sum payment to compensate for the loss, or a specified number of weeks of compensation, irrespective of the time period during which the injury actually disables the employee. The law also provides for the payment of medical expenses and often covers therapy and retraining costs for an employee who can no longer perform his or her previous job due to the injury.

Q 8:181   What if the company disagrees with the worker about the compensability of an on-the-job injury?

State systems vary with respect to how disputes under their workers' compensation laws are handled. Many states have a workers' compensation bureau or board with referees whose job it is to hear disputes over such issues as whether the injury really occurred in the course of employment and whether the employee is still disabled or has recovered enough to return to work. Other states stipulate that such disputes should be settled within the state court system.

Q 8:182   How can an employer prevent workers' compensation "scamming"?

With the cost of workers' compensation claims climbing, even more than group health insurance premiums by most estimates, preventing workers' compensation scams and malingering is an essential part of most companies' loss control programs. Many experts suggest the following as essential to a successful loss prevention program:

1. Employee safety training to prevent legitimate workplace injuries;

2. Creation of light duty programs for workers who are either recovering from, or who are particularly susceptible to certain injuries;

3. Insistence upon early reporting of all job-related injuries, with severe disciplinary penalties (such as termination of employment) for failure to make an early and accurate report of any injury sustained; and

4. Consistent, regular contact with off-work employees who are collecting workers' compensation benefits, such as through hand delivery of their benefit checks, and even, when appropriate, video surveillance (see Q 5:23).

Some companies have gone so far as to investigate the possibility of setting up a workers' compensation claim, intercorporation reporting service to red flag scammers. However, such a system could conceivably run afoul of the Americans with Disabilities Act (ADA). [See Qs 4:86, 4:87; see also, Castagnera and Szvetitz, "Off-the-Job Scamming," *Convenience Store Decisions*, Mar 1992, at 28]

Q 8:183 Is an injury sustained while commuting to work covered by workers' compensation insurance?

Generally, commuting time is not work time. However, if an employee is injured while working out of the home as a salesperson, taking work home on the instructions of the boss, or traveling directly from home to a remote job site, it is possible that the travel will be considered work time and the employee will therefore be eligible for workers' compensation benefits. Also, many state courts have held that injuries occurring while driving a car on the employer's property, such as in an employee parking lot, are on-the-job injuries and are eligible for workers' compensation benefits.

Q 8:184 Is an injury sustained during a lunch hour or other free period covered by workers' compensation insurance?

In general, injuries occurring during lunch or other break times on the premises of the employer are covered by workers' compensation insurance. This could include a twisted ankle suffered while playing basketball in a court provided in the employee parking lot. This rule also extends to workers who are injured while eating their lunches at a remote job site. For instance, if a truck driver stops by the side of the road, gets out to eat lunch at a roadside picnic table, and is hit by another motorist, that injury probably is covered by workers' compensation insurance.

Q 8:185 What if an employee is injured by a piece of equipment manufactured by a third party?

If an employee is injured by a piece of machinery or equipment that was manufactured by someone other than the employer, the employer must still provide the employee with workers' compensation benefits. However, the employer's liability is limited to the remedies under the workers' compensation law; the manufacturer of the equipment is subject to a third-party lawsuit under personal injury and products' liability law in a state or federal court.

Q 8:186 If the employee sues a third party for his or her injuries, can the employer recover any of the workers' compensation benefits paid to that employee?

The employer and/or its insurance carrier has a subrogation right to money that is recovered by the employee in a third-party action against the manufacturer of the machinery or other product that was directly responsible for the employee's injury. Moreover, in many states, the insurance carrier or the employer has the right to confront the third-party manufacturer directly to exercise this subrogation interest.

Q 8:187 How does the ADA impact on workers' compensation?

Just as the ADA affects an employer's discretion with respect to which benefits will be provided under group health insurance plans (see Q 4:94), it can also be expected to have an impact on workers' compensation. First, it's important to bear in mind that while an employee injured on the job is afforded the exclusive remedy of workers' compensation benefits against the employer under state law, workers' compensation exclusivity/immunity provisions cannot preempt an employee's right to be free from disability discrimination under the provisions of the ADA.

Second, just as employers are not permitted to make disability or medical inquiries prior to a conditional offer of employment (see Qs 4:86, 4:87), so, too, the employer may not inquire into an applicant's workers' compensation history. An employer may make such an inquiry if the same inquiry is regularly made of all applicants after the conditional offer of employment has been made and accepted. (The condition, of course, is that the subsequent medical inquiry or examination does not reveal a disability that prevents the new employee from performing the major functions of the job, even with a reasonable accommodation.)

One reason that an employer might want to have a regular program of post-employment inquiries concerning workers' compensation claims is to be able to substantiate when post-employment injuries are in fact second injuries (i.e., prior on-the-job injuries only aggravated by the new employment experience) subject to a state's workers' compensation second injury fund.

At least one group of experts writing for Panel Publishers contends that a good case management program for job-related injuries can both control workers' compensation costs and keep a company in compliance with the ADA.

> A recent example of a successful program that not only ensured compliance with the ADA but also drastically reduced the company's workers' compensation costs was created by the Community Hospitals of Central California. [T]his group reduced its compensation costs by 47 percent in one year with an internal case management program that consisted of an aggressive, modified, light-duty program. There was also a $365,000 reduction in the cost of first year claims and a 10 percent insurance claims reserve reduction. [Bannon et al, *Company Policy Manual Special Report: How to Cut Workers' Compensation Costs* at 30 (1993)]

Q 8:188   How do workers' compensation and the ADA relate to mental injuries and diseases?

Two U.S. district court decisions early in 1995 illustrate how workers' compensation and the ADA, respectively, affect employee mental illness and injury.

In deciding a motion to dismiss filed by the defendant corporation, Senior Judge Shane Devine in federal court in New Hampshire decided that the plaintiff's claim of intentional infliction of emotional distress, related to his termination of employment, was subsumed by the exclusivity provision of the state's workers' compensation law. According to the court, Plaintiff Herbert Kopf had been hired as a regional sales manager by Chloride Power Electronics Inc. early in 1991. About 18 months later he tumbled from a ladder while repairing his home and suffered a hematoma of the brain. After brain surgery, Kopf could work only about an hour a day. Despite his medical condition he received disciplinary letters in December 1992 and again in February 1993. The company set sales goals upon which Kopf's continued employment was contingent. Not long after these goals were set, the plaintiff's employment was terminated, allegedly for insubordination in a meeting with his boss to discuss the sales goals. While the court relied on a long line of New Hampshire precedents in holding that Kopf's state law tort claim of emotional distress was a workers' compensation claim, and thus subject to dismissal early in the legal action, his ADA claim survived Chloride's preliminary motion. [Kopf v Chloride Power Electronics Inc, 1995 US Dist LEXIS 384 (D NH 1995)]

By way of contrast, one of the nation's most bizarre ADA cases concerning mental illness came to an end early in 1995, but not before going to trial in a federal court in Florida. The case concerned an employee who was a successful team leader for GTE's computer programming division, in Temple Terrace, until he allegedly began stealing people's purses on the way to work. He eventually was accused of stealing thousands of dollars from co-workers until finally being led away from his office in handcuffs by the local police in July 1992. After the plaintiff was arrested, one of his co-workers searched his briefcase, where the colleague found a loaded derringer pistol. GTE fired the plaintiff for violating a rule against possessing firearms in the workplace.

The plaintiff sued, alleging a violation of the ADA in that he was diagnosed as suffering from a mental imbalance brought on by the antidepressant Prozac. He and his counsel hotly contended that, like any heart attack or cancer victim working for GTE, he should have been accorded an opportunity to recover from his mental illness. In June 1994 a federal judge seemed to agree, denying GTE's motion to end the case in the corporation's favor. [Hindman v GTE Data Serv Inc, 1994 US Dist LEXIS 9522 (MD Fla 1994)] The judge's decision outraged many management-side employment lawyers; even the Equal Employment Opportunity Commission (EEOC) expressed its doubts about the soundness of the decision.

When the case finally went to trial early in 1995, a different judge, U.S. District Judge George Woods, visiting the mid-Florida bench from his normal venue in Detroit, granted GTE's motion for a directed verdict. [Steve Huettel, "Fired GTE Supervisor Loses Federal Lawsuit," *The Tampa Tribune*, Jan 24, 1995, at 6]

His ADA assault upon GTE's decision to terminate his employment having failed, Hindman might consider a workers' compensation claim, provided the time has not expired to assert such a claim. This comment assumes that his underlying depression was job-related. Certainly his case underlines the intimate relationship between a federal claim under the ADA, a state-law tort claim, and a workers' compensation claim whenever an employee contends mental injury, illness, or imbalance. The employer that wishes on the one hand to protect employees and customers from a mentally ill worker—an obligation imposed both by state tort law concerning negligent hiring and by the Occupational Safety and Health Act—and to avoid an ADA action such as Hindman's on the other, might do well to consider treating the problem as a worker compensable temporary, total disability.

Q 8:189 How does workers' compensation deal with injured athletes?

In a landmark decision in 1993, the Texas Workers' Compensation Commission ruled that a scholarship football player at a university was that university's employee and therefore was eligible for workers' compensation benefits when injured "on the job." The player, who was actually injured in 1974 while playing for Texas Christian University, has been confined to a wheelchair since he was hurt two decades ago, and is now the president of the National Paralysis Foundation. He says he filed the claim in 1991 not for the money, but to raise the issues of players' rights and related problems in athletics.

The reasoning behind the Texas award was that the student met the criteria of a statutory employee despite being classified by the school purely as a student. In labor and employment law, the courts and government agencies have always looked past the form of a relationship to its substance, particularly at the statutory employer's right to control the employee (see Qs 2:63, 2:64). "A finding that he's an employee for purposes of workmen's compensation does not necessarily mandate that a student-athlete be considered an employee for other purposes." [Lederman, "Texas Panel Awards Workers' Compensation to Injured Athlete; First Such Case in the 1990s May Have Broad Ramifications," *Chronicle of Higher Education*, Apr 7, 1993, at A34]

According to one publication following the case, "In the last 30 years, with mixed results, agencies and courts in a half-dozen states have ruled on whether college athletes are entitled to workers' compensation benefits." [Lederman at A33]

Reportedly, professional athletes are also increasingly seeking to take advantage of workers' compensation benefits when their careers are cut short by permanent injuries, or even when "old age" renders them "disabled" from playing any longer at the professional level. Since such injured college and professional players are likely to live a long time after sustaining such game or practice-related injuries, the cost to teams, universities, and state funds can be substantial.

In one such case, decided early in 1995, an Illinois court of appeals held that former Chicago Bears lineman Ted Albrecht is entitled to workers' compensation benefits because a football injury shortened his professional career. Albrecht, who graduated from the University of California in 1977, was the Bears' first-round draft pick and started every game for five years, until he injured his back in training in April 1982. Albrecht earned $130,000 on the injured reserve list in 1982, then saw his income decline to $80,000 the following year. As a travel-business owner and sometime sportscaster he earned as little as $36,000 one year in the mid-1980s.

The appellate court's decision in favor of the former football player overturned previous rulings by the state workers' compensation commission, an NFL arbitrator, and the Cook County Circuit Court. However, under Illinois law, Albrecht is entitled to less than $300 per week, so that he will not come close to recouping all the income his injury cost him. Nonetheless the decision has been heralded as precedent setting. [Jim Merriner, "Ex-Bears Player Albrecht Wins Workers Compensation Ruling," *Chicago Sun-Times*, Mar 18, 1995, at 11]

Unemployment and Health Insurance

Q 8:190   What is unemployment insurance?

Unemployment insurance is a publicly funded insurance plan that provides compensation to people who are out of work through no fault of their own, but who are available and willing to take a job. Almost all employers are required to pay unemployment tax to the state(s) in which they do business. The rate of this tax is usually determined by the amount of money needed by the state to pay benefits to unemployed workers, as well as the amount of benefits the laid-off employees of the particular employer have collected in the recent past. Often employees are taxed to support this fund as well. (Unemployment compensation issues are covered in detail in chapter 13.)

Q 8:191   Is the Clinton administration striving to reform the unemployment compensation system?

The Reemployment Act of 1994, which made its first appearance in 1993 as the Workforce Security Act, if enacted would "revamp the unemployment system by creating an employment and training system that would help American workers build skills and find jobs." ["Labor Department Focused on Encouraging 'New Economy,' Says DOL Deputy Secretary," 1994 *BNA Daily Labor Report* 35, Feb 23, 1994, at D18] Labor Secretary Robert Reich told the Senate Budget Committee on February 22, 1994, that the federal-state unemployment insurance system, which was conceived and created a half century ago, was intended only to provide an income supplement to employees on temporary layoff status. By contrast, many workers laid off in today's economic environment "face structural displacement," claimed Reich, who declared the available programs and services overlapping and confusing. The Act was not enacted in 1994 and its chances of passage in the next two years is slight given the Republican control of Congress.

Q 8:192   What is a health maintenance organization?

A health maintenance organization (HMO) is a type of health insurance plan that developed relatively recently. Under a typical health insurance plan, a patient goes to a doctor of his or her choice and the insurance company pays some or all of the medical or hospital bills. Under an HMO plan, a member's medical care is reimbursed only if it is obtained from participating health care providers. Under some HMO plans, HMO members must go to a clinic or hospital that has been established by the HMO specifically to provide services under the plan. Generally, all medical expenses are covered by the plan; usually, there are no deductibles or upper limits. Also, an HMO may result in lower or more stable employer-paid premiums. However, the disadvantage of an HMO is that employees lose some discretion in choosing health care providers.

Q 8:193   Must an employer provide employees with the option of joining a health maintenance organization (HMO)?

A company must offer an HMO option if the following factors apply:

- The company offers a traditional health insurance plan
- The company comes under the minimum-wage requirements of the federal FLSA
- During the previous calendar quarter, the company employed at least 25 workers
- The company receives a written request from a qualified HMO that covers a service area in which at least 25 of the company's employees live

These requirements are set by the Health Maintenance Organization Act (HMO Act). However, the employer is not required to pay more for health benefits as a result of offering a qualified HMO option than it would otherwise pay for health benefits under a collective bargaining agreement or other employer-employee contract in effect at the time the HMO is included in the health benefit plan.

Q 8:194   What is meant by the term "to offer a health benefits plan" under the HMO Act?

This term means that an HMO will be available to employees who live in a service area in which at least 24 co-workers reside. The employer must make a financial contribution to the HMO on behalf of the participating employees that is at least the equivalent of the contribution made on behalf of other employees to a traditional health insurance plan.

Q 8:195   When must an HMO file a request to be included in a company's health benefits plan?

An HMO wishing to be included in a company's health benefits plan must file a request with the company no more than 365 days and no less than 180 days before the expiration or renewal date of a health insurance contract, an employer-employee contract, or a collective bargaining agreement covering these types of benefits.

Q 8:196   How are problems with U.S. health care being addressed?

A major problem of the current U.S. health care system is rising costs, which annually outpace inflation. For example, it has been predicted that rising costs have left the Medicare trust fund with only enough money to pay hospital bills for senior citizens and disabled persons for the next several years. A second concern is the need to provide health insurance to the millions of Americans without it today. Third, many believe that it is unfair and too uncertain to connect health insurance to employment.

While health care reform remained the hottest topic on the Congressional agenda in 1994, the issue of rising costs began to be addressed in some more immediate, and perhaps more practical, ways.

> While President Clinton, Congress, and various state governments are overhauling the health care system, the Justice Department is marshaling its resources to correct widespread and systematic abuses in the current system. . . . Criminal prosecutions by U.S. attorneys have become a vital weapon in

the government's arsenal. Health care abusers have been convicted under federal mail fraud, wire fraud, the federal Racketeer Influenced and Corrupt Organizations Act, antikickback and bribery statutes, as well as for violations of the Internal Revenue Code. A rise in the number of prosecutions appears imminent. [Marc S Raspanti, "Health Care Fraud: The Government's Next Campaign," *The Philadelphia Lawyer*, Spring 1994, at 24-25]

A General Accounting Office study says that the two most common types of health care fraud are (1) so-called "pill mills" in which doctors and allied health professionals bill Medicaid for tens of thousands of dollars for unnecessary office visits, diagnostic tests, and prescription drugs, and (2) pharmacy "cash for scrips" schemes in which the government program is billed for prescriptions that are never filled. [Id]

In 1995 the Executive Office of the U.S. Attorneys reported a major success involving a pilot project. The White Collar Fraud Civil Enforcement (WCFCE) Pilot Project was established in three judicial districts across the country—the Central District of California, the Western District of New York, and the Middle District of Pennsylvania—considered to be large, medium, and small in size and case loads, respectively. The WCFCE program in mid-Pennsylvania focused on Medicare fraud.

Using the False Claims Act, [31 USC §§ 3729-3733] the Pennsylvania task force targeted health care providers in Harrisburg and Scranton. Emulating the IRS, the unit conducted computerized audits of the so-called common procedural terminology (CPT) codes on claims submitted by those hospitals to Medicare and Medicaid. The computer spotted irregularities, some as bizarre as charges for procedures dated after the patient's death. Because the False Claims Act requires no proof of specific intent to defraud the government to affix liability and because a conviction carries a mandatory fine of $5,000 per occurrence, U.S. attorneys assigned to the task force found that in virtually all instances in which irregularities were found, health care providers paid without a fight. Most agreed to pay treble damages on the strength of a demand letter. None chose to be brought to trial. The U.S. Attorney's office reported in April 1995, "During the course of the last 36 months, this office has generated approximately $24 million. . ., [making] the White Collar Fraud Civil Enforcement Unit's time worth $4,375 per hour." [Andrew S Quinn, "Health Care Providers and the False Claims Act" in *Federal Civil Litigation Practice* (Widener University School of Law Continuing Legal Education Program, 1995)]

Reportedly this federal program will be extended to more federal judicial districts and eventually will become a nationwide activity of the Justice Department.

Q 8:197   What are the states doing with regard to health care reform?

From coast to coast, a number of states are experimenting with health care reform, and some have taken the lead. While Oregon is looking at a form of minimum health care services that would be available to all residents, Massachusetts has enacted one of the most drastic reform measures, a law calling for a 12 percent surcharge, called a "medical security contribution," on the first $14,000 of wages (about $1,680 per employee) to be paid by all employers of six or more workers. The surcharge would be levied on behalf of each employee who works 30 or more hours per week, or who puts in at least 20 hours a week and is the head of his or her household.

However, it is unclear whether the Massachusetts statute will ever take effect. Its effective date has been postponed several times and is finally scheduled for 1995. Additionally, there looms the issue of ERISA preemption, which is also haunting the Oregon state health care reform project. [See Massachusetts Gen L ch 151A, Massachusetts Health Security Act (1988)]

Until recently, state reform of health care was essentially prohibited under ERISA. ERISA Section 514(a) provides that ERISA would preempt, or supersede, state laws that "relate to any employee benefit plan." An exception to preemption exists for a state law that regulates insurance. Thus, ERISA has denied states the opportunity to adopt health care reforms since such efforts are preempted under the law.

This situation changed in 1995 with a decision of the U.S. Supreme Court in a closely followed case, *New York State Conference of Blue Cross & Blue Shield Plans v. Travelers Insurance Co.* [63 LW 4372 (Apr 26, 1995)] The court's unanimous decision has destroyed existing wisdom on preemption of state health care reforms and could remove the shackles on state experimentation that have existed until now. [Prince, *Managing Employee Health Benefits* 3:3, Summer 1995]

The case arose out of a New York statute that imposed a surcharge of 13 percent on hospital charges paid by commercial health insurers, except for Blue Cross and Blue Shield plans and HMOs. These funds were to be paid to the hospitals. The law also imposed a surcharge of as much as 9 percent, to be paid to the State of New York, on hospital charges paid by HMOs. Hospital charges paid by Medicare were exempted from both surcharges. Further, for one year, hospitals were permitted to charge an additional 11 percent surcharge for commercially insured patients. This money also was turned over to the state.

The purpose of the law was to make the cost of Blue Cross and Blue Shield plans less expensive in relation to other commercial insurance plans and therefore more attractive. Also, the surcharges would provide additional money to hospitals to cover the cost of care for patients without insurance. Finally, the law was adopted as a way for New York to raise revenue.

Immediately, several insurers and insurance trade association brought suit to invalidate the surcharges. They claimed that since many of the patients affected by the surcharges received insurance through their employers, ERISA preempted New York from passing any law that affected these plans.

The insurers prevailed in the U.S. District Court for the Southern District of New York and on appeal in the Second Circuit Court of Appeals, also in New York. Both courts agreed that the surcharges were intended to increase the cost of certain types of health insurance, imposing a significant economic burden on them. This relationship with ERISA-covered health plans was sufficient to trigger the preemption provision in ERISA.

The Supreme Court accepted the case on the appeal brought by the State of New York and Blue Cross and Blue Shield. Oral argument was held before the Supreme Court on January 18, 1995. The unanimous decision of the court, written by Justice David Souter, reversed the decision of the Second Circuit and upheld the New York statute. The court acknowledged that the purpose and effect of the law is to make commercial insurance plans and HMOs more expensive than the Blues. However, the court said that such indirect economic effect is not enough to trigger preemption. The reasoning was that the price difference does not bind plan administrators to any particular choice. Plan administrators will use the price differential in determining which insurance plan to use. However, a plan administrator is free to choose a commercial insurer over the Blues despite the price, because a commercial insurance plan might offer superior benefits or have other advantages over the Blues. The court compared the surcharge to other state laws that concern quality standards or employment in hospitals. These laws also have an indirect effect on the cost of medical services but are not preempted by ERISA.

Justice Souter pointed out that simply because the law causes different plans to have different costs does not preclude uniform administration of plans throughout the country, the goal of ERISA. He reasoned that plan administrators always have shopped among plans looking for the one with the best price. Plan administrators simply will consider the surcharges when shopping for a plan.

The court dismissed the arguments of the commercial insurers, saying their arguments would "bar any state regulation of hospital costs." The court also stated "nothing in the language of the act or the context of its passage indicates that Congress chose to displace general health care regulation, which historically has been a matter of local concern."

The court cautioned, however, that just because a state law affects only the costs of benefit plans does not mean it is beyond the reach of the preemption provision. Such a law might be subject to preemption if it leaves "consumers with a Hobson's choice" forcing "all health insurance consumers to contract with the Blues."

The decision has opened the door for states to regulate health care, at least to the point of making some plans more expensive than others. The Clinton administration, which submitted an amicus brief on behalf of the state of New York, may feel that it can hasten health care reform by loosening the ERISA stranglehold over the states. The effect could be the creation of 50 laboratories for reform.

The Republican Congress also must be pleased with the decision. Republicans defeated President Clinton's health care bill in 1994 and it is unlikely they would attempt any significant reform this year. The decision could relieve pressure on the federal government to make some reform by instead placing the burden, and political heat, on the states.

Q 8:198   May an employer alter its health care coverage to save money?

In 1991, the U.S. Court of Appeals for the Fifth Circuit held in *McGann v. H&H Music Co.* that an employer is permitted by ERISA to exclude AIDS from the conditions covered by its $1 million major medical plan, relegating HIV/AIDS to a far more modest amount ($5,000) of major medical insurance. The Supreme Court denied *certiorari* (i.e., review) to McGann. The EEOC has since predicted a different result (namely a finding of illegal discrimination against a disabled person) under the ADA (see Q 4:94).

A ruling in March 1994 by the U.S. Court of Appeals for the Eleventh Circuit that Section 510 of ERISA must be interpreted "both to protect employees'" rights to receive benefits according to the terms of the applicable plan and employers' "right to modify the benefits they offer" also chipped at, if not swept away, the short-lived *McGann* decision. Thus, distinguishing *McGann*, the court concluded that "ERISA prohibits employers from discharging employees to avoid paying benefits but permits employers to reduce or terminate nonvested benefits simply by changing the terms of the plan." [1993 *BNA Daily Labor Report* 51, Mar 18, 1993, at 1] The case involved a real estate sales agent who contended that her brokerage firm tried to force her to change her status from employee to independent contractor so that it could stop paying her health insurance benefits. (See generally Qs 2:63, 2:64 for a discussion of the distinctions between employees and independent contractors. ERISA is not much help with making this distinction, because it defines employee as "any individual employed by an employer." [29 USC § 1002(6)])

Between the EEOC's invocation of the ADA in opposition to the outcome under ERISA in *McGann* and the Eleventh Circuit's distinguishing of *McGann* from the real estate agent's situation, it seems unlikely that *McGann* will be successfully invoked in similar factual circumstances (for example, to carve out an exclusion for HIV/AIDS or some other dread disease from a group health insurance policy's coverage of a corporation's employees). On the other hand, it seems clearer that employers retain the right under ERISA to alter nonvesting employee benefit plans for nondiscriminatory reasons, when the change is aimed at a category of coverage or services rather than at particular individual(s) in the company's workforce. Indeed, the Eleventh Circuit in another 1993 decision followed the Fifth Circuit in *McGann*, permitting a Georgia-based chain of furniture stores to set a $25,000 cap on AIDS-related claims. [1993 *BNA Daily Labor Report* 40, March 3, 1993, at 1]

The real question about the future vitality of any part of *McGann* and its progeny, is whether an employer or insurer can entertain and articulate a nondiscriminatory reason for carving out an exception from usual coverage limits for a particular malady, such as AIDS, which is expressly listed as a disability in the ADA's implementing regulations. [29 CFR Part 1630] The EEOC has hinted that some defenses to a charge of disability discrimination may exist. [See Bender and Derewicz, "Health Insurance and the ADA: Some Preliminary Guidance," *Employment Law Update*, Apr 1993 at 3; McGann v H&H Music Co, 946 F 2d 401 (5th Cir 1991); compare, 29 USC § 1002(1) (defining "employee welfare benefit plan") and 29 USC § 1002(2)(A) (defining "employee pension benefit plan") for a clearer understanding of which benefits are subject to vesting and which are subject to nondiscriminatory revisions and reductions under ERISA; see also Qs 8:110, 8:111 for a discussion of the distinction; and, finally, see *Analysis of the Americans with Disabilities Act and Implementing EEOC Regulations* (RIA 1991) at 22, and Q 4:81 for discussion of "undue hardship" under the ADA, which may in fact be one possible defense to a charge of disability discrimination based upon reduction in health benefits for AIDS-related conditions]

Given all of the foregoing discussion, a new decision handed down by the Fifth Circuit in 1995 may be an historical curiosity as soon as it hits the case reporters. Involving a lawsuit initiated before the ADA had taken effect, *Hines v. Massachusetts Mutual Life Insurance Co.* [43 F 3d 207 (5th Cir 1995)] was initiated in 1988 by the legal guardian of a worker who was permanently disabled in an auto accident six years earlier. The defendant employer, GECO Geophysical Co., changed insurers shortly after employee Bobby Alan Parker's accident, so that his preexisting conditions ceased to be covered by group health insurance. GECO itself picked up Parker's medical bills until 1988, after which Hines instituted her action. Based solely upon ERISA, Hine's suit was disposed of by the Fifth Circuit under the rule in *McGann*. The appellate panel said, "Parker because of his condition was not covered by [GECO's] new policy. Nevertheless, Hines offers no positive evidence to prove a specific intent to discriminate against Parker. Under *McGann*, her evidence of a specific intent to discriminate cannot withstand summary judgment." [Id]

Disability Insurance

Q 8:199 Are employees entitled to disability insurance?

As a general rule, employees are not entitled as a matter of law to disability insurance. However, a number of states tax employers and employees to provide disability insurance under programs analogous to unemployment compensation plans.

Q 8:200 Are pregnant employees entitled to disability insurance?

Under the Pregnancy Discrimination Act (PDA), if employees who are injured or ill are eligible for short- and long-term disability benefits, employees disabled by pregnancy must be accorded the same benefit. Similarly, if the employer provides unpaid or paid leaves of absence to employees for any reason, that employer is well-advised to offer maternity leave as well.

Leave

Q 8:201 What types of paid time off do companies usually provide the employees?

Typically, companies provide paid time off to employees in the form of vacations, sick leave, and holidays. Paid extended leaves of absence are much more rare. For example, many colleges and universities provide paid sabbaticals for their faculty members. Some companies provide paid maternity leaves to pregnant employees. However, these types of paid leaves are more the exception than the rule.

Vacation

Q 8:202　Is an employee entitled to paid vacation time?

No state or federal law requires an employer to give employees paid vacation time. However, once paid vacations are offered, state wage payment and collection laws may come into play and require that when vacation time is earned it is in fact given; otherwise compensation is given to the employee in lieu of the paid time off.

Q 8:203　Why should a company offer employees paid vacation time?

There are two reasons for giving an employee paid vacation time. First, it is a reward for services rendered. Second, it is a chance for the employee to become refreshed and to prepare to work well in the future.

Q 8:204　How much paid vacation time should a company give to its employees?

The amount of paid vacation time generally depends on seniority and status. Often employees are not entitled to vacation time until they have been on the job at least a full year. After a full year, employees may get a week or two of paid vacation time in the following year. As seniority in the job increases, employees usually get increased vacation time, generally up to a maximum of four or five weeks. On the other hand, management employees may start off with as much as a month's paid vacation time, but their vacation entitlement may or may not increase as time goes on.

Leaves of Absence

Q 8:205　What are the various types of leaves of absence?

Leaves of absence can be classified in at least two general ways: by the benefits provided, and by the reasons for providing these benefits.

1. By benefit:

    Leave with pay. It is somewhat unusual (but not unheard of) in this country for a leave of absence to be with pay. However, such leaves (called sabbaticals) are common in higher education.

Leave without pay, but with guaranteed reinstatement. More common is a leave of absence during which current employees, perhaps supplemented by temporary help, absorb the absent employee's workload, while the company keeps the position available. A less difficult alternative, from the company's perspective, is a leave policy that guarantees the employee the same or a comparable job upon returning from leave.

Leave without pay or guaranteed reinstatement. The most common and least secure form of leave policy is that during which the employee is replaced and will only be reemployed if an appropriate position happens to be available when the leave ends. Generally, although reinstatement when desired is not a sure thing, such a leave does preserve for the leave-taking employee a preferential position as against new applicants. Also, if and when the employee is reinstated, no new probationary period is required by the company. Finally, once reinstated, the employee picks up benefit entitlements (such as vacation, pension, and sick leave) right where they left off.

2. By reason:

Disability leave. An employee disabled by injury or illness (including pregnancy, see Q 8:206), whether job-related or not, may be accorded a leave during which to recover and convalesce. Such leave may be in conjunction with, but is different from, disability insurance. The latter provides income supplements (at least partial) usually starting within a week or two from when the disability commences. Neither leave nor benefits are required by law; however, job-related injuries must be covered by workers' compensation benefits. Nonetheless, except where specified in a collective bargaining agreement or where the employer voluntarily commits to do so, even an on-the-job injury does not legally require the employer to keep the job open for the injured and absent employee.

Education leave. As noted above, sabbaticals are quite common in higher education. Typically, they are paid leaves of a semester or two with reinstatement virtually ensured (since, usually, they are available only to tenured faculty). In other industries, they are much less widely accepted and, where available, may be without pay. More commonly, employers tend to provide tuition assistance for courses taken on a part-time basis that are job-related and do not interfere with work schedules.

Military leave. Federal law requires employers to hold jobs open for employees fulfilling their active duty obligations in the National Guard or U.S. military reserves. These obligations typically entail one weekend per month plus two weeks of active duty. Although not required by law, many companies go a step further and pay employees the difference between their regular salaries and what the armed forces pay while they are on active duty. Employees who are drafted or enlist in the armed forces for extended periods are also usually entitled to reinstatement upon release from active duty, if they demand it.

Q 8:206　What is the difference between maternity disability leave and parental leave?

The PDA requires that employee group health and/or disability plans (whether implemented by insurance, self-insurance, or otherwise), if any such plans are provided, must provide the same benefits to employees disabled and requiring medical services due to pregnancy as are provided to any other sick or disabled worker. This is a legal requirement.

An employer may offer paid parental leave or unpaid parental leave. Such leave, when offered, is to afford the new parent time to spend with the infant; it is not correlated to, nor is it dependent upon, the parent's pregnancy-related disability.

Q 8:207　Are employees entitled to unpaid leaves of absence?

On February 4, 1993, Congress passed, and a day later President Clinton signed, the Family and Medical Leave Act (FMLA). The act took effect six months later. It applies to certain private sector employers and allows eligible employees as much as 12 weeks of unpaid leave in a 12-month period. The new federal statute joined 12 state statutes that provide some form of unpaid leave to workers employed by private corporations.

Q 8:208   What are the highlights of FMLA?

1. The statute applies to private employers with 50 or more employees.
2. Federal civil service employees, state and local government workers, and employees of Congress also are covered.
3. To be eligible under the act, an employee must have worked for the company for at least 12 months prior to applying for an unpaid leave of absence and must have logged at least 1,250 hours on the job during that 12-month period.
4. Eligible employees are entitled to 12 weeks of unpaid leave during a 12-month period.
5. The company can require the eligible employee to first use any paid sick leave or accrued vacation time as part of the 12-week unpaid absence from work.
6. An employee on leave under the new law is entitled to continue receiving health benefits under the same terms and conditions as when not on leave.
7. Such an unpaid leave must be granted for an employee's own serious illness, the care of a seriously ill parent, spouse, or child, or in connection with the birth or adoption of a child.
8. Intermittent periods of leave of less than 12 weeks are available only by mutual agreement of employer and employee.
9. Upon return from the leave of absence, the employee must be given the same or an equivalent position as that held prior to the unpaid absence.

Q 8:209   Does FMLA preempt state leave laws?

In many respects, the FMLA of 1993 is patterned after the federal FLSA, which for more than half a century has governed minimum wage and overtime pay. Like the FLSA, the new act does not preempt any state statute that provides more advantageous leave of absence provisions than the federal law.

Furthermore, FMLA, since it has a remedy of its own, cannot be used to support a wrongful termination action under state common law. [Gall v Quaker City Castings Inc, 874 F Supp 161 (ND Ohio 1995)]

Q 8:210   How will FMLA be enforced?

As with the FLSA, the FMLA will be administered and enforced by the DOL. Besides giving the secretary of labor enforcement powers, the act gives employees a private right of action to sue for damages under the new statute.

Q 8:211   What is the history behind the enactment of the federal FMLA?

Representative Pat Schroeder is credited with having introduced the forerunner of the 1993 statute on April 4, 1985. If that bill had been enacted, it would have required employers to provide at least 18 weeks of unpaid leave within any two-year period, but only to employees electing to stay home to care for a new baby, a newly adopted child, or a seriously ill child. During the next five years, other senators and representatives proposed different versions of a federal leave act. These assorted bills and amendments were the subject of numerous arguments in various congressional committees.

Finally, in 1990, the first full-blown FMLA emerged from Capitol Hill, only to be shot down by President George Bush's veto at the opposite end of Pennsylvania Avenue. On September 22, 1992, President Bush exercised his veto power for a second time to ensure that he left office without the enactment of a federal leave statute. A week later, while the Senate mustered sufficient votes to override the president's rejection of the bill, House Democrats were unable to rally the two-thirds majority needed to upset the president's veto.

Q 8:212   Does the FMLA of 1993 require employers to permit "stacking" of short- or long-term disability leave with unpaid leaves of absence for serious illnesses?

The act itself does not specifically answer this question. But it does give one clue: employers are permitted to require leave-taking employees to use paid sick leave and accrued vacation time as part of the total 12-week absence from the job. This statutory provision seems to imply that employees will not be permitted to insist upon being allowed to stack paid and unpaid leave in conjunction with a serious illness.

Employers should also note that the FMLA will not preempt any more favorable state enactment on this issue. Nor is a voluntary stacking policy or collective bargaining arrangement in which a particular employer may acquiesce prohibited.

Q 8:213   Which states have unpaid leave acts similar to FMLA?

Eleven states and the District of Columbia currently have leave laws similar to the federal act.

California. In 1978, California was the first state to pass a law governing unpaid leave for pregnant workers. The U.S. Supreme Court upheld the constitutionality of the law and also held that it was not preempted by the federal Pregnancy Discrimination Act of 1978. Today, California's statute allows as much as 16 weeks of leave over a two-year term of employment. It covers private concerns with 50 or more employees but does not apply to an employee's own serious illness.

Connecticut. This state statute ensures eligible employees as much as 16 weeks of leave in a 24-month span. However, it only applies to private corporations with at least 75 employees.

District of Columbia. DC's law provides for 16 weeks of unpaid leave over two years and originally applied to organizations with 50 or more employees. In April 1994, the law dropped its threshold to include companies with as few as 20 workers. To be eligible for the act's benefits, an employee must have worked at least 1,000 hours during a one-year span. By mutual agreement between employer and employee, the unpaid leave can be in the form of partial work weeks or other intermittent absences spread out over a maximum of 24 weeks.

Hawaii. This state's leave law provides for four weeks of leave over a one-year period for employers of 100 or more employees. It became effective on January 1, 1994. It does not cover an employee's own illness. To be eligible, an employee must have worked for the company for at least six months. Intermittent leaves are not allowed.

Maine. This state's law provides 10 weeks of leave in a two-year period. The law covers employers of 25 or more. Twelve consecutive months with the same employer creates eligibility. Benefits may be maintained during the leave of absence, but at the employee's own expense, unless a different arrangement is negotiated between the parties or by a labor union on behalf of a bargaining group.

Minnesota. Minnesota's pregnancy leave act was the subject of U.S. Supreme Court scrutiny along with the more widely publicized California act of the same type. Minnesota still provides for as much as six weeks of child care leave for a newborn or newly adopted child. Employers of 21 or more persons are subject to the statute.

New Jersey. The Garden State's leave act provides 12 weeks of leave over 24 months and covers companies with 50 or more workers. Note that in 1991, a New Jersey court held that the state's leave act, to the extent that it required employers to maintain health insurance for employees on leave, was preempted by ERISA. [New Jersey Business & Indus Assn v State of New Jersey, 592 A 2d 660 (NJ Super 1991)] However, the new federal law now imposes a similar requirement nationally.

Oregon. This state provides 12 weeks of leave within a 24-month time period for employees of companies with 50 or more workers, and no coverage for an employee's own illness.

Rhode Island. This state legislated 13 weeks of leave within 24 months for employees at companies with 50 or more workers. An unusual feature of this state's act requires the leave-taking employee to give the leave-granting employer a lump sum deposit, equal to health care premiums anticipated during the term of the leave, prior to commencing the sabbatical. If the employee returns from the leave as anticipated, the deposit must be returned within 10 days.

Vermont. The law provides 12 weeks of leave per year, covering companies employing 15 or more workers who average 30 hours or more of work per week. The employer is required to pay the cost of continuing all benefits during the otherwise unpaid leave of absence.

Washington. Up to 12 weeks of leave is available every two years for employees of 100-plus companies. Interestingly, covered companies are entitled to deny leave to designated "key personnel" or to the 10 percent of most highly paid employees working within the state.

Wisconsin. A maximum of six weeks of leave for the birth or adoption of a child is provided and up to two weeks of leave to care for a seriously ill child. The law applies to employers of 50 or more workers.

Q 8:214   Are all employers with 50 or more employees bound by the FMLA?

An employee is entitled to an unpaid leave under the FMLA only if 50 or more co-workers are employed by the company within a 75-mile radius of the leave-seeking employee's worksite. Thus it is possible that some employers of 50-plus employees may escape coverage if their business is highly decentralized. For instance, certain retail chains, for example, grocery or convenience food stores, may not, in some sales regions, have 50 workers within 75 miles, and therefore fall outside the purview of the act.

Q 8:215   How does the FMLA of 1993 define "parent" and "son or daughter"?

Congress expressly opted for broad definitions of these terms for purposes of determining eligibility for leave under the act. The terms "son or daughter" are defined to include "biological, adopted, or foster child, legal ward, or a child of a person standing *in loco parentis.*" The relevant congressional committee report explains that "the terms 'parent' and 'son or daughter' [should] be broadly construed to ensure that an employee who actually has day-to-day responsibility for caring for a child is entitled to leave even if the employee does not have a biological or legal relationship to that child." Children include dependents under 18 years of age and older offspring who cannot care for themselves due to a mental or physical disability.

Q 8:216   Has the DOL issued regulations implementing FMLA?

The DOL published its final regulations, implementing FMLA of 1993, in the Federal Register on January 6, 1995. These regulations took effect on April 6, 1995. Under the statute, employees of covered employers (those with 50 or more employees) enjoy three fundamental rights:

1. Eligible employees are entitled to unpaid leave for as long as 12 weeks in any 12-month period for birth or care of a child, adoption or receipt of a child for foster care, the serious health condition of a family member (such as child, spouse, or parent), or the employee's own serious health condition preventing job performance.

2. While on leave the employee is entitled to continuation of health insurance on the same terms as before the leave.

3. The employee gets reinstatement to the same or an equivalent job as the one held prior to taking the leave of absence.

Under the regulations, designation of absences as FMLA leaves is a burden shared by the employer and the employee. The employee is obliged merely to provide the employer with sufficient, timely information to enable the boss to determine how to designate the leave properly. The employer may require that this information include certification from a health care provider. Upon receiving sufficient information, the employer must designate the absence as an FMLA leave within two days and notify the employee accordingly.

On-the-job injuries, which result in absences from work, may be counted concurrently as FMLA-related serious health conditions. However, if the employer fails to tell the worker that the compensable absence is being counted as an FMLA leave, then the employee may be eligible for a subsequent FMLA period of absence for the same injury.

An employee unable to resume the same or an equivalent job following an injury may turn down a "light duty" assignment offered by the company. Although declining a light-duty post may result in cessation of workers' compensation benefits under applicable state law and the insurance policy involved, this result will not affect the employee's right to opt for a full 12-week leave of absence under the FMLA.

The new regulations contain a model notice of FMLA rights, which covered employers should post prominently at each worksite. The regulations may be found in Title 29 of the *Code of Federal Regulations*, as well as in the April 6, 1995, issue of the *Federal Register*.

Q 8:217   What is a "serious health condition" allowing for an unpaid leave under FMLA?

The question of what constitutes a "serious health condition" has been the subject of substantial litigation. In general, a serious health condition is "an illness, injury, impairment, or physical or mental condition" that demands either inpatient care at a health care facility or continuous treatment by a health care provider. The issue is clarified further under the regulations issued on January 6, 1995. Under these regulations, a "serious health condition" is defined as:

- A condition involving continued treatment by a health care provider, which condition includes incapacity in excess of three days

- Certain chronic health conditions, such as asthma and diabetes, which are episodic rather than continuing, but which extend over time and require periodic visits to health care providers for treatment

- Pregnancy or prenatal care, which may involve periodic visits to health care providers, as well as episodes of severe morning sickness

In late 1994, a federal judge in Philadelphia held that a child's ear infection was not a serious illness, so that the mother's absence from work to care for the boy did not come under the coverage of FMLA. Consequently, her termination for excessive absenteeism did not offend the federal act. [Seidle v Provident Mutual Life Ins Co, 871 F Supp 238 (ED Pa 1994)]

Q 8:218　What particular problems have emerged since FMLA has been in effect?

According to Eric Paltell, "While the FMLA is clearly well-intentioned, the intermittent leave provisions will be a burden for many employers." [Paltell, "Intermittent Leave Under the Family and Medical Leave Act of 1993: Job Security for the Chronically Absent Employee?" 10 *The Labor Lawyer* 1, (Winter 1994)]

While not all leaves allowed under FMLA can be taken on an intermittent basis—birth or adoption of a child cannot under normal circumstances—"[t]he FMLA allows covered employees to take intermittent leave for their own or a family member's serious health condition. There is no limit on the length of an increment of leave. Additionally, the FMLA does not require that employees give advance notice of absences caused by an unforeseeable serious health condition." [Id at 4]

Consequently, management-side labor attorneys worry that "employers must be prepared to accommodate employees who will repeatedly miss time from work, with no advance notice to their employer, to attend to their own or a family member's serious health condition." [Id]

Since "serious health condition" is very broadly defined under the act [Id at 5; see Q 8:217, above], employers may find themselves providing accommodations to chronically absent employees that would not be deemed reasonable accommodations under the ADA (see Q 4:80), seemingly the more burdensome law of the two on its face.

Indeed, the FMLA may prove to be more of a burden to employers than many lawyers and human resources professionals anticipated when it went into effect. The intermittent leave difficulty is one of the first signs that this may be so.

Sick Leave

Q 8:219　Are employees entitled to paid sick leave?

No state or federal law requires paid sick leave. However, most employers provide this benefit to maintain employee morale and to keep valued employees from changing jobs.

COBRA

Q 8:220   Which employers are subject to COBRA?

An employer that employs 20 or more persons on a typical business day and maintains a group health plan is required to provide continuation coverage. [IRC § 4980B(d)] Under COBRA legislation, the definition of "employee" can include an independent contractor.

Q 8:221   What is a qualifying event under COBRA?

A qualifying event is any event that would normally result in a loss of coverage for the covered employee or qualified beneficiary were it not for the application of COBRA. These events are:

- The death of the covered employee
- The termination (other than by reason of gross misconduct) or reduction of hours of the covered employee's employment
- Divorce or legal separation
- The covered employee's becoming entitled to Medicare benefits
- A dependent child ceasing to meet dependency requirements
- A proceeding in a case under federal bankruptcy law with respect to the employer from whose employment the covered employee retired at any time

[IRC § 4980B(f)(3)]

Q 8:222   Who is required to receive continuation coverage when a qualifying event occurs?

Continuation coverage must be offered to any covered employee to whom a qualifying event occurs. A covered employee is any individual who is (or was) covered under a group health plan by virtue of that individual's employment or previous employment with the employer.

Continuation coverage must also be offered to any qualified beneficiary. A qualified beneficiary is any individual who is (or was) a beneficiary under the plan as the spouse or the dependent child of the covered employee. Also, when the qualifying event is termination of employment or reduction of hours, a covered employee will be considered a qualified beneficiary. [IRC §§ 4980B(f), 4980B(g)]

While an employer need not pay health care insurance costs for employees while they are on strike, strikers do not forfeit their COBRA rights. They are entitled to notice and opportunity to continue their group health insurance at their own expense. Furthermore, according to the court, the 45-day grace period for the initial premium payment could not be shortened by New York Telephone in the case of its striking workers. [Communications Workers of America v NYNEX Corp, 12 EBC Cas 1049 (2d Cir 1990)]

Q 8:223   How long must the continuation coverage last?

Generally, continuation coverage must last at least 36 months. However, when the coverage is triggered by a termination of employment or a reduction of hours, continuation coverage must last only 18 months. If a second qualifying event occurs before expiration of this 18-month period, the period is extended to 36 months. The above notwithstanding, coverage can also be terminated when the qualified beneficiary becomes covered by another group health plan or becomes eligible for Medicare benefits. [IRC § 4980B(f)(2)(B)] However, COBRA continuation need not end when the beneficiary becomes covered by a new employer's plan if the new plan excludes preexisting medical conditions. This change in the law took effect for qualifying events occurring after December 31, 1989, and for people who elected COBRA coverage after December 31, 1988— or who tried to pay and were rejected. Effective since mid-December 1989, a COBRA amendment allows workers on Social Security disability benefits to stretch COBRA coverage another 11 months, for a total of 29 months of eligibility. Additionally, if an employee becomes eligible for Medicare during the 18-month COBRA eligibility period, any beneficiary under the COBRA coverage can continue the coverage for 36 months from the date of the employee's entitlement for Medicare benefits.

Q 8:224   What are the various notice requirements under COBRA?

When an employee begins coverage under a group health plan, written notice of COBRA rights must be given to the employee and his or her spouse. If a qualifying event occurs (other than a change in dependency status of a child, a divorce, or a legal separation), the employer is required to give notice to the plan administrator within 30 days of the qualifying event. In the event of divorce or legal separation or when a child ceases to be a dependent, the covered employee or qualified beneficiary must notify the plan administrator within 60 days of such event. Within 14 days of receipt of that notice, the plan administrator must notify the covered employee and/or qualified beneficiary of his or her COBRA rights. [IRC § 4980B(f)(6)]

Q 8:225   What are the sanctions for failure to comply with COBRA?

An employer will be assessed a tax of $100 per day for each failure to properly notify a qualified beneficiary of his or her COBRA rights. (The tax for failure with respect to family coverage is $200 per day per family.) The noncompliance period may extend six months after the date on which the continuation coverage could be terminated. For example, if an employee is terminated, and the employer failed to provide the COBRA notice, the noncompliance period would be 24 months (18 months continuation for terminated employees plus six months). Under certain circumstances, a third party that administers the health plan for the employer may be held liable for this tax.

No excise tax will be assessed if the failure is not the result of willful neglect, and is corrected within 30 days. Furthermore, there is an aggregate dollar limit on the tax when the failure is due to reasonable cause. This limit is equal to the lesser of 10 percent of aggregate cost the employer pays or incurs in providing for health coverage or $500,000. Finally, if it is shown that the failure would not have been discovered by an employer exercising reasonable diligence, no tax will be imposed. [IRC §§ 4980B(c) and 4980B(f)]

Chapter 9

Government Contractors

Thousands of American corporations and individuals contract with federal, state, and local governments. For some, government contracts are the bulk of or even all of their business; for others, the occasional government contract rounds out their business in the private sector. The general public most often hears about government contracting when the U.S. Department of Defense, usually in conjunction with the U.S. Department of Justice, charges a defense contractor with contract fraud. In addition, government contracting has been in the news since the Cold War ended and forced Fortune 500 companies to lay off employees and reduce the size of their operations.

However, contracting by the Defense Department, while a major part of government contracting, is not the whole picture. Federal, state, and local governments are also major players in the construction industry, building everything from prisons to highways across the nation. The privatization of government functions, spanning the spectrum of traditional government functions from trash collection to (in a few instances) the experimental private operation of prisons, has become a major trend in government contracting. In short, a great many corporate and individual tax dollars flow back to private corporations and individuals in the form of consulting and other service contracts, construction contracts, and government purchase orders for all manner of goods, ranging from tanks and aircraft carriers to paper clips and personal computers.

One major employment issue of concern to many government contractors is the question of security clearances; this issue is covered at the beginning of this chapter. Also briefly touched upon in this chapter is the requirement that government contractors take steps to hire women and minorities. This portion of the chapter should be read in conjunction with chapter 4, Employment Discrimination. Next, and perhaps most important to government contractors, is coverage of special wage and fringe benefit requirements that companies contracting with the federal government must follow. Note that most states have their own laws analogous to the federal Walsh-Healey, Davis-Bacon, and Service Contract acts. These state laws regulate the payment of wages and fringe benefits on state and municipal contracts. Finally, the chapter discusses restrictions on government contracting and debarment.

Security Clearances

Q 9:1　What steps must a contractor take to protect classified information that it obtains pursuant to bidding for a contract or in performing a contract for the U.S. Department of Defense?

A contractor is required to follow numerous steps to protect classified information, including appointing a U.S. citizen to direct and supervise appropriate security measures, limiting the disclosure of information to authorized persons only, providing suitable methods for safeguarding classified information, performing security checks within its facility, and providing limited access to restricted areas. The extensive list of duties the contractor is required to perform is set forth in the Industrial Security Manual for Safeguarding Classified Information, published by the U.S. Department of Defense. Non-citizen employees are generally restricted from access to classified information.

Q 9:2   Is it sufficient for a contractor to certify that it has complied with or will comply with the Industrial Security Manual for Safeguarding Classified Information?

No. The manual requires a contractor to establish standard practices and procedures for implementing the safeguards explained in the manual. Employees should be educated regarding the handling of classified materials, including the retention, destruction, and transfer of such classified materials, and the methods that can be employed for internal and external reporting of unauthorized divulgence of information.

Q 9:3   What are the basic requirements for security clearance for a contractor's employees?

Generally, only U.S. citizens can be granted a standard security clearance. A naturalized U.S. citizen whose country of origin is determined to have interests adverse to the United States must have been a U.S. citizen for five years or have resided in the United States for the past ten years. To be cleared for confidential information, an individual must be at least 16 years old; to be cleared for secret or top secret information, an individual must be at least 18 years old; and any non-U.S. citizens must be at least 21 years old to be cleared for secret or top secret information.

Q 9:4   Who grants security clearances?

Clearances for top secret, secret, or sensitive information or restricted data are granted solely by the U.S. Department of Defense. A contractor may grant a clearance for confidential information only.

Q 9:5   May immigrants be granted security clearances?

An immigrant alien may be granted a limited access authorization if:

1. His or her access is limited to a specific government contract;

2. He or she possesses a rare or unusual expertise;

3. A qualified U.S. citizen cannot be hired in sufficient time to meet the contractual requirement the individual will fulfill; and

4. He or she resides permanently in the United States, has a green card, and certifies his or her intent to become a U.S. citizen as soon as possible.

Affirmative Action

Q 9:6   Is a government contractor required to provide affirmative action programs?

Procuring agencies must include in all contracts a clause requiring the contractor to certify whether it has established an affirmative action program at its facilities. Exemptions to the requirement may be made for contracts that the contracting agency determines to be essential to national security, contracts for goods or services totaling less than $10,000 in value, contracts for work outside of the United States, contracts with state or local governments, or other contracts that the director of the Office of Federal Contract Compliance Programs (OFCCP) determines to be subject to special circumstances that justify exemption.

Q 9:7   What sanctions may a contractor suffer for failure to comply with affirmative action requirements?

The contract may be canceled, terminated, or suspended for failure to comply with the government's affirmative action requirements. Further, the contractor's name may appear in a public list of "nonawardable prospective contractors," which is tantamount to a suspension or debarment from performing government contracts.

**Q 9:8   Which government agency enforces affirmative action
programs with government contractors?**

Like most U.S. employers, government contractors are subject to
the Equal Employment Opportunity Commission's (EEOC's) jurisdiction. But in addition to the EEOC, the OFCCP is charged with ensuring that contractors comply with their affirmative action
requirements. A disappointed employee or job applicant not only can
file a discrimination charge with the EEOC, but also can file a
complaint with the OFCCP, which may then review the contractor's
entire affirmative action program. It is questionable, however,
whether the OFCCP vigorously investigates such complaints. The
OFCCP was cited in the late 1980s for failure to perform its investigative duties adequately.

Following the GOP's triumph in the November 1994 Congressional
elections, federal affirmative action requirements came under fire.
Then on June 12, 1995, the U.S. Supreme Court issued a decision
involving highway construction contracts in Colorado in which the
court held that "[a]ll racial classifications, imposed by whatever
federal, state, or local governmental actor, must be analyzed by a
reviewing court under strict scrutiny." [Adarand Constructors, Inc v
Pena, 115 S Ct 2097, 1995 US LEXIS 4037, 132 L Ed 2d 158, 63 USLW
4523, 67 FEP Cas (BNA) 1828, 66 *Empl Prac Dec* (CCH) P43, 556
(1995)] While this decision may sound to the non-lawyer like legal
jargon, the implications may be highly significant to proponents and
opponents of affirmative action alike.

What the "strict scrutiny" standard of judicial review implies is
that minority set-asides in government contracting and affirmative
action initiatives in hiring and promotion in favor of minorities and
women will be just as suspect in the eyes of federal judges from now
on as are alleged acts of invidious job discrimination. No longer will
federal agencies or government contractors engaging in affirmative
action enjoy a judicial presumption that their behavior is legitimate.
Rather the governmental entity requiring contractors to subcontract
to disadvantaged firms or to engage in affirmative action hiring likely
will have to be prepared to show that the minority or female preference is designed to remedy actual past discrimination.

The *Adarand* decision inspired new efforts by conservatives in
Congress to end affirmative action entirely. Under heavy fire, Presi-

dent Bill Clinton announced on July 19, 1995, the results of a five-month review of federal affirmative action programs and vowed to maintain his support for such efforts in the future. In a speech Clinton claimed, "The job is not done. . . . We should reaffirm the principle of affirmative action and fix the practices. We should have a simple slogan: Mend it, but don't end it."

Additionally, in a directive to federal bureaucrats, Clinton ordered an examination of existing programs for evidence of quotas, preferences for unqualified individuals, or continuation after their goals have been fulfilled—all clearly illegal in light of *Adarand*.

White House advisor Christopher Edley, who wrote the report with George Stephanopoulos, another advisor, was quoted immediately after Clinton's remarks as saying, "What you see is a strong endorsement of the program as a whole." The report concludes that "empirical literature indicates that affirmative action generally, and specifically the OFCCP Executive Order program, does create opportunity." The report should hasten long-overdue OFCCP reform, which was being discussed in the early 1990s.

The report calls for the U.S. Department of Labor to:

1. Reduce employer paperwork associated with affirmative action initiatives;

2. Revise OFCCP regulations, guidelines, and technical assistance materials to "underscore and reinforce current law and policy regarding nondiscrimination, the illegality of quotas, the enforcement focus on 'good faith efforts,' and the relationship of equal opportunity to legitimate qualifications"; and

3. Collaborate with leaders in the private sector to "promote the best practices in providing equal employment opportunity."

More specifically, the report recommends that a more difficult test be used to determine whether employers are truly disadvantaged, and that mechanisms be established whereby such legitimately disadvantaged companies eventually graduate into the mainstream of business activity and are no longer eligible for preferential treatment in contract and subcontract contexts. This recommendation specifically cites *Adarand*.

On the litigation front, the OFCCP shifted emphasis from handicap-discrimination cases to Executive Order 11246, the original proclamation mandating affirmative action by government contractors issued by President John Kennedy.

However, just as OFCCP was preparing to enforce affirmative action more vigorously, the Republicans captured a majority in Congress in November 1994. By June 1995, the U.S. Department of Labor Deputy Assistant Secretary Shirley J. Wilcher, who heads OFCCP, was justifying OFCCP's mission to the Senate Labor Committee. (See "Shirley J. Wilcher's Statement to Senate Labor Committee," 1995 *BNA Daily Labor Report* 116, June 16, 1995, at d31)

Q 9:9 What is the OFCCP's mission?

The Office of the Federal Contract Compliance Programs (OFCCP) enforces Executive Order 11246, Section 503 of the Rehabilitation Act of 1973, and the affirmative action provisions of the Vietnam Era Veterans' Readjustment Assistance Act of 1974. Approximately 22 percent of the American workforce, or about 26 million workers, are employed by federal contractors and subcontractors subject to these laws. In fiscal 1993, federal contractors included 92,500 non-construction establishments and some 100,000 construction companies. The federal government in that year awarded 176,000 prime contracts. [Id]

Q 9:10 What is Executive Order No. 11246?

While the U.S. Constitution gives Congress law-making powers, the executive branch has the power to issue orders controlling its own activities, including its contracting activities with private companies. Executive orders have been defined as "laws of the executive branch of the federal government [that] deal with those matters under the direct control of that branch. For example . . . during his presidency, Jimmy Carter issued executive orders that required government contractors to employ a certain percentage of minority workers in their businesses in order to qualify for federal projects." [Jennings, *Business and the Legal Environment* 15 (2d ed, 1991)] The president's power to do so stems from Article II of the Constitution, which states in pertinent part that the president "shall take Care that the Laws be faithfully executed."

The president's power to rule by executive order is not unlimited, and must derive either from the chief executive's role as commander in chief of the armed forces under Article II, (see, e.g., Youngstown Sheet and Tube Co v Sawyer, 343 US 579 (1952)) which held that, despite the Korean conflict, President Harry Truman lacked the constitutional power to seize privately owned steel mills that had been closed by a strike], or incident to the enforcement of laws duly passed by Congress.

President Kennedy is credited with the initial conception of both the 1964 Civil Rights Act and Executive Order 11246. Both were adopted after his assassination under his successor, Lyndon B. Johnson, who signed the executive order in 1965, thereby requiring all government contractors to agree to refrain from job discrimination.

Executive Order 11246 states at Section 202(d) that:

> [T]he contracting agency or the Secretary of Labor may direct that any bidder or prospective contractor or subcontractor shall submit . . . a statement in writing . . . to the effect that the signer's practices and policies do not discriminate on the grounds of race, color, religion, sex or national origin, and that the signer either will affirmatively cooperate in the implementation of the policy and provisions of this order or that it consents and agrees that recruitment, employment, and the terms and conditions of employment under the proposed contract shall be in accordance with the purposes and provisions of the order.

Section 201 empowers the secretary of labor to adopt rules and regulations deemed "necessary and appropriate to achieve the purposes" of the order. Among the rules and regulations adopted and promulgated by the Labor Department are those requiring contractors and subcontractors to develop and implement affirmative actions plans. [See 29 CFR § 1608 and 41 CFR § 60-2; see also Castagnera, *Employment Law Answer Book: Forms & Checklists* (New York: Panel Publishers 1994) at 9-3 for a model affirmative action plan]

Q 9:11   What happens if a contractor violates Executive Order 11246?

An employee or applicant wishing to charge a government contractor with a violation of Executive Order 11246 can file a complaint with the Office of Federal Contract Compliance Programs (OFCCP) of the U.S. Department of Labor within 180 days of the alleged violation. OFCCP either can investigate the complaint itself or refer it to the Equal Employment Opportunity Commission. If OFCCP investigates, the inquiry must be completed within 60 days.

If, as a result of the OFCCP investigation, the agency finds reason to believe that the executive order was violated, the contractor is served with a "show cause" notice, directing the company to provide a response as to why enforcement proceedings should not be instituted against it. The contracting firm is afforded 30 days in which to proffer any such evidence. During this same 30-day period, OFCCP has the obligation to try and resolve the case through mediation and conciliation efforts between the parties.

If neither the company's show-cause response nor the agency's conciliation efforts brings the case to a conclusion, the director of OFCCP may refer the complaint to the office of the secretary of labor for the initiation of administrative enforcement proceedings, or alternatively to the U.S. Department of Justice for judicial enforcement proceedings. The complaining employee or applicant cannot initiate a private lawsuit against the government contractor, but can sue the OFCCP to force the agency to elect one of these two enforcement alternatives in the event that the agency fails to act of its own volition. [Legal Aid Society v Brennan, 608 F 2d 1319 (9th Cir 1979)]

Administrative enforcement proceedings include a hearing before an administrative law judge (ALJ), whose decision is open to review by the secretary of labor. The secretary's disposition of the ALJ's decision in turn is subject to review in an appropriate federal district court. [Firestone Co v Marshall, 507 F Supp 1330 (ED Tex 1981)]

Among the available remedies are injunctions against further violations by the employer; hiring or reinstatement (with or without back pay); or the awarding of retroactive seniority or promotion to the complaining employee or applicant, as deemed by the ALJ or court as necessary to make the aggrieved person whole. Additionally, the offending firm may have its government contract suspended or canceled and may be declared ineligible to compete for future contracts (see Q 9:7).

Q 9:12   What is the *Adarand Constructors* case and how does it affect OFCCP's affirmative action mission?

A bare majority of five U.S. Supreme Court justices, led by Justice Sandra Day O'Connor, announced in June 1995 that from now on federal affirmative action programs must be reviewed by the courts under the "strict scrutiny" standard, which had been announced by the high court a mere five years earlier. The case concerned a guardrail subcontractor that was the low bidder but lost a highway contract in Colorado to an Hispanic competitor due to a federal program that gave a bonus to a prime contractor for hiring a minority-owned firm as a subcontractor. In reinstating the disappointed subcontractor's claim, Justice O'Connor wrote for the majority that the Fifth and Fourteenth Amendments to the U.S. Constitution "protect persons, not groups." [Adarand Constructors, Inc v Pena, 63 USLW 4523, 1995 US LEXIS 4037 (1995)]

Writing for the four dissenters, Justice John Paul Stevens decried what he termed the majority's deviation from established precedent. He disparaged Justice O'Connor's opinion as a "disconcerting lecture about the evils of governmental racial classifications." Calling the majority's demand for equal treatment for all "the difference between the 'No Trespassing' sign and a welcome mat," he warned that the opinion in essence "would treat a Dixiecrat Senator's decision to vote against Thurgood Marshall's confirmation in order to keep African-Americans off the Supreme Court as on a par with President Johnson's evaluation of his nominee's race as a positive factor."

The court's sole African-American, Justice Clarence Thomas, voted with the majority, casting the fifth and deciding vote. Justice Thomas wrote a separate opinion in which he called affirmative action "racial paternalism" which "can be as poisonous and pernicious as any other form of discrimination." In his own concurring opinion, Justice Antonin Scalia opined that the government "can never have a 'compelling interest' in discriminating on the basis of race in order to 'make up for' past discrimination."

Justice O'Connor noted that strict scrutiny, while a difficult evidentiary standard for a governmental entity touting a preference to overcome, is not intended by the Court to be an impossible Constitutional hurdle. Nonetheless, liberals and minority groups criticized the decision as a step backward in American race relations and minority-group progress.

While the opinion does not come from an employment case, it has implications for affirmative action decisions affecting hiring, promotion, and firing. Employers, such as government contractors and universities, long distinguished for their vigorous affirmative action initiatives, may have to reexamine their policies in light of the new tougher standard enunciated by the Supreme Court.

In testimony before the Senate Labor Committee following the *Adarand* decision, however, OFCCP head Shirley J. Wilcher insisted that the ruling would not affect the agency's affirmative action mandate. Stating that OFCCP's "goals and timetables" program for hiring minorities, veterans, women, and the disabled are not a subterfuge for quotas, she commented, "The decision has significant implications for federal programs that accord minority preferences. However, Executive Order 11246 does not require the use of racial or gender preferences. The numerical goals approach, which implements the affirmative action provision of Executive Order 11246 . . . is a mechanism designed to measure the success of a contractor's good faith efforts at broadening the pool of qualified candidates for entry-level or promotional opportunities. Quotas are expressly prohibited by OFCCP's regulations. . . ." ["Shirley J. Wilcher's Statement to Senate Labor Committee," 1995 *BNA Daily Labor Report* 116, June 16, 1995, at d31]

Q 9:13   Is there such a thing as affirmative action in favor of unions with regard to federal government contracts?

In the words of political commentator George Will:

> Clinton has rescinded the executive order that required federal contractors to post notices telling nonunion workers that they are not obligated to join unions and that they have a right to

stop unions from using money collected in lieu of dues for political activities the workers oppose. Clinton also rescinded the order forbidding federal agencies and contractors hired by the feds from requiring workers on construction projects to be unionized. [Will, "The Core of Clintonism Is an Ideology Demanding a Vast Expansion of Government," *Philadelphia Inquirer*, Apr 24, 1993, at A8; see also, "Reich Endorses Rescission of Bush Executive Orders," 1993 *BNA Daily Labor Report* 19, Feb 1, 1993, at 1]

Rescission of the executive orders of the prior administration comports with the new administration's often-asserted intention to level the labor relations playing field, which President Bill Clinton and Secretary of Labor Robert Reich believe became tilted in management's favor during the 12 years of Republican presidents (1981–1992). Other related measures favored by the Democrats include a striker replacement bill that, if enacted, would prevent employers from permanently replacing their striking employees. [See "Striker Replacement Bill Faces Tough Battle in Senate," 1993 *BNA Daily Labor Report* 71, Apr 15, 1993, at 1; "Workplace Fairness Bill Benefits U.S., Reich Says," 1993 *BNA Daily Labor Report* 60, Mar 31, 1993, at 1; Karr, "Union Leaders See Their First Chance in Years for Substantial Legislative Gains," *The Wall Street Journal*, Nov 5, 1992, at A4; and Q 11:9]

Q 9:14 Does the federal government engage in affirmative action by means of the contracts it awards?

The federal government is capable of engaging in affirmative action not only by requiring its myriad agencies, contractors, and subcontractors to act affirmatively to engage minority group members as employees and subcontractors, but also by the content of the contracts that are let out for bids. For instance, in mid-1993 the 17 National Institutes of Health unveiled their long-awaited strategic plan, which included such key projects as the Women's Health Initiative and the Minority Health Initiative—major undertakings that cut across the constituent institutes. [Burd, "Director's Strategic Plan for NIH Faces an Uncertain Future," *Chronicle of Higher Education*, May 19, 1993, at A19]

Similarly, Secretary of Labor Robert Reich has described his department's mission as one dedicated to reversing the "disturbing trend" of declining wages, benefits, and working conditions for non-college educated workers. He says there is no doubt the government "can play a constructive role both in educating and training non-college educated [workers] for the workplace of the future and also encouraging the private sector to better utilize" these workers. [1993 *BNA Daily Labor Report* 19, Feb 1, 1993, at 1]

Any such initiatives in retraining will include the letting of numerous contracts to private corporations and will undoubtedly include affirmative action components (see Q 14:3).

However, the U.S. Supreme Court's decision in *Adarand Constructors Inc. v. Pena* [63 USLW 4523, 1995, US LEXIS 4037 (1995)] calls into serious doubt the continued vitality of affirmative action programs in the federal contracting arena in the future (see Q 9:12).

Q 9:15   What is President Bill Clinton's national service program?

One way the Clinton administration engages in affirmative action by means of government contracting is through a national service program for disadvantaged youth. This is in addition to such existing programs as the Job Corps. [See 29 USC § 1501 and Q 14:5 for more on the Job Corps] This program, which the administration hopes will enroll 100,000 students by 1997, selected its first 1,500 participants in June 1993. [Birnbaum and Trost, "Clinton's Program for National Service Would Start Small, Expand Gradually," *The Wall Street Journal*, Mar 2, 1993, at A9; Jaschik, "First 1,500 Participants to Be Selected for Service Program," *Chronicle of Higher Education*, May 19, 1993, at A21]

From 430 applicants, the national service program selected 16 contractors to conduct community service projects using the first 1,500 enrollees. The Commission on National and Community Service awarded a total of $10 million to these successful government contractors, including the following:

1. City College of New York and the Borough of Manhattan Community College were chosen to start five "one-room schoolhouses" where children from Harlem would get meals

and remedial instruction from national service program participants during the summer recess from the regular school year.

2. Clark Atlanta University launched a program to clean up a school and a neighboring public housing project and then to use the school to tutor children from the housing project over the summer of 1993.

3. Nursing students drawn from eight colleges in Philadelphia and its vicinity were employed during the summer of 1993 in immunizing 8,000 infants under the age of two in that urban area.

As these examples suggest, institutions of higher education lead the list of government contractors that reaped the benefits of the national service program. However, the debate remains heated as to what is the best model for the program. One possible model is the Civilian Conservation Corps of the New Deal era; another is the Peace Corps. Depending on what form the full-blown program ultimately takes, private industry may find itself in line for its share of the contracts in the future. (See Birnbaum and Trost, supra; Bernstein and Cock, "The Appropriate Models for National Service," *Chronicle of Higher Education,* May 19, 1993, at A44)

As the Clinton administration prepared to repeat the experiment during the summer of 1994, international events suggested that something be done to aid the youth of industrialized nations as they go into the workforce. Notably, the French government was forced by students taking to the streets (a sort of echo of May 1968) to back off its plan to allow employers to pay workers age 26 and younger something less than the nation's minimum wage. Trade unions joined students in protesting the plan, which "was developed as a way to help reduce youth unemployment, which now stands at 24 percent" in France. ["France Drops Minimum-Wage Plan in Face of Mass Protests," *Chronicle of Higher Education,* Apr 13, 1994, at A36]

However, the Republican's capture of both houses of Congress in November 1994, their efforts to cut federal spending, and the U.S. Supreme Court's *Adarand Constructors* decision (see Q 9:12) combined to jeopardize the national service program.

Q 9:16 How have government contractors responded to requirements imposed by the Americans with Disabilities Act in conjunction with Section 503 of the Rehabilitation Act?

The Associated General Contractors of America has taken the lead in 1994 in protesting labor department rules concerning recordkeeping requirements regarding disabled individuals. The AGC has called for the deletion of "punitive provisions" which could result in debarment for a variety of undefined violations, included so-called "paperwork deficiencies."

"Both AGC and the Constructors Association of Western Pennsylvania urged OFCCP to raise the thresholds for application of the proposed rules [aimed at bringing the ADA and § 503 into line with one another] to employers of 250 or more employees and to contracts valued at $500,000 or more." ["Contractors Seek Changes in ADA Proposed Rules," 58 BNA *Federal Contracts Report* 23, Dec 21, 1992, at D10]

Commentators on the proposed rules also protested the extension of record retention from one to two years and the expansion of records to be retained to include such things as interview notes. "OFCCP has offered no valid justification for extending either the duration of the recordkeeping requirement or the quantity of records that must be kept," declared Jeffrey Norris, president of the Equal Employment Advisory Council, an association of major government contractors, which opposes the proposed rules.

Q 9:17 Must a government contractor make light-duty work available to disabled employees in order to comply with Section 503 of the Rehabilitation Act?

In *OFCCP v. Cissell Manufacturing Co.*, [Case No 87-OFC-26 (Feb 14, 1994)] the assistant secretary of labor, sitting as a sort of appellate court judge, couched the issue and answer as follows:

> The central issue in this case is whether a government contractor may refuse to comply with the obligation to make reasonable accommodation to the physical limitations of an employee under Section 503 of the Rehabilitation Act of 1973 . . . because

it has a company policy of no 'light duty' jobs. . . . I find that such a refusal violates Section 503.

In this case, which dates back over a decade, complainant Larry Brown suffered an on-the-job injury in 1983, when he was a production welder assembling parts for commercial clothes dryers. Three doctors independently diagnosed a condition which constituted a form of arthritis. The company's doctor suggested that the complainant "try to avoid jobs with excessive bending and lifting at the knees." An independent orthopedist recommended that Brown "avoid kneeling, deep knee bending, and stairs as much as possible."

When Brown reported to work with a doctor's note containing such recommendations in October 1984, his foreman told him to "hit the clock." His union steward was told by Cissell's personnel office that no light-duty work was available for Brown. Brown next took 26 weeks of paid sick leave and two successive 90-day leaves of absence without pay. Finally, on July 11, 1985, the director of corporate relations wrote a letter to the complainant, advising him that "if you are not released to perform regular duties with no restrictions by 10/10/85 your employment status will become termination." Brown then filed his OFCCP complaint.

Following a hearing, an administrative law judge held that Brown was disabled under the Rehabilitation Act, because Cissell had treated him as unable to hold any job at the plant, that he was actually qualified to hold several welder jobs, and that Cissell's failure to accommodate him violated Section 503. Consequently, the ALJ proposed reinstatement with back-pay, but no debarment for Cissell provided the contractor complied.

Reviewing the ALJ's ruling, the DOL assistant secretary found that "given the actual functioning and circumstances of Cissell's business, Cissell did not show that making reasonable accommodation to Mr. Brown's handicap by assigning him to jobs that did not require excessive stooping and bending would impose an undue burden." [Id]

Cissell in some ways is not an ideal case from which to draw conclusions about OFCCP's attitude toward light-duty jobs, as reasonable accommodations, going forward. The decision mildly chides the complainant for failing to consult his union about its attitude concerning the status of light duty in light of the labor contract and for failing to avidly seek jobs outside the welding trade with his employer. The company, too, was criticized for creating confusion concerning Brown's employment status between 1984 and 1988.

However, the decision makes it clear that government contractors must at least explore light-duty accommodations of disabled employees or risk back-pay exposure under the Rehabilitation Act.

Wages and Benefits

Q 9:18   What laws govern wages and benefits of government contractors?

One law is the Walsh-Healey Act, which applies to manufacturers and so-called "regular dealers" who sell goods to the U.S. government. In recent years the U.S. Department of Labor (DOL) has limited enforcement of wage and hour issues under this law to minimum wages, overtime pay, and essentially the same fundamental issues covered by the Fair Labor Standards Act (FLSA), which applies to almost all employers.

The Davis-Bacon Act controls wages, benefits, and working conditions of "laborers and mechanics" employed by contractors in the construction, alteration, or repair of public buildings and public works. The act requires contracts in excess of $2,000 to set forth the minimum wages to be paid to all classes of laborers that a contractor employs under the contract. Contractors and subcontractors may not pay less than the federal minimum wage. Davis-Bacon's rules and regulations generally also apply to construction contracts under a group of more narrow federal statutes, and are supplemented by other laws aimed at preventing cheating in the payment of construction contract workers.

In 1965, a gap in this federal scheme was filled by the enactment of the Service Contract Act (SCA). Apparently anticipating the post-industrial transition to a service economy, the act applies to the wide range of services, from janitorial to sophisticated consulting, which the federal government contracts for.

Q 9:19   How does the DOL enforce proper payment of wages and fringe benefits by government contractors?

There is no private right of action for employees under either Davis-Bacon or the Service Contract Act (SCA), the legal rationale being that privity of contract runs between the contractor and the government, and therefore it is to the government that any such right accrues.

Administrative enforcement of Davis-Bacon and SCA is entrusted to various administrative boards, such as the Wage Appeals Board and the Armed Services Board of Contract Appeals. Such boards, and their administrative law judges who hear cases, are empowered to adjudicate challenges by government contractors and would-be contractors of the DOL's wage determinations when the procurement process is initiated. While the decisions of these boards can often be taken to the appropriate U.S. Court of Appeals, federal courts have limited jurisdiction (at best) to interfere with this administrative process.

In auditing contractors and their reports, the DOL is concerned primarily with ensuring that contributions were made at least quarterly, irrevocably to the employee or the benefit plan, and following an accurate computation. Relevant records include payroll records and contractor statements of compliance.

When a violation is found to be minor—for example, less than $1,000—and non-willful, and future compliance is not in doubt, restitution alone (to the eligible employees) may be acceptable to the DOL.

When larger amounts or more egregious circumstances are detected, the DOL may:

- Withhold unpaid funds under the contract pending resolution of the claim
- Terminate the contract
- Seek liquidated (double) damages
- Seek debarment from further federal contract work against the offending contractor for as much as three years or
- In some instances, seek criminal penalties

Q 9:20   What are wage determinations?

Before the DOL can prescribe minimum wages and fringe benefits for employees doing work under Davis-Bacon and Service Contract Act (SCA) contracts, it must have a way to determine the appropriate wages and benefits for a particular part of the country.

Like other government agencies, the DOL has divided the nation into ten geographic regions and established regional headquarters in ten major cities. Regional staff in each of these offices use mail and telephone surveys of contractors subject to Davis-Bacon in their particular region to learn what these contractors are paying in wages and benefits. Under the guidance of a manual developed for this purpose, government wage specialists may select "any rate that is paid more than the majority of the time," according a top DOL wage administrator in Philadelphia.

Under the SCA, the DOL's Bureau of Labor Statistics (BLS) in Washington conducts such surveys under an interagency contract with the DOL's Wage and Hour Division. The explanation for this dichotomy between Davis-Bacon and the SCA regarding survey techniques apparently relates to the DOL's perception of the trades and professions involved. Experience has taught the government's wage experts that in the building trades, there is a great deal of variance depending on geography.

Under the SCA, there is an ongoing effort to extend wage determinations geographically and temporally both for uniformity and cost efficiency of the BLS surveys. Thus, a current pilot program is testing the efficacy of "blanket wage determinations" that will stay in place at a major facility, such as a military post or federal building in a major city, for an extended period—for example, one year—rather than preparing a Standard Form 98 wage determination for every procurement of a new contract.

Q 9:21   Can a government contractor substitute one fringe benefit for another?

Yes. The DOL recognizes that it is not always practical, or even possible, for a particular contractor to provide precisely the type and mix of benefits found to be prevalent in the relevant geographic area.

For example, the current legal limit on the portability of pension plans means that contributions to an employer plan, especially in construction, in which workers move from project to project and employer to employer, would benefit the employer's long-term employees only. Thus, the DOL permits substitution of one benefit for another, and even the substitution of the cash equivalent applied as a supplement to the hourly rate. The most striking example can be found in SCA wage determinations that permit in place of a health and welfare plan, 59 cents per hour, $23.60 per week or $102.26 per month. Currently, 59 cents per hour is the amount the DOL requires as a substitute for a bona fide health and welfare plan nationwide. However, under a 1970 amendment to the SCA, if an incumbent contractor has provided certain fringe benefits under a collective bargaining agreement, the successor contractor must match the wages and fringes under the agreement. In general, the SCA requires more precise identification, communication to employees, and recordkeeping as to fringe benefits and substitution than does Davis-Bacon.

Q 9:22 How should government contractors determine which benefits to provide or which substitutions should be made?

In determining which benefits to provide, and which substitutions to make, contractors must calculate the values of both prevailing benefits and the benefits (if any) that they propose to offer in substitution. Strategically, they must consider not only the dollars and cents issue, but such broader corporate concerns as the effect of a given mix of pay and benefits on recruitment, morale, work incentive, and retention of the workforce; the value of a given compensation package in preventing unionization; and the long-term effect on the company of the introduction of certain benefits that may outlive the particular contract.

Contractors do not have absolute discretion in making these tactical and strategic determinations. Fringe benefits on the DOL's "menu" include the following:

- Medical and hospital care
- Pension plans
- Compensation for work-related injuries
- Life and accident insurance

- Disability benefits
- Vacation and holiday pay and
- Apprenticeship programs

The DOL also accepts substitution of other bona fide fringe benefits not otherwise required by federal, state, or local law to be provided.

The "not otherwise required" phrase has been interpreted by the DOL's Wage and Hour Administrator to exclude credit for such mandatory payments as the contractor's contributions to social security. Furthermore, an employer's own contributions (such as co-payments to a group health insurance plan) and fringe benefit payments by the employer itself that are tied to non-government contract work by the particular employee cannot be counted toward equating the prevailing fringe benefit package. And these substitution decisions, once made, must be maintained throughout the term of the particular contract.

Q 9:23   How does a government contractor calculate cash equivalency?

Sometimes the wage determination itself sets the cash equivalent. When the DOL states the value of a fringe benefit as a specific dollar amount per week or month, the contractor paying the cash equivalent will do so on an hourly basis. This is done by multiplying (for example) the monthly amount by 12, dividing that amount by 52 (the weeks), and dividing it again by 40 to obtain the hourly amount. This amount is then added into the employee's hourly wage rate.

Calculating the cash equivalent of a paid vacation is a bit more complex. Assume the DOL's determination calls for a week of paid vacation after a year of service with the contractor or any successor corporation. Work performed by the employee before and after the wage determination is issued must be counted in calculating that employee's eligibility for the vacation benefit.

Next, if the contractor prefers to pay the employee the cash value of the week's vacation, it multiplies that worker's hourly wage rate by the number of hours of vacation time. If the vacation benefit is not specified in hours by the wage determination, the contractor should assume a standard 8-hour day and a 40-hour work week. Again, the contractor is permitted to pay this cash equivalent to the employee on an hourly basis, spread across the whole year. To make this calculation, the contractor divides the dollar value of a week's vacation by 2,080 (the standard number of working hours in 52 weeks), and the quotient of this calculation is added into the employee's hourly wage rate.

One more example may be helpful. If the DOL's applicable wage determination includes holidays, the contractor can give days off with pay of its choosing; it need not adhere strictly to the list of holidays in the determination. Alternatively, the contractor can require an employee to work the designated holiday and pay double-time. Or, the contractor can multiply the number of holidays on the list by eight (the hours in the workday), divide by 2,080, and add the result of this calculation to the employee's hourly wage rate.

There may be a distinct cash flow (and, therefore, competitive) advantage in spreading some or all of these fringe benefit costs across 2,080 work hours since any savings for the contractor would be enhanced by employee absenteeism. However, labor unions, competition with other companies for skilled employees, and workforce morale combine to restrict a contractor's ability to replace such popular benefits as vacations and holidays with cash equivalents.

Q 9:24 How should a government contractor treat temporary and part-time employees with respect to fringe benefits?

Whenever a wage determination fails to distinguish between full-time, part-time, and temporary employees, these latter two categories are entitled to their pro-rata share of the contractor's benefit package. Of course, if a requirement for a paid vacation is a full year of employment, a temporary employee of lesser tenure would not qualify for paid vacation. However, if the contractor chooses not to provide paid holidays to temporary and part-time employees, then these workers must be proportionately compensated with the cash equivalent or some substitute fringe benefit.

As with the FLSA and virtually all the other federal contract laws, the fringe benefit requirements of the SCA are based on the central concept of the "work week." Thus, the concept affects the contractor's obligation to pay part-timers pro-rated holiday pay, which is covered in the regulations as follows:

> All employees, including part-time and temporary employees, are entitled to a proportionate share of the required holiday fringe benefits to which full-time employees are entitled under a determination, if they perform any work in the workweek in which the holiday occurs. [*Wage and Hour Admin Op*, Jan 28, 1970]

Q 9:25   What are bona fide benefits and prohibited offsets?

For an employee fringe benefit to be bona fide (in other words, to count toward the employer's fringe benefit obligations under the DOL's applicable wage determination), the benefit must be provided at the employer's expense. A timely illustration of this principle involves employee health insurance. With increasing frequency in the 1990s, employers require their employees to contribute to the insurance premiums for their group health plans. These employee contributions cannot be counted toward the employer's overall fringe benefit obligation.

Additionally, most employer payments that are already required by some other federal, state, or local law cannot be counted towards the employer's obligation under the wage determination. This prohibition covers social security (FICA) contributions by the employer, as well as the company's share of such payments as state unemployment taxes. In New Jersey, for example, this requirement would include payments for unemployment taxes and for a state disability fund.

Some employees may spend a part of their workday on a government contract, while devoting other working hours to non-government work. In such circumstances, fringe benefit payments attributable to non-government contract work cannot be counted toward setting off the government contractor's obligations under the wage determination attached to the government contract.

Q 9:26   What are "sunshine funds" and does the U.S. Department of Labor view them as fringe benefits?

The term "sunshine funds" has broad application in America. Almost any fund set aside for miscellaneous charitable work or good deeds can be labeled sunshine funds. In the context of government contracting, the term typically refers to any of the following:

- Funds expended by an employer for such events as company picnics, Christmas parties, and other social functions

- Money spent for flowers for hospitalized employees, magazine subscriptions, professional association and club dues, incentive awards, bonuses for recruiting new employees or

- Provision of employee lounges and recreation rooms

All of these expenditures are considered the contractor-employer's business expenses. [See Wage and Hour Admin Op No WH-358 of Nov 7, 1975]

Sunshine funds are not considered fringe benefits under the DOL wage determination.

Of course, the contractor's provision of tools, uniforms, or safety gear, such as respirators and ear plugs, cannot qualify as a bona fide fringe benefit.

Q 9:27   What are the restrictions on wage deductions?

The skyrocketing cost of health insurance has led many employers in recent years to press for or raise employee contributions. Other traditional deductions from wages include union dues pursuant to a collective bargaining agreement; U.S. Savings Bond purchases; credit union contributions; and repayment of employee loans such as vacation pay advances. The Copeland Anti-Kickback Act makes it essential that government contractors performing public works comprehend which deductions they can and cannot make legally, whether for employee benefits or otherwise. This act covers virtually all construction projects, whether financed in whole or only in part by federal funds.

Q 9:28 Why has the federal government enacted the Copeland Anti-Kickback Act for the construction industry in particular?

Attorneys and human resources familiar with the federal labor laws, notably the National Labor Relations Act (NLRA) and the closely connected Labor Management Relations Act (LMRA), know that the construction industry has received special treatment in several significant respects regarding the Copeland Anti-Kickback Act. For example, the LMRA permits employers and unions in the construction trades to enter pre-hire agreements under which such a union is automatically recognized as the bargaining representative of the contractor's employees, without the formalities of an organizing drive and a National Labor Relations Board (NLRB) election. The rationale behind this unique exception to the formalities normally imposed by the NLRB upon both unions and employers is not unrelated to the Copeland Anti-Kickback Act's reason for being.

The pre-hire provisions of the LMRA recognize that construction projects, in contrast to factories and other places of business, are of relatively short duration. Consequently, in many instances a project would be completed, and the contractor and its subcontractors long gone, before a trade union could organize the employees and the NLRB could hold an election.

A similar appreciation of this unique aspect of the construction industry—its mobility and the concurrent mobility of its workforce— were among the rationales underlying enactment of the Copeland Anti-Kickback Act. Today kickbacks are infrequent. Typically, in a blatant instance, a foreman or other supervisor simply tells the employees something like, "I have to pay you $15 per hour under this contract. But you normally get $13 per hour from us so we expect you to turn back $2 per hour after you cash your paycheck."

Q 9:29 Are there types of kickbacks other than cash?

Yes. Fringe benefit kickback schemes exist, but are believed to be rarer than cash kickbacks. They are also more difficult for the DOL to detect, since they usually involve deposits to an employee welfare benefit plan on paper and siphoning of the funds into operating capital in reality. Such siphoning is possible since DOL regulations requiring all trustees to be unaffiliated with the employer-contractor have been superseded by the Employee Retirement Income Security Act of 1974 (ERISA), which allows a company, its officers, or managers to be trustees without invalidating the plan. Thus, the DOL no longer enforces contrary regulations under Davis-Bacon, albeit they remain on the books. Due in part to this situation, there reportedly is increased interest within the DOL in revitalizing the Copeland Anti-Kickback Act criminal enforcement program.

Q 9:30   What sorts of payroll deductions are excluded from the act?

Bona fide payroll deductions for employee contributions into benefit plans are permissible under the Copeland Anti-Kickback Act. Likewise, employee-authorized deductions for U.S. Savings Bonds and United Way contributions are allowed under the act and relevant DOL regulations.

Union dues and initiation fees constitute legal deductions under the act, if made in connection with a check-off clause in the collective bargaining agreement, but union fines and special assessments are not.

Repayment of bona fide short-term loans by the employer to certain employees may be legally acceptable, but a notarized statement of each employee's freely given consent should be obtained before the deductions are taken. Deductions connected with long-term loans, such as a mortgage loan, are less likely to be countered by the DOL and therefore, if done to accommodate a relocating new-hire, for example, should be transferred to an arm's-length commercial lender as soon as possible.

Q 9:31   May a government contractor recover the costs of recruiting and training employees?

Pursuant to restrictions set forth in the federal acquisition regulations [*BNA Wage and Hour Manual*, 99:1551], a contractor may charge recruitment costs against a contract, including educational testing programs and travel and relocation costs connected with recruiting new employees. Also subject to restrictions, the contractor may charge the government for the costs of training and educating employees, including those incurred for materials, textbooks, tuition, and fees.

Restrictions

Q 9:32 May a contractor charge the government for employee wage rates that are beyond those charged to commercial customers?

No. Discriminatory pricing against the government is forbidden, and costs that include greater compensation payments to employees than they would be paid for non-government work are prohibited. Further, fringe benefits such as insurance premiums and holiday pay are not direct costs of a particular contract; they are overhead costs that are negotiated separately under the contract. Overhead may include the cost of providing employee health and welfare activities, such as first aid classes or income tax information.

Q 9:33 Are contractors required to inform the government if they have used consultants to aid in obtaining government contracts?

Yes. The federal acquisition regulations require a contractor to report to the government any arrangement it makes with a non-employee individual or entity whereby the individual obtains or solicits a contract and is paid contingent on success. When the contractor provides a guarantee that it has not employed any such individual or entity, a breach of the guarantee may result in contract annulment or deduction from the contract price of any contingent fee paid.

Q 9:34 What restrictions are placed on the hiring of former government employees by government contractors?

A former government employee employed by a contractor is forbidden by federal criminal law to represent the contractor with regard to any judicial proceeding or to attempt to obtain a contract or pursue another particular matter in which he or she participated personally while a government employee. Further, a former government employee will commit a criminal act if, within two years after being employed by the government, he or she represents a government contractor before the U.S. government to obtain a contract, ruling, or determination if such a determination pertains to a matter that was actually pending under his or her official responsibility as a government employee within one year prior to his or her termination or in which he or she participated personally as a government officer or employee. The prohibition also extends to partners of the former government employee and carries with it substantial criminal penalties. However, the law does not prohibit a former government employee from performing certain acts on behalf of the contractor, such as giving testimony or furnishing scientific or technological information under procedures that the particular government agency considers acceptable. In addition, a recent regulation requires that the contractor certify that it has not offered employment or inducement to a government employee in return for a contract or otherwise sought selection or proprietary information.

Q 9:35   Are conflicts of interest involving current and former government employees a concern for government contractors?

The federal government can enter into contracts with its own employees or business organizations controlled by such employees only when it can demonstrate a compelling reason for doing so, such as no alternative reasonable method of getting the job done. [Federal Acquisition Regulations (FAR) 3.602; Keyes, *Government Contracts in a Nutshell* at 41 (1990)] In other words, in a typical situation, a government contracting officer is prohibited from "knowingly making an award of a contract to a government employee or to a business concern or other organization owned or substantially owned or controlled by one or more government employees." [FAR 3.601]

Government employees themselves are prohibited by statute and are subject to serious penalties from representing the federal government in any matter in which they have a personal financial interest. Obvious examples of such conflicts of interest include those in which a federal employee participates in letting a government contract under which the employee will ultimately receive a share of the government contractor's profits. [See, e.g., K&R Engineering Co, Inc v US, 222 Ct Claims 340, 616 F 2d 469 (1980)]

In contrast to such a blatant example, involvement of former government employees is often not so clear-cut. While federal law does restrict former employees' involvement in contracts that were actually pending when they were employed by the federal government (see Q 9:34, above), the use by government contractors of retired military officers and other such former government workers as consultants has not always resulted in disqualification for a given contract or punishment of the retired or resigned federal employee. [See, e.g., NKF Engineering, Inc v US, 9 Claims Ct 585 (1986), vacated, 805 F 2d 372 (Fed Cir 1986) (use of retired deputy director of Naval Sea Systems Command as consultant on contract for which he had done the evaluation of contractors' initial proposals before retiring did not disqualify contractor, according to U.S. appellate court, which vacated the Claims Court's contrary holding)]

Q 9:36   What other labor restrictions apply to government contractors?

Under the Walsh-Healey Act, contractors may not employ children or convicts when fulfilling government contracts. Children are defined in the federal acquisition regulations as persons under 16 years of age. Convicts do not include those persons convicted but on parole or otherwise discharged from prison. A contractor must also maintain and make available for inspection employment records listing the name, address, sex, and occupation of each employee, as well as wage and employment records for each. A contractor must stipulate that the performance of the contract for the government does not entail working conditions that are unsanitary or hazardous to the health and safety of employees. Contractors may satisfy this requirement by showing compliance with the health and safety laws of the state in which the contract is performed.

Q 9:37   Do the federal acquisition regulations (FAR) place any restrictions on collective bargaining agreements between government contractors and labor unions?

Government contractors are typically subject to an assortment of requirements and restrictions with respect to the subcontracting of portions of their prime contracts with the U.S. government. For example, government contracts in excess of $500,000 typically contain a provision requiring the prime contractor to carry out its subcontracting activities in a way calculated to ensure that small businesses are afforded a fair opportunity to compete for their share of the subcontracted work. [Keyes, *Government Contracts in a Nutshell* at 454 (1990)] Furthermore, subcontracts cannot result in labor compensation costs "to the extent they result from provisions of labor-management agreements that, as they apply to work in performing government contracts, are determined to be unreasonable because they are either unwarranted by the character and circumstances of the work or discriminatory against the government." [FAR 31.206(b)(4)(c); (see also Q 9.35 above)] Additionally, where a union forces a prime contractor to enter subcontracts only with unionized subcontractors, such subcontracts may result not only in a violation of the foregoing FAR, but also of the federal antitrust laws as well. [Connell Construction Co v Plumbers Local 100, 421 US 616 (1973)]

Consequently, although the National Labor Relations Act requires employers to bargain in good faith with unions representing their employees (see Q 11.43), a government contractor or subcontractor cannot avoid the restrictions placed on it by the FARs. [Keyes at 453] Thus, the federal courts have held that union proposals that would violate such federal regulations are not subject to collective bargaining.

Debarment

Q 9:38   On what grounds may a contractor be debarred or suspended from performing government contracts?

The government may debar a contractor if the contractor is convicted of fraud or a criminal offense in connection with obtaining or attempting to obtain a contract, for embezzlement, for any offense indicating a lack of business integrity or honesty, or for violation of the terms of a contract, such as a willful failure to perform or a history of failure to perform. A contractor can be held liable for an employee's acts of criminal fraud or other acts justifying debarment or other penalties if the contractor in any way encouraged or condoned the employee's acts.

Q 9:39   Should a contractor require its employees to report infractions of time charging or other cost accounting rules and regulations?

Yes. Government contractors are held accountable for failures to charge the government accurately for time employees spend on government contracts. Accordingly, a mischarging of time by an employee or a number of employees to a contract on which they have not actually worked is considered a serious infraction. A contractor should therefore educate employees about the importance of correctly charging their time to contracts on which they have worked, preventing inadvertent or intentional mischarging of time, and of reporting infractions of time charging rules and regulations both internally and externally, auditing accounting records to determine whether contracts have been accurately and appropriately charged, and reporting to the government any infractions along with recommendations for corrective or restitution actions.

Q 9:40   Will the commission of a crime or an infraction by an individual employee automatically subject a contractor to debarment or other penalties?

No. Although the government may seek to prosecute the corporation if it believes a wrongful act was a result of or was otherwise condoned by the corporation's lack of internal controls, education, and efforts at compliance, the government may also seek to prosecute only an individual employee for his or her wrongful acts. Thus, an individual employee acting in contravention of the company's established policy and without the company's knowledge may be subject to individual prosecution for his or her wrongful acts.

Q 9:41   What is the difference between debarment and non-responsibility?

Federal agencies are allowed to award their contracts only to "responsible" bidders, meaning those government contractors that meet all the basic qualifications for fulfilling the requirements of the contract. Some of these qualifications are fundamental to all government contracts, such as a record of integrity and business ethics. Consequently, a determination that a contractor or its employees lack such fundamental qualities would be a basis not only for an agency to find that contractor non-responsible but also to debar the company from bidding for and performing all government contracts.

On the other hand, a particular company may simply lack the technical skills or organizational ability to perform under a particular contract, and therefore would be ruled non-responsible with respect to that contract only, leaving the firm free to compete for other government contracts let for bids by the same or different government agencies. [FAR 9.104-1]

Q 9:42　Can a government contractor be debarred for failure to comply with the Drug-Free Workplace Act?

The Drug-Free Workplace Act went into effect in March 1989 and applies to federal contractors and grant recipients (see Q 1:19). The act outlines a series of specific steps that companies covered by it must follow to ensure that they are creating and maintaining drug-free workplaces (see Qs 7:138–7:142). Failure to follow these steps can result in suspension of current contracts and debarment from future bidding on federal projects (see Qs 7:143, 7:144). "In addition debarment or suspension may result from an offeror's submission of a false certification: that he has a drug-free workplace . . ." [Keyes at 78]

The way the government usually demonstrates a false certification or a contractor's failure to make a good-faith effort to fulfill its obligations under the act is through evidence of convictions of a number of that contractor's employees for drug-related crimes. Generally, a Drug-Free Workplace Act debarment will not exceed three years, but can be as high as five years.

Q 9:43　Is a contractor that is debarred by one government agency debarred from all federal contracts?

Yes. The General Services Administration is charged with maintaining a comprehensive list of all debarred contractors. This list is made available to all agencies in the executive branch of the U.S. government. Absent highly compelling reasons stated in writing by a particular agency for wanting to deal with a debarred contractor, no such agency can solicit bids from, award contracts to, or permit subcontracts with a debarred contractor during the term of the debarment. [FARs 9.405, 9.405-1, and 9.405-2]

Q 9:44   Can a federal agency continue an existing contract with a debarred contractor?

Yes. An agency can, but is not required to, continue an existing contract with a debarred contractor. The agency that chooses to continue an existing contract is not empowered to renew the contract for any additional term, absent a written statement by the agency head of a compelling reason, such as national security considerations. [FAR 9.405-1]

Q 9:45   What are the legal procedures for debarring a government contractor?

All federal agencies are required to establish and to maintain procedures for debarment that protect the contractor's constitutional right to due process of law. In particular, the targeted company must be afforded an opportunity to submit information and argument in opposition to the debarment. [FAR 9.406-3] The specific procedures are as follows:

1. A contractor targeted by a federal agency for debarment will receive a notice of the proposed action via certified mail and copies will be sent to any affiliated company named in the contract.

2. The debarment notice will advise the contractor that it has 30 days from receipt of the notice to file any information and arguments the company chooses to offer in opposition to the proposed action. The notice also will explain the contracting agency's specific procedures for handling a debarment and the effect that the debarment will have upon the contractor.

3. The agency's debarment procedures may include a public hearing. If no hearing is held, the contractor will be afforded the opportunity to present in writing, such as by way of relevant

affidavits of potential witnesses, all the information it might have proffered at the hearing.

4. Debarment proceedings may be accompanied or followed by parallel civil or criminal proceedings by the government against the contractor. In fact, the U.S. Supreme Court has held that the federal government's simultaneous pursuit of administrative, civil, and criminal actions does not frustrate the contractor's constitutional right to due process of law. [US v Kordel, 397 US 90 (1970)]

5. The same government official who proposed the debarment also may serve as the debarring official, who will make the debarment decision. This official will review the contractor's information and arguments in opposition to debarment, decide whether a debarment should be imposed, and if so, the length of the debarment. The decision to debar need only be based upon a preponderance (51 percent or more) of evidence.

6. If the debarring official determines that genuine issues of material fact exist between the agency and the contractor, a hearing may be held. The hearing may be informal, however, and some courtroom rights, such as cross examination, need not be accorded to the contractor. The hearing need not conform to the complicated and extensive federal rules of evidence.

7. The debarring official's decision will be in writing, including findings of fact, which should include due consideration of the evidence presented by the contractor, as well as consideration of the contractor's arguments.

8. The debarring official's decision will be conveyed to the contractor by certified mail, and if the contractor is to be debarred, the time period of the debarment and its effective dates will be included.

9. A debarred contractor can submit additional evidence, such as the reversal of a related criminal conviction, and request reconsideration or reduction of the debarment by the debarring official.

(See FAR 9.405, 9.406; for a more detailed discussion of the debarment process, see Keyes at 76)

Q 9:46 Besides debarment proceedings, what other contract dispute procedures exist in federal contracting?

In addition to debarment, a federal agency may refuse to pay a portion of the contract price; cancel the contract before it is complete; award the contract, perhaps unfairly, to another bidder; or impose wage and employee benefit requirements upon an unwilling contractor. While these types of disputes (with the exception of the last) more properly fall within the purview of books on government contracting, it may be useful to know what some of these procedures and their statutory or regulatory sources are:

1. The Contract Disputes Act of 1978 [41 USC §§ 601–613] generally lays down the procedures to be used by contractors in attempting to collect unpaid claims from the federal bureaucracy under government contracts. The act applies to most contracts, express or implied, entered by an agency of the federal executive branch for—

   • The procurement or disposal of personal (chattel) property

   • The purchase of services

   • Construction, alteration, repair, and maintenance of real estate

   The first level on which a contractor can pursue a claim against a federal agency under a contract is via written request to the contracting officer responsible for administering the contract. A dissatisfied contractor may appeal the contracting officer's decision to the agency's board of contract appeals. [41 USC §§ 605(c)(4), 606] Much the same procedure pertains to claims by the agency against the contractor. (With respect to wage determinations under government contracts, see Qs 9:19–9:32.) Administrative enforcement of Davis-Bacon and SCA is entrusted to various administrative boards, such as the Wage Appeals Board and the Armed Services Board of Contract Appeals. Such boards and their administrative law judges who hear cases also are empowered to adjudicate challenges by government contractors and would-be contractors of the DOL's wage determinations when the procurement process begins. [Castagnera and Littell, *Federal Regulation of Employee Benefits* (1992) at 318; see also BNA, *Wage and Hour Manual* (1977) at 99:1095, 99:1325]

2. The decisions of contract appeals boards can be appealed to an appropriate federal court under most circumstances. [See, e.g., Home Improvement Corp v Brennan, 22 *BNA Wage & Hours Cas* 295 (ND Ohio 1974); Curtiss Wright v McLucas, 364 F Supp 750 (D NJ 1973); Descomp Inc v Sampson, 21 *BNA Wage & Hours Cas* 999 (D Del 1974)]

Q 9:47   For what sorts of violations might OFCCP be seeking more debarments in 1995 and 1996?

In early 1994, Shirley J. Wilcher, then the incoming director of OFCCP, threatened more debarments as sanctions for government contractors found to practice "systemic discrimination." Wilcher pledged to focus agency efforts on the "most egregious violators," adding that she intended to "send a signal" under the agency's "targeted enforcement" strategy by means of debarments and other harsh sanctions. Citing her boss, Secretary of Labor Robert Reich (who also ordered her to clean up OFCCP's backlog of 10- to 15-year-old cases), Wilcher added that, "Those who take the low road should not be given a competitive advantage." ["New Director of OFCCP Promises to Beef Up Efforts to Address Systemic Discrimination," 1994 *BNA Daily Labor Report* 20, Feb 1, 1994, at D26]

Taking charge of an agency whose enforcement activities sharply declined during the Reagan and Bush era, Wilcher stated, "Not to fully utilize all of our available resources, especially women and people of color, in this day and age is short-sighted." [Id]

But by June 1995, Wilcher found her agency beleaguered in the face of Republication-controlled Congress and a new U.S. Supreme Court decision undercutting federal affirmative action decisions (see Q 9:12).

Q 9:48   May government contractors permanently replace striking employees?

For many years, organized labor has lobbied hard for a new law that would forbid employers to replace unionized employees permanently while they were engaged in an economic strike, meaning a work stoppage aimed at obtaining better wages, fringe benefits, or working conditions.

The Clinton administration entered office with an avowed purpose of granting labor its wish. The Republican's capture of both houses of Congress in November 1994, however, made the enactment of such a law virtually impossible in the foreseeable future. Consequently, the president made an "end run" around Congress by signing Executive Order 12954 that would deny government contracts to private companies that replace striking workers.

Q 9:49   What is Executive Order 12954?

Signed by President Bill Clinton on March 8, 1995, Executive Order 12954 prohibits federal contractors from replacing striking workers on pain of having their contracts canceled or being denied new contractual opportunities with Uncle Sam. The National Labor Relations Act already allows for the reinstatement of workers who join a picket line in protest of unfair labor practices by the employer. But since the U.S. Supreme Court ruled on the question back in the 1940s, the rule has been that strikers were subject to being replaced permanently. While labor enjoyed the allegiance of one American worker in every three during the 1950s and 1960s, permanent replacement workers were the exception, not the rule.

In 1981, however, one of President Ronald Reagan's first official acts was to replace the government's striking air traffic controllers permanently. Many private enterprises took their lead from this presidential action throughout the 1980s and into the 1990s, leading organized labor to make the striker replacement bill a priority. Naturally, Clinton's executive order was welcomed by the AFL-CIO, when it was announced by Vice President Albert Gore. Of course, the order was denounced by the GOP. However, Senate Republications fell one vote short of the two-thirds majority needed to repeal the executive order. Therefore, at least for the time being, the tens of thousands of corporations doing business with the federal government must refrain from permanently replacing employees who take to the picket lines (although these strikers may be temporarily replaced while the strike is active) or risk loss of their business with Uncle Sam.

Executive orders are implicitly permitted by the U.S. Constitution, which placed the president in charge of the executive branch of the federal government. While not expressly permitted by the Constitution, executive fiats have been approved by the U.S. Supreme Court on the legal theory that the president could not do his job without such authority. However, such orders have been described as being in a gray order between executive and legislative power.

George Washington was the first to use an executive order to overrule the will of the recalcitrant Congress in 1793, when he declared that the United States would remain officially neutral in the war between England and France. Lincoln's 1863 Emancipation Proclamation was an executive order, as was Franklin D. Roosevelt's order in 1942 requiring the internment of Japanese-Americans, an action since denounced but at the time approved by the U.S. Supreme Court.

In 1952, during the Korean War, organized labor was threatening to halt steel production. President Harry Truman used an executive order in an attempt to seize major steel mills. But the high court ruled against the attempt. [Youngstown Sheet and Tube Co v Sawyer, 343 US 579 (1952)]

Perhaps the best known executive order still in effect is President John Kennedy's Executive Order 11246, which predated the 1964 Civil Rights Act by more than a year in forbidding job discrimination by federal contractors. President Jimmy Carter later supplemented Kennedy's long-standing order with one of his own, requiring federal contractors to employ prescribed percentages of minority workers in order to qualify for Uncle Sam's patronage, once again invoking Article II of the Constitution, which says the president "shall take Care that the Laws be faithfully executed." Clinton's March 1995 order is more in the tradition of Kennedy's famous, and still effective, executive decree, (see Q 9:10) and having survived by one vote the Senate's attempt to repeal it is unlikely to cause a constitutional crisis. Nonetheless, a group of plaintiffs, led by the U.S. Chamber of Commerce, has initiated a legal action challenging the validity of Clinton's order. [Chamber of Commerce v Reich, Civil Action No 95-0503 (USDC, District of Columbia, 1995)]

Q 9:50   How has the Chamber of Commerce challenge to Clinton's striker replacement order fared in the federal courts?

The U.S. District Court for the District of Columbia dismissed *Chamber of Commerce v. Reich* [Civil Action No 95-0503], ruling that the challenge to President Clinton's Executive Order 12954 was unripe for adjudication until the secretary of labor initiated actual proceedings against a government contractor to enforce it. [See Chamber of Commerce v Reich, 1995 *BNA Daily Labor Report* 91, May 11, 1995]

In May 1995, however, the chamber and its co-plaintiffs filed an appeal of this dismissal with the U.S. Court of Appeals for the District of Columbia Court. (See "Motions Filed with D.C. Circuit Concerning Striker Replacement Executive Order," District of Columbia Court. [See "Motions Filed with D.C. Circuit Concerning Striker Replacement Executive Order," 1995 *BNA Daily Labor Report 99*, May 23, 1995, at d39] This appeal was pending as this third volume went to press.

Chapter 10

Public Employees

A century ago, employment at will was as much a part of public as private employment. One expert on public employment has rightly observed:

> The public employee's stake in the job was . . . not much more secure than that of his or her private counterpart. Indeed, it was less so because personal efficiency and honesty were attributes of considerably less value in a system where governmental services were not competitive and were not measured by efficiency scales.

[Silver, *Public Employee Discharge and Discipline*, at v–vi (New York: John Wiley & Sons, 1989)]

Before progressives such as Theodore Roosevelt championed the changes known as civil service reform, political partisanship was the primary basis of tenure and promotion. Decade by decade, as the federal and state legislatures and courts chipped away at the edifice of at-will employment, they also narrowed politicians' discretionary treatment of public employees to the sphere of their inner circles of top aides and advisers.

While the development of public employees' legal rights have paralleled those of private employees, the controlling legal principles are sufficiently different to justify this chapter's special treatment. Furthermore, organized labor's precipitous decline in the private sector has been balanced to some extent by the growth of union ranks in state and local government. Consequently, employers interested in union avoidance may do well to study the success of organized labor among white collar public employees.

Public sector employees are supported by taxation and charged with civic responsibilities including the general population's health and safety. Therefore, job termination, collective bargaining, and economic pressures from strikes and lockouts present special problems and issues in the public sector. When the United Auto Workers strikes General Motors, new car buyers may have to wait a month for the models they want, or they can buy Fords, Chryslers, or Toyotas. But if a community's police and fire fighters walk out, the citizenry is ill prepared to meet emergencies in alternative ways. Consequently, public employment issues require special consideration and regulation.

The 1990s brought hard times not only to the private sector—where re-engineering (see chapter 14), the end of the Cold War and much of its related defense contracting, and a recession combined to create significant unemployment in the first years of the decade—but also to public employees, as many states were hard-pressed to meet their budgets and Uncle Sam moved to close unneeded military bases across the nation.

The Clinton administration's effort to shut down military facilities and control the federal deficit led to some litigation in 1994. "In a rare U.S. Supreme Court appearance by a member of Congress, Sen. Arlen Specter (R-Pa.) told the justices on March 2 [1994] that the Defense Base Closure and Realignment Act of 1990 was an effort by Congress and the president to distance themselves from a political 'hot potato' while at the same time achieving a fair process to decide which obsolete bases to close." ["Pennsylvania Senator Asks Justices to Let Courts Review Base Closings," 32 *BNA Government Employee Relations Report* 1555, Mar 7, 1994, at 319]

Specter went on to claim that the decision to close the Philadelphia Naval Shipyard and the resultant threat to the 7,000 federal jobs there was the result of "fraud and chicanery" by the Defense Base Closure and Realignment Commission. (See Dalton v Specter, 114 S Ct 1719, 128 L Ed 2d 497, 1994 US LEXIS 3778 (1994), *reh denied* 114 S Ct 2771 (1994)) Ironically, while the senior senator from the Keystone State was making his case before the high court, others in Philadelphia were finding creative ways to privatize and to preserve the aging shipyard. With the end of a half century of the Cold War, the former Soviet Union also was strapped with expensive and partially obsolete military machinery. Negotiations are underway that could lead to contracts under which the former Soviet Union will sail unwanted naval vessels to Philadelphia, where shipyard employees would carve them up for scrap metal for private sale.

Sen. Specter's 1994 lawsuit against the secretary of the U.S. Navy was dismissed by the U.S. Supreme Court on the grounds that the recommendations of the Defense Base Closure and Realignment Commission under the 1990 closure act were not reviewable by the federal courts. [Dalton v Specter, 114 S Ct 1719 (1994)] In June 1995, as this edition went to press, the commission's work continued apace, and additional military installations were scheduled to be closed. The total number of civilian jobs to be lost in the U.S. Department of Defense is 34,000 over the past six years. ["Air Force Bases Closed and Re-aligned, Labs Spared on First Day of Voting," 1995 *BNA Daily Labor Report* 121, June 23, 1995, at d13]

The job preservation plan for the Philadelphia navy yard is just one example of the public sector taking a page from the book of private enterprise in an effort to become more economically relevant and efficient, and thus offset some of the job losses. Other areas in which public sector employment mirrors the private sector are discussed in this chapter. Also discussed are discrimination and drug testing in public employment.

10-3

Collective Bargaining

Federal Employees

Q 10:1   Do public employees have the right to join unions, bargain collectively, and strike?

The rights of public sector employees to organize and to bargain collectively are relatively recent legal developments. The National Labor Relations Act (NLRA), which structures labor relations in the private sector, excludes employees of federal, state, and local governments from its coverage. Only in the last few decades have Congress, the executive branch, and the states adopted legal provisions allowing public employees some rights to organize and to bargain collectively.

Although many labor relations issues in the public sector are similar to those in the private sector, there are also significant differences. Actions taken by government employers with regard to their employees may raise issues of the constitutional rights of those employees. Both the U.S. Constitution and the various state constitutions regulate and limit governmental action affecting citizens. Because public sector workers are citizens and employees, their constitutional rights must be respected by their employers. Therefore, the public sector employer may be limited in its attempts to discipline or to regulate its employees by constitutional provisions. The private sector employer faces no similar constitutional problems.

A second area in which public sector employment differs from the private sector is in the right to strike. The right to strike is protected by Section 7 of the NLRA for private sector workers. Public sector workers, in general, do not have the right to strike. The activities of the government employer are generally vital to the public interest; disruptions of those activities because of labor disputes could imperil the welfare of the public. For that reason, the right to strike by public sector workers may be prohibited (as in the federal government and most states) or limited to certain employees whose refusal to work would not endanger the public safety or welfare.

The third area in which public sector relations differ from the private sector is the scope of issues for collective bargaining. In the private sector, the duty to bargain encompasses the broadly defined matters of "wages, hours, and other terms and conditions of employment." In the public sector, however, matters relating to terms and conditions of employment also may affect the legally required activities or duties of the public sector employer. To bargain over such issues could, in effect, involve delegating to the union the determination of functions and the exercise of authority legally given to the government. Therefore, the scope of collective bargaining must be limited on such issues so that the governmental employer does not abdicate its authority. For this reason, the scope of collective bargaining is more restrictive than in the private sector; the various federal and state provisions narrowly define "terms and conditions" of employment. Indeed, some state legislation does not provide for bargaining at all, but rather for consultation or "meeting and conferring" on such issues.

Q 10:2 When did federal employees receive the right to unionize?

It is not known precisely when federal employees began negotiating over the terms of their employment, but informal bargaining began as early as 1883. In that year the Pendelton Act, known as the Civil Services Act, was passed. It granted Congress the sole authority to set wages, hours, and other terms and conditions of federal employment. This act led to informal bargaining and congressional lobbying by federal employees seeking higher wages and better conditions.

In 1906, President Theodore Roosevelt halted informal bargaining by issuing an executive order forbidding federal employees, or their associations, from soliciting increases in pay, either before Congress, its committees, or before the heads of the executive agencies. Employees violating the order faced dismissal.

In the years following the executive order, Congress passed several laws that gave limited rights of organization to some federal workers. The Lloyd-La Follette Act of 1912 gave postal workers the right to join unions. In 1920, the federal government negotiated the terms of a contract with the union representing construction workers building the government-sponsored Alaskan Railroad.

It was not until 1962, with the issuing of Executive Order 10988 by President John Kennedy, that large numbers of federal employees were given the right to organize and to present their views on terms and conditions of employment to the agencies for which they worked.

Executive Order 10988 was supplemented by Executive Order 11491, which was issued in 1969 by President Richard Nixon. That order placed the entire program of employee-management relations under the supervision and control of the Federal Labor Relations Council.

The Federal Service Labor-Management Relations Act of 1978 (FSLMRA), which was enacted as part of the Civil Service Reform Act of 1978 and took effect in January 1979, was the first comprehensive enactment covering labor relations in the federal government.

Q 10:3 What is the FSLMRA?

The FSLMRA, which was modeled after the NLRA, established a permanent structure for labor relations in the federal public sector. It created the Federal Labor Relations Authority (FLRA) to administer the act, and it granted federal employees the right to organize and to bargain collectively. It also prohibited strikes and other specific practices.

The FSLMRA covers federal workers employed by a federal agency or who have ceased to work for the agency because of an unfair labor practice. Most federal agencies are covered, but some are specifically exempted. Those agencies excluded from FSLMRA coverage are the FBI, the CIA, the National Security Agency, the General Accounting Office, the Tennessee Valley Authority, the Federal Labor Relations

Authority, and the Federal Service Impasse Panel. Furthermore, any agency that the president determines is investigative in nature, or has a primary function of intelligence and would thus not be amenable to FSLMRA coverage because of national security, may be excluded. The FSLMRA also excludes certain employees from coverage. Noncitizens working outside of the United States for federal agencies, supervisory and management employees, and certain foreign service officers are exempted. In addition, the act excludes any federal employee participating in an illegal strike.

The Thurmond Act of 1969 prohibits military personnel from belonging to a union. That act makes it a felony for enlisted personnel to join a union or for military officers or their representatives to recognize or to bargain with a union. The Thurmond Act does not apply to civilian employees of the military.

Those employees covered by the FSLMRA are granted the right to form, join, or assist any labor organization, or to refrain from such activity, freely and without reprisal. Employees may act as representatives of a labor organization and present views of the organization, or refrain from such activity. Employees may act as representatives of a labor organization and present views of the organization to the heads of agencies, the executive branch, and Congress.

Q 10:4   How is the FSLMRA administered?

The FSLMRA created the FLRA, which assumed the duties of the Federal Labor Relations Council created by Executive Order 11491. The FLRA is the central authority responsible for the administration of the FSLMRA.

The FLRA is composed of three members nominated by the president and confirmed by the Senate. The members serve five-year terms. The FLRA is empowered to determine the appropriateness of units for representation, to supervise or conduct elections to determine if a labor organization has been selected as the exclusive representative by a majority of the employees in the appropriate unit, to resolve issues relating to the duty to bargain in good faith, and to resolve complaints of unfair labor practices.

The FLRA has the authority to hold hearings and issue subpoenas. It may order any agency or union to cease and desist from violating the provisions of the FSLMRA, and it can enlist the federal courts in proceedings against unions that strike illegally. The FLRA may take any remedial actions it deems appropriate in carrying out the policies of the act.

Q 10:5   How are bargaining units determined for federal employees?

Under the FSLMRA, a union becomes the exclusive representative of an appropriate unit of employees when it has been selected by a majority of votes cast in a representation election. When selected, the union becomes the sole representative of the employees in the unit and is authorized to negotiate the terms and conditions of employment of the employees in the unit. The union must fairly represent all employees in the unit, without discrimination or regard to union membership. The FLRA is authorized to settle issues involving representation, such as the determination of the appropriate unit and the holding of representation elections.

The FLRA ensures employees the fullest possible freedom in exercising their rights under the FSLMRA in determining the unit and ensures a clear and identifiable community of interest among the employees in the unit to promote effective dealing with the agency involved. The FLRA may determine the appropriateness of a unit on an agency, plant, installation, functional, or other basis.

Units may not include any management or supervisory employees, confidential employees, employees engaged in personnel work, except those in a purely clerical capacity, employees doing investigative work that directly affects national security, employees administering the FSLMRA, or employees primarily engaged in investigation or audit functions relating to the work of individuals whose duties affect the internal security of an agency. Any employees engaged in administering any provision of law relating to labor-management relations may not be represented by a labor organization that is affiliated with an organization representing other individuals under the act. An appropriate unit may include professional and nonprofessional employees only if the professional employees, by majority vote, approve including nonprofessional employees.

Q 10:6   How are representation elections conducted in the federal sector?

The procedures for representation elections under the FSLMRA closely resemble those for elections under the NLRA. The act allows for holding consent elections to determine the exclusive representative of a bargaining unit. It also provides that the FLRA may investigate the question of representation, including holding an election, if a petition is filed by any person alleging that 30 percent of the employees in a unit wish to be represented by a union for the purpose of collective bargaining. When a petition alleging that 30 percent of the members of a bargaining unit no longer wish to be represented by their exclusive representative union, the FLRA will investigate the representation question.

If the FLRA finds reasonable cause to believe that a representation question exists, it will provide, upon reasonable notice, an opportunity for a hearing. If, on the basis of the hearing, the FLRA finds that a question of representation does exist, it will conduct a representation election by secret ballot. An election will not be held if the unit has held a valid election within the preceding 12 months.

When an election is scheduled, a union may intervene and be placed on the ballot if it can show that it is already the unit's exclusive representative, or that it has the support of at least 10 percent of the employees in the unit. The election is by secret ballot, and the employees choose between the union or unions and "no representation." If no choice receives a majority of votes cast, a runoff election is held between the two choices receiving the higher number of votes. The results of the election are certified; if a union receives a majority of votes cast, it becomes the exclusive representative of the employees of the unit.

A union that has obtained exclusive representation status can be present at any formal discussions between the agency and unit employees concerning grievances, personnel policies and practices, or other conditions of employment. The exclusive representative also must be given the opportunity to be present at any examination of an employer in the unit in connection with an agency investigation that the employee reasonably believes may result in disciplinary action against the employee, provided that the employee involved has requested such representation. (This right is the equivalent of the Weingarten rights established by the NLRB for organized employees in the private sector.)

Q 10:7   What are union consultation rights in the federal sector?

If the employees of an agency have not designated a union as their exclusive representative on an agency-wide basis, a union that represents a substantial number of agency employees may be granted consultation rights. Consultation rights entitle the union to be informed of any substantive change in employment conditions the agency proposes. The union is to be permitted reasonable time to present its views and recommendations regarding the proposed changes. The agency must consider the union's recommendations before taking final action, and it must provide the union with written reasons for taking the final action.

Q 10:8   How is collective bargaining conducted with federal employees?

The FSLMRA requires that agencies and the exclusive representative of agency employees meet and negotiate in good faith. Good faith is defined as approaching the negotiations with a sincere resolve to reach a collective bargaining agreement, meeting at reasonable times and convenient places as frequently as may be necessary, and being represented at negotiations by duly authorized representatives prepared to discuss and negotiate on any condition of employment.

The act defines "conditions of employment" as including personnel policies, practices, and other matters, whether established by rule, regulation, or otherwise, that affect working conditions. However, the act excludes the following from being defined as conditions of employment: policies relating to prohibited political activity, matters relating to the classification of any position, and policies or matters that are provided for by federal statute. Wages are not subject to collective bargaining. Federal "blue-collar" employees are paid under the coordinated Federal

Wage System, which provides for pay comparable to pay for similar jobs in the private sector. Federal "white-collar" employees are paid under the General Schedule (GS) and increases and changes in GS pay scales are made by presidential order.

The FSLMRA contains a strong management's rights clause, which also restricts the scope of collective bargaining. According to that clause, collective bargaining is not to affect the authority of any management official or any agency to determine the mission, budget, organization, number of employees, or the internal security practices of the agency. Furthermore, management's right to hire, assign, direct, lay off, retain or suspend, reduce in grade or pay, or to take disciplinary action against any employee is not subject to negotiation. Decisions to assign work, to contract out work, or to select candidates to fill positions are not subject to negotiation. The act also precludes bargaining over any actions necessary to carry out the mission of the agency during emergencies.

The duty to bargain extends to matters that are the subject of any rule or regulation, as long as the particular rule or regulation is not government-wide. However, if the agency determines that there is a compelling need for such a regulation, it can refuse to bargain over that regulation. The exclusive representative must be given an opportunity to show the FLRA that no compelling need exists.

The agency's duty to bargain includes the obligation to furnish, upon request by the exclusive representative, data and information normally maintained by the agency. Such data must be reasonably available and necessary for full and proper discussion of subjects within the scope of bargaining. Data related to the guidance, training, advice, or counsel of management or supervisors relating to collective bargaining are excluded from the obligation to provide information. The duty to bargain in good faith also includes the duty to execute a written document embodying the terms of agreement, if either party so requests.

Q 10:9 Can federal employees be disciplined for improper behavior, amounting to sexual harassment, during collective bargaining activities?

In American Federation of Government Employees Local 3254 and Grissom Air Force Base [FMCS Arb No 93-19558 (Jan 17, 1994)],

Federal Mediation and Conciliation Service arbitrator B.J. Speroff ruled that, while rough language may be a legitimate part of the give-and-take across the negotiating table, a continuation of such language outside the negotiating sessions was inappropriate and subject to disciplinary action by the employer-agency. The arbitrator therefore denied a union grievance filed on behalf of a union representative who was given a 14-day suspension from work for his crude language directed at a female agency representative outside the building at the conclusion of a negotiating session.

Speroff noted that "robust debate" around the bargaining table justifies some rough language, and the presence of more women on both sides of the table does not alter negotiators' free speech right to express themselves in terms that might be viewed as inappropriate or offensive to females in some other context.

Although the federal chief negotiator may have been offended by the local union president's remarks at the bargaining session, Speroff said, she had no sexual harassment claim based upon hostile environment (see Q 4:49), since the remarks were made spontaneously in the heat of collective bargaining. But once the parties had left the building, the president's lewd remarks, "spoken in public and away from the negotiating table, being uttered sans provocation, can in no way constitute a privileged or protected activity, and, indeed, become a form of sexual harassment."

Q 10:10   How are bargaining impasses resolved under the FSLMRA?

The FSLMRA created the Federal Service Impasse Panel, which is authorized to take any action necessary to resolve an impasse in negotiations. The Federal Mediation and Conciliation Service (FMCS), created by the Taft-Hartley Act, also assists in the resolution of impasses by providing mediation service for the parties. If the mediation efforts fail to lead to an agreement, either party may request that the Federal Service Impasse Panel consider the dispute. The panel may recommend procedures for resolving the impasse or assist the parties in any other way it deems appropriate. The formal impasse resolution procedures may include hearings, fact finding, recommendations for settlement, or directed settlement. With the approval of the panel, the parties also may seek binding arbitration of the impasse.

Q 10:11   How is the Federal Service Impasse Panel (FSIP) dealing with drug testing in the federal government?

Although federal and state government employees have constitutional rights which must not be violated by drug testing programs (see Q 10:30), in 1994 the Federal Service Impasse Panel resolved an impasse at the Norfolk Naval Shipyard in favor of the employer, in the process writing into the collective bargaining agreement between the facility and a technical employees' union employer-proposed random drug testing language. [Norfolk Naval Shipyard and International Federation of Professional and Technical Engineers Local 1, Case No 93 FSIP 239, Mar 11, 1994)]

The FSIP panel rejected union contentions that the Navy's plan to place some segments of the workforce into a "random pool" for testing purposes violated neither the relevant Supreme Court decisions on random testing of public employees or the standard set by the Drug-Free Workplace Act. (See Qs 1:19, 3:70, 7:138)

Relying on a federal district court decision in another jurisdiction, which upheld the Navy's program on the West Coast, (see American Federation of Government Employees Local 1533 v Cheney, 754 F Supp 1409 (ND Cal 1990), *affd*, 944 F 2d 503 (9th Cir 1991)) the panel adopted this precedent, which it claimed "established strict criteria for determining whether a [job category] should be subject to random testing so as not to violate employees' Fourth Amendment rights." Under the *Cheney* standard, a position may not be designated for random drug testing unless the job has an impact on public safety, national security, or some other compelling governmental interest.

The panel concluded that the agency-employer's proposal "strikes a better balance between employees" privacy interests and the employer"s concerns over the costs, logistics, and overall administration" of the drug testing activity.

While this case, like the various federal court decisions aimed at defining the parameters of public employee drug testing, is grounded in part on constitutional considerations, courts seeking to establish the boundaries of employee privacy interests in the sensitive realm of drug testing are increasingly turning to such cases for guidance in the private sector too. [See, e.g., Borse v Piece Goods Shop Inc, 963 F 2d 611 (3d Cir 1991)] (Qs 7:151, 13:27)

Q 10:12   Is grievance arbitration allowed under the FSLMRA?

The FSLMRA provides that all collective agreements under it must contain a grievance procedure that provides for binding arbitration as the final step in resolving grievances. If arbitration is invoked, either party may appeal the arbitrator's decision to the FLRA for review within 30 days of the granting of the award. Upon review, the FLRA may overturn the arbitrator's award only if it is contrary to a law, rule, or regulation, or is inconsistent with the standards for review of private sector awards by the federal courts. If no appeal is taken from the arbitrator's award within 30 days of the award, the arbitrator's award is final and binding.

When a grievance involves matters subject to a statutory review procedure, the employee may choose to pursue the complaint through the statutory procedure or through the negotiated grievance procedure. Grievances alleging discrimination in violation of Title VII of the Civil Rights Act of 1964 provide the grievor such a choice. The grievor can pursue the complaint through the grievance process or through the Title VII procedure. Performance ratings, demotions, and suspensions or removals that are subject to Civil Service review procedures may be pursued either through the Civil Service procedures or a grievance.

Q 10:13   Are there unfair labor practices under the FSLMRA?

The FSLMRA prohibits unfair labor practices by agencies and unions. The unfair labor practices defined in the act are similar to those defined by Section 8(a) and (b) of the NRLA.

Unfair labor practices by agencies under the FSLMRA include interference or restraint of the exercise of employees' rights under the act, encouraging or discouraging union membership by discrimination in conditions of employment, sponsoring or controlling a union, disciplining or discriminating against an employee for filing a complaint under the act, refusing to negotiate in good faith, and refusing to cooperate in impasse procedures. It is also an unfair labor practice for an agency to enforce any rule or regulation that conflicts with a preexisting collective bargaining agreement.

Union unfair labor practices under the FSLMRA include interfering or restraining the exercise of employees' rights under the act; coercing or fining a member for the purpose of impeding job performance; discriminating against an employee on the basis of race, color, creed, national origin, sex, age, civil service status, political affiliation, marital status, or handicap; refusing to negotiate in good faith; and refusing to cooperate in impasse procedures. It is also an unfair labor practice for a union to call or condone a strike, work slowdown or stoppage, or to picket the agency if the picketing interferes with the agency's operations. Informational picketing that does not interfere with agency operations is allowed.

Q 10:14   What unfair labor practice procedures are there under the FSLMRA?

Upon the filing of a complaint alleging unfair labor practices with the FLRA, the General Counsel's Office of the FLRA investigates the complaint and attempts to reach a voluntary settlement. If no settlement is reached and the investigation uncovers evidence that the act has been violated, a complaint will be issued. The complaint contains a notice of the charge and sets a date for a hearing before the FLRA. The party against whom the complaint is filed has the opportunity to file an answer to the complaint and to appear at the hearing to contest the charges.

If the FLRA finds, by a preponderance of the evidence, that a violation has occurred, it will issue written findings and an appropriate remedial order. FLRA decisions are subject to judicial review by the federal courts of appeals.

Q 10:15   What are the remedies for unfair labor practices under the FSLMRA?

The FLRA has broad authority for fashioning remedial orders for unfair labor practices. Remedial orders may include cease and desist orders, reinstatement with back pay, renegotiation of the agreement between the parties with retroactive effect, or any other action deemed necessary to carry out the purposes of the act.

When a union has been found by the FLRA to have intentionally engaged in a strike or work stoppage in violation of the act, the FLRA may revoke the exclusive representation status of the union or take any other disciplinary action deemed appropriate. Employees engaging in illegal strikes are subject to dismissal. The FLRA may also seek injunctions, restraining orders, or contempt citations in federal courts against striking unions.

Q 10:16   Can the courts review FLRA decisions?

Final orders, other than bargaining unit determinations and arbitration awards, are subject to review in the U.S. courts of appeals. The party seeking review has 10 days from the issuance of the FLRA decision to file a petition for review with the court of appeals for the appropriate circuit. Unless specifically authorized by the appeals court, the filing of a petition for review does not stay an FLRA order.

Upon review, the court may affirm, enforce, modify, or set aside an FLRA order. Findings of fact by the FLRA are deemed conclusive if supported by substantial evidence. The order of the court of appeals is subject to discretionary review by the U.S. Supreme Court.

Q 10:17   Do federal job terminations affect some groups more severely than others?

Yes. A recent study by a professor at Brown University says African-Americans and native American Indians who work for the federal government are twice as likely as white federal employees to lose their jobs. ["Minority Federal Workers Fired at Twice the Rate of Nonminorities," 1995 *BNA Daily Labor Report* 76, April 26, 1995, at d13] Commissioned by the federal Office of Personnel Management, the study was released April 19, 1995. In it, researchers reviewed 12,000 termination actions involving more than 2.1 million federal employees in the executive branch. The researchers found that minority employees are fired at the rate of 10 per thousand, while white employees are dismissed at the rate of only about 3 per thousand. [Id]

State Employees

Q 10:18 Do the states have public sector labor laws?

In 1954, Wisconsin adopted a public employee labor relations law covering state, county, and municipal employees. Since that first legal provision for state public sector labor relations, approximately 40 states have adopted provisions relating to public sector labor relations. The various state laws differ widely in their treatment of issues such as employee coverage, impasse resolution procedures, and restrictions on the scope of bargaining. Because of the diversity of statutes, it is not possible to discuss them in detail. The remaining portion of this chapter, therefore, will discuss certain general features of state public sector labor relations statutes.

Q 10:19 What is the coverage of state public sector labor laws?

As noted, some 40 states have provisions for some labor relations activity by state or local employees. Most of those states have adopted statutes that provide for organizing rights and for collective bargaining by public employees. Some states that have no statutes dealing with public sector labor relations allow voluntary collective bargaining by public employees based on court decisions. Other states, while not restricting the rights of public employees to join unions, prohibit collective bargaining by public employees, based on statutory prohibitions or court decisions.

In those states having public sector labor relations statutes, the pattern of coverage of those statutes varies. Some statutes cover all state and local employees. Others cover only local or only state employees. Some states have several statutes, including separate laws covering teachers, police, and fire fighters. Some states also allow for the enactment of municipal labor relations legislation. New York City, for example, has established, by means of a city ordinance, an Office of Collective Bargaining.

The courts have generally held that there is no constitutionally protected right to bargain collectively. For that reason, the courts have upheld restrictions or prohibitions on the right to bargain. The right to join unions or to organize, however, has been held to be protected by the constitutional freedom of association under the First and Fourteenth amendments. Because the right to organize is constitutionally protected, restrictions on that right of public employees have consistently been struck down by the courts.

But while public employees in general may have the right to organize, many states exclude supervisors and managerial or confidential employees from unionizing. Other states may allow those employees to organize, but provide for bargaining units separate from other employees. The courts have generally upheld exclusions of managerial, supervisory, and confidential employees from organizing and bargaining.

Q 10:20 Are state and municipal employees permitted to unionize?

Most of the state statutes authorizing public sector labor relations provide for exclusive bargaining representatives of the employees. The statutes generally create a Public Employee Relations Board (PERB) to administer the act and to determine representation issues and unfair labor practice complaints.

The determination of appropriate bargaining units is generally the function of the PERB agency created by the particular statute. Some statutes provide for bargaining by all categories of public employees, while other statutes may specifically define appropriate units, such as teachers within a particular school district. When the PERB is entrusted with determining the appropriate unit, it generally considers community interest factors such as the nature of work, similarity of working conditions, efficiency of administration, and the desires of the employees. Some statutes require determination based on efficiency of administration. Police and law enforcement officers and firefighters generally are in separate district-wide units (or state-wide units for state law enforcement officers). Faculty at public universities may be organized in state-wide units or may bargain on an institutional unit basis. In general, PERB agencies seek to avoid a proliferation of small units.

The procedures for holding representation elections for units of public employees generally resemble those under the FSLMRA and the NLRA. The union seeking representation rights petitions the PERB requesting an election. The union must demonstrate some minimum level of employee support within the unit. If the parties fail to reach agreement on the bargaining unit definition, the eligibility of employees to vote, and the date and other details of the election, the PERB settles such issues after holding hearings on them.

The elections are by secret ballot, and the results are certified by the PERB. Either party may file objections to the election, in which case the PERB will review the challenges and could order a new election if the challenges are upheld.

Q 10:21 Are some state and municipal employees not entitled to unionize?

An important new federal appellate court decision holds that some countervailing governmental interests are so significant that they outweigh public employees' First Amendment rights of speech and assembly, which rights form the basis of a constitutional right to organize. [Gregorich v Lund, 1995 US App LEXIS 10281, 149 BNA LRRM 2278 (7th Cir 1995)] The plaintiff in this case was a research attorney for the Illinois' Fourth District Court of Appeals. The defendant was the presiding judge of that court. When attorney Gregorich attempted to unionize his fellow attorneys, Judge Lund fired him. Gregorich sued in federal district court, contending that the termination violated his First Amendment rights. The federal trial judge agreed, but on appeal, the Seventh Circuit, which sits in Chicago, said that the staff attorneys' privity "not only to internal memoranda and draft opinions, but also to the judges' very thought processes," justified Judge Lund's decision to dismiss the plaintiff and squelch the unionization effort. [Id; see also, "Court Attorney's Attempt to Unionize Justifies Firing, Seventh Circuit Says," 1995 *BNA Daily Labor Report*, 101, May 25, 1995, at d10]

Q 10:22 How is collective bargaining handled at the state and local levels?

A majority of states have provisions requiring, or at least permitting, some form of collective bargaining. Some statutes may use the term "meet and confer" rather than collective bargaining, but in actual operation the process is not substantially different from collective bargaining.

The scope of bargaining subjects may be restricted to protect the statutory authority of, or to ensure the provision of essential functions by, the public employer. Additionally, the public employer may be legally prohibited from agreeing with the union on particular subjects. For example, if state law requires a minimum number of evaluations of employees annually, the employer may not agree to a lesser number of evaluations.

Public sector labor relations statutes generally have broad management-rights clauses. As a result, the subjects of "wages, hours and other terms and conditions" of employment may be defined more narrowly than in the private sector under the NLRA.

The state PERBs generally classify subjects for bargaining into mandatory, permissive, and illegal subjects. Mandatory topics involve the narrowly defined matters relating to wages, hours, and other terms and conditions of employment. Permissive subjects generally are those related to government policy, the employer's function, or matters of management rights. Illegal subjects may include those matters to which the employer is precluded by law from agreeing. Some states may prohibit bargaining over certain terms that may be classified as permissive in other states.

Q 10:23 Are any trends discernible in public sector collective bargaining in 1995?

If the state of Oregon is any example, the trend for the second half of this decade is to reduce the collective bargaining rights of unionized public employees. As this edition went to press in June 1995, Oregon Gov. John Kitzhaber and the Oregon legislature agreed on a bill that would "narrow the scope of bargaining, eliminate mandatory fact-finding from the dispute-resolution process, and redefine which state workers are considered management and thereby [are] excluded from bargaining units." ["Legislature, Governor Agree on Bill to Restrict Public Sector Bargaining," 1995 *BNA Daily Labor Report* 109, June 7, 1995, at d10] Once enacted, the bill also would "establish new criteria for resolving public-safety-employee contracts through binding arbitration, including a new requirement for the last-best-offer method of arbitration." [Id]

According to State Representative John Watt, a Republican proponent of this dramatic change in Oregon's public sector bargaining scheme, the revisions are necessary to restore public sector management rights that have been eroded over the years by Oregon's courts and the state's Employment Relations Board.

Q 10:24   What are "sunshine" laws?

Some states have adopted open-meeting, or "sunshine," laws that require meetings of public bodies to be open to the public. Such laws may present a problem for collective bargaining by public employers because they may allow members of the general public to take part in the bargaining process. In some states, such as Ohio, collective bargaining is exempted from the open-meeting or sunshine law. In other states, however, the right of the public to participate in the bargaining process is legally protected.

Q 10:25   How are bargaining impasses handled at the state and local levels?

Because most state laws restrict or prohibit strikes by public employees, they must provide some alternative means for resolving bargaining impasses. Most statutes provide for a process that includes fact-finding, mediation, and ultimately, interest arbitration.

Mediation is generally the first step in the impasse resolution process; the mediator may be appointed by the PERB at the request of either party. The mediator attempts to offer suggestions and to reduce the number of issues in dispute.

If mediation is unsuccessful, fact-finding is the second step. Each party presents its case to the fact-finder, who issues a report defining the issues in dispute and establishing the reasonableness of the positions of each side. The fact finder's report may be released to the public in an attempt to bring the pressure of public opinion on the parties to force a settlement.

If no resolution is reached after mediation and fact-finding, the statutes generally provide for interest arbitration. The arbitration may be either voluntary or compulsory and may be binding or nonbinding. Compulsory, binding arbitration is generally found in statutes dealing with employees who provide essential services, such as fire fighters and police. Nonbinding arbitration awards may be disregarded by the public employer if it so chooses; binding arbitration awards bind both parties to the arbitrator's settlement of the dispute.

In several states, the arbitration of bargaining disputes has been challenged as being an illegal delegation of the public employer's legal authority to the arbitrator. Most state courts have upheld the legality of arbitration, including New York, Michigan, Minnesota, Maine, Washington, and Pennsylvania. In some states, such as Texas, South Dakota, Colorado, and Utah, however, courts have held compulsory arbitration to be illegal.

Some statutes allow for judicial review of arbitration awards, generally to determine if the award is unreasonable, arbitrary, or capricious.

Q 10:26　Are state workers allowed to strike?

Most state public sector labor relations statutes prohibit strikes by public employees. Other states, such as Pennsylvania, Michigan, Vermont, and Hawaii, allow strikes by employees whose jobs do not immediately affect the public health, safety, and welfare of the citizens. Still other states allow strikes in situations in which the public employer refuses to negotiate or to abide by an arbitration award.

Penalties for illegal strikes vary from state to state. New York's Taylor Law, which prohibits all strikes by public employees, allows fines and loss of dues and check-off provisions for unions involved in illegal strikes. Employees who participate in illegal strikes in New

York may face probation, loss of job, and loss of pay. Courts may issue injunctions or restraining orders against illegal strikes.

Disciplining public sector employees, even those who have taken part in illegal strikes, may pose constitutional problems for public-sector employers. The employer must ensure that any disciplinary procedure ensures the employees "due process," including adequate notice of and an opportunity to participate in a hearing on the proposed penalty.

Constitutional and Civil Rights

Federal Employees

Q 10:27 Do public employees enjoy workplace rights under federal and state constitutions?

Federal, state, and local government agencies must conform their actions to the Bill of Rights and later U.S. constitutional amendments. State constitutions also contain constraints on government activities. Courts have long held that such constitutional rules as due process of law apply to government agencies in their roles as employers. For example, when the U.S. Supreme Court renders a decision restricting police officers' powers of search and seizure respecting crime suspects, courts will likely require supervisors of government employees to observe the same restrictions when investigations lead them into employees' desks or lockers. Perhaps most significant in recent years has been the legal battle revolving around mandatory drug tests for government workers. Additionally, First Amendment rights of speech and assembly have been used to support public employee unionization efforts; however, a recent federal court decision has undercut these rights (see Q 10:21).

Q 10:28 What is meant by "due process of law"?

The Fifth and Fourteenth amendments to the U.S. Constitution forbid government entities, such as the police and the courts, to deprive people of their liberty or property without following appropriate legal procedures. The Fifth Amendment, which is part of the

10-23

original Bill of Rights, applies to the federal government. The Fourteenth Amendment, adopted shortly after the Civil War, places similar restraints upon state and local government.

When, for instance, a government agency proposes to discipline, or perhaps even to discharge, an employee, the agency typically must advise the employee of the accusations against her and afford her the opportunity to respond, possibly in the context of a formal disciplinary proceeding. Often there are appeal rights or recourse to an adversarial hearing before a forum such as the Merit System Protection Board in the federal civil service.

Q 10:29   What does "equal protection of the law" mean?

Closely related to the due process clause of the Fourteenth Amendment to the U.S. Constitution is the so-called equal protection clause. This provision requires state and local governments to apply their laws evenly to all citizens.

For purposes of public employment, the clause can be used to restrict the government's use of affirmative action programs. For instance, in *Krupa v. New Castle County*, [732 F Supp 497 (D Del 1990)] a group of white police officers challenged the promotion of black counterparts under the county's affirmative action plan. Holding that absent evidence of past discrimination the county could not favor the black police, the federal judge observed. The equal protection clause of the Fourteenth Amendment provides that "[N]o State shall make or enforce any law which shall . . . deny to any person within its jurisdiction the equal protection of the laws." [citation omitted] Judicial review of racially preferential state employment actions under this clause requires an equal application of its provisions regardless of whether the allegedly aggrieved individual is a member of a minority or majority class.

[732 F Supp at 506]

Q 10:30   Does drug testing violate the due process and equal protection clauses of the Constitution?

On March 21, 1989, just five days after the effective date of the Drug-Free Workplace Act, the Supreme Court announced two closely related decisions that together seek to limit drug testing by the federal government, both within the bureaucracy and the regulated private sector. By implication, these two cases give important clues as to what government contractors and grantees can or cannot do, bearing in mind that private employers are not directly subject to the restrictions in the Bill of Rights (for drug testing purposes, the Fourth, Fifth, and Fourteenth Amendments).

National Treasury Employees Union v. Von Raab, [489 US 656 (1989)] concerns the constitutionality of a drug testing program announced by the Commissioner of the U.S. Customs Service in 1986. The program called for urinalysis, designed to detect marijuana, cocaine, opiates, amphetamines, and phencyclidine. Any employee seeking promotion or transfer to any one of the following three job categories had to submit to the test:

- Jobs directly involving interdiction of illegal drugs
- Positions requiring the carrying of a firearm
- Assignments involving classified materials

The courts disagreed on the program's constitutionality. The federal district court enjoined its operation, but a divided panel of the U.S. Court of Appeals for the Fifth Circuit reversed. The case then went to the U.S. Supreme Court.

The U.S. Supreme Court affirmed in part and reversed in part. First, the Court found that the collection and analysis of employees' urine samples was a search, which therefore had to meet the reasonableness requirement of the Fourth Amendment. Consequently,

> [T]he public interest in the Customs Service program had to be balanced against the privacy concerns implicated by the tests, without reference to the usual presumption in favor of the warrant and probable cause procedures specified in the Fourth Amendment, because the program was not designed to serve the ordinary needs of law enforcement.

Next, in applying the reasonableness test, the Court held that the U.S. Customs Service needed no search warrants to collect the samples, and with regard to jobs involving firearms or drug interdiction, the policy was reasonable even absent probable cause or individualized suspicion. On the other hand, regarding jobs requiring access to classified documents, the drug-testing program struck the Court's majority as an overly broad response to the commissioner's concerns. Therefore, on remand, the Fifth Circuit was instructed to ascertain what Customs Service materials were considered "classified" and which employees might be tested under this category.

Skinner v. Railway Labor Executives' Association [489 US 602 (1989)], involved the imposition of federal drug rules on the employees of private, but heavily regulated, corporations, specifically railroads.

The Federal Railroad Administration (FRA), responding to evidence (notably a much-publicized Amtrak wreck involving fatalities) indicating that railroad employees' drug and alcohol abuse posed a threat to public safety, promulgated drug and alcohol testing regulations. Subpart C of these regulations required railroads to test employees involved in train accidents.

Subpart D allowed, but did not require, testing when supervisors had "a reasonable suspicion" that an employee was "under the influence" or had contributed to an accident or dangerous incident. The federal district court that first judged the regulations decided that the regulations were reasonable intrusions of employees' privacy interests. The U.S. Court of Appeals for the Ninth Circuit reversed the trial court, finding that, because the regulations did not require a showing of individualized suspicion, they were constitutionally invalid.

The U.S. Supreme Court held that:

1. The Fourth Amendment applied to FRA regulations, even though it was left to private employers to apply them;

2. The tests were reasonable under the circumstances, reflecting the government's interest in public safety; and

3. A search warrant was not essential for the regulations to pass constitutional muster, since this procedure would delay necessarily prompt testing.

Q 10:31   Have due process of law and equal protection under the law become statutory?

After the Civil War and the adoption of the Thirteenth, Fourteenth, and Fifteenth amendments to the Constitution, Congress passed a series of civil rights statutes, today codified at Title 42, sections

1981-1985, of the U.S. Code. Among these laws, 42 USC § 1983 forbids state action that deprive citizens of due process and equal protection of the law. A Section 1983 lawsuit is among the most common means for a public employee to challenge a governmental employer's alleged deprivation of that employee's constitutional rights. Successful employee-litigants can obtain compensatory, and even punitive damages, plus attorneys' fees in some circumstances.

Q 10:32 Can 42 USC § 1983 be the basis of a lawsuit by an employee against a private employer?

Like the Bill of Rights itself, Section 1983 is directed only at wrongdoing by state actors, meaning governmental entities. Therefore, this section is not usually available to private-sector employees. However, among highly regulated industries and certain classes of government contractors, the nexus between the private employee and the regulating or contracting agency of federal or state government may be so close that the employer's deeds amount to state action. For instance, in *Skinner v. Railway Labor Executive's Association* (see Q 10:30), the U.S. Supreme Court held that FRA drug testing rules for railroad workers were subject to Fourth Amendment search and seizure limits, even though the FRA rules were enforced by privately run railroads. By contrast, private colleges and universities usually have been held not to be state actors, even when substantially supported by state funding.

Q 10:33 How much "due process of law" is enough?

When public employees are purely probationary, most states do not require that disciplinary proceedings be lengthy or elaborate. For example, in *Harrington v. U.S.,* [673 F 2d 7 (1st Cir 1982)] the federal appeals court ruled that the Federal Personnel Manual required that a disciplined or discharged probationer was entitled only to a written notice of the employing agency's conclusions and decision, not written detailed reasoning for the result, which the plaintiff-employee had demanded. In another example of probationers' limited due process rights, a Massachusetts state appellate court held in *Ruggieri v. City of Somerville,* [405 NE 2d 982 (Mass App 1980)] that the Comprehensive Employment Training Act did not provide for the right to a formal hearing.

By contrast, once a public employee has passed the probationary stage, a sort of "property right" in the position may accrue. An excellent example is tenured faculty at state universities. However, even where probationary public employees are concerned, the courts usually will not countenance arbitrary and capricious employment decisions.

Q 10:34   Does sovereign immunity affect the public employee's right to sue a government employer?

State legislatures have the right to accord sovereign immunity to state and local government agencies. During the second half of this century, however, many states have elected to abrogate sovereign immunity, that is to permit citizens to sue, at least for some causes of action. More significantly, state sovereign immunity statutes cannot affect federally created legal rights, such as the right to sue under 42 USC § 1983 (see Q 10:31). However, the U.S. Supreme Court has held that employees seeking to sue the state itself may be prohibited by the Eleventh Amendment to the U.S. Constitution. [See Quern v Jordan, 440 US 332 (1979)] Thus, while public employees enjoy constitutional rights of due process and equal protection of law with respect to their jobs, their right to sue presents complex procedural questions relating to the separation of powers between the state and federal governments.

Q 10:35   Are government employees protected by antidiscrimination laws?

Federal, state, and local government employees are covered by Title VII of the 1964 Civil Rights Act, the Equal Pay Act, the Age Discrimination in Employment Act, and the Americans with Disabilities Act. Additionally, state and municipal workers in many states and larger cities across the country are covered by state human relations acts and antidiscrimination ordinances. Consequently, most of chapter 4, Employment Discrimination, applies to public employees under these laws with equal accuracy.

Q 10:36   Are federal employees treated any differently than other workers under federal antidiscrimination laws?

When the Civil Rights Act of 1964 was enacted, Title VII excluded the federal government from its definition of employer. The statute also stated, however, that all employment decisions in the United States be discrimination-free and authorized the president to issue executive orders. In fact, a series of executive orders were issued over the years. Additionally, the U.S. Constitution arguably prohibits job discrimination (see Q 10:29), as does the Code of Federal Regulations. Yet, as late as the early 1970s, federal courts disagreed over whether or not sovereign immunity (see Q 10.34) denied federal workers a private cause of action for employment discrimination. In 1972, Congressional hearings and reports revealed under-representation of minorities and females in the federal bureaucracy, and poor administrative procedures for addressing the problem. In the 1972 amendments to the Civil Rights Act of 1964 and the Civil Service Reform Act of 1978, Congress placed the federal government under Title VII's jurisdiction and transferred enforcement jurisdiction from the Civil Service Commission to the Equal Employment Opportunity Commission (EEOC).

Q 10:37   Does the EEOC enforce the federal antidiscrimination laws in the federal sector in the same manner as in private employment?

Even after Congress extended Title VII's coverage to the federal bureaucracy and gave jurisdiction to the EEOC (see Q 10:36), the federal government continued to enjoy significant advantages over other employers covered by federal antidiscrimination laws. Enforcement also was burdened by some unique complications. On one hand, federal workers were required to initiate the administrative process within 30 days of the discriminatory employment action or lose the right to do so. Many federal workers lost legitimate discrimination claims as a consequence of this brief limitation period. On the other hand, depending on the facts and circumstances of the case, the federal worker would have been able, up to a point, to pursue parallel remedies under EEO and civil service procedures (see Q 10:38). Consequently, treatment of federal employees under federal antidiscrimination acts came under substantial criticism by civil rights advocates, federal workers and their unions, and the advocates who represented them. Congress finally reacted to this criticism in 1991.

Before November 1991, Congress was itself exempt from the very civil rights acts it has passed. But part of the Civil Rights Act of 1991 (CRA '91) extends significant protection to federal employees. Sections 301-320 of CRA '91 are entitled the Government Employment Rights Act of 1991 (GERA). GERA establishes a fair employment office for congressional employees. This office will handle discrimination complaints, initiated by congressional employees within 180 days, under a four-part procedure, consisting of

- Counseling
- Mediation
- Formal complaint and hearing before a board
- Review by the select committee on ethics

Q 10:38   How does CRA '91 alter the way federal job discrimination cases are administered?

Section 114 of CRA '91 extends from 30 days to 90 days the period for federal employees to initiate a charge of job discrimination. This is still only half the time (180 days) accorded private employees to institute discrimination complaints with the EEOC. (Private sector employees may have up to 300 days in the majority of states, referred to as "deferral states' because they offer a state law alternative.) Likewise, federal workers now have 90 days to initiate a lawsuit after termination of EEOC proceedings, instead of the mere 30 days they previously had; this is the same 90 days given private employees after they receive an EEOC "letter to sue." Since most complainants come before the EEOC without representation, and legal representation is often hard to obtain in contingent-fee job discrimination cases, 30 days could be too short a time even for a meritorious plaintiff to obtain competent legal counsel. Furthermore, a new study indicates that minority employees of the federal government are fired at three times the rate of firing for white employees of the government, perhaps suggesting the need for still more reform of the process of federal discrimination cases (see Q 10:17).

State Employees

Q 10:39 Does the Civil Rights Act of 1991 extend rights to any state employees?

Members of an elected state official's personal staff and key policy makers, previously exempt from the protections of the federal antidiscrimination acts, will now be permitted to pursue a remedy before the EEOC with limited judicial review in lieu of a full-blown right to a federal lawsuit.

Q 10:40 How do state antidiscrimination acts protect state workers?

Almost every state has enacted its own civil rights or human relations act. By and large, state and municipal employees enjoy the same rights and procedures as their private-sector counterparts. These rights and procedures vary widely from state to state. Most states have established commissions which, through work-sharing agreements and interlocking regulations, cooperate closely with the EEOC. Beyond the investigation stage, the multitude of state statutes may require conciliation efforts, administrative hearings, or recourse to state courts. The remedies and damages can range from back wages, through reinstatement, to compensatory and punitive damages, these latter remedies having become available under Title VII only with passage of the CRA '91.

Q 10:41 What is being done to make public-sector employees more efficient?

Where the buzzwords in the private sector are "employee participation programs," (see Q 14:17) in the public arena the current talk is of "enterprise compacts," a term coined by Irving and Barry Bluestone in their 1992 book, *Negotiating the Future: A Labor Perspective on American Business*. Key points of the enterprise compact, according to Barry Bluestone, are:

- Labor and management should negotiate productivity targets for each year of their collective bargaining agreement

- Quality standards should be set jointly by labor and management
- No lay-offs should be allowed
- Some sort of profit- or gains-sharing approach should be taken toward meeting or surpassing productivity targets
- The traditional management-rights clause should be replaced by cooperative language, reflecting the goals outlined above

["Joint Efforts Needed to Rectify Problems Endemic to Public Sector Workforce, Speakers Say," 32 *BNA Government Employee Relations Report* 1559, Apr 4, 1994, at 468]

In a step seemingly aimed at implementing this concept of enterprise compacts, in 1994 the U.S. Department of Veteran Affairs and five labor unions signed an agreement establishing the VA National Partnership Council, "a joint labor-management partnership designed to improve VA services." ["Veterans Affairs, Five Unions Sign National Partnership Pact," 32 *BNA Government Employee Relations Report* 1561, Apr 18, 1994, at 510]

The five unions reportedly represent 98 percent of the huge agency's 170,500 organized employees. The council has been established ostensibly in response to Executive Order 12871, which created the National Partnership Council and directs the components of the federal bureaucracy to evolve a new version of labor-management relations to achieve the objectives of the National Performance Review. The review, in turn, was aimed at reducing red tape and waste while cutting costs and enhancing bureaucratic efficiency. [Id]

According to a spokesperson for one of the five participating unions, the American Nurses Association, the partnership process offers VA nursing professionals their first chance to participate in agency decision-making. The pact aims at least in part at meeting the anticipated challenges of health care reform and dealing with outsourcing of some government services to the private sector, according to the spokesperson for the Service Employees International Union. [Id]

Chapter 11

Labor Unions

The rights conferred upon labor unions and union employees are generally derived from the authority of the National Labor Relations Act, which followed closely on the heels of the Norris-LaGuardia Act. An employer confronted with efforts to organize a union must be aware of the statutory mandates and prohibitions that apply to labor organizations. This chapter provides the background to the development of labor unions and covers various procedures and events that should be followed when a company becomes the target of a union organizing drive. It also covers collective bargaining and employment practices, deals with the effects of bankruptcies, mergers, and acquisitions on labor contracts, and discusses the numerous bills now pending before Congress which aim at amending the NLRA. ["Much Labor Law Reform Debate Expected in 1994," 1993 *BNA Labor Relations Reporter*, 144 LRR 495-97, Dec 20, 1993]

Background

Q 11:1   What is a labor union?

A labor union is an organization (which may be incorporated but usually is not) formed under the authority of the federal labor laws (notably the National Labor Relations Act (NLRA) or the Railway Labor Act for railroads and airlines) for the purpose of representing eligible and interested employees when negotiating the terms and conditions of their employment. The largest combination of labor unions in the United States is the American Federation of Labor-Congress of Industrial Unions (AFL-CIO).

Q 11:2   Do employees have the right to belong to a labor union?

Yes. The NLRA (amended by the Taft-Hartley Act in 1947) gives employees the right to join a labor union and to authorize that union to negotiate with the employer on their behalf. Note, however, that the NLRA also affords employees the right to refrain from joining and participating in a labor union. This right has been strengthened in states that have passed right-to-work laws pursuant to a provision in the Taft-Hartley Act.

Q 11:3   What is the AFL-CIO?

The AFL was founded in 1879 as a confederation of trade unions, each of which focused on the representation of a particular craft. The CIO has been in existence since 1938 and focused on organizing rank-and-file employees in particular industries (such as steel, rubber, and glass). The AFL and CIO rivaled each other for employee loyalty. Eventually, however, they united to form what is probably the most powerful confederation of organized labor in history.

Q 11:4   Are all unions members of the AFL-CIO?

Most major unions are members. The Teamsters left the AFL-CIO in the 1950s but rejoined in 1987. However, there are some small, independent unions, some limited to the employees of only one company or one plant. Such independents are legal under federal law, provided they are not controlled by their employer companies.

Q 11:5   Is labor unionism on the decline in the United States?

Union membership has steadily declined from a peak of 35 percent of the U.S. workforce in the 1950s to less than 20 percent in the early 1990s. However, there has been growth in union affiliation among public employees (e.g., police and teachers), many of whom were not allowed to unionize until about 20 years ago. Union leaders seemed optimistic about a resurgence in membership stemming from the growing dissatisfaction among white-collar workers (both clerical and professional) in the service and information sectors of the economy. Thus far, however, union success in these sectors has been very limited.

In fact, union membership dropped to just 16.1 percent of the U.S. workforce in 1990, accounting for 16.74 million members, a decline of 1.3 percent from the year before, according to the Bureau of Labor Statistics. Work stoppages in 1990 were also almost a record low, according to the Bureau. "Stoppages" are defined as including both strikes and lockouts, and the Bureau tracks incidents of either that involve at least 1,000 workers. There were only 45 stoppages in 1990, affecting a total of 202,000 workers; the only year the figure was lower was 1988. In 1989 51 major work stoppages involved some 452,000 workers, with close to three times the lost work days (17 million versus 6.6 million). The longest strike of 1990 involved the International Longshoremen's Association against companies employing about 1,600 tugboat and barge workers in the Port of New York, which ran for more than a year. [See Cynthia L Gramm, "Empirical Evidence on Political Arguments Relating to Replacement Worker Legislation," *Labor Law Journal*, August 1991, at 491-496]

Meanwhile, a report released by the Economic Policy Institute, written by Economics Professor Thomas Karier of Eastern Washington University, casts some doubt on the common assumption that union wages and work rules reduce the competitiveness of U.S. companies. Professor Karier found higher rates of unionization in the three top competitors to the United States: Japan, Germany, and Canada, which together account for 65 percent of the U.S. trade deficit. The report concludes that higher wages and higher rates of unionization are usually accompanied by higher levels of capital investment, and that all three are characteristic of countries with increasing productivity and improving competitiveness.

Q 11:6 How well did organized labor perform on the organizing front during the past decade?

Organized labor did not fare well during the 1980s, according to an April 1990 article in Cornell University's Industrial and Labor Relations Review by Professors Gary N. Chaison and Deleep G. Dhavole. The professors reported that since 1982, union certification elections in the private sector have yielded annual average net increases in union membership of only 43,000 employees per year. They comment that this number is "an almost inconsequential addition to the stock of 10.7 to 12 million union members in the private sector," and conclude that their study "confirms that the decline in union organizing is severe." They suggest that this decline "should give a new sense of urgency to ongoing debates over the barriers to union organizing, the effectiveness of the National Labor Relations Board (NLRB) in protecting employee free choice, and the future directions of a substantially smaller labor movement."

However, the unions' success rate did improve somewhat in 1989. Unions reportedly won nearly half of their representation elections as the decade came to a close. According to NLRB statistics, the unions' success rate was 45.9 percent in 1985, climbing to 48.6 percent in 1988 and 49.8 percent in 1989. The absolute number of representation elections also increased, to 3,506 in 1988 and to 3,644 in 1989.

These numbers can be misleading, however. The 1989 increase was shored up by a 71.8 percent rate of victory for local, independent unions in 195 elections. Unions successfully resisted only 31.2 percent of decertification efforts in 1989. These statistics hardly herald a major rebound by "big labor" in the 1990s. [See "Union Election Win Rates Fell in First Half of Year," 1991 BNA Daily Labor Report 200, Oct 16, 1991, at a15]

Union Organizing and Employer Response

Q 11:7   Are there any union organizing tactics that seem to be particularly effective?

During the 1980s, a movement began within organized labor that was little noticed or remarked upon by the news media or the general public. The effect of this movement was that by 1993, an estimated 500,000 workers who had once eschewed labor unions per se had joined employee associations sponsored by those very labor organizations. One such association that has garnered some media attention is 9 to 5, The National Association of Working Women, based in Milwaukee and boasting about 15,000 members nationwide. The name 9 to 5 inspired a popular movie of the same name, which drew attention to sexual harassment in the workplace. The group 9 to 5, however, is one of many employee associations. The far West has its Montana Family Union and the California Immigrant Workers Association (1,400 and 6,000 members, respectively), while Cincinnati is home to the National Association of American Workers (1,700 members at last published count). In New York, where the decades-long migration of the garment industry to offshore locations has eroded the International Ladies Garment Workers Union (ILGWU), Associate ILGWU Members (AIM) has reclaimed about 2,500 to the union fold, sort of.

Employee associations are not labor unions, although almost all are affiliated with the AFL-CIO or some subsidiary union, such as the ILGWU or the Service Employees International Union. Associations tend to differ from traditional unions by the association's goals and members. First and foremost, the goal of organized labor has been higher wages. Writing about "The Philosophy of Trade Unionism" 90 years ago, one of its most famous leaders, John Mitchell, laid it out this way:

> In its fundamental principle, trade unionism is plain and clear and simple. Trade unionism starts from the recognition of the fact that under normal conditions the individual, unorganized workman cannot bargain advantageously with the employer for the sale of his labor. [John Mitchell, *Organized Labor* 2 (1903)]

Certainly, anyone who has ever read a collective bargaining agreement knows that the typical labor contract covers many terms and conditions of employment. Experienced labor negotiators also know that the bottom line, wage rates, remains the main consideration and the most frequent cause of work stoppages. In recent years, issues closely related to that bottom-line concern, such as the cost of group health insurance and who will pay for it (see chapter 8), have, with increased frequency, taken center stage along with fundamental wage issues. The issue is not one of exclusivity but of emphasis. Employee associations tend to emphasize issues historically viewed by unions as peripheral to their main mission.

Focusing on issues that were, and often still are, viewed as of secondary concern to traditional labor unions, employee associations have attracted a nontraditional membership. Perhaps the genesis of such associations can be found in a category of employees who are excluded from the ranks of organized labor by law—front line managers: "The term 'employee' . . . shall not include any individual employed as . . . a supervisor." [29 USC § 152(3)] Front line supervisors, often enjoying less job security than the unionized workers they supervise, formed organizations outside the protection of the National Labor Relations Act, such as the Federal Managers Association, a long-established group for first-level supervisors in the U.S. government. "[W]orker associations appeal to growing segments of the workforce, often women and immigrants in low-wage jobs, and to nontraditional members, such as supervisors and workers in nonunion shops." [Milbank, "Labor Broadens Its Appeal by Setting Up Associations to Lobby and Offer Services," *The Wall Street Journal*, Jan 13, 1992, at B1]

Some union leaders decry employee associations as a dilution of the labor movement, just as they criticize employee cooperation programs (see Qs 11:107–11:110). Others see these associations as the means of revitalizing unions and overcoming their becalmed condition. A quarter century ago, Harvard economist John Kenneth Galbraith had already recognized that, "modern technology opens the way for a massive shift from workers who are within the reach of unions to those who are not." [JK Galbraith, *The New Industrial State* at 267 (1967)] In the words of one member of the National Association of American Workers, who actually voted to decertify the union where she worked, "All unions don't operate the way I'd like them to, but employees need an organization so they have some degree of muscle . . . . I don't have any illusions about what NAWA can do for me, but it's my way of standing up and being counted." [Milbank, supra]

Q 11:8 Are there any current trends that may stimulate greater union organizing activity and enhance unions' prospects for success in that activity?

U.S. Secretary of Labor Robert Reich, referred to by organized labor as "the perfect choice" for that position in the Clinton administration, has called the current upswing in the American economy a "jobless recovery," contending that structural changes in U.S. business and industry have eliminated many jobs forever. [Gordon, "White House's $37.6 Billion Labor Budget Proposal Stresses Job Training," Associated Press, Apr 7, 1993; see, generally, Reich, *The Work of Nations* (1991); (see also chapter 14)]

Whether Reich had it in mind, reengineering is a new concept that has caught the attention of the news media recently and seems to be catching on with top management in America's manufacturing sector and threatens to eliminate many jobs permanently.

Reengineering embraces such techniques as work teams, training employees in multiple skills so that they can perform more than one job. . . . In one sense, it is the application of just-in-time inventory controls to all phases of a company's operations. . . . The bad news comes in the dislocation of all those people whose current jobs will disappear. [Ehrbar, "Re-Engineering Gives Firms New Efficiency, Workers the Pink Slip," *The Wall Street Journal*, Apr 16, 1993, at A1]

According to Harvard labor economist Richard Freeman, the category facing the biggest threat "is middle-aged men without college degrees who had union jobs and were earning more than a competitive wage." Middle managers are also being hit hard by reengineering efficiencies, as are white-and pink-collar clerical workers in such industries as banking and financial services, which were once thought to be more or less immune to extensive union organizing.

Combine this apparent restructuring of American industry with Secretary Reich's stated intent to amend the National Labor Relations Act to enhance organized labor's ability to wage successful organization and economic strikes, and a resurgence of labor organizing efforts may very well be seen, as well as an increasing success rate on the unions' part. (See, "Striker Replacement Bill Faces Tough Battle in Senate," 1993 *BNA Daily Labor Report* 71, Apr 15, 1993, at 1; "Workplace Fairness Bill Benefits US, Reich Says," 1993 *BNA Daily Labor Report* 60, Mar 31, 1993, at 1; Karr, "Union Leaders See Their First Chance in Years for Substantial Legislative Gains," *The Wall Street Journal*, Nov 5, 1992, at A4)

A fundamental reason may exist for a resurgence of unionism, a reason which could conceivably make sense to thoughtful business owners and managers. A controversial book published late in 1994 argues that class structure in America during the last few decades has been driven increasingly by IQ levels. Those with lower IQs have lost income as well paying but relatively simplistic, repetitive manufacturing jobs have disappeared, only to be replaced by lower-paying service jobs. In other words, well-compensated assembly line workers, whose jobs have been re-engineered away in the names of technology and competitiveness, find themselves slinging french fries or waiting tables for wages at or near the statutory minimum. These are often the souls who were, or historically would have been, represented by organized labor. While these people struggle to make a living, the class called the "cognitive elite" is enjoying genuine affluence. [Richard J. Herrnstein and Charles Murray, *The Bell Curve: Intelligence and Class Structure in American Life* 515-16 (Free Press 1994)]

But why should this "cognitive elite," whose CEOs for instance are enjoying previously unimagined salaries and bonuses (see Robert Reich, *The Work of Nations: Preparing Ourselves for 21st Century Capitalism* 204-05 (Knopf 1991)), care about "the other half"? And certainly one might wonder why these "top dogs" should embrace organized labor. To appreciate why they might, one can recall economist John Kenneth Galbraith's argument of a quarter century ago, when unionism was near its zenith, that organized labor was, together with Big Business and Big Government, a force for stability and prosperity. [JK Galbraith, *The New Industrial State* (1969)] Then one might ask whether it was a mere coincidence that, as unionism declined and suffered drastic membership losses during the ensuing 25 years, this period also saw the ever-increasing intrusion of government into the workplace.

When fully a third of all workers were represented by unions, most employment disputes were handled by grievance and arbitration under a procedure outlined in a collective bargaining agreement. Labor arbitration was (and still is, where it hangs on) sufficiently flexible to deal with tough evidentiary questions such as an employee's refusal to take an employer-mandated lie detector test. Arbitrators could hear medical testimony and determine whether a worker had been improperly denied a promotion or job transfer due to an alleged disability. (See Dennis R. Nolan, *Labor Arbitration Law and Practice in a Nutshell* 512-14 (West 1979)) By contrast today, both polygraph exams and handicap discrimination are the subjects of complex legislation. (See chapter 3 for a comprehensive discussion of the federal Polygraph Protection Act and chapter 4 for extensive coverage of the Americans with Disabilities Act.)

Until 1991, some federal discrimination laws at least mirrored the labor arbitrator's approach to an unjust firing, both limiting damages to reinstatement with back pay (See Nolan, supra, at 182-91). But the 1991 Civil Right's Act (Q 1:8) changed all that; today plaintiffs in Title VII and ADA cases can claim compensatory and punitive damages, just like any other tort claimants; they can also get reasonable attorneys' fees, something even plaintiffs in malpractice, product liability and personal injury cases usually cannot.

In a landmark decision, the U.S. Supreme Court ruled that an employee who knowingly and voluntarily agreed to arbitrate all employment disputes, must submit his age discrimination in employment case to binding arbitration, prior precedents to the contrary notwithstanding. [Gilmer v Interstate, 111 S Ct 1647 (1990)] (See Qs 4:153, 11:56, 13:2, 15:3.)

A decrease in the hostility to organized labor may be expected, enhancing organized labor's prospects for a resurgence near the turn of the century. Regardless of future prospects, the realities of the present for organized labor are that (1) the perennially proposed striker replacement bill was struck down on July 13, 1994, when Senate Democrats failed to get the 60 votes needed to end a GOP filibuster on the measure, (2) the U.S. Supreme Court ruled in a 5-4 decision that nurses functioning as "working foremen" on hospital floors were supervisors under the NLRA and therefore could not be members of bargaining units, and (3) the Republican party took control of both houses of Congress in the November 1994 elections. ["Year in Review: Board Appointments, Court Rulings Brought Changes in Labor Field in '94," 1995 *BNA Daily Labor Report* 17, Jan 26, 1995, at d17]

Q 11:9   Assuming that organized labor enjoys enhanced opportunities to organize American workers during the remainder of the 1990s, will labor unions be able to seize the perceived opportunities?

Despite the early success of the relatively new notion of employee associations affiliated with labor unions (Q 11:7), the threat to American workers posed by re-engineering and the Clinton administration's promise of workplace fairness legislation (Q 11:8), there are those who doubt organized labor's ability to seize the opportunities these trends appear to present. In fact, some labor consultants and union officials believe organized labor may continue to be marginalized and its membership continue to decrease. In the words of one, "If tomorrow, workers had the right to organize and really had a free choice, you'd see some more unionization. . . . But unions still have to have a strategy that will make employees want to join." [1993 *BNA Daily Labor Report* 38, Mar 1, 1993, at 1]

Not long ago, two leading labor scholars, writing in a prestigious publication, suggested the following factors as components of a union recovery formula:

1. Formation of coalitions between organized labor and other groups in American society which share the same or similar concerns, such as corporate governance, the American standard of living, income inequities, and human resource development and utilization;

2. Greater political activism;

3. New forms of employee representation (Q 11:7);

4. Increased centralization and improved management of unions; and

5. Perhaps most important, the emergence of new leaders who are unafraid to criticize openly and consistently the status quo and propose a clear agenda for the future.

Absent these components, these two commentators state:

> [L]abor will neither be ready to react appropriately to a changed environment, if and when it may emerge, nor to play any significant role in spawning its emergence. Instead, workers and their unions will continue to be buffeted by changing economic and social events. As such, they can only play a reactive, increasingly invisible role.

> [Kochan and Wever, "American Unions and the Future of Worker Representation," The State of the Unions, Industrial Relations Research Association (1992); see also, "Union Recovery Formula," *BNA Collective Bargaining Negotiations and Contracts*, Jan 9, 1992, at 4]

While work stoppage remains a union weapon, strikes stayed at a low level in 1993, the most recent complete year for which statistics are available. The U.S. Department of Labor's Bureau of Labor Statistics reported that in that year only 35 strikes involved 1,000 or more employees across the nation, as compared with 187 in 1980 and 381 in 1970. ["Labor Unions Turn More Often to Strategies Other Than Strikes," 1994 *BNA Daily Labor Report* 204, Oct 25, 1994, at d19] According to the AFL-CIO's Director of Organizing and Special Projects Joseph Uehlein, "The strike is still a weapon. It's not dead, but it has to be considered as part of a wide array of weapons."

Adds Richard Trumka, president of the militant United Mine Workers of America, which has suffered major fines for violating strike injunctions in recent years (Q 11:62), "We're not negotiating with ma and pa companies anymore. We can't just strike one facility or even a group of plants in one country" and expect to win against a multinational corporation. [Id] Instead, unions are trying to use so-called "comprehensive campaigns." Such campaigns, or limited variations of the concept, have been used by unions in recent years against the Walt Disney World Dolphin Hotel, Hertz Corp., British-owned Peabody Coal, and the Ravenswood Aluminum Corp., to name a few. [Id]

The Peabody Coal action was by Trumka's coal miners, whose union has not only been historically among the most militant, but also among the leaders in organized labor for more than a century now. (See John Mitchell, *Organized Labor: Its Problems, Purposes and Ideals and the Present and Future American Wage Earners* (1903)) The campaign grew out a protracted collective bargaining dispute between the UMWA and the Bituminous Coal Operators Association in 1993. Elements of the campaign included "in-plant" actions and a proxy battle involving Hanson PLC, Peabody's British parent, plus an alliance between the union and local religious leaders. Trumka contends that the pressure brought to bear by these broad-spectrum activities helped end a bitter seven-month work stoppage and win a satisfactory settlement. ["Labor Unions Turn More Often to Strategies Other Than Strikes," supra]

Trumka also cites the Ravenswood Aluminum Corp. as the target of a successful UMWA comprehensive campaign. According to Charles Perry, a professor of industrial relations at the University of Pennsylvania's Wharton School, the prospect of the long and expensive litigation of an unfair labor practice charge pending before the National Labor Relations Board, was one of the key pressure points that led the company to give Trumka's miners "an apparent clear victory." [Id]

Additionally, preliminary data for 1994 indicates that the trend toward fewer major strikes may have halted, and even reversed, itself during that year. Eleven months' worth of data reflected 45 strikes and lockouts involving 186,000 employees. Major stoppages included a 24-day walkout by some 24,000 Teamsters from major trucking concerns and a stoppage by 14,000 auto workers at Caterpillar Inc. ["Year in Review: Board Appointments, Court Rulings Brought Changes in Labor Field in '94," 1995 BNA Daily Labor Report 17, Jan 26, 1995, at d17]

But, as management consultant John Sheridan points out, unions must still make their main gains through one-on-one vote getting [Id], a traditional process mandated by the National Labor Relations Act and which has been frustrated by management and management consultants such as Sheridan with substantial success in recent years (Qs 11.27–11.35).

Q 11:10   What is the Dunlop Commission and what does it portend for organized labor?

Formed early in the Clinton administration, this study group's formal name is the Commission on the Future of Worker-Management Relations. Headed by Assistant Secretary of Labor John Dunlop, the body consists of nine experts appointed to review the nation's labor laws. The commission has been asked to submit a report of its findings to the secretary of labor. ["Workplace Cooperation Commission Reflects Organized Labor's Views," 54 *Apparel Industry Magazine* 10, October 1993, at 34]

Hearings continued into 1994 with a range of labor and management advocates expressing their varied views. Among the pro-labor people appearing before the commission was Professor Emeritus Charles J. Morris of Southern Methodist University, best known as the main author of the American Bar Association's two-volume Developing Labor Law, perhaps the leading treatise on the National Labor Relations Act. Morris contended in a lengthy statement to the commissioners in January 1994:

> It is a truism that the United States does not have a coherent labor relations system. We have a patchwork of employer-employee practices that contain scattered elements of a system, or perhaps even several systems. Although we can boast of some of the most advanced protective employment laws of any country in the world, our laws relating to employee representation and employee participation in determining conditions of employment are the most complex and legalistic of any in the industrial democracies. And we are certainly the most litigious in the application and enforcement of our labor and employment laws. Considering the way in which the NLRA and its enforcement agency, the NLRB, have functioned, it is little wonder that approximately 88 percent of the employees in the private sector have no organized means with which to share decision-making about conditions of their employment. Such an institutional void is not a healthy state of affairs, considering the need for an efficient work environment in today's sophisticated world-market economy."
>
> [Charles J. Morris, "In Search of a National Labor Policy," Statement to the Dunlop Commission, January 1994, at 1]

"Because Reich and commission members, who include three former labor secretaries, favor collective bargaining with unions, it is likely they will advocate legislative and regulatory changes to expand union influence." ["Workplace Cooperation Commission Reflects Organized Labor's Views," *54 Apparel Industry Magazine* 10, October 1993, at 34] The commissioners seem likely to share Morris's opinion that fostering workplace cooperation programs in the wake of the

NLRB's *Electromation* decision (Qs 11:8, 11:108, 11:109, 11:111, 14:17, 15:15) does not require amendment of provisions of the NLRA which outlaw company-created and company-controlled labor organizations.

Nonetheless, while the commission continued to contemplate the testimony of Morris and others (see, e.g., "Panel Told Silicon Valley Experience Supports Change in Workplace Relations," 1994 *BNA Daily Labor Report* 18, Jan 28, 1994, at D17; "Workplace Participation Improves Productivity But Cannot Be Legislated, Speakers Tell Panel," 1994 *BNA Daily Labor Report* 51, Mar 17, 1994, at D18; "Dunlop Panel Urged To Consider Special Needs of Working Women," 1994 *BNA Daily Labor Report* 66, Apr 7, 1994, at d10), congressional proponents of amending or repealing provisions of the NLRA to overcome any impediment to workplace cooperation programs posed by the labor board's *Electromation* decision submitted bills to accomplish that goal in 1994. (See, e.g., HR 1529, Teamwork for Employees and Management Act; HR 1341, a bill which would repeal the right of unions to represent all the employees in a bargaining unit, whether or not they have joined the union)

The Dunlop Report was issued in January 1995. Its relative merits may be judged from the fact that neither business nor labor embraced it wholeheartedly. "In a typical business reaction the U.S. Chamber of Commerce says it supports only three of the 23 recommendations." [William H Miller, "Dunlop Report Won't Go Far," *Industry Week*, Jan 23, 1995, at 77] And Teamster President Ron Carey was quoted as saying, "The Dunlop Commission turned out to be better at identifying problems than at recommending real solutions." [Philip Dine, "Neither Labor Nor Management Raves Over New Workplace Report," *St. Louis Post-Dispatch*, Jan 11, 1995, at 1C]

Chairman Howard Knicely of the Labor Policy Association, which includes top human resource experts from 225 big corporations, criticized the report's recommendations aimed at amending the National Labor Relations Act to enhance union organizing opportunities. "By focusing its recommendations on strengthening union organizing, we feel the final report represents a lost opportunity," he stated. [Id] Organized labor for its part focused on the commission's endorsement of workplace cooperation committees, arguing that adoption of its recommendations on employee participation programs would in the words of Steelworkers President George Becker "turn back the labor law clock 60 years, suggesting that the boss can decide who speaks for workers on workplace committees." [Id]

With the GOP now in charge of both houses of the Congress and President Clinton seeking cooperation with Congress plus the fact that Labor Secretary Robert Reich has long been a vocal proponent of workplace cooperation programs, the likelihood is that two central notions contained in the Dunlop Report will be enacted into law in the not-too-distant future. They are the commission's strong endorsement of alternative dispute resolution and amending the NLRA to eliminate the problems posed by the *Electromation* decision, thus boosting workplace participation and cooperation programs. According to Jerry Hunter, a former NLRB general counsel and now a consultant:

> Those are the two measures that I think would have a chance of passing in this Congress. Those are excellent ideas. I think in the employment area that litigation has just exploded so much that it is hurting the competitiveness of business in this country. And I firmly believe that we need to encourage more employee participation in the workplace. [Id]

With all the talk today of the so-called "virtual corporation," the time may fast be coming when employers will want to create the "virtual union." This term is intended here to suggest a combination of workplace cooperation committees combined with an effective ADR program, thereby providing most of what organized labor has to offer employees, while at the same time taking advantage of the opportunity posed by the U.S. Supreme Court's decision in *Gilmer v. Interstate*, [111 S Ct 1647 (1990)] to include binding ADR in the employment relation, thereby cutting off access to the 'money pit' of courtroom litigation.

The "virtual union" is a window of opportunity for American business. If ignored, then there exists the very real possibility that organized labor will leap into the breach, and we will witness a resurgence of union organizing successes, which combined with burgeoning employment litigation, will present business with the worst of all possible worlds (Q 11:9).

Q 11:11   Why does a labor union conduct an organizing drive at a company?

There are several reasons a labor union might organize the employees of a particular company. First, the company may be particularly large and visible, with many employees. Second, the company may be involved in a heavily organized industry in which the employees traditionally have been represented by a particular union (for example, steel, automobile, and coal mining). Third, the company may have a large percentage of dissatisfied employees, which makes it more susceptible to unionization.

Q 11:12   How can a company avoid being unionized?

One of the best ways to avoid becoming unionized is to provide employees with some or all of the things that a union can provide them. Many research studies have shown that job security and compensation are the two main concerns of most employees. Therefore, many companies provide nonunion employees with competitive compensation packages and a workplace due-process program that provides them with a sense of job security. Open communications, fair and evenhanded treatment, and predictable behavior by the employer all help to increase employee security. Secure, well-paid employees should have no reason to pay union dues to put a union between themselves and their companies.

Q 11:13   Is an employee stock ownership plan (ESOP) an effective union-avoidance tool?

Private-sector unionization peaked at approximately 35 percent of wage earners in the 1950s, when American manufacturing likewise reached its zenith. By 1990, only about 17 percent of the private-sector workforce was unionized. While unionism was riding high in 1958, Louis Kelso published *The Capitalist Manifesto* [NY: Random House] which laid out the political economics underlying employee stock ownership plans (ESOPs). (See also, Louis O. and Patricia Hetter Kelso, *Democracy and Economic Power: Extending the ESOP Revolution* (New York: Ballinger 1986); Robert B Reich, *The Work of Nations* (New York: Knopf 1991)) Then, beginning in 1973 under the leadership of Senator Russell Long, Congress passed some 20 pieces of legislation aimed at facilitating establishment of ESOPs. ESOPs have increased from a handful 30 years ago to thousands today, as unionism has languished.

Is this apparently inverse relationship between unionization and employee ownership a mere coincidence? The labor movement's decline has many causes, and recent reports indicate ESOPs are among them. (See, e.g., Blasi and Kruse, *The New Owners* (New York: Harper Business 1991) and "Strategic Problems and Tactical Promise: Unions and Employee Ownership," *Labor Law Journal*, August 1991, 498-507)

Many people associate ESOPs historically with union buyouts of failing firms. Widely publicized examples, such as Weirton Steel and Rath Packing, have reinforced this view. Yet a 1985 General Accounting Office survey found that only 4 percent of all ESOPs were set up to bail out floundering companies. [Malon Wilkus, "Union Considerations in Employee Buyouts," *Labor Law Journal*, August 1991, 508-514] Furthermore, two other 1980s studies showed that 60-70 percent of ESOPs excluded unionized employees from participating. [Hammer & Stern, "A Yo-Yo Model of Cooperation: Union Participation in Management at the Rath Packing Company," 30 *Industrial and Labor Relations Journal* 3, 337–349; Stern, "Participation by Representation: Workers on Boards of Directors in the US and Abroad," 15 *Work and Occupations* 4, 1988, 396–422] A reasonable conclusion can be drawn that ESOPs are mainly used as employee incentives: an employee who feels like an owner or future owner of the firm might prefer cooperation in the boardroom to confrontation across the collective bargaining table.

Q 11:14 What should a company do if it becomes the target of a union organizing drive?

First, a company should not: interrogate employees about their interest in the union or union activities; discharge or otherwise punish employees who are trying to organize for the union; make threats or promises to employees; or conduct surveillance of employees at organizing meetings or other union activities. A company should, however, conduct a meeting of supervisors and managers to explain what actions to avoid, and should try to determine the grievances or problems that led employees to seek a union's help or that may lead employees to join the union. It should also plan a management campaign to diffuse the organizing drive, preferably before an election petition has been filed with the National Labor Relations Board.

Q 11:15 How does a union organize a company's employees?

Disgruntled employees will often approach the labor union with an invitation to organize them and their co-workers. The union will then ask these employees to be inside organizers. Additionally, the union may call organizing meetings, or a business agent may visit the job site to distribute union authorization cards and other union literature.

Organized labor recently revealed that:

> In analyzing the reasons for winning or losing an election, generally we can track the outcome back to the early days of the campaign. Although organizers sometimes claim "we lost the election in the last two days," this is rarely the case. Since we know that companies will unleash major issues in the last days or weeks of the campaign . . . it is incumbent upon the organizers to build a foundation that will withstand this inevitable assault. This means building a strong committee, made up of a representative group of key leaders, who can prepare their co-workers for the management campaign.

> [*The Blitz, A Manual for Organizers on How to Run Fast-paced Pre-petition Campaigns*, AFL-CIO]

The book quoted above is published by the AFL-CIO as a handbook on a relatively new union organizing technique known as the "blitz." Credit for development of the blitz technique is given to organizer Richard Bensinger of the Amalgamated Clothing and Textile Workers Union. ["Labor's Newest Strategy for Winning Elections," I *Labor Relations Ink* 4, February 1993, at 3] Although the handbook doesn't contain anything truly revolutionary, it is described as a blueprint for doing what unions have always done during organizing drives, but doing it faster and more efficiently.

Blitz campaigns are divided into two phases. The first phase is the preparation phase, which involves building a list of employees and recruiting volunteers to help the organization effort. This phase can take weeks or months. Regardless of the time involved, the key to success is believed to be absolute secrecy. Management should keep in mind that the unions themselves have concluded that when the corporate hierarchy becomes aware of this phase of the organization effort, the blitz is probably doomed to failure. The union in this phase will be using a small but ever-growing committee to build a list of eligible voters.

The next phase is the action phase. This, too, is divided into steps; the first consists of training as many volunteers as available to make house calls on all eligible voters. These house calls are planned to be made within a two- to three-day period. Consequently, the volunteer committee may be supplemented and supported by paid workers, generally union members from other corporations, within the general geographic area, or union staffers. Phase two ideally occurs during a "blitz week." Monday and Tuesday of a typical week are devoted to training the house callers; note that during an organizing drive or election campaign, union representatives, but not employer representatives, are permitted by the NLRA to make house calls (see Q 11:21 for additional discussion of the employer's right to communicate with its employees). Wednesday, Thursday, and Friday are usually devoted to house calls. The goal is to make contact with at least 60 percent of all eligible voters. By the following Monday, a representation petition will have been filed with the NLRB (Q 11:27). In a well-executed blitz, management will not know the drive is underway until the first day of home visits, at the earliest.

Labor claims its win rate using the blitz has increased from 45 percent to 65 percent or better.

Q 11:16 What is the significance of President Clinton's executive order regarding striker replacements?

For many years organized labor has lobbied hard for a new law that would forbid employers to replace unionized employees permanently while they were engaged in an economic strike (i.e., a work stoppage aimed at obtaining better wages, fringe benefits, or working conditions.) The Clinton Administration entered office with an avowed purpose of providing labor with this wish. However, the

Republican's capture of both houses of the Congress in November 1994 made the enactment of such a law a virtual impossibility in the foreseeable future. Consequently, the president made an "end run" around the Congress by signing an executive order which will deny government contracts to private companies which replace their striking workers.

Signed on March 8, 1995, the executive order prohibits federal contractors from replacing striking workers on pain of having their contracts canceled or of being denied new contractual opportunities with Uncle Sam. (See Qs 9:38–9:47 for an explanation of debarment.) The National Labor Relations Act already allows for the reinstatement of workers who join a picket line in protest of unfair labor practices by the employer. But since the U.S. Supreme Court ruled on the question in the 1940s, the rule has been that strikers seeking only to improve their economic conditions were subject to being permanently replaced. While labor enjoyed the allegiance of one American worker in every three during the 1950s and 1960s, permanent replacement workers were the exception, not the rule.

However, in 1981 one of President Reagan's first official acts was to replace the government's striking air traffic controllers permanently. Many private enterprises took their lead from this presidential action throughout the 1980s and into the 1990s, leading organized labor to make the striker replacement bill a top priority. Naturally, Clinton's executive order was welcomed by the AFL-CIO, when announced by Vice President Albert Gore. [Uchitelle, "Gore Says Clinton Will Move to Help Striking Workers," *The New York Times*, Feb 21, 1995, at A1, A16]

Of course, the order was denounced by the GOP. However, Senate Republicans fell one vote short of the two-thirds majority needed to repeal an executive order. [Stan Crock, "The Presidency: Clinton May Be Playing a Risky Game of Solitaire," *BusinessWeek*, Mar 27, 1995, at 41] Therefore, at least for the time being, the tens of thousands of corporations doing business with the federal government must refrain from permanently replacing employees who take to the picket lines (although these strikers may be temporarily replaced while the strike is active) or risk loss of their business with Uncle Sam.

Q 11:17   What is an executive order, such as President Clinton's striker replacement edict?

Executive orders are implicitly permitted by the U.S. Constitution, which places the president in charge of the executive branch of the federal government. While not expressly permitted by the Constitution, executive fiats have been approved by the Supreme Court on the legal theory that the president could not do his job without such authority. However, such orders have been described as being in "the twilight zone where the executive and legislative branches share power . . ." [Stan Crock, "The Presidency: Clinton May Be Playing a Risky Game of Solitaire," *BusinessWeek*, Mar 27, 1995, at 41]

George Washington was the first to use an executive order to overrule the will of a recalcitrant Congress in 1793, when he declared that America would remain officially neutral in a war between England and France. Lincoln's 1863 Emancipation Proclamation also was an executive order, as was Franklin Roosevelt's 1942 internment of Japanese-Americans, an action now denounced but at the time approved by the U.S. Supreme Court. [Id]

In 1952 with the Korean War in full fury and organized labor threatening to halt U.S. steel production, Harry Truman used an executive order to seize major steel mills, but the high court ruled against the attempt. [Id; see Youngstown Sheet and Tube Co v Sawyer, 343 US 579 (1952)]

Perhaps the best known executive order still in effect is President John Kennedy's Executive Order 11246, which predated the 1964 Civil Rights Act by more than a year in forbidding job discrimination by federal contractors (Qs 9:10, 9:11). President Carter later supplemented Kennedy's long-standing order with one of his own, requiring federal contractors to employ prescribed percentages of minority workers to qualify for Uncle Sam's patronage, once again invoking Article II of the Constitution, which says the president "shall take Care that the Laws be faithfully executed."

Clinton's March 1995 order is more in the tradition of Kennedy's famous and still effective executive decree, and, having survived by one vote the Senate's attempt to repeal it, is unlikely to cause a constitutional crisis. Nonetheless, such executive orders continue to trouble constitutional scholars who believe that the three branches of the federal government should respect the separation of powers concept. [See Crock, supra]

Q 11:18 Can a union representative enter company premises?

The general rule is that a union organizer who is not an employee of the company cannot enter company premises, but the National Labor Relations Board (NLRB) has carved out some exceptions. For example, if the site is remote or if safety considerations make it difficult or impossible for the union to contact the employees any-where but on the job site, an organizer may enter company premises. At times, union organizers have been permitted to enter a lumber camp or to board a ship, but this right is carefully circumscribed by the NLRB, and especially the board appointed by Ronald Reagan. The NLRB has also permitted union organizers to distribute literature in company parking lots when street traffic outside the company's gates would endanger the organizers.

In a 1992 decision involving an organizing drive by the United Food and Commercial Workers, the U.S. Supreme Court upheld the right of a Connecticut company to keep union organizers from pass-ing out leaflets and placing fliers on windshields of cars at a parking lot it owned. By a 6 to 3 vote, the Court found that the NLRB erred in granting union organizers the right to trespass on private property to get their message to employees. The case involved a department store owned by Lechmere Inc. located in a shopping mall in New-ington, Connecticut.

In one of his first opinions since joining the high court, Justice Clarence Thomas said that federal labor law, by its plain terms, confers rights only on employees, not on unions or organizers. Therefore, as a rule, an employer cannot be forced to allow distribu-tion of literature by labor organizers on its property. "Access to employees, not success in winning them over, is the critical issue—although success, or lack thereof, may be relevant in determining whether reasonable access exists," he wrote. [Lechmere, Inc v NLRB, 1992 BNA Daily Labor Report 18, Jan 28, 1992 at A-A; (see also James O Castegnera & Thomas J Bender, Jr, "Justice Thomas and NLRB Refine Unions' Rights to Organize and Picket," Employment Law Update (Philadelphia: Saul, Ewing, Remick & Saul) April 1992 at 1)

Q 11:19   Can employees engage in organizing efforts and hand out literature on company property?

Yes. Employees are permitted to discuss unionism and to solicit their co-workers, provided that these activities are done before and after their shifts or during lunch and break times; employees are not entitled to engage in these activities when they should be working. Also, it may be permissible for an employee to give co-workers union flyers or authorization cards in a lunchroom or a locker room, or in the parking lot. However, they do not have the right to distribute literature on the work floor where the paper could create a hazard.

Q 11:20   How can an employer ensure that employees do not abuse their rights to discuss the union and to solicit one another at the workplace?

An employer should adopt a "no-solicitation rule." A valid, legal no-solicitation rule might read as follows:

> Persons not employed by this company will not be permitted to solicit on behalf of any cause or organization at any time on company property. No person employed by this company will be permitted to solicit on behalf of any cause or organization during working time or in work areas during work time. Working time is defined as all hours of work exclusive of authorized break or rest periods, meal periods, and other authorized nonworking periods. Any nonemployee found violating this rule will be removed from company property. Any employee found violating this rule will be subject to discipline up to and including discharge.

However, if other employee solicitation activity is permitted, such as selling Girl Scout cookies or using interoffice mail to advertise the sale of an automobile, it is likely that a no-solicitation rule will be considered invalid by the Labor Board if later applied to union organizing activities.

Q 11:21   Does an employer have the right to communicate its views about unions to employees?

Yes. An employer can do so in employee meetings and through letters and other literature distributed to employees. However, an employer may not threaten employees with discipline, or discharge, or closing of the plant if they support a union. An employer cannot make promises incumbent on employees avoiding the union. The information disseminated about the union and unionism, as well as information about the company, must be truthful. Also, a statement claiming that a union is dominated by a particular racial group, even if true, may constitute an unfair labor practice. Allegations that a union is dominated by organized crime or is inclined to lead its members into long and bitter strikes may be permissible but must be handled carefully to ensure its accuracy.

NLRB

Q 11:22　How does the NLRB fit into the organizing process?

The NLRA was passed in the 1930s and prohibited unfair labor practices. Most notably, employers' interference with their employees' right to engage in union activity was forbidden. In 1947, the Taft-Hartley Act additionally prohibited unfair union practices. The NLRB is the independent governmental agency empowered by Congress to enforce these laws. Among its many duties, the NLRB must accept representation petitions filed by labor unions and employees, investigate the validity of those petitions, and conduct secret ballot elections. If a union wins a secret ballot election, the NLRB has the authority to certify that union as the bargaining representative for that group (bargaining unit) of employees.

Q 11:23　Is the National Labor Relations Board a fair and efficient government agency?

Recently, the NLRB has come under criticism both for the pace at which it renders its decisions and, from the union camp, for being biased in favor of management. The allegation of bias arises from 12 years of Reagan/Bush appointments to the Board. Board members firmly deny any such management favoritism. For instance, NLRB member Clifford R. Oviatt has commented: "I have serious questions as to whether or not the board is the reason for the claim of an uneven playing field, if there is an uneven playing field. . . . I think this board has consistently stayed within the law. There has been no overriding desire to go out and write new law and we've honored the process of stare decisis" (i.e., following the rules laid down in prior board decisions). [Remarks to LABNET Conference, as quoted in 1993 *BNA Daily Labor Report* 48, Mar 15, 1993, at 1]

The NLRB's decision in the *Electromation* case, involving the issue of whether so-called employee action committees were really illegal company-sponsored unions (Q 11:108), tends to support Oviatt's contentions. In declaring such action committees to be illegal, the labor board engaged in an extensive analysis of its relevant decisions going back to the first opinion published. (See Pennsylvania Greyhound Lines, 1 NLRB 1 (1935), *enforcement denied in part*, 91 F 2d 178 (3d Cir 1937), rev, 303 US 261 (1938)) However, while coming down in favor of the complaining union's contention that Electromation's action committees constituted an unfair labor practice, the present labor board took pains to reassure corporate America that its decision was a narrow one, not intended to outlaw employee participation programs or labor-management cooperation generally (Q 11:110 and chapter 14). Oviatt himself, in a concurring opinion in the case, offered these comments:

> American companies, their employees, and labor unions representing those employees are at present confronted with diverse competitive forces requiring an array of different responses if those companies are to remain competitive in the world economy. To the extent present laws are interpreted to apply restrictions and roadblocks to companies' ability to perform more efficiently and to respond promptly to competitive conditions, the more difficult will be the common task of achieving or retaining equality. This is a time of testing for the American and world economies and we must proceed with caution when we address the legality of innovative employee involvement programs directed to improving efficiency and productivity.
>
> [Electromation Inc, 309 NLRB 163, 1992 NLRB LEXIS 1417 (1992)]

The NLRB has also come under criticism for its "glacial" proceedings. (See, e.g., "Ninth Circuit Scores Injunction Against Hospital," *1993 BNA Daily Labor Report* 72, Apr 16, 1993, at 1 ("Suggesting that interim steps to afford relief may be worse than awaiting the ultimate outcome of 'glacial' proceedings at NLRB, the U.S. Court of Appeals for the Ninth Circuit set aside a preliminary injunction requested by the agency on behalf of the California Nurses Association")) The *Electromation* decision was itself the subject of long delay and, presumably, significant behind-the-scenes wrangling before the board rendered its decision. Indeed, the pace at which the labor board performs its mission, as well as the cumbersome structure of proceedings under the NLRA (Q 11:24), have for decades been the subject of periodic congressional and private sector criticism. Undoubtedly, as opportunities arise, the Clinton administration will appoint board members more congenial to organized labor, while reform of labor act procedures may be much more than a mere "pipe dream" of Labor Secretary Robert Reich. [See Q 11:111; see also, "Striker Bill Seen As Start to Wider Labor Law Reform," 1992 *BNA Daily Labor Report* 221, Nov 16, 1992, at 1]

In his January 1994 appearance before the Dunlop Commission on the Future of Labor-Management Cooperation (Q 11:10), the distinguished labor law expert Professor Charles Morris proposed the following reforms with regard to the NLRB:

- Expansion of the board's seldom-used administrative rule-making powers

- Reorganization and streamlining of union organizing procedures

- Increased use of the board's ability to seek federal court injunctions, especially in cases in which employers are accused of firing employees because of their union affiliations or activities

- More frequent use of injunctive relief to enforce board orders more speedily

- Reorganization of the administrative law judge's (ALJ) division of the agency, giving ALJs powers as comprehensive as those of traditional judges, plus involvement in labor board cases before commencing an unfair labor practice hearing

- Creation of pre-hearing discovery methods similar to those used in federal district courts (Q 15:7)

[Charles J Morris, "In Search of a National Labor Policy," Statement to the Dunlop Commission, January 1994]

Morris's views were reflected in a number of the pro-labor bills introduced in Congress in 1994 that were aimed at amending the National Labor Relations Act. [See Q 11:8; "Much Labor Law Reform Debate Expected in 1994," 1993 *BNA Labor Relations Reporter*, 144 LRR 495-97, Dec 20, 1993] However, the November 1994 elections resulted in Republican dominance of both houses of Congress for the first time in four decades. Furthermore, the Dunlop Commission's report favors Labor Secretary Robert Reich's view that the National Labor Relations Act needs to be loosened up to allow for greater employee participation in the form of employer-sponsored committees on productivity and the like (Q 11:10). Critics of the report from organized labor have argued with Steelworkers President George Becker:

> We will fight any attempt to legislate this recommendation. . . . It would be the same as having the employer sit on both sides of the bargaining table. Incomes and working conditions have been declining steadily for two decades. The problem is employers have too much power and workers too little. The solution is laws that strengthen workers' rights to organize and bargain collectively, not reduce them.

> [Philip Dine, "Neither Labor Nor Management Raves Over New Workplace Report," *St. Louis Post-Dispatch*, Jan 13, 1995, at 1C]

But the reality is that the new GOP majority is unlikely to add new powers and duties that will help the NLRB overcome labor's critique.

Q 11:24   Are NLRB procedures unduly drawn out and cumbersome?

For decades, Congress, the federal courts, and labor and management alike have criticized the NLRB for taking too long to render decisions and resolve disputes (Q 11:23). Statistics suggest that the NLRB, like most court systems and other agencies (see Q 4:94 with respect to the backlog of ADA cases at the EEOC at present), labors under a backlog of cases, some of which take years to resolve. However, statistics also indicate that, as with most court systems, the vast majority of cases are disposed of fairly quickly at an early stage.

Under the National Labor Relations Act, any person can file an unfair labor practice charge against a company or a union. [29 USC

§ 158] Historically, of all such charges filed in NLRB regional offices across the country, 33 percent are voluntarily withdrawn by the charging parties; another 33 percent are dismissed by the NLRB regional director after investigation by a board agent finds them to be without merit; and 33 percent are found to be meritorious, thus resulting in the issuance of a complaint by the labor board against the accused company or union. Of these complaints, 60 percent are settled, usually long before the parties ever appear before an administrative law judge (ALJ) in a public hearing. [Cihon & Castagnera, *Labor and Employment Law* 69 (2d ed 1992)]

On the other hand, a party determined to delay a decision under the National Labor Relations Act, and willing to expend the legal fees necessary, can achieve significant delays. Consider the example of a company that loses a representation election but does not desire to bargain with the successful union. That firm might first file objections to the election itself, contending union improprieties during the election campaign. If the board rejects these objections, a determined employer might then refuse to bargain in good faith toward a collective bargaining agreement (see Qs 11:43–11:45). The union would then have no choice but to file an unfair labor practice charge (Q 11:95). If the relevant NLRB regional director issues a complaint against the company, following the board agent's investigation, then a public hearing will be held in front of an ALJ. If the company loses at this stage in the procedure, it can appeal the ALJ's decision to the NLRB itself in Washington, where it will be reviewed by a three-member panel of the board. Losing again at this level, the firm might appeal to the U.S. Court of Appeals having jurisdiction over the case. All of this can take several years and in the interim the union's majority support among the company's employees may erode or even evaporate due to turnover and discouragement with the collective bargaining process. While arguably unethical, such tactics have been used with some success by companies determined to remain union-free.

In 1994, the board took steps to clean its own house, perhaps in anticipation of a poor report card from the Dunlop Commission. A new chairman and general counsel, plus two new members, came onboard relatively early that year. In March the U.S. Senate confirmed the chairmanship of Stanford Law Professor William B. Gould and approved President Clinton's nomination of long-time House Education and Labor Committee staff member Fred Feinstein as general counsel. Newly appointed members were prominent Philadelphia labor lawyer Margaret A. Browning, who had founded and built her own firm, and Charles I. Cohen of a well-known District of Columbia law firm.

Not awaiting guidance from the Dunlop panel, Gould formed his own labor and management advisory bodies and set them to work examining a range of procedural issues from the performance of the board's administrative law judges to whether the NLRB should conduct representation elections using mail ballots. ["Year in Review: Board Appointments, Court Rulings Brought Changes in Labor Field in '94," 1995 BNA *Daily Labor Report*, 17, Jan 26, 1995, at d17]

By year-end the board had announced a year-long experiment in which the chief judge can assign an ALJ to mentor settlement talks between the parties in an unfair labor practice case before a hearing on the complaint occurs. Also, for 1995, ALJs were given the authority to dispense with briefs, hear oral arguments and issue bench decisions in appropriate cases. [Id] Obviously these steps are aimed at expediting ALJ decisions in unfair labor practice (ULP) cases.

Similarly, Feinstein promised a more "user friendly" agency, less hierarchical and more efficient. Targets for the handling of representation cases were set in an effort to speed their handling, too. But, though a public hearing was held on the proposal, no action was taken to initiate balloting by mail in representation elections. [Id]

Q 11:25 Is an arbitration award enforceable when it contradicts an NLRB decision?

An arbitration award that contradicts an earlier NLRB ruling is unenforceable according to a case decided by the U.S. Court of Appeals for the Ninth Circuit. The union claimed that two related corporations under a double-breasting arrangement (whereby separate union and nonunion operations are run by a common owner) were alter egos; that is, the arrangement was created to avoid the employer's obligations under the National Labor Relations Act (NLRA). The NLRB agreed. Later, in the context of a grievance arbitration, the arbitrator ruled that the two firms did not meet the test of common or joint control. According to the federal court, the NLRB holding was binding. [A Dariano & Sons Inc v District Council of Painters, 869 F 2d 514 (9th Cir 1989)]

This case touches upon an issue that periodically haunts the grievance arbitration environment: How much attention must (or should) an arbitrator pay to public law when resolving a grievance and fashioning an award? Certainly an award that runs contrary to the law is unenforceable. But the arbitrator's charge is to fashion the award from the four corners of the labor contract. Sometimes public law and private law (the contract) are incompatible. Some arbitrators acknowledge a controlling public policy. Others adhere to the mandate of the contract and let a court overrule them on public law grounds in a later action to enforce or vacate the award. [Castagnera, "Using Statutory Law to Resolve Labor Contract Ambiguities," *Employee Relations Labor Journal*, Sept 2, 1983, 194-203]

Q 11:26   When will the NLRB defer an unfair labor practice charge to arbitration?

When an employee files an unfair labor practice charge, but the employer demands an arbitration under the labor contract, the current NLRB practice is to defer the matter to the arbitrator if the unfair labor practice claim "implicates" a parallel provision in the collective bargaining agreement. However, some federal courts of appeals, which are charged with reviewing and enforcing labor board orders, have demonstrated their disagreement with this standard of deferral. (See, e.g., NLRB v Motor Convoy, Inc, 673 F2d 734 (4th Cir 1982); Richmond Tank Car Co v NLRB, 721 F2d 499 (5th Cir 1983); American Freight Systems, Inc v NLRB, 722 F2d 828 (DC Cir 1983)) In other words, just because some clause in the labor contract may be parallel to language in the Taft-Hartley Act (e.g., a clause forbidding discrimination by the employer based on employees' union affiliation—a common clause) that clause does not free the board to defer its obligation to the private-party grievance procedure.

Elections

Q 11:27   What must a union do to get an NLRB election?

The union must show that at least 30 percent of the employees in the appropriate bargaining unit want representation. In practice, a union will rarely file a representation petition with the NLRB until a substantial majority of the employees have signed authorization cards.

Q 11:28   Can a union offer free medical tests to workers prior to a representation election?

In 1989 the NLRB took the position that free medical testing offered two days before an election so tainted the vote that the union victory had to be set aside. The union offered screenings for high blood pressure, lung functions, cholesterol level, and diabetes. The tests were given in two vans bearing the union logo. The NLRB concluded that workers who availed themselves of the tests believed they had gotten a gift from the union and that it was a benefit they would lose if they did not retain the union. This, the NLRB felt, was no different than an employer giving gifts during the campaign period. [Mailing Services, Inc., 293 NLRB No 58 (1989)]

Q 11:29   What is an authorization card?

A union authorization card usually states that the employee seeks union representation in collective bargaining with the employer. Although employees are often told by union organizers that the card merely indicates their desire for a representation election, generally the card actually signifies that the employee wants that union to be the group's representative.

Q 11:30   Can a union become the collective bargaining representative of the employees on the basis of authorization cards alone?

Yes. A union can become the collective bargaining representative of a company's employees without a secret ballot election if the union presents authorization cards signed by a majority of the employees, and the employer or one of the managers reviews those cards and perceives that the union has obtained a majority. Supervisors should therefore be instructed at the start of a union organizing effort to refuse to touch, take possession of, or review authorization cards that might be offered by a union representative, since this might be construed as a review by the employer.

Q 11:31 Can the union picket a business when trying to organize its employees?

As a general rule, a union can picket an employer for up to 30 days before filing an election petition with the NLRB. A union may also be entitled to picket for a longer period in order to protest the employer's poor wages or benefits; this is called "area-standards" picketing.

Q 11:32 What happens after a union files a petition with the NLRB?

The NLRB first will determine whether the union is supported (e.g., through signed authorization cards) by at least 30 percent of the workers that the union seeks to represent. If so, a board agent will begin laying the groundwork for a secret ballot election. Either by mutual agreement of the company and the union or by the board's decision following a hearing, the appropriate bargaining unit, list of eligible voters, date and place of the election, and other details will be outlined.

Q 11:33 Is there an election campaign?

Yes. The length of the campaign period is generally about 30 days. During this election campaign the company has a chance to defend itself and to attempt to persuade the employee voters to vote against the union.

Q 11:34 Is it possible for a company to win a union representation election?

Yes. Unions lose more elections than they win; thus, the chances of winning are probably high enough for an employer to invest the time and money necessary to conduct an effective campaign to win employees back from the union. This generally means hiring a professional consultant or labor lawyer.

Q 11:35 Can a company's efforts defeat a union organizing effort?

Yes. A company that vigorously opposes unionization enjoys a substantially better chance of defeating a union than a company that does not address the issue of organizing. First, companies that practice effective employment policies are more likely to have satisfied employees with no desire to unionize. Second, labor unions have long held that, as in Canada, companies in the United States should remain neutral during union organizing efforts. To the contrary, the National Labor Relations Board under Ronald Reagan's administration in the 1980s expanded employers' rights to question employees about union interest and to communicate the company's views to the workers.

Bargaining Units and Employment Practices

Q 11:36 What constitutes an appropriate bargaining unit of employees?

All employees in a bargaining unit should share common work interests, such as similar pay, status, and benefits. The NLRB tends to prefer single location bargaining units, especially if the company's several facilities are geographically distant from one another. Supervisors, confidential secretaries, and security guards are generally excluded from units representing other categories of employees. Supervisors and managers are not covered by the protection and organizing rights of the National Labor Relations Act. Professional employees may be allowed, if they choose, to form their own separate unit, although they may be represented by the same union.

Q 11:37 What is the current status of the NLRB's rules on health care bargaining units?

In mid-1989 the American Hospital Association (AHA) filed a lawsuit challenging the NLRB's asserted power to mandate appropriate bargaining units by means of the administrative rule making process. The 6,000-member trade association contended that Section 9(b) of the Taft-Hartley Act requires that bargaining units be determined on a case-by-case basis. [American Hospital Assn v NLRB, 718 F Supp 704 (ND Ill 1989)] A small irony in this lawsuit is that in the NLRB's more than 50 years as an independent agency, the health care case is one of the few times the NLRB invoked its rule-making power. Historically, the NLRB has been content to develop its rules through case precedents.

In July 1989, the federal district court in *American Hospital Association* issued a permanent injunction, preventing the NLRB from enforcing its rules on health care bargaining units. The trial court held that these rules were inconsistent with the Congressional admonition against the "undue proliferation" of bargaining units within a single company contained in legislative history dating back to a 1974 amendment of the NLRA. However, this court order was not long-lived. In April 1990, the U.S. Court of Appeals for the Seventh Circuit vacated the lower court's order and gave the NLRB the authority to implement this historic rule-making.

On April 23, 1991, the Supreme Court unanimously upheld the NLRB's general rule defining the eight bargaining units appropriate for health care workers in private acute care hospitals and dramatically altered the ground rules for organizing in the health care industry. In *American Hospital Association v. NLRB*, the Supreme Court endorsed the Board's use of its broad rule making powers, thereby making clear that unions attempting to organize in hospitals may automatically break down the workforce into eight separate units for the purposes of organizing and collective bargaining. Union leaders' immediate reaction to the Supreme Court's opinion has been exuberant; they pledged to increase their organizing efforts in the industry immediately. [111 S Ct 1539 (1991)]

Q 11:38   To which employers does the NLRB's health care bargaining unit rule apply?

The Board rule upheld by the Supreme Court applies to acute care hospitals and provides, with three exceptions, that eight and only eight units shall be appropriate in any such hospital. The eight units are as follows:

- Registered nurses
- Physicians
- Professionals other than registered nurses and physicians
- Technical employees
- Skilled maintenance employees
- Business, office, and clerical employees
- Guards
- Other nonprofessional employees

The three exceptions to application of the rule are as follows:

- Cases that present extraordinary circumstances
- Cases in which nonconforming units already exist
- Cases in which labor organizations seek to combine two or more of the eight specified units

Therefore, hospitals that are already unionized and whose bargaining units do not conform to the rule are exempt from the rule's application. Further, hospitals in which the eight-unit rule will produce a unit of five or fewer employees automatically come within the extraordinary circumstances exception.

Q 11:39 What arguments of the AHA were rejected by the Supreme Court when it affirmed the NLRB's hospital bargaining unit rules?

The Supreme Court rejected the AHA's argument that Section 9(b) of the NLRA prevents the NLRB's promulgating this type of rule by its language requiring that "the Board shall decide in each case whether . . . the unit appropriate for the purposes of collective bargaining shall be the employer unit, craft unit, plant unit, or subdivision thereof." The AHA emphasized the "in each case" phrase, arguing that the phrase amounted to a mandate that the NLRB consider the appropriateness of bargaining units on a case-by-case basis. The Supreme Court rejected the AHA's reading of this language, choosing instead to interpret the phrase as simply an indication that whenever there is a disagreement about the appropriateness of a unit, the NLRB shall be the entity to resolve the dispute. The Supreme Court concluded that the language in Section 6 of the NLRA granting the NLRB the "authority from time to time to make, amend, and rescind . . . such rules and regulations as may be necessary to carry out the provisions" of the NLRA unquestionably provides sufficient support for the promulgation of this rule by the NLRB.

The AHA also argued that the eight-unit rule results in a proliferation of bargaining units in acute care hospitals, in opposition to a congressional warning against such proliferation (found in the legislative history of the amendments to the NLRA that brought hospitals under the Board's jurisdiction). The Supreme Court rejected this argument on the grounds that the congressional warning did not rise to the level of legislation, and that the presence of eight bargaining units in a hospital does not constitute proliferation. Hospitals and management groups have been opposed to the Board's eight-unit rule since its inception, primarily because the possibility of strikes increases with the number of bargaining units. Additionally, the rule has been opposed because unions find it markedly easier to organize among smaller groups of employees; therefore, the greater number of units translates into easier organizing.

Q 11:40 How should hospitals respond to the Supreme Court's ruling on health care bargaining units?

In response to both the Supreme Court's ruling and the unions' plans to organize, hospital employers and management representatives must be prepared to deal with the unions and their organizing drives. Hospitals must concentrate on creating a work environment that makes employees less likely to look to a union. In order to do this, hospitals must review their personnel policies and their policies on solicitation, distribution, and access to their premises by outside organizers, on bulletin board postings, and on the wearing of buttons and insignia. Unions have not wasted any time in targeting vulnerable hospitals; all hospitals should take all precautionary steps available and be prepared to meet head-on the unions' organizing efforts.

Q 11:41   Are independent contractors covered by the NLRA?

The easy answer is that independent contractors are not employees covered by the protection of the NLRA; the tougher answer is defining the difference between independent contractors and actual employees. As a general proposition, the definition depends on whether the company has the right to control how such workers perform their jobs.

Some of the factors that indicate a person is an employee include working for only one employer, being provided work space, tools, and materials by the employer, and/or being required to be on the job at certain times on specified workdays. Factors suggesting an independent contractor status include allowing the worker to come and go as he or she pleases, allowing the worker to decide how to best accomplish the general goals set, and providing no fringe benefits to the worker. In a given situation, if most factors suggest an independent status, the worker has no NLRA protection with respect to labor organizing activities.

In 1989, a group of rabbis who performed "kosher kills" for a Chicago meat packer were determined to be independent contractors after they sought to be represented by Local 100-A of the United Food and Commercial Workers Union. The rabbis, known as "schoctim," were compensated based on the number of kills they performed in accord with Orthodox Jewish principles, received no fringe benefits from the company, were not subject to the firm's disciplinary policy, and were accorded complete discretion on how they handled their task.

Another interesting case, involving independent contractors in a different context, was decided by the NLRB early in 1991. The Board found that the Coca-Cola Company had violated the Taft-Hartley Act by forbidding a janitorial worker at its Atlanta headquarters from distributing literature about a Service Employees Union's organizing drive. The janitorial work was subcontracted by Coca-Cola to Southern Services, Inc., who actually employed the janitor. Using the slogan "Justice for Janitors," SEIU Local 679 had begun organizing Atlanta-area janitors in 1987. Since the SSI janitor was distributing information at her normal place of employment, and was not a trespasser, the NLRB held that the NLRA protected the janitor's right to distribute the information. [1991 *BNA Daily Labor Report* 15, Jan 23, 1991, at 2]

Q 11:42   If a union is certified by the NLRB to represent some of a company's employees, what legal responsibilities does the company have?

The company has the legal duty to bargain in good faith with the union.

Q 11:43   What does bargaining in good faith mean?

Briefly, bargaining in good faith involves listening to the other side, keeping an open mind, and being motivated to reach an agreement. It involves being available to meet and confer at reasonable times and places. However, it does not mean that a company has a legal obligation to make a concession. A company has the legal right to bargain to an impasse, if good-faith negotiating does not bring the two sides together.

Q 11:44   Is collective bargaining necessarily an adversarial exercise?

Typically in contract negotiations, both sides (or at least the union representatives) come to the bargaining table with a list of demands. The posture on both sides ranges from mildly to stridently adversarial, but this stance is not necessarily inevitable. For the past two years, the Department of Labor's (DOL's) Bureau of Labor-Management Relations and Cooperative Programs has been working to develop a new collective bargaining model that seeks to emphasize mutual interests over confrontation. Deputy Under Secretary John R. Stepp, who heads the Bureau, announced in 1990 that research was close to completion. He cited the 1986 negotiations between General Motors and the United Auto Workers Union as a touchstone example in which the parties set forth common issues, rather than demands, for discussion. For the first time in the auto industry's history, a contract agreement was reached "without ever having to set a strike date," according to Stepp. [See Castagnera, "To Confront or Cooperate? The Lesson of Anthracite Coal," *Labor Law Journal*, March 1990, 158-164]

Q 11:45 What is a collective bargaining agreement?

Commonly called a labor contract, a collective bargaining agreement is a pact between the union and the company that covers the terms and conditions of employment of the unionized employees.

Q 11:46 Is an employer's refusal to execute a collective bargaining agreement a continuing violation of the NLRA?

In 1989, the NLRB set aside an 11-year-old precedent when it ruled that it no longer intended to treat refusal to execute a labor contract as a continuing violation of the Act. From now on an employer's initial refusal to sign will start the clock ticking on a six-month NLRA statute of limitations. In other words, the aggrieved union must file its unfair labor practice charge within that six-month period or risk losing its opportunity for a remedy thereafter.

Q 11:47 Does the National Labor Relations Act preempt a state law claim?

The common law recognizes a tort action for injurious interference with a contractual relationship. For example, a tort action has occasionally been invoked by one college or professional sports team against another for pirating away a coach. In 1989, a member of the Teamsters Union was able to sue the Seaboard Railroad System for allegedly getting him fired by his employer, a subcontractor of Seaboard's, in retaliation for filing Occupational Safety and Health Act (OSHA) charges against Seaboard. Even though the union had grieved the discharge and an arbitrator had ruled against the employee, the employee was allowed by a federal court to proceed with his action against Seaboard, which was not a party to the Teamster labor contract under which the arbitration was brought. The plaintiff's tort theory was that Seaboard wrongfully interfered with his employment relationship with the subcontractor. [Dougherty v Parsec, Inc, 872 F2d 766, 4 BNA IER Cas 417 (6th Cir 1989)]

By contrast, another federal court in 1990 refused to allow a coal miner to pursue a state law action against the United Mine Workers of America for alleged negligence in carrying out a mine inspection. The union's duty, said the court, came from the collective bargaining agreement. Consequently, the miner-member had to sue for breach of that agreement under Section 301 of the Taft-Hartley Act, if he sued at all. [Sluder v UMW Intl and District 12, 892 F 2d 549, 5 BNA IER Cas 187 (7th Cir 1989)]

It is well settled under several Supreme Court decisions that employment discrimination suits are not preempted by the grievance arbitration procedures in labor contracts. Beyond that, however, at what point a disgruntled unionized employee can sue the employer and/or union outside the umbrella of the labor acts, the NLRB, and the collective bargaining agreement continues to evolve on a case-by-case basis.

Recently the U.S. Court of Appeals for the Fourth Circuit held that a West Virginia statute, which sought to prevent local police from enforcing the state's criminal trespass law in the context of a labor dispute, was preempted by federal labor law. In an appeal that grew out of a 1989 United Mine Workers strike, the court ruled that a motion for preliminary injunction by Rum Creek Coal Sales, ordering the state police to enforce the trespass act, should have been granted. [Rum Creek Coal Sales, Inc v Caperton, 926 F 2d 353 (4th Cir 1991)]

Q 11:48   What is a union shop?

A union shop is a company or company facility in which employees who come under a labor contract between the employer and a union must join that union and begin paying dues sometime (typically 30 days) after being hired.

Q 11:49   Is a union shop legal?

In most states, union shops are legal. Closed shops, which hire only those who already belong to the union, are illegal. However, states are allowed by the Taft-Hartley Act to pass right-to-work laws.

In a right-to-work state, union shops are illegal. Sometimes these laws make agency shops illegal as well.

Q 11:50 What is an agency shop?

An agency shop is one in which employees covered by a collective bargaining agreement can choose whether or not to join the union. But if an employee decides not to become a union member, that employee must still pay an agency fee to the union in return for the services (negotiating, grievance representation, etc.) performed by the union.

Q 11:51 Can the union that represents a company's employees force the company to collect fees from the employees?

A union checkoff clause, requiring the employer to deduct dues directly from paychecks, is a subject for collective bargaining. In states where such a clause is legal, unions usually bargain extensively to include such a clause in their labor contracts.

Q 11:52 Do unionized employees have a right to union representation in disciplinary matters?

Union employees have "Weingarten rights" (named for a famous NLRB case); these rights allow a union representative (for example, a steward or an officer) to be present whenever an employee interview could lead to disciplinary action by the employer.

Q 11:53 What is the union's duty to the employees it represents?

The union must represent all of its members fairly and without discrimination.

Q 11:54 What does the union's duty of fair representation mean?

The duty of fair representation means that the union must treat all members equally. Fair representation also means that the union must investigate employee grievances and represent all aggrieved members in a responsible and reasonable manner in relation to the employer. However, the union's duty does not prevent the union from settling grievances, even if the settlement does not please every concerned member-employee. The union also has an obligation to conduct every employee grievance or disciplinary matter through arbitration.

With the sharp decline in traditional union membership recently, fair representation cases appear to have been on the rise. A number of these cases have involved abuse by union officials of local hiring halls to favor their supporters at the expense of their opponents among the rank-and-file members. In once recent case, this author was co-counsel to some 30 carpenters who had voted for the wrong candidate in a marked-ballot election for president of their local. Thereafter, they were sent out to jobs less often and for shorter durations than their fellow members. [See Brenner v Local 514, 927 F 2d 1283 (3d Cir 1991)]

Q 11:55   How far is a union entitled to go to protect employees' health and safety?

In 1989, the NLRB ruled that Glass Workers Local 193 in Wilson, NC, had the right to enter a glass container plant and take heat measurements. [American Natl Can Co, Foster-Forbes Glass Division, 293 NLRB No 110 (Apr 28, 1989)] The NLRB derived its decision from a close analysis of the labor contract. One provision granted the union's international representative the right to visit plants to investigate grievances arising out of the interpretation or application of the contract. Another provision, entitled "Relief," called for "additional relief . . . where heat or cold conditions warrant." Yet another clause required the company to "provide adequate heat, light, and ventilation to employees" and to "continue its best effort to devise systems to control drafts, noise, fumes, dust, grease, and job hazards." Putting all these provisions together, the NLRB concluded that the union had the right to collect the heat data.

Two observations, one practical and the other legal, may be appropriate here. First, heat levels constitute a very serious health concern in the glass-making industry. Second, the NLRB looked to the collective bargaining agreement for guidance, not to OSHA or anywhere else outside its area of expertise.

Q 11:56 Can the provisions of a collective bargaining agreement supersede the requirements of the federal discrimination statutes?

The federal scheme of discrimination statutes, Title VII, the Age Discrimination in Employment Act, the Americans with Disabilities Act, and some lesser enactments (see Qs 1:1–1:8) appear to permit labor contracts to supersede federal discrimination statutes in two general situations. First, when a collective bargaining agreement contains, as almost all do, a grievance arbitration procedure, the federal courts require an aggrieved employee to submit the grievance, even one based on employment discrimination, to the arbitrator. Historically, such union members have been permitted to pursue remedies concurrently or subsequently under Title VII or the ADEA. In 1990, the U.S. Supreme Court signaled the possibility of a break in that historic tradition when it held that a stockbroker, who had agreed in his employment agreement to arbitrate all disputes arising under it, had to submit his age discrimination claim to final and binding arbitration. [Gilmer v Interstate, 111 S Ct 1647 (1990); (see Q 4:120)] Whether the Court will apply the *Gilmer* rule to arbitration under collective bargaining agreements remains to be seen.

In the area of seniority, the terms of a labor contract may prevail over the requirements of federal discrimination statutes.

Two major discrimination acts expressly recognize the historic importance of seniority in labor-management relations. Title VII of the 1964 Civil Rights Act states in pertinent part:

> Notwithstanding any other provision of this subchapter, it shall not be an unlawful employment practice for an employer to apply different standards of compensation, or different terms, conditions, or privileges of employment pursuant to a bona fide seniority or merit system . . . provided that such differences are not the result of an intention to discriminate because of race, color, religion, sex, or national origin.

[42 USC § 2000e-2(h)(1981)]

Similarly, the Age Discrimination in Employment Act reads as follows:

> It shall not be unlawful for an employer, employment agency, or labor organization . . . to observe the terms of a bona fide seniority system or any bona fide employee benefit plan such as retirement, pension, or insurance plan, which is not a subterfuge to evade the purposes of this chapter, except that no such employee benefit plan shall excuse the failure to hire any individual.

> [29 USC § 623(f)(2) (1978)]

The effect of these two provisions, plus the relevant parts of the Civil Rights Act of 1991 and various federal court decisions upon arguably discriminatory job decisions within unionized corporations, is the subject of the questions and answers that follow.

Q 11:57 How might a collective bargaining agreement affect the application of the Americans with Disabilities Act (ADA) to discriminatory employment decisions?

Put simply, the ADA prohibits employment decisions based on disabilities that either do not prevent the applicant or employee from performing the job or can be overcome by an applicant or employee who is accorded a reasonable accommodation (see Qs 4:79–4:96). At first glance, the ADA appears to apply with equal force in all employment situations, whether there exists a collective bargaining agreement or not. Section 102(b)(2) of the ADA declares that illegal job discrimination includes "participating in a contractual or other arrangement or relationship that has the effect of subjecting a covered entity's qualified applicant or employee with a disability" to discriminatory treatment. The act expressly includes in this section "a relationship with a . . . labor union."

But this is not the end of the analysis. The ADA's legislative history, carefully researched by a number of labor lawyers and scholars, indicates that Congress was concerned with how the new law might inappropriately affect well-established labor-management relations. (See, e.g., Stahlhut, "Playing the Trump Card: May an Employer Refuse to Reasonably Accommodate under the ADA by

Claiming a Collective Bargaining Obligation?" 9 *The Labor Lawyer* 1, Winter 1993, at 75) For example, a 1989 report of the Senate Committee on Labor and Human Resources observed:

> The collective bargaining agreement could be relevant, however, in determining whether a given accommodation is reasonable. For example, if a collective bargaining agreement reserves certain jobs for employees with a given amount of seniority, it may be considered as a factor in determining whether it is a reasonable accommodation to assign an employee with a disability without seniority to that job.
>
> [S Rep No 101-116, 101st Cong, 1st Sess at 32 (1989)]

Of course, a collective bargaining agreement can be negotiated, or renegotiated, to contain a provision permitting the employer to take all necessary actions to comply with the requirements of the ADA or, even more explicitly, to make reasonable accommodations notwithstanding the disabled applicant's or employee's rank in seniority.

Q 11:58 Is any guidance available to help unionized employers ascertain how best to balance competing requirements of their collective bargaining agreements and the ADA?

The final regulations published by the Equal Employment Opportunity Commission, pursuant to its mandate to do so under the ADA, are not particularly helpful to employers faced with resolving conflicts that may arise between the ADA's requirement of according reasonable accommodation and their own labor contracts' emphasis upon seniority as the controlling factor in promotions, transfers, and other job-related decisions. However, what the EEOC did not do provides a clue as to how the agency is likely to respond to such disputes in the future. "[T]he EEOC did not follow the suggestion of various labor and management groups who advocated that collectively bargained rights should automatically trump the rights of a disabled employee." [Stahlhut at 76] Instead, the EEOC promised further guidance in the future. [29 CFR § 35727 (1991); see also, Feldblum, Americans with Disabilities Act: Selected Employment Requirements (1992) at 37]

A second source of guidance for this issue, as with virtually all questions concerning how the courts will interpret and apply the

ADA, is the Federal Rehabilitation Act, which has been around for much longer and applies ADA-like requirements to government contractors. (See Vocational Rehabilitation Act of 1973 §§ 503, 504; Q 1:5) Some cases decided by federal courts under this law indicate that it is not reasonable to require an employer to favor a disabled individual over a union member with greater seniority when making a job assignment. For example, in *Shea v. Tisch* [870 F 2d 786 (1st Cir 1989)], the court upheld the refusal of the postmaster general to accommodate a Vietnam veteran with an anxiety disorder by assigning him closer to his home, where the labor contract required employees to bid on open job assignments, which were then to be awarded on the basis of seniority. In another postal service case, a custodian who began to suffer asthmatic attacks two months after he had commenced employment applied for a permanent light-duty position in which he would not be exposed to dust. The request was denied on the basis of the applicable collective bargaining agreement, which reserved permanent light-duty assignments for union members with at least five years of accrued seniority. Upholding the postmaster general, the court ruled that an "employer cannot be required to accommodate a handicapped employee by restructuring a job in a manner which would usurp legitimate rights of other employees under a collective bargaining agreement." [Carter v Tisch, 822 F 2d 465 (4th Cir 1987); accord, Daubert v US Postal Service, 733 F 2d 1367 (10th Cir 1984); Jasany v US Postal Service, 755 F 2d 1244 (6th Cir 1985); Bey v Bolger, 540 F Supp 910 (ED PA 1982)] If the reasoning of these cases is extended to lawsuits brought under the ADA, it would then seem that seniority provisions in collective bargaining agreements may sometimes render accommodations unreasonable where such accommodations conflict with the clear seniority rights of the firm's unionized employees.

Q 11:59   Can a bona fide seniority system supersede the requirements of Title VII of the 1964 Civil Rights Act?

As pointed out in Q 11:56, Section 703(h) of Title VII says, "it shall not be an unlawful employment practice for an employer to apply different standards of compensation, or different terms, conditions, or privileges of employment pursuant to a bona fide seniority . . . system . . ." [42 USC § 2000e-2(h)(1981)] The U.S. Supreme Court has twice rendered significant interpretations of this exception to

Title VII's general prohibition against job discrimination. In a 1977 decision, the Court was confronted with a situation in which a TWA employee belonged to the Worldwide Church of God, which forbade working from sundown Friday to sundown Saturday. Under the applicable collective bargaining agreement the plaintiff was subject to a seniority system that gave more senior employees first choice of job and shift assignments. When plaintiff was assigned a Saturday shift and refused to work it, the airline agreed to allow the union to switch shifts, but the union refused to go against the seniority system. Plaintiff complained that a reasonable accommodation by the airline was to buck the terms of the labor contract and make the shift change. The issue became a federal lawsuit, and when it eventually reached the Court, seven justices disagreed with the plaintiff's position, saying in their majority opinion:

> Both the union and TWA had agreed to the seniority system; the union was unwilling to entertain a variance over the objections of men senior to Hardison; and for TWA to have arranged unilaterally for a swap would have amounted to a breach of the collective bargaining agreement. . . . Hardison and the EEOC insist that the statutory obligation to accommodate religious needs takes precedence over both the collective bargaining contract and the rights of TWA's other employees . . . but we do not believe that the duty to accommodate requires TWA to take steps inconsistent with the otherwise valid agreement.

[Trans World Airlines v Hardison, 432 US 63 (1977)]

Next came *Lorance v. AT&T Technologies Inc.* [490 US 900 (1989)], in which the Supreme Court rendered a very narrow interpretation involving the time period in which the seniority system itself could be challenged as illegally discriminatory. The court held that employees had to mount a legal challenge immediately against any seniority rules, even though the provisions might only directly affect them in the future, or run the risk of having their later lawsuit or discrimination charge held to be untimely. *Lorance* was expressly overruled by a provision of the 1991 Civil Rights Act, which states in Section 205(a)(2) that the statute of limitations for filing Title VII charges of discrimination (usually 300 days, see Q 4:10) will begin to run with regard to an unlawful employment practice, such as a discriminatory seniority system, on the date the illegal practice is initiated or "has been applied to affect adversely the person aggrieved, whichever is later." Section 205(b) of the act then explicitly addresses seniority systems themselves, saying that if a system is included in a collective bargaining agreement with the intent by the parties to discriminate, either its adoption or its application to particular persons can constitute the discriminatory act for purposes of triggering a cause of action and starting the running of the statutory time limitation.

While *Lorance* is clearly overruled by the above-cited provisions of the 1991 Civil Rights Act, *TWA v. Hardison* remains good law under Title VII, apparently allowing employers and unions to rely on bona fide seniority provisions in their labor contracts as a sound basis for denying reasonable accommodations that go against such contract clauses.

Q 11:60   Can a bona fide seniority system supersede the prohibition of age discrimination contained in the Age Discrimination in Employment Act?

As with Title VII, the ADEA contains a clause that provides limited protection to bona fide seniority systems against the act's otherwise sweeping prohibition of age discrimination. (See Q 11:56; 29 USC § 623(f)(2) (1982)) In *United States v. McMann* [434 US 192 (1977)] the Supreme Court held that a bona fide seniority system could lawfully mandate involuntary retirement of union members. This case was overruled a year later, when the ADEA was amended to forbid mandates of involuntary retirement in seniority clauses and retirement plans. Since the concept of reasonable accommodation is not a legal consideration in age cases, the only thing this provision of the ADEA does is clarify the fact that seniority systems in collective bargaining agreements remain a legal part of the labor-management landscape.

Illegal Activities

Q 11:61   What happens to a labor union when its leadership is guilty of racketeering?

In 1990, Roofers Union Local 30-30B was placed under a federal court "decreeship" in Philadelphia after 14 officers were found guilty of violating the Racketeer Influenced and Corrupt Organizations Act (RICO) for bribing local judges and for threatening nonunion roofing contractors within the union's jurisdiction. [US v Local 30, United

Slate, Tile and Composition Roofers, Damp and Waterproof Workers Assn, 1989 US Dist LEXIS 6853, 135 LRRM 3113 (ED Pa 1989)] As a result, a court liaison officer was appointed by the federal judge to oversee the local union's affairs. Other requirements were imposed as well: the union must adopt a grievance/arbitration procedure; all collective bargaining agreements must now be countersigned by the liaison officer; and the convicted former officers are barred from having any further contact with the union or any roofing job. The court took ultimate control of all union expenditures. It could have gone even further, by imposing a trusteeship and ousting the local's newly elected contingent of officers. Other unions that have been under Department of Justice scrutiny involving allegations of corruption include the Teamsters and Laborers. The Philadelphia Roofers Union posed a particularly egregious example of such corrupt activity, because the U.S. attorney's net caught judges who had accepted union favors and bribes.

Q 11:62 What happens to a labor union when it directs or condones a violent strike?

In 1989, national news media attention turned to a strike by the United Mine Workers of America (UMWA) against the Clinchfield Co. in southwest Virginia. When the company attempted to mine coal with replacement workers, the strikers, acting under union direction, conducted sit-ins to block traffic in and out of the struck mines, occupied a coal breaker (processing plant), put together convoys to block the transport of coal over state highways, threw rocks and shot at coal trucks, and subjected "scabs" to threats and assaults.

When the company obtained a labor injunction from the circuit court for Russell County (VA), the union and its members defied the injunction, ultimately incurring fines totaling $52 million for contempt of the court's order. When the strike was finally settled, a term insisted upon by the union was Clinchfield's consent to the vacating of the huge contempt fines. The court, however, surprised the parties by refusing to go along with their joint request to vacate the citations. Instead the court appointed a special commissioner with authority to collect the fines on behalf of the commonwealth and the relevant counties. In a benchmark decision, *John L. Bagwell, Special Commissioner v. United Mine Workers of America* [244 Va 463 (1992)], the

Virginia Supreme Court in late 1992 upheld the enormous penalties against the union, finding that they were neither excessive nor a violation of the UMWA's due process of law rights or the federal labor laws and policies. [Morse, "Virginia Supreme Court Affirms Fines Against UMWA," 1 *Labor Relations Ink* 3, January 1993, at 1]

However, in 1994 the U.S. Supreme Court unanimously vacated the $52 million fine. Had the high court failed to do so, the UMWA would have had to declare bankruptcy. ["Year in Review: Board Appointments, Court Rulings Brought Changes in Labor Field in '94," 1995 *BNA Daily Labor Report* 17, Jan 26, 1995, at d17] The court's decision is no surprise to students of labor history or of the American common law's evolving attitude toward "union busting." Since the second half of the nineteenth century, when courts declared that unions were not illegal conspiracies, through the early years of this century when exemptions were carved out of our antitrust acts for organized labor, to the present, when preemption has been the usual reason for overturning state court sanctions of union activities, the trend against such devastating sanctions as the $52 million fine has been clear cut. [See James O. Castagnera, "The Doctrines of Civil and Criminal Conspiracy as 'Union Busting' Techniques in Labor Law Past and Present," 8 *Thurgood Marshall Law Review* 1, Fall 1982, 1-63]

Q 11:63　Is an employee entitled to a jury trial in a Section 301 action?

In 1989 at least one federal court decided that the jury trial right adhered to a breach of labor contract case brought under Section 301 of the Taft-Hartley Act against his employer, which also enables members to sue a union for breach of fair representation. But, strangely, the court also held that the employee had no jury trial right on the other side of the coin—his fair representation action against the union. Usually, breach of the collective bargaining agreement and breach of the duty of fair representation go together in a Section 301 suit by a union member claiming denial of his or her contract rights. Consequently, employers might reasonably expect both aspects of the suit to go to the jury, or both to be decided by the judge. But federal District Judge Mencer of Western Pennsylvania ruled that, although the breach of contract claim would have been recognized by eighteenth century common law, and thus must be accorded a Seventh Amendment jury trial, the duty of fair representation half of the suit is analogous to an unfair labor practice charge under the NLRA and therefore cannot be decided by a jury. [Nicely v USX Corp, 706 F Supp 646, (WD Pa 1989)]

The federal appeals courts are in disagreement about whether or not the Seventh Amendment jury trial right applies to fair representation cases. Recent decisions suggest a tilt against the right to a jury trial, but it remains for the Supreme Court to resolve the controversy when it is presented with the right case. Meanwhile, there is speculation regarding whether juries will be more likely to favor labor unions or individual workers in such cases.

Q 11:64 Can union members sue their union for leading them to commit illegal activities?

Yes. A group of former employees of Royal Harvest Foods, a poultry processing plant in Springfield, MA, is suing the United Food and Commercial Workers Union (UFCW) because a business agent induced them to conduct a wildcat strike that cost them their jobs. According to the evidence at trial, the business agent encouraged nonstrikers to join in once the wildcat was underway, saying that more participants were needed for the strike to succeed. The hapless members sued the UFCW for breach of its duty of fair representation under Taft-Hartley. The case is somewhat unique in the annals of fair representation cases, which more typically revolve around a union's poor handling of a member's grievance or some internal union discrimination tactic, such as mismanaging the hiring hall for political gain (Q 11:54). For example, in December 1989, the Supreme Court held in *Breininger v. Sheet Metal Workers, Local 6* [493 US 67 (1989)] that discrimination in union hiring hall referrals gave rise to a "duty of fair representation" case. Overall, there seems to be a willingness within the federal court system to expand these causes of action by union members against their unions when abusive practices occur. This willingness is perhaps one more sign of the declining influence of labor unions in national policy.

Q 11:65 What happens to a union that violates a court order with respect to illegal picketing and strike activities?

In 1989 the state courts in Virginia imposed and upheld fines totaling $52 million against the UMWA for disobeying court orders regarding UMWA members' illegal activities directed against the Pittston Coal Group during the course of a violent 10-month strike. In May 1993, the U.S. Supreme Court agreed to review the propriety of these massive contempt fines. The labor union's contention is that the criminal contempt fines are so excessive as to amount to a denial of UMWA's due process of law rights under the federal constitution, as well as being cruel and unusual punishment in violation of the Eighth Amendment.

The fines were imposed originally by a state court trial judge to punish the union for allegedly permitting its pickets to obstruct ingress and egress to mines, intimidating non-strikers, shooting at coal trucks, throwing rocks, and puncturing tires. The Virginia Supreme Court upheld the fines, holding that settlement of the strike did not moot the fines and that courts must have the power to enforce their orders by "employing coercive, civil sanctions if the dignity of the law and public respect for the judiciary are to be maintained." ["Justices Vote to Review $52 Million Contempt Fine," 1993 *BNA Daily Labor Report* 104, June 2, 1993, at 1]

In 1994 a unanimous U.S. Supreme Court overturned the fines in their entirety. Had the high court failed to do so, the UMWA would have had to go bankrupt. ["Year in Review: Board Appointments, Court Rulings Brought Changes in Labor Field in '94," 1995 *BNA Daily Labor Report* 17, Jan 26, 1995, at d17]

Q 11:66 Can a union member sue the union for unfair operation of its hiring hall?

In *Breininger v. Sheet Metal Workers, Local 6*, (Q 11:64) the Supreme Court held that a union member, who claimed to be a victim of hiring hall discrimination, could either file an unfair labor practice charge with the NLRB or a lawsuit in federal court under Section 301 of the Labor-Management Relations (i.e., Taft-Hartley) Act.

On March 18, 1991, the U.S. Court of Appeals for the Third Circuit took the *Breininger* holding a step farther. The appeals court ruled that, when union members sue their local union for discriminatory hiring hall practices in breach of its duty of fair representation, the most appropriate state statute of limitations (and not the six-month limitation for unfair labor practice charges before the NLRB) should be applied by the federal court. [Brenner v Local 514, United Brotherhood of Carpenters and Joiners of America, 927 F 2d 1283 (1991)]

Q 11:67 What is a grievance arbitration?

Almost all collective bargaining agreements (labor contracts) contain a grievance procedure. The grievance procedure may call for several steps aimed at resolving the problem. An employee subject to disciplinary action, or who has some other grievance (for example, denial of a vacation request), usually must start the procedure within a specified time (for example, within three days of the event) by bringing the matter, either orally or in writing, to the attention of his or her immediate supervisor. If the issue is not settled at this stage, the grievance moves to the next step, consisting of a meeting between the shop steward and the department manager, and then to a third meeting, perhaps between the union business agent and the company's personnel director. If all the steps are followed without a resolution, the union may submit the grievance to the American Arbitration Association (AAA) to obtain an outside arbitrator. The AAA will provide a list of professional arbitrators from which the union and the company can choose. The arbitrator will hold a hearing and reach a decision that with few exceptions, will be final and binding on the parties.

Q 11:68 What is "interest arbitration"?

"Interest arbitration" signifies the arbitrator's role in breaking a deadlock between the company and the union in negotiating one or more issues of a collective bargaining agreement. Interest arbitration is rare in the private sector in the United States, but is much more common in public employment, especially if safety forces (for example, police and firefighters) are involved. Interest arbitration is often used in the public sector to break deadlocks on wages and other contract terms, in lieu of the employees' right to strike or lock out.

Disputes and Decertification

Q 11:69   What is a lockout?

A lockout occurs when an employer refuses to allow employees to work without a signed contract. A lockout is used to pressure the union into agreeing to the company's position on a new labor agreement.

Q 11:70   When can a union call a strike?

The vast majority of labor contracts contain no-strike clauses. Therefore, the union cannot call for a work stoppage during the term of the agreement. Once the collective bargaining agreement has expired, however, the union can call a strike if a new contract has not been made with the company. The strike is the union's principal economic weapon.

Q 11:71   Can the company continue to operate during a strike?

From a legal standpoint, the employer is entitled to keep operating during a strike, even if this means hiring replacement workers. As a practical matter, the company may find it unrealistic to do so, perhaps because of a lack of available replacement employees, or a desire not to antagonize the union or the strikers.

Q 11:72   Once unionized, can a company ever get rid of the union?

It is not easy to get rid of a labor union, but it is legally possible. This is generally accomplished by demonstrating to the NLRB's satisfaction that the union no longer enjoys the loyalty of a majority of the employees it claims to represent. The most common method of proving this is by a decertification petition and election.

Q 11:73   What is a decertification petition?

A decertification petition is a request for a representation election, filed by employees who are currently represented by a labor union but who desire to decertify (get rid of) the union as their collective bargaining representative. As with the representation petition that initially elected the union as bargaining representative, the decertification petition must be supported by at least 30 percent of the represented (unionized) employees.

Q 11:74   When can a company's unionized employees file a decertification petition?

Employees who are covered by a current collective bargaining agreement can file a decertification petition at two times: between the ninetieth and sixtieth day prior to the expiration of the current collective bargaining agreement (the so-called window period), or after the collective bargaining agreement expires, provided no new agreement has been negotiated between the employer and the union.

Q 11:75   Can an employer encourage its unionized employees to file a decertification petition?

It is illegal for an employer to encourage unionized employees to eliminate their union. However, if one or more of these employees questions management about the procedure for eliminating the union, management is free to advise such employees to visit the NLRB to become informed about a decertification election.

Q 11:76   Can a company ever withdraw recognition from the union?

If the employer has a good-faith belief, based on objective evidence, that the union no longer enjoys the support of a majority of the unionized employees, that employer may be able to withdraw recognition from the union. This rarely happens during the term of a collective bargaining agreement, unless the union has virtually abandoned the enforcement and maintenance of the agreement (e.g., ceased to investigate and negotiate grievances, to collect dues, or to perform other basic functions under the collective bargaining agreement). During the period between the

90th and 60th day prior to the expiration of the collective bargaining agreement, an employer that has objective evidence that the
union has lost a majority of support may file a petition for a new
election with the NLRB. Following expiration of the collective
bargaining agreement, and prior to negotiation of a new one, the
employer may likewise seek a representation election or withdraw
recognition from the union, based on objective evidence of the
union's loss of majority support.

Q 11:77 What objective evidence supports an employer's good-faith belief in the union's loss of majority support among the employees?

Factors and events that may be considered by the NLRB in determining whether the employer has legally withdrawn recognition
from the union are:

1. Extensive, rapid turnover of employees in the bargaining unit,
   especially as the result of hiring permanent replacements for
   striking workers;
2. Withdrawal of dues checkoff authorization by a majority of the
   employees in the bargaining unit;
3. A petition presented to the employer by a majority of the
   employees, requesting the company to withdraw recognition of
   the union; and
4. Failure of the union to enforce the union contract, investigate
   grievances, hold meetings, or otherwise function normally.

As a general rule, no single factor will support withdrawal of
recognition. Rather, the board decides whether the employer had
sufficient grounds for harboring a good-faith belief in the union's loss
of majority support.

Q 11:78 Can the hiring of replacement workers during a strike give rise to a good-faith doubt about the union's continuing majority support?

It is well established in labor law that a struck employer can hire
replacement workers, assuming it can find new employees willing to
cross the picket line. The company can even hire replacement work-

ers on a permanent basis, not just for the duration of the strike. Major examples of hiring replacement workers in recent memory include the air traffic controllers' strike in the early 1980s and, more recently, the Greyhound bus strike (Q 11:79).

Whether such permanent replacements can be considered pro- or anti-union has been a subject of substantial controversy for many years. The NLRB's view has shifted back and forth over the decades, as the makeup of the NLRB has been altered by expiring terms and new presidential appointments. As of 1990, the NLRB and the Supreme Court are in full accord that replacement workers will not be presumed to be either for or against the union. Consequently, if an employer has permanently replaced a majority of the striking workforce it does not mean that the company can withdraw recognition from the union, claiming a good-faith doubt about the union's continued majority support.

Good-faith doubt has, in fact, become a very difficult position for a company to maintain. It cannot be based on a "nose count" of replacement employees, nor can it be based on a secret-ballot private poll, since such a poll can itself only be justified by a good-faith doubt.

Q 11:79 Can employers still hire permanent replacements for their striking employees?

Yes. As of this writing, organized labor has not yet succeeded in lobbying Congress to overrule the Supreme Court's historic decision in *Mackay Radio & Tel. Co. v. NLRB*, [304 US 333 (1938)] holding that a company can legally replace economic strikers. Under *Mackay*'s long-standing "rules of the game" the employer can hire permanent replacements for striking employees if the strike is about wages and other economic aspects of their employment, but must reinstate strikers who protest their employer's unfair labor practices. Unions have long argued that, since most strikes are strictly economic, the *Mackay* rule gives companies an unfair advantage. When unions claimed a third of all U.S. workers and nearly 100 percent of blue-collar employees in some key U.S. industries (e.g., steel and autos), *Mackay* was rather academic, since organized labor had ample clout to compel reinstatement without loss of seniority at the end of a strike. But, as the air traffic controller and Greyhound strikes have demonstrated in recent years, the waning of union power (see Qs 11:5, 11:6) has made the 16 percent or so of unionized U.S. workers very vulnerable to permanent replacement whenever they take to their picket lines.

Nonetheless, so far Congress has resisted organized labor's efforts to pass a new labor law that overrules *Mackay*, although bills have been introduced in virtually every session of Congress in recent years. Consequently, organized labor has turned to the state legislatures for relief. For instance, in 1991 the Delaware legislature passed a striker replacement bill that insured striker reinstatement rights for six months from the inception of a work stoppage. The bill, however, was vetoed by Governor Castle, who said that in his view it was preempted by federal labor law.

Bankruptcies, Mergers, and Acquisitions

Q 11:80 During the term of a labor contract, what company business decisions must be negotiated with the union?

A company that has a collective bargaining relationship with a union must bargain about decisions that affect wages, hours, and conditions of employment. Some of the company's business decisions that are closely related to these categories must be negotiated also, unless the union waives its right to negotiate clearly and unequivocally, such as by an unambiguous provision in the collective bargaining agreement. The decision to subcontract work normally performed by the unionized employees is an example of a business decision that must be negotiated. On the other hand, the company's decision to close a plant or department is fundamental to "entrepreneurial control" and usually need not be negotiated with the union, although the company is probably obligated to discuss the effects that a closing or similar decision may have on the unionized workers.

Q 11:81 When must a company open its financial books to a union during labor negotiations?

The general rule is that when a company claims during labor negotiations that it is financially unable to pay the wages and benefits being demanded by the union, the union has a right to demand disclosure of financial information to support the company's contention. This is a long-established doctrine in labor law. [See NLRB v Truitt Manufacturing Co, 351 US 149 (1956) ("[I]t is settled law that when an employer seeks to justify the refusal of a wage increase upon an economic basis . . . , good faith bargaining under the act requires that upon request the employer attempt to substantiate its economic position by reasonable proof.")]

However, the National Labor Relations Act expressly states that neither party to labor negotiations must make a particular concession to be viewed as bargaining in good faith. (See Q 11:43; 29 USC § 158(d)) Consequently, a company can always contend that it is unwilling to agree to the union's wage demands, without going so far as to say that the firm is unable to agree to those increases.

During the 1980s, walking the line between claiming unwillingness, as opposed to inability, to pay became a part of the fine art of concession bargaining, as more firms demanded rollbacks in wages and benefits from their unionized employees. In the 1990s, a new twist is being witnessed in the fine art of walking the tightrope with regard to whether the company's books must be opened to the union. With increasing frequency, employers are arguing not that they necessarily are unable to accede to union wage and benefits demands, but rather that by doing so, the corporation places itself in an uncompetitive position in the marketplace, where the higher wage costs will affect sales adversely.

The NLRB was confronted with such an argument in a case involving Nielson Lithographing Co. [305 NLRB No 90, 138 LRRM 1441 (1991)] The case has a long and tortured history. [See 279 NLRB 877 (1986), *enforcement denied*, 854 F 2d 1063 (7th Cir 1988), on remand, 305 NLRB No 90; Q 11:24]

In this case, the company and the union, which had a collective bargaining history dating back three decades, entered contract negotiations in 1985. The company confronted the union with 76 proposals, including lengthening the workday, reducing wages and health insurance benefits as well as shift premiums and holiday pay, and reducing job retraining programs.

In making these proposals, the company never claimed that it was unable to pay more than what was proposed. Rather, it contended that "the costs in our contract were prohibitive, and [we] needed to have concessions . . . to compete with the competitors. . . . The trends showed [us] that [we] would have a worse problem in the future."

The labor board said: "[Nielson went] beyond the expression of a mere unwillingness to continue paying the costs of its collective-bargaining agreement; by its words and conduct [Nielson] conveyed to the union an inability to pay . . . and thus triggered a duty to disclose financial information.

On appeal, the federal court disagreed, citing one of its own precedents on the issue:

> Nielson . . . never claimed that it was unable to pay the existing scale of wages and benefits. It admitted to being profitable but said it wanted to bring its wage bill into line with the wages paid by competitors to whom it was losing sales. A company can survive, certainly in the short run and often in the long run, even though it is paying higher wages than its competitors. The company may have some other cost advantage; its competitors may price above their costs; the market may be expanding rapidly. The company will grow less rapidly than if its costs were lower and may stagnate and decline, but it need not die. There is thus no contradiction in a company's stating on the one hand that it is profitable and on the other hand that its costs are higher than its competitors' and it wants to reduce them. The board concedes that if this is all Nielson said, Nielson had no duty to open its books to the union.

[129 BNA LRRM 2367, 2368 (1992)]

The court remanded the case for the board's further consideration, and the second time the board ruled that a claim "of competitive disadvantage is not the same as a claim of financial inability to pay . . . and does not raise any obligation . . . to turn over the requested information."

The *Nielson* case began in the mid-1980s, when leveraged buyouts, mergers, and union-busting were the order of the day. The board brought the case to a close in the present decade, when its significance to corporations, struggling to climb out of one of the longest and deepest recessions of this century and to compete in an increasingly competitive marketplace, makes *Nielson* an important decision. *Nielson* frees companies to focus employees' and their unions' attention on hard international and national realities without having to bare all confidential financial information, thereby risking leaks to the competition in the process.

Q 11:82 Is a company required to negotiate with a union over its decision to close its doors?

The NLRB has held that a company is not required to bargain over management decisions that affect the basic nature or direction of the business. When labor costs are the basis for a decision to close, however, the employer is required to bargain over its decision to do so. [Otis Elevator Company (Otis II), 269 NLRB 891 (1984)]

When an employer decides to close a plant entirely, as opposed to subcontracting or transferring work, the law permits the employer to make such a decision without bargaining with the union. Once the decision to close a plant is made, the employer is obligated to bargain with the union over the effects of the closure on bargaining unit employees. Employees' rights to job security, severance pay, pensions, and other accrued benefits are the types of issues that might be addressed in "effects bargaining." As with any other negotiation with a union, an employer that has the duty to engage in effects bargaining is not required to grant any benefits or make any concessions. The only requirement is that the employer bargain in good faith. [NLRA § 8(d); see also, JD Lunsford Plumbing, Heating and Air Conditioning, 254 NLRB 1360 (1981)]

Q 11:83 Can a union's right to negotiate survive the termination of the collective bargaining agreement?

The union's right to bargain on behalf of the employees it represents is a right separate and distinct from rights contained in the collective bargaining agreement. Unless the employees vote to decertify the union (Qs 11:74, 11:75) or the employer legally withdraws recognition (Qs 11:76, 11:77), the right to negotiate survives not only the expiration of the labor contract, but also the closing of a part of the employer's business, such as a particular plant.

Q 11:84 What happens to the bargaining duty if the company goes out of business?

A complete discontinuation of the business terminates the employer's duty to bargain. However, a sham discontinuation, such as a mere change of name and location, is not sufficient. The NLRB will brand a firm a "runaway shop"; the new firm and the old company and location will be treated as a single employer and the union's labor contract will be imposed on the "new" enterprise.

Q 11:85 What happens to the collective bargaining agreement when a unionized company goes into bankruptcy?

A bankrupt company can ask the U.S. bankruptcy judge handling its case to allow it to reject or modify its collective bargaining agreement(s). Under the Bankruptcy Amendments and Federal Judgeship Act of 1984 [11 USC § 1113], the bankruptcy judge can grant the debtor-company's request only upon a showing by the company that:

1. The company first made a proposal to the union for modification of the labor agreement;

2. The proposal to the union was based on the best available information at the time it was made;

3. The proposed modifications are necessary for the company's successful reorganization;

4. All parties will be treated fairly under the proposal;

5. The union has been provided all the information it needs to evaluate the proposal;

6. The company has met with the union to discuss the proposal;

7. At such meetings, the company conferred in good faith with the union;

8. The union rejected the proposal without good cause; and

9. The circumstances on balance favor unilateral implementation of the proposed rejection or modification of the collective bargaining agreement by the company.

These statutory requirements have created some tough questions for bankrupt companies, unions, and the federal courts. For instance, must a company show that modification or rejection of a collective bargaining agreement is absolutely necessary to the success of the firm's plan of reorganization? And does a union have "good cause" to reject a proposal if a less drastic modification of the labor contract might suffice to help save the company? Courts have reached differing conclusions on these questions since Congress passed the act seven years ago. For example, in *Wheeling-Pittsburgh Steel Corp. v. Steelworkers* [791 F 2d 1074 (3d Cir 1986)], the court held that the word "necessary" in part 3 of the above test must "be construed to signify only modifications that the trustee is constrained to accept because they are directly related to the company's financial condition and its reorganization." But in *Teamsters Local 807 v. Carey Transportation* [816 F 2d 82 (2d Cir 1987)], a sister appeals court held that the test permits "necessary, but not absolutely minimal changes that will enable the debtor to complete the reorganization process successfully." In other words, one court interpreted the act as limiting modification of union contracts essentially to what is absolutely necessary for a successful company reorganization, while the other court allowed the debtor-company greater flexibility to propose broader modifications.

Q 11:86   Do the automatic stay provisions of the Bankruptcy Code apply to arbitrations under a collective bargaining agreement?

The code's "stay" provisions say that, as soon as a voluntary or involuntary bankruptcy petition is filed, all other lawsuits (whether in state or federal court) must be placed on hold, pending the resolution of the bankruptcy case. Usually litigants with claims against the debtor-company will file proofs of claim with the bankruptcy court and pursue their claims in that arena; those who fail to do so risk losing their claims through the debtor's discharge by the bankruptcy court. Although the judicial trend is to apply the code's stay provisions to lawsuits by unions against debtor-companies, the courts appear willing to permit arbitrations under collective bargaining agreements to proceed, at least up to the point where the bankruptcy court permits a debtor to reject the labor contract itself.

Q 11:87 What happens to the labor contracts in a unionized company if it is purchased by another company?

If the acquiring company buys the stock of the unionized firm, under corporate law the buyer steps into the shoes of the former shareholders. Therefore, the buyer gets all of the seller's assets and liabilities, including its labor agreements and union relationships. However, if the buyer purchases a unionized company's assets only and not the common stock, then liabilities do not automatically follow. In this case, the buyer does not automatically assume the seller's labor contracts, nor does the buyer necessarily have a duty to recognize and bargain with the seller's unions.

Q 11:88 When must the buyer of a unionized company's assets recognize and negotiate with the seller's union?

The asset purchaser becomes the seller's successor and must recognize and bargain with the seller's union(s) if and when a majority of the buyer's relevant bargaining unit consists of unionized employees of the former owner.

Q 11:89 Can the asset buyer that hires a majority of the workforce from among the asset seller's employees ever avoid being a successor?

If a lengthy hiatus takes place between the time the seller closes the facility and the time the purchaser buys and reopens the facility, the buyer may be insulated from successorship status. Similarly, if the asset purchaser uses the assets, such as a plant or warehouse facility, to engage in a completely different line of business from the seller's, or integrates the assets and employees into a much larger organization, the buyer may be insulated from successorship status because of the drastic operational change.

Q 11:90   Can a union ever picket a nonunion company?

A union can set up a picket line as part of its efforts to organize the employees of a nonunion company. The picket line may remain for 30 days, after which a union must either file an election petition with the NLRB or cease picketing. A union can also picket a nonunion company to protest low wages that are inconsistent with union standards for the geographic area, or a company that has allied itself with a "primary employer" with which the union has a legitimate labor dispute.

Q 11:91   Can labor unions picket employers' homes?

In 1988 the Supreme Court ruled that a Milwaukee municipalities law that banned picketing in front of a private home was constitutional. [Frisby v Schultz, 487 US 474 (1988)] The case arose from the picketing of a doctor's home by antiabortion activists. Although it was not a labor law case per se, the same principles seem to apply with respect to a union picketing an employer's home in the course of a labor dispute or organization drive.

Q 11:92   How does a company become an "ally" that may be picketed?

An ally is a company that agrees to do work and fill orders on behalf of a company whose employees are on strike.

Q 11:93   What is a secondary employer?

The primary employer is a company with which the union has a legitimate labor dispute; a secondary employer is any other company with which the union has no dispute but that the union may picket in order to force the primary employer to meet the union's demands. For instance, a union on strike against a steel manufacturer might picket the car producer that buys the sheet metal for the car bodies, thus attempting to convince the car maker to pressure the steel manufacturer to settle the strike. This is a secondary boycott. It is usually illegal unless the secondary employer is the primary employer's ally (Q 11:92).

Q 11:94   How can a company protect itself in the event of a labor dispute?

Under the NLRA, both companies and unions can file unfair labor practice charges (ULPs) with the NLRB. Usually, if the NLRB issues a complaint after promptly investigating a ULP charge, it will refer the case to an administrative law judge for trial and resolution. However, in the case of secondary boycotts and similar illegal picketing and work stoppages, the NLRB may have both a right and a duty to ask a federal judge for an injunction against the illegal union activity.

Unfair Labor Practices

Q 11:95   Is the decision of the NLRB's general counsel to drop an unfair labor practice complaint, after the administrative law judge hearing has begun, reviewable?

The general counsel's withdrawal of a complaint even after the hearing had started, but before any evidence on the merits had been introduced, was determined by Court of Appeals for the Ninth Circuit to be an unreviewable, unappealable decision. This ruling expands the historically well-settled proposition that the general counsel's decision not to issue a complaint on an unfair labor practice charge is without appeal. [Intl Brhd of Boilermakers v NLRB, 872 F 2d 331 (9th Cir 1989)]

Q 11:96   Is it an unfair labor practice to fire unionized employees testing positive for drug use?

Yes. The NLRB general counsel has announced a policy of seeking reinstatement of employees who are fired after testing positive for drug use if the NLRB discovers that the employer failed to engage in good-faith bargaining with the employee's union before instituting the drug testing policy. This pronouncement appears to be part of a coalescing policy position of the NLRB's general counsel, the effect of which is that implementation of a drug-testing program without collective bargaining will in most cases constitute an unfair labor practice. This policy has been upheld by two decisions of the five-member NLRB. [Johnson-Bateman Co, 295 NLRB No 26, 131 LRRM 1393 (1989); Star Tribune, 295 NLRB No 63, 131 LRRM 1404 (1989)] Some labor specialists believe that a particularly strong management rights clause in a collective bargaining agreement may permit implementation of a drug testing policy without prior union negotiation. At a bare minimum, however, employers must be aware that NLRB regional offices will closely scrutinize any unfair labor practice charges by unions that involve drug programs in the absence of negotiation. However, the NLRB has shown a willingness to defer these cases to arbitration. [See Inland Container Corp, 298 NLRB No 97 (1990)]

Q 11:97 What have been recent labor union responses to employers' drug testing policies?

As noted in Q 11:96, the NLRB considers an employer's drug testing program to be a mandatory subject of collective bargaining. Consequently, the NLRB general counsel has announced a policy of seeking reinstatement of employees who are fired after testing positive for drug use if the NLRB discovers that the employer did not bargain with the employee's union before instituting the drug testing policy.

This position has been upheld by the NLRB itself in the Johnson-Bateman Co. and Star Tribune decisions. In these two cases, drug testing was declared to be a mandatory subject for collective bargaining. Consequently, under most circumstances unionized employers cannot unilaterally implement a drug testing program for employees without first bargaining with its union(s) to impasse over that issue. Indeed, the NLRB majority was clear that only the most unequivocal waiver of the union's bargaining rights will permit an employer to institute testing in the absence of good faith negotiations; most management rights and so-called zipper clauses in labor contracts will not suffice, nor will prior unilateral implementation of a "no drugs/no alcohol" work rule.

However, the NLRB does not require bargaining over a policy of testing job applicants as part of a preemployment screening program, because "applicants are not bargaining unit employees and . . . preemployment drug and alcohol testing is not encompassed within the statutory duty to bargain about terms and conditions of employment. . . ." The union still enjoys the right, however, to request information from the company concerning this preemployment testing.

Where the company's right to test is clearly one of contract interpretation, the NLRB has recently demonstrated a willingness to refer the case to arbitration. (See Inland Container Corp, 1991 NLRB LEXIS 1281 (Sept 18, 1991) (allegation that employer unilaterally modified labor contract by implementing substance abuse program deferred to grievance arbitration)) At arbitration it appears employers are being severely tested. For instance, in one award reported in 1990, a Houston bus driver was reinstated with full back pay and benefits because the arbitrator found the collection site and chain of custody procedures for testing to be too lax. The arbitrator noted that the employer, Houston Metropolitan Transit Authority, was required to follow U.S. Department of Transportation standards [49 CFR Part 40], which place heavy emphasis on chain of custody safeguarding of samples. He found the collection procedures at St. Joseph Hospital, where the driver provided a urine sample following an accident with his bus, to be remiss in many respects, including failure to give the driver written instructions, failure to take the temperature of the specimen immediately following collection, and overall laxity at the collection site, according to four union witnesses. (See Metro Transit Auth, Houston, Texas and Transp Workers Union, Local 260 (Arb Barry J Baroni, Jan 8, 1990), reported in 28 *BNA Government Employee Relations Report*, 1355, Mar 12, 1990 at 324)

Thus, even if an employer has the right to test its unionized employees—either by virtue of waiver or negotiation (whether to agreement or impasse)—this will not do the employer much good if proper procedures are not established and stringently followed.

Q 11:98   Do employees have the right to engage in concerted activities to protest drug testing in the workplace?

Although Section 7 of the National Labor Relations Act provides employees with the right to engage in concerted activity, whether or not they are unionized, the U.S. Court of Appeals for the Fifth Circuit, which sits in New Orleans, ruled in 1993 that the Motorola Company did not commit an unfair labor practice (ULP) when it forbade its workers in Austin, Texas, from distributing leaflets and wearing T-shirts in support of Citizens Advocating Protection of Privacy (CAPP). CAPP was formed by employees of another Austin-based electronics firm, Texas Instruments (TI), when TI announced plans to start testing employees for drugs in 1989.

"Warning that an NLRB holding (that Motorola had committed a ULP) would force employers to open the workplace to an array of political splinter groups," the Fifth Circuit overturned the labor board's ruling against the corporation, adding that "not every interference with employee rights rises to the level of an unfair labor practice" and that the NLRB was being "simply unrealistic." ["Court Favors Motorola Right to Curb Leaflets," 1993 *BNA Daily Labor Report* 103, June 1, 1993, at 1]

Q 11:99 How are unions faring in labor arbitrations challenging the discharge of members for illicit drug use?

A small sampling of cases suggests that, while arbitrators are demonstrating some inclination to uphold grievances and reinstate workers fired for illicit drug use, at least under some circumstances, the federal judiciary is not prepared to permit such arbitration awards to stand. In two separate cases, U.S. appeals courts sitting in New Orleans and Philadelphia overturned arbitrators' awards reinstating employees fired for illegal drug abuse. In cases involving a refinery in Texas and an oil tanker that ran aground on the Mississippi River, the arbiters had relied upon post-firing good conduct and rehabilitation of the grievants as the basis for reversing their terminations and reinstating them. In setting aside these arbitration awards, the two federal appellate panels said that public safety and environmental concerns were sufficiently strong considerations to sustain the companies in their contention of just cause (Q 13:2) for imposing the severe penalty of discharge upon the two employees. ["Courts Tighten Standards for Drug Infractions," 1993 *BNA Daily Labor Report* 101, May 27, 1993, at 1]

Additionally, it is worth noting that in considering the discharged employees' post-termination conduct, the arbitrators arguably were going outside their mandate under the respective collective bargaining agreements, because implicit in arbiters' review of just cause for discharge is the limitation upon them to reconstruct a "snapshot" of the circumstances at the time the employers made their decisions. Subsequent behavior by the grievants is irrelevant to the existence or nonexistence of just cause at the time the terminations took place.

Q 11:100   Will the NLRB defer drug testing cases to arbitration?

The NLRB's tendency to defer drug testing charges to arbitration, noted at Q 11:97, where the grievance and arbitration clause of a labor contract permits arbitration of such issues, has been reinforced by recent labor board decisions. In a case involving the San Onofre, CA, nuclear power plant, a majority of board members deferred to an arbitrator's decision that the management rights clause of the collective bargaining agreement between the Southern California Edison Co. and Utility Workers Local 246 was broad enough to permit the company's unilateral institution of a drug and alcohol testing program. ["NLRB Defers to Arbitration Allowing Drug, Alcohol Tests," 1993 *BNA Daily Labor Report* 93, May 17, 1993, at 1]

If any larger trend can be discerned from this and other cases being decided by governmental agencies and courts, it is that the more dangerous the industry, either in terms of employee safety or environmental concerns involving the general public, the more likely it is that the employer will be permitted to implement a unilateral policy for mandatory drug testing, even randomly. On the other hand, when the setting poses little danger of harm to co-workers, the general public, or the environment, courts and boards are more reluctant to permit involuntary drug tests and more likely to impose liability upon employers for invasion of privacy where such plans are implemented and employees punished for refusing to participate in them. [See Qs 2:14, 3:70, 4:89, 4:90, 5:15, 7:138–7:151, 11:97–11:101; compare Hennessey v Coastal Eagle Point Oil Co, 589 A 2d 170 (NJ Super 1991) (no violation of employee's privacy right in subjecting him to a random drug test where he handled massive quantities of petroleum products in storage tanks) with Borse v Piece Goods Shop Inc, 963 F 2d 611 (3d Cir 1991) (employee has cause of action for wrongful discharge for refusing to agree to random drug testing in retail store setting)]

Q 11:101   Have labor unions accepted employer drug testing of their members?

In light of all the apparent protection afforded unionized employees by the NLRB and neutral arbitrators, one might expect organized labor's acceptance of drug testing, since big labor has in recent years made serious efforts to stake a claim to job safety as a raison d'etre for the survival of labor unions in this post-industrial, predominantly white-collar era; however, such has generally not been the case.

Still many companies, including some of the nation's major unionized employers, have gone forward with drug testing programs because of the significant risks and costs associated with drug abuse in the workplace. In fact, nearly 50 percent of the Fortune 500 companies have implemented or are considering drug testing.

One recruit to these ranks is the Boeing Company, which in December 1990 instituted a drug and alcohol testing program affecting all 150,000 of its employees. This program was implemented over the objection of the company's largest union.

At the time Boeing instituted the program, which called for "reasonable suspicion" testing and company-run rehabilitation, the president of the local union was quoted in the BNA Daily Labor Report of December 17, 1990, as observing: "What's ironic about this is, how does Boeing expect its employee assistance program to work when (the company has) a 'we don't care what you think' attitude. The company has unilaterally implemented its drug plan in spite of the opposition of its employees." This statement suggests that unions and union members may resist even programs that are clearly beneficial to their members, if the leadership believes that its influence is being undermined by either the programs or its manner of implementation.

Therefore, both from the standpoint of labor peace, as well as litigation (arbitration, unfair labor practice) avoidance, unionized employers must involve union leadership at the onset of planning a drug-free workplace, and especially a drug testing program.

Q 11:102   Have labor unions accepted employer smoking bans?

In the United States, smoking in the workplace has become a subject of substantial controversy (see Qs 7:84–7:95). Many employees have insisted upon smoke-free workplaces and have sued when secondary smoke aggravated their asthmatic conditions and their employers have refused to take remedial measures sufficient to solve the problem. Some employers have felt "damned if I do and damned if I don't" as smokers have also brought legal actions, claiming that nicotine addiction is a disability and demanding reasonable accommodation in otherwise smokeless workplaces. A number of public employers, such as major U.S. cities, have enacted ordinances forbidding smoking in parts of public buildings or mandating smoke-free areas in restaurants and other public accommodations.

In the midst of this controversy, a significant subsidiary issue is whether a ban on smoking in the workplace is a mandatory subject for collective bargaining. As unions have, at times, insisted upon collective bargaining with regard to drug testing programs by employers (Q 11:101), so, too, have they sometimes challenged corporate decisions to mandate smoke-free workplaces. In one recent case, the Connecticut Supreme Court ordered the Connecticut State Board of Labor Relations to go back and reconsider the American Federation of State, County and Municipal Employees (AFSCME) Union's request for collective bargaining with regard to a local school board's smoking ban. While not providing a smokers' lounge, the New Britain Board of Education banned all smoking by teachers, even when classes were not in session and outside the school building on all school grounds. The court agreed with the union that such highly discretionary restrictions triggered a duty to bargain about these rules. ["Impact of Smoking Ban Held Subject to Bargaining," 1993 BNA Daily Labor Report 43, Mar 8, 1993, at 1]

Q 11:103   Can related corporations be drawn into a labor dispute?

Parent, subsidiary, and brother and sister corporations generally cannot be picketed by a union that has a dispute with a related corporate entity, nor can such a separate but related company be forced to share legal liability for an unfair labor practice brought to the attention of the NLRB by a union. Only by becoming involved in the related, unionized company's labor relations and corporate affairs can the parent or sister company be made to share labor law liability under the same labor contract as a single employer.

Q 11:104   Can one owner, shareholder, or holding company acquire and operate unionized and nonunionized companies simultaneously?

Yes. The unionized firms' labor contracts and bargaining duties will not spill over into the nonunionized entities, provided that day-to-day labor relations, corporate labor policies, and the normal indicia of corporate integrity and separateness are carefully maintained, and provided that the nonunionized entity was not created merely to avoid or circumvent the unionized company's labor contract commitments.

Q 11:105   Can a labor union have an ownership interest in a company in which it represents the employees?

ESOPs are offered with increasing frequency to unionized employees in return for wage and fringe benefit concessions or in lieu of a pension plan. When the employees are unionized, ESOPs cause a problem for the union, which in essence may find its members represented on both sides of the bargaining table. Yet sometimes, the sale, merger, acquisition, and, indeed, continued operation of a company or plant will hinge on the union's willingness to become involved in the transaction through an ESOP or stock trust. If care is taken to separate the interests of the employee-shareholders as owners from their interests as unionized employees, such arrangements can be legal and functional and include union participation.

Q 11:106   Is the team approach to production legal under the NLRA?

In 1990, an NLRB administrative law judge ruled that a DuPont "design team" was actually an illegal labor union, created with the intent to undermine the union legally certified to represent team members. The design team included supervisors and dealt with issues that touched on mandatory subjects for collective bargaining. The Chemical Workers Association of the International Brotherhood of DuPont Workers challenged the arrangement. However, by the time that the administrative law judge pronounced the team to be an unfair labor practice, the design team had completed its objectives and had been dissolved, according to a DuPont spokesperson.

The DuPont design team experience raises the issue of whether other sorts of innovative team approaches might run afoul of labor laws. Presumably, collective bargaining of team concepts could solve the illegalities found in the DuPont case by the administrative law judge. A union may not always visualize at the bargaining table the sweeping changes in the labor-management relationship that a team concept can cause. A truly successful and effective team approach can undermine the traditional power of union business agents and stewards, short-circuiting the traditionally vivid lines of authority. Yet the team concept is highly conducive to the kind of labor-management cooperation many labor experts believe is essential for U.S. industry to be competitive in an international marketplace.

Q 11:107   What is an employee participation program?

The term "employee participation program" is the label used to describe a broad spectrum of workplace cooperation and quality methods that have caught on across this country, in response to Japan's reputed success in using such methods to become a world-class competitor, especially in manufacturing, where the United States was once the undeniable leader. As one expert recently observed:

"It is currently fashionable to embrace labor-management cooperation programs to rebuild our industrial base. Everywhere you look some arm of the government and some major corporations are extolling the virtues of cooperation programs. And why not? Serious and legitimate labor-management cooperation may be just the solution we have been looking for." [Herrnstadt, "Why Some Unions Hesitate to Participate in Labor-Management Cooperation Programs," 8 *Labor Law J* 71 (1992)]

In March 1993, U.S. Labor Secretary Robert Reich announced the creation of a joint commission with the Department of Commerce to explore ways to increase labor-management cooperation and employee participation in the workplace. The mandate of the 10-member panel is to ascertain whether there are any new institutions, structures, or methods that should either be legally required, or at least encouraged by government, to enhance productivity through labor-management cooperation and employee participation in the workplace. [1993 *BNA Daily Labor Report* 56, Mar 25, 1993, at f1] According to Reich, "The goal here . . . is to improve this economy, to increase the standard of living of Americans."

Q 11:108   Does the National Labor Relations Act impose any legal restrictions upon employers' discretion in creating employee participation programs in their workplaces?

In a long-awaited decision, the NLRB held that at least some employee participation programs violate the NLRA's restraint upon employers establishing or supporting labor organizations. In *Electromation Inc.* [309 NLRB No 163 (Dec 16, 1992)], the labor board found the so-called action committees set up by a small electrical parts manufacturer in Elkhart, IN, to be illegal. In the words of one commentator, "In late 1988, after a year of heavy losses, management skipped wage hikes for its 200 workers. When employees objected, the company set up committees, each with up to six hourly workers and one or two managers, to deal with problems such as absenteeism and pay scales for skilled workers." [Bernstein, "Putting a Damper on the Old Team Spirit," *BusinessWeek*, May 4, 1992, at 60] When a union sought to represent these same hourly workers, the company gave the action committees the option of disbanding or continuing to meet as the company saw fit. Meanwhile, at least one of the committees, charged with "Pay Progression for Premium Positions," had submitted a proposal under the guidance of the company's controller. The union filed an unfair labor practice charge, and after hearing the case, an NLRB administrative judge found the company's committees violated the NLRA. Electromation took exception to the ruling, and the case proceeded to the NLRB in Washington.

In reviewing the administrative judge's decision, the labor board took into consideration two provisions of the act. Section 2(5) defines a "labor organization" as "any organization of any kind, or any agency or employee representation committee or plan, in which employees participate and which exists for the purpose, in whole or in part, of dealing with employers concerning grievances, labor disputes, wages, rates of pay, hours of employment, or conditions of work."

Section 8(a)(2) makes it an unfair labor practice for an employer:

> [T]o dominate or interfere with the formation or administration of any labor organization or contribute financial or other support to it; provided that subject to rules and regulations made and published by the board pursuant to section 6, an employer shall not be prohibited from permitting employees to confer with him during working hours without loss of time or pay.

Meticulously reviewing its own precedents, as well as leading opinions of the U.S. Supreme Court, and even the 50-year-old legislative history of the NLRA, the board majority held, ". . . we find, in agreement with the judge, that the Action Committees constitute a labor organization within the meaning of 2(5) of the act; and that the respondent dominated it, and assisted it, i.e., contributed support, within the meaning of section 8(a)(2)," in violation of the NLRA.

Q 11:109 Does the NLRB's *Electromation* decision mean the end of employee participation programs?

It is highly unlikely that the NLRB's *Electromation* decision will greatly affect, much less end, the proliferation of and continued interest in employee participation programs in this country, for several reasons.

First, the majority opinion and the concurring opinions in the *Electromation* decision go to great lengths to make it clear that the decision is limited to the particular facts of the case. For instance, footnote 28 of the majority's opinion expressly states:

> We find no basis in this record to conclude that the purpose of the Action Committees was limited to achieving "quality" or "efficiency" or that they were designed to be a "communication device" to promote generally the interests of quality or efficiency. We, therefore, do not reach the question of whether any

employer-initiated programs that may exist for such purposes
. . . may constitute labor organizations under section 2(5).

NLRB member Devaney's concurrence states clearly that, "It is my
position . . . that legislative history, binding judicial precedent, and
Board precedent provide significant latitude to employers seeking to
involve employees in the workplace." Furthermore, ". . . a 'pure'
employee participation plan was not before Congress in 1935 and has
never been before the Supreme Court."

Similarly, NLRB member Oviatt stated:

> American companies, their employees, and labor unions repre-
> senting those employees are at present confronted with diverse
> competitive forces requiring an array of different responses if
> those companies are to remain competitive in the world econ-
> omy. To the extent present laws are interpreted to apply restric-
> tions and roadblocks to companies' ability to perform more
> efficiently and to respond promptly to competitive conditions,
> the more difficult will be the common task of achieving or
> retaining quality. This is a time of testing for the American and
> world economies and we must proceed with caution when we
> address the legality of innovative employee involvement pro-
> grams directed to improving efficiency and productivity.

Second, Labor Secretary Reich and various members of Congress
have indicated their view that *Electromation* is an extremely narrow
holding. They have also suggested their willingness to amend the
labor laws, if need be, to remove any legal impediments to employee
workplace cooperation programs that prove themselves competitively appropriate. Consequently, it seems clear that employee participation programs will be a permanent part of the American labor
scene, the *Electromation* case notwithstanding.

Nevertheless, at the 1993 national conference of the Society of
Human Resource Management, NLRB member John Raudabaugh
commented that *Electromation* has at least made it riskier for companies to set up employee participation programs. In his view the
decision should not be read as meaning that "employee committees
are great with few exceptions." To avoid committing unfair labor
practices, companies setting up committees of employees should
have committee members steer clear of wages, hours, and other such
terms and conditions of employment, focusing their energy and
attention instead upon product quality. However, he warns some-

what ominously that even consideration of safety issues by such committees may run afoul of the NLRA. ["Employee Participation Groups at Risk After Electromation," 1993 *BNA Daily Labor Report* 100, May 26, 1993, at 1]

Q 11:110   What are some general categories of employee participation programs?

Although employee participation programs are very diverse, three general approaches have been identified, arranged according to power and purpose:

1. *Problem-Solving Teams.* Typically, these consist of five to 12 volunteers who gather for a few hours each week to explore new ways to improve quality, efficiency, and the on-the-job environment. Problem-solving teams do not usually have power to implement their ideas. "Quality circles," depending upon who is using the term, are either a subset of or are synonymous with problem-solving teams.

2. *Special-Purpose Teams.* These may function to come up with and introduce new technologies or to reform particular workplace practices. A team may even deal with a company's customers or suppliers directly.

3. *Self-Managed Teams.* This is probably the model that enters most people's minds when the word "team" is mentioned. Typically, a team consisting of five to 15 employees learns all relevant production tasks for a particular product. For example, in the assembly of an automobile, team members rotate jobs, learning each position, including managerial duties, such as work schedules and purchasing functions, which are an integral part of the self-managed teams' approach.

Q 11:111   Will the National Labor Relations Act be amended during the Clinton administration?

With regard to employee participation programs (see Qs 11:108–11:110), Labor Secretary Robert Reich has stated that, if the NLRB's *Electromation* decision or any subsequent decisions render labor-management cooperation illegal in the workplace, he ". . . will do what's necessary, up to and including amending the National Labor Relations Act" in order to legalize such programs. [See Frank Swoboda, "Reich Vows to Preserve Workplace Cooperation," *Washington Post*, Mar 9, 1993, at D3]

Additionally, President Clinton has indicated sympathy for organized labor's goal of requiring reinstatement of economic strikers following termination of a labor dispute. Under long-standing Supreme Court and labor board precedents, employees who strike for better wages can be replaced permanently, as the air traffic controllers were by President Reagan in 1981.

Pursuant to this stated sympathy toward organized labor and labor-management cooperation, in 1993 the Clinton administration established the Dunlop Commission on the Future of Worker-Management Relations. The commission held hearings into 1994 and submitted its report in January 1995 (Q 11:10.) However, since the commission membership included three former labor secretaries, its recommendations were widely anticipated to be in line with Secretary of Labor Reich's views on how American labor policy ought to evolve in the 1990s. ["Workplace Cooperation Commission Reflects Organized Labor's Views," 54 *Apparel Industry Magazine* 10, Oct 1993, at 34]

Numerous bills are pending before both houses of the Congress, many unabashedly pro-labor, or at least clearly aimed at amending what are perceived by liberal members of Congress as provisions of the National Labor Relations Act which inhibit labor-management cooperation or organized labor's ability to unionize more of the private-sector workforce. [See Q 11:8; "Much Labor Law Reform Debate Expected in 1994," *BNA Labor Relations Reporter*, 144 LRR 495-97, Dec 20, 1993] Already the North American Free Trade Agreement's supplemental North American Agreement on Labor Cooperation has been enacted into law by the U.S. Senate and arguably supersedes some aspects of the NLRA, where for example a company tries to escape its obligations to a labor union by establishing a "runaway shop" south of the U.S. border with Mexico (Q 1:28).

However, some commentators have suggested that legitimate employee participation programs (i.e., those that are not company-controlled labor unions in disguise) are not rendered illegal by *Electromation* [see, e.g., Charles J. Morris, "In Search of a National

Labor Policy," Statement to the Dunlop Commission on the Future of Worker-Management Relations, January 1994] and that the labor laws have already anticipated and will readily accommodate even participation programs of questionable legality if they are packaged properly by management. [See, e.g., "Little-known Teamwork Provision Touted as Solution to Electromation Problems," 1993 BNA *Daily Labor Report* 154, Aug 12, 1993, at page d19, citing the Labor Management Cooperation Act of 1978]

While such arguments may make problematic the revision of the NLRA to more clearly accommodate employee-management cooperation programs, the existence of so many bills before the House and Senate makes many lawmakers nervous, because once the seldom-amended labor statute is thrown open to change, no one is certain that the process can be guided in any particular direction. The various proposals are simply too diverse to ensure the outcome desired by any side in the labor law debate (Q 11:8.)

In summation, despite, or in part, even because of, the plethora of bills to amend the NLRA before Congress in 1994, gridlock may prevent any significant tampering with an act that has not undergone radical revision since the Taft-Hartley Act of 1947.

Chapter 12

Immigration and Naturalization

The United States has traditionally professed a policy of welcoming foreigners as prospective citizens. However, the government has acted from time to time to restrict immigration to prevent an adverse impact on the nation's economy and employment. The Immigration Act of 1990 attempted to address long-standing grievances among certain nations and national groups that believed they were poorly represented in recent immigration quotas. Notably, the act increases the number of visas to be issued to Irish and other European nationalities. The act also anticipated the widely predicted shortage of certain categories of skilled labor in this country in the next decade and into the 21st century. A substantial number of visas are earmarked under the act for highly educated professionals and others willing to bring their talents and skills to this country. Furthermore, recognizing that the island state of Hong Kong will soon be part of Communist China, Congress has allowed, under the law, a large number of additional citizens of Hong Kong to immigrate to the United States in the years ahead.

On the other hand, 1994 saw continued controversy over the U.S. policy of turning back refugees from Haiti.

The adoption of NAFTA (chapter 1) has focused attention on the chronic problems of illegal immigration into the U.S. from Mexico. With economic recovery in 1994, the Federal Reserve saw fit to raise interest rates slightly to dampen the threat of inflation, yet the jobless rate remained tenaciously stuck at around 7 percent. Unemployment lines led to increasing clamor about the dangers NAFTA may pose to Americans' jobs, which is but a variation on the theme, heard again in 1995, that immigrants take jobs from the least fortunate stratum of American workers. This contention also kept the spotlight on illegal immigration along our southern border.

This chapter reviews the development of immigration legislation (Qs 12:1–12:5); employer responsibilities in complying with the immigration statutes (Qs 12:6–12:26); and the application of the statutes to specific categories of workers (Qs 12:27–12:45).

Immigration Reform and Control Act of 1986

Q 12:1   What are the purposes of the Immigration Reform and Control Act of 1986?

The Immigration Reform and Control Act of 1986 (IRCA) has three main purposes:

1. Provide a solution for controlling illegal immigration to the United States;

2. Make limited changes in the system for legal immigration; and

3. Provide a controlled legalization program for undocumented aliens who entered the United States before 1982.

Q 12:2   How does IRCA control illegal immigration?

IRCA changed a 1952 federal law that allowed employers to hire illegal aliens without penalty. Under the current law, employers are subject to civil and/or criminal penalties if they hire undocumented aliens or continue the employment of undocumented aliens. Congress believed that most undocumented aliens enter the country to find jobs. Therefore, it created a system whereby employers share the responsibility of controlling illegal immigration. An employer that fails to carry out this responsibility will be penalized. The philosophy behind this approach is that the imposition of penalties for violating the act will deter employers from hiring illegal aliens. The employers' reluctance to hire will, in turn, deter aliens from illegally entering the United States.

Q 12:3   From where do illegal immigrants come and how do they harm the U.S. labor force?

Undocumented aliens usually come from countries with high population growth but few employment opportunities. Unfortunately, the United States cannot correct this imbalance by absorbing these workers into its economy, because the large-scale influx adversely affects the unemployment ratio. Unemployment in the United States is much higher among the minority groups with whom undocumented workers directly compete for most jobs. The NAACP has found that black workers are forced from employment rolls by undocumented workers who will work for wages below minimum wage. Since the undocumented worker knows he or she is in the United States illegally and cannot be protected by the minimum wage requirement, the alien will accept "starvation" wages.

Q 12:4   How did IRCA change the way predecessor laws classified immigrants?

IRCA altered several immigration provisions of the Immigration and Naturalization Act of 1952. First, a new immigrant category for dependents of employees of international organizations was created. IRCA recognized the unique position of children and spouses of long-term international organization employees when those employees die, transfer, or retire. It is often difficult for children and spouses to become reoriented to their original society and culture. For all purposes, these individuals are "Americanized." The special immigrant category recognizes their Americanization and allows the individuals to remain in this country if they meet certain residence requirements.

Second, IRCA restricted the ability of many foreign students to adjust their status to that of lawful permanent resident aliens. This modification was aimed at reducing the number of foreign students who remain in the United States. IRCA also altered the allocation of visas and created a visa waiver program.

Finally, IRCA modified the former H-2 program for temporary workers by adding the H-2A program for temporary agricultural workers. It also established a mechanism by which "special agricultural workers" are admitted to perform field work in perishable crops. Under this mechanism, agricultural workers move freely between employers without penalty and are fully protected under all federal, state, and local labor laws. This mechanism creates a legal workforce without decreasing the number of workers available to harvest perishable crops.

Q 12:5   Did IRCA legalize undocumented aliens already in the United States?

IRCA provided a one-shot amnesty program under which illegal aliens who entered the United States before January 1, 1982, could become legalized. Applications for the amnesty program were accepted for an 18-month period that ended in April 1988.

Q 12:6   Must an employer fire undocumented employees hired prior to the effective date of IRCA?

No. IRCA "grandfathers" workers hired prior to November 6, 1986. However, although the employer will not be subject to sanctions, the grandfather provisions of IRCA do not make it lawful for an unauthorized alien to accept employment. Consequently, the alien is still subject to deportation for accepting employment.

Q 12:7   Is an employer allowed to fire undocumented employees hired prior to the effective date of IRCA?

No. A Chicago area hospital recently had to pay civil damages and a fine because it fired an illegal alien who had lied on his employment application. After Congress passed IRCA in 1987, the employee, Rodriguez, pursued the amnesty provision available under the act. When he asked the hospital to provide him with a letter confirming his employment, he was terminated for having falsified his job application.

The Mexican-American Legal Defense and Education Fund instituted a suit on Rodriguez's behalf, maintaining that his termination was illegal and seeking civil damages. The Justice Department's Office of Special Counsel also participated in this suit to enforce IRCA's antidiscrimination provisions. In announcing the settlement, Siskind of the Department of Justice stated that the hospital had "discriminated against Rodriguez by treating him differently from citizens that have falsified their employment applications but who had not been fired."

Q 12:8   What employees are affected by IRCA?

The act applies only to unauthorized aliens hired after November 6, 1986. It does not apply to employees hired before that time.

Q 12:9   Who are unauthorized aliens?

Unauthorized aliens are aliens who enter the United States illegally or whose immigration status does not permit employment in the United States.

Q 12:10   What happens to an unauthorized alien employee?

The worker who is not authorized to be in the United States can be arrested and deported.

Q 12:11　Is there any way to "legalize" an unauthorized alien employee?

Yes, through a process called "labor certification." This process requires a lawyer.

Business Considerations and Compliance

Q 12:12　How does IRCA affect employers?

Employers can no longer hire illegal aliens with impunity. Any employer that recruits or hires unauthorized aliens and/or continues to employ unauthorized aliens is subject to civil and possibly criminal penalties.

Q 12:13　Are all employers covered by the antidiscrimination provisions of IRCA?

No. Employers with three or fewer employees are exempt from IRCA's antidiscrimination provisions. Those employers with more than three but fewer than 15 employees are covered exclusively by the antidiscrimination provisions of IRCA. Employers with 15 or more employees are prohibited from discriminating on the basis of national origin and citizenship status by Title VII of the Civil Rights Act of 1964 and are subject to the new provisions of IRCA only with respect to citizenship status claims filed with the Office of Special Counsel.

Q 12:14　What must employers do to comply with IRCA?

Employers must verify the employment eligibility of any employee hired.

Q 12:15　What preemployment question must be asked?

The preemployment question that must be asked is: Is the employee a U.S. citizen or lawfully authorized to work in the United States?

Q 12:16 How does an employer verify an employee's employment eligibility?

To comply with verification requirements, an employer must show that it has examined documents that establish both (1) the employment authorization and (2) the identity of the employee. A U.S. passport, certificate of U.S. citizenship, certificate of naturalization, or certain resident alien cards establish both. Employment authorization documents include a Social Security card or a birth certificate. Identity documents include a driver's license, other state-issued card, or, under certain circumstances, other documentation approved by the Attorney General.

Q 12:17 What records must be kept for verification?

The employer and employee must fill out an Immigration and Naturalization Service (INS) form called an I-9. The I-9 form must be kept for (1) three years after the person is hired or (2) one year after the person is terminated, whichever is later. The I-9 contains a document checklist showing the evidence used to verify the employee's legal right to work. The I-9 form does not require that copies of the documentation be retained, but the employer may make copies and keep them on record. However, if copies of the inspected documents are retained, it may be possible for the INS to second-guess the good faith of the employer in accepting such documents if they are later found to be forgeries.

The employer must also sign a sworn statement, under penalty of perjury, that, to its knowledge, the employee's documents are genuine.

Because IRCA limits the uses to which the I-9 forms and backup documents can be used, employers may have to keep such information in a file separate from employee personnel files to avoid any claim of their improper use by law-enforcement agencies or the employer.

Q 12:18 Where can an I-9 form be obtained?

The INS mails the form to all employers. The form can also be obtained from a Border Patrol Station or an INS district office.

Q 12:19 Must an employer verify every employee?

Yes. If only foreign-looking employees are checked, the employer is guilty of discrimination. The act contains an antidiscrimination provision stating that it is an unfair employment practice for an employer to discriminate on the basis of citizenship status or national origin. This provision applies only to employers with four or more employees.

The employer must make a verification check at the time of hiring. Only agricultural employers get a 24-hour grace period; agricultural employees must be verified within 24 hours of hiring.

If an employer hires an unauthorized alien or continues employment of an unauthorized alien hired after November 26, 1986, that employer will be fined, and may even be imprisoned. IRCA provides both civil and criminal penalties. Beginning in 1988, fines for all offenses were imposed without first-offense warnings. An employer who failed to obey the preceding regulation was subject to penalties. The following is a listing of civil penalties that may be imposed:

1. First offense: $250 to $2,000 for each unauthorized alien hired;
2. Second offense: $2,000 to $5,000 for each unauthorized alien hired; and
3. More than one prior offense: $3,000 to $10,000 for each unauthorized alien hired.

Failure to verify employees subjects the employer to a fine of $100 to $1,000 for each unverified employee.

Any employer that engages in "pattern or practice" violations is subject to a maximum fine of $3,000 for each unauthorized alien, six months imprisonment, or both. Pattern or practice violations are regular, repeated, and intentional activities. They do not include isolated or accidental acts. The criminal penalties cited above apply only to employers who have employed, recruited, or referred undocumented aliens. The penalties do not apply to verification violations.

Q 12:20 What must an employer do upon learning that an illegal alien has been hired?

In *Mester Manufacturing Co. v. Immigration and Naturalization Service* [879 F 2d 561 (9th Cir 1989)], the court held that where the employer had notice from the Immigration and Naturalization Service (INS) that the alien identification numbers provided by the employees on their I-9 forms could not be verified by the agency as authentic, that employer in effect had constructive knowledge of the employees' illegal status (see Q 12:17 for a definition of the I-9 form). The constructive notice triggered the employer's duty to suspend or terminate the employees or risk legal sanctions.

Q 12:21 How can an employer verify an alien's right to work in the United States?

As of Aug. 3, 1993, all permanent resident aliens must possess the newest version of the Alien Registration Receipt Card (Form I-551). [See J Castagnera, *Employment Law Answer Book: Forms & Checklists* (New York: Panel Publishers 1994) at chapter 12 for samples of the latest INS forms] The old Form I-551 is no longer valid; only the new version is valid documentation of lawful admission into the United States for permanent residency purposes.

Employers have received some additional assistance from the federal Social Security Administration (SSA). As of June 29, 1992, the SSA affixes the notice "VALID FOR WORK ONLY WITH INS AUTHORIZATION" on Social Security cards issued to aliens with temporary work authorization only. This type of limited-use Social Security card should be accepted by employers only in conjunction with appropriate INS-issued work authorization documents. This should prevent an alien whose work authorization has expired from trying to get new employment by using the Social Security card as one form of identification, thereby misleading the prospective employer. [See 57 Federal Register 28700 and 28872 (June 29, 1992)]

In 1995 the Clinton administration announced that a major immigration initiative would include a focus on what has been termed "the major flaw in the 1986 Immigration Reform and Control Act, the lack of a verification method that allows employers to comply." INS Commissioner Doris Meissner says the administration will ask Congress to appropriate funds to test a nationwide data base. INS also plans to expand its telephone verification system in the near future, thus enabling employers to call the agency to verify whether an employee or applicant is authorized to work in the United States.

["Administration's Immigration Effort More Likely to Succeed, INS Chief Says," *BNA Daily Report for Executives*, Apr 13, 1995]

Meissner added, "What we have now is a situation of documented undocumented immigrants." By that she meant that counterfeit documents are being manufactured, particularly in Los Angeles and have been tracked by INS to "30 or 40 cities in the country." [Id]

Q 12:22 What documents constitute acceptable verification of an applicant's eligibility for employment?

Two types of documentation are required by the INS Form I-9: proof of employment authorization and proof of identity (Q 12:16). Without exception, the documents must be originals, not photocopies or other facsimiles.

Certain documents can be used to help establish both identification and employment eligibility:

- An unexpired or an expired U.S. passport
- A certificate of U.S. citizenship
- An unexpired foreign passport with an INS employment authorization affixed to it
- An unexpired reentry permit (Form I-327) (See Castagnera, *Employment Law Answer Book: Forms & Checklists* (New York: Panel Publishers 1994) at chapter 12)
- An alien registration card with photo affixed
- A standard INS Employment Authorization Document (Form I-688B)
- An unexpired temporary resident card (Form I-688)
- An unexpired employment authorization (green) card (Form I-688A)
- An unexpired Refugee Travel form (Form I-571)

Under the INS regulations, the following documents help establish identity, but not employment eligibility:

- State-issued driver's license with photo affixed
- School ID card with photo affixed
- Voter registration card

- Dependent's ID card with respect to a member of the U.S. armed forces
- Merchant mariner card issued by the U.S. Coast Guard
- American Indian tribal documents
- Canadian driver's license
- Any other ID card issued by a federal, state, or local governmental entity that either has a photo affixed to it or gives physical information about the holder (such as name, date of birth, address, height, weight, and eye color)

The following documents, according to the regulations, establish employment eligibility, but do not verify the applicant's identity:

- Citizenship Identification Card (Form I-197)
- Certificate of Birth Abroad (Form FS-545)
- Resident Citizen Card (I-179)

In the "Chinese menu" approach adopted by the INS regulations, the employer must have from the applicant one item from the first list or one each from the second two lists. Finally, note that in using documents from the first list (those that are acceptable for both identity and right to work purposes), if the applicant presents two documents attached to one another (e.g., foreign passport plus employment authorization form), the employer must record the ID numbers and expiration dates of both. [See 56 Federal Register 41767 (Aug 23, 1991)]

INS Commissioner Doris Meissner has stated that "it's not difficult for [employers] to comply with the law and still hire illegal aliens," due to a burgeoning market in counterfeit documents. She indicated the Clinton administration's resolve to stop the flow of such documents and detect their use in hiring. ["Administration's Immigration Effort More Likely to Succeed, INS Chief Says," *BNA Daily Report for Executives*, Apr 13, 1995]

Q 12:23   Can an employer specify which documents are acceptable to verify applicant identification and right to work?

Under INS regulations, applicants can submit the documents of their choice to meet the identification and right-to-work requirements of the immigration act. However, if the employer finds the initial documents submitted to be inadequate, the company has the right to request additional documentation. [28 CFR § 44.200(a)(3)] Furthermore, no person representing an employer should sign the certification at the bottom of the I-9 form unless and until any doubts have been resolved concerning the authenticity of the proffered documentation. The INS and Justice Department have attempted to prosecute employer representatives for allegedly making false certifications, which is illegal under 8 USC § 1546.

These efforts may increase in 1996, if recent statements by the INS Commissioner concerning the Clinton administration's resolve to crack down on the flow and use of counterfeit documents by illegal aliens prove to be an accurate prediction of federal activity. ["Administration's Immigration Effort More Likely to Succeed, INS Chief Says," *BNA Daily Report for Executives*, Apr 13, 1995]

Q 12:24   Must an employer verify an employee referred by a state employment agency?

No, this is unnecessary as long as the employer has documentation of the agency's referral that specifically certifies that the agency has satisfied such requirements. If this documentation is not available, the employer must verify the employee.

Q 12:25   Must employment agencies and other persons or entities recruiting for a fee verify a prospect's employment eligibility?

Yes. Prior to recruiting for a fee or referring for employment for a fee, the entity must complete an I-9 form even though the entity is not an employer per se.

Q 12:26   Can the Immigration and Naturalization Service enter a business to look for I-9s?

Yes. The INS may enter a place of business without a subpoena or a search warrant, if it provides three days' warning. If the INS has probable cause to believe an employer is violating the law, it can enter the workplace without warning after obtaining a subpoena or search warrant.

Q 12:27   How does IRCA affect alien skilled and unskilled temporary workers?

IRCA revised prior law regarding temporary workers by dividing these workers into agricultural workers and nonagricultural workers. The previous H-2 program was left intact and pertains to nonagricultural temporary skilled and unskilled workers. Under IRCA, temporary workers can enter the United States if there is a shortage of U.S. workers and if the employment of alien workers will not adversely affect the working conditions and wages of workers in the United States. This is determined by the secretary of labor. As under previous law, the temporary workers must obtain a valid nonimmigrant visa in order to be temporarily employed. This IRCA provision is called the H-2B program. The provision regarding temporary agricultural workers is called the H-2A program. Temporary agricultural workers are eligible for nonimmigrant visas under this program.

Q 12:28   How does IRCA affect alien skilled and unskilled permanent workers?

IRCA does not affect the substance of previous law allowing skilled and unskilled workers to enter the United States permanently. The employees must obtain a valid visa for permanent status.

Q 12:29   What about seasonal agricultural workers?

Aliens who worked 90 "man-days" in agricultural positions involving perishable crops from May 1, 1985, to May 1, 1986, can apply for lawful temporary resident status. These aliens remain in this status for two years, at the end of which they can apply for adjustment to lawful permanent status. Aliens that satisfied the 90-day requirement during May 1, 1983–1984, or May 1, 1984–1985, have temporary status for one year before adjusting to lawful permanent resident status.

Q 12:30 Can an employer use day labor to avoid the need to comply with IRCA?

Although employers are presumed to be in compliance with IRCA's verification procedures for the first 24 hours after an employee has been hired in order to give the employee time to produce the required documents, IRCA specifically forbids employers from using day labor to avoid compliance.

Q 12:31 Must companies verify that independent contractors are authorized to work in the United States?

Companies need not verify the employment qualifications of bona fide independent contractors. (See Qs 2:63, 2:64 for a general discussion of the differences between employees and independent contractors.) The INS regulations set out the following test of independent contractor status:

- Contractor offers services to the general public, not just a single employer
- Contractor provides the tools and materials
- Contractor can control the priority and sequence with which the work gets done
- Contractor determines the days and hours of work
- Contractor bears the risk of profit or loss on the project

Employers beware: knowingly employing an illegal alien as an independent contractor or subcontractor is a violation of the "knowing hire" prohibitions of the act. [8 CFR § 274(a)(5)]

Q 12:32 How does IRCA affect long-time employees of international organizations and their immediate families?

Under IRCA, special immigrant status is granted to long-time employees of international organizations and their immediate families at the time of the employee's death, transfer, or retirement. This status allows the employee and his or her family to remain in the United States. In order to acquire this status, however, the alien must have resided in the United States for a certain period of time. If the alien is an unmarried son or daughter of the principal alien (the principal alien being the employee or official of the international organization, for example), then the child must have lived in the United States for a period of seven years between the ages of 5 and 21. The surviving spouse of the deceased employee must have lived in the United States 15 years prior to the death of the employee and must apply for benefits within six months of the employer's death. A retired officer must have lived in the United States for 15 years in order to gain this special immigrant status.

Q 12:33 What is an "employer sanctions" investigation?

The INS may initiate an employer sanctions investigation any time the agency receives a lead from the local police or other source or obtains other information giving its agents the basis to form a reasonable suspicion that an employer is violating the act. Often a tip comes from a disgruntled employee or ex-employee or from a business competitor. The typical stages of an investigation include:

- Surveillance of the work site
- Gathering of evidence from state employment agencies, employees, and other sources
- A workplace raid based upon probable cause (Q 12:26)
- Subpoena of employment records
- An I-9 inspection

Q 12:34 What is an I-9 inspection?

Employers are required to complete and retain I-9s (Q 12:17). Therefore, one good way for the INS to detect employer violations as part of an employer sanctions investigation is to review that employer's I-9 files. No subpoena or search warrant is necessary (Q 12:26), even though no probable cause (as is required for a broader workplace raid) exists. However, INS regulations require three days' notice prior to an I-9 inspection. The INS *Field Manual for Employer Sanctions* dictates that the three-day notice be in writing. However, at least one INS administrative law judge (ALJ) has ruled that the field manual does not create a substantive right to written notice. Consequently, according to this judge, failure to give the notice in writing does not invalidate any violations that the INS may subsequently uncover during the inspection. [US v Big Bear Market, No 88100038 (Office of the Chief Administrative Hearing Officer, Mar 30, 1989)]

Nevertheless, an employer does have the right to insist upon three days' notice prior to an I-9 inspection. As soon as the notice is received, the employer would be wise to get all I-9s together and have the company's legal counsel review them before the INS arrives. Experts recommend that the inspection of the I-9s occur at a location away from the work site, such as at a lawyer's office. This way the employer avoids the risk of having the inspector observe some other on-site violation while conducting the inspection. [Gordon & Gordon, *Immigration Law and Procedure* § 158.04(3)(a), (1992)]

Other advance preparations that are sometimes recommended include:

- Preparing a list of all employees hired after the act's effective date, November 6, 1986

- Striking from the list all grandfathered employees (Q 12:6), independent contractors (Q 12:31), and seasonal workers (Q 12:29)

- Gathering all I-9s

- Reviewing all I-9s

- Correcting all incorrect and incomplete I-9s for current employees, but make the corrections obvious, so that there is no possible accusation of fraud or cover-up

- Suspending any employee whose records look questionable, pending further investigation

Discrimination Against Aliens

Q 12:35   What do the antidiscrimination provisions of IRCA do that Title VII has not already done?

The antidiscrimination provisions of IRCA supplement those of Title VII in three important ways:

1. They extend civil rights protections to aliens, a group not covered by Title VII.
2. They expand the number of employers covered by antidiscrimination provisions from those with 15 or more employees (Title VII) to employers with three or more employees.
3. They create an Office of Special Counsel and provide an alternative to an Equal Employment Opportunity Commission (EEOC) determination of the presence or absence of discrimination in the workplace.

Q 12:36   What conduct is prohibited by the antidiscrimination provisions of IRCA?

IRCA prohibits discrimination on the basis of an individual's national origin or citizenship status with respect to hiring, recruitment, or referral for employment. However, the antidiscrimination provisions do not apply when an employer's employees must be U.S. citizens for the employer to comply with federal or state law or regulations.

Q 12:37   What preemployment questions cannot be asked?

Preemployment questions that cannot be asked are as follows:

1. Where were the employee or the employee's parents born?
2. What is the employee's nationality, parentage, or ancestry?
3. What language is spoken in the employee's home or what is the employee's first language?
4. What are the names and addresses of any relative other than spouse or children who are dependents of the applicant?

Q 12:38   As currently interpreted, are employers liable for unintentional acts of discrimination against illegal aliens under the antidiscrimination provisions of IRCA?

The Special Counsel charged with enforcement of IRCA's antidiscrimination provisions has said that employers would be liable only if they intended to discriminate on the basis of a person's national origin or "alienage." Employers are not liable for unintentional acts that nevertheless have a harmful effect on aliens.

Q 12:39   What constitutes a prima facie case of discrimination against an alien under IRCA?

The same general legal standard applies to alien discrimination cases under IRCA as has historically been applied by the federal courts in Title VII and ADEA cases. This test was enunciated by the Supreme Court in two major cases, *McDonnell Douglas Corp. v. Green* [411 US 792 (1973)] and *Texas Department of Community Affairs v. Burdine.* [450 US 248 (1981)] (See Q 4:24; see also 28 CFR § 44.200(a)) The *prima facie* case consists of the plaintiff showing:

1. Membership in one of the groups protected from discrimination by IRCA (i.e., U.S. naturalized citizen, permanent resident alien, refugee, person granted asylum, or otherwise legalized alien) (Q 12:40)
2. Application for position
3. Rejection by the employer
4. A continued search by the employer followed by the filling of the job with someone having similar qualifications as the rejected plaintiff, but not in the protected class.

Q 12:40   Are other groups protected by antidiscrimination legislation?

Yes, under the terms of IRCA, U.S. naturalized citizens, permanent resident aliens, refugees, individuals who have been granted asylum, and newly legalized aliens are covered.

Q 12:41   What are the possible sanctions for violation of the antidiscrimination provisions of IRCA?

For the first violation, an employer can be ordered to provide back pay for up to two years and to pay civil fines of up to $1,000 for each individual discriminated against. For subsequent violations, the fine can increase to $3,000 for each individual discriminated against. In addition, if the employer is found to have been "unreasonable in law and in fact," attorney fees may be awarded to successful claimants.

Q 12:42   Did the Immigration Act of 1990 add anything to IRCA's protection of aliens against discrimination?

The Immigration Act of 1990 (see Q 12:50) expanded the protection of aliens against discrimination in two new ways:

1. It is an unfair employment practice for a company to require an alien to produce different or more documentation than is required by IRCA (see Q 12:22) [see 28 CFR § 44.200(a)(3)]; and

2. Coercion, intimidation, or retaliation against a person who seeks to exercise rights under IRCA, files a charge under IRCA, or assists in an investigation or testifies at an INS hearing is also an unfair employment practice. [28 CFR § 44.200(a)(2)]

Q 12:43   How do the INS and the EEOC share jurisdiction in cases involving charges of national origin discrimination?

Under Title VII of the 1964 Civil Rights Act [42 USC §§ 2000e-17], the Equal Employment Opportunity Commission has jurisdiction over employers of 15 or more employees and, therefore, can investigate charges of national origin discrimination involving such entities. If an employer has at least three employees but fewer than 15, a victim of national origin discrimination can file a charge with the Office of Special Counsel of the Immigration and Naturalization Service. Additionally, the INS General Counsel's Office has jurisdiction over charges of discrimination based upon citizenship status as opposed to national origin, such as, naturalized citizens, permanent and temporary residents, refugees, and those seeking asylum in the United States. [Compare Qs 4:38, 12:40; see also Wisniewski v Douglas County School District, No 88200037 (OCAHO, Oct 17, 1988); 8 USC § 1324b(a)(1)]

A victim of discrimination cannot pursue charges before the EEOC and the INS simultaneously. However, if an alleged victim of national origin or citizenship discrimination files a charge with the wrong agency, and that agency ultimately dismisses the charge for lack of jurisdiction, under a work-sharing agreement between the EEOC and INS each agency has appointed the other as its respective agent for receipt of such charges, thereby keeping the accusation from becoming untimely due to such an error. [17 *Federal Register* 15904 (May 4, 1988); (see also Qs 4:140-4:150 for further discussion of the INS' role in preventing employment discrimination)

Q 12:44　What are the penalties for violation of IRCA's antidiscrimination provisions?

The penalties and sanctions initially provided under IRCA (Q 12:41) were enhanced by the 1990 Immigration Act (Q 12:50) to permit a fine of as much as $5,000 for a second violation and as much as $10,000 per violation in a case of repeated offenses. [Immigration Act of 1990 § 536]

Q 12:45　How do the INS' discrimination procedures compare to those used by the EEOC?

The EEOC's investigative procedures are detailed at Qs 4:8–4:20. Briefly, the EEOC can subpoena documents, interview witnesses, hold fact-finding conferences, and negotiate conciliations (make-whole settlements) of meritorious charges. Except in the case of charges filed by federal workers, the EEOC does not use hearing examiners or administrative law judges (ALJs), nor does it hold hearings. If the EEOC finds probable cause that Title VII was violated and the employer refuses to conciliate the claim, EEOC's options are to file suit in federal court on the charging party's behalf or issue a letter authorizing the individual who was discriminated against to file a Title VII claim as a private litigant.

The INS procedures are more closely analogous to those of the National Labor Relations Board (Qs 11:19, 11:80). Under the National Labor Relations Act, the NLRB General Counsel is authorized to investigate unfair labor practice (ULP) charges. [29 USC § 1539(d)] In actual practice this power is delegated to the NLRB's 10 regional offices, where board agents perform investigations of ULP charges under the supervision of the respective regional directors. Meritorious charges that are not settled at the investigative stage result in the issuance of unfair labor practice complaints, which are litigated before ALJs.

Similarly, the Special Counsel's Office of the INS is empowered to investigate discrimination charges, which, if unresolved, are turned over to ALJs within the INS. However, while the NLRB General Counsel's decision to dismiss a ULP charge is unappealable and ends the case (Q 11:95), a victim of discrimination has the right to bring a charge before an ALJ under the immigration statutes. In either situation, the procedures for the conduct of such hearings can be found at 28 CFR Part 68.

While the discovery process with respect to both EEOC investigations of discrimination charges and NLRB adjudications of ULP complaints before ALJs is limited, Immigration Act adjudications of citizenship discrimination claims allow for a full range of discovery techniques permitted by the Federal Rules of Civil Procedure: deposition by oral examination or written questions; written interrogatories; requests for production of documents and things; physical and mental examinations; and requests for admissions. (Compare Federal Rules of Civil Procedure 26 through 37 with 28 CFR § 68.18)

Like an ALJ in an NLRB unfair labor practice case, an ALJ in an immigration discrimination case can order a losing employer to take affirmative acts, such as hiring or reinstating, as well as order an employer to pay fines and damages, notably back pay (see Q 12:41, 12:42). The dissatisfied employer in an NLRA case can take exceptions to the ALJ's decision on appeal to the presidentially appointed National Labor Relations Board in Washington, which will assign a panel of three board members to review the ALJ's decision. A disappointed employer in an immigration discrimination case can appeal the ALJ's ruling to the Chief Hearing Officer for review. [28 CFR § 68.53(a)(1) and(2)] Under both the NLRA and Immigration Act, subsequent review is by the appropriate U.S. Court of Appeals. [28 CFR § 68.53(a)(3)] If no such appeal is taken, the INS Special Counsel or the victim of discrimination can appeal to an appropriate federal district court for enforcement of the ALJ's order. [28 CFR § 68.53(b); (see also related sample forms in Castagnera, *Employment Law Answer Book: Forms & Checklists* at chapter 12 (New York: Panel Publishers (1994))]

Fair Labor Standards Act

Q 12:46   Can illegal aliens sue employers for violations of the Fair Labor Standards Act (FLSA)?

At least one U.S. appellate court has held that even though an illegal alien may be working in the United States in violation of IRCA, he or she is still entitled to sue a company that improperly pays minimum wages or overtime under the FLSA. The rationale behind this ruling is that IRCA and the FLSA have essentially the same purpose: preventing exploitation of employees.

Q 12:47   Are undocumented aliens protected by the minimum wage and overtime provisions of the FLSA?

Yes. In spite of IRCA's passage, the Eleventh Circuit has held that an undocumented alien worker can recover lost wages under the minimum wage and overtime provisions of the FLSA. The court reasoned that bringing undocumented aliens within the scope of the FLSA would reduce the incentive to hire such workers at wage rates less than that demanded by law for documented aliens. [Patel v Quality Inn South, 846 F 2d 700 (11th Cir 1988)]

Q 12:48   Do illegal aliens enjoy any other rights under U.S. law?

An excluded or illegal alien cannot be held indefinitely in a federal prison. This is the gist of a 1994 decision by the U.S. Court of Appeals for the Ninth Circuit concerning a holdover case from the Mariel boatlift from Cuba in 1980. [Barrera-Echavarria v Rison, 21 F 3d 314 (9th Cir 1994)]

The plaintiff in this case is the classic example of the "man without a country." When in 1980 the Castro regime permitted a mix of legitimate political refugees and outright criminals to sail from Cuba's shore in the Mariel boatlift, Barrera-Echavarria was one of those arrivals found by U.S. authorities to be unacceptable and therefore excludable. However, the Cuban government has refused to repatriate him. Consequently, he remained in a federal prison for eight years.

Finally, in 1994 the Ninth Circuit held that, "Incarcerating an excluded alien in federal prison for eight years merely because the government deems him dangerous to society violates substantive due process." [62 USLW 2609] In so holding, the appeals court observed:

> The suggestion is made that the extent of the government's obligation to an alien castaway is to provide food, clothing, and shelter, exactly what slaves were once furnished. Times have changed, and so has what any person has a right to expect from our government. Liberty from bodily confinement has been repeatedly recognized as "the core" of the liberty protected from arbitrary government action. The attorney general's zeal for the protection of society is laudable. But in our society no person may be imprisoned for many years without prospect of termination. [Id at 2610]

While this case involves an excludable alien, the same principle certainly applies to all aliens, legal and illegal, who reach America's shores for whatever reasons and under whatever circumstances.

Q 12:49   Does state law apply to defining aliens' rights?

In 1994 the U.S. Court of Appeals for the Ninth Circuit, sitting in San Francisco, said that the Immigration and Naturalization Service erred in ordering the deportation of a Canadian woman due to a drug conviction. While the woman was vulnerable to being deported because of the crime, family ties in the United States are grounds recognized by the INS as sufficient to counterbalance the conviction. The deportee's boyfriend testified that the couple had established the equivalent of a common-law marriage and would formalize the relationship, if given the opportunity.

INS rejected the "family ties" argument because California, where the couple resided, does not recognize common-law marriage. Reversing the agency's decision, the Ninth Circuit, citing a Supreme Court decision, said that "in the absence of a plain indication to the contrary . . . Congress when it enacts a statute is not making the application of the federal act dependent on the state law." [Kahn v Immigration and Naturalization Service, 20 F 3d 960 (9th Cir 1994), citing Jerome v United States, 318 US 101 (1943)]

However, aliens (illegal or not) probably enjoy the right to prosecute tort claims where their state law rights are violated by private entities. This is one conclusion that reasonably can be drawn from a case in which the public's seemingly insatiable hunger for "real life" reporting led CBS into the apartment of a group of plaintiffs who are now suing CBS for invasion of privacy and infliction of emotional harm. The case concerns the search of the plaintiff's apartment by U.S. Treasury agents investigating a possible credit card fraud scheme. The agents were accompanied by a news crew from the CBS program "Street Stories." According to the court, "The CBS crew followed and taped the agents as they searched the apartment and [the plaintiffs'] belongings. They took close-up pictures of the interiors of closets, personal letters, family pictures, and even a homey maxim on the wall." [Ayeni v CBS, Inc, 848 F Supp 362, 1994 US Dist LEXIS 3023 (EDNY 1994)]

Although the court does not say so specifically, the facts of the case imply that the plaintiffs may well have been recent arrivals to the United States. Clearly they were uncertain about their privacy rights under U.S. constitutional and state tort law. No evidence of credit card fraud was found. However, when the plaintiffs sued the federal agents and CBS, the latter contended that the suit must be dismissed because the TV crew was shielded behind the agents' qualified immunity from suit. Finding that the videotaping of the plaintiffs' apartment amounted to a search and seizure under the U.S. Constitution and that the agents' search warrant did not permit them to extend its authorization to a private entity to participate in the otherwise legal search, the court held that CBS was not entitled to use an affirmative immunity defense to defeat the plaintiffs' action. [Id]

The principles enunciated in the *Ayeni* case can be extended by analogy to a situation in which, for example, an employer attempts to ascertain the authenticity of an applicant's employment documentation by means of some sort of private investigation. The quasi-official nature of such a background investigation cannot be expected to immunize the employer from a state court privacy action, should the investigation overstep its bounds. Thus, while we have indications of increased pressure by the INS in 1996 to crack down on document fraud by illegal immigrants (see "Administration's Immigration Effort More Likely to Succeed, Says INS Chief," *BNA Daily Report For Executives*, Apr 13, 1995), employers would be ill-advised to respond to this pressure by taking steps which result in the invasion of even an illegal alien's privacy. [See chapters 5 and 6; see also Castagnera & Szvetitz, "The Search for a 'Hire' Authority," *Convenience Store Decisions*, January 1995, at 38]

Immigration Act of 1990

Q 12:50 What is the Immigration Act of 1990?

Primarily, the Immigration Act of 1990 constitutes a restructuring of this nation's priorities in admitting skilled immigrants. This landmark legislation increases the annual maximum of employment-based visas from 54,000 to 140,000. Also, the act replaces the 20,000-visas-per-country standard with new calculations that are intended to benefit citizens from countries considered by Congress to have been affected adversely by prior legislation. Additionally, total family-based visas have been annually increased to 465,000 for each of the next three federal fiscal years, then to 480,000 thereafter.

Q 12:51 When did the Immigration Act of 1990 take effect?

The new law went into effect on October 11, 1991.

Q 12:52 What categories of skilled immigrants does the Immigration Act of 1990 favor?

The new law authorizes the annual increase in permanent resident visas from 54,000 to 140,000 in five categories:

Priority workers. These are defined as immigrants with "extraordinary ability" in the arts, athletics, business, education, or the sciences. The application must reflect a national or international reputation, extensively documented achievements, and the stated intention to continue working in the field of high accomplishment plus the potential to "substantially benefit" the United States. Also included in this category are internationally recognized professors with substantial teaching or research experience, plus an offer of tenure or a tenure-track position at a U.S. institution. Executives sponsored and employed by multinational corporations are also included. In short, this category allots at least 40,000 visas to the best and the brightest applicants available.

Professionals with advanced degrees and aliens of exceptional ability. This category is also accorded 40,000 visas per year, plus any "trickle down" of surplus visas from the Priority Workers category. In lieu of the "extraordinary ability" required of priority workers, "exceptional ability," plus labor certification, such as a job offer, is required. A bachelor's degree plus five years of experience is likely to be the bare minimum to meet this category's alternative criterion of an advanced degree.

Other professionals and skilled workers. Another 40,000 visas are allotted to this category, plus any "spillover" from the prior two categories. However, only 10,000 of these visas can be accorded to aliens who will fill jobs demanding less than two years of prior experience. Along with having labor certification, applicants must offer some special skill or a bachelor's degree.

Special immigrants. With 10,000 visas available, this category includes, for example, ministers and other religious workers.

Investors. As many as 10,000 aliens, each of whom is willing and able to invest at least $1 million in a business that will employ at least 10 Americans are eligible for these visas. The requisite investment can be more modest for as many as 3,000 of these applicants who intend to put their money in certain targeted areas, such as rural regions or locales with high unemployment.

Q 12:53 What does the Immigration Act of 1990 require with regard to family-based immigration quotas?

The act increases the number of available visas overall and, in particular, increases visas allotted to the spouses and minor children of permanent resident aliens.

1. First preference is accorded to the unmarried sons and daughters of U.S. citizens. (The act earmarks 23,400 such visas annually, augmented by any "spillover" from the fourth preference below.)

2. Second preference, amounting to 114,200 visas with potential for significant supplementation of this number, is for spouses,

minor children, and unmarried sons and daughters (regardless of age) of permanent resident aliens.

3. Third preference, 23,400 plus spillover from the first two categories, goes to the married sons and daughters of U.S. citizens.

4. Fourth preference provides 65,000 visas, plus spillover from the top three categories, for sisters and brothers of adult U.S. citizens.

Q 12:54 Are there any regulations interpreting and enforcing the Immigration Act of 1990?

Yes. The regulations are published at 8 CFR Parts 1, 103, 214, 274n, and 299; 22 CFR Part 44; 24 CFR Part 49; and 29 CFR Part 501.

Q 12:55 What is the main goal of the DOL's proposed immigration regulations?

According to Deputy Assistant Secretary David O. Williams, as quoted in the May 17, 1991, *BNA Daily Labor Report*, "The department recognizes that some dissatisfaction exists with administrative processes that have sometimes impeded the ability of employers to obtain needed workers within reasonable time limits." He emphasized that the DOL intends to accelerate the certification process, which he characterized as "cumbersome and lengthy" in the past.

Q 12:56 Does the Immigration Act of 1990 provide any protection against displacement of U.S. employees by immigrants?

The new law requires the DOL to balance its increases in employment-based immigration with specific new protections for U.S. citizens. These protections include employer notification to employees in advance of hiring aliens. Such an employer will have to notify either the affected employees' union, or post notices in the plant if the employees are not organized. A second protection mandated by the new law is "attestation-like processes" to protect the wages and working conditions of Americans when companies hire certain categories of nonimmigrant aliens, such as D-Visa crews to perform longshoremen's work, H-1B specialty occupations, and students with F-visas who accept off-campus employment. Employers hiring such temporary employees must file attestations with the DOL to the effect that they will pay prevailing wages and provide appropriate working conditions. Employees will have a grievance procedure through which to challenge these hiring practices.

A third mandate requires the DOL to develop a labor market information pilot program to identify shortage and surplus skilled occupations for streamlining visa processing while hopefully protecting Americans who might otherwise be displaced from overstocked occupations.

The law also calls for state grants to be used to educate and train U.S. workers to fill shortage categories that would otherwise be filled by alien employees. Underemployed Americans are to be the special targets for these grants.

Q 12:57　What is the public policy underlying the expanded employment-related programs in the Immigration Act of 1990?

The policy behind the act appears to be revitalization of the economy and culture through immigration.

Q 12:58　Does the Immigration Act of 1990 reflect a motive of aiding alien workers from any particular countries?

Yes. Hong Kong, which reverts to mainland China in 1999, has had its quota increased from 5,000 to 10,000 immigrants for each of the next three fiscal years, starting with the act's effective date of October 1, 1991. The law also allows issuance of up to 12,000 additional visas annually during this same three-year period for employees of U.S. businesses operating in Hong Kong. Additionally, persons seeking political asylum have been permitted to convert to permanent residence status in greater numbers as of October 1, 1991. For this same three-year period, Irish immigrants are in line for 40 percent of some 40,000 transition visas per year to offset perceived adverse impact of prior legislation. Then, starting October 1, 1994, 55,000 so-called diversity visas can be allocated annually to other countries and regions found by the DOL to have been under-represented by past immigration practice.

Q 12:59 Does immigration pose a threat to American workers, and if so, what should be done about it?

In his 1991 book, *The Work of Nations: Preparing Ourselves for 21st Century Capitalism*, Secretary of Labor Robert Reich pointed out that an influx of immigrant workers was likely to be good for the most skilled and affluent segment of the workforce (i.e., the top 20 percent, whom he labeled "symbolic analysts"), but not so good for the 40 percent of the workforce that provides more mundane services, whose jobs are immediately threatened by immigrant labor. Reich asked, "Is unrestricted immigration good for the American economy?" He answered:

> If you happen to be a symbolic analyst in America, an influx of new immigrants is likely to save you money, particularly if they already have good basic education and possess useful skills. If you are an in-person server and already in the American labor force, however, immigration is a more qualified blessing. . . . [T]o the extent that their presence remedies pending "labor shortages," it reduces the pressure on other Americans to pay more for your services.

American factory workers, a diminishing breed in any event, would seem to be equally threatened by an influx of large numbers of immigrants. Add to this the North American Free Trade Agreement and the result is substantial worker and union nervousness about an acceleration in the erosion of manufacturing jobs in the United States. This has placed Reich and organized labor at loggerheads for the first time since labor unions initially applauded his appointment by President Clinton. [Salwen, "Labor Secretary, Despite Opposition of Unions, Backs Mexico Trade Pact," *The Wall Street Journal*, Apr 30, 1993, at A14; see also Moffett, "Mexicans Anticipate Passage of Trade Pact Will Lift Economy," *The Wall Street Journal*, Apr 20, 1993, at A1]

Additionally, some experts have begun to express concern about the effect of immigration and the commensurate population increases on the environment, and especially on remaining open land and wilderness areas in states such as California, which are experiencing a disproportionate share of the influx. These critics would require environmental impact statements analogous to those required under our federal environmental statutes. [Burke, "An Environmental Impact Statement for Immigration," *The Wall Street Journal*, Apr 1, 1993, at A15]

To quote Secretary Reich again:

> For these reasons, immigration policy will become a point of growing contention . . . in coming years. As the debate over how wide to open the American market to foreign goods and services loses much of its force, the debate over how wide to open it to foreign workers can only intensify. [Reich at 289]

Reich's comments appear to have been prescient. In testimony before the House Judiciary Subcommittee on Immigration, witnesses told Congress that American minorities and low-skilled, low-paid workers are disproportionately hurt by illegal immigration. ["Minorities, Low-Income Workers Hurt by Illegal Immigration, Witnesses Say," *BNA Daily Report for Executives*, Apr 6, 1995] While the focus of this testimony was on illegal immigration, the clear implication is that even legal immigration is hurting minority and low-income workers. For example, 38 percent of Los Angeles' population is foreign-born, according to Professor Vernon M. Briggs Jr. of Cornell University. "[S]uch immigrants will often do whatever it takes to survive. They will work multiple jobs, double or triple up families in housing, and work in violation of child labor laws and other employment standards. Literally speaking, no citizen or permanent resident alien can compete with such workers," he testified. [Id]

These facts pose a difficult issue for politicians such as Reich, who traditionally champion both constituencies. We are now witnessing the phenomenon of poorer African Americans, among others, speaking out against continued immigration, both legal and illegal, in such regions as central and southern Florida and Southern California. While affluent Republicans may favor expanded immigration to ensure low wages for the industries they own and run, liberal Democrats are faced with espousing continued immigration at the peril of incurring the wrath of key segments of their constituencies. Additionally, politicians and government servants of all political persuasions appear to be reacting to the growing threat posed by population pressures along all our borders. This response is reflected in the following recent events:

- Clinton's 1995 budget request included $1 billion to stem illegal immigration. The money will be spent to enhance both border deterrence and workplace enforcement efforts by the INS. ["Administration's Immigration Effort More Likely to Succeed, Says INS Chief," *BNA Daily Report for Executives*, Apr 13, 1995]

- As this edition went to press, the Clinton administration also had indicated its intent to submit an immigration reform bill to the Congress. According to INS Commissioner Doris Meissner, noting unprecedented public interest in the immigration issue, said the nation is "in a period of historically high levels of immigration," including "substantial illegal immigration," which is occurring "at a time when we're going through a substantial amount of economic restructuring." [Id] Thus, immigration is "fundamentally a bipartisan issue." [Id]

- The U.S. Court of Appeals for the Eighth Circuit held that an immigrant was not denied due process of law in violation of her constitutional rights where she lost the right to challenge an INS deportation order because her appeal was filed one day after the 10-day filing period. [Talamantes-Penalver v Immigration and Naturalization Service, 1995 US App LEXIS 6318 (8th Cir. 1995)]

- The U.S. Court of Appeals for the Ninth Circuit, whose venue includes California, held that persons born in the Philippines while those islands were a U.S. territory were not automatically U.S. citizens. [Rabana v Immigration and Naturalization Service, 35 F 3d 1449 (9th Cir. 1994), US *cert granted*, 63 USLW sec 3 (Apr 18, 1995)]

- The Labor Department issued stringent standards for the granting of visas to professional workers under the H-1B visa program. These stringent regulations immediately were challenged by the National Association of Manufacturers. ["Expert Immigrant Worker Rule Challenged by National Association of Manufacturers," *BNA Daily Report For Executives*, Apr 17, 1995] The NAM's challenge underlines the point made above that capital and management tend to favor open immigration policies which enable them to heighten competition in the labor markets, thus keeping down salaries and wages, while the Democratic administration in Washington finds itself harking to the concerns of their labor union and worker constituencies.

Q 12:60 Is the immigration issue heating up between the U.S. and Mexico?

Although the North American Free Trade Agreement (NAFTA) and its supplemental understanding on labor issues (see chapter 1) ostensibly will resolve the issue of illegal alien workers from south of the border, during 1994, this issue in fact warmed up, as our southern neighbor experienced significant political turmoil. "Many Republicans have argued that both legal and illegal aliens unfairly burden American social services. . . . But now, even Democrats, who stayed clear of such debates as they relied on ethnic and civil rights groups for support, are joining the chorus, albeit cautiously." [Berke, "Politicians Discovering an Issue: Immigration," *The New York Times*, Mar 8, 1994, at A19]

The story was published about half a year after the Clinton administration took steps to stop illegal movement along our lengthy border with Mexico. "In the seven months since hundreds of Federal immigration agents were deployed along the banks of the Rio Grande . . . , the traffic of illegal workers from Mexico has all but stopped." [Id]

In addition to tightening security on our borders, conservatives in the Congress in 1994 called for denial of social services to illegal aliens who do slip into the U.S., and even introduced a bill to reduce the annual influx of legal immigrants from 675,000 down to about 500,000. [Id]

Although NAFTA is supposed to help protect American workers from unfair competition from cheap labor, events in Mexico in 1994 and 1995 did little to reassure U.S. observers of the Mexican government's ability to accomplish the kinds of reforms required to make Mexican labor and employment standards reasonably comparable to those of the United States and Canada. (See "Mexico Union Registration Process Faulted in US NAO Report on Sony Charges," *BNA Daily Report for Executives*, Apr 13, 1995) Consequently, skepticism remains high that improved working conditions in Mexico will discourage workers to illegally emigrate to the United States at any time soon. Thus it falls to the INS to stop these trespassers at the border. Clearly, this is what the vast majority of Americans, and especially lower-paid Americans, want and desperately need, (See "Minorities, Low-Income Workers Hurt Most by Illegal Immigration, Witnesses Say," *BNA Daily Report for Executives*, Apr 6, 1995)

Chapter 13

Employment Termination

Chapters 1 through 4 of this book reflect the creation of numerous new protections for employees during the past quarter-century by federal and state legislators and state and federal court systems. The employment-at-will doctrine, once the absolute standard of employment outside the four corners of a written employment contract, has been pared down by common-law theories of wrongful discharge. Title VII of the 1964 Civil Rights Act, the Age Discrimination in Employment Act, the Americans with Disabilities Act, and the 1991 Civil Rights Act are four examples of federal statutes that have created new protection for employees by declaring illegal many reasons used in the past for job termination.

In the realm of union-management relations, the National Labor Relations Act makes it equally illegal for an employer to fire an employee based upon the employee's union affiliation, sentiments, or activities. Additionally, the Occupational Safety and Health Act and other labor legislation expressly forbid job terminations in retaliation for employees exercising their rights under such laws. Consequently, managers are justified in feeling that an involuntary job termination accomplished without triggering a lawsuit is a difficult and precarious task.

The purpose of this chapter is to alert the employer to potential legal hazards in employment termination. A caveat is in order: There is no single action or procedure that will absolutely ward off every wrongful discharge suit and

employment discrimination charge. But the human resources professional or other company executive who
recognizes where the dangers lie has vastly increased the
odds in favor of litigation prevention. One of the most
important tools of the trade with respect to litigation prevention may be a valid and binding release, knowingly and
voluntarily executed by the exiting employee, perhaps in
conjunction with a severance agreement. The Older Workers Benefits Protection Act sets up a series of conditions
that must be met successfully to have a valid and binding
release with respect to an over-40 employee or a group
of employees being asked to buy into an early retirement
package.

Particular attention is paid to the most recent developments involving federal Worker Adjustment and Retraining Notification Act (WARN Act) requirements in the face
of plant closings and layoffs, whether these come as a
consequence of NAFTA (see chapter 1), re-engineering
of the corporate structure (see chapter 14), or otherwise.

Prerequisites and Grounds for Termination

Q 13:1   What is termination for cause and is it necessary in order to terminate an employee?

There is no single simple definition of what constitutes "good
cause" for the termination of an employee. Courts and arbitrators
recognize that certain conduct is outside the realm of appropriate
behavior and justifies discipline, sometimes including immediate
termination or termination after a progressive disciplinary process.

Examples of good cause for immediate termination are intoxication on the job, fighting on the job, theft of employee property, and gross insubordination. Conduct that normally requires progressive discipline to constitute good cause for termination includes absenteeism and tardiness, minor instances of negligent job performance, and inappropriate dress or language on the job. In states where employment at will is still the norm, the employer generally need not demonstrate good cause for terminating an employee. Rather, the burden is on the employee to demonstrate an illegal motive on the part of the employer underlying the termination.

Unionized employers, however, are almost always subject to a "good cause" requirement within the collective bargaining agreement. Today, many individual employment contracts specify that termination of the agreement can only be for good cause, and a few employers have incorporated a good-cause requirement into their employee handbooks.

Q 13:2   Are there any new court decisions involving just cause for termination of employment?

The U.S. Supreme Court's decision in *Gilmer v. Interstate* [111 S Ct 1647 (1990)] heralded a new era in alternative dispute resolution (ADR) of employee discharges. The court required Gilmer to abide by the arbitration provision of his employment contract, even though he alleged that he had been fired in contravention of the Age Discrimination in Employment Act (ADEA). Prior to this decision, employment lawyers had always assumed that an arbitration clause could not be used by an employer to circumvent federal discrimination statutes (see Q 4:120).

Predictably, more employment agreements will contain arbitration provisions in the wake of Gilmer. If this prediction has merit, then it is incumbent on companies intending to join the trend toward ADR, such as mediation and arbitration, to understand how labor arbitrators view the concept of just or good cause for termination, because such a concept is likely to play a part in any ADR procedure.

Typically, arbitrators require that the employer prove that the employee violated a well-known and sensible rule for a finding of just cause for dismissal. In the words of the leading commentators on labor arbitration, "Where suspension or discharge is a possible penalty for violation of a rule, the rule must be reasonable, consistently applied and enforced, and widely disseminated." [Elkouri and Elkouri, *How Arbitration Works* 183 BNA (1991)]

What is reasonable will depend on the circumstances. However, some conduct is widely recognized among labor arbitrators and other human resources professionals as so wrong as to require termination of employment on the first offense, regardless of the nature of the business or the workplace environment. (Some examples of such offenses can be found at Q 13:4.) Even if the employer does not publicize rules against such conduct, an arbitrator will probably sustain a discharge based on such egregious behavior.

However, "[u]nless the conduct proscribed is so clearly wrong that it need not be specifically referenced, an arbitrator will usually refuse to sustain a discharge where management did not give an employee adequate notice."[Elkouri and Elkouri at 183]

Even if the rules are thoroughly disseminated, many arbitrators are reluctant to find a discharge to be just unless one of two factors are found: either the offense is so serious as to justify firing on the first occasion or the employee has received counseling on prior occasions but has nonetheless persisted in the inappropriate conduct. Some examples of when arbitrators have sustained a termination for just cause on the first offense are the following:

- *Burger Iron Co.* [92 *BNA LA* 1100 (Arbitrator Dworkin 1987)]: using and selling drugs on the company's premises.
- *OK Grocery Co.* [92 *BNA LA* 441 (Arbitrator Stoltenberg 1989)]: extortion of money from co-workers.
- *Eastern Air Lines* [90 *BNA LA* 272 (Arbitrator Jedel 1987)]: use of the company's E-mail system to send messages disparaging the company and its management (for further discussion of the E-mail issue, see Qs 5:26 and 6:30).
- *Safeway Stores* [89 *BNA LA* 627 (Arbitrator Staudohar 1987)]: negligent sale of alcoholic beverages to minors.

Sometimes the seriousness of the offense will be relative to the work environment. The courts are also sensitive to this consideration. An excellent example is *Borse v. Piece Goods Shop.* [963 F 2d 611 (3d Cir 1991) (discussed in greater detail at Q 2:14)] In this case, which is pending in the federal district court, the plaintiff contended that she was fired for refusing to agree to be a target of random drug testing by her employer. The federal appeals court, overruling a decision by the trial court dismissing the case, held that under the Pennsylvania common law of invasion of privacy (see Qs 5:14–5:15) Borse had enunciated a proper cause of action. In reaching this conclusion, the court compared Borse's situation to that of the plaintiff in *Hennessey v. Coastal Eagle Point Oil Co.* [589 A 2d 170 (NJ 1991)], where the court had held that drug testing was permissible. In *Hennessey*, the New Jersey Supreme Court held that an oil company was within its legal rights to fire a lead pumper who had tested positive for marijuana use in a random urinalysis. The Third Circuit distinguished *Borse* from *Hennessey* on the basis that, while the oil company was justified in firing the employee, who had handled large quantities of petroleum products, a retail store had no right to terminate a sales clerk for refusing to have her privacy invaded by something so intrusive as a random urine test.

While *Borse* was decided on the basis of a public policy exception to employment at will, it aptly illustrates how arbitrators and judges will often decide whether an offense was sufficiently serious to constitute just cause within the context of the job site and the nature of the employment.

One of the most interesting wrongful termination cases to be decided in 1995 was *State of New York v. Wal-Mart Stores* [1995 NY App LEXIS 17], which involved the highly publicized discharge of two employees, one of whom was married, for dating one another. The pair sued the discount retailer and subsequently were joined by the New York Attorney General, who sought to enforce a newly enacted and untested statute. The statute, one of the so-called "lifestyle" laws that have become popular in recent years around the nation (see Qs 2:14, 2:15), forbids discriminating against or disciplining employees for engaging in off-the-job "recreational activities," which are defined to include "any lawful leisure time activity, for which the employee receives no compensation and which is generally engaged in for recreational purposes. . . ."

Wal-Mart said it terminated the dating employees because it has a policy against potentially adulterous relationships, it being a self-described family-oriented organization. The trial court held that

Wal-Mart violated New York's life-style law, but an appeals panel reversed the decision. The panel ruled that dating went beyond mere recreation into the area of romance. Construing the statute strictly, the court held that, therefore, the statute did not forbid what Wal-Mart did. [Castagnera & Sprang, *Termination of Employment,* Bulletin 4, Apr 4, 1995 (NY: Warren, Gorham & Lamont) at 13] This decision suggests a very broad, implied standard of what can constitute good cause for discharge. However, Wal-Mart bolstered its moralistic explanation for the termination by alleging co-worker complaints that the dating relationship had proved to be a distraction for the two terminated employees from their duties in store as well. [See Randall Samborn, "Love Becomes a Labor Law Issue," *The National Law Journal,* Feb 14, 1994, at 33; Q 2:15]

Q 13:3   Will arbitrators consider an employee's prior work record in deciding whether there exists just cause for termination?

Obviously, where an employer's work rules require progressive discipline (see Q 13:5), an arbitrator will almost always require that the procedure have been faithfully followed, unless the employee's offense was so serious as to compel immediate termination on the first occurrence (see Qs 13:2, 13:4). Furthermore, if a collective bargaining agreement or a company's disciplinary policy states that prior discipline will be expunged from an employee's personnel file after a specified time period, such as a year or two, an arbitrator will usually refuse to give any weight to past infractions that should have been expunged when determining if the most recent infraction merited termination of employment. [See, e.g., Trailways Computer Transit, 92 *BNA LA* 503 (Arbitrator Marcus 1989); Southern California Permanente Medical Group, 92 *BNA LA* 41 (Arbitrator Richman 1989)]

On the other hand, an arbitrator might consider an employee's work record to determine if it merits mitigation of the punishment. [See, e.g., Babcock & Wilcox Co, 90 *BNA LA* 607 (Arbitrator Ruben 1987)] However, if a labor contract or employer work rules do not permit an arbitrator to do this, a decision reversing a termination based on past work history may be overturned in a court challenge. [See, e.g., Georgia-Pacific Corp v Paperworkers Local 27, 864 F 2d 940

(1st Cir 1988); Pennsylvania Liquor Control Board v Independent State Stores Union, 553 A 2d 948 (Pa 1989)]

The length of service with the company, standing alone, usually won't save an employee who has committed a serious offense. For instance, in the case of an employee who was fired for engaging in sexual harassment, the arbitrator sustained the termination as just, despite the employee's 32 years with the company, because of the seriousness of the offense and the company's history of firing managers and nonsupervisors for such conduct. [Schlage Lock Co, 88 *BNA LA* 75 (Arbitrator Wyman 1986)]

Q 13:4 Can an employee be discharged for a single incident of inappropriate behavior?

If the employment is at-will, an employee can be terminated for any reason or no reason at any time. However, where the employer operates under a "good cause" requirement, whether in a collective bargaining agreement with the union, an employee handbook, or an individual employment contract with a particular employee, not every infraction of disciplinary rules will constitute such good cause for termination after only one instance. Furthermore, unemployment compensation referees and other bureaucrats who may have occasion to review the termination decision tend to question seriously termination decisions that are based upon single minor infractions of disciplinary rules. Nevertheless, certain serious violations of company policy or the law certainly mandate immediate termination. The most common examples of such infractions are the following:

- Possession or use of alcohol or drugs on the job
- Being under the influence of alcohol or drugs on the job
- Fighting on the job
- Stealing on the job
- Committing a serious safety violation
- Sexual harassment
- Gross insubordination
- Sabotage

Q 13:5   What is a progressive discipline system?

In a typical progressive discipline system, sometimes known as a punitive discipline system, minor infractions of work rules, such as absenteeism, tardiness, and minor neglect of job duties, subject the employee to increasingly severe levels of discipline. Typical steps in a progressive discipline system are the following:

- Nondisciplinary counseling
- First verbal warning
- Second verbal warning
- First written warning
- Second written warning
- Suspension of one to three days without pay
- Discharge from employment

The number and types of these progressive disciplinary steps will vary from company to company. Generally speaking, for an employee's disciplinary situation to move from one step to the next, the employee need not have violated the same work rule. On the other hand, corporations generally will expunge employee work records after a certain period without incident, e.g., a rolling 12-month period. For example, an employee receiving a first verbal warning would have the record of that warning expunged from his or her personnel record after 12 months have elapsed.

Q 13:6   What is the positive discipline approach?

A variation of punitive, progressive discipline is the "positive discipline" approach. A positive discipline system typically includes meetings between supervisor and employee, or human resources representative and employee, at which time the parties attempt to reach a written agreement on the nature of the problem and the nature of the solution. If two or more such meetings do not succeed in solving the problem, then a day off with pay may be mandated for the employee, during which time he or she is required to reflect upon the nature of the problem and his or her willingness and interest in continuing in the position. If all of these efforts ultimately fail, termination from employment is still the end result.

Q 13:7   What critical steps can be taken before discharge?

Common sense and fair treatment are the best guidelines for the avoidance of employment litigation. Traditionally, there are any number of practical steps that an employer can take before discharging an employee to guard against a subsequent lawsuit. These include the following:

1. It is almost always a good idea to have clear and fair work rules in place;

2. Work rules should be clearly communicated to all covered employees;

3. Work rules should be uniformly enforced within the organization;

4. Disciplinary action should be documented (this does not mean that every disciplinary action needs to include a written warning or a memorialization directed to the employee; with respect to verbal warnings and counseling sessions, a simple note to the file is often sufficient);

5. Upper management or the human resources professional in the organization must monitor the enforcement of work rules to ensure that individual supervisors are enforcing these rules in a fair and nondiscriminatory manner, and that supervisors across the organization are administering these rules consistently with one another;

6. When discharge of an employee appears to be in order, a specific review of that employee's personnel file, the relevant work rules, and any other pertinent information should be conducted by the human resources professional in the organization together with the supervisor who is recommending or making the termination decision;

7. The manner in which the employee is informed of the discharge should be worked out in advance. This plan should include:

   a. determining who will meet with the employee and discuss the discharge decision;

   b. when and where the decision will be communicated to the employee;

   c. what the employee will be expected to do following that meeting;

   d. whether a waiver and release of claims will be requested from the employee;

   e. which confidential information in the possession of the employee must be recovered following that meeting;

   f. which third parties (e.g., which co-workers, customers of the corporation, or others) must be informed of the employee's departure and in what manner.

Q 13:8   What guidelines can employers follow to avoid employment-related suits?

The following list provides guidelines employers can follow to help avoid lawsuits for wrongful discharge:

1. It may be unwise for an employer to oppose an unemployment insurance claim by a discharged employee because such opposition may antagonize the individual, stimulating subsequent legal action against the employer; however, in some states, successful opposition to such a claim may bar a subsequent wrongful discharge claim. Employers should consult legal counsel before deciding whether to oppose an unemployment insurance claim.

2. Do not force or badger a discharged employee into signing a release of any legal claims.

3. Resist terminating a long-term employee unless there is evidence of serious wrongdoing; try counseling instead.

4. Do not violate either the letter or the spirit of company personnel policies, even if they do not constitute a part of any employment contract.

5. It is unwise to fire an employee for poor performance unless it can be documented thoroughly and the employee has received prior notice of unsatisfactory performance.

6. Before terminating an employee, try to get relevant information from more than just the supervisor urging termination.

7. Do not ignore employee grievances.

8. Avoid conveying any information regarding the discharge of an employee to others who have no interest in the proceedings. Only those employees who have a reason to participate in these

procedures, such as supervisors or personnel administrators, should be involved in the termination process.

9. Document all termination actions, and keep this documentation confidential.

Q 13:9   **Should an employer consider using employment contracts with arbitration clauses as a means of avoiding employment-related lawsuits?**

ADR is becoming an increasingly popular method of keeping employment disputes out of court (see Qs 2:49–2:54). The U.S. Supreme Court's decision in *Gilmer v. Interstate* [111 S Ct 1647 (1991); see Qs 4:120, 13:2] permits employers to rely on arbitration requirements in employment contracts to circumvent discrimination suits in federal court. The question becomes whether what is legally possible is, as a practical matter, advisable. The following factors, at least, should be taken into consideration in trying to answer this question:

- Obtaining an arbitration agreement from an employee will require the company to give good consideration to the employee. In other words, the employer must give the employee something in return, or the employee won't be held to the promise to arbitrate an eventual termination of employment. And the arbitration agreement will ordinarily be just one provision in a broader employment contract. Such a contract does not necessarily have to commit the company to keeping the employee for a specified term of employment. However, even a marginally sophisticated employee will probably demand that the contract contain some statement of the standards or rules the employer will follow in determining whether to terminate the contract and the employment relationship. Typically, the employee will want to be subject to termination only for good or just cause (see Q 13:2). Thus, the employer who agrees to such a provision in return for an arbitration clause will have relinquished whatever employment-at-will rights it enjoyed under the common law of the state or states where it is doing business (see Qs 2:3–2:10), and this is good consideration.

- While many employees may be dissuaded from suing their employers, these same employees may find arbitration much less forbidding. Consequently, the company that decides to institutionalize arbitration in its employment relationships may actually find itself facing more challenges to its discharge decisions than it faced otherwise. However, experience in the unionized sector of the economy suggests that this problem can be avoided at least partially by requiring that both sides share the costs of the arbitration or that the loser pay all. Individual employees, like labor unions, will not want to spend their limited dollars on an arbitration that has little or no chance of succeeding.

Even so, a company with little history of employment litigation may not wish to institutionalize an ADR program that may alter the litigation-averse culture of its workforce.

On the other hand, a company that has experienced frequent court and agency challenges by employees to discharge and discipline, or a company that has been the target of union organizing drives in the recent past, may want to institute an ADR program through arbitration clauses in employment contracts.

[See James O. Castagnera, "Alternative Dispute Resolution: Construction Industry," 52 *Am Jur Trials* 209 (Lawyers Cooperative Publishing 1994)]

Q 13:10 Is an arbitration requirement or other alternative dispute resolution method contained in an employee handbook enforceable against a company's employees?

Unlike a collective bargaining agreement or individual employment contract, the status of an employee handbook or personnel manual as an enforceable contract is often unclear. For one thing, many employers expressly include disclaimers in their handbooks precisely because they do not want to be held to have made such publications a part of a contractual relationship with their employees (see Qs 2:31, 2:32). At a bare minimum, the employer that wants to hold its employees to an arbitration or ADR provision in a handbook must probably be willing to abide by all the other terms of the handbook as well. However, this requirement may not necessarily rule out a reservation in the handbook of the right to revise it from time to time, provided employees are given appropriate and prompt notice of the revisions if and when they occur.

In 1995 the Vermont Supreme Court released a decision for publication, which had been decided earlier, in which it expressly "join[ed] the many courts that have held that personnel manual provisions inconsistent with an at-will relationship may be used as evidence that the contract of employment requires good cause for termination despite the fact that the manual was not a part of the initial employment agreement." [Taylor v National Life Insurance Co, 652 A 2d 466 (Vt 1993), *overruling* Larose v Agway Inc, 508 A 2d 1364 (Vt 1986); see Castagnera & Sprang, *Termination of Employment,* Bulletin No. 4, Apr 4, 1995, at 14-15]

With respect to ADR methods that fall short of binding arbitration (see Qs 2:55–2:57 for examples of peer review systems in some corporations), it seems unlikely that the Supreme Court's *Gilmer* decision can be stretched so far as to cover these forms of dispute resolution as substitutes for employees' rights to seek adjudication of their discrimination and wrongful termination claims in federal and state courts. Nevertheless, such ADR methods may prove useful in resolving disputes before they reach litigation, thus potentially saving employers tens of thousands of dollars in legal costs. Furthermore, it is conceivable that some courts will at least view such ADR procedures as mandatory threshold proceedings before an employee is entitled to initiate a lawsuit. [Compare ERISA, 29 USC § 1133, which requires an employee benefit plan to afford an employee or former employee "a reasonable opportunity. . .for a full and fair review" of the denial of benefits; federal courts have held that this review is a prerequisite to an ERISA lawsuit to challenge the denial of the benefit; see also, Haertl Wolff Parker Inc v Howard S Wright Construction Co, Civil Action No 89-1033-FR (D Or 1989)(a contract calling for ADR should be enforced, and therefore a party should not be permitted to evade the contract by prematurely resorting to the federal courts for relief); Schultz v Nienhuis, 152 Wis 2d 434, 448 NW 2d 655 (1989)(dismissing the plaintiff's malpractice complaint for failure to participate in statutorily mandated mediation first); Helms v Duckworth, 249 F 2d 482 (DC Cir 1957) (analogizing a private agreement to engage in good faith negotiation of contract disputes to the National Labor Relations Act's good faith bargaining requirement and ordering the parties to do so before resorting to litigation); Q 4:13

(concerning the EEOC's April 1995 decision to use ADR more often in settling charges of employment discrimination); James O. Castagnera, "Alternative Dispute Resolution: Construction Industry," 52 *Am Jur Trials* 209 (1994) at 239-40]

Q 13:11   What are "reasonable termination procedures"?

A generally acknowledged set of reasonable expectations in procedures applicable to both disciplinary and nondisciplinary terminations has evolved in the personnel management area.

Reasonable termination procedures include the following:

1. Termination should take place early in the week to avoid undue stress and counterproductive behavior.

2. Termination should be discussed face-to-face and privately. Notifying an employee by mail or memo denies the employee a chance to raise questions regarding the termination. The indirect method of termination may result in added stress, anger, and loss of self-esteem.

3. Explain the reason for termination.

4. Allow the employee to remove personal items from a desk, locker, and work area without embarrassment.

5. Appropriate co-workers and/or customers should be told of the termination directly by the proper management source.

6. Provide severance benefits to help reduce the pressure and anxiety the employee feels regarding finances.

7. Prepare letters summarizing severance benefits. This eliminates needless confusion and allows the employee to leave without having to contact the employer again to clarify the severance benefits.

8. Outplacement assistance may be appropriate, but this depends on the reasons for discharge and the size of the employer.

9. In terms of references, an employer should generally provide only titles held and dates of employment.

Q 13:12   How should the company handle a terminated employee who refuses to leave the premises?

Q 13:11 outlines reasonable termination procedures. These procedures presuppose reasonable responses and reactions by the terminated employee each step of the way. In some situations, the employee's emotions may take over, and out of anger or resentment, the employee may refuse to cooperate. Another possible situation involves the employee who is terminated on Monday but reports back to work on Tuesday morning as if nothing happened. Such employees may be sincerely distraught, disoriented, or confused, or may be faking the whole thing. The first thing the employer should remember is that the roles of management and security are not that of amateur psychologists. If a lawsuit ensues from mistreatment or defamation of the discharged employee, a jury will hear only of the objective manifestations of the employee's confusion or emotional distress and the objective responses of the company's representatives. Therefore, every such situation should be treated as if the employee's behavior is authentic.

The employee who refuses to vacate the workplace after being told of the termination and the requirement to leave should be given a written notice, and this notice should be read aloud before being handed over to the fired worker.

Then, unless theft or sabotage of company property is feared, the employee should be given a reasonable amount of time to gather up personal possessions or even just to be alone in that employee's office to regain emotional control and prepare to leave the premises in quiet dignity. Even if theft or sabotage are concerns, the employee can be accorded reasonable time but in the presence of a security guard or manager.

The written notice that is read and handed to the employee should also state that no company property can be taken or used by the employee. In other words, not only must all handbooks, manuals, printouts, diskettes, and other company property be left behind, but they cannot be duplicated on the company's copy machine. Company keys and credit cards must be turned over to the human resources department or to security. If the employee fills a carton or briefcase with personal items, either the process should be observed by a company representative or the containers should be examined before they leave the premises.

Finally, the written notice that is read aloud to the employee should contain a warning that, if departure from the premises fails to occur by the required deadline, forcible escort will occur, to be carried out either by the company's own security personnel or the local police if the company doesn't have appropriately trained and qualified security professionals.

The employee who refuses to vacate the premises, stating, for example, "You have no right to fire me," should be isolated from other employees of the company, except for security and management personnel assigned to accomplish an efficient but dignified removal of the employee from the premises. The recalcitrant dischargee may believe that the employment contract, labor agreement, or employee handbook prevents the termination of employment. The individual may also think that leaving the premises voluntarily somehow prejudices the legal right to challenge the removal later. One such circumstance in which this might occur is when the employee has said in an emotional pique, "I quit," then thought better of it, while management has taken the employee literally and proceeded with the termination process (see Q 13:13). Or the dischargee may want to put on a show for as many witnesses as possible so as to bolster a defamation or emotional distress claim later. In either situation, removing the employee's secretary from the area, disconnecting the employee's extension from the phone system, and otherwise isolating the employee should result in a sense of futility, even a feeling of foolishness, in persisting with a refusal to vacate.

At each step in the process of removing the employee from the premises, the employee should be advised verbally of exactly what the employer's representatives intend to do. Under no circumstances should the employee be touched by any company representative. If the employee cannot be talked into leaving when the deadline arrives, even if the employer has first-rate security personnel, the local police should be summoned to accomplish any forcible removal or arrest of the employee. While the police should be a last resort, it's almost always better to have them involved when physical contact seems to be the only alternative.

In a case involving the firing of a chemically unbalanced employee, who blamed his erratic behavior on the controversial drug Prozac, the plaintiff was removed from the employer's premises in handcuffs by police after he was found to have stolen money from co-workers. After the plaintiff was arrested, a colleague searched his briefcase and found a loaded gun. The plaintiff was discharged for bringing the derringer pistol to work. The ex-employee brought suit under the Americans with Disabilities Act (see Qs 4:88–4:97), contending that he should have been accorded the opportunity to be hospitalized to recover from his mental condition. Although the controversial case survived the defendant-company's motion for summary judgment and made it to trial in a central Florida federal courthouse, the federal district judge took the case away from the jury and granted a directed verdict to the employer in February 1995. [See Hindman v GTE Data Services Inc, 1994 US Dist LEXIS 9522 (MD Fla 1994) (denying defendant's summary judgment motion); Castagnera & Sprang, *Termination of Employment,* Bulletin No. 5, May 6, 1995 (NY: Warren, Gorham & Lamont) at 15; compare, Fehr v McLean Packaging Corp, 860 F Supp 198 (ED Pa 1994)(ADA applies whether plaintiff's mental condition is directly disabling or the disability arises from the side effects of medication)]

Once the employee is off the premises, all access codes of any kind must be immediately altered. Even though the employee has surrendered a set of company keys, the employer should consider whether some locks can be changed conveniently as added insurance against intrusion. Security personnel should be alerted that the employee is not welcome to return to the premises, and the dischargee should not be permitted to do so, except by prior appointment with appropriate personnel who should be summoned to meet the employee upon arrival for the appointment and should be required to stay with the employee throughout the return visit. In situations in which the employee was particularly recalcitrant about vacating the premises in the first instance, it is preferable for any necessary, face-to-face meetings to be held at an off-site, neutral location. This advice applies with equal force in situations in which the employee has been guilty of dishonest behavior, which came to light either before or after the discharge.

Q 13:13   Does "I quit" really mean "I quit"?

One reason an employee may refuse to leave the company's premises after termination of employment or may report back to work the next day is that the employee said "I quit," but didn't mean it. The employee may even have stormed out of the building, cleaned out the locker, punched the time card, or otherwise indicated that the "quit" was voluntary and intended. The employee may even have meant it at the moment but reconsidered later, during a long night or upon awaking to the harsh light of unemployment the following morning.

In a pure employment-at-will relationship (see Qs 2:3–2:10) whether the employee quit or was fired may be theoretically irrelevant. However, if a collective bargaining agreement with a grievance and arbitration procedure, an individual employment contract, a possible allegation of employment discrimination, or a mandate of public policy is involved, the issue of constructive discharge may be of concern to the company (see Q 13:15). Thus, if the evidence indicates that the employee had been harassed or goaded by a supervisor into storming off the job, the requisite intent to quit may later be found to have been lacking and the legal principle of constructive discharge may be applied. Even absent company concern about constructive discharge, at a minimum, the corporation may want to oppose the employee's subsequent claim for unemployment compensation by being able to argue that the claimant voluntarily abandoned the job and therefore is ineligible for benefits.

Consequently, the employee's behavior and the context of the quitting are important facts in many situations. Words spoken by the employee in anger or under duress are less likely to count as evidence of a genuine intent to quit than words spoken calmly in circumstances that are not charged with confrontation or emotion. Indicia of a genuine intent to quit include an employee:

- Following the procedure of the human resources department
- Cleaning out the office, desk, or locker
- Turning in keys and company property
- Filling out forms to receive pension contributions

- Proceeding directly from the place of employment to the state unemployment compensation office to apply for benefits

- Reporting to a new job the next day

Q 13:14   Can an employer lock a terminated employee's desk drawers, files, and office?

In the typical situation where the employee's office, desk, and file cabinets are all the property of the company, the company certainly has the legal right to secure this property at any time. Where there exists a risk that the employee, having been informed of his or her termination, will remove company property, such as confidential information in the nature of trade secrets or customer information, the employer is well-advised to secure its property from the employee. However, several cautionary notes are in order.

First, the employer must be careful that such actions, which may be viewed by the terminated employee's co-workers, will not communicate a message to those third parties that amounts to constructive defamation of the terminated employee.

Second, the employee does have the right to retrieve personal property that may be in the office, file cabinets, or desk drawers.

Third, to the extent that the termination can be carried out in a civil manner without unnecessary destruction of whatever goodwill may remain between the employer and employee, it may be a poor personnel practice to subject the employee to the annoyance and humiliation of having his or her office, desk drawers, and file cabinets locked up. For all of these reasons, a better human resources policy is for the employee, following the termination meeting, to be accompanied to his or her office by the director of security, the terminated employee's immediate supervisor, or the human resources director, where the terminated employee and the company representative together examine the contents of the desk and file cabinets. These individuals can then sort out company property from personal property, so that the employee can leave the premises with all personal possessions and a modicum of personal dignity as well. With respect to public employees, the restrictions in the Bill of Rights, and perhaps the relevant state constitution as well, against unlawful searches and seizures may apply in these circumstances. Under present Supreme Court doctrine, an individual may not be subjected to unreasonable search and seizure. Therefore, when an employee has a reasonable expectation of privacy, it is a violation of that employee's constitutional rights to engage in a search and seizure even on the employer's premises. What is reasonable under the circumstances will vary from employer to employer and facility to facility. For example, depending upon the personnel practices of a particular public employer, a terminated employee may have a reasonable expectation of privacy with respect to his or her locked desk drawers or personal automobile, but may have no reasonable expectation of privacy with respect to file cabinets in or around the office.

Q 13:15 Can an employee be required to sign an agreement not to sue as a condition of receiving severance benefits?

Many courts have manifested great reluctance in enforcing employees' waivers and releases of employment claims. A number of barriers have been erected by the law, which employers must successfully surmount in order to enforce such releases.

First, under most circumstances, the release must be executed "knowingly and voluntarily." Second, any such release of claims must be supported by valid consideration. This means, for example, that the employer cannot condition the receipt of benefits to which the employee is already legally entitled upon the execution of such a release. Thus, if an employee has vested pension rights that are protected by ERISA, a release that conditioned receipt of those benefits upon its execution would not only be unenforceable by law, but might constitute a violation of ERISA, subjecting the employer to potential legal action under that law. In the case of severance payments, if such payments are given to all employees pursuant to a severance plan or policy or an employee handbook, then singling out some employees and conditioning their receipt of these same benefits upon the execution of a release of claims would not result in an enforceable waiver and release agreement.

Q 13:16 What is meant by the "knowing and voluntary" release of claims?

A release is knowingly executed when the employee clearly understands that he or she is releasing certain specific causes of action that may otherwise be available to him or her after termination. Federal courts traditionally have tended to require that statutes such as Title VII be specifically identified in the language of the release. Indeed, the Older Workers Benefits Protection Act (OWBPA) makes this a statutory requirement with respect to the Age Discrimination in Employment Act (ADEA). OWBPA also requires that a valid release of rights under the ADEA provide the employee the opportunity to consult an attorney. A release is voluntarily executed when the knowledgeable employee signs the release without undue duress or pressure from the employer. Thus, the OWBPA requires that an older worker signing a waiver under the ADEA, or a group of such workers in the case of an early retirement scheme or reduction in force, be accorded a substantial amount of time to consult legal counsel and otherwise become knowledgeable with regard to their rights.

Q 13:17   How much must an employee know in order for a release of claims to be enforceable?

In 1993, a federal trial judge in Minneapolis ruled that a former cafeteria manager, who was paid $5,000 in return for a full release of claims, could not rescind the release on the basis of alleged ignorance as long as he admitted to being "aware of its terms and allege[d] no fraud." [Somora v Marriott Corp, 812 F Supp 917 (ED Minn 1993)] The release Somora signed said he released "Hamline, its subsidiaries and affiliates, if any, its attorneys, agents, successors, assigns, trustees, directors, officers, administrators and employees. . .from any and all liability, claims, demands of any kind in tort, contract or equity." [See "Settlement and Release Held Binding on Employee," 1993 BNA Daily Labor Report 31 (Feb 18, 1993) at 2] In noting that Somora was represented by legal counsel, the court may have been implying that if the plaintiff had a cause of action against anyone, perhaps it was his attorney for failure to fully explain the ramifications of the release to him.

It is crucial to note that the above-quoted release would not be sufficient under the Older Workers Benefits Protection Act to release an employee's Age Discrimination in Employment Act rights effectively, as it does not specifically recite those rights as subject to waiver or release (see Q 4:118). Indeed, an employer seeking to enforce such release language in the context of a discrimination claim of any variety might find the EEOC, an analogous state discrimination agency, or a federal or state court reluctant to infer a knowing waiver of such claims, even if the ex-employee had the advice of counsel. [See Runyan v National Cash Register Corp, 787 F 2d 1039 (6th Cir 1986), *cert denied,* 479 US 850 (waiver and release agreement executed by corporation's in-house legal counsel was not binding upon him)] Consequently, the prudent employer will have the employee execute a release that recites all the federal and state statutory rights the employee is waiving, as well as any particular claims, such as bonus payments, that the terminating worker is releasing.

Q 13:18　Can employers require signing of termination agreements on the spot?

With respect to virtually all releases, in situations where the terminated employee is suddenly confronted with a release and informed that the offer of severance benefits in return for execution of the release is open only during the course of the termination meeting, such a release will rarely be considered voluntary. The OWBPA expressly prohibits such "on the spot" execution of releases of ADEA claims. With respect to the release of other claims, whether such a document is enforceable may depend upon the bargaining power and sophistication of the employee executing it. For example, if the employee being terminated is the company's general counsel, vice president for human resources, or other highly placed and knowledgeable individual, even an "on the spot" release might ultimately be enforceable against that individual. But in most instances, where the employee is less sophisticated and not highly placed in the organization, and where that individual is suddenly confronted with termination and an ultimatum to sign a release in return for severance benefits on the spot, the likelihood that the release will ultimately be enforced is slight.

Q 13:19　Can a former employee who later challenges a waiver and release of claims in court be required to return the severance benefits paid in consideration of that release?

Under traditional rules of contract law, a plaintiff challenging the validity of a release of legal claims is generally required to tender back the consideration that was paid by the releasee for the agreement. However, the trend in federal common law seems to be not to require plaintiffs who sue under federal antidiscrimination laws (such as Title VII and the ADEA) to tender back early retirement benefits, severance pay, or other consideration received for the release of claims.

In an effort to combat this apparent trend in the federal common law, many companies are including express provisions in severance agreements to the effect that:

- Upon breach or challenge of the agreement by the employee, the employer may immediately cease making any deferred payments not yet paid to the employee; and

- The employee, upon initiating an action to rescind the release or to pursue a cause of action subject to the release provision of the severance agreement, will immediately tender back to the corporation the consideration already paid by the company under the agreement.

Q 13:20 Is it important for the employer to calculate promptly and carefully the money due and owing to a terminated employee?

There are at least two reasons why it is important for an employer to calculate carefully and pay promptly all money due and owing to a discharged employee:

- Failure to make prompt and proper payment can constitute a violation of the relevant state's wage payment and collection act, a violation that, if without good excuse, can result in serious penalties and the award of attorney's fees in the wake of a successful collection action. Some state statutes even include criminal penalties, although these tend to be rarely invoked.

- A release of claims will not be enforceable unless the employee has received some meaningful consideration over and above what the employer already owes. While no statute or case has set a minimum payment as constituting adequate consideration, where the employer and employee have made a mutual mistake about the actual amount of money being paid in excess of wages and benefits or severance pay under a preexisting policy, on challenge a court is likely to allow the employee to rescind the release.

The severity of the first of these two concerns is amply illustrated by a 1995 Maine decision in which the failure of an employer to pay a terminated employee's wages promptly on demand exposed that employer to triple damages. [Community Telecommunications Corp v Loughran, 651 A 2d 377 (Me 1995), enforcing 26 Maine Rev Stats Ann § 626]

Similarly in Connecticut in 1995 real estate agents, although specifically exempt from unemployment and workers' compensation laws of the state, were employees entitled to have the labor commissioner sue on their behalf for double their unpaid wages. The Commission of the Connecticut Department of Labor brought the case on behalf of two salespersons, one of whom claimed unpaid real estate commissions, and the other of whom was a sales manager seeking unpaid overrides on her subordinates' commissions. [Tianti v William Raveis Real Estate, 651 A 2d 1286 (Conn 1995), *enforcing* Conn Gen Stats §§ 31-71, 31-72; see Castagnera & Sprang, *Termination of Employment,* Bulletin No. 4, Apr 4, 1995 (NY: Warren, Gorham & Lamont) at 10–12]

Q 13:21   Are severance payments subject to ERISA?

The Employee Retirement Income Security Act (ERISA) governs pensions and many other types of employee benefit plans (see Qs 8:110, 8:111). Whether ERISA governs severance payments has been the subject of courtroom controversy for many years. Recently, the U.S. Court of Appeals for the Second Circuit held that a breach of contract claim for severance pay was not preempted by ERISA. In a case in which a group of employees sued for severance payments they were promised if they stayed with the defendant company until it closed its office, the court reasoned that the employer's promise of 60 days of severance pay did not amount to a plan subject to the terms of ERISA. [See "Suit Over Severance Pay Is Not Preempted by ERISA," 1993 *BNA Daily Labor Report* 92 (May 14, 1993) at 1] Apparently, the court's decision was motivated at least in part by its recognition that, absent the right to pursue their state law contract claims, the former employees might have been without a remedy, because under recent case law the employer could unilaterally alter a nonvesting employee welfare benefit plan in order to defeat the employees' rights. [See McGann v H&H Music Co, 946 F 2d 401 (5th Cir 1991), discussed in detail at Q 4:109] Thus it may be that special, one-time promises of severance pay are not plans subject to ERISA.

The employer's right to alter nonvesting benefits unilaterally received significant judicial support in 1995. The U.S. Supreme Court struck down an appellate court opinion that cast doubt on the traditional "reservation of rights" clause used in most such plans. The high court held that the clause in question—"The Company reserves the right at any time and from time to time to modify or amend, in whole or in part, any or all of the provisions of the Plan."—was valid and enforceable under ERISA. [Curtiss-Wright Corp v Schoonejongen, 63 USLW 4201 (1995), *reversing* 18 F 3d 1034 (3d Cir 1994)] Additionally, the Fifth Circuit reaffirmed its holding in *McCann,* supra. [Hines v Massachusetts Mutual Life Insurance Co, 43 F 3d 207 (5th Cir 1995)]

However, true severance pay plans are employee welfare benefit plans governed by ERISA. Consequently, employers must be sensitive to the interplay of ERISA with the federal discrimination statutes and other state and federal laws. For example, with regard to ERISA and the ADEA, leading commentators have observed:

> A consensus of circuit court decisions holds that severance policies are governed by the Employee Retirement Income Security Act (ERISA). Pursuant to ERISA requirements, employers carrying out a reduction in force or voluntary early retirement program may adopt and publish termination allowance plans under which severance payments are often fixed in amount or computed by standard formulas causing the severance payments to increase with increasing salary or seniority or both. Such termination allowance plans are intended both to satisfy ERISA requirements of publication of plan administration and ADEA requirements that severance payments not be computed or paid on a discriminatory basis with respect to age. The release of claims frequently required as part of such plans is also intended to provide the employer with protection against employment termination claims under state law.

[Schlei and Grossman, *Employment Discrimination Law* at 204 (1989); see also Castagnera and Littell, *Federal Regulation of Employee Benefits* (NY: John Wiley & Sons 1992) at 98]

In 1995 employers posted a significant victory in *Hickey v. Digital Equipment Corp.* [43 F 3d 941 (4th Cir 1995)], a decision in which the appellate panel held that, upon a change of ownership, when the former employer had negotiated provisions protecting jobs, salaries, seniority, and benefits of the plant employees, the sale of the facility did not trigger an obligation to pay severance benefits under the seller's plan. The ERISA-governed plan called for severance pay upon termination of employment due to a plant closing. The court held that under the foregoing facts no such closing had occurred. [Castagnera & Sprang, *Termination of Employment*, Bulletin No. 4, Apr 4, 1995, at 7-8]

Q 13:22   What terms, conditions, and benefits should be included in a severance package?

Whether severance is being paid in a lump sum to a particular employee or under a severance plan governed by ERISA (see Q 13:21), there exist some rules, plus a great deal of lore and legend, that should be taken into consideration. Among the rules recommended are:

1. If the company adopts a severance plan, all severance payments to be made under the plan should be contingent on a release of claims reflected in the plan document itself.

2. Similarly, all sui generis severance agreements should contain a release of claims provision that meets the requirements of applicable state and federal statutes (see Q 13:17).

3. The severance plan or agreement should also require the return of all severance immediately upon the employee's initiation of an attempt at rescission of the release or initiation of a lawsuit in contravention of it (see Q 13:20).

4. The severance plan or agreement should clearly spell out what benefits the employee will receive to which there already exists a vested entitlement (e.g., vested pension or savings plan funds) and which benefits are being made available only under the terms of the severance plan or agreement in return for the

release and other consideration required from the employee (see Q 13:21).

5. Even if the Older Workers Benefits Protection Act is not implicated in the severance arrangement (see Q 4:116), the employee should be instructed by the express terms of the plan or agreement to take some time to reflect on its terms and to consult counsel (see Q 13:18).

6. If the severance agreement is one of a kind, the employer may wish to include a confidentiality provision permitting the employee to discuss its contents only with a spouse, attorney, and a tax advisor.

Concerning the type and the amount of severance the employer should offer an employee, the following items may be considered:

1. The reason(s) for the termination of employment; for example, if the employee is quitting voluntarily, many companies deny severance entirely, and greater longevity usually merits greater severance benefits. But the cause of the termination (e.g., a plant closing or elimination of a position as opposed to negligent performance of the job or willful misconduct) may also affect the amount of severance pay.

2. Some companies will consider the tightness of the job market at the time of termination; however, if severance is extended to allow for a lengthy job search, early cessation of payments may be permitted if the ex-employee finds new employment faster than expected.

3. Unless the severance amount is modest, most firms prefer to spread the payments out over time rather than making a lump-sum award, for two good reasons:

   — The employee is encouraged to abide by the terms of the severance agreement at least so long as payments remain to be made by the company, and particularly if the agreement expressly permits immediate cessation of future payments upon a breach by the employee.

   — The company's cash flow situation is usually less heavily impacted by periodic payments than by a lump-sum payout; however, sometimes tax considerations favor a lump-sum payment in a particular tax year rather than stretching out the payments (the employee may have some similar tax considerations to place on the table during severance negotiations).

4. What constitutes an appropriate amount of severance for an employee in a particular position for a specified time is subject to many opinions in the human resources profession; for instance, one commonly stated rule of thumb is that an employee should receive a month of severance for every year of prior employment with the company; the American Bar Association has promulgated a model policy for large law firms that indicates that an associate being separated from the firm should receive at least three months of severance. It must be emphasized that none of these rules has the force of law, unless and until the employer incorporates them into a severance plan or promise subject to potential enforceability under ERISA or state contract law.

5. Many times departing employees will request severance benefits of questionable legality or requiring amendment of a pension plan or other employer plan or policy:

— An employee may seek, for example, an extension of COBRA benefits (see Qs 8:222–8:227) beyond the limits allowed by the law with respect to continued participation in group health insurance. An employer may have to clear such a contractual extension of rights with its insurer or risk being unable to fulfill its promise to the employee when the time comes.

— An employee may seek a lump-sum payout of pension funds, where the plan does not allow such payouts. To accommodate this request, the employer may have to amend the plan.

Q 13:23 What roles do human resources managers play in an employee's initial decision to file a lawsuit?

Human resources managers may have the best opportunity to forestall litigation at an early stage by providing the plaintiff's lawyers with all the facts involved in the termination. This often prevents the discharge from developing into a legal dispute.

The human resources manager's response to an initial inquiry from the plaintiff's attorney is vital because the information the employer provides allows the attorney to evaluate the case and settle at an early stage. However, the human resources manager must be discreet and understand the legal issues involved; otherwise, he or she should be silent.

From an employer's point of view, the case can be disposed of with the least expense during the initial stage when a terminated employee has not yet begun to accrue consequential damages (e.g., damages arising from lost pay, such as overdue bills) following the discharge, and the employer has yet to incur large legal fees. For example, if the human resources manager can provide the potential plaintiff's lawyer with copies of disciplinary records that justify the discharge, the attorney may conclude that the threatened lawsuit lacks merit and advise the client accordingly.

Q 13:24   Can an employer fire an employee based solely on a lie detector test?

Even when an employer can legally give a worker a lie detector test, the Employee Polygraph Protection Act of 1988 prevents an adverse employment action based solely on the results of that test. There must be some other evidence supporting the decision to terminate or otherwise discipline the tested employee. For more on the Polygraph Protection Act, see Qs 3:40–3:61.

Q 13:25   Can an employer fire an employee because he or she has AIDS?

The Department of Justice (DOJ) ruled in a memorandum dated September 27, 1988, that Section 504 of the Rehabilitation Act of 1973 covers people with AIDS, and that no justification exists to single out AIDS as a basis for discharge. This DOJ opinion supersedes an opinion issued earlier that said that if an employer believed AIDS might be contagious, it could lawfully discriminate against the affected individual.

Although the protections under the Rehabilitation Act are extended to people with AIDS, a federal employer or federally financed program may, in individual circumstances, exclude an AIDS-infected individual from the workplace. If an individual poses a threat to the health and safety of others, or is unable to perform his or her job or satisfy the requirements of the program, that individual may be excluded if there is no reasonable way to accommodate these health and safety performance conditions.

Q 13:26 Can firing an employee on the basis of a positive drug test give rise to a wrongful discharge suit?

The "war on drugs" has resulted in the proliferation of drug tests in U.S. companies. Government contractors are required to maintain drug-free workplaces (see chapter 9). Many federal, state, and local agencies, especially those involved with public safety or transportation, have also embraced various types of drug testing. Some private employers, though not required by law to test employees, have chosen to do so, at least in some limited circumstances. Not surprisingly, much of this testing has resulted in litigation. Most cases have been directed at government agencies by their employees or the unions that represent them. However, there have been a few private civil actions reported. In Pennsylvania, the mid-level appellate court ruled in June 1989 that an employer did not violate any clear mandate of public policy by terminating an employee who had tested positive on a drug screening, the results of which were not reconfirmed by a second drug test. Therefore, the termination did not amount to an exception to the employment-at-will rule. [Hershberger v Jersey Shore Steel Co, 575 A 2d 944 (Pa Super Ct 1990)] In New York, however, an investment banker has been permitted to proceed with his suit against Bear Stearns, in which he alleges that a positive drug test was the result of blood-level traces of poppy-seed rolls he had eaten instead of narcotics in his bloodstream. [Doe v Roe, Inc, 553 NYS 2d 364 (S Ct NY 1990)]

Q 13:27 Can firing an employee for refusing to submit to a drug test give rise to a wrongful discharge suit?

In *Borse v. Piece Goods Shop Inc.* [963 F 2d 611 (3d Cir 1991) (discussed at Q 2:14)], the court held that termination of a longtime employee by a retail establishment because she refused to sign a waiver agreeing to random drug testing violated a clear mandate of public policy under Pennsylvania law and therefore supported a wrongful discharge action.

Despite cases such as *Borse*, a survey by the American Management Association, completed in March of 1993, revealed that 73.5 percent of America's largest corporations were screening job applicants for drug use. The survey of 630 companies found that about a third of them also were doing random drug testing of current employees. [Odom, "Drug Testing by Employers Still on the Rise," *Philadelphia Inquirer,* Apr 27, 1993, at F1] While testing, especially random testing, clearly entails some risk of legal liability, as *Borse* attests, the dangers and costs associated with drug use and addiction by employees apparently pose a more substantial threat in the workplace. Testing, while obviously intrusive, is also effective.

Furthermore, a plaintiff who sought the protection of the federal Rehabilitation Act because he claimed to be addicted to marijuana had his cause of action rejected by a federal judge before whom he brought his action. [Grimes v US Postal Service, 3 *BNA AD Cases* 1764 (WD Mo 1994)] And an employee who sought relief under the Americans with Disabilities Act, claiming that his workplace theft and gun-toting behavior was induced by the anti-depressant Prozac, while managing to make it to trial, suffered a directed verdict against him in February 1995 in the U.S. District Court for the Middle District of Florida. [Castagnera & Sprang, *Termination of Employment,* Bulletin No. 5, May 6, 1995, at 15; see Hindman v GTE Data Services Inc, 1994 US Dist LEXIS 9522 (MD Fla 1994)(denying defendant-employer's earlier summary judgment motion)]

Wrongful Discharge

Q 13:28   What legal basis might a discharged employee use to assert a claim against an employer?

An employee who believes that his or her employment was wrongfully terminated may file suit against an employer based on such alleged claims as violation of federal or state antidiscrimination or other employee protection statutes, breach of an employment contract, or state common-law exceptions to the employment-at-will doctrine. Liability under any one of these can prove costly to an employer. Even if an employer ultimately avoids liability, the costs incurred in defending such lawsuits can be exorbitant.

The two most often used laws to protect employees are the National Labor Relations Act (NLRA), which prohibits employers from discharging employees for union activities, and Title VII of the 1964 Civil Rights Act (Title VII), which prohibits terminations based on a person's race, color, religion, sex, or national origin.

Other federal laws containing restrictions on an employer's right to fire employees include the following:

1. The Age Discrimination in Employment Act (ADEA). Employers may not discharge workers over 40 years old solely because of age.

2. The Vocational Rehabilitation Act. This Act prohibits federal contractors from discriminating against handicapped workers.

3. The Fair Labor Standards Act (FLSA). FLSA prohibits employers from discharging employees for exercising their rights guaranteed by the Act's minimum wage and overtime provisions.

4. The Occupational Safety and Health Act (OSHA). OSHA prohibits employers from discharging employees in reprisal for exercising rights under the Act.

5. The Employee Retirement Income Security Act (ERISA). Employers cannot discharge employees to prevent them from receiving vested pension benefits.

6. The Judiciary and Judicial Procedure Act. This Act prohibits employers from discharging workers for serving on a jury.

7. The Bankruptcy Code. In keeping with its mission to grant debtors a "fresh start," the Code prohibits employers from discharging employees who file for bankruptcy.

8. The Immigration Reform and Control Act (IRCA). IRCA prohibits employers from discharging employees because of national origin or citizenship.

Q 13:29 Are freedom of speech and due process of law employee rights?

Employees who work for federal, state, or local government agencies are protected by the Bill of Rights. Specifically with respect to job terminations, such public employees are entitled to due process of law (e.g., an informal hearing) before being terminated. Additionally, such rights as free speech must be respected by the employer. (However, the federal Hatch Act is an example of legislation restricting public employees' right to engage in certain political activities.)

In the private sector, the Bill of Rights does not restrict private parties' actions. However, this old rule may not be as clear-cut today as it once was.

A number of state constitutions (e.g., the Alaska Constitution) project civil rights, similar to some of those in the U.S. Bill of Rights, into the private sector. Also, the old civil rights acts (e.g., Civil Rights Act of 1866) [42 USC §§ 1981–1985] incorporate the concept of due process of law in statutory form; thus, for example, race discrimination in a private corporation's hiring practices could fall prey to a Section 1981 action for compensatory and possible punitive damages. Furthermore, employment actions by private corporations regulated by the government may be deemed "state action" for purposes of applying the Bill of Rights. For instance, random drug tests by railroads, pursuant to Federal Railroad Administration regulations (when challenged by the railroad unions) were viewed by the courts as state action, but ultimately were approved as reasonable intrusions into employees' privacy interests. [Skinner v Railway Labor Executives' Ass'n, 489 US 602 (1989)]

Finally, due process and other constitutional rights have been brought into the private workplace through the back door in a few cases. For example, in one case, a plaintiff fired for refusing to submit to a random urinalysis won a $485,000 jury verdict on the ground that her discharge was wrongful because the California constitution established a public policy against invasion of privacy. [Luck v Southern Pacific Transportation, 218 Cal App 3d 1, 267 Cal Rptr 618 (1990); *accord,* Novasel v Nationwide Ins Co, 721 F 2d 894 (3d Cir 1983) (clear mandate of public policy found in free speech provisions of federal and Pennsylvania constitutions); *contra,* Johnson v Carpenter Technology, 723 F Supp 180 (D Conn 1989) (no clear mandate of public policy against random drug testing found in Connecticut constitution)]

Q 13:30   What is "constructive discharge"?

Constructive discharge occurs when an employer causes or allows an employee's working environment to be so difficult or unpleasant that a reasonable person would feel compelled to resign. The law views the employee as having been fired by the employer under such conditions.

Q 13:31   What is "constructive demotion"?

Constructive demotion is similar to constructive discharge. Constructive demotion occurs when an employer makes the working conditions so unbearable that a reasonable person in the employee's place would feel compelled to accept a demotion rather than remain in his or her current position or when the employer leaves the employee's title unchanged but reduces his or her salary and/or strips the employee of his or her former job responsibilities.

Q 13:32   Is an employer liable for intolerable working conditions caused by others?

To hold the employer liable for the hostile environment created by the employee's co-workers or immediate superior, the employee must establish that the employer knew or should have known about the conditions and failed to take appropriate action to remedy the situation.

Q 13:33   Should employers voluntarily adopt binding arbitration procedures for handling wrongful discharge claims?

Adoption of binding arbitration is an alternative to the time, expense, and risk of substantial damage awards presented during litigation over wrongful discharge claims.

The trend in U.S. common law is to enforce arbitration agreements in employment contracts. Notably, in 1991 the Supreme Court ruled in *Gilmer v. Interstate/Johnson Lane Corp.* [111 S Ct 1647] that a stockbroker whose contract contained an arbitration clause that is fairly standard in the securities industry must arbitrate his age discrimination claim.

Q 13:34 Should an employer reinstate a terminated employee who has filed a lawsuit?

An employer can attempt to stop the plaintiff/former employee from accruing additional damages by offering reinstatement after he or she has filed a suit. However, the plaintiff can reject the offer if the workplace would be so hostile that his or her return would be intolerable, he or she would displace another employee, or he or she has already accepted another job.

The employer should be aware, however, that an insincere reinstatement offer could backfire if a genuinely unsatisfactory former employee accepts the offer to return to his or her old job or the plaintiff rejects the offer and the employer has to explain later to a court why it offered to rehire an employee who was considered unsuitable a short time earlier.

Discrimination

Q 13:35 What factors should an employer consider in deciding whether to settle a wrongful discharge suit?

An employer should consider the following noneconomic factors:

- The demeanor and potential jury appeal of the plaintiff
- The anticipated testimony and credibility of all probable witnesses
- The nature of the forum (e.g., jury or nonjury trial, federal or state court, liberal or conservative community)
- The experience and skill of the plaintiff's attorney

An employer should also consider certain economic factors, including:

- Potential recovery for the plaintiff
- Whether the plaintiff has found or unsuccessfully attempted to find a new job
- Whether the plaintiff realistically may recover punitive damages or an award for pain and suffering
- The cost of litigating the case through trial and possible appeals

Q 13:36 What remedies might a court award an employee who has proven a discriminatory discharge?

Once a court has determined that an employee was the victim of a discriminatory discharge or discipline, the court may order:

- Reinstatement
- Back pay
- Retroactive seniority
- Monetary damages
- Protective orders
- Attorneys' fees

Q 13:37 When might a court order reinstatement?

The trial court has discretion to grant reinstatement under most federal and state labor and employment laws. The general purpose of reinstatement is to eradicate discrimination. If the employee's former position is no longer available, the court may order the employee to be placed in a comparable position.

Q 13:38 Can a court award punitive damages in a discriminatory discharge or discipline case?

Punitive damages are punishment damages; that is, the judge and jury can consider whether the employer's behavior was so outrageous that a special sanction is required. Such damages are not available under the NLRA. However, the Civil Rights Act of 1991 allows punitive damages under Title VII and the ADA. The FLSA allows an award of liquidated damages at the court's discretion in an amount equal to the back-pay award. In wrongful discharge actions under state law, punitive damages may be awarded for malicious or outrageous conduct in connection with the tortious termination. In 1991, the Supreme Court held in an appeal by Pacific Mutual Life Insurance Company that punitive damages do not violate the due process of law clause of the Fourteenth Amendment.

Q 13:39   What damages and remedies are available for improper discipline, termination, or layoff?

Federal laws (e.g., the NLRA, ADEA) provide for a "make whole" remedy retrospectively, meaning back pay and benefits. Prospectively, these laws permit a court to order reinstatement or front pay in lieu of reinstatement, where reinstatement is not a practical alternative due to the hostile work environment or other circumstances, such as the company having moved out of state.

Some federal employment laws allow for liquidated damages. For example, the FLSA permits the doubling of damages under some circumstances.

Other federal and state laws allow for compensatory and even punitive damages. Compensatory damages are typically broader than the "make-whole" remedy in that they allow for the award not only of back pay and benefits lost due to a wrongful discharge or layoff, but also allow a judge or jury to award additional damages for pain, suffering, humiliation, and consequential monetary losses, such as medical bills. If punitive damages are permitted, the jury is normally instructed to consider the size and wealth of the employer and the seriousness of the malicious or outrageous conduct to reach a figure that will predictably dissuade the employer from engaging in such conduct in the future. In a few cases involving Fortune 500 corporations, multimillion dollar punitive damage awards have been upheld.

Equitable repeal remedies might include reinstatement (with or without back pay), promotion to an appropriate new position, expungement of false material from personnel records, or other remedial relief having the effect of placing the employee in the same position as if the wrongful or discriminatory termination, layoff, or discipline had not occurred.

Q 13:40   What is a protected class?

Federal antidiscrimination laws, and many similar state laws and municipal ordinances, identify race, color, national origin, sex, religion, age, and handicap (or disability) as protected classifications that can form the basis of employment discrimination suits. While the courts recognize causes of action for such things as reverse discrimination (e.g., a suit by a white male employee claiming he was adversely treated in comparison to a black, female co-worker), as a practical matter courts most closely scrutinize cases involving plaintiffs who are clearly members of minorities, for example, blacks, females, workers age 50 and older, and members of traditional, mainstream religious groups, such as Jews (as opposed to plaintiffs claiming religious discrimination due to their adherence to a fringe group with bizarre or esoteric rituals). Thus, realistically, employers and human resource professionals must pay closer attention to treatment of members of such groups because the Supreme Court has directed courts to be more suspicious of discrimination in cases concerning these minorities. For a detailed discussion of employment discrimination, see chapter 4.

Public Policy

Q 13:41 What special limitations are placed on employers in terminating employees from a protected class?

As a general rule, the law places no special limitations on terminating such minority employees. Minority employees can be held to the same standards of job performance as nonminority employees, with just a few, narrow exceptions. First, the Americans with Disabilities Act (ADA), which took effect in July 1992 for employers of more than 25 workers, requires "reasonable accommodation" of disabled employees. Second, employers subject to an affirmative action plan or an affirmative action order issued by a court may have to provide minority employees with special training or special protection in the event of a layoff or reduction in force. Third, under some circumstances, employees may be entitled to reasonable accommodations of their religious practices. Generally, special treatment need not be accorded to members of protected classes; however, human resource professionals should act as surrogate judges, closely scrutinizing managerial decisions to terminate such employees. All procedural steps should be scrupulously followed and appropriately documented.

Q 13:42   May an employee sue an employer for wrongful discharge based on the theory that his or her dismissal violated public policy?

Yes. The public policy exception to the employment-at-will doctrine is rapidly expanding to provide greater protection for the large numbers of employees who are considered employees at will. (See Qs 2:11–2:13.)

Q 13:43   What is "public policy"?

Public policy is generally characterized as a legal requirement that prohibits individuals from acting in any manner that may be harmful to the public or the public good. In determining whether a particular discharge violates public policy, courts examine whether the discharge would violate a person's basic rights, duties, and/or obligations.

The California courts, which pioneered this cause of action, have restricted the public policy interest involved in a wrongful dismissal case by requiring it to be fundamental and substantial, as well as distinctly public. [Foley v Interactive Data Corp, 47 Cal 3d 654 (1988)]

Q 13:44   What legal rights might an employee assert that would be protected by the public policy exception?

Although courts differ, generally an employee cannot be discharged for asserting his or her legal right to:

- File a workers' compensation claim
- File for bankruptcy
- Assert compensation rights
- Assert stock option rights
- Assert political beliefs
- Refuse to take a lie detector test
- Vote
- Serve on a jury or as a witness

Q 13:45 What types of employer motives justify an employee's assertion that his or her discharge violated public policy?

Generally, employer motives that may support a public policy violation include:

- Retaliating against an employee's exercise of a legal right
- Penalizing an employee for performing a legal duty
- Retaliating against an employee for protesting an employer's illegal or unethical activities
- Penalizing an employee for "blowing the whistle" on improper company activity

In 1991, the U.S. Court of Appeals for the Second Circuit, in a case involving whistleblowers, held that a plaintiff demoted for financial wrongdoing in the New York State Department of Education's Office of Vocational Rehabilitation was entitled to punitive damages under the Civil Rights Act of 1971, if the adverse personnel action was motivated by "an evil intent." [Vasbrinder v Ambach, 926 F 2d 1333 (2d Cir 1991)] (See Qs 2:16–2:20 for a full discussion of whistleblowing and the federal Whistleblower Protection Act.)

Q 13:46 What is the range of state law regarding wrongful discharge based on public policy?

There remain few, if any, states that do not recognize a cause of action for wrongful discharge resting upon violation of a "clear mandate of public policy." The public policy exception to the employment-at-will doctrine is not only the most common, but also the most conservative approach to the doctrine of wrongful discharge. At the opposite end of the legal spectrum are states such as California and Massachusetts that have adopted the doctrine of good faith and fair dealing. Good faith and fair dealing originate from insurance law, which has for a long time required that insurance companies meet this high standard in their dealings with their policyholders. Since employers in states where the courts have adopted the doctrine of good faith and fair dealing must meet the same high standard of behavior, even in the absence of a written employment contract, it is easier for a plaintiff-employee to plead and prove a wrongful discharge case. In the majority of states where only the public policy exception to at-will termination exists, the plaintiff must point to some clearly articulated public policy in a state's statute or its case law that was undercut by that plaintiff's job termination. (A good example is the termination of an employee for missing work to serve as a juror or a witness in a trial.) Most courts demand that the public policy be fundamental, substantial, and distinctly public (see Q 13:44). By contrast, in a state that recognizes the good faith and fair dealing standard, a plaintiff pleading bad faith and unfair dealing may prevail if he or she can articulate almost any conduct that reasonable jurors might find offensive, whether or not the allegedly improper conduct undercuts a clear mandate of public policy.

The result of the adoption of good faith and fair dealing as the common law of several states was a deluge of wrongful discharge litigation. In many instances, juries awarded staggering sums in compensatory and punitive damages. Nowhere was this flood of litigation more debilitating to business than in California. In an effort to stem the deluge, the California Supreme Court ruled retroactively that plaintiffs successfully pursuing good faith and fair dealing claims were limited to contract damages, such as lost wages and benefits, rather than compensatory damages for such alleged harm as humiliation, emotional suffering, or punitive damages. [Newman v Emerson Radio Corp, 4 BNA IER Cas 609 (Cal 1989)] The aim of decisions such as *Newman* was not only to eliminate the previously open-ended nature of the employer-defendant's exposure to damages, but, by making such wrongful discharge cases less lucrative, to discourage plaintiffs and attorneys from bringing these actions in numbers that overwhelm the courts' limited resources.

Q 13:47 In what types of situations might an employee allege he or she was discharged for refusing to commit illegal or unethical acts?

Courts have held that an employer's authority over its employees does not extend to requiring employees to commit criminal acts. Employees will typically raise wrongful discharge claims if they are terminated because they refuse to:

- Falsify records
- Commit perjury

- Participate in antitrust price-fixing schemes
- Engage in activity that would endanger the employee's health or safety
- Commit acts that would harm the environment
- Engage in conduct that would violate a professional code of ethics

Q 13:48 Can the courts penalize former employees who bring frivolous lawsuits?

Yes, but this rarely happens in practice. In the federal courts, Federal Rule of Civil Procedure 11 permits the award of the other party's costs and attorneys' fees for frivolous and bad faith actions. For example, in 1991 the U.S. Court of Appeals for the Fourth Circuit approved on appeal a $10,000 sanction imposed by the trial judge upon a plaintiff who had filed employment claims against his former employer. The plaintiff was a pharmacist who happened to have some legal training. The district judge found that he had persisted in pursuing repetitive, spurious conduct throughout the action. After it won the suit, the defendant-hospital moved for $43,000 in fees and expenses accrued in the district court and an appeal. A U.S. magistrate considered the motion and recommended $10,000. In affirming this award against the plaintiff-pharmacist, the Fourth Circuit found that he was guilty of a "total failure . . . to do any investigation whatsoever into the relevant facts of law." The court also concluded that, as the plaintiff had become the owner of a pharmacy, he had the means to pay the sanction. In another 1991 decision, the U.S. Court of Appeals for the Sixth Circuit required the plaintiff's attorney to pay $36,000 to the other side for forcing the employer to defend two frivolous reverse-discrimination cases. [See 1991 *BNA Daily Labor Report* 63 (4-2-91)]

Many states have enacted statutes or adopted procedural rules similar to Federal Rule 11. Some federal statutes, such as ERISA, permit the award of attorneys' fees to either side at the trial court's discretion. However, statutes such as Title VII are meant to be remedial and the award of fees to successful plaintiffs was expressly allowed by Congress to encourage wronged employees to act as "private prosecutors," helping to eradicate job discrimination. Consequently, most courts, including the Supreme Court, have concluded that it should not be easy for successful defendant-employers to win their fees and expenses from employee-plaintiffs and their attorneys. The majority of courts that have considered the question have found that to make such recoveries easy or frequent would be to defeat or at least undercut the remedial mission of such statutes. Consequently, while the two appellate decisions reported above may encourage beleaguered employers, they are likely to remain the exception to the rule in employment litigation.

Q 13:49 What standard will the Supreme Court follow for sanctioning plaintiffs and their attorneys who pursue frivolous employment-related lawsuits?

The Supreme Court has not yet had an opportunity to rule on this matter, but agreed in late June 1991 to hear an appeal by an employee-plaintiff against whom a federal judge imposed $19,000 in attorneys' fees against the plaintiff under Federal Rule 11. The Supreme Court will review this aspect of the case; out of this appeal should come dispositive guidance on when employers subjected to frivolous employment lawsuits reasonably can expect to recover their attorneys' fees and other costs of a successful defense. [Willy v Coastal Corp, 855 F 2d 1160 (5th Cir 1990), *cert granted,* 111 S Ct 2824 (1991)]

Plant Closings, Mass Layoffs, and WARN

Q 13:50 Does any federal law require a company to notify the union of its decision to close its operations?

Until recently, a company was required by the Labor Management Relations Act (LMRA) to give reasonable notice to the union of its decision to close its operations. What constituted "reasonable" notice depended on the circumstances of each case.

The Worker Adjustment and Retraining Notification Act (WARN), which took effect February 4, 1989, generally requires employers that are planning a plant closing or mass layoff to give affected employees at least 60 days' notice of its employment action. The Department of

Labor (DOL) has recently interpreted WARN and has attempted to clarify some questions that have arisen concerning it.

Q 13:51   Which employers are covered by WARN?

All companies with 100 or more employees, excluding part-time employees, or those with 100 or more employees, including all part-time employees who work, in the aggregate, at least 4,000 hours per week exclusive of overtime, are covered by WARN whether or not their employees are represented by a union. Employees on temporary layoff or on leave who have a reasonable expectation of recall are included as employees for purposes of WARN. A worker has a reasonable expectation of recall when he or she is notified, or understands through industry practice, that his or her employment with the company has been only temporarily interrupted and that he or she will be recalled to the same or a similar job.

Q 13:52   What constitutes a "plant closing" under WARN?

A plant closing is a permanent or temporary shutdown of a single site of employment, or one or more facilities or operating units within a single site of employment, resulting in 50 or more employees (excluding part-time employees) losing employment during any 30-day period. Any employment action resulting in the effective cessation of production or the work a unit performs, even if a few employees remain, is a shutdown.

Q 13:53   What is a "mass layoff" under WARN?

A mass layoff is a reduction in workforce that is not due to a plant closing but results in an employment loss at a single site of employment during any 30-day period of at least 33 percent of the active employees, excluding part-time employees, or at least 50 employees, excluding part-time employees. If 500 or more full-time employees are affected, notice is required even if the affected number of employees is less than 33 percent of the workforce.

The difference between a plant closing and a mass layoff is that a plant closing involves an employment loss resulting from the shutdown of one or more distinct units within a single site or the entire site; a mass layoff occurs when an employment loss occurs, regardless of whether one or more units at the site are shut down.

Q 13:54 Who are "affected employees"?

Affected employees are those employees who may reasonably be expected to lose their jobs as a result of their employer's proposed plant closing or mass layoff. These employees include individuals who are likely to lose their jobs because of bumping, seniority rights, or other factors, to the extent that these individuals can reasonably be identified at the time the employer is required to give notice. Unlike "employees" within the meaning of the NLRA, "affected employees" under WARN include managerial and supervisory employees. Business partners, consultants, contract employees who have a separate employment relationship with another employer and are paid by that other employer, or those who are self-employed are not affected employees under WARN.

Q 13:55 What is a "single site of employment"?

The term "single site of employment" under WARN can refer to either a single location or a group of contiguous locations. For example, buildings that form a campus or industrial park, or separate facilities across the street from one another, may be considered a single site of employment. Separate buildings or areas that are not directly connected or are not in immediate proximity to one another may be considered a single site of employment if they are in reasonable geographic proximity, are used for the same purpose, and share the same company equipment. An example is an employer that operates several warehouses within a geographic area and transfers or rotates the same employees from one facility to another. When two plants that are managed by a single employer are located on opposite sides of a town, each plant is a separate site if it employs different workers. Similarly, contiguous buildings that are owned by a single employer but that have separate management, produce different products, and employ separate workforces are separate single sites of employment.

Q 13:56   Who must give 60 days' notice?

The employer is responsible for designating the most appropriate person within its organization to prepare and serve the required notice.

In the case of the sale of all or part of a business, the seller is responsible for providing notice of any plant closing or mass layoff that occurs up to and including the effective date of the sale. The buyer must provide notice of any plant closing or mass layoff that takes place after the date of sale.

If the buyer plans on effecting a plant closing or mass layoff within 60 days of purchase, the seller may give notice to the affected employees as the buyer's agent. If the seller fails to give notice, the buyer is nevertheless responsible for giving notice. Under these circumstances, buyer and seller should determine the impact of the sale on workers and arrange to give notice to affected employees if the parties to the transaction anticipate a mass layoff or plant closing.

Q 13:57   Who must receive notice?

If affected employees are represented by a union, written notice must be served on the union's chief elected officer. If there is no union at the time notice must be given, notice must be served on each affected employee individually. Notice must also be served on the state's dislocated-worker unit and the chief elected official of the local government within which a closing or layoff is to occur.

Q 13:58   What must the notice contain?

When the affected employees are represented by a union, the notice must contain:

1. The name and address of the employment site at which the closing or layoff will occur;
2. The name and telephone number of a company official to contact for further information;
3. A statement indicating whether the closing or layoff is expected to be permanent or temporary;

4. Whether the entire plant is to be closed;

5. The schedule for making separations from service, including the anticipated date of the first separation; and

6. The names and titles of the individuals currently holding affected jobs.

When the affected employees are not represented by a union, the notice must be written in language employees can understand and must indicate:

1. Whether the layoff will be permanent or temporary;

2. Whether the entire plant will be closed;

3. When the plant closing or mass layoff will commence;

4. The date on which the individual employee will be separated;

5. Whether or not employees have bumping rights; and

6. The name and telephone number of a company official to contact for further information.

The notice that is provided both to the state's dislocated-worker unit and to the head of the local government must contain all of the information in the notice to the union or individual employee and, in the case of a union, the name of each union representing affected employees and the name and address of the chief elected officer of each union.

Q 13:59   How is the notice to be served?

The notice may be served in any way that ensures receipt of the notice at least 60 days before the plant closing or mass layoff. For example, first-class mail or personal delivery with optional signed receipt are acceptable methods of delivery. Another viable option, when affected employees must be notified directly, is inserting the notice into pay envelopes.

Q 13:60   May notice be given less than 60 days in advance?

WARN's notification period may be less than 60 days in three circumstances:

- A faltering company
- An unforeseeable business circumstance
- A natural disaster

Q 13:61   When is a company a "faltering company" for purposes of WARN?

The faltering company exception to the 60-day notice requirement permits a financially troubled business to avoid the 60-day advance warning if the company is actively seeking financing through any commercially reasonable method with a realistic opportunity of obtaining such financing, or is seeking new business at the time notice would have been required. This exception applies only to plant closings, not mass layoffs. The amount of capital or volume of new business sought, if obtained, must be sufficient to have enabled the company to avert or postpone the shutdown.

Because of the fact-sensitive nature of the inquiry into what is reasonable or realistic, employers seeking to invoke the faltering company exception under WARN are especially cautioned to consult an attorney to ensure that they are not running afoul of WARN.

Q 13:62   When does the "unforeseeable business circumstances" exception apply?

Business circumstances that were not reasonably foreseeable at the time that the 60-day notice would have been required excuse the employer from the 60-day notice in the case of plant closings and mass layoffs. An important indication of a business circumstance that is not reasonably foreseeable is a sudden, dramatic, and unexpected action or condition outside the employer's control. For example, a strike at the employer's major supplier, an important client's unexpected withdrawal from a major contract with the employer, an unexpected and severe economic downturn, and a government-ordered closing of an employment site without prior notice might be considered business circumstances that cannot be reasonably foreseen.

Q 13:63 When does a natural disaster exempt an employer from the 60-day notice requirement?

Advance notice may be precluded when a plant closing or mass layoff is caused by a flood, earthquake, drought, storm, tidal wave, or similar natural disaster. The information stated in the notice, however, must still be given as soon as practicable, whether before or after the occurrence of an employment loss caused by a natural disaster.

The natural disaster exception does not apply when a natural disaster indirectly causes a plant closing or mass layoff. However, the employer may be able to avail itself of the unforeseeable business circumstance exception under such conditions.

Q 13:64 What is an employer's liability if it fails to give the required notice under WARN?

In the event of a plant closing or mass layoff, an employer that fails to give the required notice under WARN may be assessed back pay for each affected employee for each day of violation, up to a maximum of 60 days. The employer is further liable for the cost of employee benefits for each day of violation.

When an employer fails to provide the required notice to the local government, it is subject to a civil penalty of up to $500 for each day of violation.

Q 13:65 Are there any court interpretations of the WARN requirements?

The first case to be brought under WARN was filed in April 1989 by former employees of a New York brokerage house. [Finnan v LF Rothschild, 726 F Supp 460 (SDNY 1989)] In what was also the first class action suit under WARN, the complaint asserted that more than 250 employees were laid off without warning. According to the complaint, L. F. Rothschild Holding Co. distributed termination notices on March 10, 1989, that were effective immediately, despite WARN's requirement that employers of 100 or more people give 60 days' advance notice. Rothschild claimed that it could not give advance notice because it was seeking funding that might have allowed it to continue operations. WARN does not require a company to provide notice if it is actively seeking capital to prevent or postpone the shutdown.

In 1991, litigation under WARN and the LMRA proceeded apace. The International Association of Machinists (IAM) sued McDonnell Douglas and General Dynamics on behalf of some 2,000 members laid off in January 1991, when production of the A-12 stealth bomber was canceled. IAM President George Kourpias was quoted as contending that the defense contractors "knew months ago" that the $4.8 billion project was subject to soaring costs and technical problems that placed its future in serious jeopardy. The suit seeks 60 days' back pay for each plaintiff. [1991 *BNA Daily Labor Report* 17 (Jan 25, 1991)]

Meanwhile, in New Jersey a U.S. district judge upheld an arbitrator's award of more than $2 million in severance benefits for members of a glassblowers' union local against Owens-Illinois. Owens sold its Glassboro, New Jersey, plant to Anchor Hocking Corporation. The relevant collective bargaining agreement by its terms remained "in full force and effect" and was "binding upon the purchaser." Under federal labor law, such a successorship clause places a contractual obligation upon the selling employer to induce the buyer to assume the labor contract or face liability for failing to so persuade it. According to the federal judge: "When Owens sold the plant to Anchor and expressly agreed that the purchaser would not be bound by the collective bargaining agreement, it breached this obligation to the union, and the union was damaged thereby. Consequently, the arbitrator's conclusion that Owens had an affirmative obligation to secure the assumption by the purchaser, is grounded in sound principles of contract construction." As the United States moves through the 1990s, marked by a recession and the savings and loan crisis, more plant closings and corporate failures are to be anticipated. WARN and other federal and state labor laws cannot be ignored in these circumstances. As the cases discussed above suggest, companies that believed they were finding a solution to an economic problem by closing an unprofitable plant discovered instead that they had created new legal liabilities by failing to follow the legal requirements.

Q 13:66   What are the most recent court interpretations of the WARN requirements?

In 1993, the U.S. Court of Appeals for the Third Circuit held that a Pennsylvania company, the Warehouse Club, did not violate the Worker Adjustment and Retraining Notification Act (WARN) when it failed to give employees at its North Versailles, Pennsylvania, location the requisite 60-day notice of the corporation's intent to close that facility in 1992. Although the plaintiffs contended that 52 people lost their jobs due to the closing, the evidence indicated that a few of these full-time employees were reemployed by the company at other locations, so that the total of those actually terminated due to the closing fell below the threshold number for invoking the act's notice requirements. ["Third Circuit Rules on WARN Act Threshold," 1993 *BNA Daily Labor Report* 87 (May 7, 1993) at 1]

Meanwhile, federal judges sitting in St. Louis and Los Angeles, ruling in separate cases, have found that corporate defendants' business situations were in such states of uncertainty that they were excused from WARN's notice provisions. In one of the cases, General Dynamics convinced the trial judge that in the defense industry traditionally, few contracts are canceled, even if over budget or behind schedule, and that therefore the company was not obliged to give 60-day notice to 1,200 employees laid off when the Navy surprised the contractor by canceling the $4.4 billion A-12 fighter plane project. ["Federal Judges Expand WARN Act Exception," 1993 *BNA Daily Labor Report* 102 (May 28, 1993) at 1]

In central California, a federal district judge ruled that a company called Santa Fe Terminal Services did not have to give the 60-day WARN notice when its parent company canceled a service agreement without warning. [Id]

In 1994 the following federal cases were among the more significant decisions concerning the WARN Act:

The U.S. District Court for eastern Oklahoma held that a uranium conversion facility was excluded from the notice requirements of WARN when it conducted a mass layoff without advance warning to its workers. The layoff involved permanently letting go 107 workers in Gore, Oklahoma, in November 1992. The plant, which purifies and converts natural uranium ores into uranium hexafluoride, was shut down for nine months by the Nuclear Regulatory Commission between September 1991 and April 1992 pending investigation and cleanup of contaminated soil on the property. The company claimed to have lost $18 million in anticipated revenue during the shutdown.

No sooner had the NRC given the facility a clean bill of health when the accidental release of toxic nitrogen dioxide gas on November 17, 1992, led to a second government-mandated shutdown and investigation. Due to anticipated additional revenue losses, and the fact that the company was in secret negotiations with another company concerning a merger that might render the troublesome Gore facility redundant, the defendant firm decided on the layoffs. The court concluded that, under these circumstances, the layoffs were the result of a sudden and unexpected event, constituting a "business circumstance" not reasonably foreseeable when the 60-day WARN notice would be required otherwise. Consequently, the company incurred no liability to its workers in failing to give such notice. [Bradley v Sequoyah Fuels Corp, Civil Action Nos. 93-252-S and 93-514-S (ED OK 1994); see, "Closing of Uranium Processing Facility Falls Within Exception to WARN Act Notice," 1994 *BNA Daily Labor Report* 62, April 1, 1994, at D5]

In its first WARN Act ruling, the U.S. Court of Appeals for the Fifth Circuit in New Orleans found that a department store in that city violated WARN when it failed to give the employees of a company it was acquiring the required 60-day notice.

The court rejected the defendant's claim that uncertainty about exactly when the merger would take place constituted a "business circumstance" that could excuse the company from the notice requirement in the act.

However, the appeals court gave the retailer some relief, reducing the damages awarded to the workers by the federal trial court. The Fifth Circuit ruled that workers were entitled to wages only for the days they actually would have worked from the date notice should have been given, not for every calendar day during the notice period. [Carpenters District Council of New Orleans & Vicinity v Dillard Department Stores Inc, No 92-3419 (5th Cir 1994); see, "Fifth Circuit Finds WARN Act Violations, but Orders Reduction of Employee Damages," 1994 *BNA Daily Labor Report* 35, Feb 25, 1994, at D3]

The *Dillard* decision creates a split between the federal appellate circuits on the proper measure of damages in cases concerning a company's failure to give workers written notice. In February 1994, the same month the Fifth Circuit announced its *Dillard* decision, the U.S. Supreme Court refused to review the Third Circuit's earlier determination in *United Steelworkers of North America v. North Star Steel Co.* that terminated employees should be paid damages calculated according to all the calendar days when they should have had advance notice of the closing or layoff. [See 1994 *BNA Daily Labor Report* 35, Feb 23, 1994, at A5]

A federal judge in Detroit was poised to award damages in what has been heralded as the first jury trial under the WARN Act. The case had been filed on behalf of some 160 workers who lost their jobs when the Detroit Coke Corp. closed its plant in September 1991. The defendant raised the "faltering company" defense for its failure to give the salaried and nonsalaried employees (and the latter's union) the requisite 60-day notice. But a jury found that the owners knew at least 22 days in advance of the shutdown that the closing by then was inevitable. [Wallace v Detroit Coke Corp, Civil Action No 92-CV-72890-DT (ED MI 1994); see, "Federal Judge to Set Damages on Jury Finding of WARN Violations," 1994 *BNA Daily Labor Report* 36, Feb 24, 1994, at D6]

In 1995 U.S. Courts of Appeals rendered three significant rulings, all responding to the granting of defendant-employers' motions by federal district judges in the courts below. The success of the employers in defeating WARN Act claims in the federal trial courts seems to stem from union attempts to mold and adapt the WARN Act into a weapon of substantial firepower through creative arguments concerning its interpretation, much as the civil provisions of the Racketeer Influenced and Corrupt Organizations Act (RICO) have been used in ways the Congress seems never to have intended. [For an explanation of RICO and union racketeering see Q 11:61; for more on organized labor's response to the GOP victory in the November 1994 Congressional elections and its efforts to use weapons such as WARN in creative new ways, see, generally, "Republican Congress Changes Debate Over National Labor Policy," 1995 *BNA Daily Labor Report* 19, Jan 30, 1995, at d26]

In *International Alliance of Theatrical and Stage Employees and Moving Picture Machine Operators v. Compact Video Services Inc.* [1995 US App LEXIS 5821, 95 Cal Daily Op Service 2145, 95 Daily Journal DAR 3669 (9th Cir 1995)], the court was faced with a summary judgment granted to the defendants on the ground that the sale of a business is not a WARN Act event. Seller had sold out its unionized business to a nonunion entity, which had proceeded to reduce wages and fringe benefits of those employees who stayed with the company. Some employees either quit or were not retained by the buyer. Noting that whether the buyer was just an alter ego of the seller and whether the purging of the union was an unfair labor practice were both issues for the National Labor Relations Board to resolve, the appellate panel affirmed the trial judge, who had ruled that "employees who find themselves transferred from the payroll of one company to the payroll of another as the result of a sale have not suffered a compensable 'employment loss' under WARN, whatever may be the consequences of that scheme for purging a workforce of its unionized character in appropriate proceedings before the NLRB. . . ." [Id] Thus, the Ninth Circuit rejected the union's implied invitation to make WARN a surrogate weapon for attacking an employer's alleged unfair labor practices.

In a non-WARN case worthy of note here, the U.S. Court of Appeals for the Fourth Circuit rejected a claim for severance benefits by employees of a company that sold out to another, after first having negotiated with the buyer sales provisions that protected the employees' jobs, salaries, seniority, and fringe benefits. The court rejected the plaintiff-employees' demand for severance pay under an ERISA-governed plan, since the sale had nothing to do with workforce reduction, which was the plan's stated purpose, and no plaintiffs had lost their jobs. Thus the appellate panel implicitly viewed the triggering of the severance plan as a windfall for these plaintiffs, whose claims therefore were rejected. [Hickey v Digital Equipment Corp, 43 F 3d 941 (4th Cir 1995)]

The union-plaintiff faired better before the U.S. Court of Appeals for the Ninth Circuit in *International Brotherhood of Teamsters v. American Delivery Service Co.* [1995 US App LEXIS 5820, 148 BNA LRRM 2841, 95 Cal Daily Op Service 2149, 95 Daily Journal DAR 3658 (9th Cir 1995)], a case in which defendant Montgomery Ward & Co. sought to escape liability for the alleged acts of its wholly owned subsidiary. When American Delivery closed its "Big Ticket Distribution Center" in Garden Grove, California, the union sued under Section 301 of the National Labor Relations Act, the WARN Act, and state tort law. The tort claims involved allegations of fraud, the union claiming that American Delivery had assured the union that, if its members acceded to a new collective bargaining agreement, "Ward would not cancel its contract with ADS." [Id] Under WARN the union sought 60 days' salary and benefits for the displaced workers in the wake of the warehouse closing.

The federal district judge granted Ward's motion for summary judgment. Reversing, the Ninth Circuit said that the union had successfully enunciated a Section 301 breach of contract claim; that because the union's fraud claim did not require interpretation of the terms of the new collective bargaining agreement, it was not preempted by federal labor laws; and, there were genuine issues of fact to be resolved by a jury concerning the WARN Act count of the complaint.

The union-litigant did not do so well before the Eighth Circuit in *United Food and Commercial Workers International Union, Local 751 v. Brown Group Inc.* [1995 US App LEXIS 6608 (8th Cir 1995)], in which Brown Shoe had mailed a letter to the international union, but not Local 751, advising of its plan to close a plant employing some 277 union members. The local sued for WARN damages on behalf of the displaced workers. The trial judge dismissed for lack of union standing to sue. The local, however, neglected to pray for the relief to which it was entitled, that is, proper notice. Instead it asked only for the back pay and fringe benefits owed to its members. In a decision bound to cause much controversy, the appellate court panel distinguished between the union's WARN Act right to be a plaintiff and its standing in the particular suit at hand. Parsing the act carefully, the panel ruled that, while the union was a "representative of employees" entitled to bring an action under the act, it had not itself been directly aggrieved by the defendant's failure to pay wages and benefits to the displaced employees, and therefore under general federal common-law rules of standing, had no right to sue for back pay.

The foregoing four new cases suggest that plaintiffs, especially unions, are pushing the theories of liability under WARN and other laws related to plant closings and sales, and that the federal courts forced to respond to these novel legal theories and aggressive litigation efforts are, by and large, construing the relevant statutes narrowly and resisting their expansion into new aspects of employer liability.

Q 13:67　If a company hires employees to work on contracts for the rebuilding of Kuwait, can the employment contracts specify that any disputes arising under the contracts be resolved in Kuwaiti courts under Kuwaiti laws?

In early 1991, the U.S. Court of Appeals for the Ninth Circuit held that a forum selection clause in an employment contract involving a job in Saudi Arabia, which chose Saudi Arabian law to govern all disputes, was reasonable and enforceable. The appeals court affirmed the trial court's dismissal of a wrongful discharge claim filed in California by the plaintiff after he had returned from overseas. The court's decision noted that the plaintiff failed to present evidence, such as allegations of excessive travel costs, unavailability of appropriate legal counsel, or location of witnesses, that would render a Saudi Arabian forum unreasonably inconvenient. The appellate court also rejected the appeal for lack of evidence of fraud or undue influence upon the plaintiff-appellant at the time he entered his employment contract. [Spradlin v Lear Siegler Management Services Co, 926 F 2d 865 (9th Cir 1991)]

The Ninth Circuit's decision may lead some to wonder why a company might choose a Saudi Arabian (or Kuwaiti) court and the laws of an alien nation for the resolution of employment contract disputes. One reason might be the location of the relevant records and witnesses in the foreign nation. Another reason may be that in Saudi Arabia, for instance, although citizens are ruled at least in part by traditional Muslim laws with their underlying religious tradition, Saudi Arabian labor law is quite modern and relatively streamlined, being somewhat analogous procedurally to the U.S. National Labor Relations Board.

Q 13:68　What is the statute of limitations for filing a WARN Act lawsuit?

In the two cases that dealt with the issue, federal trial courts concurred that the six-month statute of limitations in the National

Labor Relations Act [29 USC § 160(b)] applied to WARN lawsuits, rather than a state statute of limitations. The general rule is that if Congress fails to state a statute of limitations in a law, the federal courts should look to the most closely analogous state statutory limitation of actions and adopt that limit for actions under the federal act brought within that particular jurisdiction. Both federal district judges who have thus far considered the WARN Act have found it to be so closely related to the NLRA as to compel adoption of the NLRA's six-month limit. [See "Six-Month Filing Deadline Applies to WARN Act Claims," 1993 *BNA Daily Labor Report* 46 (Mar 11, 1993) at 1]

The U.S. Supreme Court had heard arguments in cases accepted for the purpose of resolving this important WARN Act issue. [See Crown Cork & Seal Co Inc v United Steelworkers; North Star Steel Co v Thomas, Nos 94-835 and 94-834, argued Apr 25, 1995] According to one report, "The U.S. Supreme Court responded with apparent skepticism . . . to management arguments favoring a six-month limitations period for [WARN Act] suits stemming from mass layoffs or plant closings." ["Justices Ponder Time Limit for Lawsuits Under WARN Act," 1995 *BNA Daily Labor Report* 80, Apr 26, 1995, at d25]

Q 13:69   Are there any efforts in Congress to amend the WARN Act?

Early in 1994, outgoing Senator Howard Metzenbaum (D-OH) introduced a bill aimed at amending the coverage, compliance, and enforcement problems he saw in the WARN Act. His proposed Worker Adjustment and Retraining Notification Amendments Act (S 1969) tracked the provisions of a companion HR 4072 introduced into the House of Representatives by William Ford (D-MI).

If enacted, these measures would "lower the thresholds for determining employer coverage, set a sliding scale for notification periods in layoff situations, and require that notice be given to all affected employees, not just their union representatives." ["Metzenbaum Introduces Bill to Address Issues Related to Federal WARN Statute," 1994 *BNA Daily Labor Report* 60, Mar 30, 1994, at D17] However, the GOP capture of majorities in both houses of the Congress in the November 1994 elections makes the enactment of any such liberalization of WARN requirements extremely unlikely in the foreseeable future. [See "Republican Congress Changes Debate Over National Labor Policy," 1995 *BNA Daily Labor Report* 19, Jan 30, 1995, at d26] Additionally the federal courts appear to be interpreting WARN narrowly at least when faced with novel theories of liability being posed by WARN Act plaintiffs such as labor unions (see Q 13:66).

Termination Interviews and Letters

Q 13:70   Who should conduct the termination interview and how should it be handled?

In most corporations the termination interview is conducted by a member of management—often the employee's direct supervisor or someone in the employee's chain of command. Sometimes it is handled by a member of the human resources department. Regardless of who handles the interview, usually a one-on-one format is preferable. The place where the interview occurs, whether in the human resources department or the supervisor's office, should afford sufficient privacy to ensure that the termination is not overheard by the dischargee's co-workers or others. Defamation or unnecessary embarrassment of the employee to be terminated should be carefully avoided.

With respect to timing, most experts believe a Monday morning is preferable to a Friday afternoon, as it provides the unlucky employee with a full workweek to hit the job market running, rather than leaving the dischargee with a weekend to brood over the termination. The company, too, may benefit from conducting the termination first thing Monday morning, so that any follow-up activities that may be necessary can be carried out while the company's full staff, including security professionals, are available.

Q 13:71   What should a termination letter say?

A termination letter should clearly spell out the fact that the employee has been fired and reiterate the effective date. Often, the human resources department prefers to hand this letter to the employee during the termination interview (see Qs 13:12, 13:68). The letter also should spell out clearly the severance package being offered to the employee. If a severance agreement is required for the employee to qualify for the severance package, this should be stated, and the agreement should be attached, although it is also acceptable to forward the agreement to the employee a day or two later.

The termination letter should not rehash the reasons reviewed in the termination interview that underlie the discharge. It is preferable to state simply that the discharge is for the reasons discussed in the interview and leave it at that. Otherwise, the company will be held to the reasons enunciated in the letter, even if the drafter of the letter inadvertently overlooked some of the reasons. Furthermore, the company does not want to place in the employee's hands a document that, if viewed by third parties, could give rise to a defamation claim.

Chapter 14

Worker Retraining, Quality, and Productivity

As a result of a deep and lengthy recession in the early 1990s, the experience of termination has been all too common. Early in 1993, as the Clinton administration, whose leader and many of the cabinet members constitute the first full-fledged contingent of the postwar "baby boom" era to lead this nation, took office, America seemed to be haltingly emerging from the economic trough. But Harvard Professor Robert Reich no sooner assumed his office as Clinton's secretary of labor than he decried what he called a "jobless recovery." Reich suggested that persistently high unemployment reflected structural changes in the U.S. economy. A new idea called re-engineering, based on the concept of just-in-time inventory control, received front-page coverage in *The Wall Street Journal* and is sweeping through companies, permanently eliminating, in particular, middle-management jobs. Even in "Japan Inc.," millions are being idled, some with no hope of holding a real job again between now and retirement age. [See, Ono, "Unneeded Workers in Japan Are Bored, and Very Well Paid," *The Wall Street Journal,* Apr 20, 1993, at A1]

Where once many workers, especially unionized employees in the mighty manufacturing sector, could anticipate retiring from the firm where they had once been apprentices, today many if not most Americans must anticipate a half-dozen job changes in their careers, possibly including geographic reallocations. Experienced professionals such as attorneys are taking up to three months to get a first job interview, whether because they wish to change jobs or find themselves involuntarily terminated. [Dean, "Six New Rules for Getting and Keeping a Job in the '90s," 56 *Philadelphia Lawyer* 1, 28, Spring 1993]

Job changes, whether the result of company failures stemming from international trade competition or job elimination due to corporate re-engineering, will demand retraining with ever-increasing frequency. Meanwhile, young people entering the working world for the first time can no longer count on unions to provide the apprenticeship training they need. Indeed, even college graduates may need on-the-job training to fit into the new, fast-paced, high-tech entrepreneurial environment.

Success in world competition, as trade wars replace the Cold War as the defining arena of international conflict in the late 1990s and early 21st century, also demands ever-increasing efficiency, especially in manufacturing. "Employee empowerment," a term that encompasses employee participation (e.g., quality circles), and labor-management cooperation programs are increasingly acknowledged as key ingredients in the efficiency formula.

This chapter goes beyond employee termination, which is no longer the end of the spectrum of employment law issues, to cover these issues of intense concern today—retraining, quality, and productivity.

Role of the United States in the Global Marketplace

Q 14:1   Has the United States lost its preeminence in the global marketplace?

In early 1993, the United States emerged, if only haltingly, from a two-year recession that some commentators suggest reflects not merely a swing in the traditional economic cycle, but a structural change in the American socioeconomic landscape. [See, e.g., Reich, *The Work of Nations: Preparing Ourselves for 21st Century Capitalism* (NY: Random House 1991) at 224 ("[B]y the 1990s. . .the core American corporation was vanishing. The links between top executives and the American production worker were fading. An ever-increasing number of subordinates and contractees were foreign, and a steadily growing number of American routine producers were working for foreign firms. An entire cohort of middle-level managers, who had once been deemed 'white collar,' had disappeared; and, increasingly, American executives were exporting their insights to global enterprise webs."); see also, Olgeirson, "Economic Data Raise Questions Over Recovery," *The Wall Street Journal,* Apr 1, 1993, at A2]

Powerful new players in the world market, such as Japan and South Korea, are not the only reasons for possibly irreversible structural changes in the American economy. Some have pointed to the orgy of merger-mania that characterized the 1980s but seems to have died down in the more austere 1990s. [See, e.g., Demick, "Now, Buyout Burnout?" *Philadelphia Inquirer,* Jan 21, 1990, at 1C; "Fall of the House of Drexel," *The Wall Street Journal,* Mar 19, 1990, at A26; Drucker, *The New Realities* at 228 (1989) (the hostile takeover was "the most serious assault on management in its history—a far more serious assault than any mounted by Marxists or labor unions. . . .[T]he 'raider' with his hostile takeover bid prevails—and only too often immediately dismantles or loots the going concern, sacrificing long-range, wealth-producing capacity to short-term gains.")] The end of the Cold War is also causing disruptions to America's manufacturing sector. [See, Gnoffo, "Making a Bomb Plant Suitable for Business," *Philadelphia Inquirer,* Apr 4, 1993, at D1 ("The plant brought a boom-or-bust economy. . . .Booms came during World War II and the wars in Korea and Vietnam, when as many as 20,000 workers were employed in the plant. . . .But the end of the Cold War brought the biggest bust of all. Without the Soviet threat, and faced with growing budget deficits, the Army determined in 1990 that it no longer needed the Indiana plant.")]

Other observers are suggesting that in the face of these permanent structural changes in our economic landscape, American public policy is failing to face up to the reinvestment in human resources that competitors in other parts of the world have recognized as crucial to continued competitiveness and maintenance of a traditional standard of living. For example, Professor Samuel Estreicher of the New York University School of Law has observed that:

> There is no one cause for the relative decline in the U.S. position. [But] I would place under-investment in human resources high on the list of causes. In the words of a Massachusetts Institute of Technology study by leading economists and scientists, Americans systematically under-value "how much difference it can make when people are well educated and when their skills are continuously developed and challenged." [Estreicher, "Laws Promoting Worker Training, Productivity and Quality," 9 *The Labor Lawyer* 19, 20 (1993), citing Dertouzos et al., *Made in America: Regaining the Productive Edge* at 82 (1989)]

Calling the 1993 recovery from the prior years' deep recession a "jobless recovery," Secretary Reich repeatedly harped on a view that he first voiced in his 1991 book *The Work of Nations,* that is, that the U.S. economy is undergoing "fundamental structural change" that transcends the current economic weakness, and that is resulting in a "structural mismatch" between workers' skills and existing jobs. He also claims that the United States is "developing a two-tier society in terms of wages, with highly skilled people doing well and low-skilled people finding themselves in competition with workers worldwide." ["Reich says U.S. in Jobless Recovery," Reuters, Apr 7, 1993; Racz, "Labor Department Budget Would Cut Outlays but Create or Expand Programs," *The Wall Street Journal,* Apr 8, 1993; 1993 *BNA Daily Labor Report* 66 (Apr 8, 1993) at 1; see also, Dempsey, "The Bitter Fruits of Airline Deregulation," *The Wall Street Journal,* Apr 8, 1993 at A15]

In 1994 a controversial book weighed into the debate, contending that, indeed, a two-tiered America is evolving, and that IQ is determining this new class structure. [Herrnstein and Murray, *The Bell Curve: Intelligence and Class Structure in American Life* (Free Press 1994)] Although harshly attacked by its critics [see, e.g., Malcolm W.

Browne, "What Is Intelligence, and Who Has It?" *The New York Times Book Review,* Oct 16, 1994, at 3; Charles Lane, "The Tainted Sources of 'The Bell Curve'," *The New York Review of Books,* Dec 1, 1994, at 14], the book is part of a broader debate that questions such sacred cows of an earlier era as affirmative action. In the wake of the GOP's capture of the Congress in November 1994, even such staid liberals as Senator Daniel Patrick Moynihan (D-NY) suggested that affirmative action programs were ripe for being revisited. More conservative legislators and jurists seemed prepared to end affirmative action as a social program entirely. [See, e.g., Robert A. Rankin, "New Environment Could Spell the End of Affirmative Action," *The Philadelphia Inquirer,* Feb 24, 1995, at A1; Charles B. Craver, "Radical Supreme Court Justices Endeavor to Rewrite the Civil Rights Statutes," 10 *The Labor Lawyer* 4, Fall 1994, at 727] In the most controversial part of their book, Herrnstein and Murray flatly state, "[O]ur largest reason for wanting to scrap job discrimination law is our belief that the system of affirmative action, in education and the workplace alike, is leaking a poison into the American soul." [*The Bell Curve,* supra, at 508] In sum, these various critiques of affirmative action appear to contend that the concept in practice hurts America's competitive posture, while failing to eradicate the ills it is aimed at curing. [See id, Appendix 7 at 655]

However, others argue that the key to economic equal opportunity at home and American competitiveness abroad lies not in IQ scores or scrapping affirmative action programs, but in empowering the poorer portion of our society by ensuring equal access to the information highway. "The stakes are high. Access to the information highway may prove to be less a question of privilege or position than one of the basic ability to function in a democratic society. It may determine how well people are educated, the kind of job they eventually get, how they are retrained if they lose their job. . . ." [Suneel Ratan, "A New Divide Between Haves and Have-Nots," *Time,* Spring 1995 Special Issue, at 25]

In sum, it seems that America's stature in the global marketplace is intimately intertwined with the plight of that segment of our society that is experiencing information "disenfranchisement." [Id, quoting Mitch Kapor, co-founder of Lotus Development Corp. and president of the Electronic Frontier Foundation]

Q 14:2   What do America's leading competitors in the global marketplace do to ensure the training and retraining of their workers?

Beginning at age 15, German teenagers destined for the blue-collar workforce can enroll in a formal apprenticeship system during which they spend four days on the job and only one day in school each week. Their skills are sharpened and given greater depth through on-the-job training and continuing education once they are full-time workers. German companies are reported to be investing, on the average, twice as much in worker training as their American counterparts and about 17 times as much per apprentice as U.S. employers put into training the average worker. [Hilton, "Shared Training: Learning from Germany," *Monthly Labor Review* 33 (Mar 1991)]

Japanese workers are also benefiting from a managerial culture committed to the concept of continuous learning because it considers it critical to ultimate economic success. [Estreicher, "Laws Promoting Worker Training, Productivity and Quality," 9 *The Labor Lawyer* 20 (1993)]

Q 14:3   What is the United States doing to train American workers to meet the challenges of industrial restructuring and global competition?

The federal 1993 budget listed more than 60 vocational, education, and training programs funded by the federal government and administered by seven agencies. Many of these are components of broader statutes and programs, such as:

- Community Development Block Grants administered by the U.S. Department of Housing and Urban Development
- Title 9 of the Public Works Act of 1965, administered by the U.S. Department of Commerce
- The Job Opportunities and Basic Skills (JOBS) program, which the U.S. Department of Health and Human Services controls under the Family Support Act of 1988
- The Vocational and Adult Education program of the U.S. Department of Education

- The Job Training Partnership Act, which created the Job Corps, run by the U.S. Department of Labor
- The Defense Conversion Adjustment Act, which aims at retraining veterans of the armed services
- The Omnibus Trade and Competitiveness Act of 1988, which created the trade adjustment assistance program for workers displaced by the ravages of foreign competition
- The Economic Dislocation and Worker Adjustment Assistance Act of 1988
- The Carl D. Perkins Vocational Education Act of 1984, as amended in 1990

Additionally, a number of federal offices, agencies, and commissions have studied, and consequently urged, reformation of the U.S. approach to educating, training, and retraining American workers to help them overcome the disruptive effects of restructuring and dislocation and to meet more effectively the challenges of global competition. These studies include:

- A report published by the Commission on Workforce Quality and Labor Market Efficiency, appointed by Labor Secretary Ann M. McLaughlin in 1989, titled "Investing in People: A Strategy to Address America's Workforce Quality," U.S. Department of Labor (1989)
- "America's Choice: High Skills or Low Wages!" National Center on Education and the Economy (June 1990) issued by the Commission on Skills of the American Workforce, chaired by former labor secretaries William Brock and Ray Marshall

As a result of such studies, the U.S. Office of Technology Assessment, which comes under the control of Congress, has concluded that it is necessary for total employer investment in formal training programs to be about $30 billion to $44 billion, or at least $263 per worker per year for U.S. companies to be competitive.

Finally, provisions of the Internal Revenue Code also have been enacted by Congress to encourage greater worker participation and investment in their employment opportunities through such devices as employee stock ownership plans (ESOPs). [See Qs 8:159–8:167; Blasi and Kruse, *The New Owners: The Mass Emergence of Employee*

Ownership in Public Companies and What It Means to American Business at 31 [NY: Harper Business 1991)]

However, since the GOP triumph in November 1994, these training programs are under attack, and many, if not all of them, may be casualties of the cost-cutting aspects of the Republicans' Contract with America. On March 16, 1995, the U.S. House of Representatives voted 227-200 in favor of $17 billion in rescissions, a package of cuts that included trimming the U.S. Labor Department's fiscal 1995 budget by $2.3 billion. The largest piece of this proposed cut is the elimination of the Job Training Partnership Act's (JTPA) summer jobs program, which previously had been funded at $867 million for 1995 and $871 million for 1996. This total funding of $1.7 billion was intended to help provide summer jobs for 1.2 million disadvantaged young Americans. Assistance for displaced workers under Title III of the JTPA and other aspects of adult job training under the DOL were also high on the GOP list of spending reductions. ["House Passes Rescission Package, Cuts Labor Department $2.3 Billion," *BNA Pensions & Benefits Daily,* Mar 20, 1995]

Additionally, the House Budget Committee approved budget cuts for future years, intended to offset the tax reductions promised to voters as part of the Contract with America. "Focusing on elimination of duplication and waste, the package includes five-year cuts of $9.2 billion in ineffective training and employment programs, $723 million through reductions in Goals 2000 and school-to-work programs, and $122 million through a freeze on operations of state unemployment insurance programs and the Employment Service." [Id]

These deep cuts were met with anticipated opposition by both politicians and the news media. For example, a Florida newspaper asked, "No one disputes the need to bring federal spending in line with revenues. But should the budget be balanced on the backs of 2,700 youths in Palm Beach County. . .?" [Robert Douglas, "Contract 'on' America Hitmen Target Youth Jobs," *The Palm Beach Post,* Mar 10, 1995, at 9B] Not surprisingly, the most vociferous opponent of the cuts is DOL Secretary Robert Reich, who came into office two years ago hoping to streamline the diverse group of training programs outlined above; however, Reich may be a lone voice as others in the administration, including President Clinton, seem to be vying with the GOP to sell their own package of budget reductions to voters who last November were—in the words of Republican Party Chairman Haley Barbour—"anti-Democratic, anti-liberal, anti-big government, and anti-Clinton." [John A. Farrell, "Reich Redux," *The Boston Globe Magazine,* Apr 2, 1995, at 26] Consequently, at least some substantial cutting of the DOL job training budget seems certain, and other programs may be eliminated.

Q 14:4   Does the United States have any apprenticeship training programs?

In 1987, the Department of Labor launched an "Apprenticeship 2000" initiative to seek ways to apply the concept of apprenticeship to the task of raising the general skill levels of the U.S. workforce. An apprentice is commonly considered a person learning a craft or trade from an employer. In early times, an apprentice was "usually a minor, bound in due form of law to a master, to learn from him his art, trade, or business, and to serve him during the time of his apprenticeship." [*Black's Law Dictionary* at 80 (2d ed West 1910)] During this century, the concept of apprenticeship most commonly occurred in conjunction with representation of a workforce by a labor union. Numerous collective bargaining agreements still contain apprenticeship provisions, especially among the building trades. The Labor Department's establishment of an Office of Work-Based Learning in 1987 was at least in part a tacit recognition of the declining influence of organized labor in the training of the workforce, as in other aspects of the American labor scene (see Qs 11:5–11:6).

Yet, some are wary of such government attempts:

> [H]owever laudatory the goals of this initiative, the prospects for expanded apprenticeship training are unclear. This is due in part to the fact that non-construction industry associations in this country either have not been interested in, or are not well structured to provide, apprenticeship training. A 1976 effort by the Labor Department's Bureau of Apprenticeship Training to promote similar programs had little lasting effect once funding ended in 1979.

> [Estreicher, "Laws Promoting Worker Training, Productivity and Quality," 9 The Labor Lawyer 1 at 25 (1993)]

The Job Corps, a part of the Job Training Partnership Act [29 USC §§ 1501-1991j], operates out of Job Corps Centers around the country in training disadvantaged young people to become productive members of the workforce. It is, in effect, offering surrogate apprenticeship programs. [See 29 USC §§ 1691–1709, creating company-sponsored programs under which, "The Secretary [of Labor] may contract with private for-profit businesses and labor unions to provide intensive training in company-sponsored training programs, combined with internships in work settings." 29 USC § 1698(d)(3)]

Additionally, a number of states are striving to fill the apprenticeship vacuum left by the decline of organized labor in the American economy. For example, consider the following brief case study:

> [A]s a pioneer student in Maine's . . . Youth Apprenticeship Program, which is run by the Maine Technical College System, [Michael] Moody's experiences are of keen interest to the Clinton Administration.
>
> Mr. Clinton and his Secretaries of Education and Labor have repeatedly promised to shore-up job-training programs and pay more attention to non-college-bound students. While the Administration is divulging few details of its plans, hundreds of millions of dollars have been pledged for apprenticeship programs.
>
> As the politicians wring out policy details, Michael Moody is enjoying life away from the traditional vocational school. . . .He now spends one day a week in regular high school classes with other apprentices, taking academic classes specially designed to dovetail with experiences from work.
>
> [Lively, "Maine's Month-Old Youth Apprenticeships Show How a National Plan Might Work," *Chronicle of Higher Education*, Mar 31, 1993, at A20]

Students such as Moody spend the other four days working at a participating company, earning a $5,000 stipend during the course of the school year, which presumably is good economics for the employer as well as the apprentice. Other states with such programs include Arkansas, Pennsylvania, and Wisconsin, along with cities such as Boston, Tulsa, Oklahoma, and Binghamton, New York.

However, the GOP-controlled Congress has proposed deep reductions in current and future federal budgets with regard to virtually all aspects of federally funded job training, including "Apprenticeship

2000" and the Job Training Partnership Act. [Robert Douglas, "Contract 'on' America Hitmen Target Youth Jobs," *The Palm Beach Post,* Mar 10, 1995, at 9B; "House Passes Rescissions Package, Cuts Labor Department $2.3 Billion," *BNA Pensions & Benefits Daily,* Mar 20, 1995; John A. Farrell, "Reich Redux," *The Boston Globe Magazine,* Apr 2, 1995, at 26]

Q 14:5 Does the American workforce require government intervention to achieve retraining, quality, and productivity?

The answer to this question involves many sub-issues. First, while most Americans are likely to agree that this country faces fierce international competition and has just been through a painful recession, not all will subscribe to the description of the structural nature of our economic problems as viewed by Labor Secretary Robert Reich and others cited in Q 14:1. Quality circles and other employee participation and cooperation programs (see Q 14:19) remain somewhat controversial in this country, although they are widely accepted among some of the United States' most successful international competitors, notably Japan. For instance, one labor leader was quoted in a national magazine as complaining that, "What the company wants is for us to work like the Japanese. Everybody go out and do jumping jacks in the morning and kiss each other when they go home at night. You work as a team, rat on each other, and lose control of your destiny. That's not going to work in this country." [*Business Week,* Jul 10, 1989; see also, Castagnera, "To Confront or to Cooperate? The Lesson of Anthracite Coal," *Labor L J* 158 (Mar 1990)]

Those who find employee participation programs appropriate may nevertheless oppose government involvement in such programs in the private sector. For example, Professor Samuel Estreicher raises the following concerns:

> The argument for government intervention is that firms will underinvest in worker training. Because of the job mobility of U.S. workers, firms cannot fully capture the benefits of training, and hence forego optimal investment in the human capital of their workers. However, in evaluating the force of this argument, we should ask whether the training investment in question

concerns "firm specific" skills. . .or "general" transferable skills. Under human capital theory, there is no reason to believe that investments in firm-specific skills will be underproduced. Both workers and firms share the costs and benefits of specific training, and turnover is made less likely because of deferred compensation practices. Moreover, some studies suggest that firms that invest in both general and specific training are also less likely to lose their investments through turnover. Indeed, companies like IBM, Xerox, and Motorola. . .engage in "high performance" strategies without any need for government prodding.

[Estreicher, "Laws Promoting Worker Training, Productivity and Quality," 9 *The Labor Lawyer* 1 at 28 (1993)]

However, others are highly skeptical of Estreicher's optimistic view of corporate America, saying American corporations reward the accumulation of capital, not the development of human resources. Thus, top CEOs, such as Disney's Michael Eisner, and investment experts, have reaped multi-billion-dollar rewards from corporate shareholders in recent years (see Q 8:84), while average American workers have experienced declining real wages during the past decade and a half. [John A. Farrell, "Reich Redux," *The Boston Globe Magazine*, Apr 2, 1995, at 26]

For those who support not only employee participation, but government support of such programs, the remaining question becomes how much support and what sort. Training and quality programs can be government-sponsored, as the Jobs Corps (see Q 14:8) is today; they can be private-sector based or a combination of the two, as with apprenticeship training in Maine (see Q 14:4). But how should they be funded then? Should U.S. business or workers be asked to bear yet another payroll or excise tax? Should only those companies that do not establish voluntary training and retraining efforts be forced to support such a fund? The GOP-controlled Congress was signaling strongly that worker training would not receive much, if any, federal funding in the next couple of years. [Farrell, supra; Robert Douglas, "Contract 'on' America Hitmen Target Youth Jobs," *The Palm Beach Post*, Mar 10, 1995, at 9B; "House Passes Rescissions Package, Cuts Labor Department $2.3 Billion," *BNA Pension & Benefits Daily*, Mar 20, 1995]

Government Involvement

Q 14:6   What new legislation is being considered by Congress with regard to the retraining, productivity, or quality of the American workforce?

A number of workforce training or retraining bills were introduced during the 102nd Congress. For instance, Senate Bill 1790, sponsored by the senators from Massachusetts, incorporated many of the recommendations of the Commission on Skills of the American Workforce (see Q 14:3). Labeled the "High Skills and Competitive Workforce Act," its aim was to appropriate $580 million to train workers and to encourage companies to adopt "high performance" workplace policies. The specific components of SB 1790 were:

- To develop a voluntary system of occupational certification by a proposed national board of professional and technical standards

- To link high school instruction with on-the-job training under a mentor (see Q 14:15)

- To promote high-performance organization of job tasks and increase the level of employment-based training

- To encourage the private sector to create high skills training consortia among companies in the same industry or those that use the same or similar technologies; doing so would involve the award of matching grants and probably the easing of antitrust restraints

- To coordinate federal, state, and municipal government unemployment and training programs

SB 1790 contained a so-called pay or train provision that would have levied a 1 percent payroll tax on employers of 20 or more workers for the creation of a High Skills Training Trust Fund. Organized labor supported the bill.

Meanwhile, the Clinton administration drafted legislation aimed at creating a new school-to-work program, another form of apprenticeship program for non-college students. [*BNA Daily Report to Executives* (Apr 8, 1993) at 66]

The Republicans in Congress had proposed "Job Training 2000," a bill aimed at, among other things, establishing a job-training clearinghouse to coordinate the 60-plus training and retraining programs administered by seven federal agencies, to develop a more uniform certification system to ensure quality, and to improve local delivery of the training services. However, Congress, dominated by the GOP since the November 1994 elections, was seriously considering deep immediate and mid-range cuts in job training programs, including the elimination of some of these programs. [See Qs 14:3, 14:4; "House Passes Rescissions Package, Cuts Labor Department $2.3 Billion," *BNA Pensions & Benefits Daily,* Mar 20, 1995]

Q 14:7 Does federal legislation provide any financial incentives for employers to participate in the training or retraining of workers?

Most proposed federal legislation aimed at improving the competitive position of the American worker in the world market, either by training, retraining, or otherwise, contained incentives for corporations to participate in the legislative program. For example, employee stock ownership plans (ESOPs) afford sponsoring companies, their major shareholders, and often even the owner's estate substantial potential tax advantages in return for creating broad-based employee ownership in the enterprise (see Qs 8:163 and 8:166).

Similarly, current federal programs directed toward worker training or retraining, as opposed to outright equity participation in the business, also typically include either outright funding or tax relief for corporations that choose to participate in such programs. Some of these programs are voluntary, while others contain mandatory participation provisions that can be triggered by certain circumstances. Examples of these federal programs are discussed in greater detail in Qs 14:5 et seq.

However, all such programs, whether in force or merely proposed, are under attack as the GOP's Contract with America legislative program seeks to cut such budgetary expenditures to fund a middle-class tax cut (see Qs 14:3–14:5).

Federal Legislation

Note: All of the federal programs outlined in this section were targeted by the Republican-dominated Congress for cuts or elimination. [See Qs 14:3–14:7; see also Robert Douglas, "Contract 'on' America Hitmen Target Youth Jobs," *The Palm Beach Post,* Mar 10, 1995, at 9B; "House Passes Rescissions Package, Cuts Labor Department $2.3 Billion," *BNA Pensions & Benefits Daily,* Mar 20, 1995; John A. Farrell, "Reich Redux," *The Boston Globe Magazine,* Apr 2, 1995, at 26]

Job Training Partnership Act

Q 14:8   What is the federal Job Training Partnership Act?

The Job Training Partnership Act (JTPA) [29 USC § 1501 (1982)] was enacted in 1982 with the expressed purpose of establishing "programs to prepare youth and unskilled adults for entry into the labor force and to afford job training to those economically disadvantaged individuals and other individuals facing serious barriers to employment, who are in special need of such training to obtain productive employment." The core program was dubbed the "Job Corps," and participation by eligible disadvantaged youths was conditioned on compliance with the registration requirements of the Military Selective Service Act. [29 USC §§ 1504 et seq] The secretary of labor was charged with distributing grants of federal funds to the states for the educational assistance and training of American workers, while private industry councils were created to help ensure adequate private-sector participation.

While the act always contemplated the allocation of some funds for the training of older individuals, the statute was significantly amended in 1988 by the Economic Dislocation and Worker Adjustment Assistance Act (EDWAA) for the specific purpose of training and relocating workers dislocated by plant closings and the like. [29 USC §§ 1651–1662e]

Economic Dislocation and Worker Adjustment Assistance Act

Q 14:9　What are the major provisions of the Economic Dislocation and Worker Adjustment Assistance Act (EDWAA) of 1988?

Under EDWAA, workers who have lost their jobs or who have been notified that they will lose their jobs, and who have no expectation of being able to find new employment in their occupation or industry, are potentially eligible for assistance. The act requires states that accept federal funds under this statute to spend at least 50 percent of those funds on retraining services for dislocated workers. [29 USC § 1661d(a)] Workers receiving plant-closing notices pursuant to the WARN Act (see Qs 13:50–13:65) are entitled to on-site assistance from their respective states under the act. [29 USC §§ 2101 et seq]

Compared to other federal entitlement programs, EDWAA is not heavily funded. The basic statutory program was allocated $377 million by Congress for 1993, plus an additional $200 million for workers who have lost their jobs due to the requirements of the 1990 Clean Air Act. [Estreicher, "Laws Promoting Worker Training, Productivity and Quality," 9 *The Labor Lawyer* 1 at 25 (1993)]

The assistance provided under EDWAA must be spent by the states and their municipal subdivisions in accordance with plans submitted by the states to the federal government. The act specifies four categories of appropriate uses for the funds:

1. *Rapid Response Assistance.* Theoretically, within as little as 48 hours of the announcement of a major plant closing, the dislocated (or about-to-be-dislocated) workers should be provided with:

   a. On-site information and access to public programs and services, such as unemployment compensation,

   b. Emergency assistance tailored to the particular closure or layoff,

   c. Promotion of the formation of labor-management committees by means of financial aid to cover start-up costs; technical advice, such as information about public and private services that may be available; aid in the selection of worker representatives in instances in which no union is available, and

d. Funding of a preliminary assessment, if appropriate, of the feasibility of having a company or group (including a union or other worker group) buy the plant and keep it running.

2. *Basic Readjustment Services.* This can include:

a. Job and career counseling,

b. Evaluation of skills, aptitudes, education, and interests,

c. Job placement assistance and labor market information, or

d. Child care, commuting assistance, or relocation aid.

3. *Retraining Services.* This can involve:

a. Classroom training,

b. On-the-job training,

c. Out-of-area job searches,

d. Basic remedial education,

e. English as a second language, or

f. Entrepreneurial training.

4. *Needs-Related Payments.* This includes supplemental payments for displaced workers who have exhausted their unemployment compensation entitlement.

Q 14:10   How is workers' eligibility for EDWAA assistance triggered?

Typically, the corporation that is closing a plant or conducting a mass layoff has an obligation to notify the appropriate state office or agency about the impending action. For example, the WARN Act requires a 60-day notice under most such circumstances (see Qs 13:50–13:60). If a union represents the affected rank-and-file employees, it, too, is typically entitled to notice. One would assume a faltering company would have every incentive to give such notice at the earliest opportunity. However, in reality, corporations typically are involved in behind-the-scenes negotiations or financial maneuvering, which may be aimed at selling the faltering facility or moving it to Mexico, offshore, or another part of the United States. Under such common scenarios, premature disclosure may scuttle the deal. When the secret negotiations are aimed at keeping the threatened plant open under new owner-ship, premature disclosure hurts employees as well as the current owner. WARN allows for these circumstances by permitting shorter notice in such situations (see Qs 13:60, 13:61).

Trade Adjustment Assistance Act

Q 14:11   What is the Trade Adjustment Assistance Act?

The Trade Adjustment Assistance Act (TAA), or Trade Act of 1974 [19 USC §§ 2101–2495], as amended by the Omnibus Trade and Competitiveness Act of 1988 [19 USC §§ 2251–2395], is comprehen-sive legislation that empowers the president, the International Trade Commission, and the U.S. trade representative to represent the United States in the world marketplace, and in particular, to take steps to protect American businesses and workers from unfair trade competition. For example, the act empowers the president, acting on advice from the International Trade Commission, to facilitate positive adjustments to import competition. This section of the statute states, in part:

> If the United States International Trade Commission . . . deter-mines . . . that an article is being imported into the United States in such increased quantities as to be a substantial cause of serious injury, or the threat thereof, to the domestic industry producing an article like or directly competitive with the im-ported article, the President, in accordance with this chapter, shall take all appropriate and feasible action within his power which the President determines will facilitate efforts by the domestic industry to make a positive adjustment to import competition and provide greater economic and social benefits than costs.

Q 14:12   Who is eligible to receive benefits under the TAA?

Eligibility is determined by the secretary of labor, who must certify a group of workers as eligible for TAA benefits if:

> [A] significant number or proportion of the workers in such workers' firm or an appropriate subdivision of the firm have

become totally or partially separated . . . sales or production, or both, of such firm or subdivision have decreased absolutely, and increases of imports of articles like or directly competitive with articles produced by such workers' firm or appropriate subdivision thereof contributed importantly to such total or partial separation, or threat thereof, and to such decline in sales or production.

[19 USC § 2272(a)(1988)]

Q 14:13 What benefits can displaced workers receive under the TAA, and how are they administered?

In the words of one knowledgeable commentator, "Retraining displaced workers is touted as an important feature of federal trade adjustment assistance programs. The basic trade adjustment assistance [TAA] program, as most recently amended by the Omnibus Trade and Competitiveness Act of 1988, provides that eligible workers receive 78 weeks of unemployment benefits provided that they are enrolled in training." [Estreicher, "Laws Promoting Worker Training, Productivity and Quality," 9 *The Labor Lawyer* 1 at 24 (1993)]

Typically, TAA benefits are dispersed through state agencies. The following is an illustrative statement from one state's brochure dealing with the issue:

> Trade Adjustment Assistance (TAA) is available to workers who lose their jobs or whose hours of work and wages are reduced as a result of increased imports. TAA benefits include re-employment services such as funded training, job search allowances, relocation benefits, and, after you exhaust your unemployment compensation, weekly benefits of Trade Readjustment Allowances (TRA). Each benefit under the TAA program has distinct eligibility requirements, and each benefit must be applied for separately. Also there are separate time limitations to apply for each benefit.
>
> [Commonwealth of Pennsylvania, Department of Labor and Industry, Pennsylvania Unemployment Compensation Handbook 11 (Harrisburg 1990)]

Q 14:14   How are workers certified as eligible for Trade Adjustment Assistance benefits?

A petition for certification must be filed with the secretary of labor. Any group of workers or their authorized representative, such as a labor union, may file such a petition. When the labor secretary receives such a petition, it must be promptly published in the Federal Register, after which an interested party has 10 days in which to request a hearing on the petition. The secretary then has 60 days to determine eligibility and, if found, issue a certification and publish the determination in the Federal Register.

Q 14:15   What can petitioning employees do if the secretary of labor refuses to certify them as eligible for Trade Adjustment Assistance benefits?

The disappointed employees can appeal the denial of their petition to the U.S. Court of International Trade. By way of illustration, in *Former Employees of Hawkins Oil and Gas Inc. v. U.S. Secretary of Labor* [No 90-02-00083, Slip Op 93-27 (Feb 18, 1993)], the court held that the department's repeated denials of the plaintiffs' petitions for adjustment assistance were not supported by substantial evidence. In this case, three employees on the exploration staff in Hawkins Oil's geology department filed a petition on behalf of all the workers of Hawkins/Tulsa. The three petitioners had lost their jobs in mid-1989. The Department of Labor (DOL) denied their initial petition in late December of that year, finding that increased imports had not "contributed importantly" to their job loss. (Under the TAA Act, "contributed importantly" means "is important but not necessarily more important than any other cause".)

The three challenged the DOL's finding in the Court of International Trade, which initially remanded the case to the department for a new investigation. DOL again denied the petition. The second time around, the court again ruled in favor of the ex-employees of Hawkins, holding that:

> Labor's investigation was deficient. Among other factors, the court pointed out that Labor only requested data regarding the customers' purchases from Hawkins and did not solicit data or opinions regarding the overall condition of the domestic oil and gas market. Further, Labor did not inquire about the role imports have played in this condition.

Labor also failed to evaluate and investigate the connection between oil and gas imports and the decline in prices of oil and gas.

["CIT Orders Labor Secretary to Certify Plaintiff as Eligible for TAA Benefits," *BNA International Trade Reporter,* Mar 31, 1993, citing Former Employees of Hawkins Oil and Gas Inc v US Secretary of Labor, No 90-02-00083 (Slip Op 93-27, 2/18/93)]

Q 14:16   Is the Trade Adjustment Assistance program considered to be an effective public policy for helping displaced American workers?

One well-regarded expert has observed:

The TAA program suffers from a number of problems: eligibility for assistance is restricted to certification requirements; payments are made after displacement has occurred; and funds for training or relocation assistance are quite limited. . . .It is thus better to view TAA as a compensation program rather than one that truly provides readjustment assistance.

[Estreicher, "Laws Promoting Worker Training, Productivity and Quality," 9 *The Labor Lawyer* 1 at 24 (1993)]

In fact, while the DOL's 1994 budget proposal heavily emphasizes job training and assistance for displaced workers, it also suggests the elimination of TAA as a separate program. Criticizing such "categorical programs," Labor Secretary Robert Reich said the result has been a bureaucratic nightmare because of the need to certify the particular cause of the dislocation to render the workers eligible for aid. According to one report:

The administration currently expects to continue its requests for sizable increases through fiscal 1997, as it implements the plan to improve on EDWAA and replace the Trade Adjustment Assistance program. According to a DOL spokesperson, funding levels of about $2.7 billion are anticipated in fiscal years 1995 through 1997. The budget requests lower funding for TAA benefits and allowance payments because the administration will be asking Congress to repeal the entitlement program effective July 1, 1994.

["Job Training, Aid for Displaced Workers Emphasized in Administration Budget Plan," *BNA Daily Report for Executives*
(Apr 8, 1993) at 66]

Employee Participation Programs

Q 14:17   Does the Clinton administration plan to promote workplace cooperation programs?

Despite the National Labor Relations Board's rejection of an employee participation program in *Electromation Inc.* [309 NLRB No 163
(Dec 16, 1992)] (see Qs 11:108–11:111), Labor Secretary Reich has
made it clear that workplace cooperation programs will be a part of
this administration's program, even if it means approaching Congress
to amend the National Labor Relations Act. [See Swoboda, "Reich
Vows to Preserve Workplace Cooperation," *Washington Post*, Mar 9,
1993, at D3]

In confirmation of the sincerity of his vow, Reich and Commerce
Secretary Ron Brown subsequently announced the creation of a
10-member panel to consider labor-management cooperation and
employee participation in the workplace. The purpose of the panel's
year-long investigation is to explore new methods and institutions to
improve productivity through labor-management cooperation and
employee participation; determine if such programs should either be
encouraged or mandated by federal law and regulation; and consider
whether current laws, such as the NLRA, need to be changed to
promote these administration goals. Prospects for more frequently
solving workplace problems in the workplace, rather than in the
courts and regulatory agencies, is another goal of the new panel.
[1993 *BNA Daily Labor Report* 56 (Mar 25, 1993) at 1-2]

Q 14:18   What is the difference between "labor-management cooperation" and "employee participation" programs?

The term "labor-management cooperation" is usually intended to
designate situations in which organized labor (a labor union) is
involved in a cooperative effort with the management of a company.
Such programs are encountered, for example, when a union has

invested in an employee stock ownership plan (ESOP) (see Q 11:105). By contrast, employee participation programs occur more commonly in nonunion companies and can take on a variety of forms (see Q 11:110).

Q 14:19   Are employee participation programs practical only for large corporations?

To the contrary, a number of smaller companies have proven in well-publicized studies that employee cooperation programs such as quality circles can enhance productivity and profitability. Here are three cases, for example:

1. Moog Inc., a manufacturer in Erie County, New York, received regional recognition when it embarked on a program of total quality management (TQM) among its 2,000 workers at four locations in the Buffalo area. Moog established "continuous improvement teams." One of the first areas addressed was shipping costs, which annually exceeded $1 million. In one situation, equipment being made at Moog for a plant in the Philippines was slated to be shipped by air. The team in charge of examining this issue discovered that careful scheduling, together with ocean shipment instead of air, would save Moog about $1.50 per pound of goods shipped. Because "continuous improvement" are the teams' watchwords, this group then went on to make other shipping suggestions estimated to be able to save about $250,000 per year. [Hartley, "Commitment, Not Lip Service, Makes Quality Programs Work," *Business First-Buffalo,* Oct 21, 1991 at 1]

2. Thor-Lo Inc., a North Carolina manufacturer of athletic socks, was founded by a patriarch and taken over by a son, who came into the family enterprise after 20 years of working for large apparel manufacturers. The 54-year-old inheritor of Thor-Lo was quoted as saying, "Corporate America uses the team concept, but the structure and culture subverts the process— people are still rewarded for their individual contributions. Until you build a living structure, the teamwork will not happen." Acting on this philosophy, Thor-Lo's 350 employees were called "partners." Production partners were scheduled to work three 12-hour shifts per week and spend the remaining

four hours of their normal workweek on education. The reported goal is the creation of a "truth-telling culture" where the "partners" feel free to discuss ways to improve the product. [Cranford, "Sock Maker Marching to Workers' Order," *Business J-Charlotte,* Nov 4, 1991, at 1]

3. Wallace Co., a Houston-based piping distributor, seems to be somewhat of a Cinderella story. Teetering on the brink of financial disaster in 1985, the company came all the way back to win the Malcolm Baldridge National Quality Award in 1990. Between 1987 and 1990, the Houston, Texas, concern reportedly spent $2 million, or about $8,000 per employee, on training programs, even though sales were in a slump. The company's total quality management (TQM) program included a corporate mission statement: immediate follow-through from quality training to quality reform. The TQM structure followed the lines of the Baldridge Award criteria:

- Leadership
- Information and analysis
- Strategic quality planning
- Human resource utilization
- Quality assurance of products and services
- Quality results
- Customer satisfaction

[Altany, "Cinderella with a Drawl," *Industry Week* (Jan 6, 1992) at 49]

New Developments in Employee Compensation, Retraining, and Welfare Reform

Welfare

Q 14:20   Are middle-class workers losing ground in American business and industry?

Secretary of Labor Robert Reich ably illustrated in his 1991 book *The Work of Nations* (see Q 14:1) that the gap between compensation paid to the CEOs of America's top corporations and that paid to these companies' average workers has grown dramatically since the 1950s, when the after-tax income of the average CEO was only about 12 times that of the average rank-and-file worker. Now the average chief executive pockets after-tax revenues some 70 times greater than those realized by ordinary workers in the same companies.

In the years since Reich wrote *The Work of Nations,* the trend has not been reversed. In fact, the gap may be widening. Despite a proposal by the Financial Accounting Standards Board (FASB) to require companies to treat stock options as current liabilities deductible from reported earnings (see Q 8:85), stock options remain the key to mega-compensation packages for top corporate executives. According to a compensation survey by William M. Mercer, Inc., consultants in New York, as reported in *The Wall Street Journal,* April 11, 1994, the big winners in 1994 were Walt Disney's Michael Eisner, who earned $203 million, most of it from the exercise of stock options, and Travelers' Sanford Weill, who is described as "an ardent proponent of stock compensation and relatively low salaries," at $52.6 million, including an exercise of options worth $46.9 million.

From those two mega-earners, the figures drop precipitously into the $10 million to $20 million range. [Id] But there may be those who would consider even the relatively paltry $11.8 million realized by Whirlpool's David Whitman to be good money. According to *The Wall Street Journal:*

> For America's corporate chiefs, this is the year of politically correct pay. Many chief executive officers, confronting increased regulation and criticism of their sky-high compensation, are embracing a new mantra: "I should only get richer when investors get richer." Some business leaders are skipping salary raises amid good times. More CEOs now collect stock awards only if they significantly drive up their companies' share price—rather than just for coming to work. Others have begun to give up part of their generous cash bonuses for stock.
>
> "You are seeing the pendulum swing in reaction to executive pay abuses in the past," says Carl L. Campbell, president and CEO of Keystone Financial, Inc.. . . ." But the pay pendulum only swings so far. "We aren't politically correct to the point where we are reducing anybody's pay," says Jude Rich, chairman of consultants Sibson & Co. in Princeton, New Jersey. That's why CEO compensation keeps rising. "Chief executives'

salaries and bonuses rose 8.1 percent in 1993," reported Joann S. Lublin.

["Looking Good: For CEOs, the Pay Gains Haven't Stopped," *The Wall Street Journal*, Apr 13, 1994, at R1]

Since FASB acceded to the wishes of the Securities and Exchange Commission and numerous corporations and, thus, backed away from its proposed treatment of options as current corporate obligations (see Q 8:85), we may anticipate even more widespread use of the stock option as a compensation device.

By contrast, ordinary working people continue to be buffeted by declining wages and salaries, if not the outright threat of layoff and permanent job loss. Consider for example:

When Mary Gumpper started at Frankford Hospital's School of Nursing in 1991, she thought she'd be making $17 an hour as a graduate nurse in the Philadelphia area. Three years later, she's at the Ridge Crest Nursing & Rehabilitation Center and she's making $6 an hour.

[Anthony S. Twyman, "Health-Care Shifts: Job Seekers Find the Market Is Changing," *Philadelphia Daily News*, Apr 13, 1994, at 19]

The plight of ordinary working folk, and particularly those Americans at the lower end of the socioeconomic spectrum, was spotlighted in a book published in 1994 that created controversy due to its questioning of affirmative action programs. [See Herrnstein and Murray, *The Bell Curve: Intelligence and Class Structure in American Life* (1994)] Although their conclusions have been criticized sharply, [see, e.g., Charles Lane, "The Tainted Sources of 'The Bell Curve'," *The New York Review of Books*, Dec 1, 1994, at 14] the authors point relates to this topic:

From the end of World War II until the early 1970s, average family income rose. Then in 1973, median family income hit a peak. Part of the reason for the subsequent lack of progress has been the declining real wages for many categories of blue-collar jobs. . . .Part of the reason has been the decline in two-parent families. . . . In any case, the average American family has been stuck at about the same place economically for more than 20 years.

[Herrnstein and Murray, supra, at 516]

Average family income has been stuck at around $36,000 a year for several years and actually declined modestly by $700 in 1993. One may wonder whether this tough situation facing so many American workers helps explain the proliferation of theft and other dishonesty in the workplace (see Qs 6:1–6:12), or the fact that homicide is now the second highest cause of workplace fatalities. ["Workplace Violence: OSHA Should Hold Employers Accountable for Taking 'Reasonable Measures,' Labor Says," *BNA Occupational & Health Daily,* Jan 26, 1994]

But knowledgeable commentators have begun to worry what effect this widening gap between the haves and have-nots will have on the American democratic process. "[A] coalition of the cognitive elite and the affluent class now represents something well in excess of 5 percent of families and, because of their much higher than average voting rates, somewhere in the vicinity of 10 percent to 15 percent of the voters." [Herrnstein and Murray, supra, at 517-18]

They worry that differing degrees of access to the information highway will serve to exacerbate both the widening workplace remuneration gap and the lower half's ability to participate in the democratic process.

> In an era in which success is increasingly identified with the ability to use computers and to gain access to cyberspace, will the new technology only widen the gap between rich and poor, educated and uneducated, blacks, whites, and Hispanics? As Commerce Secretary Ron Brown puts it, 'How do you create an environment so that once we've built this information infrastructure, you do not create a society of haves and have-nots?'
>
> [Suneel Ratan, "A New Divide Between Haves and Have-Nots?" *Time,* Special Issue, Spring 1995, at 25]

While these commentators worry about such issues, however, policymakers in Washington, D.C., where the GOP now controls both houses of Congress, are questioning the continued viability of affirmative action as a means of addressing these issues. [See, e.g., Robert A. Rankin, "New Environment Could Spell the End of Affirmative Action," *The Philadelphia Inquirer,* Feb 24, 1995, at A1]

Q 14:21   What federal labor, employment, and welfare legislation is needed to aid in this nation's transition from the Industrial to the Information Age?

What changes ought to be made to America's legal system to meet the challenges of the Information Age may depend on one's political and economic orientation. For example, organized labor contends that a striker replacement statute, aimed at preventing employers from permanently replacing striking employees seeking improved wages and benefits, will strengthen labor unions and save jobs (see Q 11:8). Opponents of such an amendment to the National Labor Relations Act protest that such a rule would merely perpetuate inefficiencies and damage American companies' competitively. Nonetheless, faced with a Republican-dominated Congress, the Clinton administration in 1995 provided labor a large part of what it wanted by promulgating an executive order that forbids government contractors from replacing their striking employees on pain of being debarred. (See chapter 11 for a more extensive discussion of that executive order, and Qs 9:41–9:47 for an explanation of the significance of debarment.) The GOP legislators were unable to overturn Clinton's order, which now stands as part of the law of the land, applicable to the tens of thousands of private corporations doing business with Uncle Sam.

There are also those who support sharply increased tax rates presumably to raise revenue to assist those requiring retraining or other assistance to cope with job displacement. But available information indicates that taxing the Michael Eisners of the nation would not result in increased revenue (although such taxation might create a feeling of greater fairness in the way free enterprise compensates its employees, because it might have the effect of closing the after-tax gap in compensation between the lowest- and highest-paid people in America's corporations) (see Q 14:20). To the contrary, the historical data from the early part of this century indicate that steeply increased tax rates raise little additional revenue. One reason may be the phenomenon we are witnessing in the mid-1990s of billionaires actually renouncing their American citizenship to avoid paying any U.S. taxes at all.

Perhaps more promising are plans to substitute the current welfare system with a new scheme aimed at training, or retraining, welfare recipients and getting them into paying jobs in the private sector. Such a scheme, typically called the Graduated Income Supplement (or GIS), was proposed some 20 years ago by President Nixon, and was supported by many knowledgeable observers and welfare experts. [See, e.g., Castagnera, "GIS: A Welfare Substitute," *Texas Observer*, Jul 23, 1982, at 16] Under a GIS program, welfare recipients would be trained to fill anticipated openings in the job market and then receive income supplements to the extent that their new jobs failed to provide at least a minimum annual income pegged at keeping them above the poverty level. A similar approach was proposed in 1994 by the Clinton administration. However, what hope the proposition may have had is placed in grave doubt in light of the Republican capture of majorities in both houses of the Congress in the November 1994 elections.

Supplementation of U.S. laws, such as the Trade Adjustment Assistance Act (see Qs 14:11–14:16), may be required to offset the impact of the North American Free Trade Agreement (NAFTA) on American workers. Although the United States pushed through a supplementary agreement called the North American Agreement on Labor Cooperation (see Q 1:30), many commentators believe that NAFTA will result in a net loss of U.S. jobs to Mexico at least in the near term, which the Labor Cooperation accord and its dispute mechanisms would be powerless to prevent. [See, e.g., "NAFTA Displaced Workers Program Criticized," *BNA Labor Relations Reporter-Analysis*, 145 BNA LRR 217, Mar 22, 1994]

Nevertheless, two complaints are pending under the Labor Cooperation supplement's dispute-handling provisions, each alleging a violation of NAFTA by Mexican subsidiaries of U.S. companies, General Electric and Honeywell, by the Teamsters Union and the United Electrical Workers, respectively. [See, *BNA Labor Relations Reporter-Analysis*, 145 LRR 205 (1994); *CCH Labor Law Reports* para 9499-9500 (1994)] These complaints are being processed by the U.S. Department of Labor's National Administrative Office (NAO). In 1995 the NAO was faulting Mexico's handling of these complaints. ["Mexico Union Registration Process Faulted in US NAO Report on Sony Charges," *BNA Daily Report for Executives*, Apr 13, 1995]

Already enacted by Congress is the NAFTA Transitional Adjustment Assistance Program, created to provide training in new occupational skills, job search assistance, and trade adjustment allowances to employees whose job losses are demonstrated to be NAFTA-related. As this volume goes to press, some 55 petitions from 21 states have been generated under this program.

The Clinton administration sent a proposed Reemployment Act of 1994 to Capitol Hill, which, if enacted, would have brought the older Trade Adjustment Assistance Act [19 USC §§ 2101–2495; see Q 14:11] and the NAFTA-TAAP together under a single, comprehensive dislocated workers program. Ideally, such a synthesis of diverse dislocated-workers programs would be more effective than the current patchwork of programs.

All such legislation may amount to no more than stopgap measures, easing the impact of the Information Age with its restructuring of work and compensation in America. A distinct possibility, subscribed to by many conservative economists, is that—as was the case two centuries ago in England and to a lesser extent in the United States at the outset of the Industrial Revolution—displacements in the labor market will be corrected only when the new technologies of the Information Age create sufficient numbers of new jobs to replace those being lost to the re-engineering of U.S. enterprises and the flight of industrial jobs to Third World nations only now experiencing their own Industrial Revolutions.

During this difficult transition period, and perhaps also into the 21st century, the situation of the middle and lower classes might be substantially advanced by the extension of enterprise ownership by means of ESOPs (see Qs 8:168–8:171), stock options (see Qs 8:84, 8:85, and 14:20), and employee participation programs (see Qs 14:17–14:9). The fact that strikes seem to have lost their effectiveness even for millionaire baseball players suggests that the Clinton Administration may be right in arguing that some revamping of the National Labor Relations Act is required to make that law a meaningful part of the federal labor and employment law. [James O. Castagnera, "Millionaires' Strike Sounds Sour Note," *Philadelphia Daily News,* Aug 12, 1994, at 38] And affirmative action also may require substantial revision, if it is to have significance in the Information Age, as even such liberal proponents as Senator Daniel Patrick Moynihan of New York appear to recognize. [Robert A. Rankin, "New Environment Could Spell the End of Affirmative Action," *The Philadelphia Inquirer,* Feb 24, 1995, at A1; see, generally, Herrnstein and Murray, *The Bell Curve: Intelligence and Class Structure in American Life* (1994) at Appendix 7]

Chapter 15

Managing Labor and Employment Litigation

To say that the United States is a litigious society may be an understatement. The corporation that has not experienced some form of employment litigation is the exception rather than the rule. Despite all the advice that an employer may glean from attorneys, accountants, and other outside advisers—and despite all the best intentions of management—a lawsuit is likely. Labor unions face similar risks as suits by members charging breach of the duty of fair representation (see Qs 11:53, 11:54) are common. Even employees find themselves on the receiving end of litigation, as when they seek to switch employers and find a noncompete agreement, signed at the time they first took their previous employment, standing in the way of their performing in the new position (see Qs 6:35–6:41). In short, all the participants in employee relations—companies, employees, and unions—are subject to the anxiety, disruption, expense, and risks of litigation.

The inauguration of President Clinton also inaugurated a pro-employee and pro-union administration in Washington for the first time in more than a decade. Clinton's near-immediate signing of the Family and Medical Leave Act and the posture of Labor Secretary Reich on issues such as permanent replacement of strikers may encourage those inclined to initiate increased labor litigation.

This point was underlined by Clinton's controversial executive order of March 8, 1995. In the words of one commentator, "[A]fter months of hibernation following his party's November [1994] pasting [at the polls], Clinton has discovered a potent weapon, one often brandished by presidents to bypass an opposition-controlled Congress: executive fiat." [Stan Crock, "Clinton May Be Playing a Risky Game of Solitaire," *Business Week,* Mar 27, 1995, at 41] The order forbids private companies doing business with Uncle Sam from permanently replacing their striking employees on pain of being debarred from further federal contracts. With the GOP-controlled Congress having failed to overturn the order, we may reasonably anticipate that its invocation by Secretary of Labor Robert Reich's Labor Department will precipitate federal court challenges in 1996.

Litigation by Employees against Employers

Q 15:1   What are the various grounds upon which an applicant, employee, or former employee might sue a potential, current, or former employer?

The grounds upon which an applicant or employee (whether current or former) might sue an employer (that is, an individual, partnership, corporation, or joint venture that employs, or seeks to employ, individuals) can be divided into statutory and common-law causes of action. Nearly all of the federal statutes discussed in chapter 1 provide individual employees and job applicants with a cause of action. A notable exception is the Occupational Safety and Health Act (OSHA), which provides individuals with administrative recourse by filing a charge with OSHA (see Q 7:29), but provides no private cause of action. The National Labor Relations Act is something of a hybrid; unfair labor practice charges are initiated with the National Labor Relations Board, and if the board refuses to issue a complaint based on a charge and such refusal is affirmed by the NLRB's general counsel, a charging party has no recourse to any court (see Q 11:95). But an employee can sue a company for breach of a collective bargaining agreement or a union for breach of its duty of fair representation. [29 USC § 301] However, most federal labor and employment statutes (e.g., the Fair Labor Standards Act, Title VII, the Age Discrimination in Employment Act, the Americans with Disabilities Act, and the Immigration Reform and Control Act) create private rights of action and even permit successful plaintiff-employees to recover their attorney fees from defendant-employers. Numerous analogous state statutes in such areas of the law as job discrimination and wage payment do likewise.

Common-law causes of action have been recognized or created by the judiciary in most of the 50 states and the District of Columbia in the areas of wrongful discharge and such related tort claims as defamation, infliction of emotional distress, and breach of express or implied employment contracts (see Qs 2:11–2:23, 13:28–13:49).

With regard to job safety, not only does OSHA not provide a private right of action, but as a general proposition, state workers' compensation laws restrict employee claims to the benefits prescribed in those laws (see Qs 8:172 et seq.). However, lawsuits may arise with regard to smoking in the workplace (see Qs 7:84–7:95), intentional (as opposed to accidental) injuries inflicted by employers upon employees, and invasions of an employee's privacy in the course of maintaining a safe workplace, notably with respect to drug abuse and testing issues. [See Qs 7:151, 13:26; Borse v Piece Goods Shop Inc, 963 F 2d 611 (3d Cir 1991), discussed in detail at Q 2:14]

Additionally, in states such as Texas, where participation in the workers' compensation system is optional rather than mandatory, employers opting out of the program have been sued successfully for failure to maintain safe workplaces. "Last year, a Texas jury returned a record $30 million verdict against the owner-operator of a convenience store where an employee was raped twice in two weeks after her boss refused her request for a transfer or for increased security." [Claudia H. Deutsch, "Returning to the Scene of the Crime, to Sue the Owner," *The New York Times,* June 3, 1994, at B8]

Q 15:2　Can an applicant, employee, or former employee seeking to sue an employer proceed directly into a court of law?

Many of the federal and state statutes that create private rights of action as discussed in chapter 1 and summarized in Q 15:1 require the potential plaintiff-employee to initiate an administrative charge against the employer before proceeding into an appropriate state or federal court. In fact, when the statute requires such a threshold administrative proceeding, the courts have typically held that failure to exhaust administrative remedies divests the courts of jurisdiction, and therefore the plaintiffs' complaints have usually been dismissed (see Qs 4:8–4:20). Statutes that require filing of a complaint or charge with an administrative agency before proceeding into court include Title VII, the Age Discrimination in Employment Act, the Americans with Disabilities Act, and most analogous state job discrimination statutes. Wage payment and collection laws or whistle-blower statutes in some states may likewise require initial recourse to an administrative agency before the employee seeks recourse from a court. Consequently, employers faced with employee lawsuits should determine, as an initial consideration, whether some or all of the suit is subject to dismissal on the basis of failure to exhaust an administrative procedure. Employers and legal counsel also should be sensitive to the possibility that a cause of action packaged by opposing counsel as, for example, a wrongful discharge action, may in fact be a discrimination claim that should have been initiated in the appropriate state or federal administrative agency.

Thus, for example, in 1995 the federal court in Cleveland ruled that the federal Family and Medical Leave Act (see chapter 8) could not be used as the public policy source in support of a state-law wrongful discharge action, since the FMLA provided its own statutory right of action. [Gall v Quaker City Castings Inc, 874 F Supp 161 (ND Ohio 1995)] And the U.S. District Court for Eastern Pennsylvania dismissed a "shotgun blast" style complaint filed by a postal worker, alleging a variety of federal and state claims, where the U.S. Postal Service attorneys in a Federal Rule 12 motion demonstrated repeated failures by the plaintiff to exhaust administrative remedies and initiate action within the time constraints of the agency's "right to sue" requirements. [Abdullah-Johnson v Runyon, 1995 US Dist LEXIS 3233 (ED Pa 1995)] These two new decisions illustrate the opportunities often afforded determined employers with competent employment attorneys to narrow or even defeat employment-based lawsuits, where counsel is better versed than the opposition in the procedures of labor and employment litigation.

Q 15:3   Can an employer avoid employee litigation through alternative dispute resolution?

Yes. The most common methods of alternative dispute resolution (ADR) are:

Arbitration. This term typically refers to a proceeding in which one or more arbitrators, designated and accepted by the parties, renders a decision following an arbitration hearing. This decision is binding on the parties and is enforceable by the prevailing party in a court of law. Grievance arbitration is most commonly associated in this country with labor unions and collective bargaining agreements, which typically contain grievance arbitration clauses (see Q 11:67).

Brokerage firms operating under the rules of the New York Stock Exchange and other major exchanges have included arbitration clauses in their employment contracts for many years. Recently, the U.S. Supreme Court ruled that such a clause bound an employee to arbitrate a job termination, even if the employee contended that the firing violated federal job discrimination laws. [Gilmer v Interstate/Johnson Lane Corp, 111 S Ct 1647 (1991); Q 2:49] The *Gilmer* case has led to speculation that a clause calling for binding arbitration in almost any employment contract is enforceable, even in the adjudication of a discrimination claim, and that such a clause in an employee handbook, if the handbook constitutes a binding part of the employment relationship, might be upheld by a federal or state court (see Qs 2:31–2:37). And, in following *Gilmer,* numerous federal courts have held exactly that. [Piskorski and Ross, "Private Arbitration as the Exclusive Means of Resolving Employment-Related Disputes," 19 *Employee Relations Law Journal* 2 (Autumn 1993) at 205; see, e.g., McNulty v Prudential-Bache Securities Inc, 871 F Supp 567 (ED NY 1994) (demotion and reduction in pay were subject to mandatory arbitration); O'Donnell v First Investors Corp, 872 F Supp 1274 (SD NY 1995) (ambiguity concerning arbitration provision's applicability to employment disputes resolved in favor of arbitration); Bungard v Rural Mutual Insurance Co, 1995 Wisc App LEXIS 479 (Wis Ct App 1995) (age discrimination claims subject to binding arbitration); but see, Prudential Insurance Co v Lai, 42 F 3d 1299 (9th Cir 1994) (sexual harassment claims not subject to arbitration clause in employment manual that was not shown to employees prior to signing their contracts); Turner v IDS Financial Services Inc, 1994 US App LEXIS 29461 (7th Cir 1994) (arbitration clause not broad enough to cover plaintiff's Title VII claim against employer)]

Mediation. While arbitration typically is binding on the participating parties and can be overturned only in a court by showing extreme bias or misbehavior on the arbitrator's part, mediation usually is a nonbinding procedure in which a skilled ADR professional attempts to bring the parties to a mutually agreeable resolution. Based on the *Gilmer* doctrine that arbitration clauses in employment contracts will be enforced by the courts, a clause in a contract calling for mediation probably will be upheld by federal and state judges. [See AMF Inc v Brunswick Corp, 621 F Supp 456 (EDNY 1985) (parties must fulfill their contractual promise to engage in good faith, nonbinding ADR efforts before bringing their case into court); James O. Castagnera, "Alternative Dispute Resolution: Construction Industry," 52 *Am Jur Trials* §§ 13–16 (1994); Robert M. Rodman, "ADR Contract Clauses," in Wilkinson (ed.), Donovan Leisure Newton & Irvine *ADR Practice Book* 268 (1990)] Often, mediation under the tutelage of a skilled and sensitive mediator results in a final resolution of the dispute, which is made binding by a subsequent mediation-settlement agreement.

Other grievance resolution procedures. A variety of other dispute resolution mechanisms also are available. These come under the general heading of "workplace due process" and include an "open door policy," as well as far more complex ADR techniques (see Qs 3:112–3:122). Again, under *Gilmer*, professionals have speculated about whether courts will go so far as to enforce against an employee an ADR outcome under such a due process procedure, which the company contends is final and binding. Regardless of how the common- (court-made) law develops on this issue, the fact remains that most such ADR procedures as a practical matter do result in resolution of employee claims and therefore generally save employers substantial legal fees and litigation risks.

Q 15:4 Can an employee and an employer agree that a mediation or other workplace due process proceeding will be final and binding?

Even in the absence of a preexisting employment contract that contractually binds the employee and employer to binding arbitration, the parties can always enter into an agreement, even subsequent to the employee's discharge, that whatever ADR method selected will be final and in lieu of any subsequent potential lawsuit. In fact, sometimes the parties to an employment litigation agree, even after the employee has filed a lawsuit, to short-circuit the expensive and time-consuming court proceedings in favor of an arbitration, mediation, or other ADR proceeding. When such a procedure results either in a binding decision by an arbitrator or in a settlement agreement between the parties, the court having jurisdiction of the underlying lawsuit will, on request of the parties, enter the decision or agreement as the judgment in the case. Courts are prepared to enforce such agreements and may even subject the recalcitrant party to penalties, such as paying the other party's attorney fees when a court order is needed to compel participation in the ADR proceeding. [See, e.g., O'Donnell v First Investors Corp, 872 F Supp 1274, 1995 US Dist LEXIS 387 (SD NY 1995) (plaintiff ordered to submit to arbitration, but no Rule 11 sanctions imposed, since contract clause was ambiguous and his resistance to ADR was made in good faith)]

Q 15:5 When faced with employment litigation, how should an employer select legal counsel?

If the corporation already enjoys a working relationship with an attorney, that lawyer is the first person outside the company who should be consulted concerning representation in the employment lawsuit. Corporate counsel may not be the appropriate lawyer to handle the representation, but usually should be asked to recommend an attorney specializing in such work. The reasons for this recommendation are: (1) the company's regular corporate counsel may not be an experienced litigator or appear regularly in court, and (2) even if a good litigator, he or she may not be sufficiently conversant with the vagaries of labor and employment law to defend the corporation efficiently and effectively.

Upon selecting counsel, the company will want to discuss the following issues before retaining a particular attorney:

- Number of similar cases handled by the attorney, and more important, the number of such cases tried to verdict and the results

- Whether the attorney will handle the case personally or assign part or all of it to a subordinate, and if so, the difference in billing rates between them

- The attorney's hourly rate or other method of billing for services

- The attorney's estimate of the cost of the litigation, preferably broken down as follows:

    — Preliminary work: investigation of the facts, preliminary legal research, answering the complaint, preliminary motions, if any

    — Discovery stage: number and cost of oral depositions, interrogatories, requests for documents, and responding to the other side's requests for the same

    — Pretrial motions: motion for summary judgment motions in limine; pretrial memorandum or order

    — Trial and post-trial motions

    — Whether settlement overtures might be advisable and if so, the attorney's view as to what an appropriate settlement agreement might look like

One additional issue should be considered as a result of revisions to Federal Rule of Civil Procedure 26, which took effect at the end of 1994. Numerous federal courts have adopted the mandatory disclosure requirements in the new rule. These courts control about 37 percent of the federal civil litigation docket. This arrangement may make it difficult for corporations to continue using the same legal counsel in each case. The risk the company runs is that the experienced attorney or firm will have developed broad knowledge of the company's employment practices, placing a burden on such counsel to make early, mandatory disclosures that the company itself might not be called on to make until much later in the discovery phase, if ever. For example, suppose a sexual harassment claim is brought by an employee at one location of a multi-plant manufacturing company. If the plant's manager or human resources director is subpoenaed for a deposition or to produce relevant personnel records, he or she might not be aware of other such cases that occurred at another of the company's facilities. But the outside labor counsel hired to defend this claim may be well aware of prior claims. In light of this possibility, corporations and their in-house counsel may want to consider spreading employment litigation across a spectrum of outside litgators and law firms. [James M. Sheehan, "Recent Changes in the FRCP and Their Impact Upon Litigation," *Federal Civil Litigation Practice* (Widener University School of Law 1995)]

Q 15:6 What factors should an employer consider in deciding whether a case should be settled with an employee-plaintiff?

Each case is unique and will have specific factors to be considered. A competent labor attorney will be able to assist the employer in identifying and evaluating the factors to be considered in evaluating every case for settlement. They include the following:

Merits of the case. Is this a case in which the employee is in the right? Is it fair to make the employee whole for a wrong by the company, whether intentional, negligent, or merely inadvertent?

Likelihood of success. Whether the employee is in the right, is the employee-plaintiff likely to succeed? Sometimes this is a difficult issue for management. The company may be convinced that the former employee's cause of action is meritless or even frivolous; indeed, management may believe the case is grounded in perjured testimony. But counsel may nonetheless advise an early settlement, especially if it can be achieved for nuisance value. Nuisance value may be something less than the cost of defending the action to a resolution by the court, possibly at an early stage in the proceedings. If so, that decision would be one made as a pure dollars-and-sense business judgment. In some cases, it may be wise to swallow hard and make the settlement overture to the plaintiff's attorney.

Company policies and managerial morale. The company must consider—even if on a dollars-and-sense basis it makes sense to settle a meritless lawsuit cheaply—long-term issues that may transcend the immediate bottom-line considerations for settling the case:

- Is an important company policy at stake in the case that could be undermined by a settlement?

- Will a settlement, even for a small amount of money, send a message to workers that the corporation is an easy mark, encouraging others to bring similar suits?

- Will a settlement send a message to management that the company's top executives are not prepared to expend legal fees and mount a defense to back up front-line supervisors' personnel decisions? In other words, will management morale suffer from a settlement?

Q 15:7 What are the typical phases and procedures in a lawsuit brought by an employee or former employee against a corporation?

The phases and procedures in a lawsuit brought by an employee are:

Pre-litigation discussions. Rarely does an employee or former employee commence an action without that potential plaintiff's attorney first contacting the company's management or in-house counsel, usually by letter, stating the employee's claims, threatening suit, and demanding damages. This pre-litigation phase may be brief or may extend over several months of discussion, depending on the company's response, the proximity of the running of any statute of limitations relating to any threatened action, and a host of other factors including the employee's temperament.

Complaint. If the claim is not resolved during the pre-litigation phase (which may accompany, precede, or follow an administrative charge, such as in a discrimination case, in which the Equal Employment Opportunity Commission or a state agency is involved), the plaintiff-employee's attorney may file a complaint with a federal or state court with jurisdiction over the alleged cause of action. The complaint must be filed before the statute of limitations on the employee's cause(s) of action expires. Although statutes of limitation vary from state to state, some typical ones include:

- Breach of contract: four years
- Wrongful discharge: two years

- Defamation or fraud: one year

In other words, if the ex-employee doesn't sue within the statutory time after termination, the cause of action is lost to that plaintiff.

The level of detail of the facts pled in the complaint will vary among jurisdictions. Under the Federal Rules of Civil Procedure, which have been adopted in large part by many state court systems, "A pleading which sets forth a claim for relief . . . shall contain (1) a short and plain statement of the grounds on which the court's jurisdiction depends . . . , (2) a short and plain statement of the claim showing that the pleader is entitled to relief, and (3) a demand for judgment for the relief the pleader seeks." [FRCP 8(a)] This is called "notice pleading," since the plaintiff needs to plead only enough facts to put the defendant on notice of the nature of the action and permit that defendant to admit or to deny. By contrast, some states still hold to so-called fact pleading, which requires much more detailed statements of the underlying facts supporting the alleged cause of action.

Answer. Once the complaint has been served properly, the company and any individually named managerial defendants must file an answer within the time allowed by the court's procedural rules. In lieu of an answer, the company's attorney may file a motion, such as to dismiss the action if on its face the complaint does not state a cause that the court recognizes as a valid basis to recover damages. For example, in a state that does not recognize a cause of action for wrongful discharge based on breach of an implied covenant of good faith and fair dealing (see Qs 2:21–2:25) or where the complaint makes clear on its face that the appropriate statute of limitations has expired, a motion to dismiss would be an appropriate response to the complaint. The court in reaction to such a motion may dismiss the complaint outright or permit the plaintiff to redraft the complaint to correct inadequacies raised by defense counsel.

As with the complaint, the answer will have to be as detailed or sketchy as the rules of civil procedure in the particular jurisdiction demand. The defendants also are permitted in the answer to:

- Make a counterclaim against the plaintiff, for instance if a former salesperson owes unearned draw against commissions
- Join other parties as additional defendants, such as if two companies are in a joint employer relationship, a labor union

shares responsibility for the alleged wrong raised in the complaint, or if an insurer ought to be defending the company

- Make a cross-claim against one of the other defendants, as if the company decides to argue that, if it is liable to the plaintiff-employee, then a manager individually named ought to make the company whole for any damages it has to pay

Discovery. In general, discovery is the process through which the two sides in a lawsuit learn more about one another's case and the evidence that will be used to prove the case. As with almost all aspects of litigation, the rules of discovery vary somewhat among states. However, the Federal Rules of Civil Procedure have become something of a standard across the nation, and almost all states have adopted or adapted them. The major tools attorneys use in conducting discovery are:

Interrogatories. These are written questions demanded of the other party, which that party must answer under pain of perjury within a specific time.

Requests for production of documents and things. In conjunction with, or separate from, a party's interrogatories, that party's attorney can require opponents to produce documents that relate to the lawsuit. Some examples in employment litigation typically include the personnel file of the plaintiff, and perhaps those of other employees of the defendant-corporation; payroll records; the company's employee handbook, other personnel policies, and employee benefits plans; disciplinary records; medical records; correspondence; and date books, telephone logs, and computer records (whether in hard copy, on diskette, or otherwise). The inspection of premises also may be demanded. Other items that may be examined include tools, vehicles, computers, drugs, or lockers.

Admissions. These are statements that one side can require the other side to admit or deny under pain of perjury or other possible court sanctions for dishonesty in answering. If a party admits a particular statement, the admission can be used as evidence by the other side at the trial of the case.

Depositions. Typically, when a party to the lawsuit or a third-party witness is summoned to an oral deposition, that individual is placed under oath by a court reporter who then makes a transcript of the proceeding in which the opposing counsel questions that witness. Counsel for the party being questioned as well as anyone who plans to call the witness at trial also is accorded an opportunity to ask questions after opposing counsel has finished with the witness. Usually a deposition is taken only for purposes of discovering what the party or witness contends are the facts of the case. However, a discovery deposition also can be used at trial to impugn the integrity of a party or other witness who tells a different version of the facts on the witness stand. Occasionally, when a third-party witness will be out of the country, is old or ill, or otherwise may be unavailable for trial, the deposition will be taken in lieu of the testimony that the witness would normally be expected to give in court. If, indeed, the witness becomes unavailable, the deposition will be read to the jury by the attorney whose witness the deponent was.

Automatic Disclosure/Mandatory Discovery. Available for adoption as of December 31, 1993, Federal Rule of Civil Procedure 26 was amended to include a lengthy prefatory provision requiring early identification of discoverable materials and potential witnesses, plus a meeting among counsel to resolve potential discovery problems and to set a discovery schedule. The rule permits federal judicial districts to opt out of the new provisions or to adopt them in modified form. Its adoption stirred controversy with a Supreme Court justice and a former attorney general leading the opposition to it. [See Griffin B. Bell, "Automatic Disclosure in Discovery—The Rush to Reform," 27 *Ga L Rev* 1 (1992); 61 USLW at 4391 (Scalia, J, dissenting)] The status of new FRCP 26 was reportedly as follows:

> According to monitoring by Alfred W. Cortese, Jr. and Kathleen L. Blaner, both of [the] Washington, D.C., office of Philadelphia's Pepper, Hamilton & Sheetz, as of Oct. 1, 1994, only 19 out of 94 federal districts, representing just 19 percent of the federal courts' 1993 civil caseload, had fully implemented Rule 26(a)(1). Another 18 districts, representing 13 percent of the caseload, adopted Rule 26(a)(1) but have exempted such cases as bankruptcy, appeals, prisoner petitions, administrative agency appeals, government collections and Social Security from its purview. . . . Twenty-nine districts, representing 30 percent of the caseload, have no mandatory disclosure, and 28 districts, representing 37 percent of the court[s'] civil docket, have adopted some form of mandatory [early] disclosure, either by local rule or as part of their . . . Rule 26(a)(1) formula.

[James M. Sheehan, "Recent Changes in the FRCP and Their Impact Upon Litigation," in *Federal Civil Litigation Practice* (Widener University School of Law 1995)]

Thus, though few of the federal judicial districts have adopted new Rule 26(a) entirely, two-thirds have moved to some form of early, mandatory disclosure in supplementation of the traditional, long-familiar discovery practices. [Id]

Motion practice. Among the motions that may be filed by the parties during the course of the litigation are:

Motion for judgment on the pleadings. When the complaint, answer, any counterclaims, and replies to those counterclaims have been filed, the pleadings are considered closed. If one of the parties believes that the other party's pleadings are inadequate to sustain, or conversely to deny, the cause of action at issue in the suit, that party may ask the court to grant judgment against the pleader on the basis of those early court filings. The court will grant the motion only if, on viewing all the pleaded facts in the light most favorable to the party against whom the motion is filed, clearly, there seems to be no way that party could win the case. More often, even when that party's pleadings are in fact inadequate, the court will give the party 30 days to amend the pleadings and correct the errors or inadequacies.

However, this is not always so. By contrast, in a case decided by the federal court in Philadelphia in 1995, the plaintiff was a former employee of the U.S. Postal Service. He sued Postmaster General Marvin T. Runyon, Jr., alleging a variety of federal civil rights violations plus a state claim of intentional infliction of emotional distress. According to the court, "Plaintiff's claims in this action allegedly arose from a series of events that occurred during the plaintiff's employment by the USPS Frankford Station in Philadelphia, Pennsylvania. According to the plaintiff, a USPS employee attacked him on April 20, 1990, and the USPS and its representatives have harassed and discriminated against him and his family ever since the incident. Specifically, plaintiff contends the USPS and its representatives refused to place him in a safe working environment after the incident; forced him to resign; refused to submit his personnel file to another branch of the USPS; forwarded 'unjust' evaluations to that branch so that plaintiff would not receive a transfer; and terminated his health and other benefits . . . [and] tried to intimidate other postal employees into reducing his evaluations and reduced the severity of disciplinary action . . . for the employee who assaulted plaintiff. . . ." [Abdullah-Johnson v Runyon, 1995 US Dist LEXIS 3233 (ED Pa 1995)]

Notwithstanding FRCP 12's admonishment to regard all of a plaintiff's well-pleaded facts as true when challenged by a defendant's motion to dismiss, the court sifted carefully through all of Abdullah-Johnson's pro se complaint and ultimately rejected every claim, dismissing the lawsuit in its entirety. First, the federal judge agreed with the USPS that plaintiff's Title VII claims were barred because he had failed to file suit within 90 days of either of the "right to sue" letters from the Equal Employment Opportunity Commission. The court next rejected the plaintiff's contention that an earlier, timely filed federal suit, dismissed without prejudice by the U.S. District Court for the Middle District of Florida, had somehow halted the running of the 90-day limitation period in the letters. As for an early incident also alluded to, the court agreed that the plaintiff had entirely failed to avail himself of the administrative remedies required by law to be exhausted before bringing the matter to the attention of a federal court. His Americans with Disabilities Act claim was dismissed along with the rest of his suit because the USPS is a federal agency not covered under the ADA. The postmaster general and other individually named defendants were accorded immunity from suit, because the court found that at all times they were acting in official capacities. The state claim was then dismissed under the court's discretionary authority when it has held that all the related federal causes of action are without merit on their face. [Id] This case illustrates how a determined employer can attack a employee action and sometimes succeed early in the process.

Motion to compel discovery/motion for a protective order. Sometimes the parties don't agree on what documents should be provided to the other side or which questions should be answered in interrogatories or oral depositions. At other times, one of the parties may simply be slow in responding to a request for documents or a set of interrogatories. In such circumstances, the court usually requires the parties to work out their discovery disputes amicably without bothering the judge. However, if an amicable resolution is impossible, the party seeking the discovery can move the court to order the recalcitrant party to cooperate with the discovery requests. On the other hand, the party refusing to respond to the discovery request, perhaps believing it to be unduly burdensome or that it violates the attorney-client privilege, may file a motion asking the judge in the case (or the motion court judge in some jurisdictions) to forbid the other side from demanding the documents or answers requested; this is termed a protective order.

Motion for summary judgment. When the discovery process is complete, or nearly complete, one of the parties may file a motion contending that based on the facts that both sides admit to be true, a judgment should be entered in the moving party's favor without a trial. Although summary judgment motions are more often granted than motions for judgment on the pleadings, the burden on the moving party is great: if there are any facts remaining in dispute on which a jury might find in favor of the other party, the moving party's summary judgment motion will be denied.

Here, too, recent case law ably illustrates an employer's ability to use motion practice to dispose of a meritless case prior to a trial. In *Seidle v. Provident Mutual Life Insurance Co.* [871 F Supp 238 (ED Pa 1994)], the court granted the defendant's motion for summary judgment after the plaintiff had invoked the federal Family and Medical Leave Act (see chapter 8) to challenge her termination based on excessive absenteeism. The plaintiff, a single mother, argued that she stayed home to care for a child with an ear infection and thus her employment could not be terminated under the terms of the FMLA. The court, carefully examining the legislative history of the "serious health conditions" language of the act, noted that "heart attacks, . . . heart bypass, . . . most cancers, back conditions requiring extensive therapy or surgical procedures, strokes, severe respiratory conditions, spinal injuries, appendicitis, pneumonia, emphysema, severe arthritis, [and] severe nervous disorders . . ." were among the conditions Congress had considered when writing the law. The court further found that Congress had specifically chosen not to include "minor illnesses which last only a few days." Given this legislative record, the court ruled that as a matter of law the child's ear infection did not rise to the level of a serious health condition permitting the plaintiff to invoke the protections of the FMLA. Therefore the defendant-employer's motion for summary judgment was granted, ending the action. [Id]

Motion in limine. Before a case comes to trial, one or both litigants may request that the court forbid opposing counsel from presenting certain evidence, or evidence on certain issues, to the jury, for example, because the evidence is irrelevant or prejudicial.

A good example of when a motion in limine might work well for an employer-defendant on the eve of trial is *Preston v. Phelps Dodge Copper Products Co.* [35 Conn App 850, 647 A 2d 364 (1994)] In this wrongful-discharge case, the defendant-corporation learned during discovery that the plaintiff had engaged in wrongdoing that, if known to the employer prior to plaintiff's termination, would have provided independent grounds for firing. Specifically, the plaintiff had rubbed poison ivy on his supervisor's toilet seat. The defendant asked the court to dismiss the action in its entirety, based on this wrongdoing, revealed belatedly. The court refused to do so, but stated that the after-acquired evidence involving the poison ivy would be used at trial to limit the amount of damages that the jury would be allowed to award the plaintiff, should the jurors decide to find in his favor. [Id]

Trial. Although in some jurisdictions as much as 90 percent of all litigation ends in settlement before trial, some cases must be resolved in a courtroom. Trial may take place before a jury or a judge alone; the latter is called a bench trial. Since the passage of the Civil Rights Act of 1991 (see Q 1:8), litigants in Title VII cases are no longer limited to bench trials, but may demand trial by jury. The same right applies to age and disability discrimination suits under federal and many state laws. Wrongful discharge and breach of employment contract actions also carry the right to jury trial in most instances. However, if neither party demands a jury, the right is not enforced automatically, but rather may be deemed to have been waived. Whether a bench or jury trial, the major components of the proceeding are:

- Opening statements by the parties' legal counsel
- Presentation of the plaintiff's case
- Possible motion by defense counsel for a directed verdict at the close of the plaintiff's case
- Presentation of defendant's case
- Counsel's closing arguments

- If a jury trial, jury instructions by the judge followed by the jury's deliberations

- If a bench trial, the judge may enter a verbal "bench decision" after hearing both sides' arguments, or may deliberate, perhaps even requiring post-trial briefing by both sides, before rendering a written decision and verdict

Q 15:8   Has a directed verdict ever been successfully obtained by an employer?

In 1995 a U.S. District Judge in Florida's Middle District provided a fine example of how a directed verdict could be used. The judge used this technique to end a bizarre case involving the Americans With Disabilities Act that had survived defendant's summary judgment motion to the collective outrage of the employment law defense bar. In *Hindman v. GTE Data Services* [1994 US Dist LEXIS 9522, 8 Fla Law W Fed D259 (MD Fla 1994)], the plaintiff is described as a successful team leader who had performed his job well until he began exhibiting criminal tendencies, such as stealing co-workers' money, which resulted in his being taken away from the workplace in handcuffs by the local police. After the plaintiff's arrest, a colleague examined the plaintiff's briefcase and found a loaded pistol. GTE fired the plaintiff for bringing a loaded weapon to work. The plaintiff brought his ADA action, contending that like any cancer or heart attack victim, he should have been accommodated until he recovered from his mental imbalance, which he blamed on the anti-depressant drug Prozac. While the judge who handled GTE's summary judgment motion agreed that the case deserved to go to trial, a second federal judge, who handled the trial, granted GTE's motion for a directed verdict after all evidence was presented. [Steve Huettel, "Fired GTE Supervisor Loses Federal Lawsuit," *The Tampa Tribune*, Jan 24, 1995, at 6] Of course, a directed verdict—while it may be a sweet win for both client and lawyer—is less desirable than disposing of a case via a summary judgment motion. Summary judgment is awarded by the judge when the facts in evidence *prior to trial* demonstrate that no reasonable group of jurors could come out in favor of the non-moving party. A directed verdict can only come after the parties have endured the time, anxiety, and expense of an actual jury trial.

Q 15:9 What happens after a judge or jury has rendered a verdict?

A disappointed party may file one of several motions following a verdict. If the trial had been before a judge sitting without a jury, a party may file a motion for reconsideration or for a new trial. If a jury verdict, the loser may ask the judge to enter a contrary judgment notwithstanding the jury's verdict or may request a new trial.

Whether post-trial motions are filed, the parties have the right to file an appeal to the next highest court in the state or federal court system. Ordinarily an appeal must be based on a serious procedural error made by the trial judge, or some misinterpretation of the law that the judge applied in deciding the case or in sending it to the jury for determination.

The federal and most state court systems include an intermediate and a supreme court of appeals. While in most civil cases a dissatisfied party (note that both parties may be dissatisfied with a portion of the judgment ultimately entered by the court and so there may be cross appeals) has the right to appeal to the intermediate court such as the appropriate U.S. Court of Appeals, most supreme courts are not required to take all cases appealed beyond the intermediate level. For instance, the U.S. Supreme Court grants "certiorari" (i.e., certification of the case from the appellate court to it for further consideration) to only a tiny percentage of the cases in which one or both parties request the court's consideration.

Most court decisions cited in this book are appellate court rulings. When lawyers speak of the common law, they are referring to the vast body of collected decisions in the thousands of case reporters that often fill a floor or more of a law library. Cases decided by the supreme and mid-level appeals court of a state or a federal circuit are mandatory precedents in that jurisdiction, and the trial judges in these jurisdictions are supposed to follow the rules laid down in these cases. Other published decisions may be viewed by these judges as persuasive, even though the rule of *stare decisis* ("follow the decision") does not require them to take such ruling into account in rendering their own decisions. With regard to procedural matters, such as those discussed above, the opinions of trial judges, too, are sometimes published in case reporters. Most trial courts have a local rule that says that the decisions of its own judges will be treated by all the judges of that venue as binding precedents in future cases.

Q 15:10   How much does it cost a company to litigate a lawsuit?

The cost of litigating a case varies greatly from one lawsuit to another and is difficult to predict. Obviously, as the foregoing materials suggest, a lawsuit may settle early or drag on through trial and even appeal. A lawyer may require many depositions and lots of other discovery to prepare for trial, or there may be only a few witnesses and documents necessary to prepare the case properly.

Nonetheless, experienced labor lawyers will have some idea, after initial consultation, or at least following further investigation, of how much work will be required to bring a particular employment case to conclusion and what the approximate cost will be in legal fees and other expenses. One attorney who has left the private practice of law to specialize in counseling corporations on buying legal services has suggested the following steps in ascertaining legal fees, whether for litigation matters or otherwise:

- Obtain a layperson's understanding of the main legal issues involved in the case, such as by reviewing materials readily available from trade associations, government agencies, and other human resource professionals in the same industry, as well as publications written for nonlawyers

- Gather the relevant documents together and understand them thoroughly before taking them to the attorney to be consulted

- Define the company's economic and noneconomic goals in the case

- Try to determine how much the company is willing, or can afford, to spend in defending or in settling the suit

- Determine if there is a relevant timetable for the company to resolve the dispute, because of a pending merger, for example, or other transaction in which pending litigation could be debilitating

- Ask about the likely sequence of activities and events and explore areas in which corporate personnel might participate to keep legal fees and expenses down, by searching for additional relevant documents or investigating facts, for example

- Discuss the specifics of the law firm's billing practices: when and how often the matter is billed and how the work of the various personnel (associate attorneys, paralegals, private investigators) will be monitored

- Tell the law firm that the company will not pay for time spent educating inexperienced associate attorneys who may be involved

- Commit preparatory work and discussions with legal counsel to writing

[Harwi, "Dealing Effectively with a Lawyer," *Legal Triage News,* January 1993, at 2]

Only recently have some large-volume users of legal services begun treating the legal profession like any other group of vendors. There is a growing trend away from hourly billing toward billing by case or other project, much as other independent contractors are required to bid and perform at their own risk of misapprehending the difficulties involved. Furthermore, organizations such as Structured Benefits, which is affiliated with Aetna Insurance Co., are discovering that data over a wide range of litigations can be collected and used to model the likely costs and liability exposures in future, similar lawsuits. The bottom line is that soon we may see a change in legal fees and other litigation costs at least by major users of such services, such as insurers. The result for these major buyers of legal services will be reduced unit costs. Also helping to push prices down is the trend toward expanded use of alternative dispute resolution techniques. [See Q 15:3; James O. Castagnera, "Alternative Dispute Resolution: Construction Industry," 52 *Am Jur Trials* 209 (Lawyers Cooperative Publishing 1994)]

Q 15:11   Are attorneys willing to represent employee-plaintiffs on a contingent fee basis?

Personal injury lawyers, who normally make much of their living on a contingent fee basis, may be reluctant to take employment cases on a basis of no recovery, no fee. In the past, employees have sometimes found it hard to obtain competent counsel, when laws such as Title VII and the Age Discrimination in Employment Act permitted only back pay and reinstatement as remedies in a typical case. However, the 1991 Civil Rights Act permits juries to award compensatory and punitive damages (see Q 1:8).

Furthermore, to encourage employees to act as "private prosecutors" with regard to the violation of federal and state employment laws, many of these statutes either mandate or permit the award of reasonable attorney fees to prevailing plaintiffs. Where such statutes are involved in employment law litigation, contingency fee agreements normally will be written to allow such court-awarded fees to be factored into the overall fee arrangement.

Lawsuits by and against Labor Unions

Q 15:12   Can a labor union be sued by a union member?

Although union members must generally pursue their grievances against labor unions under the auspices and procedures of the particular union's constitution, if the union violates its duty to represent all its members fairly and in an unbiased manner, an unfairly treated member may turn to the federal courts for recourse. A variety of federal statutes give union members a right of action against their unions under appropriate circumstances. For example:

- 29 USC § 185 (commonly called Section 301 of the NLRA) allows suits against labor unions for, among other things, breach of a collective bargaining agreement or the duty of fair representation of its members (see Qs 11:64, 11:66)

- 29 USC § 623 (c) makes labor unions responsible for their acts of age discrimination with respect to their members, whether with respect to membership in the union or with respect to their employment by third parties

- 42 USC § 2000e-2(c) imposes Title VII restrictions (employment discrimination) upon labor unions

- 29 USC §§ 401–531, the Labor-Management Reporting and Disclosure Act, sometimes called the union member's bill of rights, encompasses the main body of members' rights against their unions and provides a private right of action for the enforcement of those rights

Q 15:13   Can a company sue a labor union?

Under the National Labor Relations Act (and specifically the later portion of the act passed in 1947, often referred to as the Taft-Hartley or Labor-Management Relations Act), an employer can sue a union for breach of a collective bargaining agreement.

An employer also can sue a union to stop illegal activities on an otherwise lawful picket line, such as blocking ingress and egress to the plant, damaging company property, and for money damages resulting from such illegal activities. A union also can be sued for trying to force a company to deal only with unionized subcontractors, if such a union demand violates federal antitrust laws. [Connell Construction Co v Plumbers Local 100, 421 US 616 (1973)]

Q 15:14   Can a union ever sue an employer?

Although the National Labor Relations Act and the grievance and arbitration procedures in collective bargaining agreements are the major forums in which union-management disputes must be resolved, there are some limited circumstances in which a union may sue an employer:

- As with employees and companies, unions can sue for breach of collective bargaining contracts under Section 301 of the NLRA

- Some collective bargaining agreements provide that the contracting unions can go into state or federal court to sue employers for failure to make timely payment into union-operated employee benefit funds

- Under some discrimination statutes, a union may be able to establish standing to sue on behalf of its members

Q 15:15 Can a party to a grievance and arbitration provision in a collective bargaining agreement take a grievance to court?

There are a variety of ways that a grievance, subject to the grievance and arbitration provision of a collective bargaining agreement, may end up in court:

- One of the parties to the labor contract may sue to compel the other to submit the grievance to arbitration if the other party refuses to do so

- The successful party to an arbitration that has resulted in an arbitrator making an award may sue to force a recalcitrant loser to abide by the award, by reinstating the successful grievant in a termination case with back pay, for example

- A disappointed party may sue to overturn an arbitration award in those rare cases in which the arbitrator was biased or rendered an award in clear violation of statutory law or clearly outside the terms of the arbitration provision

Most federal courts now hold that employees may agree in individual employment contracts to subject their claims to binding arbitration (see Q 15:3). Nevertheless, union members continue to be covered by an earlier U.S. Supreme Court decision, which says that a grievance or arbitration provision in a collective bargaining agreement cannot deprive an individual union member of the right to pursue a Title VII claim before the Equal Employment Opportunity Commission and the federal district court. [Alexander v Gardner-Denver Co, 415 US 36 (1974)]

Q 15:16 Can attorney fees be awarded to union members who successfully sue their unions?

In duty of fair representation cases (see Q 11:66, for example) courts can award reasonable attorney fees to members who successfully sue their unions. However, such awards are not mandatory. For example, in a case in which former employees of John Morrell & Co. packing plant won $4.7 million in damages against the United Food & Commercial Workers Union, the U.S. Court of Appeals for the Tenth Circuit reversed the trial judge's additional award of $2.2 million in attorney fees. ["Court Finds UFCW Breached Duty, But Vacates Fee Award," 1993 *BNA Daily Labor Report* 101 (May 27, 1993) at 1]

The case illustrates that the question of whether a reasonable attorney fee is justified—and, if so, the amount of such fee—can be a major part of the litigation of an employment law case. Indeed, an enormous amount of litigation has resulted at the trial and appellate court levels concerning this issue. [See, e.g., Summit Valley Industries v Local 112, Carpenters, 456 US 717 (1982) (attorney fees incurred by employer/charging party during NLRB proceedings were not a proper element of damages under the NLRA in a subsequent civil action for damages due to the union's unfair labor practices pursuant to 29 USC §§ 185, 187); Christiansburg Garment Co v EEOC, 434 US 412 (1978) (trial court can award fees to corporate defendant under Title VII, 42 USC § 2000e-5[k] where the court finds the plaintiff's action to have been frivolous, unreasonable, or without foundation, even if the action was not brought in bad faith)]

Attorney fee provisions in federal labor and employment statutes vary from those that provide that the courts "may" award reasonable fees to prevailing parties [see, e.g., Title VII, 42 USC § 2000e-5(k)] to those that mandate fees to a prevailing employee-plaintiff. [See, e.g., 29 USC § 216(b), which applies to successfully prosecuted private actions under the Fair Labor Standards and Age Discrimination in Employment acts] Under some of these statutes, in rare instances of frivolous lawsuits, courts have awarded fees to the prevailing employer-defendant. [See, e.g., Christiansburg Garment Co v EEOC, supra; see also Federal Rule of Civil Procedure 11 ("The signature of an attorney or party constitutes a certification that . . . to the best of the signer's knowledge, information, and belief . . . it is well grounded in fact and is warranted by existing law, and that it is not interposed for an improper purpose. . . . If a pleading, motion, or other paper is signed in violation of this rule, the court, upon motion or upon its own initiative, shall impose upon the person who signed it . . . an appropriate sanction. . . .")]

Typically, after judgment has been entered by the trial court, a prevailing party, who arguably is entitled to attorney fees under the relevant statute, will prepare and file a fee petition with the trial judge. The losing party will then have the opportunity to file a brief in opposition to the fee petition.

The prevailing party can even request, as part of the fee award, the additional fees incurred by that party's attorneys in preparing the fee petition itself. But, as with all other parts of the judgment, the trial judge's decision on fees is subject to appeal if the lower court makes a legal error in formulating the award.

Q 15:17   What is a class action suit?

The Federal Rules of Civil Procedure permit one or more plaintiffs to commence a lawsuit on behalf of all persons who allegedly have the same claim against one or more defendants, even though not every such person has been contacted and agreed to join in the action, if the litigants meet the following criteria:

- The proposed class is so numerous that actual joinder of all members in the action is impracticable

- There exist questions of law or fact common to all members of the proposed class

- The claims or defenses of the representative litigants are typical of the claims of all the class members

The U.S. Department of Labor frequently prosecutes class actions on behalf of large groups of employees and former employees of companies, which DOL contends failed to pay minimum wages or appropriate overtime premiums over a period of years. The EEOC has brought class actions against corporations that have discriminated against employees or applicants of a particular race or sex. Private litigants can sometimes do so as well. [See Qs 7:154–7:156, for example, concerning UAW v Johnson Controls Inc, 111 S Ct 2238 (1991)(successful challenge of company's fetal protection policy under Title VII); Q 4:54, relating to a successful class action with regard to sexual harassment involving a hostile workplace situation]

Two noteworthy class actions that garnered national news media attention in 1994 were directed at the major cigarette manufacturers. One, commenced in Louisiana by Melvin Belli and 25 other prominent attorneys, seeks $5 billion on behalf of all Americans allegedly addicted to cigarettes. The other is being brought in federal court in Manhattan on behalf of shareholders of Philip Morris for the company's alleged propping up of its stock price by keeping negative information about cigarettes secret (see Q 7:96).

New Developments in Litigation

Q 15:18   What are the latest techniques in court-mandated alternative dispute resolution?

As indicated (see Qs 15:3, 15:4), alternative dispute resolution (ADR) appears to be gaining in popularity among employers as an option to long and costly lawsuits. This trend has been given a boost by the U.S. Supreme Court's decision in *Gilmer v. Interstate/Johnson Lane Corp.* [111 S Ct 1647; Q 2:49] that plaintiffs complaining of job discrimination who have arbitration clauses in their employment contracts must arbitrate their discrimination claims.

Not only employers but even the courts themselves are striving to streamline the administration of justice by mandating ADR proceedings. These procedures, while usually mandatory (meaning the litigant who refuses to participate in good faith risks an adverse outcome in the lawsuit), usually result in judgment, awards, or recommendations that may be appealed as a matter of right; in other words, the loser in an ADR proceeding generally can demand a de novo trial before a judge or a jury. However, the parties may stipulate in advance that the ADR proceeding will be final and binding.

The main types of ADR procedures mandated by various state and federal courts include the following:

Court-annexed arbitration. The most common ADR technique used by federal and state courts today, arbitration usually is mandated in cases in which the plaintiff is claiming a relatively modest amount of money damages, such as $50,000 or less. The arbitration often will be scheduled at the time the complaint is filed and will occur nine months to a year after the filing. Arbitrators usually are practicing attorneys within the court's jurisdiction who are paid modest fees to sit in panels of three to decide cases assigned to them. Court administrators will try to create panels of one plaintiff-side lawyer, one defense attorney, and a neutral party, such as an attorney who represents plaintiffs and defendants regularly or who does not litigate cases at all (perhaps a business lawyer, law school professor, or professional arbitrator).

Under typical local rules, parties who fail to appear for court-annexed arbitration risk having default judgments entered against them. But a losing party almost always has a specified period after the rendering of the arbitrators' award (such as 30 days) in which to demand trial de novo before a jury.

Arbitration hearings include the presentation of witnesses and documentary evidence. However, no court reporter is present, unless one of the parties pays a reporting service to make a transcription. Arbitrations can last less than an hour in small cases, and the arbitrators confer and render awards immediately after the litigants leave the hearing room. Despite the parties' absolute right to demand a jury trial, the vast majority of court-annexed arbitrations result in the entry of final judgments or the voluntary settlement of cases after the parties learn how the arbitrators weighed the merits.

Mini-trial. Credit for invention of the mini-trial is given to U.S. District Judge Robert E. Keeton of the federal court in Massachusetts. The lawsuit that spawned the groundbreaking technique involved a Boston real estate firm and the Insurance Company of North America (INA). Faced with a trial that could take two months, Judge Keeton persuaded the parties to agree to a procedure that would place the case before him for binding decision expeditiously.

The court's order, which was accepted by both sides, contained the following procedures and conditions:

- Each side designated an officer to attend the proceeding armed with full authority to settle the case
- Each side was bound to disclose every claim and defense and all grounds for each such assertion
- Counsel for each side was given four and a half hours to present its case to Judge Keeton
- These major presentations were followed by rebuttals and, finally, summations
- Presentations were followed by negotiations, requiring each party to present settlement offers in sealed envelopes

The whole proceeding took about two and a half days and ended with a $5.9 million settlement on a claim carrying a top demand of $20 million. A jury trial would have required about two months.

Summary jury trial. The summary jury trial is the most modern of the court-annexed ADR techniques. Again, a federal judge is credited with pioneering the concept. In this instance, U.S. District Judge Thomas Lambros of the Northern District of Ohio, sitting in Cleveland, had come to the conclusion after many years on the federal bench that parties bound for trial frequently "have an unrealistic view of the law and facts surrounding their cases, either because they have been poorly advised by counsel or have refused to consider the facts from their opponent's standpoint." [Lambros, "The Summary Jury Trial—An Alternative Method of Resolving Disputes," 69 *Judicature* 286, 290 (Feb–Mar 1986)]

Summary jury trial may be termed a variation on the mini-trial described above. The proceeding is designed for an abbreviated presentation of each side's case to a mock jury especially impanelled for this purpose. Typically, the attorneys for the parties present their positions in one or two hours. The presentations are followed by rebuttals and then brief deliberation by jurors. The idea is that the mock jury will give both sides a realistic simulation of what a real jury would do with the case if a full-fledged trial ensued. This healthy dose of realism frequently moves the parties into realistic settlement positions.

Numerous federal courts have adopted local rules of civil procedure enabling their judges to use this technique. For example, Local Rule 513 of the U.S. District Court for Central Pennsylvania reads as follows:

> A judge may in his discretion set any civil case for summary jury trial, provided, however, he gives consideration to any reasons advanced by the parties as to why such a trial would not be in the best interests of justice.

In the 1990s many forces are pushing hard toward the greater use of these techniques in place of full-blown litigation. In employment law, the 1991 Civil Rights Act expressly encourages the use of ADR (see chapter 1), and the EEOC and U.S. Department of Labor have conducted pilot projects aimed at using ADR more frequently. While a criminal matter, the O.J. Simpson double murder case has convinced many thoughtful observers that the American litigation system has become hopelessly confused with mass media and the entertainment business. [See "A Star on Trial: O.J. Simpson and a National Obsession," *The Philadelphia Inquirer,* Jan 1, 1995, at G3] Observers of labor-management relations are calling for dispute resolutions that will benefit all sides to a labor dispute. [See Samuel Estreicher, "Win-Win Labor Law Reform," 10 *The Labor Lawyer* 4 (Fall 1994) at 667]

Q 15:19 What are the recent significant changes in the Federal Rules of Civil Procedure?

A substantial package of some 30 amendments to the Federal Rules of Civil Procedure (FRCP) was adopted on December 1, 1993. Although labor lawyers and other attorneys who practice in the federal courts will need to familiarize themselves with all these rule changes, human resources professionals need to keep several of the more significant changes in mind when working with their companies' labor counsel on investigating and preparing lawsuits and defenses.

Rule 11. Probably the most controversial changes were made to what was already the most controversial of the FRCP. "Barrels of ink have been spilled over [Rule 11], the rule that empowers federal judges to impose sanctions for frivolous litigation and misconduct. Each time Rule 11 is amended, most recently this past December and before that in 1983, the debate over sanctions captures the attention of the legal profession." [Thomas E. Baker, "The Inherent Power to Impose Sanctions: How a Federal Judge Is Like an 800-Pound Gorilla," *Legal Opinion Letter,* Mar 25, 1994]

Concerning this most recent revision of the rule, "[a]lthough the revision broadens the scope of the Rule 11 obligation, the new rule places greater restraints on the imposition of sanctions, which are now discretionary only, and expressly directs courts to consider nonmonetary sanctions for rule violations." [*New Jersey Lawyer,* Jan 24, 1994]

Briefly, Rule 11 has been changed as follows:

1. While federal judges can fine litigants and their lawyers for filing frivolous lawsuits, or motions within lawsuits, those fines no longer go to opposing parties to offset legal fees. Rather, Rule 11 fines are now paid to the court.

2. Where the evidence indicates that a party's attorney acted frivolously, without the informed consent of the client, only the attorney will suffer the monetary fine or other sanction, whereas under the earlier rule the party and the lawyer were usually sanctioned.

3. The "full heart, empty head" defense to a Rule 11 motion will no longer work. In other words, an attorney's subjective belief that a motion, legal position, or cause of action has merit will not suffice if objectively the position taken is frivolous and without merit.

4. However, a party and legal counsel accused by the other side of violating Rule 11 is accorded a 21-day "safe harbor" under the revised rule. That is, when the opposition files its Rule 11 motion, contending, for example, that a cause of action in a complaint is so novel or so contrary to existing legal precedent as to be obviously untenable, the party proposing the cause of action has three weeks in which to voluntarily withdraw that cause of action and thereby avoid sanctions.

5. A federal judge may *sua sponte* (of his or her own accord) initiate a Rule 11 action against a party, but if so, must accord that party an opportunity to respond and be heard before imposing any sanction.

Rule 26. "As the U.S. Senate rushed to adjourn in 1993, it left unfinished one piece of procedural business that has had important consequences for federal civil litigation. The Senate failed to act on H.R. 2814, thereby allowing the most controversial amendment in the half-century history of the FRCP to go into effect on Dec. 1. That change to Rule 26 prescribes mandatory pre-discovery, or automatic disclosure, a procedure that requires parties to disclose significant information relating to their cases before the litigants may commence formal discovery." [Carl Tobias, "The Back-Door Route for Changing Federal Discovery Rules," *The Recorder,* Feb 3, 1994, at 8]

The major tools of discovery in typical labor and employment lawsuits are described in Q 15:7. The changes mandated by Rule 26, as amended, are the following:

1. The parties in the lawsuit disclose to one another early in the proceedings the identities and locations of all documents they believe to be relevant to their claims or defenses; the identities of witnesses, including experts; and their knowledge "relevant to disputed facts alleged with particularity in the pleadings."

2. This early disclosed information must be supplemented automatically any time new or different information of the same kind comes to a party's attention.

3. A motion to dismiss the lawsuit under Rule 12 does not supersede or slow this early-disclosure process.

4. The parties must file a discovery plan with the federal court. If the two sides cannot get together on a single plan, then each side must provide the judge with its proposal for such a plan.

5. Each side is limited to 10 depositions and 25 interrogatories.

6. A second mandatory disclosure, this time of witness lists, must occur 30 days before trial.

The impact of these major changes in the federal rules is mitigated by the option accorded to the various federal jurisdictions to opt out of the amendments. "For various reasons, a large number of the nation's 94 federal district courts have opted out of the controversial prediscovery disclosure requirement in the newly amended [Rule 26], according to two recent monitoring efforts." [Coyle and Lavelle, "Half of Districts Opt Out of New Civil Rules," *National Law Journal,* Feb 28, 1994, at 5]

Other courts, such as the U.S. District Court for the Eastern District of Pennsylvania, reportedly prefer not to limit the number of depositions and interrogatories each party can demand.

About two-thirds of the nation's 94 federal judicial districts have adopted some or all of the changes to Rule 26 or, alternatively, local rules embodying the courts' own versions of the same general principles and concepts. [Cortese and Blaner, "Districts' Discovery Rules Differ," *National Law Journal,* Nov 14, 1994, at A1]

United States Code

[References are to question numbers.]

United States Code

[References are to question numbers.]

17 USC

101 et seq 6:21
101 . . . . 6:22–6:26
201(b) 6:24

18 USC

2314 . . . . 6:34

19 USC

2272(a) 14:13

29 USC

152(3) 8:170, 11:7
158 . . . . 11:24
158(d) 11:81
160(b) 13:68
185 . . . . 15:12, 15:16
187 . . . . 15:16
201–219 . . . . 8:25
203(d) 4:96
207(i) 8:26
207(j) 8:26
207(m) 8:26
207(o) 8:26
207(p) 8:26
207(q) 8:26
216 . . . . 8:54
216(b) 4:115, 15:16
260 . . . . 8:54
301 . . . . 15:1
401–531 . . . . 15:12
541.113(e) 8:29

623(c) 15:12
623(f)(2) 11:56, 11:60
630(b) 4:96
660(a) 7:16
666(a) 7:126
666(c) 7:126
666(e) 7:126
706(7)(b) 4:68
1002(1) 8:198
1002(2)(A) 8:198
1056(d) 8:112
1133 . . . . 13:10
1539(d) 12:45
1661(d)(a) 14:9
1691–1709 . . . . 14:4
1698(d)(3) 14:4
2101 et seq 14:9

41 USC

605(c)(4) 9:46
606 . . . . 9:46

42 USC

300ee(2) 7:112
1983 . . . . 10:31, 10:32, 10:34
2000e(b) 4:96
2000e-2(c) 15:12
2000e-2(h) 11:56, 11:59
2000e-5(k) 15:16
12111(5)(A) 4:96

Code of Federal Regulations

[References are to question numbers.]

[References are to question numbers.]

Internal Revenue Code

[References are to question numbers.]

State Statutes and Constitutions

[References are to question numbers.]

[*References are to question numbers.*]

Massachusetts

Massachusetts Gen L ch 151A, Massachusetts Health Security
Act (1988) 8:197

Michigan

Mich Comp Laws Ann § 445.774(a)
(1989) 6:35

Montana

Montana Human Rights Act
§ 49-2-310 . . . . 8:103

Montana Wrongful Discharge from
Employment Act, Mont Code
§§ 392901–392914 (1988) . . . 2:36

New Jersey

New Jersey Family Leave Act, 34 NJ
Stats §§ 11B-1–11B-16 . . . 8:103

New York

NY Criminal Code § 155.00(6) . . 6:34

North Dakota

ND Cent Code §§ 9-08–06 . . . . 6:35

Oklahoma

Okla Stat title 15 §§ 217–219
(1981) 6:35

Pennsylvania

43 Pa Cons Stat Ann §§ 1321, 1322
(1978) 5:2, 5:6

18 Pa Stats Ann § 3930 . . . . . 6:34

35 Pa Stat Ann § 655.7 . . . . . 7:130

42 Pa Stat Ann §§ 260.1 et seq . . 2:36

Table of Cases

[References are to question numbers.]

[References are to question numbers.]

B

Table of Cases

[References are to question numbers.]

[References are to question numbers.]

Table of Cases

Table of Cases

[References are to question numbers.]

Hopkins, Price
  Waterhouse v 3:88, 4:32,
    4:42, 4:89
Howard S Wright Construction Co,
  Haertl Wolff Parker Inc v . . 13:10
Hudspeth Mental Retardation Center,
  Roosevelt Jackson and Annie
  Grant v 3:45
Hughey, New Jersey Chamber of
  Commerce v 7:51
Hutchcraft Van Service Inc v City of
  Urbana Human Relations
  Comm'n 3:21
Hyatt Legal Services,
  Cain v 4:99, 4:110,
    7:104, 7:107, 7:131

I

IDS Financial Services Inc,
  Turner v 15:3
Illinois v Chicago Magnet
  Wire Co 7:46, 7:47
Illinois v O'Neil 7:46, 7:47
IMI Systems Inc, Bernard v 2:9
Immigration and Naturalization
  Service, Kahn v 12:49
Immigration and Naturalization
  Service, Mester Manufacturing
  Co v 12:20
Immigration and Naturalization
  Service, Rabana v 12:59
Immigration and Naturalization
  Service, Talamantes-
  Penalver v 12:59
Independent State Stores Union,
  Pennsylvania Liquor Control
  Board v 13:3

Independent Steelworkers Union,
  Gilliam v 8:171
Ingram, Central Adjustment
  Bureau v 6:37
Inland Container
  Corp 11:96, 11:97
Interactive Data Corp,
  Foley v 13:43
International Alliance of Theatrical
  and Stage Employees and Moving
  Picture Machine Operators v Com-
  pact Video Servs, Inc 13:66
International Assn of Machinists v
  Meagher 8:154
International Brotherhood of
  Boilermakers v NLRB 11:95
International Brotherhood of Team-
  sters v American Delivery
  Service Co 13:66
International Schools Services, Inc,
  Bryan v 4:5
Interstate/Johnson Lane Corp,
  Gilmer v 2:49, 3:118,
    4:120, 4:153, 11:8, 11:10, 11:56,
    13:2, 13:9, 13:33, 15:3, 15:18
Iredell Digestive Disease Clinic v
  Petrozza 6:35

J

Jackson v Ferrand 6:7
Jackson State University,
  Langley v 4:36
Jacksonville Shipyards, Inc,
  Robinson v 4:52
James v Commonwealth of Pennsylva-
  nia, Unemployment Compensation
  Board of Review 2:34

Table of Cases

[References are to question numbers.]

M

Table of Cases

[References are to question numbers.]

Table of Cases

Table of Cases

[References are to question numbers.]

Table of Cases

Index

[References are to question numbers.]

A

Accident insurance
amendment reducing or
eliminating, 9:30
benefits as compensation, 6:3
Accountants and accounting
administering qualified plans, role
in, 16:23
adoption of plan, 1:23
fiduciary status, 19:6
Form 5500 series return/report,
audit and opinion on, 17:14
malpractice, 19:4
Service Provider and Trustee
Information (Schedule C)
accompanying Form 5500, 17:4
Account balance
amounts payable to alternate payee
under qualified domestic relations
order, 30:17, 30:18
generally, 11:15
vested, 13:5
Accrual rate
age of participants, dependent on,
9:23
flat benefit plans, 4:15
most valuable accrual rate, 4:17

normal rate for plan year, 4:17
Accrued benefits
age of employee, cessation related
to, 9:23
amending plan to reduce, 9:24
amendment to reduce or stop
accruals, 21:59
annual benefit limitation, 6:15
anti-cutback rule. *See* Anti-cutback
rule
change after freeze date, 9:26
copy of statement furnished
participant, 18:13
defined benefit offset plans, 7:16
distribution of offset amount, 28:12
eliminating or reducing, 9:28–9:30,
10:63, 21:59
excess distribution tax, 13:38
generally, 9:2
loans secured by, 13:48
maximum offset allowance, 7:16
multiemployer plans, of, 22:5
nonforfeitability of, 9:2
normal retirement age, benefits
determined with reference to, 9:2,
10:55
present value determination rules,
9:25–9:27

[References are to question numbers.]

Accrued benefits *(cont'd)*
pro rata increases in, 21:53
reporting and disclosure, 9:2
retroactive reduction of, 8:25, 10:63
Section 411(d)(6) protected benefit,
as, 10:42
Tax Reform Act of 1986 limitations,
6:15
terminated plan, 21:4, 21:42, 21:43
top-heavy plans. *See* Top-heavy
plans
vested, 13:5

Acquisition of property for resale
deduction for contributions, 12:22
uniform capitalization rules, 12:22

Acquisitions. *See* Mergers and
acquisitions

Active employees
highly compensated employees
defined, 3:3
family aggregation rule, 3:14, 5:22
multiple categories, 3:7
non-highly compensated
employees, 3:13

Active participation. *See* Individual
retirement plans (IRAs)

**Actual contribution percentage
(ACP) test**
calculation of ACP, 23:49
contributions included in, 23:50
excess aggregate contributions,
23:53
generally, 23:48
mandatory employee contributions,
applied to, 6:17
plan year, 23:51
voluntary employee contributions,
applied to, 6:20

**Actual deferred percentage (ADP)
test**
actual deferral ratio, 23:9, 23:10
aggregation of plans, 23:42
calculation of, 23:9
compensation for purposes of, 23:11

elective contributions for purposes
of, 23:12
excess contributions, 23:16, 23:17
excess deferrals, 23:30
generally, 23:8
matching contributions, 23:12
multiple plans, 23:10
notice for current plan year, 23:8
qualified contributions, 23:14
qualified nonelective contributions,
23:12
safe harbor, 23:8
satisfaction of, 23:15

Actuaries and actuarial assumptions
administering qualified plans, role
in, 16:21
adoption of plan, 1:23
deduction for contributions, 12:19
defined benefit plans. *See* Defined
benefit plans
disclosure requirements, 16:16
fiduciary status, 19:6
funding costs, determining, 8:8
interest rate assumption, 8:8
investment growth and earnings,
8:13
IRS actuarial examination program,
8:8
malpractice, 19:4
optional forms of benefit,
calculating, 10:33
pension liabilities, 8:10
retirement age assumptions, 2:35,
8:8, 8:11
Schedule B accompanying Forms
5500 and 5500-C/R, 17:4
Standard Termination Certification
of Sufficiency, 21:34

Administration costs. *See* Costs

Administration of plan. *See* Plan
administration

**Administrative Policy Regarding
Sanctions**
generally, 15:16

[References are to question numbers.]

[References are to question numbers.]

[References are to question numbers.]

Index

[References are to question numbers.]

[References are to question numbers.]

Assignment or alienation (*cont'd*)
distributed plan benefits, 4:27
execution. *See* Execution
future benefit payments, 4:24
garnishment. *See* Garnishment
loan treated as, 4:24
nonassignment provision, 4:1
qualified domestic relations orders, 4:24, 30:4
qualified plan benefits, 4:24, 4:25
tax levy, effect on, 4:26
voluntary and revocable, 4:24

Assumption of debts
basis, as, 13:2

Attachment
IRS levy. *See* Tax levy
IRS lien. *See* Tax lien
qualified domestic relations orders enforcement, 30:23
qualified retirement plan benefits, 4:27

Attorneys
fees and costs. *See* Attorneys' fees and costs
fiduciary status, 19:6
malpractice, 19:6
party in interest, as, 20:2

Attorneys' fees and costs
administrative proceedings, 19:41
breach of fiduciary duty, 19:41
lodestar/multiplier method of calculating, 19:41
prejudgment interest, 19:41
reasonable, 19:31

Audits
Form 5500 series return/report, accountant's audit and opinion on, 17:14
IRS Examination Division, 15:12
PBGC audit of defined benefit plan records, 16:6
post-termination compliance audits, 21:46

Automatic survivor benefit rule
401(k) plans, 10:6
annuity contracts used to provide benefits, 10:15
crime by spouse, effect of, 10:19
death benefits, applicability to, 10:18
defined benefit plans, 10:18
defined contribution plans, 10:18
effective date of, 10:32
exemption from, 10:7
floor-offset plans, 10:6, 10:14
frozen plans, 10:16
generally, 10:1
insurance contract proceeds, applicability to, 10:18
life annuity, 10:6
life insurance benefits, applicability to, 10:18
loan made by qualified plan, spousal consent to, 13:47
misconduct by spouse, effect of, 10:19
one-year marriage requirement, 10:19
profit sharing plans
exemption from rule, 10:7
generally, 10:6
qualified domestic relations order, effect of, 10:19, 10:21
spousal consent rule
effective date of, 10:32
general consent, 10:26
plan document detailing, 10:28
stock bonus plans, 10:6
terminated plans, 10:16
transferee plans, 10:6, 10:13
vested benefits, 10:18
waiver of benefits
alternate beneficiary mandated where, 10:23
antenuptial agreement, in, 10:22
general consent, 10:26
generally, 10:20

[References are to question numbers.]

Index

[References are to question numbers.]

[References are to question numbers.]

Construction industry
qualified separate lines of business, 5:54
withdrawal liability, 25:23

Consultants
fiduciary status, 19:6
malpractice, 19:6
personal service corporations, 5:39

Continuance of plan
permanent basis requirement, 1:23, 4:1
voluntary obligation, 1:22

Contract with America Tax Relief Bill of 1995. *See* Tax Fairness and Deficit Reduction Bill of 1995

Contribution
breach of duty by co-fiduciary, 19:39

Contributions. *See also* Funding requirements
401(k) plans. *See* 401(k) plans
age as factor in determining, 2:28
age-based profit sharing plans, 2:7, 2:8
allocation dates, amendment altering, 9:30
amendment reducing or eliminating right to make after-tax, 9:30
annual, 1:25
bankruptcy estate, inclusion of improper contributions in, 4:24
basis, as, 13:2
breaching co-fiduciary, from, 19:29
business owner, by, 1:32, 2:31
choices in, 2:38
complete discontinuance of, 21:56, 21:57
constructive, 12:16
cost-of-living increases, anticipated, 12:25
defined benefit plans. *See* Defined benefit plans
defined contribution plans. *See* Defined contribution plans

discrimination in favor of highly compensated employees, 2:29
earmarking of employer contributions, 19:55
elective. *See* 401(k) plans
excess. *See* Excess contributions
failure to make
generally, 8:18
liability for, 8:19
Notice of Failure to Make Required Contributions (Form 200), 17:26
flexibility where fluctuating profits, 2:26
frozen plan, 1:10
full funding limitation, 8:16
funded plans, 1:12
funding standard account, 8:15
health insurance benefits, 1:34
inclusion in income
coverage rule, failure to satisfy, 5:30
nondiscrimination rule, failure to satisfy, 4:23
participation rule, failure to satisfy, 5:30
income earned on, 1:8
individual retirement plans (IRAs). *See* Individual retirement plans (IRAs)
insurance plans, allocation to, 1:9
insured qualified plans, 2:22
investment gains and losses affecting, 2:34
leased employees, by, 5:64
maximization of, 2:33
money purchase pension plans, 2:4, 2:5, 2:33
net operating loss created by, 1:9
nondeductible. *See* Excess contributions
nondiscrimination rule. *See* Nondiscrimination requirements
participation, as condition of, 5:6

[References are to question numbers.]

Contributions *(cont'd)*
permitted disparity. *See* Permitted disparity
plan assets, 19:24
profit sharing plans. *See* Profit sharing plans
recurring and substantial, 1:23
returned contributions, 6:1
return following adverse determination, 4:6
rollovers. *See* Rollovers
self-employed individuals, by, 6:34
simplified employee pension contributions, 27:6
simplified employee pensions (SEPs). *See* Simplified employee pensions (SEPs)
suspension of, 21:56
target benefit plans, 2:5
taxation of, 1:6, 1:12
thrift or savings plans, 2:10, 5:6
timing of, 1:35
top-heavy plans, 4:1
trusts, to, 4:4
voluntary nondeductible. *See* Voluntary contributions
waiver of, 8:24
Control
defined, 5:34
Controlled group
annual compensation limit, 6:28
contributions, liability for, 8:19
coverage requirements, 5:33
defined, 5:33
employer securities, 24:9
funding standard accounts, 8:17
limitation year, 6:16
loans made by, 13:44
management corporation in, 5:36
minimum funding standards, waiver of, 8:20
reimbursement of PBGC for underfunded terminated plan, 21:47

simplified employee pensions (SEPs), 27:2
years of service with, 5:11, 9:10
Conversion of plan
termination, as, 21:4
Conversion of plans
amendment of plan, 21:6
defined benefit and defined contribution plans, 21:6
insurance contract plan, to, 8:6
profit sharing plan converted to ESOP, 24:19
qualified plan converted into comparable plan, 21:6
Cooperative hospital service organization
Section 501(c)(3) organization, 29:3
Cost-of-living adjustments
401(k) plans, 23:11
amendments eliminating, 9:24
annual addition limitation, 6:2
annual benefit limitation, 6:8
annual compensation ceiling, 6:24, 6:25
anticipated, in calculating contributions, 12:25
cap on compensation, 4:1
reduced compensation limit, to, 1:17
Costs
adoption of plan, 1:23
attorneys. *See* Attorneys' fees and costs
deduction for administrative expense payments, 12:26
defined benefit plans, 2:17
defraying of plan administration costs, 4:24, 19:25
determination letter, fee for, 15:2
excess retirement accumulation, 14:27
Social Security changes resulting in changes in, 8:13
Coverage requirements
401(k) plans, 5:23

Custom-designed plans (*cont'd*)
  simplified employee pensions
    (SEPs), 27:12

D

Damages
  breach of fiduciary duty
    direction action against fiduciary,
      19:28
    generally, 19:27
    punitive damages, 19:40
Dealers
  fiduciary status, 19:1, 19:3
  prohibited-transaction class
    exemption, 20:12
Death benefit exclusion
  tax-sheltered annuity death benefit
    payments to beneficiary, 29:45
  See also Death benefits
Death benefits
  ancillary benefit, as, 4:18
  annuity purchased with, 14:18
  automatic survivor rule applied to,
    10:18
  death benefit exclusion, 14:11, 14:18
  disclaimer by designated
    beneficiary, 4:24
  election of form of benefit, 14:19
  estate tax, 14:12
  excess distributions, computation
    of, 13:29
  incidental death benefit rule
    benefit distributions affected by,
      11:21
    violation of, 10:57
  lack of designated beneficiary, 14:10
  preretirement death benefits as
    ancillary benefit, 4:18
  preretirement survivor annuity. *See*
    Qualified preretirement survivor
    annuity
  qualified retirement plan, 1:31

  requirement to provide, 14:1
  surviving spouse, to, 14:1
  taxation of
    estate tax, 14:19
    forward averaging tax treatment,
      14:18
    income tax, 14:18
    lump-sum distributions, 14:18
    marital deduction, 14:20
  under tax-sheltered annuity, 29:45
  top-heavy plans, 22:18
  transfer to administrator of estate,
    14:18
Death of employee
  aggregation of decedent's interests,
    14:23, 30:21
  American Dream Savings account
    amounts remaining, 26:37
  death benefits. *See* Death benefits
  distributions not made prior to, 11:7
  distributions to be made after
    death, 11:5
  forfeiture of vested benefits upon,
    9:22
  IRA amounts remaining, 26:37
  IRA distributions following
    inherited IRAs, 26:38, 26:39
    minimum distribution
      requirements, 26:40
  life insurance. *See* Life insurance
  lump-sum distribution following,
    13:4
  premature penalty tax exception,
    26:41
  separation from service, 13:9
  Special IRA amounts remaining,
    26:37
  surviving spouse. *See* Surviving
    spouse
  transfer from deceased participant's
    estate as taxable distribution, 13:1
  vesting upon, 9:12
Deduction
  compensation, for, 2:32, 12:1

[References are to question numbers.]

Defined benefit excess plans *(cont'd)*
base benefit percentage *(cont'd)*
defined, 7:11
excess benefit percentage
calculated to, 7:9
maximum excess allowance
calculated to, 7:12
defined, 7:2
excess benefit percentage
base benefit percentage,
calculated to, 7:9
defined, 7:10
maximum excess allowance,
calculated to, 7:9
exemptions from DOL reporting
requirements, 17:19
integration level
defined, 7:6
general rules for, 7:15
lump-sum distributions, 7:9
maximum excess allowance
base benefit percentage,
calculated to, 7:12
defined, 7:12
excess benefit percentage
calculated to, 7:9
integration levels calculated to,
7:15
optional benefits provided, 7:9
permitted disparity tests, 7:9, 7:13
Social Security retirement age,
benefits commencing prior to, 7:14
uniform disparity, 7:25
Defined benefit offset plans
accrued benefits, reduction of, 7:16
average annual compensation
benefits based on, 7:16
defined, 7:21
maximum offset allowance
calculated to, 7:17
compensation history, 7:21
covered compensation
defined, 7:22
offset level calculated to, 7:20

table, 7:22
defined, 7:2
maximum offset allowance
accrued benefits reduced to, 7:16
average annual compensation,
calculated to, 7:17
defined, 7:17
offset level calculated to, 7:20
offset level, 7:20
permitted disparity tests, 7:16, 7:18
Social Security retirement age,
benefits commencing prior to, 7:19
taxable wage base, 7:22
uniform disparity, 7:25
Defined benefit plans
actuarial assumptions
generally, 2:17, 2:34
IRS examination program, 8:8
reasonableness of, 8:8
specification in plan, 2:18
advantages of, 2:33
age of essential employees, 2:28
age of participant, 2:33
asset valuation, 8:14
benefiting for a plan year, 5:20
benefits
business owner, to, 2:31
limitation on. *See* Annual benefit
limitation
cash balance plans, 2:21
contributions
actuarial determination of, 2:3
annual, 2:31
deduction for. *See* Deduction for
contributions
equivalent contributions, 4:10
nondiscrimination rule, 4:10
quarterly, 8:28
conversion to defined contribution
plan, 21:6
cost of funding, 2:17
cross-tested, 4:20
defined, 1:5, 2:3
early termination of plan, 2:3

[References are to question numbers.]

[References are to question numbers.]

[References are to question numbers.]

The Pension Answer Book

[References are to question numbers.]

Educational expenses
American Dream Savings accounts used for, 26:42
qualified higher education expenses, 26:42
Educational institutions
adoption of TSA by, 29:14
age requirement, 1:27
exclusion allowance. *See* Tax-sheltered annuities
public educational systems defined, 29:4
eligible employer, as, 29:2, 29:4
employer-employee relationship, 29:5
Section 501(c)(3) organization, 29:4
tax-sheltered annuities. *See* Tax-sheltered annuities
years of service, 29:24
Education expenses
IRA distribution used for, 26:43
Special IRA distribution used for, 26:43
Electrical industries
qualified separate lines of business, 5:54
Electronics industries
qualified separate lines of business, 5:54
Eligibility requirements. *See also* Participation requirements
changes in, 21:5
choices in, 2:38
nondiscrimination test. *See* Nondiscrimination requirements
partial plan termination following changes in, 21:5
qualified plans, 1:24
Eligible individual account plan
investments authorized by, 19:41
Embezzlement
pension benefits not used to satisfy judgment, 4:24

union pension plan, from, 4:24
Employee
active. *See* Active employees
age of. *See* Age of participants
allocation of, 5:56
common-law, 6:44
defined, 5:1
dishonest, 9:19
employer-employee relationship, 29:5
essential. *See* Essential employees
excludible employee, 5:26
former. *See* Former employees
highly compensated. *See* Highly compensated employees
hourly. *See* Hourly employees
independent contractor for same organization, as, 29:5
leased. *See* Leased employees
partner's status as, 5:1
party in interest, as, 20:2
qualified separate lines of business, of, 5:56
residual shared, 5:56
retired. *See* Retired employees
salaried. *See* Salaried employees
self-employed individual as, 6:35
shareholder's status as, 5:1
spouse as, 5:1
substantial service, 5:56
termination of employment. *See* Termination of employment
turnover
discrimination in favor of permanent employees, 2:30
forfeiture caused by. *See* Forfeitures
union. *See* Union employees
Employee benefit plans
defined in ERISA, 4:25
Employee-owner. *See* Business owner
Employee Plan Closing Agreements Pilot Program (CAP), 15:15

I-26

[References are to question numbers.]

[References are to question numbers.]

Fiduciaries *(cont'd)*
  bonding requirements *(cont'd)*
    plan officials, 16:24–16:29
  breach of duty
    arbitration of claim, 19:30
    co-fiduciary, by, 19:37–19:39
    contribution from breaching
      co-fiduciary, 19:39
    delay in transferring benefits,
      19:12
    direct action for damages, 19:28
    DOL penalties, 19:34
    employer benefited by
      transactions, 19:15
    failure to act, 19:32
    improper use of plan assets, 19:26
    indemnification, 19:39, 19:43
    insurance to cover, 19:42
    joint and several liability, 19:35
    jury trial, 19:29
    misleading communications or
      misrepresentations, 19:12
    nonfiduciary's liability, 19:35
    omission, acts of, 19:32
    personal liability for, 19:28
    prior fiduciary, breach by, 19:31
    proportional fault among
      fiduciaries, 19:39
    punitive damages, 19:40
    purchase of insurance contract or
      annuity as, 1:17
    recovery of attorney's fees and
      costs, 19:41
    release, 19:44
    relief from personal liability, 19:42
    remedy of breach by co-fiduciary,
      19:38
    restitution, 19:35
    setoff of liability against benefits,
      .19:33
    standing to use, 19:28
    successor fiduciary, liability of,
      19:31
    third parties, liability to, 19:27

  brokers as, 19:1, 19:3, 19:4
  consultants as, 19:6
  dealers as, 19:1, 19:3
  defined under ERISA, 19:1
  delegation of duties, 19:45
  diversification requirement, 19:38
  employer functions distinguished
    from fiduciary duties, 19:2
  former plan fiduciaries barred from
    acting as, 19:12
  good faith reliance on expert
    advice, 19:13
  insurance agents as, 19:6
  insurers as, 19:6
  investment advice
    generally, 19:4
    investment manager, given by,
      19:46
    status of fiduciary dependent on
      giving, 19:1
  investment in other entities, plan
    assets where, 19:17
  Keogh plans, 19:7
  lifetime appointment, 19:11
  look-through rule. *See* Look-through
    rule
  ministerial functions distinguished
    from fiduciary duties, 19:3
  mutual fund prospectus furnished
    to, 20:1
  named, 19:5
  officer-shareholders, 19:5
  party in interest, as, 20:2
  prohibited individuals, 19:10
  prohibited transactions. *See*
    Prohibited transactions
  recordkeeping by, 19:51
  segregation of plan assets, 19:16
  self-directed account plans, 19:9
  settlor functions distinguished from
    fiduciary duties, 19:2
  standard of care
    conversion of plans, in, 24:19
    generally, 19:13, 19:51

[References are to question numbers.]

[References are to question numbers.]

[References are to question numbers.]

[References are to question numbers.]

Index

[References are to question numbers.]

[References are to question numbers.]

[References are to question numbers.]

Governmental plans
401(k) plans, 23:1
acceleration election, 13:33
active participation in, 26:8
attained age method, 13:34
computation of recovery of initial
grandfather amount, 13:32
discretionary method, 13:33
DOL reporting requirements
exemption, 17:19
excess distribution tax calculation,
13:35
excess retirement accumulation
calculation, 14:25
funding standard exemption, 8:4
generally, 13:31
lump-sum and nonlump-sum
distributions in same year, 13:36
participation requirements, 5:25
PBGC exemption, 21:13
qualified domestic relations order
(QDRO), 30:5, 30:21
salary reduction SEPs, 27:9
surviving spouse using, 13:33, 14:26

Gross income
adjusted gross income, 26:10–26:12
annuity contract, exclusion of
amounts used to purchase, 29:1
cash-or-deferred election, 23:2,
23:3, 23:5
cash surrender value of insurance
policy included in, 14:11
distributions included in, 13:1,
13:15, 23:25
excess aggregate contributions,
23:55
excess contributions, 23:20
excess deferrals included in, 23:29
forfeitable and nonforfeitable rights,
29:12
individual retirement annuity, 26:3
individual retirement plan active
participants, of, 26:10

individual retirement plan payment
or distribution, 26:34
present benefit of life insurance
included in, 14:6
qualified domestic relations orders
tax consequences, 30:17, 30:18
tax-sheltered annuity contribution
exclusions, 29:21
Group insurance contracts. *See*
Insurance contract plans
Guarantee agreement, 24:38

H

Hardship test
waiver of minimum funding
standards, for
application process, 8:21
generally, 8:20
Hardship withdrawal
401(k) plans, 23:34–23:39
circumstances constituting
hardship, 23:35
facts and circumstances test
defined, 23:35
immediate and heavy financial
need, 23:36
necessity of withdrawal, 23:38
foreseeable or voluntarily incurred
financial needs, 23:36
immediate and heavy financial need
facts and circumstances test,
23:36
generally, 23:35
safe-harbor test, 23:37
necessity of withdrawal
facts and circumstances test,
23:38
generally, 23:35
safe-harbor test, 23:39
profit sharing plan, 1:31
resources of participant, 23:38
safe-harbor test

[References are to question numbers.]

[References are to question numbers.]

Home health service agenciesK
(*cont'd*)
special election to increase overall
limitation, 29:30
tax-sheltered annuities. *See*
Tax-sheltered annuities
Hospitals
exclusion allowance, 29:26, 29:27
special election to increase overall
limitation, 29:30
tax-sheltered annuities. *See*
Tax-sheltered annuities
Hostile takeovers
employee stock ownership plans
used against, 24:18
Hotels
qualified separate lines of business,
5:54
Hourly employees
exclusion from qualified plan, 1:29
Hours of service
defined, 5:9
multiemployer plans, 25:4
Household goods moving industry
withdrawal liability, 25:23
H.R. 10 plans. *See* Keogh plans
Husband and wife. *See* Spouse or
other relative

I

Income tax. *See* specific taxable
benefits or distributions
Incorporation
advantages of, 1:9
requirements for qualified plans, 1:7
self-employed individuals, of, 1:9,
1:10
Indemnity
breach of fiduciary duty, 19:39,
19:43

Independent contractors
employee for same organization, as,
29:5
status as, 29:5
**Individual level premium funding
method**
target benefit plans, 4:21
Individually designed plans. *See*
Custom-designed plans
Individual retirement accounts. *See*
Individual retirement plans (IRAs)
Individual retirement plans (IRAs)
active participants
active participation defined, 26:8
deduction limits, 26:11
determination of, 26:9
income level of, 26:10
limitation on deductible
contributions, 26:7
actual contribution percentage test.
See Actual contribution percentage
test
actual deferred percentage test. *See*
Actual deferred percentage test
Additional taxes attributable to
qualified Retirement plans
(including IRAs), 17:16
American Dream Savings account.
See American Dream Savings
account
annuity, 26:3
banks providing reduced or no-cost
services to customers, 26:23
brokerage commissions, 26:21
community property reclassified
into separate property, 26:34
compensation, 26:5
conduit IRAs, 28:37, 29:42
contributions
borrowed money, 26:24
cash advances using credit card,
26:25
cost-of-living increases, 26:5
deadline, 26:19

Index

[References are to question numbers.]

[References are to question numbers.]

[References are to question numbers.]

[References are to question numbers.]

[References are to question numbers.]

[References are to question numbers.]

Loans (*cont'd*)

shareholder-employee, to, 13:48

shareholders, from, 24:52

simplified employee pension
participants, to, 27:17

spousal consent to, 13:47

spouse of owner-employee, to, 1:38

survivor annuity

effect of loan on annuity amount,
10:11

spousal consent for loan, 10:12

tax-sheltered annuity to employee,
from

generally, 29:44, 29:47

prohibited transaction, as, 29:48

withholding on participant loans
from qualified plans, 16:13

Long-term care insurance

ADS accounts used for, 26:42

IRA distribution used to purchase,
26:34

medical expenses, treatment as,
26:42, 26:43

tax-sheltered annuity distribution
used for, 29:38, 29:44

Look-back year

5 percent owner, 3:4

defined, 3:11

dollar amount inflation
adjustments, 3:9

family aggregation rule, 3:14

former employees, 3:12

highly compensated active
employees, 3:7

highly compensated employees, 3:3

officers, 3:6

Tax Simplification and Technical
Corrections Bill of 1993, 3:15

top-paid group, 3:5

Look-through rule

benefit plan investor defined, 19:22

equity interest

defined, 19:19

operating company, in, 19:18

significant level of participation,
19:18, 19:21

exceptions to, 19:18

generally, 19:17

operating company

defined, 19:20

equity interest in, 19:18

real estate operating company,
19:20

venture capital operating
company, 19:20

underlying assets of entity invested
in, plan assets being, 19:23

Lump-sum distributions

after termination of employment,
1:9, 13:7

amendments eliminating rights to,
9:24

balance to the credit of employee,
13:5

beneficiary, to, 1:8, 13:12

business owner, to, 1:2

death benefits, 14:18

defined, 13:4

defined benefit excess plans, 7:9

disabled employee, to, 13:10

employer securities as, 13:17

events mandating, 10:56, 13:4

final distribution from plan as, 13:7

good health standard for
determining eligibility for, 10:47

installment payment of benefits
following, 13:7

outstanding interest in pension plan
maintained by employer, 13:5

qualified domestic relations orders
tax consequences, 30:18

rollover of. *See* Rollovers

self-employed individual, to, 1:8,
13:10

taxation of. *See* Taxation of
distributions

withholding rules. *See*
Withholding

[References are to question numbers.]

Ministerial functions
fiduciary duties distinguished from, 19:3
generally, 19:3

Money purchase pension plans
401(k) plans, 23:6
active participants, 26:9
age of participant, 2:4, 2:5
benefits, 2:4
contributions
employer securities, 20:8, 24:15
generally, 2:4, 2:5, 2:33
conversion to profit sharing plans, 21:4
defined, 2:4
forfeitures, 2:4
funding requirements, 2:4, 8:1
generally, 2:4
penalty tax for failure to make contributions, 2:4
prohibited transactions, 20:8, 24:15
safe-harbor plans, 5:65
target benefit plans compared to, 2:5
thrift or savings plans, 2:10

Mortality table
annual benefit limitation, 6:10
anti-cutback rule and changes in, 9:25
in present value determinations, 10:63

Mortgages
diversification requirement, 19:38
handling of plan funds or other property, 16:26
hardship withdrawal, 23:37
qualified plan's mortgage investment program, 13:44

Moving expenses
reimbursement as compensation, 6:3

Multiemployer Pension Plan Amendments Act of 1980 (MPPAA)
generally, 1:16

Multiemployer plans
accrued benefits of key employees, 22:5
advantages of, 25:3
amendment of plan to freeze benefits, 25:43
asset valuation, 8:14
benefits
guaranteed, 25:6, 25:8
level of, 25:8
nonguaranteed, 25:9
commonly controlled employers, 25:5
contributions suspended during labor dispute, 25:19
defined, 22:5, 25:2
Form 5500 series return/report, 17:2
free-look rule, 25:44
funding requirements, 8:3, 8:18
generally, 25:1
hours of service, 25:4
insolvent, 25:7
participation requirements, 5:25
Pension Benefit Guaranty Corporation (PBGC) premiums, 21:14
termination of
liability of employer, 25:43
mass withdrawal, 25:42
top-heavy plans, 22:5
vesting requirements, 9:4
withdrawal from as termination, 21:55
withdrawal liability
20-year cap on, 25:33
amendment of plan, 25:25
amortization, 25:33
arbitration of disputes concerning, 25:34, 25:36–25:38
bankruptcy proceedings, 25:41
barring disputes of, 25:37
change in business structure, 25:18
Chapter 11 reorganization, 25:32

[References are to question numbers.]

[References are to question numbers.]

[References are to question numbers.]

older employees, by, 5:3

tax-favored status of plan, effect on, 5:29

Partnerships

401(k) plans, 23:7

bonding for single partner plan, 16:29

coverage requirements, 5:31

currently available compensation, 23:7

dissolved, SEP of, 27:14

employee status of partner and partner's spouse, 4:25

ERISA exclusion of plans covering, 4:25

liability for contributions, 8:19

loans from qualified plans to, 20:3

officers of, 22:26

owner-employee, partner as, 5:34

participation requirements, 5:31

party in interest, as, 20:2

qualified retirement plans for, 1:7

self-employed individual, partner as, 6:31

simplified employee pensions (SEPs), 27:12

withdrawal liability, 25:18

Part-time employees

participation requirements, 5:18

Party in interest

bonding requirement satisfied by, 16:28

class exemption to, 14:16

defined, 20:2

improper use of plan assets, 19:26

loans to, 20:7

prohibited transactions. *See* Prohibited transactions

services rendered to plan by, 20:7

Past service credit

defined, 4:19

safe-harbor test, 4:19

Paternity leave

service requirement, effect on, 5:14

Payroll taxes. *See* Federal Unemployment Taxes Act (FUTA); Withholding

Penalties. *See* Criminal conduct; specific violations

Penalty tax

American Dream Savings accounts premature distribution, 26:42

Double Jeopardy Clause applied to, 20:4

early distributions. *See* Early distribution tax

excess deferrals, 23:29

excess distributions

American Dream Savings accounts, 26:35

generally, 10:52, 13:1, 13:27

401(k) plans, excess contributions, 23:18

individual retirement plans (IRAs), 26:39, 26:41, 26:43

late distributions, 13:1

nonfiduciaries, imposition against, 19:26

overstatement of pension liabilities, 8:10

prohibited transactions, 1:37, 20:4

recharacterized excess contributions, 23:22

series of substantially equal periodic payments exception, 28:9

simplified employee pensions (SEPs), 27:18

Special IRA, 26:43

tax-sheltered annuities

failure to make required distribution, 29:46

premature distributions, 29:46

Pension Annuitants Protection Act (PPA '94), 1:16, 1:17

liability for failure to make annuity payments, 21:41

termination of plan, 21:11

[References are to question numbers.]

[References are to question numbers.]

[References are to question numbers.]

[*References are to question numbers.*]

[References are to question numbers.]

[References are to question numbers.]

R

Railroad Retirement Acts
government employees, 21:13

Rate groups
amount of benefits per group, 4:17
average benefit test, 4:12, 4:17
highly compensated employees, 4:17
minimum coverage requirements, 4:12
nondiscrimination rule test, 4:12
ratio percentage test, 4:12, 4:17

Ratio percentage test
classification test combined with, 5:18
generally, 5:15, 5:16
rate groups, 4:12, 4:17

Real estate
deduction for contributed property, 12:4
funds or other property of plan, 16:25
investment in employer real property, 19:52, 20:7
limits on investment in, 19:47
loans to acquire or improve, 19:48
qualifying employer real property, 19:53

Real estate industry
qualified separate lines of business, 5:54

Real estate operating company
look-through rule, 19:20

Reasonable, good-faith compliance.
See Good-faith compliance

Recapture
reemployed participant's preseparation benefits, of, 13:5
substantially equal periodic payments, 13:41

Recordkeeping and reporting
accrued benefit accounts, 9:2
active participant status, 26:8
actuarial reports, 16:16
annual report to IRS. *See* Form 5500 series return/report
Annual Return/Report of Employee Benefit Plan, 8:14
benefits records, 16:4
criminal penalties for violations of reporting requirements, 17:10
deductible employee contribution records, 16:4
determination letters, 15:7, 15:8
direct rollovers, 28:30
distributions
notice of tax effects of, 16:15
qualified plans, from, 17:17
dividend distributions, 24:13
exemptions from DOL reporting requirements, 17:19
fiduciaries, 19:51
foreign language version of plans, 16:17
Form 5310-A, 5:51
401(k) plans
corrective distribution of excess deferral, 23:28
generally, 23:52
rights and obligations under CODA, 23:8
future accruals of benefits, amendment to reduce, 9:29
IRA trustees, 26:46
merger or consolidation of qualified plans, 9:31
minimum distribution requirements, 11:23
minimum funding standards, failure to meet, 8:18, 8:19
misleading communications or misrepresentations by fiduciary, 19:14
nondeductible contribution to individual retirement plan, 26:16
nonqualified plans, 1:13

Index

nonrecognition of gain on sale of qualified securities, 24:32

Notice of Intent to Terminate. *See* Termination of plan

optional forms of benefits, amendment of plan containing, 10:41

oral inquiries from participants, 16:17

participant requests for documents, 16:16, 18:13

Pension Benefit Guaranty Corporation (PBGC). *See* Pension Benefit Guaranty Corporation (PBGC)

plan administration records
  failure to maintain records, 16:6
  generally, 16:4

prospectus furnished by mutual fund, 20:1

qualified domestic relations orders provisions, 30:11, 30:12

qualified joint and survivor annuity participants, to, 10:29

qualified plans, for, 4:1

qualified preretirement survivor annuity participants, to,
  fully subsidized plans, 10:31
  generally, 10:30

qualified separate lines of business, 5:51

registration statement. *See* Registration statement

reportable business segments safe harbor, 5:54

reportable events, notice requirement for, 21:16

Section 402(f) Notice, 16:15, 28:27

self-directed account plans, 19:8

service records, 16:4

simplified employee pensions (SEPs), 27:13, 27:15

special returns, 17:16

statement of benefits, 18:13

Statement of Financial Accounting Standards No. 14, 5:54

summary annual report. *See* Summary annual reports

summary of material modifications. *See* Summary of material modifications

summary plan description. *See* Summary plan descriptions

supplementary reports. *See* Supplementary reports

tax-sheltered annuities, 29:49

terminal reports. *See* Terminal reports

termination of plan. *See* Termination of plan

transfer of assets or liabilities between plans, 9:31

translation of pertinent documents, 18:14

vesting records, 16:4

waiver of minimum funding standards, application for, 8:21–8:23

waiver of Section 402(f) Notice, 16:15

Refund
improper tax levy, of, 4:26

Regional prototype plans
determination letter filing, 15:7

Registration statement
Form 5500-R, 17:2
Schedule SSA, Annual Registration Statement, 17:4

Regulated investment company
securities acquisition loan, 24:6

Regulatory Burden Reduction Initiative
avoidance of employee benefit requirements regulation, withdrawal of, 5:37
inside director regulation, withdrawal of, 5:45
leased employee regulation, withdrawal of, 5:61

Reimbursements
compensation, as, 6:3

[References are to question numbers.]

[References are to question numbers.]

[References are to question numbers.]

Rollovers (*cont'd*)
forward averaging treatment for
 later distributions, 28:34
inherited IRA, 26:39
IRA rollover accounts, 28:2
judgment creditors, 28:41
life insurance proceeds,
 postponement of tax on, 14:11
lump-sum distribution, of, 13:13
minimum distribution requirements
 affecting, 11:16
mode of payment, 28:17, 28:18
partial direct rollover, 28:21
pension plan benefits to profit
 sharing plan, 10:58
procedure, 28:3
qualified domestic relations order
 (QDRO), distributions pursuant to,
 30:19
qualified plan to IRA, from, 28:34
receiving plan defined, 11:16
regular, 28:1, 28:16
reporting on Form 1099-R, 17:17
required minimum distributions,
 28:11
revocation of, 28:40
Section 402(f) Notice, 16:15, 28:27
settlement payments, 28:38
simplified employee pensions
 (SEPs), 27:19, 27:20
Special IRA, to, 26:36
surviving spouse, by, 28:6, 28:33
taxation of distributions postponed
 by, 13:1
tax-free, 28:3, 28:4
tax-sheltered annuities
 exclusion allowance, 29:22
 generally, 29:42
 surviving spouse, to, 29:43
 withholding on, 29:42
terminated plans, from, 28:31
top-heavy plans, 22:19
transfers to qualified plan from
 rollover IRA, 28:37

withholding on distribution, 28:8,
 29:42
Rugs. *See* Collectibles
Rural cooperative plans
401(k) plans, 23:6

S

Safe-harbor rules
25-year rule, 4:15
140 percent rule, 29:17
180 percent rule, 29:17
administrative safe harbors, 5:53
annuity payments, taxation of, 13:3
average accrual rate of non-highly
 compensated employees, 4:15
average benefits safe harbor, 5:54
classification test, 5:18
flat benefit plans, 4:15
hardship withdrawals. *See* Hardship
 withdrawal
highly compensated employee
 percentage ratio, 5:53
industry category safe harbor, 5:54
insurance contract plans, 4:16
leased employees, 5:65
lesser disparity safe harbor, 29:17
maximum disparity safe harbor,
 29:17
merger and acquisition safe harbor,
 5:54
minimum or maximum benefits
 safe harbor, 5:54
money purchase pension plans, 5:65
no disparity safe harbor, 29:17
nondiscrimination rule
 benefits, 4:13, 4:14
 contributions, 4:11
past service credit, 4:19
personal service corporations, 5:43,
 5:44
qualified separate lines of business,
 5:52–5:54

reportable business segments safe harbor, 5:54
Section 414(s), 6:40, 6:41
statutory safe harbor, 5:53
target benefit plans, 4:21
tax-sheltered annuities, 29:7
top-heavy plans determining minimum benefits and contributions, 22:49

Salaried employees
exclusion from qualified plan, 1:29

Salaries
compensation, as, 6:3

Salary reduction agreement
IRA deduction limit, coordination with, 26:5

Salary reduction agreements
401(k) plans, 2:11
cash-or-deferred election, 23:2
compensation, as, 6:3
elective deferrals, 26:5
generally, 29:10
tax-sheltered annuities. *See* Tax-sheltered annuities

Salesmen
personal service corporations, 5:39

Savings and loan associations
exemption from bonding requirements, 16:27
prohibited-transaction class exemption, 20:12

Savings plans. *See* Thrift or savings plans

Schedule B
filing deadline, 21:61

Schedule EA-S
Standard Termination Certification of Sufficiency, 21:34

S corporations
individual retirement plans as shareholder of, 26:2
shareholder-employees of. *See* Shareholders

simplified employee pensions (SEPs), 27:12

Section 403(b) annuities or plans.
See Tax-sheltered annuities

Section 411(d)(6) protected benefits
amendment of plan
generally, 9:24
non-Section 411(d)(6) protected benefits, 9:30
amendment of plan restricting availability of, 10:48, 10:50
anti-cutback rule
generally, 9:24
non-Section 411(d)(6) protected benefits, 9:30
availability conditioned on objective criteria, 10:47
defined, 10:42
denial to participants, 10:44
effective date of rules, 10:49
list of, 10:42
nondiscrimination rule, 10:47

Section 415 compensation
alternative definition for annual addition limitation purposes, 6:4
deduction for contributions, 12:25
defined, 6:3

Section 501(c)(3) organization
defined, 29:3

Securities
acquisition loan, 24:5–23:8
controlled group issuing, 24:9
deduction for stock contributions, 24:15
diversification requirement, 19:49
dividends paid deduction. *See* Dividends paid deduction
employee stock ownership plans (ESOPs). *See* Employee stock ownership plans (ESOPs)
employer securities defined, 24:9
exchange of target stock, 24:17
fair market value of distribution, 16:11

Securities *(cont'd)*
  handling of plan funds or other property, 16:26
  investment in employer securities, 19:52, 20:7
  lump-sum distribution in form of, 13:17
  publicly offered, 19:19
  qualified securities, 24:24
  qualifying employer securities, 19:54
  subsidiary issuing, 24:9
  valuation of employer securities not readily tradable, 24:56
  withholding on distributions of, 16:11
Securities Act of 1933
  employee stock ownership plans (ESOPs), 23:47
  investment contracts under, 24:57
Securities and Exchange Commission
  401(k) plan registration, 23:47
Securities Exchange Act of 1934
  investment contracts under, 24:57
Segregation of plan assets
  forfeiture of alternate payee's segregated amounts, 30:13
  generally, 19:16
Self-directed account plans
  earmarking in, 19:44
  fiduciaries, 19:9
  generally, 19:8
  tax-sheltered annuities, 29:50
Self-employed individuals. *See also* Sole proprietorships
  401(k) plans, 23:7
  alternative definition of compensation used for, 6:44
  borrowing from qualified plan, 1:36
  contribution limits, 6:36
  deduction for contributions, 12:1, 12:13
  defined, 1:7, 6:32
  disability of, 13:4

earned income of. *See* Earned income
  employee of other entities, 6:35
  ERISA exclusion of plans covering, 4:25
  freezing of plan covering, 1:10
  incorporation of, 1:9, 1:10
  Keogh plans. *See* Keogh plans
  life insurance benefits, 1:31
  life insurance coverage of, 14:6
  lump-sum distributions to disabled self-employed, 13:10
  owner-employee, as, 5:34
  permitted disparity, 2:37
  qualification as, 6:33
  qualified retirement plans for, 1:7, 6:30
  separation from service, 13:9
  tax advantages of qualified retirement plans, 1:8
  termination of plan covering, 1:10
Self-employment taxes
  earned income computation, 6:3
Separate lines of business (SLOB)
  50-employee requirement, 5:50
    employees of, 5:56
    highly compensated employee percentage ratio, 5:53
    industry category safe harbor, 5:54
    notice requirement, 5:51
    operating, 5:46
    testing year for, 5:57
  allocation of residual shared employees, 5:56
  averaging rules for, 5:58
  coverage requirements, 5:15, 5:46
  defined, 5:48
  effective date of requirements, 5:60
  financial accountability, separation of, 5:48
  flowchart for, 5:59
  highly compensated employees, 3:10
  line of business defined, 5:47

[References are to question numbers.]

[References are to question numbers.]

[References are to question numbers.]

[*References are to question numbers.*]

Index

[References are to question numbers.]

nonrecognition of gain on sale of qualified securities, 24:32

prohibited transactions, running with regards to, 17:14

Statutory exclusions. *See* Exclusions

Stock bonus plans
401(k) plans, 23:6
active participants, 26:9
automatic survivor benefit requirements, 10:6
comparable plans, 21:6
defined, 2:12
distributions, 2:12
employee stock ownership plans compared to, 24:2
exclusive benefit requirement, 2:36
funding standard exemption for, 8:4
generally, 2:12
repurchase of stock by company, 2:12
transferee plans. *See* Transferee plans

Stock options
compensation, as, 6:3
employee stock ownership plans (ESOPs). *See* Employee stock ownership plans (ESOPs)

Stock repurchase by company
stock bonus plans, 2:12

Straight life annuity
annual benefit under, 6:9

Student-employees
tax-sheltered annuity safe-harbor exclusion, 29:17

Subsidiaries
controlled group, as, 5:33
deductible contribution made to profit sharing plan of, 12:16
employer securities, 24:9
highly compensated employees, 3:4
operating company. *See* Operating company
separate plans for, 1:30

withdrawal liability, 25:18, 25:19, 25:38

Substantially equal periodic payments. *See* Periodic payments

Substantial-service employees
defined, 5:56

Successor employers
years of service for vesting purposes, 9:10
years of service recognized by, 5:11, 5:13

Summary annual reports
copy furnished participant, 16:16, 18:13
tax-sheltered annuities, 29:49

Summary of material modifications
Department of Labor requirement, 17:18, 18:8
participant requests for documents, 16:16, 18:13
reportable material modification, 18:9

Summary plan descriptions
contents of, 18:4
Department of Labor requirement, 17:18
disclaimer clause
generally, 18:6
sample clause, 18:6
use in lawsuits, 18:7
due date for furnishing participant with, 18:2
failure to provide, 18:2
false or misleading representations in, 18:5, 18:7
generally, 18:1
legally binding nature of, 18:5
mailing address for filing, 18:3
participant requests for documents
foreign language version of SPD, 16:16
generally, 16:16
plain English used in, 18:4

I-77

[References are to question numbers.]

[References are to question numbers.]

[*References are to question numbers.*]

[References are to question numbers.]

[References are to question numbers.]

[References are to question numbers.]

[References are to question numbers.]

U

The Pension Answer Book

[References are to question numbers.]

[References are to question numbers.]

Withdrawal from multiemployer plans. *See* Multiemployer plans
Withholding
$200 floor, 16:12
aggregation of distributions for year, 16:12
Annual Record of Federal Tax Liability (Form 945-A), 17:17
Annual Return of Withheld Federal Income Tax (Form 945), 17:17
automatic
    effective date of rule, 16:14
    generally, 16:7, 16:9, 16:13
distribution of benefits, on, 16:7
elective, 16:7
elective contributions subject to, 23:46
employer securities, distributions of, 16:11
Form 1099-R filing satisfying information reporting requirements, 17:17
hardship withdrawal, 23:38
liability for failure to withhold taxes, 16:8
participant loans from qualified plans, 16:13
plans subject to rules, 16:9
property distributions, 16:10
reliance on information provided by distributee, 16:8

rollover distributions, 28:8
tax-sheltered annuity rollovers, 29:42
withholding certificate for pension or annuity payments (Form 4-WP), 16:7
Working owner. *See* Business owner
Works of art. *See* Collectibles
Wrap fees
deductibility of, 12:26

Y

Years of service
accrual limitations, for purposes of, 9:23
consecutive years, 5:4
defined, 5:8
educational institutions, 29:24
fractional year, purposes of, 9:23
consecutive years, 5:4
defined, 5:8
educational institutions, 29:24
fractional year of service, 29:24
generally, 5:8
tax-sheltered annuities
    exclusion allowance, 29:24
    generally, 29:14
vesting purposes, for. *See* Vesting